The Handbook of Antagonism

The Handbook of Antagonism

Conceptualizations, Assessment, Consequences, and Treatment of the Low End of Agreeableness

Joshua D. Miller
Professor
Department of Psychology, University of Georgia, Athens, Georgia, United States

Donald R. Lynam
Professor
Department of Psychological Sciences, Purdue University, West Lafayette, Indiana, United States

ELSEVIER
ACADEMIC PRESS
An imprint of Elsevier

Academic Press is an imprint of Elsevier
125 London Wall, London EC2Y 5AS, United Kingdom
525 B Street, Suite 1650, San Diego, CA 92101, United States
50 Hampshire Street, 5th Floor, Cambridge, MA 02139, United States
The Boulevard, Langford Lane, Kidlington, Oxford OX5 1GB, United Kingdom

Library of Congress Cataloging-in-Publication Data
A catalog record for this book is available from the Library of Congress

British Library Cataloguing-in-Publication Data
A catalogue record for this book is available from the British Library

ISBN 978-0-12-814627-9

For information on all Academic Press publications
visit our website at https://www.elsevier.com/books-and-journals

Publisher: Nikki Levy
Acquisition Editor: Nikki Levy
Editorial Project Manager: Megan Ashdown
Production Project Manager: Purushothaman Vijayaraj
Cover Designer: Miles Hitchen

Typeset by SPi Global, India

Contents

Contributors

Robert F. Bornstein School of Psychology, Adelphi University, Garden City, NY, United States

Meredith A. Bucher Department of Psychological Sciences, Purdue University, West Lafayette, IN, United States

Brian Burke Department of Psychology, Fort Lewis College, Durango, CO, United States

Callan Coghlan Emory University School of Medicine, Atlanta, GA, United States

Nicole Cosentino Department of Psychology, University of Toronto Scarborough, Toronto, ON, Canada

Michael L. Crowe Department of Psychology, University of Georgia, Athens, GA, United States

Patrick J. Cruitt Department of Psychological and Brain Sciences, Washington University St. Louis, St. Louis, MO, United States

Matt DeLisi Department of Sociology, Iowa State University, Ames, IA, United States

Sarah Fischer Department of Psychology, George Mason University, Fairfax, VA, United States

William G. Graziano Department of Psychological Sciences, Purdue University, West Lafayette, IN, United States

Patrick L. Hill Department of Psychological and Brain Sciences, Washington University St. Louis, St. Louis, MO, United States

Christopher J. Hopwood Department of Psychology, University of California, Davis, CA, United States

Nathan W. Hudson Department of Psychology, Southern Methodist University, Dallas, TX, United States

Joshua J. Jackson Department of Psychological and Brain Sciences, Washington University St. Louis, St. Louis, MO, United States

W. Keith Campbell Department of Psychology, University of Georgia, Athens, GA, United States

Joanna Lamkin VA HSR&D Houston Center of Excellence, VA South Central MIRECC; Baylor College of Medicine, Houston, TX, United States

Robert D. Latzman Department of Psychology, Georgia State University, Atlanta, GA, United States

Justin A. Lavner Department of Psychology, University of Georgia, Athens, GA, United States

James M. LeBreton Department of Psychology, Pennsylvania State University, University Park, PA, United States

Alex C. Loeks Johnson University of Minnesota Medical School, Minneapolis, MN, United States

Donald R. Lynam Department of Psychological Sciences, Purdue University, West Lafayette, IN, United States

Jessica L. Maples-Keller Emory University School of Medicine, Atlanta, GA, United States

Joanna Marino Potomac Behavioral Solutions, Arlington, VA, United States

Julia McDonald Department of Psychology, University of South Florida, Tampa, FL, United States

Brian P. Meier Department of Psychology, Gettysburg College, Gettysburg, PA, United States

Neil A. Meyer Department of Psychology, Oklahoma State University, Stillwater, OK, United States

R. Michael Bagby Departments of Psychology and Psychiatry, University of Toronto, Toronto, ON, Canada

Joshua D. Miller Department of Psychology, University of Georgia, Athens, GA, United States

Jiwon Min Department of Psychology, Oklahoma State University, Stillwater, OK, United States

Stephanie N. Mullins-Sweatt Department of Psychology, Oklahoma State University, Stillwater, OK, United States

Katharine J. Nelson Department of Psychiatry, University of Minnesota Medical School, Minneapolis, MN, United States

Joshua R. Oltmanns Department of Psychology, University of Kentucky, Lexington, KY, United States

Thomas F. Oltmanns Department of Psychological and Brain Sciences, Washington University St. Louis, St. Louis, MO, United States

Isabella M. Palumbo Department of Psychology, Georgia State University, Atlanta, GA, United States

Abigail Powers Emory University School of Medicine, Atlanta, GA, United States

Kathleen W. Reardon Department of Psychology, Northwestern University, Evanston, IL, United States

Michael D. Robinson Department of Psychology, North Dakota State University, Fargo, ND, United States

Jérôme Rossier Research Center in Vocational Psychology and Career Counseling, Institute of Psychology, University of Lausanne, Lausanne, Switzerland

Douglas B. Samuel Department of Psychological Sciences, Purdue University, West Lafayette, IN, United States

Martin Sellbom Department of Psychology, University of Otago, Dunedin, New Zealand

Allison N. Shields Department of Psychology, Northwestern University, Evanston, IL, United States

Levi K. Shiverdecker Department of Psychology, Pennsylvania State University, University Park, PA, United States

Takakuni Suzuki Department of Psychological Sciences, Purdue University, West Lafayette, IN, United States

Jennifer L. Tackett Department of Psychology, Northwestern University, Evanston, IL, United States

Amber Gayle Thalmayer Research Center in Vocational Psychology and Career Counseling, Institute of Psychology, University of Lausanne, Lausanne, Switzerland

Renée M. Tobin College of Education, Temple University, Philadelphia, PA, United States

David D. Vachon Department of Psychology, McGill University, Montreal, QC, Canada

Edelyn Verona Department of Psychology, University of South Florida, Tampa, FL, United States

Colin E. Vize Department of Psychological Sciences, Purdue University, West Lafayette, IN, United States

Brandon Weiss Department of Psychology, University of Georgia, Athens, GA, United States

Lora M.H. Wichser Department of Psychiatry, University of Minnesota Medical School, Minneapolis, MN, United States

Thomas A. Widiger Department of Psychology, University of Kentucky, Lexington, KY, United States

Benjamin M. Wilkowski Department of Psychology, University of Wyoming, Laramie, WY, United States

Aidan G.C. Wright Department of Psychology, University of Pittsburgh, Pittsburgh, PA, United States

Megan Wrona Department of Psychology, Fort Lewis College, Durango, CO, United States

Charlotte Yasinski Emory University School of Medicine, Atlanta, GA, United States

Preface

Trait-based personality models, be they 3, 4, 5, or 6 factor models, are parsimonious approaches to representing relatively stable individual differences in thinking, feeling, and acting. Developed from different perspectives (lexical, rational, biological) they include largely the same content, although their organization varies due to differences in how the models were developed and the focus on different levels of the personality hierarchy (e.g., Digman, 1997; Markon, Krueger, & Watson, 2005). The focus of this edited handbook is on the low pole of Agreeableness, referred to here as Antagonism, which represents cognitive, emotional, and behavioral approaches to interpersonal relations. Individuals who are low on Agreeableness (i.e., antagonistic individuals) tend to be more callous, immoral, arrogant, combative, and distrustful. This dimension is among the strongest trait correlates of numerous externalizing behaviors including aggression, antisocial behavior, risky sexual activity, substance use, and gambling and serves as *the* central piece of numerous psychopathological constructs of long-standing interests to mental health professionals including psychopathy, antisocial personality disorder, and narcissism.

Despite the seemingly clear implications for the importance of this construct, it has generated less interest than the other broad traits from these models. A search of PsycINFO for each of the Big Five/Five-Factor Model trait domains in the title found only 203 titles with Agreeableness in it—compared to 1938 for Neuroticism, 1548 for Extraversion, 510 for Conscientiousness, and 271 for Openness to experience. Our own research interests in this topic, paired with concern for the lack of attention to this critical personality construct, led us to develop this book project, with the hopes of demonstrating the importance of Antagonism and spurring further research. We examine not only its importance, but issues with its conceptualization and assessment, the degree to which it is found across cultures and nonhuman primates, how it develops and changes over time, its role in externalizing behavior, psychopathological constructs, and functioning in important domains (e.g., romance; work), as well as how one might change it. Understanding Antagonism and its many important implications—for antagonistic individuals and those who live with, date, befriend, work with, and are governed by such individuals—is a goal with many clear benefits. We hope this project helps shine more light on a construct that we believe has critical consequences.

The *Handbook* starts with our own chapter (Chapter 1) introducing Antagonism and synthesizing its role in numerous outcomes such as aggression and psychopathological constructs such as narcissism. In Chapter 2, Widiger and Oltmanns review the development of Big Five/Five-Factor Models of personality in which Agreeableness-Antagonism is more broadly situated. Chapter 3 by Reardon, Shields, and Tackett reviews the development of Antagonism and related constructs in early childhood through adolescence, factors that might influence its development, and its association with various forms of psychopathology. In Chapter 4, Crowe, Lynam, and Miller report on an empirical approach to identifying the underlying structure of Agreeableness-Antagonism, noting that previous facet-level models have mostly been rationally derived. Working at the item level (from many measures of the Big Five/ FFM), these authors suggest that five narrower facets underlie this construct. In Chapter 5, Samuel, Bucher, and Suzuki review various assessment options for Agreeableness-Antagonism, including both shorter and longer measures, free and copyrighted instruments, and those which do and do not include lower order facets. These authors also discuss instruments that only assess the more pathological ends of Antagonism that are most relevant for diagnostic purposes such as the Personality Inventory for DSM-5.

The next grouping of chapters tackles several different but relevant questions surrounding Antagonism. In Chapter 6, McDonald and Verona examine the biological correlates of this trait and suggest that they may differ depending on which aspects are assessed. As part of this review, McDonald and Verona discuss issues related to heritability, genes, neurohormones, and brain networks that may be implicated in Antagonism and related trait constructs. In Chapter 7, Thalmayer and Rossier tackle cross-cultural issues in the study of Antagonism including the degree to which gender differences may depend on culture the degree to which means are comparable across cultures (even while factor structures of instruments are), and the degree to which Agreeableness-Antagonism's nomological network is consistent across cultures. In Chapter 8, Palumbo and Latzman discuss what is known about Antagonism in nonprimate humans including the consequence of these traits among highly social species, as well as neurobiological and environmental correlates (e.g., serotonergic functioning, rearing strategies, frontal gray matter). These authors then go on to discuss a chimpanzee model of psychopathy, a personality disorder construct strongly rooted in Antagonism. In Chapter 9, Graziano and Tobin grapple with theoretical conceptualizations of Antagonism, noting that similar previous work has focused more specifically on the high pole of this construct. These authors place the Antagonism-Agreeableness dimension in the context of several underlying motivational systems (e.g., antisocial vs prosocial, fight/flight vs care) and offer an opponent process model as a means of integration. Although we know much about the antisocial and aggressive correlates of Antagonism (reviewed in detail in later chapters), we know less about the mechanisms that account for these relations. In Chapter 10, Robinson, Wilkowski, and Meier address these issues specifically in regard to reactive aggression. More specifically, these authors review various attitudinal and cognitive/attentional processes that support these outcomes including hostile attribution biases, blame externalization, selective and prolonged processing of Antagonism-related stimuli, as well as a potential difficulty with disengagement. In Chapter 11, Wright uses interpersonal theory and the interpersonal circumplex as a means of understanding Antagonism. He notes that Antagonism can be conceived of as a slight rotation of one of the circumplex's primary axis, affiliation (love vs hate; warm vs cold) toward the hostile-arrogant quadrant, a placement consistent with several Antagonism-related personality disorders (e.g., narcissistic and antisocial). Wright also presents data from his own lab in which electronic momentary assessments across time are used to understand interpersonal behavior; he reports that antagonistic individuals generally perceive their own behavior and others as being less affiliative (i.e., more antagonistic and quarrelsome).

The next grouping of chapters situates Antagonism in broad and narrow psychiatric taxonomies and highlights its role in specific disorders and critical areas of functioning. In Chapter 12, Sellbom reviews quantitative approaches to psychopathology, in which the vast number of psychiatric disorders are reduced to a much smaller and more parsimonious number based on their patterns of covariance, detailing where difficulties with Agreeableness-Antagonism fall. More specifically, Sellbom notes that Antagonism is an essential aspect of the superfactor of "externalizing behavior," playing a specific role in a subset of these disorders including antisocial, narcissistic, histrionic, and paranoid personality disorders. In Chapter 13, Cosentino and Bagby describe Antagonism's role in the alternative model of personality disorder included in the 5th edition of the *Diagnostic Manual of Mental Disorders* (DSM-5; APA, 2013) where it is one of five core personality domains used to describe personality pathology, along with markers of personality dysfunction. In addition, they describe how traits from this DSM-5 domain can be used "as is" or scored to recreate traditional personality disorder constructs such as narcissistic and antisocial. In Chapter 14, Vachon discusses theoretical and empirical evidence that places Antagonism as the very core of psychopathic personality. He demonstrates that Antagonism can largely recreate the nomological networks of various psychopathy inventories. In Chapter 15, Weiss, Campbell, Lynam, and Miller discuss Antagonism's role in narcissism and review their trifurcated model that situates Antagonism as the central component of narcissism while suggesting that traits related to Extraversion/agency/approach and Neuroticism/vulnerability/avoidance serve to flavor specific presentations (e.g., grandiose versus vulnerable narcissism). In Chapter 16, Meyer, Min, and Mullins-Sweatt discuss the extent to which Antagonism-related traits are found in borderline personality disorder, which is typically seen as a combination of intense negative affectivity and emotional dysregulation paired with behavioral dysregulation and impulsivity. Experts—researchers and clinicians—describe prototypical cases of borderline personality disorder as involving traits related to distrust, dishonesty, and noncompliance and meta-analytic relations support these hypotheses. The authors suggest that consideration of these interpersonal characteristics may be critical for treatment providers. In Chapter 17, Vize, Miller, and Lynam describe Antagonism's central and organizing role in the "Dark Triad" of psychopathy, narcissism, and Machiavellianism. Antagonism-related traits are found across all three Dark Triad constructs, albeit with some variance in the strength of the relations as well as their relations with more specific facets. Differentiation among the Dark Triad is explained by other basic personality dimensions, including high Extraversion (narcissism) and low Conscientiousness (psychopathy). In Chapters 18 through 20, Antagonism's role in romantic functioning, work, and engagement in criminal behavior is examined. In Chapter 18, Lamkin and Lavner note that antagonistic traits are related to decreased relationships satisfaction for both antagonistic individuals and their romantic partners and specify the processes that may account for these patterns including intimate partner violence, infidelity, poorer communication, distrust, limited empathy and forgiveness, and negative perceptions of one's romantic partner. In Chapter 19, Shiverdecker and LeBreton review evidence documenting Antagonism's positive relation to counterproductive work behaviors, negative relations with positive organizational citizenship behaviors, job satisfaction, organizational commitment, and effective leadership. The authors conclude by discussing interest in organizational settings of implicit measures of personality including Antagonism and review the nascent literature that links implicit measures of Antagonism to maladaptive work outcomes. In Chapter 20, DeLisi reviews the robust evidence linking Antagonism directly to antisocial and criminal behavior, as well as its role in personality disorders such as psychopathy, which the author argues is the key construct for understanding crime. DeLisi also reviews Antagonism's relevance in official criminal justice contexts (courtrooms; correctional facilities) and laments criminology's long-standing neglect of personality.

The final section of the Handbook finishes by discussing if, and how, change can happen in Antagonism via development, psychotherapeutic and pharmacological treatment, and volition. In Chapter 21, Hill, Cruitt, Jackson, and Oltmanns demonstrate that while there are general decreases in Antagonism from age 10 to 50, these tend to be much smaller in nature than adaptive changes observed in Emotional Stability and Conscientiousness. In fact, statistically significant change is not found until the 50s and 60s. The authors review possible reasons for the more limited change found in this dimension, namely, that decreases in Antagonism might not be as purely adaptive as similar changes would in Emotional Stability and Conscientiousness in that Antagonism can be related to some positive outcomes (e.g., higher salaries for men). The authors finish with hypothesized pathways for intervention, recommending that such intervention begin earlier in the lifecourse. In Chapter 22, Wrona and Burke review motivational interviewing as a treatment framework and discuss how it might be usefully applied to encourage adoption of a more agreeable interpersonal style. The authors discuss four central phases of MI—engaging, focusing, evoking, planning—and highlight how these phases might be used in relation to a case vignette. In Chapter 23, Hopwood and Bornstein tackle treatment of Antagonism from a psychodynamic perspective. Offering that trait and psychodynamic perspectives are complementary, these authors describe ways in which a psychodynamic approach might augment our understanding of Antagonism. They close with a discussion of specific psychodynamic strategies and techniques across three phases of psychotherapy for treating Antagonism. Next, in Chapter 24, Maples-Keller, Yasinski, Coghlan, and Powers discuss how a Cognitive Behavioral Therapy (CBT) framework might be employed to treat an individual with elevated levels of Antagonism. The authors offer several techniques for identifying and changing maladaptive schemas that may underlie Antagonism, like mistrust/abuse and entitlement/grandiosity. They also discuss more behavioral strategies, including behavioral chain analysis, behavioral experiments, behavioral rehearsal and role playing, and a variety of coping skills. In Chapter 25, Fischer and Marino apply principles of Dialectical Behavior Therapy to the treatment of antagonistic individuals. They argue that based on the co-occurrence of Antagonism and Borderline PD, the condition for which DBT was specifically developed, DBT has already been shown to be effective for antagonistic individuals. They underscore elements of DBT that might be especially helpful in reducing client hostility, increasing client collaboration, and reducing therapist burn out—problems they believe to be most important in working with antagonistic individuals. Loeks Johnson, Wichser, and Nelson, in Chapter 26, discuss potential pharmacologic avenues for intervention with patients with problematic levels of Antagonism. Noting that very little pharmacologic research has been aimed specifically at Antagonism, the authors use interpersonal dysfunction and aggression as proxies to generate hypotheses for the pharmacologic treatment of Antagonism. After reviewing individual studies and meta-analyses of studies focused on behavioral dyscontrol, affective dysregulation, and cognitive perceptual difficulties, the authors suggest that mood-stabilizing anticonvulsants consistently show the strongest reductions in domains such as interpersonal dysfunction, affective instability, and impulsivity—the domains most relevant to Antagonism. They close with a list of best practices for pharmacotherapy in patients with elevated levels of Antagonism. In the final chapter (Chapter 27), Hudson reviews theory and findings from the volitional change literature, with a focus on individuals' desires and attempts to decrease their levels of Antagonism. Hudson notes that the majority of people desire to be more agreeable, more, extraverted, more conscientious, more open, and more emotionally stable; he further suggests that the desire to be more agreeable may increase with age. Hudson also reviews studies showing that individuals desiring to increase their levels of Agreeableness were able to do so on their own, although the increases were quite modest. He concludes with a discussion of self-help interventions and why they may have proven less effective in changing Antagonism than in changing other traits.

We appreciate readers' interest in the topic of this Handbook and hope they will more fully explore these chapters in the pages that follow. Ultimately, it is our intention to convince readers that Antagonism, although relatively neglected compared to other broad personality traits, is among the most important. Antagonism is found in every personality system across cultures and even across species. It appears early in development and is relatively stable. It is linked to a variety of externalizing outcomes—antisocial behavior, aggression, externalizing psychopathology, personality disorders, and counterproductive work behavior. Importantly, there is evidence that it can be changed.

References

American Psychiatric Association. (2013). *Diagnostic and statistical manual of mental disorders – 5th Edition (DSM-5)*. American Psychiatric Pub.

Digman, J. M. (1997). Higher-order factors of the Big Five. *Journal of Personality and Social Psychology*, *73*, 1246–1256.

Markon, K. E., Krueger, R. F., & Watson, D. (2005). Delineating the structure of normal and abnormal personality: an integrative hierarchical approach. *Journal of Personality and Social Psychology*, *88*, 139–156.

On the ubiquity and importance of antagonism

1

Donald R. Lynam, Joshua D. Miller†*
*Department of Psychological Sciences, Purdue University, West Lafayette, IN, United States, †Department of Psychology, University of Georgia, Athens, GA, United States

What is antagonism?

Antagonism can be defined in many ways. Most minimally, Antagonism, in this chapter and throughout this book, is conceptualized as one end of a bipolar personality domain dealing with an orientation toward others that runs from Antagonistic to Agreeable. Slightly less minimally, we can define this domain extensionally, through more basic trait terms that comprise Antagonism. Crowe, Lynam, and Miller (2018; see chap. 4) recently examined the structure of Antagonism/Agreeableness among personality inventories designed to capture this domain. The authors administered 131 items from 22 scales to a large sample of participants ($N=1205$) recruited from Amazon's Mechanical Turk (MTurk) website. After deleting redundant items, the authors conducted a bass-ackward analysis (Goldberg, 2006) which allows one to examine the factor emergence of the domain, from a single factor to increasingly more specific factors. An optimal five-factor structure was identified through this procedure. Accordingly, the Antagonism/Agreeableness dimension can be said to include these more basic bipolar traits: callousness versus compassion, immorality versus morality, distrust versus trust, combativeness versus affability, and arrogance versus modesty. Table 1 includes these bipolar dimensions as well as traits describing both the Antagonistic and Agreeable poles.

More broadly, this domain can be characterized as individual differences in the motivation to maintain positive social relations with others; as such, Antagonism/Agreeableness is firmly grounded in an interpersonal context (Graziano & Eisenberg, 1997; Graziano & Tobin, 2017). Antagonistic individuals place less value on interpersonal harmony, being more likely to sacrifice interpersonal harmony for other goals. Agreeable individuals, on the other hand, are likely to be motivated to maintain harmonious relations across many interpersonal contexts, whether it be with a romantic partner or an acquaintance. This domain also has theoretical links to behaviors that have figured prominently in human evolutionary history, such as altruism and social cooperation (Axelrod, 1984; Brown & Brown, 2006; Riolo, Cohen, & Axelrod, 2001). Indeed, the consistent cross-cultural emergence of an Antagonism/Agreeableness domain using natural language approaches (e.g., Costa & McCrae, 1992; Heaven, Connors, & Stones, 1994) suggests that Antagonism-related traits describe fundamental ways in which human beings think, feel, and relate to one another.

The Handbook of Antagonism. https://doi.org/10.1016/B978-0-12-814627-9.00001-3

Table 1 Trait descriptors of the poles of the Antagonism-Agreeableness continuum

Facet	Antagonism	Agreeableness
Callousness vs compassion	Exploitative	Altruistic
	Callous	Empathic
	Ruthless	Tender-minded
Immorality vs morality	Manipulative	Confiding
	Deceptive	Honest
	Cunning	Straightforward
Distrust vs trust	Skeptical	Trusting
	Suspicious	Naïve
	Cynical	Gullible
Combativeness vs affability	Oppositional	Cooperative
	Aggressive	Polite
	Quarrelsome	Docile
Arrogance vs modesty	Boastful	Humble
	Egocentric	Unassuming
	Self-centered	Self-effacing

We have two goals for the remainder of the chapter. First, we review the role of Antagonism in personality, personality disorders, and general psychopathology. Second, we examine the role of Antagonism in various sorts of interpersonal problems. We seek to answer two questions. How ubiquitous is Antagonism in models of behavior? How important is it to outcomes we care about? Our answer to both questions is *very*.

Antagonism in basic models of personality

Antagonism/Agreeableness appears in all major models of personality. It has its most explicit representation in the Five-Factor Model of personality (FFM) which was derived from studies of the English language undertaken to identify the domains of personality functioning most important in describing oneself and others (Digman, 1990; John & Srivastava, 1999; Wiggins & Pincus, 1992). This research was rooted in the lexical hypothesis which posits that most socially relevant and salient personality characteristics have been encoded in the natural language and that the representation in the language is reflective of their relevance and salience (e.g., Allport, 1937). This lexical research emphasized five broad personality domains, identified, in order of their relative linguistic representation from most to least, as Extraversion, Agreeableness, Conscientiousness, Neuroticism, and Openness (John & Srivastava, 1999). Extraversion entails an individual's proneness to positive emotions and degree of sociability. Agreeableness references an individual's interpersonal relationships and strategies; people high in Agreeableness tend to be trusting, straightforward, and empathic, whereas those who score low are manipulative, arrogant, and unconcerned about others. Conscientiousness deals with the "control of impulses," and the ability to plan, organize, and complete behavioral tasks. The domain of Neuroticism includes emotional adjustment and emotional stability. The fifth domain, Openness, assesses an individual's interest in culture, and in experiencing and exploring new activities, ideas, and emotions. Each of these five broad domains can be further divided into finer-grained facets or components. Costa and McCrae (1995) proposed six facets within each domain on the basis of their research with the NEO Personality Inventory-Revised (NEO PI-R; Costa & McCrae, 1992). For example, they parse the domain of Agreeableness (vs Antagonism) into more specific facets of trust (vs suspicion), straightforwardness (vs deception), altruism (vs exploitation), compliance (vs aggression), modesty (vs arrogance), and tender-mindedness (vs tough-mindedness). Soto and John (2017) recently identified three facets under each of the five domains within the second version of the Big Five Inventory (BFI-2). The facets underlying Antagonism/Agreeableness are compassion (e.g., is compassionate, has a soft heart), respectfulness (e.g., starts arguments with others), and trust (e.g., is suspicious of others' intentions).

Antagonism/Agreeableness is also found in other major models of personality, often in combination with other basic dimensions. Eysenck's PEN model includes factors of Neuroticism, Extraversion, and Psychoticism (Eysenck & Eysenck, 1970): Neuroticism entails emotional stability and adjustment; Extraversion reflects traits related to sociability and agency; and Psychoticism encompasses egocentricity, (lack of) interpersonal warmth, (lack of) empathy, and impulsiveness. Within this model, Antagonism is combined with Conscientiousness in the Psychoticism factor (McCrae & Costa, 1985). The case is similar in Tellegen's (1985) model which also posits three basic dimensions: Positive Emotionality which refers to the tendency to be positively engaged with others and the world; Negative Emotionality which reflects an individual's tendency to experience negative emotions (e.g., fear, anxiety, and anger) and his or her tendency to break down under stress, and Constraint which assesses an individual's ability to control impulses, act deliberately, avoid potentially dangerous situations, and endorse traditional values and standards. In this model, the Negative Emotionality factor includes content from both Neuroticism (i.e., a subscale measuring stress reactivity) and Antagonism (i.e., subscales assessing aggression and alienation).

Watson, Clark, and Harkness (1994) have argued that these "Big Three and Big Five models define a common 'Big Four' space in which (a) two traits are equivalent (Neuroticism and Extraversion), (b) the third Big Three dimension (Constraint or Psychoticism) represents some combination of two Big Five factors (Conscientiousness and Agreeableness), and (c) the final Big Five trait (Openness, or imagination) is excluded" (p. 24). They label the Big Four as Neuroticism (or Negative Emotionality), Extraversion (or Positive Emotionality), Conscientiousness (or Constraint), and Agreeableness. The top half of Table 2 presents the correspondence among major dimensions of general personality functioning.

More recently, a six-factor model of personality has been introduced that largely (but not identically) captures the FFM/Big Five and adds an additional Honesty-Humility factor that comprises traits of sincerity, fairness, greed avoidance, and modesty (e.g., Lee & Ashton, 2008). This model and resultant scales (e.g., Ashton & Lee,

Table 2 Relations of general models of personality and models of disordered personality with the domains of the FFM

	Neuroticism	Extraversion	Openness	Agreeableness	Conscientiousness
Domains from models of general personality functioning					
HEXACO[a]	Emotionality	eXtraversion	Openness	Agreeableness Honesty-Humility	Conscientiousness
NEO PI-R	Neuroticism	Extraversion	Openness	Agreeableness	Conscientiousness
BFI	Neuroticism	Extraversion	Openness	Agreeableness	Conscientiousness
P-E-N[b]	Neuroticism	Extraversion		Psychoticism (−) Lie (−)	Psychoticism (−)
MPQ[c]	NEM (stress reaction)	Communal PEM	Absorption	NEM (aggression (−))	CON
Domains from models of maladaptive personality					
PID-5	Negative affectivity	Detachment (−)	Psychoticism	Antagonism (−)	Disinhibition (−)
DAPP[d]	Emotion dysregulation	Inhibition (−)		Dissocial behavior (−)	Compulsivity
CAT PD[e]	Negative emotionality	Positive emotionality	Oddity	Antagonism (−)	Disconstraint (−)
SNAP temperaments[f]	Negative	Positive			Disinhibition (−)
SNAP traits[f]	Dependency	Detachment (−) Exhibitionism	Eccentric Perceptions	Aggression (−) Manipulativeness (−)	Impulsivity(−) Workaholism Disinhibition (−)

[a]Assignments based on results from Brockleback, Pauls, Rockmore, and Bates (2015) and Gaughan, Miller, and Lynam (2012).
[b]Assignments based on results from Costa and McCrae (1995).
[c]Assignments based on Church (1994) and Gaughan, Miller, Pryor, and Lynam (2009).
[d]Assignments based on Markon et al. (2005) and Van den Broeck et al. (2014).
[e]Assignments based on Wright and Simms (2014).
[f]Assignments based on Markon et al. (2005).

2009; Lee & Ashton, 2018) were created on the basis of data that suggest that this domain is sufficiently separable from the domain of Agreeableness in lexical analyses. We would note that measures of the FFM, typically from the NEO family of measures (e.g., Costa & McCrae, 1992; Maples, Guan, Carter, & Miller, 2014) contain this Honesty-Humility content to a much greater extent than do measures from the Big Five tradition (e.g., see Miller et al., 2011). Crowe and colleagues' item-level analysis of existing Agreeableness measures included HEXACO items from Honesty-Humility but found little evidence that it formed a separate factor.

Antagonism is one of the major axes of the interpersonal circumplex

Researchers interested in interpersonal behaviors have identified two major dimensions that are useful in conceptualizing, organizing, and assessing interpersonal behavior—Agency and Communion. Agency is primarily concerned with becoming individuated and involves behaviors/traits such as dominance, status, control, and power (Gurtman, 2009). Communion is concerned with connecting with others and involves behaviors/traits such as love, friendliness, and affiliation (Gurtman, 2009). When crossed, these two dimensions yield an interpersonal circumplex on which any interpersonal behavior can be placed. High Communion (i.e., friendly) sits at 0 degrees, low Communion (i.e., hostile) sits at 180 degrees, high Agency (i.e., dominance) sits at 90 degrees, and low Agency (i.e., submission) sits at 270 degrees. Any interpersonal trait or behavior can be placed on this circle. Individuals who are both dominant and warm are placed at approximately 45 degrees. Much research suggests that the two interpersonal domains of the FFM, Extraversion and Agreeableness, represent slight (i.e., 30–45 degrees) rotations of the Agency and Communion dimensions (e.g., McCrae & Costa, 1989). Within the Agency/Communion Circumplex, Agreeableness lies in the Warm Submission quadrant (at 330 degrees) with Antagonism in the Cold Dominant quadrant (at 150 degrees; see Fig. 1).

In a recent study examining the relations between psychopathy, a personality disorder with Antagonism at its core, and Communion–Hostility, Sherman and Lynam (2017) examined the relations among self-reported psychopathy, the interpersonal circumplex, the five-factor model, and a laboratory measure of social discounting. We found that psychopathy and Agreeableness were highly correlated with one another ($r = -.75$), with a measure of Communion ($rs = -.68$ and .79 for psychopathy and Agreeableness, respectively), and with the measure of social discounting ($rs = .19$ and $-.28$ for psychopathy and Agreeableness, respectively). The social discounting results were particularly interesting as they provided a behavioral measure of the relative importance of others. These results indicated that individuals high in psychopathy and Antagonism (i.e., low in Agreeableness) were less willing to give up money for others; this was especially true when the others involved were rated as interpersonally close compared to distant. That is, whereas individuals low in psychopathy and Antagonism are less willing to give up money for individuals as the interpersonal

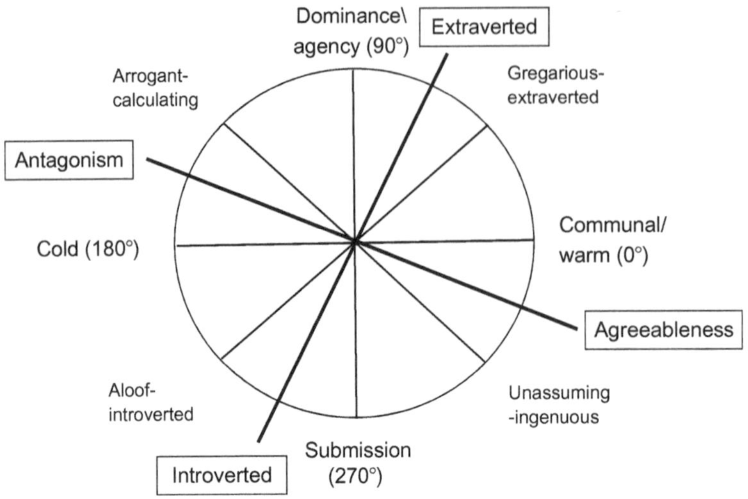

Fig. 1 Interpersonal circumplex with Agency, Communion, Extraversion, and Antagonism.

distance grows, individuals who are high in these traits show little willingness to forego money even when the individual is interpersonally close.

Antagonism in models of personality dysfunction

For a number of years, dimensional trait theorists and personality disorder researchers have sought to replace the existing categorical PD nosology with a more dimensional, trait-based approach. The categorical system has many flaws including high comorbidities, within-disorder heterogeneity, arbitrary boundaries, and no clear bridge to basic personality science (see Widiger & Trull, 2007 for a review); these problems do not exist for the dimensional system. Psychiatrists have been generally cool to this suggestion, and for years, a frequent rejoinder to the push for a more dimensional system was "which one?" In fact, the Chair of the fourth edition of the Diagnostic and Statistical Manual of Mental Disorders (APA, 1994), Allen Frances, published an article titled "Dimensional diagnosis of personality disorder – not whether but, when and which" (Frances, 1993). It is now recognized, however, that, as is the case for models of general personality functioning, various trait models of personality pathology converge around a common, four-factor structure (Widiger, Livesley, & Clark, 2009). This structure includes an explicit dimension of Antagonism versus Agreeableness in addition to constructs that are very similar to three of the remaining four dimensions of the FFM: Extraversion versus Introversion/Detachment, Emotional Stability versus Neuroticism/Emotional Dysregulation, and Constraint/Conscientiousness versus Disinhibition.

There are four commonly used inventories for assessing pathological traits, the Dimensional Assessment of Personality Pathology (DAPP; Livesley, Jackson, & Schroeder, 1992), Personality Inventory for DSM-5 (PID-5; Krueger, Derringer,

Markon, Watson, & Skodol, 2012), Computerized Adaptive Test of Personality Disorder (CAT-PD; Simms et al., 2011), and the Schedule for Nonadaptive and Adaptive Personality (SNAP; Clark, 1993). A number of studies (e.g., Markon, Krueger, & Watson, 2005; Van den Broeck et al., 2014; Wright & Simms, 2014) have examined these inventories in relation to one another and to the FFM. Results have been remarkably consistent; Antagonism versus Agreeableness appears in every system of pathological personality traits—as Antagonism in the PID-5 and CAT, Dissocial Behavior in the DAPP, and in multiple traits within the SNAP including Aggression and Manipulation. All systems also include a Detachment/Positive Emotionality dimension corresponding to Extraversion in the FFM, a Negative Affect/Emotion Dysregulation dimension that is similar to FFM Neuroticism, and a Disinhibition/Disconstraint dimension corresponding to FFM Conscientiousness. Less consistent across these models is the inclusion of an Oddity/Eccentricity dimension; this particular dimension, when it is present, is not particularly consistent with Openness in the FFM, which may be due to the inclusion of particularly heterogeneous content in the latter that includes both intelligence and apophenia—the latter of which is positively related to oddity while the former is negatively related (DeYoung, Grazioplene, & Peterson, 2012). See Table 2 for the mapping of the dimensions from models of disordered personality on to the FFM.

Antagonism in hierarchical models of psychopathology

A number of structural studies of psychopathological constructs have been conducted in an effort to refine and organize clinical symptoms and syndromes. Factor-analytic work traditionally identified two broad dimensions (or spectra) of common mental disorders—internalizing and externalizing (e.g., Achenbach, 1991; Krueger & Markon, 2006). The internalizing spectrum encompasses depression, anxiety disorders, PTSD, and eating disorders, whereas the externalizing spectrum consists of substance use disorder, antisocial behavior, aggression, and the disruptive behavior disorders (conduct disorder, oppositional defiant disorder, and ADHD). More recently, a third thought disorder spectrum has been identified (e.g., Kotov et al., 2011) which encompasses psychotic disorders, cluster A PDs, and bipolar I disorder. Within this three-factor structure, Antagonism does not emerge as a separable factor but, along with Disinhibition, comprises the higher order externalizing dimension, which is comprised of the strongest joint behavioral correlates of A and C—antisocial behavior, aggression, and drug use. Although some see Disinhibition as the core of the externalizing spectrum (Krueger, McGue, & Iacono, 2001; Venables & Patrick, 2012), empirical work demonstrates that indicators of Antagonism are as or more strongly related to externalizing than indicators of disinhibition. For example, correlations with total scores on the Externalizing Spectrum Inventory are stronger for MPQ indicators of Antagonism (i.e., $r = .45$ for higher order NEM, $rs = .30$ and .44 for lower order Alienation and Aggression) than for MPQ indictors of Conscientiousness ($r = -.22$ for higher order Constraint, $rs = -.33$, $-.17$, and .07 for lower order Control, Harm Avoidance, and Traditionalism; Venables & Patrick, 2012). Similar findings were observed by Tackett, Herzhoff, Reardon, De

Clercq, and Sharp (2014) who modeled the externalizing spectrum using aggression, relational aggression, and rule breaking. These authors found that markers of Antagonism ($rs = .72$, .47, .66, .78, and .65 for irritable-aggressive, narcissistic, affective lability, resistance, and lack of empathy; average $r = .66$) were slightly more strongly related to externalizing scores than were markers of disinhibition ($rs = .65$, .72, .51, .55, and .62 for hyperactive, impulsivity, disorderliness, distraction, and risk taking; average $r = .61$).

When studies of structure began to include separate indicators of Antagonism and Disinhibition, not just joint behavioral indicators, via the inclusion of personality disorders and/or traits in larger quantitative models, separate dimensions of Antagonism and Disinhibition emerged (Kotov et al., 2011; Wright & Simms, 2014). A recent integration of research on the structure of psychopathology, the Hierarchical Taxonomy of Psychopathology (HiTOP), explicitly includes Antagonism as one of its higher order spectra (Kotov et al., 2017). This model includes six levels arranged hierarchically with symptoms at the lowest level and an unspecified set of super-spectra that capture shared variance from the spectra at the next level below. Between symptoms and super-spectra lie components (e.g., symptom groupings and lower order maladaptive traits), syndromes/disorders (e.g., major depressive disorder, schizophrenia, conduct disorder, and narcissistic personality disorder), subfactors (e.g., fear, substance use, and antisocial behavior), and finally spectra. There are five core spectra and one provisional one (i.e., somatoform) in the HiTOP model. The five spectra are Internalizing, Thought Disorder, Detachment, Disinhibited Externalizing, and Antagonistic Externalizing. The levels below antagonistic externalizing include antisocial behavior (i.e., subfactor), antisocial PD, conduct disorder, and narcissistic PD.

Antagonism is important to multiple life outcomes

Antagonism is ubiquitous. It appears in all models of individual differences whether these models describe general personality functioning, more specific interpersonal functioning, personality pathology, or more general psychopathology. Not surprisingly, Antagonism is an important predictor of multiple negative outcomes, especially those dealing with harm to others which is not surprising given the interpersonal nature of the construct. To illustrate the importance of Antagonism, we searched the literature for meta-analyses of the relations between FFM domains and various outcomes. Effects sizes were examined to identify outcomes where Antagonism made a sizable contribution in order to ascertain the type of outcomes for which Antagonism is most important. We subjected the coefficients for the FFM domains for these outcomes to a relative importance analysis (Tonidandel & LeBreton, 2011). Such an analysis takes into account correlations among FFM domains in order to specify the relative importance of each domain in predicting the outcome, where relative importance is defined in terms of variance in the outcome attributable to each domain. The output is a series of weights that can be converted to proportions of the total variance accounted for by the set of predictors attributable to a given predictor. For example, the first row of Table 3 shows that the five domains accounted for a total of 26.3% of the variance in psychopathy in the Decuyper, De Pauw, De Fruyt, De Bolle, and De

Table 3 Results from relative importance analyses

Study	Outcome	Relative weight (%)					*R*-squared
		Neuroticism	Extraversion	Openness	Agreeable	Conscientious	
Personality disorders							
DeCuyper et al. (2009)	Psychopathy	1.69	8.77	0.51	**54.44**	34.60	0.263
Muris et al. (2017)	Psychopathy	9.41	1.42	0.35	**68.86**	19.96	0.293
O'Boyle et al. (2015)	Psychopathy	1.84	3.28	2.12	**62.77**	29.97	0.249
Vize, Collison, et al. (2018) and Vize, Lynam, et al. (2018)	Psychopathy	2.73	2.29	0.38	**75.86**	18.72	0.257
Saulsman and Page (2004)	Antisocial PD	2.11	4.11	3.38	**61.39**	29.02	0.173
Ruiz, Pincus, and Schinka (2008)	Antisocial PD	2.17	5.59	2.82	**57.57**	31.86	0.215
Samuel and Widiger (2008)	Antisocial PD	7.48	4.19	5.56	**46.38**	36.39	0.222
DeCuyper et al. (2009)	Antisocial PD	5.91	5.42	2.35	**56.16**	30.15	0.212
Saulsman and Page (2004)	Narcissism	2.67	28.11	6.52	**57.34**	5.34	0.155
Samuel and Widiger (2008)	Narcissism	4.73	8.92	4.23	**78.82**	3.31	0.172
O'Boyle et al. (2015)	Narcissism	6.86	45.6	8.08	**38.28**	3.18	0.334
Muris et al. (2017)	Narcissism	1.73	54.33	9.10	**33.52**	1.31	0.176

Continued

Table 3 Continued

Vize, Collison, et al. (2018) and Vize, Lynam, et al. (2018)	Narcissism	1.42	56.67	7.43	**33.25**	1.24	0.187
Saulsman and Page (2004)	Paranoid PD	35.12	3.75	0.35	**58.47**	2.31	0.165
Samuel and Widiger (2008)	Paranoid PD	51.60	10.18	0.56	**35.63**	2.04	0.234
Muris et al. (2017)	Machiavellianism	1.57	1.09	0.40	**77.95**	18.99	0.206
O'Boyle et al. (2015)	Machiavellianism	1.90	1.41	0.47	**80.24**	15.99	0.168
Vize, Collison, et al. (2018) and Vize, Lynam, et al. (2018)	Machiavellianism	1.52	0.59	0.51	**84.09**	13.27	0.199
Alcohol, substance use, and addiction							
Malouff, Thorsteinsson, and Schutte (2005)	Alcohol/Drug Use	24.32	2.51	4.45	**13.92**	54.79	0.166
Malouff, Thorsteinsson, and Schutte (2006)	Smoking	17.53	15.22	4.74	**20.46**	42.05	0.049
Malouff, Thorsteinsson, Rooke, and Schutte (2007)	Alcohol use	21.48	2.07	0.44	**25.92**	50.08	0.151
Ruiz et al. (2008)	Substance use D/o	30.86	1.00	0.42	**14.86**	52.90	0.140

Kotov, Gamez, Schmidt, and Watson (2010)	Substance use D/o	30.32	3.29	0.41	**15.62**	52.36	0.258
Kayis et al. (2016)	Internet addiction	22.62	16.1	1.17	**24.47**	35.64	0.074
Aggression and antisocial behavior							
Jones et al. (2011)	Aggression	12.27	1.61	4.41	**69.66**	12.06	0.125
Vize, Collison, et al. (2018) and Vize, Lynam, et al. (2018)	Aggression	10.64	2.72	0.97	**73.27**	12.39	0.184
Mitsopoulou and Giovazolias (2015)	Bullying	5.96	18.32	12.38	**49.02**	14.32	0.099
Jones et al. (2011)	Antisocial behavior	2.52	1.07	1.64	**63.69**	31.08	0.124
Miller and Lynam (2001)	Antisocial behavior	2.90	2.03	0.37	**74.38**	20.33	0.194
Vize, Collison, et al. (2018) and Vize, Lynam, et al. (2018)	Antisocial behavior	7.44	2.55	0.72	**72.78**	16.50	0.167
Malouff et al. (2005)	Externalizing	1.68	10.03	3.85	**51.20**	33.23	0.222
Grijalva and Newman (2015)	Counterproductive work behavior	13.37	1.72	0.98	**55.23**	28.7	0.265
Berry, Ones, and Sackett (2007)	Interpersonal deviance	15.19	4.85	1.89	**66.2**	11.25	0.161
Berry et al. (2007)	Organizational deviance	11.89	0.95	0.35	**26.82**	59.99	0.144

Continued

Table 3 Continued

Victimization							
Mitsopoulou and Giovazolias (2015)	Bullying victi mization	61.36	9.66	7.52	**13.05**	8.42	0.101
Nielsen, Glaso, and Einarsen (2017)	Workplace harassment	59.3	6.96	6.48	**23.05**	4.21	0.084
Accidents							
Clarke and Robertson (2005)	Work accidents	6.19	2.30	40.82	**43.38**	7.31	0.265
Clarke and Robertson (2005)	Traffic accidents	4.61	35.40	7.77	**18.93**	33.30	0.073
Clarke and Robertson (2008)	Work accidents	10.54	1.57	48.13	**27.85**	11.91	0.211
Relationship satisfaction							
Heller, Watson, and Ilies (2004)	Marital satisfaction	33.87	7.87	2.12	**35.32**	20.82	0.150
Malouff, Thorsteinsson, Schutte, Bhullar, and Rooke (2010)	Relationship satisfaction	63.78	1.84	0.34	**23.40**	10.64	0.059

Clercq (2009) study (see last column). Of this 26.3% of the variance, Antagonism/ Agreeableness accounted for over half of that (i.e., 54.6%). Because the intercorrelations among domains scores are a prerequisite for the analysis, we used the intercorrelations from a large meta-analysis by van der Linden, te Nijenhuis, and Bakker (2010).

An examination of Table 3 reveals four major findings. First, Antagonism is a major contributor to what are typically referred to as externalizing behaviors—antisocial personalities (psychopathy and APD), substance use, aggression, and antisocial behavior. In terms of relative importance, Antagonism accounts for more of the explained variance than do the other four FFM domains combined for psychopathy, antisocial PD, and all forms of aggression and antisocial PD. Antagonism makes a sizable contribution to substance use on par with Neuroticism, but about half of the relative weight of Conscientiousness in these analyses. Second, Antagonism makes substantial contributions to relationship satisfaction; it is the second largest contributor behind Neuroticism. Third, and surprisingly, Antagonism is related to accident history, especially work-related accidents. Fourth, perhaps unsurprisingly given the positive relationship between victimizing and victimization, Antagonism is the second most important correlate of victimization behind Neuroticism. In general, Antagonism is related to important outcomes.

Antagonism is especially important for antisocial behavior (ASB) and related behaviors

As was seen in Table 3, Antagonism is particularly important for antisocial behavior and personality disorders associated with antisocial behavior, including psychopathy and narcissism. In fact, Antagonism is so central to the latter two PDs, that we have argued elsewhere that it is a necessary and near sufficient condition for both PDs (e.g., Lynam & Miller, 2015; Miller, Lynam, Hyatt, & Campbell, 2017). Because Antagonism is so central to these conditions, we spend additional time explicating these relations. More specifically, we review research that indicates Antagonism is the most robust correlate of all types of antisocial behavior, that it is the central feature of psychopathy that holds inventories together and accounts for most of the intercorrelations among inventories, and that it is the central feature of narcissism, serving to define the common space shared by the grandiose and vulnerable dimensions, and that it is the "glue" that binds together the "Dark Triad" (see Vize, Miller, & Lynam, in press, chap. 17).

Antisocial behavior. In a comprehensive meta-analytic investigation of the FFM and antisocial behavior, Vize, Collison, Miller, and Lynam (in press) examined the relations between each of the FFM domains and a variety of antisocial behavior outcomes ranging from nonviolent antisocial behavior to sexually based aggression. Vize, Collison, Miller, et al. (in press) incorporated previous meta-analytic data into their work in order to expand previous research that had only examined broad-based outcomes of antisocial and aggressive behavior (Jones, Miller, & Lynam, 2011; Miller & Lynam, 2001). By expanding the number of antisocial behaviors included in the meta-analysis, the study was able to examine whether or not differences among FFM relations with antisocial behaviors were dependent on the type of antisocial behavior under investigation. The sample size was extremely large for the broadest antisocial behavior ($k = 120$, $n > 58{,}000$) and aggression ($k = 97$, $n > 33{,}000$) outcomes; even the smallest specific types of aggression (i.e., physical, relational, reactive, proactive, verbal, and bullying), except for sexual aggression and child molestation, had at least 10 studies and over 3500 participants.

The results of the meta-analysis showed that Antagonism (i.e., low Agreeableness) was the most consistent correlate of various antisocial behaviors. Additionally, the effect sizes for (low) Agreeableness were consistently larger than effect sizes observed for the other FFM domains. When collapsing across all antisocial behaviors, the average effect size for Agreeableness ($r = -.38$) was largest, followed by Conscientiousness ($r = -.22$), and then Neuroticism ($r = .15$). Across outcomes, Neuroticism showed notable variability in effect size magnitude, due to its stronger relations with outcomes like relational and reactive aggression (rs of .28 and .32, respectively). Antagonism/Agreeableness did not show a similar pattern. It was as strongly related to relational and reactive aggression (rs of $-.39$) as it was to qualitatively different outcomes like proactive aggression ($r = -.42$) and nonviolent antisocial behavior ($r = -.38$). Taken together, these meta-analytic results suggest that traits related to Antagonism are the most robust correlates of a wide variety of antisocial behaviors. These results even hold when examining antisocial outcomes, namely, aggression, in tightly controlled laboratory studies; a recent meta-analysis revealed Antagonism was the strongest correlate of laboratory aggression paradigms (Hyatt, Zeichner, & Miller, 2018). Importantly, Antagonism-related constructs are the strongest predictors of lab aggression paradigms irrespective of the various scoring approaches that are used (Hyatt, Chester, Zeichner, & Miller, in press).

Psychopathy. While descriptions of psychopathy have existed for 200 years, it was not until work by Cleckley (1941/1988) and Hare (2003) that it became the focus of sophisticated theoretical and empirical work. Behaviorally, the psychopathic individual is impulsive, risk-taking, and involved in a variety of criminal activities. Interpersonally, the psychopathic individual is arrogant, egocentric, manipulative, forceful, and cold-hearted. Affectively, the psychopathic individual displays shallow emotions; is unable to maintain close relationships; and lacks empathy, anxiety, and remorse. With descriptors like arrogant, egocentric, manipulative, cold-hearted, callous, and remorseless, it is not surprising that psychopathy is strongly related to Antagonism. As can be seen in Table 3, Antagonism accounts for the majority of the variance in psychopathy that is accounted for basic FFM traits—over 50% in DeCuyper et al. (2009), over 60% in O'Boyle, Forsyth, Banks, Story, and White (2015), almost 70% in Muris, Merckelbach, Otgaar, and Meijer (2017), and over 75% in Vize, Collison, Miller, and Lynam (2018) and Vize, Lynam, Collison, and Miller (2018).

We have argued elsewhere that Antagonism is more than just the primary FFM correlate of psychopathy—it is the core of the disorder. Antagonism is central to all descriptions of psychopathy, relates to all subscales of multiple instruments with very few exceptions, and accounts for most of the higher order psychopathy factor. From Cleckley (1941/1988) through Hare (2003), multiple theorists from different

Table 4 Ubiquity of antagonism in theoretical/clinical descriptions of psychopathy

Theorist/clinician	Antagonism-related descriptors
Cleckley (1941/1988)	Untruthfulness and insincerity Lack of remorse Pathological egocentricity/incapacity to love Unresponsiveness in interpersonal relations
Karpman (1941, 1948)	Lack of conscience Lack of guilt Lack of generous emotion
McCord and McCord (1964)	Asocial Aggressive Lack of guilt Warped capacity for love
Craft (1965)	Lacks remorse Lacks feelings for others
Buss (1966)	Fundamental incapacity for love or friendship Pathological lying Disregard for social convention
Kernberg (1984)	Malignant narcissism
Hare (2003)	Grandiose sense of self-worth (H) Pathological lying (H) Conning/manipulative (H) Lack of remorse/guilt (H) Shallow affect (H) Callous/lack of empathy (H)

perspectives have all offered descriptions and conceptualizations of psychopathy. In all such descriptions, Antagonism serves as a centerpiece (Miller & Lynam, 2015). Table 4 provides a summary of the Antagonism traits that are present in such descriptions. These descriptions focus on multiple aspects of Antagonism: untruthfulness and manipulation, a lack of remorse or guilt, grandiosity, callousness, and a general incapacity to love others.

Antagonism appears to be the trait that unifies various operationalizations of psychopathy. As reported in Miller and Lynam (2015), across 18 subscales of 6 self-report psychopathy inventories, only 3 subscales failed to show moderate to large correlations with Antagonism. The three subscales that did not show these relations assess a construct, Boldness or Fearless Dominance that we, and others, have argued does not actually belong in the definition of psychopathy (Lynam & Miller, 2012; Miller & Lynam, 2012) but rather operates more like a diagnostic specifier.

Not only does Antagonism unify different operationalizations of psychopathy, it is also the glue that holds together the subscales within an inventory. There are multiple, multifaceted assessments of psychopathy available; for most of these assessments, there is a general positive manifold, meaning that the subscales are generally positively correlated with one another. Antagonism is the substance of this positive manifold. This can be demonstrated by showing that the intercorrelations among scales are reduced once Antagonism is taken into account. For example, the Childhood Psychopathy Scale (CPS; Lynam, 1997) is an early developmental analog of the PCL-R, with two factors. Antagonism accounts for large portions of the variance in Factor 1 and Factor 2 with Conscientiousness and Neuroticism also contributing to Factor 2 (Lynam et al., 2005). When a measure of Antagonism is partialed out of the two factors, their intercorrelations are significantly reduced.

More recently, Sherman, Lynam, and Heyde (2014) showed that Antagonism was the common core of subscales from the Youth Psychopathic Traits Inventory, which consists of 10 scales that form three first-order factors (i.e., Grandiose/Manipulative [G/M], Callous/Unemotional [C/U], and Impulsive/Irresponsible[I/I]), which in turn form a second-order factor labeled "psychopathic personality" (YPI; Andershed, Ker, Stattin, & Levander, 2002). Sherman et al. (2014) demonstrated that the positive manifold in this inventory (i.e., "psychopathic personality") could be largely accounted for by Antagonism. In five of six cases, facets of Antagonism accounted for over 55% of the overlap among first-order factors; in the remaining case (i.e., I/I regressed on G/M), the Antagonism facets accounted for 45% of the overlap. Lynam and Miller (2015) repeated these analyses for the Levenson Self-Report Psychopathy Scale (LSRP; Levenson, Kiehl, & Fitzpatrick, 1995) and Self-Report Psychopathy Scale-III (SRP; Paulhus, Neumann, & Hare, 2017). Results were similar as for other inventories. In the case of LSRP Factor 1, the introduction of the Antagonism facets reduced the overlap between the two factors between 84% and 92% (depending on which LSRP factor served as the dependent variable).

The SRP-III provides a particularly interesting case for analysis, as it has been shown to have two first-order factors as well as an overarching second-order factor. The two first-order factors are made up of Interpersonal Manipulation (IPM)/Callous Affect (CA) and Erratic Lifestyle (ELS)/Antisocial Behavior (ASB). For 10 of the 12 analyses, Antagonism accounted for over 50% of the overlap. For example, in the regression of IPM on CA, the Antagonism facets reduced the overlap by 68% reduction; in the regression of IPM on ASB (an across factor analysis), Antagonism reduced the overlap by 74%. The two exceptions to this were for the regressions involving the Factor 2 scales: ELS and ASB. In these cases, Antagonism accounted for only about one-third of the overlap. When the four scales are combined to form the two higher order factors, Antagonism accounts for between 61% and 72% of their overlap, depending on the direction of prediction.

Interestingly, when clinical psychology researchers were shown unlabeled five-factor model personality profiles associated with the three triarchic psychopathy model dimensions, as well as a total score (Patrick, Fowles, & Krueger, 2009), the profile derived from meanness, a construct virtually synonymous with Antagonism as explicated here, was viewed as most strongly associated with psychopathic personality (Miller, Lamkin, Maples-Keller, & Lynam, 2016). In fact, the profile associated with meanness was viewed as equally relevant to psychopathy as the total score, which raises questions about the necessity of these other pieces.

Narcissism. Narcissism is another PD with a long history and, like psychopathy, with a strong association with Antagonism. There are three meta-analyses that report on narcissism in Table 3. The percentages of the total variance accounted for by Antagonism range from a low of 33% in Vize, Collison, et al. (2018) and Vize, Lynam, et al. (2018) to a high of 79% in Samuel and Widiger (2008). As was the case for psychopathy, Antagonism is more than the strongest FFM correlate of narcissism; it is the core feature. It is recognized that there are two relatively distinct dimensions of narcissism—Grandiose and Vulnerable (Miller et al., 2017). Grandiose narcissism refers to individuals who are explicitly and outwardly immodest, self-promotional, self-enhancing, and entitled. Conversely, vulnerable narcissism describes individuals who are self-absorbed, entitled, and distrustful of others. These two tend to be modestly to moderately correlated but have relatively distinct nomological networks (e.g., Miller et al., 2011). The feature that accounts for their overlap, the component that both dimensions share, is Antagonism. This is shown in multiple ways. In one study, Miller, Lynam, et al. (2016) used the Five-Factor Narcissism Inventory (Glover, Miller, Lynam, Crego, & Widiger, 2012), a multiscale inventory of narcissism underlaid by three higher order factors (Miller, Lynam, et al., 2016)—Interpersonal Antagonism, Neuroticism, and Agentic Extraversion. These authors showed that indices of grandiose and vulnerable narcissism were both positively related to Interpersonal Antagonism (*mean* rs = .55 and .56, respectively), but differed in their relations to Neuroticism and Agentic Extraversion. Vulnerable narcissism was strongly related to Neuroticism (*mean* $r = .57$) but grandiose was not (*mean* $r = .04$), whereas the reverse was true for Agentic Extraversion (*mean* rs = .12 and .53 for vulnerable and grandiose narcissism). These findings have been the basis for a Trifurcated Theory of narcissism (Miller et al., 2017) in which there are three basic components of narcissism that give rise to different variations depending upon how they are combined. If all three components are present, one fits the profile of narcissistic personality disorder. If Interpersonal Antagonism and Agentic Extraversion are present, one fits the profile of grandiose narcissism. If Interpersonal Antagonism and Neuroticism are present, one fits the profile of vulnerable narcissism. Importantly, if only Agentic Extraversion and Neuroticism are present, one does not match any of these classic narcissism configurations, demonstrating that Interpersonal Antagonism is a necessary condition for narcissism.

This theory was recently tested in an item-level factor analysis of all major narcissism inventories (Crowe, Lynam, Campbell, & Miller, 2018). We recruited participants through Amazon's Mechanical Turk ($N = 591$) and had them complete 303 narcissism items encompassing 46 narcissism scales and subscales. After reducing redundancy, 215 items were submitted to a bass-ackward factor analysis (Goldberg, 2006). These analyses revealed the factor structure of narcissism at a range of specificities. No more than five meaningful factors (i.e., Grandiosity, Neuroticism, Antagonism, Distrustful Self-reliance, and Attention-seeking) were identified. The most parsimonious model appeared to be a three-factor structure with factors for Antagonism, Agentic Extraversion, and Neuroticism. Interestingly, the Antagonism factor emerged from equal contributions from grandiose and vulnerable narcissism factors at the previous two-factor level.

Machiavellianism and the Dark Triad. Machiavellianism is a construct based on the writings of Machiavelli and describes individuals who are ambitious, strategic, capable of delaying gratification, manipulative, and amoral (see Collison, Vize, Miller, & Lynam, 2018). Machiavellianism, psychopathy, and narcissism together form what has been referred to as the Dark Triad of personality (Paulhus & Williams, 2002)—a set of interrelated personality constructs that share an antagonistic, callous core. Given this description, it again is not surprising to find that Antagonism is, by far, the strongest FFM correlate of Machiavellianism. Across the three meta-analyses that included Machiavellianism in Table 3, Antagonism accounts for over 77% of the variance accounted for by FFM traits; these are highest proportions for any outcome. Much of the research on the Dark Triad examines two primary questions: 1. What accounts for the high degree of overlap among the three constructs, and 2. What distinguishes the three constructs from one another. We believe the answer to the first question is rather obvious. What unites the three Dark Triad constructs is Antagonism. It sits at the core of each of the three constructs and pulls them together (Vize, Collison, et al., 2018). Vize, Collison, and Lynam (in press) explicitly examined whether Antagonism could explain the overlap between psychopathy and narcissism. Using multiple regression techniques, these authors found that Antagonism accounted for the majority of overlap between psychopathy and narcissism and nearly all of the variance in narcissism's relations with aggression outcomes, and the majority of variance in psychopathy's relations with aggression outcomes. Vize, Miller, et al. (in press), extend the analysis to all three Dark Triad traits.

Conclusions

In a seminal paper on the importance of neuroticism published in the *American Psychologist*, Lahey (2009) stated "because of its enormous significance to the public health, an intensive research effort to fully understand relations among neuroticism, mental health, physical health, and quality of life would be well justified" (p. 250). We would argue that Antagonism, like Neuroticism, has tremendous public health significance—not only for the harm it does to the individual but for the harm it does to others, both the individuals who are victims of the externalizing behaviors associated with Antagonism (e.g., antisocial behavior, aggression, bullying, substance use) and the larger society which pays a substantial price (e.g., cost of incarceration). Given these costs, we think that Antagonism deserves greater attention from researchers in personality, clinical psychology, I/O psychology, and public health. There is still much to learn about the development of Antagonism, the processes and mechanisms through which Antagonism leads to its negative outcomes, and how to treat Antagonism and its associated conditions and outcomes.

References

Achenbach, T. M. (1991). *Manual for the Child Behavior Checklist/4–18 and 1991 profile*. Burlington: University of Vermont Department of Psychiatry.

Allport, G. W. (1937). *Personality: A psychological interpretation*. New York: Holt.

American Psychiatric Association (1994). *Diagnostic and statistical manual of mental disorders: DSM-IV*. Washington, DC: American Psychiatric Association.

Andershed, H., Ker, M., Stattin, H., & Levander, S. (2002). Psychopathic traits in non-referred youths: a new assessment tool. In E. Blaauw & L. Sheridan (Eds.), *Psychopaths: Current international perspectives* (pp. 131–158). The Hague, Netherlands: Elsevier.
Ashton, M. C., & Lee, K. (2009). The HEXACO–60: a short measure of the major dimensions of personality. *Journal of Personality Assessment*, *91*, 340–345.
Axelrod, R. (1984). *The evolution of cooperation*. New York, NY: Basic Books, Inc.
Berry, C. M., Ones, D. S., & Sackett, P. R. (2007). Interpersonal deviance, organizational deviance, and their common correlates: a review and meta-analysis. *Journal of Applied Psychology*, *92*, 410–424.
Brockleback, S., Pauls, S., Rockmore, D., & Bates, T. C. (2015). A spectral clustering approach to the structure of personality: contrasting the FFM and HEXACO models. *Journal of Research in Personality*, *57*, 100–109.
Brown, S. L., & Brown, R. M. (2006). Selective Investment Theory: recasting the functional significance of close relationships. *Psychological Inquiry*, *17*, 1–29.
Buss, A. (1966). *Psychopathology*. New York: Wiley.
Church, A. T. (1994). Relating the Tellegen and Five-Factor models of personality structure. *Journal of Personality and Social Psychology*, *67*, 898–909.
Clark, L. A. (1993). *Manual for the schedule for nonadaptive and adaptive personality*. Minneapolis: University of Minnesota Press.
Clarke, S., & Robertson, T. (2005). A meta-analytic review of the big five personality factors and accident involvement in occupational and non-occupational settings. *Journal of Occupational and Organizational Psychology*, *78*, 355–376.
Clarke, S., & Robertson, T. (2008). An examination of the role of personality in work accidents using meta-analysis. *Applied Psychology. An International Review*, *57*, 94–108.
Cleckley, H. (1941/1988). *The mask of sanity*. St. Louis, MO: Mosby.
Collison, K. L., Vize, C. E., Miller, J. D., & Lynam, D. R. (2018). Development and preliminary validation of a Five Factor Model measure of Machiavellianism. *Psychological Assessment*, *30*, 1401–1407.
Costa, P. T., & McCrae, R. R. (1992). *Professional manual: Revised NEO personality inventory (NEO-PI-R) and NEO five-factor inventory (NEO-FFI)*. Odessa, FL: Psychological Assessment Resources.
Costa, P. T., & McCrae, R. R. (1995). Domains and facets: hierarchical personality assessment using the revised NEO personality inventory. *Journal of Personality Assessment*, *64*, 21–50.
Craft, M. (1965). *Ten studies into psychopathic personality*. Bristol: John Wright & Sons, Ltd.
Crowe, M. L., Lynam, D. R., Campbell, W. K., & Miller, J. D. (2018). *Developing a comprehensive narcissism structure*. Manuscript submitted for publication.
Crowe, M. L., Lynam, D. R., & Miller, J. D. (2018). Uncovering the structure of agreeableness from self-report measures. *Journal of Personality*, *86*, 771–787.
Decuyper, M., De Pauw, S., De Fruyt, F., De Bolle, M., & De Clercq, B. J. (2009). A meta-analysis of psychopathy-, antisocial PD-and FFM associations. *European Journal of Personality*, *23*, 531–565.
DeYoung, C. G., Grazioplene, R. G., & Peterson, J. B. (2012). From madness to genius: the openness/intellect trait domain as a paradoxical simplex. *Journal of Research in Personality*, *46*, 63–78.
Digman, J. M. (1990). Personality structure: emergence of the five-factor model. *Annual Review of Psychology*, *41*, 417–440.
Eysenck, S. G., & Eysenck, H. J. (1970). Crime and personality: an empirical study of the three-factor theory. *British Journal of Criminology*, *10*, 225–239.

Frances, A. (1993). Dimensional diagnosis of personality–not whether, but when and which. *Psychological Inquiry*, *4*, 110–111.
Gaughan, E. T., Miller, J. D., & Lynam, D. R. (2012). Examining the utility of general models of personality in the study of psychopathy: A comparison of the HEXACO-PI-R and NEO PI-R. *Journal of Personality Disorders*, *26*, 513–523.
Gaughan, E. T., Miller, J. D., Pryor, L. R., & Lynam, D. R. (2009). Comparing two alternative measures of general personality in the assessment of psychopathy: a test of the NEO PI-R and the MPQ. *Journal of Personality*, *77*, 965–996.
Glover, N., Miller, J. D., Lynam, D. R., Crego, C., & Widiger, T. A. (2012). The five-factor narcissism inventory: A five factor measure of narcissistic personality traits. *Journal of Personality Assessment*, *94*, 500–512.
Goldberg, L. R. (2006). Doing it all bass-ackwards: the development of hierarchical factor structures from the top down. *Journal of Research in Personality*, *40*, 347–358.
Graziano, W. G., & Eisenberg, N. (1997). Agreeableness: a dimension of personality. In R. Hogan, J. Johnson, & S. Briggs (Eds.), *Handbook of personality psychology* (pp. 795–824). San Diego, CA: Academic Press.
Graziano, W. G., & Tobin, M. (2017). Agreeableness and the Five-Factor Model. In T. A. Widiger (Ed.), *The Oxford handbook of the Five Factor Model* (pp. 105–132). Oxford University Press.
Grijalva, E., & Newman, D. A. (2015). Narcissism and counterproductive work behavior (CWB): meta-analysis and consideration of collectivist culture, big five personality, and narcissism's facet structure. *Applied Psychology: An International Review*, *64*, 93–126.
Gurtman, M. B. (2009). Exploring personality with the interpersonal circumplex. *Social and Personality Psychology Compass*, *3*, 601–619.
Hare, R. D. (2003). *The Hare Psychopathy Checklist-Revised* (2nd ed.). Toronto, Canada: Multi-Health Systems, Inc.
Heaven, P. C. L., Connors, J., & Stones, C. R. (1994). Three or five personality dimensions? An analysis of natural language terms in two cultures. *Personality and Individual Differences*, *17*, 181–189.
Heller, D., Watson, D., & Ilies, R. (2004). The role of person versus situation in life satisfaction: a critical examination. *Psychological Bulletin*, *130*, 574–600.
Hyatt, C. S., Chester, D. S., Zeichner, A., & Miller, J. D. (in press). Analytic flexibility in the laboratory aggression paradigms: relations with personality traits vary (slightly) by operationalization of aggression. *Aggressive Behavior*.
Hyatt, C. S., Zeichner, A., & Miller, J. D. (2018). *Laboratory aggression and personality traits: a meta-analytic review*. Manuscript submitted for publication.
John, O. P., & Srivastava, S. (1999). The big five trait taxonomy: history, measurement, and theoretical perspectives. In L. A. Pervin & O. P. John (Eds.), *Handbook of personality* (pp. 102–138). New York: Guilford.
Jones, S. E., Miller, J. D., & Lynam, D. R. (2011). Personality, antisocial behavior, and aggression: a meta-analytic review. *Journal of Criminal Justice*, *39*, 329–337.
Karpman, B. (1941). On the need of separating psychopathy into two distinct clinical types: the symptomatic and the idiopathic. *Journal of Criminal Psychopathology*, *3*, 112–137.
Karpman, B. (1948). The myth of the psychopathic personality. *American Journal of Psychiatry*, *104*, 523–534.
Kayis, A. R., Satici, S. A., Yilmaz, M. F., Simsek, D., Ceyhan, E., & Bakioglu, F. (2016). Big five personality trait and internet addiction: a meta-analytic review. *Computers in Human Behavior*, *63*, 35–40.

Kernberg, O. F. (1984). *Severe personality disorders.* New Haven, CT: Yale University Press.
Kotov, R., Gamez, W., Schmidt, F., & Watson, D. (2010). Linking "big" personality traits to anxiety, depressive, and substance use disorders: a meta-analysis. *Psychological Bulletin, 136*, 768–821.
Kotov, R., Krueger, R. F., Watson, D., Achenbach, T. M., Althoff, R. R., Bagby, R. M., et al. (2017). The Hierarchical Taxonomy of Psychopathology (HiTOP): a dimensional alternative to traditional nosologies. *Journal of Abnormal Psychology, 126*, 454–477.
Kotov, R., Ruggero, C. J., Krueger, R. F., Watson, D., Yuan, Q., & Zimmerman, M. (2011). New dimensions in the quantitative classification of mental illness. *Archives of General Psychiatry, 68*, 1003–1011.
Krueger, R. F., Derringer, J., Markon, K. E., Watson, D., & Skodol, A. E. (2012). Initial construction of a maladaptive personality trait model and inventory for DSM-5. *Psychological Medicine, 42*, 1879–1890.
Krueger, R. F., & Markon, K. E. (2006). Reinterpreting comorbidity: a model-based approach to understanding and classifying psychopathology. *Annual Review of Clinical Psychology, 2*, 111–133.
Krueger, R. F., McGue, M., & Iacono, W. G. (2001). The higher-order structure of common DSM mental disorders: internalization, externalization, and their connections to personality. *Personality and Individual Differences, 30*, 1245–1259.
Lahey, B. B. (2009). Public health significance of neuroticism. *American Psychologist, 64*, 241–256.
Lee, K., & Ashton, M. C. (2008). The HEXACO personality factors in the indigenous personality lexicons of English and 11 other languages. *Journal of Personality, 76*, 1001–1054.
Lee, K., & Ashton, M. C. (2018). Psychometric properties of the HEXACO-100. *Assessment, 25*, 543–556.
Levenson, M., Kiehl, K., & Fitzpatrick, C. (1995). Assessing psychopathic attributes in a non-institutionalized population. *Journal of Personality and Social Psychology, 68*, 151–158.
Livesley, W. J., Jackson, D. N., & Schroeder, M. L. (1992). Factorial structure of traits delineating personality disorders in clinical and general population samples. *Journal of Abnormal Psychology, 101*, 432–440.
Lynam, D. R. (1997). Pursuing the psychopath: capturing the fledgling psychopath in a nomological net. *Journal of Abnormal Psychology, 106*(3), 425–438.
Lynam, D. R., Caspi, A., Moffitt, T. E., Raine, A., Loeber, R., & Stouthamer-Loeber, M. (2005). Adolescent psychopathy and the Big Five: results from two samples. *Journal of Abnormal Child Psychology, 33*, 431–443.
Lynam, D. R., & Miller, J. D. (2012). Fearless dominance and psychopathy: response to Lilienfeld et al. *Personality Disorders: Theory, Research, and Treatment, 3*, 341–353.
Lynam, D. R., & Miller, J. D. (2015). Psychopathy from a basic trait perspective: the utility of a five-factor model approach. *Journal of Personality, 83*, 611–626.
Malouff, J. M., Thorsteinsson, E. B., Rooke, S. E., & Schutte, N. S. (2007). Alcohol involvement and the five-factor model of personality: a meta-analysis. *Journal of Drug Education, 37*, 277–294.
Malouff, J. M., Thorsteinsson, E. B., & Schutte, N. S. (2005). The relationship between the five-factor model of personality and symptoms of clinical disorders: a meta-analysis. *Journal of Psychopathology and Behavioral Assessment, 27*, 101–114.
Malouff, J. M., Thorsteinsson, E. B., & Schutte, N. S. (2006). The relationship between the five-factor model of personality and smoking: a meta-analysis. *Journal of Drug Education, 36*, 47–58.

Malouff, J. M., Thorsteinsson, E. B., Schutte, N. S., Bhullar, N., & Rooke, S. E. (2010). The five-factor model of personality and relationship satisfaction of intimate partners: a meta-analysis. *Journal of Research in Personality*, *44*, 124–127.

Maples, J. L., Guan, L., Carter, N. T., & Miller, J. D. (2014). A test of the International Personality Item Pool representation of the Revised NEO Personality Inventory and development of a 120-item IPIP-based measure of the five-factor model. *Psychological Assessment*, *26*, 1070–1084.

Markon, K. E., Krueger, R. F., & Watson, D. (2005). Delineating the structure of normal and abnormal personality: an integrative hierarchical approach. *Journal of Personality and Social Psychology*, *88*, 139–157.

McCord, W., & McCord, J. (1964). *The psychopath: An essay on the criminal mind*. Princeton, NJ: Van Nostrand.

McCrae, R. R., & Costa, P. T. (1985). Comparison of EPI and psychoticism scales with measures of the five-factor model of personality. *Personality and Individual Differences*, *6*, 587–597.

McCrae, R. R., & Costa, P. T. (1989). The structure of interpersonal traits: Wiggin's circumplex and the five-factor model. *Journal of Personality and Social Psychology*, *56*, 586–595.

Miller, J. D., Hoffman, B. J., Gaughan, E. T., Gentile, B., Maples, J., & Keith Campbell, W. (2011). Grandiose and vulnerable narcissism: a nomological network analysis. *Journal of Personality*, *79*, 1013–1042.

Miller, J. D., Lamkin, J., Maples-Keller, J. L., & Lynam, D. R. (2016). Viewing the triarchic model of psychopathy through general personality and expert-based lenses. *Personality Disorders: Theory, Research, and Treatment*, *7*, 247–258.

Miller, J. D., & Lynam, D. (2001). Structural models of personality and their relation to antisocial behavior: a meta-analytic review. *Criminology*, *39*, 765–798.

Miller, J. D., & Lynam, D. R. (2012). An examination of the Psychopathic Personality Inventory's nomological network: a meta-analytic review. *Personality Disorders: Theory, Research, and Treatment*, *3*, 305–326.

Miller, J. D., & Lynam, D. R. (2015). Understanding psychopathy using the basic elements of personality. *Social and Personality Psychology Compass*, *9*, 223–237.

Miller, J. D., Lynam, D. R., Hyatt, C. S., & Campbell, W. K. (2017). Controversies in narcissism. *Annual Review of Clinical Psychology*, *13*, 291–315.

Miller, J. D., Lynam, D. R., McCain, J. L., Few, L. R., Crego, C., Widiger, T. A., et al. (2016). Thinking structurally about narcissism: an examination of the Five-Factor Narcissism Inventory and its components. *Journal of Personality Disorders*, *30*, 1–18.

Mitsopoulou, E., & Giovazolias, T. (2015). Personality traits, empathy and bullying behavior: a meta-analytic approach. *Aggression and Violent Behavior*, *21*, 61–72.

Muris, P., Merckelbach, H., Otgaar, H., & Meijer, E. (2017). The malevolent side of human nature: a meta-analysis on the dark Traid (narcissism, Machiavellianism, and psychopathy). *Perspectives on Psychological Science*, *12*, 183–204.

Nielsen, M. B., Glaso, L., & Einarsen, S. (2017). Exposure to workplace harassment and the five Factor Model of personality: a meta-analysis. *Personality and Individual Differences*, *104*, 195–206.

O'Boyle, E. H., Forsyth, D. R., Banks, G. C., Story, P. A., & White, C. D. (2015). A meta-analytic test of redundancy and relative importance of the dark triad and five-factor model of personality. *Journal of Personality*, *83*, 644–664.

Patrick, C. J., Fowles, D. C., & Krueger, R. F. (2009). Triarchic conceptualization of psychopathy: developmental origins of disinhibition, boldness, and meanness. *Development and Psychopathology*, *21*, 913–938.

Paulhus, D. L., Neumann, C. S., & Hare, R. D. (2017). *Manual for the Self-Report Psychopathy scale* (4th ed.). Toronto: Multi-Health Systems.
Paulhus, D. L., & Williams, K. M. (2002). The Dark Triad of personality: narcissism, Machiavellianism, and psychopathy. *Journal of Research in Personality*, *36*, 556–563.
Riolo, R. L., Cohen, M. D., & Axelrod, R. (2001). Evolution of cooperation without reciprocity. *Nature*, *414*, 441–443.
Ruiz, M. A., Pincus, A. L., & Schinka, J. A. (2008). Externalizing psychopathology and the five-factor model: a meta-analysis of personality traits associated with antisocial personality disorder, substance use disorder, and their co-occurrence. *Journal of Personality Disorders*, *22*, 365–388.
Samuel, D. B., & Widiger, T. A. (2008). A meta-analytic review of the relationships between the five-factor model and DSM-IV-TR personality disorders: a facet level analysis. *Clinical Psychology Review*, *28*, 1326–1342.
Saulsman, L. M., & Page, A. C. (2004). The five-factor model and personality disorder empirical literature: a meta-analytic review. *Clinical Psychology Review*, *23*, 1055–1085.
Sherman, E. D., & Lynam, D. R. (2017). Psychopathy and low communion: an overlooked and underappreciated core feature. *Personality Disorders: Theory, Research, and Treatment*, *8*, 309–318.
Sherman, E., Lynam, D., & Heyde, B. (2014). Agreeableness accounts for the factor structure of the Youth Psychopathic Traits Inventory. *Journal of Personality Disorders*, *28*, 262–280.
Simms, L. J., Goldberg, L. R., Roberts, J. E., Watson, D., Welte, J., & Rotterman, J. H. (2011). Computerized adaptive assessment of personality disorder: introducing the CAT–PD project. *Journal of Personality Assessment*, *93*, 380–389.
Soto, C. J., & John, O. P. (2017). The next Big Five Inventory (BFI-2): developing and assessing a hierarchical model with 15 facets to enhance bandwidth, fidelity, and predictive power. *Journal of Personality and Social Psychology*, *113*, 117–143.
Tackett, J. L., Herzhoff, K., Reardon, K. W., De Clerq, B., & Sharp, C. (2014). The externalizing spectrum in youth: Incorporating personality pathology. *Journal of Adolescence*, *37*, 659–668.
Tellegen, A. (1985). Structures of mood and personality and their relevance to assessing anxiety with an emphasis on self-report. In A. H. Tuma & J. D. Maser (Eds.), *Anxiety and the anxiety disorders* (pp. 681–706). Hillsdale, NJ: Erlbaum.
Tonidandel, S., & LeBreton, J. M. (2011). Relative importance analysis: a useful supplement to regression analysis. *Journal of Business and Psychology*, *26*, 1–9.
Van den Broeck, J., Bastiaansen, L., Rossi, G., Dierckx, E., De Clercq, B., & Hofmans, J. (2014). Hierarchical structure of maladaptive personality traits in older adults: Joint factor analysis of the PID-5 and the DAPP: BQ. *Journal of Personality Disorders*, *28*, 198–211.
van der Linden, D., te Nijenhuis, J., & Bakker, A. B. (2010). The general factor of personality: a meta-analysis of Big Five intercorrelations and a criterion-related validity study. *Journal of Research in Personality*, *44*, 315–327.
Venables, N. C., & Patrick, C. J. (2012). Validity of the Externalizing Spectrum Inventory in a criminal offender sample: relations with disinhibitory psychopathology, personality, and psychopathic features. *Psychological Assessment*, *24*, 88–100.
Vize, C. E., Collison, K. L., & Lynam, D. R. (in press). The importance of antagonism: explaining similarities and differences in psychopathy and narcissism's relations with aggression and externalizing outcomes. *Journal of Personality Disorders*
Vize, C. E., Collison, K. L., Miller, J. D., & Lynam, D. R. (2018). Examining the effects of controlling for shared variance among the Dark Triad using meta-analytic structural equation modeling. *European Journal of Personality*, *32*, 46–61.

Vize, C. E., Collison, K. L., Miller, J. D., & Lynam, D. R. (in press). Using Bayesian methods to update and expand the meta-analytic evidence of the Five-Factor Model's relation to antisocial behavior. *Clinical Psychology Review.*

Vize, C. E., Lynam, D. R., Collison, K. L., & Miller, J. D. (2018). Differences among Dark Triad components: a meta-analytic investigation. *Personality Disorders: Theory, Research, and Treatment*, *9*, 101–111.

Vize, C. E., Miller, J. D., & Lynam, D. R. (in press). Antagonism in the Dark Triad. In J. D. Miller & D. R. Lynam (Eds.), Handbook of Antagonism.

Watson, D., Clark, L. A., & Harkness, A. R. (1994). Structures of personality and their relevance to psychopathology. *Journal of Abnormal Psychology*, *103*, 18–31.

Widiger, T. A., Livesley, W. J., & Clark, L. A. (2009). An integrative dimensional classification of personality disorder. *Psychological Assessment*, *21*, 243–255.

Widiger, T. A., & Trull, T. J. (2007). Plate tectonics in the classification of personality disorder: shifting to a dimensional model. *American Psychologist*, *62*, 71–83.

Wiggins, J. S., & Pincus, A. L. (1992). Personality: structure and assessment. *Annual Review of Psychology*, *43*, 473–504.

Wright, A. G. C., & Simms, L. J. (2014). On the structure of personality disorder traits: conjoint analyses of the CAT-PD, PID-5, and NEO PI-3. *Personality Disorders: Theory, Research, and Treatment*, *5*, 43–54.

Five-Factor Model antagonism

2

Thomas A. Widiger, Joshua R. Oltmanns
Department of Psychology, University of Kentucky, Lexington, KY, United States

Antagonism is one of the five fundamental domains of the Five-Factor Model (FFM). "The antagonistic person is egocentric, skeptical of others' intentions, and competitive rather than cooperative" (Costa & McCrae, 1992c, p. 15). Actually, much more can be said than that. The antagonistic person is characteristically suspicious, mistrustful, deceptive, manipulative, competitive, exploitative, self-centered, selfish, oppositional, aggressive, shrewd, cunning, brutal, cruel, arrogant, conceited, tough-minded, and callous. Of course, one need not have all of these characteristics to be considered antagonistic (and these are just only a few of the traits of antagonism).

The principle assessment of FFM antagonism is provided by the *NEO Personality Inventory-Revised* (*NEO PI-R*; Costa & McCrae, 1992c). Costa and McCrae though did not begin their seminal research program with an intent to assess the FFM; they actually began with just a three-factor model, assessed by the *NEO Inventory* (e.g., McCrae & Costa, 1983), confined to the domains of neuroticism, extraversion, and openness (Costa & McCrae, 1980). Another predominant model of personality at that time was provided by Eysenck (1952, 1987), whose model was confined to the three domains of neuroticism, extraversion, and psychoticism. In other words, neither of these premier models of personality structure included a distinct domain of antagonism.

Eysenck's (1987) psychoticism was not aligned with or even comparable to the domain of psychoticism as it is typically understood today (e.g., Krueger & Markon, 2014). Psychoticism, for Eysenck, was the disposition to be aggressive, cold, egocentric, impersonal, impulsive, creative, nonconformist, unempathic, independent, reckless, and tough-minded (Eysenck, 1987). In sum, this domain of personality included much of what would currently be understood to involve antagonism (albeit also including traits of disinhibition and openness).

Antagonism was also not distinctly identified as a fundamental domain of personality within the temperament model of personality developed by Tellegen (Clark & Watson, 1999), which consisted of the domains of negative affectivity, positive affectivity, and constraint. Antagonistic behavior within this model was confined to that driven by negative affect (i.e., its subscales were aggression, along with stress reaction and alienation). However, confining antagonism to the behavior driven by negative affect would fail to capture many other traits of the domain (e.g., being mistrustful, deceptive, manipulative, exploitative, self-centered, selfish, arrogant, conceited, tough-minded, and callous, irrespective and/or independent of any feelings of anger). A subsequent version though of this domain of negative affectivity does include mistrust and manipulativeness, along with self-harm, aggression, eccentric perceptions, and dependency (Clark, Simms, Wu, & Casillas, 2014).

The Handbook of Antagonism. https://doi.org/10.1016/B978-0-12-814627-9.00002-5

The failure to recognize the domain of antagonism within a structural model of personality is somewhat surprising given its clear presence within the interpersonal circumplex (IPC; Leary, 1957; see also Chapter 11 by Aidan Wright). The IPC is well recognized as covering all manner of interpersonal relatedness, independent of negative affectivity. The IPC is typically defined by the two orthogonal domains of agency (dominance vs submission) and communion (love vs hate). If one rotates the axes of the IPC by 45 degrees, one identifies the FFM domains of agreeableness versus antagonism and extraversion versus introversion (McCrae & Costa, 1989b; Wiggins & Pincus, 1989).

Soon after the development of the *NEO Inventory*, Costa and McCrae became aware of the Big Five through a conference presentation in Hawaii by Digman and Takemoto-Chock (1981) and Goldberg (1980). In 1983 they invited Goldberg to their lab in Baltimore, at which they shared that they had already begun to develop new scales to serve as markers for agreeableness versus antagonism (and conscientiousness).

Costa and McCrae were well convinced by the compelling logic and findings of the lexical paradigm. The traditional approach to identifying the basic dimensions of personality had been to review the vast body of existing theoretical, clinical, and research literature, and from that derive an opinion of the predominant personality trait domains. This was essentially the approach taken by the authors of the predominant alternative models throughout the history of personality assessment (Wiggins, 2003). In contrast, the lexical approach is more purely empirical. The lexical approach rests on the compelling premise that what is of most importance, interest, or meaning to persons when describing themselves and others will be naturally encoded within the language. The most important domains of personality are those with the greatest number of terms to describe and differentiate their various manifestations and nuances, and the structure of personality will be provided by the empirical relationship among these trait terms (Goldberg, 1993). The language is essentially a sedimentary deposit of the observations of personality made by all persons using and transforming that language over the thousands of years of its existence. The most useful and naturally compelling structural model of personality will then be evident from the inherent structure of the trait terms within a respective language.

Galton (1884) is arguably the first to propose a lexical approach to developing a model of personality structure. Allport and Odbert (1936) though are appropriately given due credit for initiating a much more thorough effort, culling 4500 trait descriptive terms from the second edition of Webster's dictionary. They considered current slang, such as "booster, rooter, knocker, hoodlum, climber, yes-man, four-flusher, crabber, cake-eater, chiseler, gigolo, flapper, racketeer, [and] Babbitt" (Allport & Odbert, 1936, p. 3) but most of these terms did not make the final list of "clearly 'real' traits of personality" (p. 26), albeit "knocker" did. Included within the final list though were such obscure trait terms as chesterfieldian, deipnosophistic, bloodshedder, foppish, soothfast, maungy, loppy, giggish, eleutheromaniac, hugger-mugger, hyppish, and jiggish (which mean, respectfully, elegant or urbane, adept conversationalist, murderer, vain, truthful, whiny, actively performing poorly, trifling, passionate for freedom, confused, rejecting conventional values, and playful or frisky).

Such an extensive list presented Allport with quite the hugger-mugger. He did not have the necessary statistical or computer support that is needed to factor analyze so many terms. The initial statistical work yielding the five-factor structure was provided by Tupes and Christal (1958), Norman (1963), Digman and Takemoto-Chock (1981), and Goldberg (1980, 1982). This early research was confined to the English dictionary, but the five domains of surgency (or extraversion), agreeableness (vs antagonism), conscientiousness, emotional instability, and intellect (or openness) have been identified within many other languages, including Dutch, German, Italian, Roman, Hungarian, Polish, Czech, Filipino, French, Greek, and Croatian (albeit the last two domains of neuroticism and openness tend to be relatively less consistent).

Indeed, antagonism, as a fundamental, distinct domain of personality, has very strong cross-cultural, cross-language support. The first two domains extracted from any language have consistently been extraversion (vs introversion), followed closely by agreeableness versus antagonism (De Raad et al., 2010; De Raad & Mlačić, 2017). The interpersonal relatedness domains are the first two factors because of their predominance within all languages. Persons consider how one relates to other people to be the most important traits to describe. Getting along with others is fundamental to any successful family, tribe, and society (Hogan, 1982).

"Costa and McCrae reacted to the events of the early 1980s with such remarkable openness to experience that by the end of the decade these investigators had become the world's most prolific and most influential proponents of the five-factor model" (Goldberg, 1993, p. 30). Indeed, once a particular structural model of personality has been published, most authors of the respective model tend to stubbornly defend it. This did not occur with Costa and McCrae. Soon after their meeting with Goldberg, they published the extension of the NEO Inventory, the *NEO Personality Inventory* (Costa & McCrae, 1985), including now domains of agreeableness versus antagonism, and conscientiousness (albeit this version of their measure did not yet include facet scales for agreeableness or conscientiousness).

"The rest, as they say, is history" (Goldberg, 1993, p. 30). Much of Costa and McCrae's subsequent research demonstrated compellingly that the scales and traits included within all other competing models were well captured by the FFM, including (but certainly not limited to) the constructs of the IPC (McCrae & Costa, 1989b), Henry Murray's 20 need dispositions (Costa & McCrae, 1988), the California Psychological Inventory (McCrae, Costa, & Piedmont, 1993), the Myers-Briggs Type Indicator (McCrae & Costa, 1989a), the California Q-Set (McCrae, Costa, & Busch, 1986), and many others (Costa & McCrae, 2017; McCrae & Costa, 2003).

The robustness of the FFM has indeed been compelling (O'Connor, 2002, 2017). O'Connor (2002), for example, conducted integrative factor analyses of previously published findings from approximately 75 studies involving FFM scales along with the scales of 28 commonly used self-report inventories of personality. He concluded that "the factor structures that exist in the scales of many popular personality inventories can be closely replicated using data derived solely from scale associations with the FFM" (O'Connor, 2002, p. 198). O'Connor (2002) further suggested that "the basic dimensions that exist in other personality inventories can thus be considered 'well captured' by the FFM" (p. 198). The robustness of the FFM is, of course, a natural result of its lexical foundation. To the extent that the Big Five includes all of the trait terms within the language (Goldberg, 1993), then it would very likely include virtually all traits. There would not seem to be many, if any, traits for which persons have not yet developed words to describe them.

The FFM eventually became a primary basis upon which to compare and integrate seemingly diverse personality constructs (Ozer & Reise, 1994). Goldberg (1993) likened the five domains of the FFM to the coordinates of latitude and longitude used to map the world, similarly plotting all other trait models within its five coordinates. Indeed, the FFM has been very useful in explaining the similarities and differences among alternative self-report inventories purportedly assessing the same personality disorder (Widiger, Gore, Crego, Rojas, & Oltmanns, 2017).

The absorption of alternative trait models within the FFM though has not always been well received (Goldberg, 1993). If your research, teaching, or clinical career was devoted or closely tied to a particular theoretical model or measure of personality, you may not appreciate being absorbed into a broader trait model with which you were not particularly familiar. It was comparable to the Borg of Star Trek, a juggernaut absorbing or assimilating anyone and everyone into a common collective (Widiger, 2010). Nevertheless, as was often the case with the Borg, "resistance was futile." The FFM has become the predominant dimensional trait model of personality structure (John, Naumann, & Soto, 2008; Widiger, 2017).

Alternative models of FFM antagonism

The predominant measure and model for the FFM is provided by the *NEO PI-R* (Samuel, 2013; Simms, Williams, & Simms, 2017; Widiger & Trull, 1997), but Costa and McCrae (2017) are forthright in their acknowledgment that their original selection of FFM facets (Costa & McCrae, 1995) may no longer represent the optimal choices. "It is clearly not the case that these 30 [*NEO PI-R*] scales exhaust the full range of traits related to each of the factors" (McCrae & Costa, 2013, p. 23). Costa and McCrae (1995) sought to develop facet scales that would "represent the more closely covarying elements within the domain" (p. 25) to maximize the domain scales' discriminant validity. They also attempted to have the facets be as consistent as possible with traits already recognized as important within the existing psychological literature. These facet selections have received criticism as some lament that their development occurred outside of the lexical tradition (Saucier & Goldberg, 2002). Nevertheless, the six *NEO PI-R* agreeableness versus antagonism facets identified by Costa and McCrae (trust vs mistrust, straightforwardness vs deception, altruism vs self-centeredness, compliance vs oppositionality, modesty vs arrogance, and tender-mindedness vs tough-mindedness) have clearly held up quite well over the years. In fact, a recent item-level factor analysis of many different measures of agreeableness/antagonism found support for five basic facets of agreeableness that overlapped nearly perfectly with the facets identified by Costa and McCrae (although combining the facets of tender-mindedness and altruism; Crowe, Lynam, & Miller, in press).

The alternative model of the *HEXACO Personality Inventory-Revised* (*HEXACO PI-R*; Ashton & Lee, 2008) warrants attention though, as it deviates in a striking manner from the Big Five and FFM, yet is also lexically based. The primary distinction with the *NEO PI-R* is that the *HEXACO PI-R* model removes honesty and humility from agreeableness to form its own distinct factor at the domain level, defined by the four facets of sincerity, fairness, greed-avoidance, and modesty (agreeableness is defined by the four facets of forgiveness, gentleness, flexibility, and patience). The primary basis for this alternative model is the suggestion that if one extracts six factors from a language, rather than just five, a new factor of honesty-humility typically appears. This argument though has been questioned. The sixth factor is consistently the weakest, least stable, and least replicable in lexical research (De Raad et al., 2010). Removing honesty-humility from agreeableness also has the effect of losing the comprehensive and compelling circular structure of the IPC. Its removal from the second domain to provide its own sixth domain is inconsistent with the understanding that the two most important domains within all languages concern all manner of interpersonal relatedness, as if persons consider honesty and humility to have considerably less importance than the other interpersonal traits. It is worth noting that honesty-humility content is found to a much greater extent in measures of the FFM than the more lexical Big Five measures and that this can have implications for studying antagonism-related constructs like narcissism (e.g., Miller, Gaughan, Maples, & Price, 2011).

Another option for conceptualizing and assessing FFM antagonism is provided by the *Personality Psychopathology-Five* (*PSY-5*; Harkness & McNulty, 1994). The *PSY-5* was constructed by Harkness and McNulty to provide an assessment of the FFM with items from the *Minnesota Multiphasic Personality Inventory* (*MMPI*; Hathaway & McKinley, 1943). There was, at the time, considerable debate, if not competition, between proponents of the *MMPI* and proponents of the FFM. Costa and McCrae (1992a) offered a number of different ways in which the FFM might be useful to a clinician. Their suggestions were accompanied by a critical review by Ben-Porath and Waller (1992b), followed by a rejoinder by Costa and McCrae (1992b), and then followed by a further response by Ben-Porath and Waller (1992a). This was a debate that was also presaged by commentaries published 5 years earlier in the *American Psychologist* (i.e., McCrae & Costa, 1986; Waller & Ben-Porath, 1987). The *PSY-5* offered a means of assessing the FFM domains without requiring an additional administration in clinical practice of an FFM measure, more specifically, the *NEO PI-R*. The *PSY-5* included the domains of negative emotionality, introversion, psychoticism, aggressiveness, and disconstraint.

It would indeed be parsimonious to administer just one measure. The *PSY-5*, however, did not have much impact within personality research or clinical practice. This was in part because it did not in fact align that well with the FFM, due in large part to the fact that the items of the *MMPI* (and *MMPI-2*), albeit large in number, do not provide adequate coverage of the traits within the FFM domains. The term "personality" is within the title of the *MMPI*, but it was constructed largely for the purpose of assessing general psychopathology, such as mood disorders, anxiety disorders, and schizophrenia. For example, its assessment of antagonism is confined largely to aggression (hence the title of this domain scale for the *PSY-5* is Aggressiveness) without a sufficient representation of other lower order facets to allow for subscales.

Included within the fifth edition of the American Psychiatric Association's (APA) *Diagnostic and Statistical Manual of Mental Disorders* (*DSM-5*; APA, 2013) is a five-domain dimensional trait model, consisting of negative affectivity, detachment, psychoticism, antagonism, and disinhibition (see also Chapter 13 by R. Michael Bagby). As stated in *DSM-5*, "these five broad domains are maladaptive variants of the five domains of the extensively validated and replicated personality model known as the 'Big Five,' or the Five Factor Model of personality" (APA, 2013, p. 773). The *DSM-5* domain of antagonism includes the traits of callousness, deceitfulness, grandiosity, manipulativeness, hostility, and attention-seeking (APA, 2013; Krueger et al., 2011).

Attention-seeking though is included within the domain of extraversion within other FFM trait models (Tomiatti, Gore, Lynam, Miller, & Widiger, 2012). Attention-seeking is readily understood as an expression of an outgoing, engaging extraversion. Indeed, attention-seeking is a diagnostic criterion for the histrionic personality disorder, which has long been associated conceptually (Millon et al., 1996) and empirically (Samuel & Widiger, 2008) with extraversion. However, it is not unusual to find that some traits of antagonism and extraversion will cross-list, occupying interstitial space between the domains of extraversion and antagonism, consistent with the continuous circular structure of the IPC (Leary, 1957). Although attention-seeking is a trait of extraversion, it does involve a degree of manipulativeness and self-centeredness (Gore, Tomiatti, & Widiger, 2011).

Perhaps more unusual is that the DSM-5 trait model includes suspiciousness yet does not place it within antagonism/agreeableness. In contrast, the *NEO PI-R* includes the facet of trust within the domain of agreeableness. The opposite of trust would clearly be mistrust and suspiciousness. Being mistrustful, cynical, skeptical, and suspicious of others would appear to be more suggestive of antagonism than (for instance) negative affectivity. The placement of trust versus mistrust within antagonism has been well established in multiple *NEO PI-R* factor analytic studies (Costa & McCrae, 2017; McCrae & Costa, 2003). Other measures and models of FFM antagonism have also included distrust, mistrust, and/or suspiciousness within antagonism (e.g., Edmundson, Lynam, Miller, Gore, & Widiger, 2011; Mullins-Sweatt et al., 2012). On the other hand, the placement of suspiciousness within negative affectivity has been supported in some factor analytic studies (e.g., Krueger, Derringer, Markon, Watson, & Skodol, 2012; Wright & Simms, 2014). Perhaps this might reflect another instance of an interstitial occupation, with suspiciousness including aspects of both antagonism and negative affectivity. Many of the *DSM-5* traits are indeed cross-listed (e.g., hostility is cross-listed within negative affectivity; depressivity is placed within the domain of detachment but cross-listed within negative affectivity). However, *DSM-5* suspiciousness is not cross-listed within antagonism. It is cross-listed instead within detachment (which in fact is its primary location in the DSM-5 model).

Perhaps the most extensive set of FFM antagonism scales is provided within the series of Five-Factor Model Personality Disorder (FFMPD) inventories (Widiger, Lynam, Miller, & Oltmanns, 2012). Widiger, Lynam, Miller, and colleagues have developed inventories to assess the traits included within the antisocial, borderline, narcissistic, avoidant, dependent, obsessive-compulsive, schizotypal, and histrionic personality disorders from the perspective of the FFM, many of which are considered to be maladaptive variants of FFM antagonism. In fact, there is at least one scale for each of the six *NEO PI-R* facets of antagonism, including low trust (e.g., Interpersonal Suspiciousness from the *Five Factor Schizotypal Inventory*; Edmundson et al., 2011, and Cynicism from the *Elemental Psychopathy Assessment* [*EPA*]; Lynam et al., 2011); low straightforwardness (e.g., Manipulation from the *EPA* and Melodramatic Emotionality from the *Five Factor Histrionic Inventory* [*FFHI*]; Tomiatti et al., 2012); low altruism (e.g., Self-Centeredness from the *EPA*, and Exploitative and Entitlement from the *Five Factor Narcissism Inventory* [*FFNI*]; Glover, Miller, Lynam, Crego, & Widiger, 2012); low compliance (e.g., Oppositional from *the Five Factor Borderline Inventory*; Mullins-Sweatt et al., 2012); low modesty (Arrogance from the *FFNI* and Vanity from the *FFHI*); and low tender-mindedness (e.g., Callousness from the *EPA* and Lack of Empathy from the *FFNI*). FFMPD studies have typically confined their attention to just the scales for a respective personality disorder (e.g., Crego & Widiger, 2014; DeShong, Lengel, Sauer-Zavala, O'Meara, & Mullins-Sweatt, 2015; Miller et al., 2013). However, Widiger et al. (2012) had recommended that the FFMPD scales also be used as measures of maladaptive variants of the FFM, with researchers selecting scales from the various inventories to assess (for instance) maladaptive variants of antagonism. This has indeed occurred in studies by Crego, Oltmanns, and Widiger (2018), Crego and Widiger (2016), DeShong, Grant, and Mullins-Sweatt (2015), Helle and Mullins-Sweatt (in press), Oltmanns and Widiger (2016), and Rojas and Widiger (2018).

Adaptive and maladaptive antagonism

The *NEO PI-R* is generally understood to be a measure of "normal" personality, but perhaps that is misleading or simply inaccurate when considering the assessment of antagonism. Many of its items keyed in the direction of antagonism refer explicitly to traits or features of personality disorder. The items "Some people think I'm selfish and egotistical," "I'm better than most people and I know it," and "I'm a superior person" are no different than items within any traditional measure of narcissism. It would be difficult for anyone to identify which of the following items are within the *Personality Diagnostic Questionnaire-4* (Bagby & Farvolden, 2004) and which are in the NEO PI-R: "Some people think of me as cold and calculating" versus "I don't care if others get hurt so long as I get what I want," and "I know that people will take advantage of me, or try to cheat me, if I let them" versus "I believe that most people will take advantage of you if you let them" (the first and second items, respectively, are from the *NEO PI-R*).

The *NEO PI-R* provides an assessment of maladaptive variants of high neuroticism, high introversion, low openness, high antagonism, and low conscientiousness (Haigler & Widiger, 2001) and these are the poles of the FFM that are primarily involved for most (but not all) of the *DSM-IV-TR* personality disorders (Lynam &

Widiger, 2001). It is largely for this reason that the *NEO PI-R* has in fact been used quite effectively for the assessment of many of the personality disorders (Miller, 2012), albeit the *NEO PI-R* does not capture the full range or degree of psychopathology that would be evident within the domain of antagonism (or neuroticism, introversion, and low conscientiousness). It was in part for these reasons that the FFMPD scales were developed (Widiger et al., 2012).

It is self-evident that it is generally and typically better to be agreeable than antagonistic. However, if it was always or invariably better to be agreeable the disposition to be antagonistic would naturally dissipate through the course of evolution (Widiger et al., 2017). Instead, there exists a considerable range in the individual differences of personality traits because "each of the Big Five dimensions of human personality can be seen as the result of a trade-off between different fitness costs and benefits" (Nettle, 2006, p. 622). "As there is no unconditionally optimal value of these trade-offs, it is to be expected that genetic diversity will be retained in the population" (Nettle, 2006, p. 622). It is apparent across multiple evolutionary and/or sociobiological models of the FFM that there are both potential costs of presumably adaptive traits, such as agreeableness, and potential benefits for what is generally considered maladaptive traits, such as antagonism (e.g., Nettle, 2006; Penke, Denissen, & Miller, 2007). Costa and McCrae (1992c) had in fact recognized this, stating that "the readiness to fight for one's own interests is often advantageous, and agreeableness is not a virtue on the battlefield or in the courtroom" (p. 15). They further added, "skeptical and critical thinking contributes to accurate analysis in the sciences" (Costa & McCrae, 1992c, p. 15). Many studies have indeed indicated that nice "guys" do at times finish last to the antagonistic "guys" (e.g., Boudreau, Boswell, & Judge, 2001; Lin-Healy & Small, 2013).

The *Five Factor Form* (*FFF*; Rojas & Widiger, 2014, 2018) is a relatively unique measure of FFM antagonism, in providing an effort to assess distinctly both the adaptive and maladaptive variants of each of the six *NEO PI-R* facets. The *FFF* includes 30 items, each of which aligns with a respective facet of the *NEO PI*-R FFM (Costa & McCrae, 1992c). The *FFF* trust item includes "cynical, suspicious" and "cautious, skeptical" at one pole; at the opposite pole is "trusting" and "gullible." "Cynical, suspicious" is considered to be a maladaptive variant of low trust, whereas "cautious, skeptical" is considered to be an adaptive variant. Additional adaptive strengths for antagonism include "savvy, cunning, shrewd" for low straightforwardness (along with "deceptive, dishonest, manipulative" for the maladaptive variant), and "strong, tough" for tough-mindedness (along with "callous, merciless, ruthless" for the maladaptive variant).

Conclusions

Antagonism is well established as a fundamental domain of personality and interpersonal relatedness. Antagonism is among the first two domains of personality extracted from most any language. There are alternative models for FFM antagonism, but it is typically understood to include such maladaptive traits as being suspicious, mistrustful, bloodshedder, deceptive, manipulative, exploitative, self-centered, entitled, selfish, oppositional, aggressive, brutal, cruel, arrogant, vain, foppish, conceited, tough-minded, and callous, as well as such adaptive traits as cautious, competitive, skeptical, cunning, shrewd, strong, and savvy.

References

Allport, G. W., & Odbert, H. S. (1936). Trait names: a psycho-lexical study. *Psychological Monographs*, *47*(1). Whole No. 211.

American Psychiatric Association. (2013). *Diagnostic and statistical manual of mental disorders* (5th ed.). Washington, DC: Author.

Ashton, M. C., & Lee, K. (2008). The prediction of honesty-humility-related criteria by the HEXACO and Five-Factor models of personality. *Journal of Research in Personality*, *42*, 1216–1228.

Bagby, R. M., & Farvolden, P. (2004). The Personality Diagnostic Questionnaire-4 (PDQ-4). In M. J. Hilsenroth, D. L. Segal, & M. Hersen (Eds.), *Comprehensive handbook of psychological assessment, Volume 2. Personality assessment* (pp. 122–133). NY: John Wiley.

Ben-Porath, Y. S., & Waller, N. G. (1992a). Five big issues in clinical personality assessment: a rejoinder to Costa and McCrae. *Psychological Assessment*, *4*, 23–25.

Ben-Porath, Y. S., & Waller, N. G. (1992b). "Normal" personality inventories in clinical assessment: general requirements and the potential for using the NEO personality inventory. *Psychological Assessment*, *4*(1), 14–19.

Boudreau, J. W., Boswell, W. R., & Judge, T. A. (2001). Effects of personality on executive career success in the United States and Europe. *Journal of Vocational Behavior*, *58*, 53–58.

Clark, L. A., Simms, L. J., Wu, K. D., & Casillas, A. (2014). *Schedule for Nonadaptive and Adaptive Personality-2nd Edition (SNAP-2): Manual for administration, scoring, and interpretation.* Notre Dame, IN: University of Notre Dame.

Clark, L. A., & Watson, D. (1999). Temperament. In L. Pervin & O. John (Eds.), *Handbook of personality* (2nd ed., pp. 399–423). New York: Guilford Press.

Costa, P. T., & McCrae, R. R. (1980). Still stable after all these years: personality as a key to some issues in adulthood and old age. In P. B. Baltes & O. G. Brim (Eds.), *Vol. 3. Life span development and behavior*. New York: Academic Press.

Costa, P. T., & McCrae, R. R. (1985). *The NEO Personality Inventory manual*. Odessa, FL: Psychological Assessment Resources.

Costa, P. T., & McCrae, R. R. (1988). From catalogue to classification: Murray's needs and the five-factor model. *Journal of Personality and Social Psychology*, *55*, 258–265.

Costa, P. T., & McCrae, R. R. (1992a). Normal personality assessment in clinical practice: the NEO Personality Inventory. *Psychological Assessment*, *4*, 5–13.

Costa, P. T., & McCrae, R. R. (1992b). "'Normal' personality inventories in clinical assessment: General requirements and the potential for using the NEO Personality Inventory": reply. *Psychological Assessment*, *4*, 20–22.

Costa, P. T., & McCrae, R. R. (1992c). *Revised NEO Personality Inventory (NEO PI-R) and NEO Five-Factor Inventory (NEO-FFI) professional manual. Odessa, FL: Psychological Assessment Resources.*

Costa, P. T., & McCrae, R. R. (1995). Domains and facets: hierarchical personality assessment using the Revised NEO Personality Inventory. *Journal of Personality Assessment*, *64*, 21–50.

Costa, P. T., & McCrae, R. (2017). The NEO inventories as instruments of psychological theory. In T. A. Widiger (Ed.), *The Oxford handbook of the five factor model* (pp. 11–37). NY: Oxford University Press.
Crego, C., Oltmanns, J. R., & Widiger, T. A. (2018). FFMPD Scales: comparisons to the FFM, PID-5, and CAT-PD-SF. *Psychological Assessment*, *30*, 62–73.
Crego, C., & Widiger, T. A. (2014). Psychopathy, DSM-5, and a caution. *Personality Disorders: Theory, Research, and Treatment*, *5*, 335–347.
Crego, C., & Widiger, T. A. (2016). Convergent and discriminant validity of alternative measures of maladaptive personality traits. *Psychological Assessment*, *28*, 1561–1575.
Crowe, M., Lynam, D. R., & Miller, J. D. (in press). Uncovering the structure of Agreeableness from self-report measures. *Journal of Personality*.
De Raad, B., Barelds, D. P. H., Levert, E., Ostendorf, F., Mlacic, B., Blais, L. D., et al. (2010). Only three factors of personality description are fully replicable across languages: a comparison of 14 trait taxonomies. *Journal of Personality and Social Psychology*, *98*, 160–173.
De Raad, B., & Mlačić, B. (2017). The lexical foundation of the Big Five factor model. In T. A. Widiger (Ed.), *The Oxford handbook of the five factor model* (pp. 191–216). New York: Oxford University Press.
DeShong, H. L., Grant, D. M., & Mullins-Sweatt, S. N. (2015). Comparing models of counterproductive workplace behaviors: the Five-Factor Model and the Dark Triad. *Personality and Individual Differences*, *74*, 55–60.
DeShong, H. L., Lengel, G. J., Sauer-Zavala, S. E., O'Meara, M., & Mullins-Sweatt, S. N. (2015). Construct validity of the Five-Factor Borderline Inventory. *Assessment*, *22*, 319–331.
Digman, J. M., & Takemoto-Chock, N. K. (1981). Factors in the natural language of personality: re-analyses, comparison, and interpretation of six major studies. *Multivariate Behavioral Research*, *16*, 149–170.
Edmundson, M., Lynam, D. R., Miller, J. D., Gore, W. L., & Widiger, T. A. (2011). A five-factor measure of schizotypal personality traits. *Assessment*, *18*, 321–334.
Eysenck, H. J. (1952). *The scientific study of personality*. London: Routledge & K. Paul.
Eysenck, H. J. (1987). The definition of personality disorders and the criteria appropriate for their description. *Journal of Personality Disorders*, *1*, 211–219.
Galton, F. (1884). Measurement of character. *Fortnightly Review*, *36*, 179–185.
Glover, N., Miller, J. D., Lynam, D. R., Crego, C., & Widiger, T. A. (2012). The Five-Factor Narcissism Inventory: a five-factor measure of narcissistic personality traits. *Journal of Personality Assessment*, *94*, 500–512.
Goldberg, L. R. (1980, May). Some ruminations about the structure of individual differences: developing a common lexicon for the major characteristics of human personality. In J. M. Digman (Chair), *Symposium presented at the meeting of the Western Psychological Association, Honolulu, HI*.
Goldberg, L. R. (1982). From Axe to Zombie; some explorations in the language of personality. C. D. Spielberg & J. N. Butcher (Eds.), *Vol. 1. Advances in personality assessment* (pp. 203–234). Hillsdale, NJ: Lawrence Erlbaum.
Goldberg, L. R. (1993). The structure of phenotypic personality traits. *American Psychologist*, *48*, 26–34.
Gore, W. L., Tomiatti, M., & Widiger, T. A. (2011). The home for histrionism. *Personality and Mental Health*, *5*, 57–72.
Haigler, E. D., & Widiger, T. A. (2001). Experimental manipulation of NEO PI-R items. *Journal of Personality Assessment*, *77*, 339–358.
Harkness, A. R., & McNulty, J. L. (1994). The Personality Psychopathology Five (PSY-5): issue from the pages of a diagnostic manual instead of a dictionary. In S. Strack & M. Lorr (Eds.), *Differentiating normal and abnormal personality*. New York: Springer.

Hathaway, S. R., & McKinley, J. C. (1943). *The Minnesota Multiphasic Personality Inventory* (rev. ed.). Minneapolis: University of Minnesota Press.

Helle, A. C., & Mullins-Sweatt, S. N. (in press). Maladaptive personality trait models: validating the five-factor model maladaptive trait measures with the Personality Inventory for DSM-5 and NEO Personality Inventory. *Assessment*.

Hogan, R. (1982). *A socioanalytic theory of personality, Vol. 30 of Nebraska Symposium on Motivation*. Lincoln: University of Nebraska Press.

John, O. P., Naumann, L. P., & Soto, C. J. (2008). Paradigm shift to the integrative Big Five trait taxonomy: history, measurement, and conceptual issues. In O. P. John, R. R. Robins, & L. A. Pervin (Eds.), *Handbook of personality. Theory and research* (3rd ed., pp. 114–158). New York: Guilford.

Krueger, R. F., Derringer, J., Markon, K. F., Watson, D., & Skodol, A. E. (2012). Initial construction of a maladaptive personality trait model and inventory for DSM-5. *Psychological Medicine*, *42*, 1879–1890.

Krueger, R. F., Eaton, N. R., Derringer, J., Markon, K. E., Watson, D., & Skodol, A. E. (2011). Personality in DSM-5: Helping delineate personality disorder content and framing the meta-structure. *Journal of Personality Assessment*, *93*, 325–331.

Krueger, R. F., & Markon, K. E. (2014). The role of the DSM-5 personality trait model in moving toward a quantitative and empirically based approach to classifying personality and psychopathology. *Annual Review of Clinical Psychology*, *10*, 477–501.

Leary, T. (1957). *Interpersonal diagnosis of personality*. New York: Ronald Press.

Lin-Healy, F., & Small, D. A. (2013). Nice guys finish last and guys in last are nice. The clash between doing well and doing good. *Social Psychological and Personality Science*, *4*, 692–694.

Lynam, D. R., Gaughan, E. T., Miller, J. D., Miller, D. J., Mullins-Sweatt, S., & Widiger, T. A. (2011). Assessing the basic traits associated with psychopathy: development and validation of the Elemental Psychopathy Assessment. *Psychological Assessment*, *23*, 108–124.

Lynam, D. R., & Widiger, T. A. (2001). Using the five factor model to represent the DSM-IV personality disorders: an expert consensus approach. *Journal of Abnormal Psychology*, *110*, 401–412.

McCrae, R. R., & Costa, P. T. (1983). Joint factors in self-reports and ratings: neuroticism, extraversion, and openness to experience. *Personality and Individual Differences*, *4*, 245–255.

McCrae, R. R., & Costa, P. T. (1986). Clinical assessment can benefit from recent advances in personality psychology. *American Psychologist*, *41*, 1001–1003.

McCrae, R. R., & Costa, P. T. (1989a). Reinterpreting the Myers-Briggs Type Indicator from the perspective of the five-factor model of personality. *Journal of Personality*, *57*, 17–40.

McCrae, R. R., & Costa, P. T. (1989b). The structure of interpersonal traits: Wiggins' circumplex and the five-factor model. *Journal of Personality and Social Psychology*, *56*, 586–595.

McCrae, R. R., & Costa, P. T. (2003). *Personality in adulthood. A five-factor theory perspective* (2nd ed.). New York: Guilford.

McCrae, R. R., & Costa, P. T. (2013). Introduction to the empirical and theoretical status of the five-factor model of personality traits. In T. A. Widiger & P. T. Costa (Eds.), *Personality disorders and the five-factor model of personality* (pp. 15–27). Washington, DC: American Psychological Association.

McCrae, R. R., Costa, P. T., & Busch, C. M. (1986). Evaluating comprehensiveness in personality systems: the California Q-Set and the five-factor model. *Journal of Personality*, *54*, 430–446.

McCrae, R. R., Costa, P. T., & Piedmont, R. L. (1993). Folk concepts, natural language, and psychological constructs: the California Psychological Inventory and the five-factor model. *Journal of Personality*, *61*, 1–26.

Miller, J. D. (2012). Five-factor model personality disorder prototypes: a review of their development, validity, and comparison with alternative approaches. *Journal of Personality*, *80*, 1565–1591.

Miller, J. D., Few, L. R., Wilson, L., Gentile, B., Widiger, T. A., MacKillop, J., et al. (2013). The Five-Factor Narcissism Inventory (FFNI): a test of the convergent, discriminant, and incremental validity of FFNI scores in clinical and community samples. *Psychological Assessment*, *25*, 748–758.

Miller, J. D., Gaughan, E. T., Maples, J., & Price, J. (2011). A comparison of Agreeableness scores from the Big Five Inventory and the NEO PI-R: consequences for the study of narcissism and psychopathy. *Assessment*, *18*, 335–339.

Millon, T., Davis, R. D., Millon, C. M., Wenger, A. W., Van Zuilen, M. H., Fuchs, M., et al. (1996). *Disorders of personality. DSM-IV and beyond*. NY: John Wiley & Sons.

Mullins-Sweatt, S. N., Edmundson, M., Sauer-Zavala, S. E., Lynam, D. R., Miller, J. D., & Widiger, T. A. (2012). Five-factor measure of borderline personality traits. *Journal of Personality Assessment*, *94*, 475–487.

Nettle, D. (2006). The evolution of personality variation in humans and other animals. *American Psychologist*, *61*, 622–631.

Norman, W. T. (1963). Toward an adequate taxonomy of personality attributes: replicated factor structure in peer nomination personality ratings. *Journal of Abnormal and Social Psychology*, *66*, 574–583.

O'Connor, B. P. (2002). A quantitative review of the comprehensiveness of the five-factor model in relation to popular personality inventories. *Assessment*, *9*, 188–203.

O'Connor, B. P. (2017). Robustness. In T. A. Widiger (Ed.), *The Oxford handbook of the five factor model* (pp. 151–172). New York: Oxford University Press.

Oltmanns, J. R., & Widiger, T. A. (2016). Self-pathology, the five-factor model, and bloated specific factors: a cautionary tale. *Journal of Abnormal Psychology*, *125*, 423–434.

Ozer, D. J., & Reise, S. P. (1994). Personality assessment. *Annual Review of Psychology*, *45*, 357–388.

Penke, L., Denissen, J. J., & Miller, G. F. (2007). The evolutionary genetics of personality. *European Journal of Personality*, *21*, 549–587.

Rojas, S. L., & Widiger, T. A. (2014). The convergent and discriminant validity of the Five Factor Form. *Assessment*, *21*, 143–157.

Rojas, S. L., & Widiger, T. A. (2018). Convergent and discriminant validity of the Five Factor Form and the Sliderbar Inventory. *Assessment 25*, 222–234.

Samuel, D. B. (2013). Assessing the five-factor model of personality disorder. In T. A. Widiger & P. T. Costa (Eds.), *Personality disorders and the five-factor model of personality* (pp. 221–232). Washington, DC: American Psychological Association.

Samuel, D. B., & Widiger, T. A. (2008). A meta-analytic review of the relationships between the five-factor model and DSM-IV-TR personality disorders: a facet level analysis. *Clinical Psychology Review*, *28*, 1326–1342.

Saucier, G., & Goldberg, L. R. (2002). Assessing the Big Five: applications of 10 psychometric criteria to the development of marker scales. In B. De Raad & M. Perugini (Eds.), *Big five assessment* (pp. 29–58). Bern, Switzerland: Hogrefe & Huber.

Simms, L. J., Williams, T. F., & Simms, E. N. (2017). Assessment of the five factor model. In T. A. Widiger (Ed.), *The Oxford handbook of the five factor model* (pp. 353–380). New York: Oxford University Press.

Tomiatti, M., Gore, W. L., Lynam, D. R., Miller, J. D., & Widiger, T. A. (2012). A five-factor measure of histrionic personality traits. In A. M. Columbus (Ed.), *Vol. 87. Advances in psychology research* (pp. 113–138). Hauppauge, NY: Nova Science Publishers.

Tupes, E. C., & Christal, R. E. (1958). *Stability of personality trait rating factors obtained under diverse conditions.* USAF WADC technical note number 58–61. Lackland Air Force Base Texas: US Air Force.

Waller, N. G., & Ben-Porath, Y. S. (1987). Is it time for clinical psychology to embrace the five-factor model of personality? *American Psychologist, 42*, 887–889.

Widiger, T. A. (2010, May). Scientific construction of a diagnostic manual. DSM-I through DSM-V. In: *Society for the Science of Clinical Psychology Distinguished Scientist Award address, 22nd annual meeting of the American Psychological Society, Boston, MA.*

Widiger, T. A. (Ed.), (2017). *The Oxford handbook of the five-factor model.* NY: Oxford University Press.

Widiger, T. A., Gore, W. L., Crego, C., Rojas, S. L., & Oltmanns, J. R. (2017). Five factor model and personality disorder. In T. A. Widiger (Ed.), *The Oxford handbook of the five factor model* (pp. 449–478). New York: Oxford University Press.

Widiger, T. A., Lynam, D. R., Miller, J. D., & Oltmanns, T. F. (2012). Measures to assess maladaptive variants of the five factor model. *Journal of Personality Assessment, 94*, 450–455.

Widiger, T. A., & Trull, T. J. (1997). Assessment of the five-factor model of personality. *Journal of Personality Assessment, 68*, 228–250.

Wiggins, J. S. (2003). *Paradigms of personality assessment.* NY: Guilford.

Wiggins, J. S., & Pincus, A. L. (1989). Conceptions of personality disorders and dimensions of personality. *Psychological Assessment, 1*, 305–316.

Wright, A. G. C., & Simms, L. J. (2014). On the structure of personality disorder traits: conjoint analysis of the CAT-PD, PID-5, and NEO PI-3 trait models. *Personality Disorders: Theory, Research, and Treatment, 5*, 43–54.

Antagonism from a developmental perspective

3

Kathleen W. Reardon, Allison N. Shields, Jennifer L. Tackett
Department of Psychology, Northwestern University, Evanston, IL, United States

Antagonism, the maladaptive variant of low agreeableness, is a complex trait with relevance for many different psychosocial outcomes. Although much work has been done to delineate its structure, function, and correlates in adults, research on personality pathology in youth has lagged far behind that in adults, and trait antagonism is no exception. Research in the past couple of decades has made great strides toward delineating what is consistent across children and adolescents compared to adults, as well as what is distinct (Caspi, Roberts, & Shiner, 2005). The goal of the present chapter is to review what is known about antagonism and its correlates from a developmental perspective.

Defining antagonism in youth

Personality trait structure in youth

Role of general personality. Most personality research, both in children and adults, has relied on the framework of the Five-Factor Model (FFM), a widely accepted approach (John & Srivastava, 1999). In this model, there are five higher order domains: Neuroticism (N), Extraversion (E), Agreeableness (A), Conscientiousness (C), and Openness to Experience (O). Although it has not yet been studied as extensively as in adults, there is substantial evidence for the validity of this same model in youth as young as 3 years old (Tackett et al., 2012). N in adults describes the tendency to experience negative emotions such as anger, depression, and worry; in youth, it is typically dominated by irritability and fear as these are the most easily reported on by outside observers (usually parents). E in adults includes the extent to which an individual is outgoing as well as assertive. In youth, this trait is predominantly about sociability and sometimes includes energy level, often omitting assertiveness. A in adults includes warmth, trust, and low aggression (Caspi et al., 2005). In youth, A focuses more heavily on disobedience or strong will (indicating *low* A), with much less emphasis on affiliation (Tackett et al., 2012). While antagonism in adults typically refers to the low pole of A broadly, some youth models have a specific facet named antagonism. Thus while A is the trait with the most obvious relevance for antagonism, it is also strongly associated with N and C in youth. C is relatively similar across development, reflecting a general tendency to be organized and dependable (De Pauw, 2017; Tackett, Kushner, De Fruyt, & Mervielde, 2013). Finally, O in adults describes

The Handbook of Antagonism. https://doi.org/10.1016/B978-0-12-814627-9.00003-7

the tendency to seek out new experiences, including intellectual, esthetic, and thrilling ones. In youth, O is controversial, and typically emphasizes intellect to the exclusion of creativity or imagination, although it is possible to recover a three-facet structure in children (Herzhoff & Tackett, 2012).

Hierarchical organization of general personality. Importantly, in both youth and adults, there is evidence that these traits are organized hierarchically. While each domain of the FFM has been shown to contain facets (more narrowly defined behavioral traits), they can be related to superordinate factors as well. At the broadest level of abstraction, there is evidence in adults and in youth for two overarching traits, often called Alpha and Beta (Markon, Krueger, & Watson, 2005; Slobodskaya, 2011; Tackett et al., 2012). Alpha is defined by behaviors that align broadly with avoidance, and comprises elements of A, C, and N (reversed), whereas Beta aligns broadly with approach behaviors and comprises E and O.

However, there are some important developmental differences. In youth, the traits that are included in the avoidance factor are less differentiable than they are in adults, with A and C being especially strongly positively related (Soto & Tackett, 2015). N and A also show a higher correlation in youth than in adults (De Pauw, 2017), indicating that internally and externally focused negative emotionality are much more intertwined, where a differentiation of both C and A from N is possible in adults at lower levels of the hierarchy. In addition, when adults report on children, C and O are strongly positively related to one another, which is in contrast to the distinction between these two traits seen in adults (Soto & Tackett, 2015). It is worth noting that even at a four-factor level of abstraction (containing E, C/O, A/N, and A/C factors), a strong association between A and N remains in youth until around age 9–11, when they finally begin to be differentiated from one another (Tackett et al., 2012). This close association of A with both C and N reflects differences in the hierarchical structure between children and adults, and implies that antagonism may be relevant in a broad way across the trait space in youth.

Personality pathology. Personality pathology traits, which capture extreme and maladaptive variations of normal personality traits, can also be represented as hierarchically organized dimensional models in adults (Markon, 2009; Wright et al., 2012); some more recent work has extended this approach to youth as well (De Clercq, De Fruyt, Van Leeuwen, & Mervielde, 2006; Kushner, Tackett, & De Clercq, 2013). Research has found a four-factor structure of personality pathology early in development that includes Disagreeableness, Emotional Instability, Compulsivity, and Introversion as reflected in the Dimensional Personality Symptom Itempool (DIPSI; De Clercq et al., 2006; Widiger, De Clercq, & De Fruyt, 2009), with some work supporting a fifth Oddity factor (Tackett, Silberschmidt, Krueger, & Sponheim, 2008; Verbeke & De Clercq, 2014).

Hierarchical organization of personality pathology. At a two-factor level of the personality pathology hierarchy in youth, there seem to be both a maladaptive approach-avoidance factor and a self-regulation factor (Kushner et al., 2013), the latter of which contains antagonism. At the four-factor level, the Disagreeableness factor captures facets of antagonism and risk-taking, but more overt aggression (hostility and rule-breaking) loads more highly on the Emotional Instability factor. This may depend somewhat on whether the measure captures more felt negative affect (which is not always apparent for parent raters) versus more expressed negative affect (which is readily observable). This again underlines the overlap between various types of negative affect (both inward- and outward-directed) in youth, as seen in normal personality hierarchy organization (Tackett et al., 2012). Disagreeableness is much broader in youth than in adults. It includes content from low A, high E, and low C, reflecting again the difficulty in differentiating cleanly between these traits at younger ages (De Clercq et al., 2006). In further support of this point, a DSM-5-based personality pathology measure (the PID-5) in adolescents showed poor discriminant validity, despite having good convergent validity (De Clercq et al., 2014). Maturational differences, specifically those relevant to Disagreeableness, highlight the critical importance of understanding antagonism from a developmental perspective, as it is suffused more broadly throughout the trait structure of youth personality pathology, whereas in adults it is more clearly differentiated from internalizing forms of negative affect.

Antagonism and FFM personality in youth

Much of the evidence regarding trait antagonism's relationship to other child personality domains comes from factor analytic or principal components studies in which normal range and maladaptive personality facets are entered jointly into a model, and higher order factor or component solutions are explored. Traits may cross-load onto more than one factor, indicating some relationship between factors.

Agreeableness. Typically, antagonism simply represents low A in adults (Suzuki, Samuel, Pahlen, & Krueger, 2015). However, in the Inventory of Children's Individual Differences (ICID; Halverson et al., 2003) model, antagonism is a specific lower order facet of normal range A; hence, the role of antagonism in A is highly salient in children, whereas antagonism as such does not emerge as a specific facet of A in normal-range adult personality models (Shiner, 2005; Tackett et al., 2012). In youth pathological personality models, antagonism reflects hostility, mistrust, callousness, and aggression (Shiner, 2009). In the Hierarchical Personality Inventory for Children (HiPIC; Mervielde & De Fruyt, 1999) facets egocentrism and dominance and the ICID facet antagonism have been found to load negatively on the same principal components or factors as A facets (De Fruyt, Mervielde, Hoekstra, & Rolland, 2000; Halverson et al., 2003).

Conscientiousness. Conceptually, C and A are related in that they are personality indicators of self-regulation (Shiner, 2009). FFM C and A are often positively correlated, and substantial research suggests that both factors contribute to temperamental effortful control (Abe, 2005). Relatedly, HiPIC C negatively correlates with DIPSI Disagreeableness (De Clercq et al., 2006). Inability to inhibit impulses is characteristic of both low C and antagonism (Shiner, 2009). Reflecting this relationship, facets associated with antagonism have been found to cross-load on factors characterized by low A/Disagreeableness and Compulsivity (seen as a maladaptive variant of C). Specific facets associated with both of these factors include hyperexpressive traits (e.g., persistently drawing negative attention from others), dominance-egocentrism (e.g., manipulating others and demanding attention), and narcissistic traits (e.g., exaggerated sense of self-importance, and (low) compliance; De Clercq et al., 2006; De Fruyt et al., 2000).

Neuroticism. Strong links between antagonism and N are consistently found in the personality and temperament literatures. Tackett et al. (2012) note that in child measures, the anger-irritability trait is generally assigned to the N/negative emotionality factor in temperament models, but more often to the A factor in personality models. Angry hostility, conceptualized as an N facet, demonstrates strong cross-loadings with both antagonism and N factors but loads more strongly on antagonism factors in adolescents (De Fruyt et al., 2000). This amalgam of A and N is reflected in the three-factor level of the personality hierarchy and is typified by antagonism-heavy facets such as easily angered, rude, and quick-tempered. Other personality traits that relate to both N and antagonism include irritable-aggressive traits, inflexibility, ineffective coping, and egocentrism (De Clercq et al., 2006; De Fruyt et al., 2000).

Extraversion. In developing the DIPSI, De Clercq et al. (2006) found that several HiPIC E traits loaded primarily on DIPSI Disagreeableness: hyperexpressive traits, hyperactive traits, impulsivity, and risk-taking. Widiger et al. (2009) note that while these traits were originally developed as a maladaptive item set for E, their item content reflects disagreeable or antagonistic tendencies. HiPIC dominance and DIPSI disinhibition also relate to both E and Disagreeableness (De Clercq et al., 2006). However, some Disagreeableness traits also overlap with Introversion. In nonreferred children, De Clercq et al. (2006) found that DIPSI facets inflexibility and lack of empathy loaded on both Disagreeableness and Introversion. These contrasting findings emphasize the importance of examining facet-level relationships when aiming to understand antagonism's relationship with E.

Openness. In general, there is little overlap between trait antagonism and O. While adult and youth measures of personality pathology sometimes include a fifth factor (e.g., DIPSI Oddity), it is unclear whether these factors represent maladaptive variants of O (De Clercq & De Fruyt, 2012). O explains little variance in psychopathology broadly (De Clercq et al., 2006), although O facet intellect is related to *lower* levels of behavior problems (Herzhoff & Tackett, 2012). The DIPSI Disagreeableness factor was uncorrelated with HiPIC Imagination, indicating no relationship between O and antagonism.

Overall, then, antagonism in youth is a relatively broad trait with far-reaching relationships to other traits, both normative and maladaptive. Although, as in adults, it primarily indexes irritable-aggressive and dominance facets, in youth some antagonism-related facets are also highly related to emotional dysregulation and negative affect, as seen by its close relationships with N and emotional instability. The work thus far on the hierarchical structure of personality pathology makes clear that pathological personality traits emerge and are relatively stable before adulthood. Because of its central role in the personality trait structure of youth, antagonism is well positioned to be an especially useful trait to leverage in our understanding of other critical constructs in youth, including psychopathology and other life outcomes.

Developmental stability and change

In addition to personality trait structure, change over time is another important dimension of understanding. Much work has been done on the stability and change of normal and maladaptive personality traits over time in adults (Roberts & DelVecchio, 2000; Roberts, Walton, & Viechtbauer, 2006). This work suggests that personality becomes increasingly stable across adulthood, and that personality change happens at the mean level in accordance with the *maturity principle*, meaning that people develop in adaptive ways (higher A and C, lower N) as they age. However, in youth, this is not the case. In fact, the *disruption hypothesis* (Soto, John, Gosling, & Potter, 2011) suggests that early adolescence may represent the nadir of A and C, suggesting particular relevance for trait antagonism at this developmental period. With regard to maladaptive personality traits, it has been found that Disagreeableness, Emotional Instability, and Compulsivity decrease slightly across childhood and early adolescence, but less so for those with higher initial levels of personality pathology (De Clercq, van Leeuwen, van den Noortgate, de Bolle, & de Fruyt, 2009). Rank-order stability for personality pathology (maintaining the same relative ranking of personality pathology with respect to others) was estimated to be about the same as is observed for normative personality dimensions in childhood (De Clercq et al., 2009), again emphasizing the idea that normal and maladaptive traits lie on the same continuum. This is critically important because, even as it changes over development and becomes more differentiated from low C and high N, antagonism remains an early indicator of personality dysfunction that deserves further research attention.

Antagonism and psychopathology in youth

As with basic personality research, investigations of connections between personality and psychopathology in youth have lagged behind those in adults. However, several efforts have made it clear that personality in youth can be an incredibly useful tool for parsing heterogeneity in complex diagnoses (e.g., De Clercq et al., 2010; Martel, Goth-Owens, Martinez-Torteya, & Nigg, 2010). In fact, disagreeable youth are found to have among the highest levels of adjustment problems even when compared to aggressive and socially withdrawn individuals (Laursen, Hafen, Rubin, Booth-LaForce, & Rose-Krasnor, 2010). This makes trait antagonism an important focus as an indicator for psychopathology, broadly construed, as well as a tool for identifying those individuals within a diagnostic category at highest risk for severe problems.

Axis I disorders

Internalizing problems. In youth, internalizing problems are typically defined as those problems related to depressed mood, anxiety, and loneliness. Youth high in internalizing problems are characterized by patterns of low E and high N (Tackett, Kushner et al., 2013). Youth internalizing problems also show a strong negative relationship with

A in a meta-analysis (Malouff, Thorsteinsson, & Schutte, 2005). It is important to note that irritability accompanying depressed mood has been identified as a core feature of depression in youth, something that is developmentally distinct from the clinical presentation most often found in adults (Stringaris, Maughan, Copeland, Costello, & Angold, 2013). The overlap of antagonism with high N in youth may contribute to this unique presentation. That is, the intertwined nature of both internally directed negative emotion and externally directed negative emotion may result in youth suffering from internalizing disorders behaving in an antagonistic or disagreeable way. Importantly, those youth who displayed both depressed mood and high levels of irritability were more likely to have comorbid disruptive behavior disorders (Stringaris et al., 2013). However, it is also worth noting that particularly extreme elevations of A may serve as a risk factor for internalizing, as well, such that a "nonantagonistic" factor was higher in adults with comorbid fear/distress disorders (Tackett, Quilty, Sellbom, Rector, & Bagby, 2008), and A had a positive relationship with an aggregated internalizing problems factor in youth after controlling for other FFM traits (Kushner, Tackett, & Bagby, 2012). This means that a low level of antagonism may actually serve as a protective factor.

It is critical for researchers to consider a developmental perspective when accounting for the interaction of self-regulation and psychopathology. Regarding internalizing problems in particular, a high level of inward distress may mean that youth are simply overwhelmed and unable to regulate themselves. Indeed, both disagreeableness and emotionality were similarly positively related to internalizing scales in preschoolers (De Pauw, Mervielde, & Van Leeuwen, 2009). Additionally, youth high in both victimization and perpetration of bullying (i.e., "bully-victims") are at high risk for internalizing problems (Reijntjes, Kamphuis, Prinzie, & Telch, 2010). This combination of poor self-regulation and distress implies that high levels of observed antagonism may serve as a reliable marker for levels of internalizing problems that may not be readily available to outside observers.

Externalizing problems. In youth, externalizing problems are defined as those related to aggression, conduct problems, rule-breaking, and disruptive behaviors. Youth high in externalizing problems are characterized by a pattern of high N, low C, and especially low A (Tackett, Kushner et al., 2013). The strong negative associations of youth externalizing problems with A and C were also found in a meta-analysis connecting personality to clinical symptoms (Malouff et al., 2005). Using a personality pathology model to better understand the personality content of externalizing problems in a sample with a wide age range (6–18) indicated that both Disagreeableness and Emotional Instability are strongly related to the general externalizing factor, as well as to a specific aggression subfactor (Tackett, Herzhoff, Reardon, De Clercq, & Sharp, 2014). Antagonistic behaviors are among the first to get attention from adults, as they are often the most disruptive (e.g., in a classroom environment). Additionally, the comorbidity of Oppositional Defiant Disorder with other externalizing disorders is accounted for by disinhibition (e.g., low C and A; Herzhoff, Smack, Reardon, Martel, & Tackett, 2017). The presence of high levels of antagonism, even at very young ages, may serve as a risk for difficult interpersonal relationships with peers, parents, and teachers, which may in turn evoke more antagonistic behaviors. Thus high levels of antagonism should be viewed as a stable risk factor for externalizing forms of psychopathology.

Axis II disorders

Although there is mounting evidence that personality pathology traits in youth are reliably measured and as stable as in adults, personality disorder diagnoses are severely understudied and underdiagnosed prior to adulthood (Conway, Tackett, & Skodol, 2017; Tackett, Balsis, Oltmanns, & Krueger, 2009). Working models of the development of Cluster B personality disorders, particularly borderline, narcissistic, and antisocial personality disorder, have emerged, and they each highlight the critical importance of trait antagonism (Barry, Pickard, & Ansel, 2009; Beauchaine, Klein, Crowell, Derbidge, & Gatzke-Kopp, 2009; Widiger et al., 2009). Specifically, oppositional personality was found to be a core feature of borderline personality pathology (Ramos, Canta, de Castro, & Leal, 2014). Relatedly, many studies have found a strong relationship between antagonism and youth psychopathy or callous-unemotional (CU) traits (Assary, Salekin, & Barker, 2015; Lynam et al., 2005; Salekin, Debus, & Barker, 2010; Sherman, Lynam, & Heyde, 2014). Similarly, among youth with conduct problems, the presence of CU traits/psychopathy has been reliably detected as early as preschool (Graziano et al., 2016). Of the four factors represented in the youth model of personality pathology, Disagreeableness shows the strongest links to both externalizing problems and Cluster B personality disorders. This suggests that in youth, as in adults, antagonism may represent one of the most promising constructs for understanding links between personality pathology and psychopathology more broadly.

Relational aggression

Although not an official psychiatric diagnosis, relational aggression (intentionally damaging someone's social relationships through the use of social exclusion and manipulation; Crick, 1996) is a behavior that has been linked to externalizing problems and postulated as a risk factor for personality disorder (Crick, Murray-Close, & Woods, 2005; Tackett, Daoud, De Bolle, & Burt, 2013). In investigations of personality profiles of personality disorders in adults, low A was a cardinal feature of Cluster B disorders (Lynam & Widiger, 2001). Extending this personality trait profile to youth, an investigation of relational aggression found the most overlap with narcissistic personality disorder and antisocial personality disorder in the realm of low A (Reardon, Tackett, & Lynam, 2017). Specifically, investigations within the trait space of DIPSI Disagreeableness have highlighted the facets narcissistic traits, dominance-egocentrism, and hyperexpressive traits, all of which point to the centrality of antagonism for relational aggression (Tackett, Kushner, Herzhoff, Smack, & Reardon, 2014). In this way, relational aggression suggests itself as a potentially relevant construct for later personality disorder, and one that encapsulates many of the core features of trait antagonism, making it a construct deserving of further study in children and adolescents to understand its role in personality problems over time.

Taken together, the relationships between personality and internalizing problems, externalizing problems, personality disorders, and relational aggression make clear that trait antagonism is a relevant risk factor for these areas. Much work remains, however, to further understand what type of dysfunction is most likely given low A.

Researchers interested in the early detection and intervention of any of these problems (which may very well include almost all clinical psychologists) would do well to incorporate consideration of a developmentally appropriate approach to antagonism into their work.

Factors influencing the development of antagonism in youth

Although antagonism has been repeatedly connected to psychopathology, there are a wider array of psychosocial variables that should also be examined in connection with personality. A thorough understanding of antagonism's correlates will enrich our knowledge of the psychological content of this trait in youth. There are several different theoretical models detailing how personality and psychopathology may interact with one another across time, adapted from adult work (Tackett, 2006). The vulnerability model suggests that personality traits may make an individual more likely to develop psychopathology; in contrast, the scar model posits that experiences of psychopathology may leave lasting changes on an individual that may alter their later personality functioning. In a similar way, research has highlighted several early occurring life experiences as potential causal factors for the development of antagonism, which may then affect the development of other, later problematic outcomes. To understand antagonism from a developmental perspective, it is critical to evaluate what we know about how it develops, as these are complex and transactional processes.

Maltreatment. Child maltreatment is a risk factor for a host of problematic life outcomes, not least of which is the development of maladaptive patterns of personality functioning. A longitudinal assessment determined that youth who had been maltreated showed lower A, C, O, and higher N than nonmaltreated youth, and that this pattern was stable across childhood (Rogosch & Cicchetti, 2004). In addition, work on maltreated youth has shown that personality can serve as a mediator for the development of adolescent psychopathology, with particular emphasis on the role of behavioral undercontrol (i.e., poor self-regulation, or low A and C; Kim, Cicchetti, Rogosch, & Manly, 2009; Oshri, Rogosch, & Cicchetti, 2013). This emphasizes that, for youth who are maltreated, the emergence of antagonism may serve as a pathway through which they are placed at increased risk for later psychological problems.

Parenting. Parenting variables are incredibly important in shaping trajectories toward or away from problematic psychosocial outcomes. Specifically, harsh parenting and low parental warmth have been found to be a risk for the development of adjustment problems. Children who display dysregulated behavior are more likely to experience maladaptive parenting (Winsper, Hall, Strauss, & Wolke, 2017), and research shows that the reciprocal relationship between harsh punishment and borderline personality disorder symptoms is stable across time (Stepp et al., 2014). Children low on A showed the highest level of aggression in the context of negative parenting (Smack, Kushner, & Tackett, 2015), and youth low on A were the only ones to show a relationship between psychologically controlling parenting and problem behaviors (Mabbe, Soenens, Vansteenkiste, & Van Leeuwen, 2016). These findings indicate that trait antagonism plays a critical role in moderating the relationship between harsh parenting and psychological problems.

Socioeconomic status. As with parenting and maltreatment variables, low socioeconomic status (SES) has been identified as a risk factor for many different deleterious outcomes. In particular, it has been shown that low SES leads to a harsher family environment, which in turn leads to poorer self-control (Hostinar, Ross, Chen, & Miller, 2015). Similarly, it has been found that lower lifetime SES is associated with higher N and lower C, indicating again the role of poverty as a causal factor for potentially maladaptive personality patterns (Jonassaint, Siegler, Barefoot, Edwards, & Williams, 2011). In a low SES school context, A moderates the relationship between school poverty and educational attainment, such that antagonistic youth have poorer outcomes than their more agreeable peers, but only in schools with high levels of poverty (Nieuwenhuis, 2018). These results make it clear that poverty, both on the family and school level, can serve as a factor influencing the development of antagonism, and provide a context in which high levels of antagonism are more likely to lead to negative outcomes.

In sum, evaluating the various factors that set the stage for high levels of antagonism to cause problems is important because it aids our understanding of where this potentially maladaptive trait may come from, and it guides our thinking around early identification and intervention. Because personality disorders in adults are often regarded as difficult to treat, great emphasis has been placed on the importance of early detection and disruption of the pathways to deeply entrenched patterns of maladaptive behaviors. To do this successfully, it is important that we identify those individuals at highest risk for exhibiting high levels of trait antagonism, and understanding more about the pathways that shaped their dispositions. Such sociocultural factors as maltreatment, parenting, and low SES present themselves as salient targets for prevention of the development of maladaptive patterns of personality functioning.

Conclusion

Overall, this chapter has illustrated that viewing antagonism from a developmental perspective provides a more well-rounded picture of the trait and its concomitants. It also reveals that antagonism is a complex trait that, before adulthood, shares connections with low A, low C, and high N. Despite its complexity and relationships to various FFM domains, it is also stable enough to measure over time. This means that we should attend to its patterns of change over time and continue to enrich our understanding of those factors that may serve as mechanisms of adaptive personality change (i.e., those things that can ameliorate early patterns of trait antagonism). Because of antagonism's robust connections to broad forms of psychopathology in youth, including internalizing and externalizing problems as well as personality pathology, identifying and monitoring this trait's development early in life will lead to targets for effective interventions. Relatedly, focusing further research attention on those contextual factors that have been found to create risk for antagonism to cause problems, including parenting and SES, will improve our ability to identify vulnerable individuals and hopefully, promote more adaptive developmental trajectories.

References

Abe, J. A. A. (2005). The predictive validity of the Five-Factor Model of personality with preschool age children: a nine-year follow-up study. *Journal of Research in Personality, 39*, 423–442.

Assary, E., Salekin, T., & Barker, E. D. (2015). Big-Five and callous-unemotional traits in preschoolers. *Journal of Psychopathology and Behavioral Assessment, 37*, 371–379.

Barry, C. T., Pickard, J. D., & Ansel, L. L. (2009). The associations of adolescent invulnerability and narcissism with problem behaviors. *Personality and Individual Differences, 47*, 577–582.

Beauchaine, T. P., Klein, D. N., Crowell, S. E., Derbidge, C., & Gatzke-Kopp, L. (2009). Multifinality in the development of personality disorders: a biology × sex × environment interaction model of antisocial and borderline traits. *Development and Psychopathology, 21*, 735–770.

Caspi, A., Roberts, B. W., & Shiner, R. L. (2005). Personality development: stability and change. *Annual Review of Psychology, 56*, 453–484.

Conway, C. C., Tackett, J. L., & Skodol, A. E. (2017). Are personality disorders assessed in young people? *American Journal of Psychiatry, 174*, 1000–1001.

Crick, N. R. (1996). The role of overt aggression, relational aggression, and prosocial behavior in the prediction of children's future social adjustment. *Child Development, 67*, 2317–2327.

Crick, N. R., Murray-Close, D., & Woods, K. (2005). Borderline personality features in childhood: a short-term longitudinal study. *Development and Psychopathology, 17*, 1051–1070.

De Clercq, B., Aelterman, N., De Pauw, S., De Bolle, M., Decuyper, M., & Tackett, J. L. (2010). Delineating childhood Autism Spectrum symptoms from a maladaptive trait perspective. *Journal of Psychopathology and Behavioral Assessment, 32*, 529–536.

De Clercq, B., & De Fruyt, F. (2012). A Five-Factor Model framework for understanding childhood personality disorder antecedents: childhood personality pathology and FFM. *Journal of Personality, 80*, 1533–1563.

De Clercq, B., De Fruyt, F., De Bolle, M., Van Hiel, A., Markon, K. E., & Krueger, R. F. (2014). The hierarchical structure and construct validity of the PID-5 trait measure in adolescence: DSM-5 trait structure in adolescents. *Journal of Personality, 82*, 158–169.

De Clercq, B., De Fruyt, F., Van Leeuwen, K., & Mervielde, I. (2006). The structure of maladaptive personality traits in childhood: a step toward an integrative developmental perspective for DSM-V. *Journal of Abnormal Psychology, 115*, 639–657.

De Clercq, B., van Leeuwen, K., van den Noortgate, W., de Bolle, M., & de Fruyt, F. (2009). Childhood personality pathology: dimensional stability and change. *Development and Psychopathology, 21*, 853–869.

De Fruyt, F., Mervielde, I., Hoekstra, H. A., & Rolland, J. P. (2000). Assessing adolescents' personality with the NEO PI-R. *Assessment, 7*, 329–345.

De Pauw, S. (2017). Childhood personality and temperament. In *The Oxford handbook of the Five Factor Model* (pp. 243–280). New York: Oxford University Press.

De Pauw, S. S. W., Mervielde, I., & Van Leeuwen, K. G. (2009). How are traits related to problem behavior in preschoolers? Similarities and contrasts between temperament and personality. *Journal of Abnormal Child Psychology, 37*, 309–325.

Graziano, P. A., Ros, R., Haas, S., Hart, K., Slavec, J., Waschbusch, D., et al. (2016). Assessing callous-unemotional traits in preschool children with disruptive behavior problems using peer reports. *Journal of Clinical Child & Adolescent Psychology, 45*, 201–214.

Halverson, C. F., Havill, V. L., Deal, J., Baker, S. R., Victor, J. B., Pavlopoulos, V., et al. (2003). Personality structure as derived from parental ratings of free descriptions of children: the Inventory of Child Individual Differences. *Journal of Personality*, *71*, 995–1026.

Herzhoff, K., Smack, A. J., Reardon, K. W., Martel, M. M., & Tackett, J. L. (2017). Child personality accounts for oppositional defiant disorder comorbidity patterns. *Journal of Abnormal Child Psychology*, *45*, 327–335.

Herzhoff, K., & Tackett, J. L. (2012). Establishing construct validity for openness-to-experience in middle childhood: contributions from personality and temperament. *Journal of Research in Personality*, *46*, 286–294.

Hostinar, C. E., Ross, K. M., Chen, E., & Miller, G. E. (2015). Modeling the association between lifecourse socioeconomic disadvantage and systemic inflammation in healthy adults: the role of self-control. *Health Psychology*, *34*, 580–590.

John, O. P., & Srivastava, S. (1999). The Big Five trait taxonomy: history, measurement, and theoretical perspectives. In *Handbook of personality: Theory and research* (pp. 102–138). (2nd ed.). New York: Guilford.

Jonassaint, C. R., Siegler, I. C., Barefoot, J. C., Edwards, C. L., & Williams, R. B. (2011). Low life course socioeconomic status (SES) is associated with negative NEO PI-R personality patterns. *International Journal of Behavioral Medicine*, *18*, 13–21.

Kim, J., Cicchetti, D., Rogosch, F. A., & Manly, J. T. (2009). Child maltreatment and trajectories of personality and behavioral functioning: implications for the development of personality disorder. *Development and Psychopathology*, *21*, 889.

Kushner, S. C., Tackett, J. L., & Bagby, R. M. (2012). The structure of internalizing disorders in middle childhood and evidence for personality correlates. *Journal of Psychopathology and Behavioral Assessment*, *34*, 22–34.

Kushner, S. C., Tackett, J. L., & De Clercq, B. (2013). The joint hierarchical structure of adolescent personality pathology: converging evidence from two approaches to measurement. *Journal of the Canadian Academy of Child and Adolescent Psychiatry*, *22*, 199–205.

Laursen, B., Hafen, C. A., Rubin, K. H., Booth-LaForce, C., & Rose-Krasnor, L. (2010). The distinctive difficulties of disagreeable youth. *Merrill-Palmer Quarterly*, *56*, 80–103.

Lynam, D. R., Caspi, A., Moffitt, T. E., Raine, A., Loeber, R., & Stouthamer-Loeber, M. (2005). Adolescent psychopathy and the Big Five: results from two samples. *Journal of Abnormal Child Psychology*, *33*, 431–443.

Lynam, D. R., & Widiger, T. A. (2001). Using the Five-Factor Model to represent the DSM-IV personality disorders: an expert consensus approach. *Journal of Abnormal Psychology*, *110*, 401.

Mabbe, E., Soenens, B., Vansteenkiste, M., & Van Leeuwen, K. (2016). Do personality traits moderate relations between psychologically controlling parenting and problem behavior in adolescents? Controlling parenting and personality. *Journal of Personality*, *84*, 381–392.

Malouff, J. M., Thorsteinsson, E. B., & Schutte, N. S. (2005). The relationship between the Five-Factor Model of personality and symptoms of clinical disorders: a meta-analysis. *Journal of Psychopathology and Behavioral Assessment*, *27*, 101–114.

Markon, K. E. (2009). Hierarchies in the structure of personality traits. *Social and Personality Psychology Compass*, *3*, 812–826.

Markon, K. E., Krueger, R. F., & Watson, D. (2005). Delineating the structure of normal and abnormal personality: an integrative hierarchical approach. *Journal of Personality and Social Psychology*, *88*, 139–157.

Martel, M. M., Goth-Owens, T., Martinez-Torteya, C., & Nigg, J. T. (2010). A person-centered personality approach to heterogeneity in attention-deficit/hyperactivity disorder (ADHD). *Journal of Abnormal Psychology*, *119*, 186–196.

Mervielde, I., & De Fruyt, F. (1999). Construction of the Hierarchical Personality Inventory for Children (HiPIC). In: I. Mervielde, I. Deary, F. De Fruyt, & F. Ostendorf (Eds.), *Personality psychology in Europe. Proceedings of the eight European conference on personality psychology*, Tilburg: Tilburg University Press, pp. 107–127.

Nieuwenhuis, J. (2018). The interaction between school poverty and agreeableness in predicting educational attainment. *Personality and Individual Differences, 127*, 85–88.

Oshri, A., Rogosch, F. A., & Cicchetti, D. (2013). Child maltreatment and mediating influences of childhood personality types on the development of adolescent psychopathology. *Journal of Clinical Child & Adolescent Psychology, 42*, 287–301.

Ramos, V., Canta, G., de Castro, F., & Leal, I. (2014). Discrete subgroups of adolescents diagnosed with borderline personality disorder: a latent class analysis of personality features. *Journal of Personality Disorders, 28*, 463–482.

Reardon, K. W., Tackett, J. L., & Lynam, D. (2017). The personality context of relational aggression: a Five-Factor Model profile analysis. *Personality Disorders: Theory, Research, and Treatment*. https://doi.org/10.1037/per0000231.

Reijntjes, A., Kamphuis, J. H., Prinzie, P., & Telch, M. J. (2010). Peer victimization and internalizing problems in children: a meta-analysis of longitudinal studies. *Child Abuse & Neglect, 34*, 244–252.

Roberts, B. W., & DelVecchio, W. F. (2000). The rank-order consistency of personality traits from childhood to old age: a quantitative review of longitudinal studies. *Psychological Bulletin, 126*, 3–25.

Roberts, B. W., Walton, K. E., & Viechtbauer, W. (2006). Patterns of mean-level change in personality traits across the life course: a meta-analysis of longitudinal studies. *Psychological Bulletin, 132*, 1–25.

Rogosch, F. A., & Cicchetti, D. (2004). Child maltreatment and emergent personality organization: perspectives from the five-factor model. *Journal of Abnormal Child Psychology, 32*, 123–145.

Salekin, R. T., Debus, S. A., & Barker, E. D. (2010). Adolescent psychopathy and the Five Factor Model: domain and facet analysis. *Journal of Psychopathology and Behavioral Assessment, 32*, 501–514.

Sherman, E. D., Lynam, D. R., & Heyde, B. (2014). Agreeableness accounts for the factor structure of the Youth Psychopathic Traits Inventory. *Journal of Personality Disorders, 28*, 262–280.

Shiner, R. L. (2005). A developmental perspective on personality disorders: lessons from research on normal personality development in childhood and adolescence. *Journal of Personality Disorders, 19*, 202–210.

Shiner, R. L. (2009). The development of personality disorders: perspectives from normal personality development in childhood and adolescence. *Development and Psychopathology, 21*, 715–734.

Slobodskaya, H. R. (2011). Two superordinate personality factors in childhood. *European Journal of Personality, 25*, 453–464.

Smack, A. J., Kushner, S. C., & Tackett, J. L. (2015). Child personality moderates associations between parenting and relational and physical aggression. *Journal of Aggression, Maltreatment & Trauma, 24*, 845–862.

Soto, C. J., John, O. P., Gosling, S. D., & Potter, J. (2011). Age differences in personality traits from 10 to 65: Big Five domains and facets in a large cross-sectional sample. *Journal of Personality and Social Psychology, 100*, 330–348.

Soto, C. J., & Tackett, J. L. (2015). Personality traits in childhood and adolescence: structure, development, and outcomes. *Current Directions in Psychological Science, 24*, 358–362.

Stepp, S. D., Whalen, D. J., Scott, L. N., Zalewski, M., Loeber, R., & Hipwell, A. E. (2014). Reciprocal effects of parenting and borderline personality disorder symptoms in adolescent girls. *Development and Psychopathology*, *26*, 361–378.

Stringaris, A., Maughan, B., Copeland, W. S., Costello, E. J., & Angold, A. (2013). Irritable mood as a symptom of depression in youth: prevalence, developmental, and clinical correlates in the Great Smoky Mountains Study. *Journal of the American Academy of Child & Adolescent Psychiatry*, *52*, 831–840.

Suzuki, T., Samuel, D. B., Pahlen, S., & Krueger, R. F. (2015). DSM-5 alternative personality disorder model traits as maladaptive extreme variants of the Five-Factor Model: an item-response theory analysis. *Journal of Abnormal Psychology*, *124*, 343–354.

Tackett, J. L. (2006). Evaluating models of the personality–psychopathology relationship in children and adolescents. *Clinical Psychology Review*, *26*, 584–599.

Tackett, J. L., Balsis, S., Oltmanns, T. F., & Krueger, R. F. (2009). A unifying perspective on personality pathology across the life span: developmental considerations for the fifth edition of the Diagnostic and Statistical Manual of Mental Disorders. *Development and Psychopathology*, *21*, 687.

Tackett, J. L., Daoud, S. L. S. B., De Bolle, M., & Burt, S. A. (2013). Is relational aggression part of the externalizing spectrum? A bifactor model of youth antisocial behavior. *Aggressive Behavior*, *39*, 149–159.

Tackett, J. L., Herzhoff, K., Reardon, K. W., De Clercq, B., & Sharp, C. (2014). The externalizing spectrum in youth: incorporating personality pathology. *Journal of Adolescence*, *37*, 659–668.

Tackett, J. L., Kushner, S. C., De Fruyt, F., & Mervielde, I. (2013). Delineating personality traits in childhood and adolescence: associations across measures, temperament, and behavioral problems. *Assessment*, *20*, 738–751.

Tackett, J. L., Kushner, S. C., Herzhoff, K., Smack, A. J., & Reardon, K. W. (2014). Viewing relational aggression through multiple lenses: temperament, personality, and personality pathology. *Development and Psychopathology*, *26*, 863–877.

Tackett, J. L., Quilty, L. C., Sellbom, M., Rector, N. A., & Bagby, R. M. (2008). Additional evidence for a quantitative hierarchical model of mood and anxiety disorders for DSM-V: the context of personality structure. *Journal of Abnormal Psychology*, *117*, 812–825.

Tackett, J. L., Silberschmidt, A. L., Krueger, R. F., & Sponheim, S. R. (2008). A dimensional model of personality disorder: incorporating DSM Cluster A characteristics. *Journal of Abnormal Psychology*, *117*, 454–459.

Tackett, J. L., Slobodskaya, H. R., Mar, R. A., Deal, J., Halverson, C. F., Baker, S. R., et al. (2012). The hierarchical structure of childhood personality in five countries: Continuity from early childhood to early adolescence. *Journal of Personality*, *80*, 847–879.

Verbeke, L., & De Clercq, B. (2014). Integrating oddity traits in a dimensional model for personality pathology precursors. *Journal of Abnormal Psychology*, *123*, 598–612.

Widiger, T. A., De Clercq, B., & De Fruyt, F. (2009). Childhood antecedents of personality disorder: an alternative perspective. *Development and Psychopathology*, *21*, 771–791.

Winsper, C., Hall, J., Strauss, V. Y., & Wolke, D. (2017). Aetiological pathways to borderline personality disorder symptoms in early adolescence: childhood dysregulated behaviour, maladaptive parenting and bully victimisation. *Borderline Personality Disorder and Emotion Dysregulation*, *4*. https://doi.org/10.1186/s40479-017-0060-x.

Wright, A. G. C., Thomas, K. M., Hopwood, C. J., Markon, K. E., Pincus, A. L., & Krueger, R. F. (2012). The hierarchical structure of DSM-5 pathological personality traits. *Journal of Abnormal Psychology*, *121*, 951–957.

The structure of antagonism

4

Michael L. Crowe, Donald R. Lynam†, Joshua D. Miller**
*Department of Psychology, University of Georgia, Athens, GA, United States, †Department of Psychological Sciences, Purdue University, West Lafayette, IN, United States

Trait taxonomies are central to progress in personality science as they provide models to systematically organize the breadth of findings in the field (John & Srivastava, 1999). Agreeableness is a domain within the most widely known personality taxonomy, the Big Five (B5)/Five-Factor Model (FFM), which also includes Neuroticism, Extraversion, Openness to Experience, and Conscientiousness. A general consensus has been reached regarding the content at this level of personality (Digman, 1990; John, Naumann, & Soto, 2008; John & Srivastava, 1999; cf., Ashton et al., 2004). However, there is disagreement on how best to organize more specific components of personality within these domains.

Much of the previous personality research has been limited to analyses conducted at the domain level, but heterogeneity within each domain and across measures of the same domain make interpretation and theory development from such research difficult (Smith, McCarthy, & Zapolski, 2009). Trait Agreeableness is composed of a number of personality facets and the strength of findings at the domain level may vary across the lower order scales. For example, in a meta-analysis of personality and antisocial behavior, the Agreeableness facets of straightforwardness and compliance were identified as better predictors of antisocial behavior than trust and tender-mindedness (Jones, Miller, & Lynam, 2011). Miller, Gaughan, Maples, and Price (2011) demonstrated that relations between Agreeableness and several criteria differed as a function of whether Agreeableness was assessed using the Big Five Inventory (BFI; John, Donahue, & Kentle, 1991) or the Revised Neuroticism-Extraversion-Openness Personality Inventory (NEO PI-R; Costa & McCrae, 1992a, 1992b). Specifically, they found the NEO PI-R Agreeableness measure was more strongly related to scales assessing honesty, humility, narcissism, and psychopathy, most likely due to the explicit inclusion of facets assessing straightforwardness and modesty.

To understand these differences, facet-level models and analyses are necessary. Such models have been included in many personality taxonomies, but these have typically been rationally (rather than empirically) identified; the absence of an empirically derived facet-level structure has contributed to disagreements on facet-level content. The need for empirically derived facet-level models has driven research within other major personality domains. Watson, Stasik, Ellickson-Larew, and Stanton (2015) used Extraversion subscales to empirically identify four lower level facets. Similarly, Roberts, Chernyshenko, Stark, and Goldberg (2005) used 36 scales conceptually related to Conscientiousness to identify six facets of the domain. This chapter will review the development of a comprehensive, empirically based model of the facets that define Agreeableness.

The Handbook of Antagonism. https://doi.org/10.1016/B978-0-12-814627-9.00004-9

Models (and measures) of Agreeableness

Research is needed to empirically identify the structure underlying the Agreeableness domain (Graziano & Tobin, 2017). Not only is there no consensual lower order structure, but most of what there is has focused on a two-level model in which a domain, representing the broadest conceptualization of the latent trait, is composed of multiple specific facets at the lower level.

Currently, only two models of Agreeableness identify factors at an intermediate level of specificity. DeYoung, Quilty, and Peterson (2007) identified two mid-range factors in the Big Five Aspects Scales (BFAS) and showed that there is value in analysis at an intermediate bandwidth. In the BFAS, Agreeableness is broken down into two "aspects": Compassion (i.e., interpersonal warmth, sympathy, tenderness) and Politeness (i.e., cooperativeness, compliance, straightforwardness). A recent revision of the commonly used Big Five Inventory (BFI; John et al., 1991), the BFI-2, also allows for analysis at a mid-range of specificity. The BFI-2 represents Agreeableness with three factors: Compassion, Respectfulness, and Trust (Soto & John, 2017). However, the BFAS and BFI-2 represent an exception to the norm, which overwhelmingly characterize Agreeableness at a broad domain level and a precise facet level. One only needs to compare the facet structures of the major Agreeableness models to see that there is not a consensual lower order structure of the domain. Here we discuss them in order of number of facets identified starting with the fewest.

The BFI, the precursor of the BFI-2 (Soto & John, 2017), is perhaps the most popular measure of the B5 and was developed using the lexical approach. Two facets of Agreeableness (Altruism and Compliance) have been identified within the BFI (Soto & John, 2009). These were developed to be congruent with the NEO PI-R facets of the same name. Lexical analyses have been used in an attempt to identify additional facets of the "Big Five" (Perugini & Gallucci, 1997; Saucier & Ostendorf, 1999). Saucier and Ostendorf (1999) identified four facets including Warmth-Affection, Gentleness, Generosity, and Modesty-Humility. Perugini and Gallucci (1997) identified five Agreeableness facets labeled Sympathy, Tender-mindedness, Friendliness, Overbearance, and Hostility. In general, however, these facets are seldom used in research employing the BFI, which is typically utilized to measure only the B5 domains.

The Faceted Inventory of the Five-Factor Model (FI-FFM; Simms, 2009) identified facets of the FFM through a construct validation approach (Simms & Watson, 2007), which includes empirical analysis of a rationally derived item pool. The FI-FFM has been less extensively used and validated than other B5/FFM assessments, but it has been successfully used in a number of studies (Naragon-Gainey, Watson, & Markon, 2009; Watson et al., 2015; Watson, Stasik, Ro, & Clark, 2013). The FI-FFM identified the following four facets of Agreeableness: Empathy (prosocial, pleasant, sensitive to the needs of others), Trust vs Cynicism (belief in the goodness of others and willingness to trust), Straightforwardness vs Manipulativeness (willingness to take advantage of or manipulate others to get ahead), and Modesty (modesty, humility).

Agreeableness, as measured by the predominant measure of the FFM, the Revised NEO Personality Inventory (NEO PI-R; Costa & McCrae, 1992a, 1992b) includes six facets identified rationally through an examination of previous literature (Costa, McCrae, & Dye, 1991). The facets were labeled Trust (the belief in the sincerity and good intentions of others), Straightforwardness (sincerity and unwillingness to manipulate others), Altruism (concern for the welfare of others), Compliance (willingness to cooperate with others, ability to inhibit aggression and forgive others when faced with a potential conflict), Modesty (humility), and Tender-mindedness (attitude of sympathy for others).

The HEXACO (Lee & Ashton, 2004) conceptualization of Agreeableness originated from more recent lexical studies in which six (rather than five) lexical factors emerge (Ashton et al., 2004; Saucier, 2009). In the HEXACO, the variance of the Agreeableness domain (as defined by Big Five/FFM) is spread across Honesty/Humility and Agreeableness factors (see Ashton, Lee, & de Vries, 2014 for a more thorough review). Facets of these domains were identified through an examination of item content (Lee & Ashton, 2004). The facets of Honesty/Humility are labeled Sincerity (interpersonally genuine, unwillingness to manipulate others), Fairness (unwillingness to cheat or take advantage of others to get ahead), Greed Avoidance (uninterested or unmotivated by possession of wealth or status symbols), and Modesty (unassuming, no desire for special treatment). The facets of Agreeableness are Forgivingness (trust and liking toward others, even after mistreatment), Gentleness (interpersonal lenience or reluctance to judge others harshly), Flexibility (willingness to compromise and cooperate), and Patience (interpersonally imperturbable or high threshold for anger). HEXACO Agreeableness does not include altruism, a facet that is primary to many other agreeableness models (John et al., 2008), as lexical analyses suggest that the factor has significant associations with multiple domains (i.e., Honesty-Humility, Agreeableness, and Emotionality). The HEXACO-PI-R includes an "interstitial" altruism scale intended to assess traits of sympathy and soft-heartedness (Lee & Ashton, 2006).

These conceptualizations of Agreeableness are difficult to integrate. There are common elements across many of them (e.g., sympathy for others, moral behavior, tendency toward cooperation), but some facets are unique to single measures (e.g., greed avoidance). More importantly, given concerns related to the jingle-jangle fallacy (e.g., Block, 1995), one cannot assume that similarly named facets measure the same construct, nor can one assume that facets with different labels measure substantively different constructs. Such uncertainties highlight the need for a comprehensive empirical investigation of the structure of Agreeableness.

Goldberg (2006) offered a methodology (i.e., the "Bass-Ackward" approach) allowing a model of personality to be studied at a range of intermediate levels of factor specificity. In this approach, factor analyses are used to extract one to any number of factors while saving factor scores from each analysis. The relationship among the factor scores across successive solutions reveals a map of factor emergence from broad domain, to intermediate construct, to specific facet. The approach allows for exploration of the intermediate facet space while accommodating and organizing previously developed facet-level models. An investigation of Agreeableness was conducted using this methodology to empirically identify the lower-level structure of the Agreeableness domain (Crowe, Lynam, & Miller, 2018). In the remainder of this chapter, we detail the methodology and findings from this study and their implications for the assessment and study of this personality domain. An important difference between the analyses of Agreeableness and those of Extraversion and Conscientiousness is that in both previous cases the research was conducted by factor analyzing scale (rather than item) scores (Roberts et al., 2005; Watson et al., 2015). A potential limitation of this scale-level approach is problems arising from item parceling (Marsh, Lüdtke, Nagengast, Morin, & Von Davier, 2013). According to Marsh et al. (2013), parcels are appropriate only when they are unidimensional and lack high cross-loadings, requirements unlikely to be met in this case. Crowe et al. (2018) conducted all analyses at the item level to avoid the risk of item parceling effects, maximize the flexibility of the potential factor structure, and increase the likelihood of identifying a stable lower order structure.

Empirical identification of Agreeableness facets

Participants ($N = 1205$; 73% female; 84% White; M age $= 35.5$, $SD = 17.26$) recruited through Amazon's Mechanical Turk (MTurk; see Miller, Crowe, Weiss, Maples-Keller, & Lynam, 2017) completed 131 Agreeableness items from 22 different scales measuring rationally derived facets of Agreeableness (Crowe et al., 2018). All items were presented in a random order to participants, who rated their agreement with each item on a 1 (*Strongly disagree*) to 5 (*Strongly agree*) scale. The strength of the factor-analytic approach rests on the assumption that all relevant aspects of the Agreeableness domain are represented in the pool of items used. With this in mind, items were sampled from the most commonly used measures of Agreeableness and related traits (e.g., Honesty-Humility). All Agreeableness scales from the following measures were included: Big Five Inventory (BFI; John et al., 1991); Big Five Aspects Scale (BFAS; DeYoung et al., 2007); Faceted Inventory of the Five-Factor Model (FI-FFM; Simms, 2009); HEXACO-PI-R (Honesty-Humility, Agreeableness, and the Altruism interstitial scale were included; Lee & Ashton, 2006), International Personality Item Pool NEO PI-R (IPIP NEO PI-R; Goldberg et al., 2006; Maples, Guan, Carter, & Miller, 2014). All Agreeableness items were correlated with one another to identify duplicate items. Twenty item pairs were identified with correlations >.65 and 18 items were removed to eliminate item redundancy. A principal factors analysis was conducted to identify items which loaded poorly (i.e., <.30) on the Agreeableness domain. The nine identified items were removed for being unrepresentative of the general Agreeableness factor (Osborne, Costello, & Kellow, 2008). The final item pool consisted of 104 Agreeableness items, which were used to represent the domain as it is currently conceptualized in the literature.

The hierarchical structure of Agreeableness was evaluated using a Principal Axis factoring method with promax rotation. A promax rotation deviates from the orthogonal rotation described by Goldberg (2006) but is appropriate given the interrelated content of the Agreeableness domain. An eight-factor solution was identified as the maximum number of unique factors; when the nine-factor solution was evaluated, no items had their primary loading on one of the nine factors. After evaluating each of the solutions, the Five-Factor Model was selected as the final stage of the proposed hierarchy. Factors that emerged in later solutions were composed of overly specific content. Factor scores from the principal factors solutions were compared to those derived with maximum-likelihood (ML) estimation (see Saucier, 2003, for similar method). The one-factor through five-factor solutions proved to be highly robust to different factor-analytic techniques as each of the principal axis factor scores had near perfect correspondence with factors derived through ML estimation. Each of the factors through the five-factor solution also had interpretable content with generally high loadings and both positively and negatively keyed items. Further analyses were conducted to evaluate the effect of acquiescence (i.e., inflated correlations among similarly keyed items) on the identified factor structure (see Soto, John, Gosling, & Potter, 2008 for a description of the approach used). All factor solutions were nearly identical after controlling for acquiescence. The factors at all levels of the hierarchy were correlated with existing Agreeableness scales and relevant external criterion variables (e.g., the remaining BFI domains).

Observed hierarchy of Agreeableness

The "Bass-ackward" analysis revealed the sequential emergence of five stable Agreeableness[1] factors (see Fig. 1 for factor score correlations across solutions). The first unrotated factor was representative of all included domain-level Agreeableness scales. The two-factor solution revealed constructs consistent with DeYoung and colleagues' Agreeableness "aspects" (2007). Compassion (vs Callousness; 2.1) emerged as a homogeneous factor that remained stable through all factor solutions. The second factor at this level was a heterogeneous construct labeled Civility (vs Incivility; 2.2) from which all other facets emerged. The three-factor solution yielded the second stable factor to emerge, Trust (vs Distrust; 3.3). Compassion (3.1) and Civility (3.2) were highly consistent with their previous counterparts (2.1 and 2.2 respectively) indicating that Trust (3.3) exists largely independent of the previous two factors. The emergence of a trust-related factor at this stage of the analysis resulted in a three-factor solution largely consistent with that of the BFI-2. In the four-factor solution, Civility (3.2) split into two factors, Morality (vs Immorality; 4.2) and Amiability (vs Rudeness; 4.4), yielding factors like those of the FI-FFM four-factor model. Morality (4.2) was homogeneous in item content and stable into the subsequent five-factor solution. Amiability (4.4) was the final heterogenous factor, which split into Affability (vs Combativeness; 5.4) and Modesty (vs Arrogance; 5.5) in the five-factor solution.

Example items for each factor in the final solution are presented in Table 1. Each of the five facets identified in the final solution of the analysis demonstrated substantial convergent validity with the overall Agreeableness domain. The five facets correlated between .65 (Trust; 5.3) and .86 (Compassion; 5.1) with the first unrotated Agreeableness factor (1.1). There do not appear to be any redundant factors. Correlations within

[1] Throughout our discussion of the observed structure of the Agreeableness domain numeric references ranging from 1.1 to 5.5 will be included when referring to particular facets of the domain. These references correspond to the labels for each of the factors presented in Fig. 1.

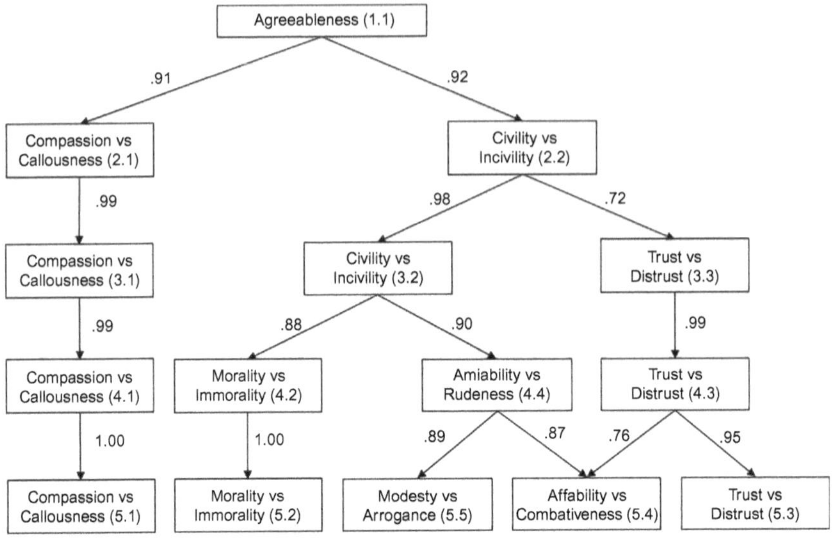

Fig. 1 Hierarchical structure of the Agreeableness domain. *Note.* Only correlations going from one level of the hierarchy to the next are identified. Correlations <.70 were removed. From Crowe, M. L., Lynam, D. R., & Miller, J. D. (2018). Uncovering the structure of agreeableness from self-report measures. *Journal of Personality, **86** (5), 771–787* with permission from Wiley Periodicals, Inc. Copyright © 2017.

Table 1 Example item content

Scale	Item	5.1	5.2	5.3	5.4	5.5
IPIPNEO	I am concerned about others.	**.78***	.30	.34	.37	.42
BFAS	I sympathize with others' feelings.	**.77***	.22	.33	.39	.40
BFAS	I can't be bothered with other's needs.	**.75***	.42	.34	.49	.37
FIFFM	I try to take others' feelings into account.	**.75***	.20	.34	.45	.46
BFAS	I like to do things for others.	**.73***	.22	.35	.32	.40
FIFFM	If I knew I wouldn't get caught, I'd be willing to break the law.	.32	**.65***	.27	.39	.23
IPIPNEO	I use flattery to get ahead.	.17	**.63***	.19	.34	.38
HEXACO	If I want something from someone, I will laugh at that person's worst jokes.	.19	**.62***	.18	.25	.31
IPIPNEO	I cheat to get ahead.	.43	**.61***	.18	.50	.35
BFAS	I take advantage of others.	.48	**.61***	.26	.52	.45
IPIPNEO	I distrust people.	.28	.27	**.70***	.33	.06

Table 1 Continued

FIFFM	I generally take people at their word.	.35	.18	**.69***	.29	.17
FIFFM	I have a hard time taking someone's word.	.28	.27	**.68***	.36	.11
BFI	I see myself as someone who is generally trusting.	.35	.16	**.66***	.31	.16
FIFFM	I think most people act in good faith.	.34	.19	**.64***	.26	.16
BFAS	I insult people.	.41	.46	.34	**.70***	.37
HEXACO	People think of me as someone who has a quick temper.	.30	.30	.35	**.69***	.37
BFI	I see myself as someone who is sometimes rude to others.	.38	.36	.32	**.69***	.32
BFI	I see myself as someone who starts quarrels with others.	.35	.40	.20	**.66***	.40
FIFFM	Some people see me as insensitive.	.56	.38	.40	**.64***	.33
FIFFM	I try to be modest about my accomplishments.	.38	.25	.18	.37	**.68***
FIFFM	I don't like to brag about my accomplishments.	.29	.26	.12	.31	**.68***
FIFFM	I'm not one to boast or brag.	.26	.22	.13	.31	**.63***
FIFFM	It is better to be modest and humble than to be proud and boastful.	.41	.27	.17	.35	**.62***
FIFFM	I like to show off whenever I can.	.30	.51	.11	.38	**.59***

Note. BFAS, Big Five Aspects Scale; *BFI*, Big Five Inventory; *FIFFM*, Faceted Inventory for the Five-Factor Model; *IPIPNEO*, International Personality Item Pool NEO Personality Inventory—Revised. For each factor, the five highest loading items that are in the table are in *bold* and *underlined*. An *asterisk* indicates that the item is among the five highest loading items for that factor.

the five-factor level ranged from .32 (Trust, 5.3; and Modesty, 5.5) to .57 (Compassion, 5.1; and Affability, 5.4) with a median association of .50. The five identified facets are quite similar to the six-facet model of the FFM, as operationalized by the NEO PI-R and IPIP NEO PI-R. NEO PI-R facets of Trust, Morality, Cooperation, and Modesty all have comparable factors in the empirically derived model. However, the empirical model suggests that a sixth facet is unnecessary as Altruism and Sympathy can be represented by a single factor. Along with being unidimensional in content, the five facets at this stage of analysis are nonredundant and they show some degree of discriminant validity in relation to the rest of the FFM and externalizing behaviors as measured by the Reactive and Proactive Aggression Questionnaire (RPAQ; Raine et al., 2006) and Crime and Analogous Behavior scale (CAB; Miller & Lynam, 2003). See Table 2 for correlations of empirically derived factor scores with existing Agreeableness measures and related criterion variables.

Table 2 Factor score correlations

	F5.1	F5.2	F5.3	F5.4	F5.5
BFI-A	.73[a]	.45[b]	.73[a]	.83[c]	.52[d]
NEO-A	.79[a]	.70[b]	.62[c]	.75[d]	.64[c]
Trust	.36[a]	.26[b]	**.82[c]**	.36[a]	.12[d]
Morality	.42[a]	**.86[b]**	.31[c]	.59[d]	.50[e]
Altruism	**.89[a]**	.38[b]	.46[c]	.57[d]	.46[c]
Cooperative	.44[a]	.57[b]	.43[a]	**.83[c]**	.47[a]
Modesty	.22[a]	.41[b]	.01[c]	.24[a]	**.55[d]**
Sympathy	**.83[a]**	.29[b]	.36[b]	.36[b]	.45[c]
HEX-A	.40[a]	.34[a]	.77[b]	.76[b]	.48[c]
Forgive	.25[a]	.20[a]	**.75[b]**	.39[c]	.23[a]
Gentle	.46[a]	.25[b]	**.65[c]**	**.66[c]**	**.54[d]**
Flexible	.30[a]	.34[a]	.50[b]	.60[c]	.34[a]
Patient	.24[a]	.24[a]	.48[b]	**.68[c]**	.39[d]
HEX-H	.43[a,c]	.82[b]	.37[a]	.45[c]	.64[d]
Sincerity	.21[a]	**.65[b]**	.23[a]	.26[a]	.40[c]
Fairness	.35[a]	**.70[b]**	.32[a,d]	.44[c]	.28[d]
Greed Avoidance	.21[a,c]	.47[b]	.26[a]	.19[c]	.48[b]
Modesty	.50[a]	.53[a]	.25[b]	.41[c]	**.76[d]**
HEX-Altruism	**.82[a]**	.45[b]	.42[b]	.58[c]	.48[b]
FIFFM-A	.74[a]	.70[a,c]	.73[a]	.79[b]	.66[c]
Empathy	**.94[a]**	.40[b]	**.51[c]**	.65[d]	.53[c]
Trust	.37[a]	.36[a]	**.87[b]**	.40[a]	.16[c]
Straightforward	.42[a]	**.82[b]**	.48[a]	**.70[c]**	.44[a]
Modesty	.50[a]	.48[a]	.24[b]	.58[c]	**.89[d]**
BFAS-A	.90[a]	.60[b]	.47[c]	.74[d]	.68[e]
Compassion	**.95[a]**	.41[b]	.42[b,d]	.55[c]	.49[c,d]
Politeness	.62[a]	**.68[b]**	.41[c]	**.79[d]**	**.73[e]**
IPC					
Love	.73[a]	.52[b]	.53[b]	.69[a]	.50[b]
Dominance	.12[a]	−.17[b]	.08[a]	−.09[c]	−.33[d]
BFI					
Neuroticism	−.06[a]	−.16[b]	−.37[c]	−.34[c]	−.08[a,b]
Extraversion	.22[a]	−.09[b]	.19[a]	.03[c]	−.23[d]
Openness	.30[a]	−.03[b]	.11[c]	.12[c]	.10[c]
Conscientiousness	.26[a,b]	.31[a]	.19[b]	.39[c]	.19[b]
Externalizing					
Proactive Aggression	−.30[a]	−.45[b]	−.19[c]	−.50[b]	−.33[a]
Reactive Aggression	−.13[a]	−.34[b]	−.34[b]	−.50[c]	−.17[a]
CAB-Drugs	.07[a]	−.21[b]	−.07[c,d]	−.10[c]	.02[a,d]
CAB-Crimes	−.10[a]	−.34[b]	−.16[a]	−.26[c]	−.11[a]

Note. IPC, Interpersonal Circumplex; *FFM*, Five-Factor Model. All correlations greater than $|r| = .074$ are significant at $P < .01$. At each factor level (i.e., F3.1, F3.2, F3.3), correlations in the same row with different superscripts are significantly different from one another at $P < .01$. Within the Agreeableness scale correlations, the five largest facet-level correlations for each factor are underlined and in bold.

Compassion vs *Callousness (5.1)*. The first factor in the five-factor solution is composed of items relating to concern for the feelings of others (e.g., "I am concerned about others"; "I sympathize with others' feelings") and was labeled Compassion due to its isomorphism ($r=.95$) with DeYoung et al.'s (2007) previously identified Compassion "aspect" related to emotional affiliation (e.g., warmth, sympathy). Compassion (5.1) emerged as a homogenous facet early in the analysis and was stable in content throughout. It is no surprise that such a factor would be one of the first to emerge as the item content represented by this facet is featured in nearly every major measure of the Agreeableness domain. Compassion (5.1) was strongly associated with scales assessing altruism (IPIP NEO PI-R, HEXACO), sympathy (IPIP NEO PI-R), and empathy (FI-FFM). Its strongest correlate was BFAS Compassion ($r=.95$).

Morality vs *Immorality (5.2)*. Morality is characterized by honest and moral interpersonal behaviors (e.g., "I would never accept a bribe, even if it were very large"), and (at the low end) interpersonal deceitfulness or willingness to manipulate others for personal gain (e.g., "If I knew I wouldn't get caught, I'd be willing to break the law"; "I use flattery to get ahead"). Its highest facet level correlations include facets of the HEXACO Honesty-Humility factor (Sincerity and Fairness), Straightforwardness (FI-FFM), and Politeness (BFAS). Its strongest single-scale predictor is the IPIP NEO PI-R Morality scale ($r=.86$).

Trust vs *Distrust (5.3)*. Trust is defined by both a willingness to trust others (e.g., "I generally take people at their word") and a willingness to forgive others when that trust has been broken ("I see myself as someone who has a forgiving nature"). Trust-related items represent a more unique factor as they have relatively modest associations with Compassion and Politeness as defined within the BFAS. This is consistent with the findings of DeYoung et al. (2007), who found that (NEO PI-R) Trust had loadings of only .42 on both (BFAS) Compassion and (BFAS) Politeness. It was, however, substantially correlated with Agreeableness-related dimensions and facets from other measures including facets from the HEXACO (i.e., Forgiveness and Gentleness), the FIFFM (i.e., Empathy and Trust), and IPIP NEO PI-R Trust. Its highest correlation was with FI-FFM Trust ($r=.87$).

Affability vs *Combativeness (5.4)*. Affability was composed of those items related to oppositional and confrontational behaviors (e.g., "I insult people"; "People think of me as someone who has a quick temper"). Its strongest correlates are measures of Cooperativeness (IPIP NEO PI-R), interpersonal leniency and patience (HEXACO Gentleness and Patience), Straightforwardness (FI-FFM), and Politeness (BFAS). Its strongest predictors are IPIP NEO PI-R Cooperativeness and BFI Agreeableness ($rs=.83$).

Modesty vs *Arrogance (5.5)*. Modesty (5.5) is composed of items related to vanity (e.g., "I like to show off whenever I can.") and humility (e.g., "I try to be modest about my accomplishments."). The most relevant scales include Modesty (IPIP NEO PI-R, HEXACO, FI-FFM), Gentleness (HEXACO), and Politeness (BFAS). The best single-scale predictor is the FI-FFM Modesty scale ($r=.89$).

Assessment implications

Facet-level distinctions are necessary to the extent that a single domain score fails to capture divergent facet-level associations with external constructs of interest. The empirically derived Agreeableness factor scores were correlated with a range of relevant criterion variables to identify where such intradomain divergence occurs (see Table 2). For instance, Crowe et al. (2018) report the first unrotated Agreeableness factor (1.1) manifested a null association with Dominance of the IAS (Wiggins, 1995). However, this null association obscured variable associations at the facet level. When Agreeableness is parsed into its component facets, Compassion, Trust, Morality, and Affability have a mixture of modest negative and positive associations whereas Modesty has a moderately sized negative association. This is consistent with the notion that immodesty/grandiosity may be a combination of low Agreeableness and high dominance (e.g., Crowe, Carter, Campbell, & Miller, 2016; Paulhus, 2001). Not surprisingly, when the facets were correlated with the remaining BFI domains (John et al., 1991), Extraversion's association with Agreeableness shows a pattern comparable to Dominance with facets of Compassion and Modesty demonstrating correlations of similar size but opposite directions. Significant facet-level variability was also observed in the magnitude of associations with measures of aggression. Facet-level correlations ranged from −.19 to −.50 and from −.13 to −.50 for proactive and reactive aggression, respectively. The data suggest that Affability (5.4) is particularly relevant for both forms of aggression, whereas Compassion (5.1) is more specifically relevant to proactive aggression and Trust (5.3) is more specifically relevant to reactive aggression. Such facet-level differences indicate the possibility of unique cognitive or motivational factors for the two types of aggressive behavior. It would be impossible to make such distinctions without facet-level analyses.

While facet-level measures of Agreeableness were developed through alternative means, many do a remarkable job of describing certain levels of the domain. Nearly all the common Agreeableness scales find counterparts within the various facets of the empirically derived model, although some parse the variance of the domain into smaller pieces than others. The BFAS seems to be largely congruent with the two-factor level, the BFI-2 has a structure comparable to the three-factor solution, the FI-FFM facets each have primary loadings on one factor at the four-facet level, and while Sympathy and Altruism do not split to become unique facets, the IPIP NEO PI-R-based representation includes primary indicators of each of the five facets identified in the final level of analyses. Interestingly, the two-factor level does not suggest an Honesty-Humility and Agreeableness split (both domains have stronger loadings on the Civility factor), both HEXACO domains can be found across different levels of the hierarchy, and the HEXACO's "interstitial" Altruism scale is among the primary indicators for the Compassion facet. Only two scales (HEXACO Greed Avoidance and Flexibility) failed to fall among the top five strongest indicators for any factor. This is likely a result of the narrowness and specificity of their scopes which have no counterparts in other popular measures of the Agreeableness domain.

Inherent to the approach taken here is the acknowledgment that variance within the Agreeableness domain can be parsed in any number of ways. While the most valuable approach will often be one that effectively balances parsimony with the goal of using narrow, unidimensional traits, there can be value to multidimensional constructs with broader bandwidths (Smith et al., 2009). Crowe et al. (2018) reveal several valid decompositions of the Agreeableness domain, all of which can be reasonably captured by one or more existing scales. The "ideal" way to measure Agreeableness can be guided by pragmatic decisions as to which level of factor specificity is most useful for the research question at hand.

Conclusions

With the importance of the Agreeableness domain well established, it is time for research to move beyond domain-level associations. Domain-only examinations are necessarily limited due to their tendency to obscure divergent facet-level relationships with outcomes of interest. While many facet-level models have been developed, none have been empirically derived through a comprehensive structural analysis of the domain. A recent analysis was conducted with this goal in mind using a comprehensive item pool of the most popular domain measures. Five unique homogenous facets were identified: Compassion vs Callousness, Morality vs Immorality, Modesty vs Arrogance, Affability vs Combativeness, Trust vs Distrust. Although there can be utility and value across a range of measurement specificity, most occasions call for increasingly specific personality measurements that allow for precise personality-based models. The identified model of Agreeableness represents an important step in the progression toward a comprehensive, flexible, and empirically informed conceptualization of the domain.

References

Ashton, M. C., Lee, K., & de Vries, R. E. (2014). The HEXACO honesty-humility, agreeableness, and emotionality factors: a review of research and theory. *Personality and Social Psychology Review*, *18*(2), 139–152.

Ashton, M. C., Lee, K., Perugini, M., Szarota, P., De Vries, R. E., Di Blas, L., et al. (2004). A six-factor structure of personality-descriptive adjectives: solutions from psycholexical studies in seven languages. *Journal of Personality and Social Psychology*, *86*(2), 356.

Block, J. (1995). Going beyond the five factors given: rejoinder to Costa and McCrae (1995) and Goldberg and Saucier (1995). *Psychological Bulletin*, *117*(2), 226–229.

Costa, P. T., & McCrae, R. R. (1992a). *Revised NEO Personality Inventory (NEO-PI-R) and NEO Five-Factor Inventory (NEOFFI) professional manual*. Lutz, FL: PAR, Inc.

Costa, P. T., & McCrae, R. R. (1992b). Normal personality assessment in clinical practice: the NEO Personality Inventory. *Psychological Assessment*, *4*(1), 5–13.

Costa, P. T., McCrae, R. R., & Dye, D. A. (1991). Facet scales for agreeableness and conscientiousness: a revision of the NEO personality inventory. *Personality and Individual Differences*, *12*(9), 887–898.

Crowe, M. L., Carter, N. T., Campbell, W. K., & Miller, J. D. (2016). Validation of the Narcissistic Grandiosity Scale and creation of reduced item variants. *Psychological Assessment, 28*(12), 1550–1560.

Crowe, M. L., Lynam, D. R., & Miller, J. D. (2018). Uncovering the structure of agreeableness from self-report measures. *Journal of Personality, 86*(5), 771–787.

DeYoung, C. G., Quilty, L. C., & Peterson, J. B. (2007). Between facets and domains: 10 aspects of the Big Five. *Journal of Personality and Social Psychology, 93*(5), 880–896.

Digman, J. M. (1990). Personality structure: emergence of the five-factor model. *Annual Review of Psychology, 41*(1), 417–440.

Goldberg, L. R. (2006). Doing it all bass-ackwards: the development of hierarchical factor structures from the top down. *Journal of Research in Personality, 40*(4), 347–358.

Goldberg, L. R., Johnson, J. A., Eber, H. W., Hogan, R., Ashton, M. C., Cloninger, C. R., et al. (2006). The international personality item pool and the future of public-domain personality measures. *Journal of Research in Personality, 40*(1), 84–96.

Graziano, W. G., & Tobin, R. M. (2017). Agreeableness and the Five-Factor Model. In T. A. Widiger (Ed.), *The Oxford handbook of the Five Factor Model* (pp. 105–132). New York, NY: Oxford University Press.

John, O. P., Donahue, E. M., & Kentle, R. L. (1991). *The big five inventory—Versions 4a and 54*. Berkeley, CA: University of California, Berkeley, Institute of Personality and Social Research.

John, O. P., Naumann, L. P., & Soto, C. J. (2008). Paradigm shift to the integrative big five trait taxonomy. O. P. John, R. W. Robins, & L. A. Pervin (Eds.), *Vol. 3. Handbook of personality: Theory and research* (pp. 114–158). New York, NY: Guilford Press.

John, O. P., & Srivastava, S. (1999). The Big Five trait taxonomy: History, measurement, and theoretical perspectives. L. A. Pervin & O. P. John (Eds.), *Vol. 2. Handbook of personality: Theory and research* (pp. 102–138). New York, NY: Guilford Press.

Jones, S. E., Miller, J. D., & Lynam, D. R. (2011). Personality, antisocial behavior, and aggression: a meta-analytic review. *Journal of Criminal Justice, 39*(4), 329–337.

Lee, K., & Ashton, M. C. (2004). Psychometric properties of the HEXACO personality inventory. *Multivariate Behavioral Research, 39*(2), 329–358.

Lee, K., & Ashton, M. C. (2006). Further assessment of the HEXACO Personality Inventory: two new facet scales and an observer report form. *Psychological Assessment, 18*(2), 182.

Maples, J. L., Guan, L., Carter, N. T., & Miller, J. D. (2014). A test of the International Personality Item Pool representation of the Revised NEO Personality Inventory and development of a 120-item IPIP-based measure of the five-factor model. *Psychological Assessment, 26* (4), 1070–1084.

Marsh, H. W., Lüdtke, O., Nagengast, B., Morin, A. J., & Von Davier, M. (2013). Why item parcels are (almost) never appropriate: two wrongs do not make a right—camouflaging misspecification with item parcels in CFA models. *Psychological Methods, 18*(3), 257.

Miller, J. D., Crowe, M. L., Weiss, B., Maples-Keller, J. L., & Lynam, D. R. (2017). Using online, crowdsourcing platforms for data collection in personality disorder research: the example of Amazon's Mechanical Turk. *Personality disorders: Theory, research, and treatment, 8*(1), 26–34.

Miller, J. D., Gaughan, E. T., Maples, J., & Price, J. (2011). A comparison of agreeableness scores from the Big Five Inventory and the NEO PI-R: Consequences for the study of narcissism and psychopathy. *Assessment, 18*(3), 335–339. https://doi.org/10.1177/1073191111411671.

Miller, J. D., & Lynam, D. R. (2003). Psychopathy and the five-factor model of personality: a replication and extension. *Journal of Personality Assessment, 81*(2), 168–178.

Naragon-Gainey, K., Watson, D., & Markon, K. E. (2009). Differential relations of depression and social anxiety symptoms to the facets of extraversion/positive emotionality. *Journal of Abnormal Psychology*, *118*(2), 299.

Osborne, J. W., Costello, A. B., & Kellow, J. T. (2008). Best practices in exploratory factor analysis. In J. W. Osborne (Ed.), *Best practices in quantitative methods* (pp. 86–99). Thousand Oaks, CA: SAGE Publications Ltd.

Paulhus, D. L. (2001). Normal narcissism: two minimalist accounts. *Psychological Inquiry*, *12* (4), 228–230.

Perugini, M., & Gallucci, M. (1997). A hierarchical faceted model of the Big Five. *European Journal of Personality*, *11*(4), 279.

Raine, A., Dodge, K., Loeber, R., Gatzke-Kopp, L., Lynam, D., Reynolds, C., et al. (2006). The Reactive–Proactive Aggression Questionnaire: differential correlates of reactive and proactive aggression in adolescent boys. *Aggressive Behavior*, *32*(2), 159–171.

Roberts, B. W., Chernyshenko, O. S., Stark, S., & Goldberg, L. R. (2005). The structure of conscientiousness: an empirical investigation based on seven major personality questionnaires. *Personnel Psychology*, *58*(1), 103–139.

Saucier, G. (2003). Factor structure of English-language personality type-nouns. *Journal of Personality and Social Psychology*, *85*(4), 695–708.

Saucier, G. (2009). Recurrent personality dimensions in inclusive lexical studies: Indications for a Big Six structure. *Journal of Personality*, *77*(5), 1577–1614.

Saucier, G., & Ostendorf, F. (1999). Hierarchical subcomponents of the Big Five personality factors: a cross-language replication. *Journal of Personality and Social Psychology*, *76*(4), 613.

Simms, E. E. (2009). *Assessment of the facets of the Five Factor Model: Further development and validation of a new personality measure* (Ph.D.). Iowa: The University of Iowa, United States. Retrieved from. http://search.proquest.com/docview/304901508.

Simms, L. J., & Watson, D. (2007). The construct validation approach to personality scale construction. In R. W. Robins, R. C. Fraley, & R. F. Kruger (Eds.), *Handbook of research methods in personality psychology* (pp. 240–258). New York: Guilford.

Smith, G. T., McCarthy, D. M., & Zapolski, T. C. B. (2009). On the value of homogeneous constructs for construct validation, theory testing, and the description of psychopathology. *Psychological Assessment*, *21*(3), 272–284.

Soto, C. J., & John, O. P. (2009). Ten facet scales for the Big Five Inventory: convergence with NEO PI-R facets, self-peer agreement, and discriminant validity. *Journal of Research in Personality*, *43*(1), 84–90.

Soto, C. J., & John, O. P. (2017). The next Big Five Inventory (BFI-2): developing and assessing a hierarchical model with 15 facets to enhance bandwidth, fidelity, and predictive power. *Journal of Personality and Social Psychology*, *113*(1), 117–143.

Soto, C. J., John, O. P., Gosling, S. D., & Potter, J. (2008). The developmental psychometrics of big five self-reports: acquiescence, factor structure, coherence, and differentiation from ages 10 to 20. *Journal of Personality and Social Psychology*, *94*(4), 718–737.

Watson, D., Stasik, S. M., Ellickson-Larew, S., & Stanton, K. (2015). Extraversion and psychopathology: a facet-level analysis. *Journal of Abnormal Psychology*, *124*(2), 432–446.

Watson, D., Stasik, S. M., Ro, E., & Clark, L. A. (2013). Integrating normal and pathological personality: relating the DSM-5 trait-dimensional model to general traits of personality. *Assessment*, *20*(3), 312–326.

Wiggins, J. S. (1995). *Interpersonal adjective scales: Professional manual*. Odessa, FL: Psychological Assessment Resources.

Self-report assessment of antagonism

5

Douglas B. Samuel, Meredith A. Bucher, Takakuni Suzuki
Department of Psychological Sciences, Purdue University, West Lafayette, IN, United States

The assessment of personality traits traces a long history back to the early adjective checklists of Cattell and Allport (Digman, 1990). Even in these early taxonomies from nearly 80 years ago, there were routinely terms such as agreeableness, aggressiveness, and assertiveness, suggesting that antagonism stretches back to the beginning of modern trait theory. The publication of this edited volume testifies to their enduring legacy and continued significance. Throughout this history, antagonism, as well as other personality traits, has been predominantly assessed by asking the target to report on their characteristic manner of thinking, feeling, and relating to others. Although other methods exist, self-reports remain a primary method by which this important construct is measured. The goal of the present chapter is to review the instruments available for this purpose. Other scholars have previously provided a survey of all possible measures of the Five Factor Model (FFM; De Raad & Perugini, 2002). In addition, we have previously written on assessments of Personality Disorder from the perspective of FFM (Samuel, 2013). In the present chapter, we lean on those basic foundations as we focus our attention on each instrument's coverage of antagonism or the maladaptively low range of agreeableness.

It is also worth noting the boundaries of coverage in this chapter. Notably, we do not attempt to cover instruments that are designed to assess the categorical constructs of personality disorder (PD) such as antisocial, narcissistic, and psychopathy (e.g., Lilienfeld & Widows, 2005; Pincus et al., 2009) or broad-band measures of psychopathology that may include such scales (e.g., Morey, 1991). Although such measures undoubtedly contain large doses of antagonism (e.g., Miller, Gaughan, & Pryor, 2008; Samuel & Widiger, 2008a), they are premised on capturing broader constructs. Thus our focus is solely on instruments, or their subscales, that are aimed at dimensional traits reasonably similar to antagonism.

General personality instruments

NEO Personality Inventory—Revised (NEO PI-R)

Any discussion of instruments assessing dimensional models of personality should begin with the NEO family of instruments, given their broad use. Presently, the NEO Personality Inventory—Revised (NEO PI-R; Costa Jr. & McCrae, 1992) remains the predominant measure and conceptualization of the FFM and, as such,

The Handbook of Antagonism. https://doi.org/10.1016/B978-0-12-814627-9.00005-0

might be considered a baseline against which other measures can be compared and contrasted. The predominance of the NEO PI-R is for a good reason as it has considerable empirical validation and a strong research foundation. The NEO PI-R contains 240 items, which are in the form of sentences. The respondent indicates their agreement with each sentence by selecting *strongly disagree*, *disagree*, *neutral*, *agree*, or *strongly agree* from a Likert-type scale. As with other FFM inventories, the NEO PI-R provides scores for the five domains including agreeableness, as well as neuroticism, extraversion, openness to experience, and conscientiousness. An important innovation of the NEO PI-R, relative to the original NEO PI or the abbreviated NEO Five Factor Inventory, is that it also provides an assessment of six facets, or subtraits, within each domain that provide finer distinctions. The domain of agreeableness is underlain by facets labeled trust, straightforwardness, altruism, compliance, modesty, and tender-mindedness; although these facets were rationally developed they align closely with the empirical structure of this domain (Crowe, Lynam, & Miller, Chapter 4).

In constructing these facets, Costa and McCrae sought to make them similar in breadth and scope so that the entire domain could be covered with equivalent precision. Additionally, although it would be impossible (and perhaps unwise) to include facets that were entirely independent of others from the same domain (as they represent components of a common underlying disposition), Costa Jr. and McCrae (1995) sought to develop facets that would "represent the more closely covarying elements within the domain, not arbitrary combinations of elements" (p. 25) to maximize the facets' discriminant validity. Finally, and perhaps most importantly, they also attempted to have the facets be as consistent as possible with traits already recognized as important within the existing psychological literature.

These facet selections for agreeableness have received criticism as some lament that their development occurred outside of the lexical tradition (Saucier & Goldberg, 2002). Additionally, there are some facets from other FFM domains that are also somewhat overlapping with agreeableness. For example, angry hostility is a facet of neuroticism, but routinely relates highly with antagonism (Costa Jr. & McCrae, 1992). Despite the potential criticisms, the NEO PI-R facets have proven to be quite useful, particularly for the assessment of personality pathology (Samuel & Widiger, 2008b). Despite the fact its items were written to assess general personality structure, the NEO PI-R also has extensive support in terms of its ability to assess maladaptive elements of these traits that capture personality disorder. The most relevant PDs when considering antagonism are antisocial and narcissistic PDs, which have obtained robust and consistent links with NEO PI-R agreeableness (Samuel & Widiger, 2008b; Saulsman & Page, 2004).

A potential limitation of the NEO PI-R to assess maladaptive levels of the traits is that it was developed as a measure of normal personality functioning. In some cases, research has indicated that the NEO PI-R may lack fidelity for capturing extremes on some traits (Haigler & Widiger, 2001). Nonetheless, this has been less of a concern for the lower levels of agreeableness (i.e., antagonism) as those limitations appear to be most salient for *higher* levels agreeableness, as well as high conscientiousness and high openness to experience (Haigler & Widiger, 2001). NEO PI-R agreeableness has routinely negatively correlated with a variety of problematic outcomes at the domain level (Jones, Miller, & Lynam, 2011) and the specific facets from the NEO have been regularly used to investigate these relations at the lower level of the hierarchy (Vize, Miller, & Lynam, 2018).

Big Five Inventory and the BFI-2

The one measure of general personality that can perhaps claim to be more commonly used than the NEO PI-R is the Big Five Inventory (BFI; John, Donahue, & Kentle, 1991). The BFI consists of 44 short phrases to which an individual rates their agreement on a five-point Likert scale ranging from *strongly disagree* to *strongly agree*. The BFI is commonly studied in basic personality research because it provides a brief, freely available, and psychometrically sound assessment of the five broad domains (John, Naumann, & Soto, 2008). Although there are major similarities between the Big Five and FFM traditions, one notable difference concerns the construct breadth of agreeableness. The BFI and inventories in the lexical tradition do not provide appreciable coverage of the degree to which individuals are honest and modest. As a result they fall short when it comes to assessing aspects central to antagonism, such as manipulativeness, deceitfulness, and arrogance (Ashton & Lee, 2001). Within the NEO PI-R this is covered by the facets of straightforwardness and modesty and allow much greater prediction of antisocial and narcissistic PDs (Miller, Gaughan, Maples, & Price, 2011).

The BFI was also considered to be limited in that it provided only a domain score. The lack of facets can be problematic both due to the inability to score lower order constructs that can have unique predictive capacity (Ashton, Jackson, Paunonen, Helmes, & Rothstein, 1995), as well as narrowing the content scope. Recently, Soto and John (2017a) created the BFI-2, which did incorporate three specific facets (compassion, respectfulness, and trust). Although initial evidence does suggest that the overall domain of A from the BFI-2 correlate somewhat higher with the NEO PI-R than did the BFI, it is not clear that the content was meaningfully altered in a way that produces greater coverage of the straightforwardness and modesty facets as those remained the lowest correlates of the BFI-2 (Soto & John, 2017a). There are also further abbreviated versions including the 30-item BFI-2 Short Form and the 15-item Extra Short Form (Soto & John, 2017b). Both measures appear to reasonably capture the BFI-2 domain content; however, faceted assessments are restricted to the BFI-2-SF.

HEXACO Personality Inventory—Revised

In contrast, the HEXACO instruments were developed with an eye trained specifically on the lack of coverage of antagonistic content on the BFI and similar instruments. Based on lexical studies in a variety of cultures, Ashton and Lee (2005b) developed a model that had six domains labeled Honesty-Humility, Emotionality, eXtraversion, Agreeableness, Conscientiousness, and Openness (i.e., HEXACO). The HEXACO

Personality Inventory—Revised (HEXACO PI-R; Ashton & Lee, 2008) is a measure of general personality that contains 200 items rated on a Likert scale ranging from 1 (*strongly disagree*) to 5 (*strongly agree*). It assesses six broad domains of general personality functioning (each containing four facets) as well as a single "interstitial" facet of altruism versus antagonism. In addition to some differences in openness, a primary distinction is the addition of the Honesty-Humility domain that split off from agreeableness. The resulting domain of agreeableness contains the facets of sincerity, forgivingness, gentleness, flexibility, and patience. This domain clearly focuses on reciprocal altruism and can be thought of as the opposite of anger, in that it emphasizes tolerance and compassion for others that is more similar to the BFI (Ashton & Lee, 2005b). The domain of honesty-humility contains the facets of sincerity, fairness, greed-avoidance, and modesty. This domain features the degree to which a person is trustworthy and fair, with low standings suggesting the tendency to exploit others for one's own gain. This content makes it well suited for capturing the pathological aspects of psychopathy and narcissism and is closely aligned with NEO PI-R facets of straightforwardness and modesty (Ashton & Lee, 2005a). There are also two abbreviated forms of the HEXACO model including a 60-item version (Ashton & Lee, 2009) that contains 2–3 items per facet (10 per domain) and a 100-item version (Lee & Ashton, 2016). In each case, the abbreviated measures have been shown to replicate the domain structure of the parent measure, although the faceted coverage may be limited by the few items.

Scales drawn from the international personality item pool

The international personality item pool (IPIP; Goldberg et al., 2006) is a collection of over 2000 personality items that are freely available within the public domain (http://ipip.ori.org) and has allowed researchers to create a variety of instruments that are relevant to the assessment of antagonism. This format has notable advantages, including free use by researchers and clinicians as well as the ability to modify items and scales to suit a given purpose. Because the IPIP contains many items that have been administered to participants who also completed existing personality instruments, researchers have created "open-source" measures that approximate scores on existing instruments. For example, there is a set of 300 items that approximates scores on the domains and facets of the NEO PI-R. This set of items has also been abbreviated to 60-item (Maples-Keller et al., 2017) and 120-item versions that maintain the assessment of the lower order facets (Johnson, 2014; Maples, Guan, Carter, & Miller, 2014).

Research to date has demonstrated that, while some facets differ in names (e.g., morality instead of straightforwardness and sympathy instead of tender-mindedness), these IPIP measures broadly share the properties of the NEO PI-R across the domains, including agreeableness (Maples et al., 2014).

Another instrument drawn from the IPIP is the 485-item version of the Abridged Big Five-dimensional Circumplex model (AB5C; Hofstee, Deraad, & Goldberg, 1992), called the IPIP-AB5C (Goldberg, 1999). It assesses the five domains as well as a total of 45 lower order facets (9 per domain). The lower order facets differ here in that they are arranged conceptually such that beyond one "pure" facet for each domain, the other eight represent blends of both high and low variants of the other four domains. Within agreeableness, those facets are understanding, warmth, morality, pleasantness, empathy, cooperation, sympathy, tenderness, and nurturance.

There are also several facets that are defined by their secondary loading with low agreeableness, including provocativeness, rationality, imperturbability, and creativity. Given its extensive length, the AB5C has not been used frequently, but Bucher and Samuel (2018) recently developed a short form. In that study they compared the facet coverage with that offered by the IPIP-120 and the HEXACO Personality Inventory—Revised (Lee & Ashton, 2004). They suggested, given its broad number of facets, the AB5C is a candidate as a template by which to compare other faceted inventories. As would be expected, they reported a broad similarity as it pertains to agreeableness, but also some evidence that the additional facets provided somewhat different coverage, such as empathy and understanding that may offer greater resolution in those areas than the IPIP-120. More work is necessary to determine if there are appreciable advantages or disadvantages to these faceted models as they assess agreeableness.

DeYoung, Quilty, and Peterson (2007) selected 100 items from the IPIP (Goldberg, 1999) that assessed "aspects" of the FFM that occupy an intermediate space between the domains and the facets. The resulting Big Five Aspects Scale (BFAS) includes two aspects for each of the five domains. Agreeableness includes compassion and politeness. These appear to remain relatively focused on adaptive aspects of the agreeableness and, although related, do not contain as much variance concerning the exploitative features of antagonism (DeYoung, Carey, Krueger, & Ross, 2016). This perhaps owes to its development within the Big Five tradition that deemphasizes these antisocial aspects of the domain.

The IPIP website also provides both 50-item and 100-item versions of Goldberg's (1992) markers for the five broad domains, in addition to an abbreviated 20-item version (Donnellan, Oswald, Baird, & Lucas, 2006). These are based on Goldberg's (1992) markers and Saucier's (1994) mini-markers for the big five, but over time the content has shifted and does not necessarily reflect the original measures (Johnson, 2005; as cited in Goldberg et al., 2006). Both Goldberg's markers and Saucier's mini-markers have been used in at least one study (e.g., Blais, 1997) and have evinced correlations with markers of antisocial PD that are reasonably consistent with theoretical expectations. However, the absence of any lower order facets may limit these instruments' utility for assessing maladaptive aspects of antagonism.

Interpersonal circumplex assessments

The interpersonal circumplex (IPC) has a long tradition as a manner of understanding human relatedness (Leary, 1957) that is organized around twin axes of agency and communion. These axes form a circle that contains various combinations of both traits. With regard to antagonism, this is primarily a rotated variant represented by a blend of dominant (vs submissive on agency) and cold (vs warm on communion) interpersonal style. The most commonly used measure of the IPC is the Revised Interpersonal Adjective Scales (IAS-R; Wiggins, Trapnell, & Phillips, 1988). On the IAS-

R the respondent rates how accurately each adjective describes himself or herself on an 8-point Likert-type scale (e.g., 1 = *extremely inaccurate* to 8 = *extremely accurate*). These 64 adjectives are then scored for eight scales that assess octants of the IPC. Although the IAS-R has displayed reasonable convergence with other measures of the FFM and expected relationships with the PDs and the octants allow for some specificity with regard to assessing pathological antagonism, its focus on normative may limit the level of pathology. However, the Inventory of Interpersonal Problems—Circumplex Scale (IIP-C; Horowitz, Alden, Wiggins, & Pincus, 2000) was designed to assess the variety of interpersonal problems that can emerge from each of the octants. In this regard, the problem most associated with the dominant-cold octant is vindictiveness (Pincus & Hopwood, 2012). These scales have shown the ability to capture personality pathology associated with antagonism and thus represent another option or assessing this construct (Hopwood, Wright, Ansell, & Pincus, 2013; Wright, Scott, Stepp, Hallquist, & Pilkonis, 2015). One of the strengths of the IPC framework is that various measures designed to assess other nuanced interpersonally oriented individual differences have been developed, such as for interpersonal values (Locke, 2000) and aversive interpersonal styles (Hopwood et al., 2011). More recently, Boudreaux, Ozer, Oltmanns, and Wright (2018) developed a new measure of interpersonal problems, the Circumplex Scales of Interpersonal Problems, which aims to augment the coverage of the IIP-C.

Maladaptive trait instruments

Personality Inventory for DSM-5

A long-anticipated advance in the diagnosis and assessment of PD was the inclusion of an alternative model in Section III of the Diagnostic and Statistical Manual of Mental Disorders, Fifth Edition (DSM-5; American Psychiatric Association, 2013). This alternative model features a list of 25 trait facets organized into five broad domains—negative affect, antagonism, disinhibition, detachment, and psychoticism—that are highly consistent with the FFM. This model was partially developed with and is assessed using the self-reported Personality Inventory for DSM-5 (PID-5; Krueger, Derringer, Markon, Watson, & Skodol, 2012). The PID-5 has 220 items answered using a four-point scale ranging from *very false or often false* to *very true or often true*. The 25 facets are each assigned to a primary domain, with manipulativeness, deceitfulness, grandiosity, attention seeking, callousness, and hostility assigned to antagonism. There are also a handful of abbreviated measures of these traits. For example, Maples et al. (2015) demonstrated that the content of the full PID-5 could largely be captured with only 100 items. The PID-5 also has an official brief form that includes 25 items that tap only the five broad domains.

The PID-5 has been the subject of considerable research to date (Krueger & Markon, 2014) and this has generally demonstrated support for its assessment of the antagonism domain. Not surprisingly, given its developmental mission, the facets included on the PID-5 have proven quite capable of capturing aspects of antisocial and narcissistic PDs (Hopwood, Thomas, Markon, Wright, & Krueger, 2012; Wright et al., 2013). In addition, the antagonism scale has evinced robust inverse relations with agreeableness as assessed by general personality measures, such as the NEO PI-R, and they appear to have largely overlapping nomological networks (Suzuki, Griffin, & Samuel, 2017).

The FFM of PD scales (FFMPD)

The FFMPD scales are a series of self-report inventory scales to assess maladaptive variants of facets of the domains of the FFM, including antagonism (Widiger, Lynam, Miller, & Oltmanns, 2012). These scales assess maladaptive variants of the traits relevant for each *DSM-IV-TR* PD. This effort entailed first using the empirical and theoretical literature to determine which traits are relevant to the description of each respective PD construct (e.g., for psychopathy this included such facets as low anxiousness, high assertiveness, low straightforwardness, and low deliberation). The measures that include scales relevant to antagonism include the Elemental Psychopathy Assessment (Lynam et al., 2013) and the Short Form of the Five-Factor Narcissism Inventory (Sherman et al., 2015). More recently, though, Crego, Oltmanns, and Widiger (2018) have reorganized the scales into the familiar FFM domains, including antagonism. This collection of scales showed strong convergence with other measures of agreeableness (although with some evidence of a split between high agreeableness and antagonism, similar to the HEXACO PI-R), as well as other dimensional measures of trait antagonism.

Computerized Adaptive Test of Personality Disorder (CAT-PD)

Simms et al. (2011) developed a novel instrument to assess a trait model of personality pathology. The CAT-PD is notable for its use of computerized adaptive testing that aims at providing an efficient and thorough assessment of personality and personality pathology, although the final version is a static one that contains 212 items that assess 33 maladaptive trait dimensions. Although the creation of the CAT-PD was guided by the integration of multiple dimensional models summarized into five broad domains (i.e., Widiger & Simonsen, 2005), it does not have a theorized structure. Nonetheless, joint factor analyses have demonstrated that it combines well with the NEO PI-R and the PID-5 including one labeled antagonism (Wright & Simms, 2014). The scales that appear most relevant to antagonism include manipulativeness, hostile aggression, domineering, callousness, norm violation, grandiosity, and rudeness.

However, an additional scale labeled risk-taking also loaded primarily on this domain, despite typically being thought of as being more affiliated with disinhibition. The CAT-PD has initial construct validity support as a measure of antagonism, such as expected relations with interpersonal outcomes (Williams & Simms, 2016).

Minnesota Multiphasic Personality Inventory—Personality Psychopathology Five (PSY-5)

Harkness and McNulty (1994) developed a model for assessing psychopathology that corresponded with the big five personality traits and has been advanced as an alternative to the FFM for assessing psychopathology. Although it was initially developed as a stand-alone measure, Harkness and McNulty identified items from the MMPI-2 that matched their conceptual model and created five scales labeled aggressiveness, psychoticism, disconstraint, negative emotionality/neuroticism, and introversion/low positive emotionality. The derivation from the MMPI-2's item pool created both advantages and limitations for the PSY-5 as it pertains to covering the domains. Nonetheless, the aggressiveness scale has fared well as a measure of antagonism as it has shown moderate correlations with both measures of general agreeableness as well as pathological variants of the domain (Harkness, Finn, McNulty, & Shields, 2012). Nonetheless, a limitation of the PSY-5 is that its assessment is confined to the broad domains described before, without any representation of the lower order facets that are necessary for adequate assessment and differentiation of personality pathology (Axelrod, Widiger, Trull, & Corbitt, 1997).

Abbreviated measures

Beyond the lengthier and more psychometrically robust instruments described before, there are also a number of abbreviated measures that can provide a relatively rapid assessment of antagonism. These abbreviated measures can be quite useful in circumstances where efficiency is of the utmost importance such as large-scale surveys that must assess a wide variety of other variables within a limited period of time, situations where participants assess multiple targets, or when individuals are being prescreened before completing a larger assessment battery.

Five Factor Model Rating Form (FFMRF) and Five Factor Form (FFF)

The Five Factor Model Rating Form (FFMRF; Mullins-Sweatt, Jamerson, Samuel, Olson, & Widiger, 2006) is a one-page rating form consisting of 30 items representing each of the 30 facets from the NEO PI-R. The 30 items are organized with respect to the 5 domains. Each item is rated on a 1–5 scale where 1 is *extremely low*, 2 is *low*, 3 is *neither high nor low*, 4 is *high*, and 5 is *extremely high*. An important property of the FFMRF, relative to the BFI and most other brief FFM measures (e.g., Gosling, Rentfrow, & Swann, 2003), is that it allows the scoring of individual facets. This allows for a more complete appraisal of antagonism, which is important for differentiation of existing PDs (Axelrod et al., 1997; Reynolds & Clark, 2001). The FFMRF has been administered as a stand-alone self-report measure in many studies (Samuel, Mullins-Sweatt, & Widiger, 2013). For example, the FFMRF facets obtained relatively similar results to the lengthier NEO PI-R (Samuel & Widiger, 2008b). A strength, and possible weakness, of the FFMRF is that it relies on a relatively face-valid assessment by referencing maladaptive adjectives to describe antagonism (e.g., manipulative, ruthless, arrogant) and so it may be limited in situations where self-presentation is relevant. Nonetheless, the FFM has proven to be a valid measure for collecting self-reports and appears able to capture the maladaptive levels of antagonism.

The Five Factor Form (FFF) was developed in order to extend assessment even further into the maladaptive range. The FFF is also a one-page rating form that considers maladaptive variants of both poles (i.e., high and low) of all 30 facets proposed by McCrae and Costa Jr. (2013), but it differs in that it uses a 1–7 scale, rather than 1–5. This is a potentially important distinction because the additional rating points are specifically aimed at the maladaptive expressions of both the high and low pole of each facet. A study on the FFF suggests that it does assess antagonism in ways comparable to other abbreviated measures and also converges well with maladaptive versions of the traits (Rojas & Widiger, 2014). Although additional research is needed to further explore the properties of the FFMRF and FFF, they appear to have validity and utility for assessing the maladaptive extremes of the FFM within a relatively brief and straightforward instrument.

Conclusions

Considering the variety of instruments that provide a measure of antagonism, which measure should one use to assess these traits? The one firm conclusion offered is that we recommend against the use of lexically derived measures such as the BFI-2, due to differences in the conceptualization of agreeableness, including the lack of some of the more antagonistic aspects. In contrast, general measures that include facets (e.g., straightforwardness, modesty on the NEO PI-R) or separate domain scales (e.g., honesty-humility on the HEXACO PI-R) that focus on this content are recommended. If an in-depth examination of a specific aspect of interpersonal constructs is desired, IPC measures may also be appropriate. Beyond that, the answer depends primarily on how much time and resources one is willing to devote to the assessment as well as the level of fidelity one desires at various levels. Assuming an unlimited time with a pure focus on providing the most valid assessment, then lengthier measures such as the NEO PI-R, HEXACO PI-R, PID-5, and CAT-PD seem a reasonable starting point. The choice of a general-range measure would provide greater fidelity across the range of the trait (including potentially normative or maladaptively low levels), whereas scales such as the PID-5 or CAT-PD are focused purely on the maladaptive levels. Although further work is necessary to fully investigate the properties, the FFMPD scales concerning antagonism hold promise for their ability to potentially provide an assessment that taps a broader array of the antagonism spectrum, given the dual aim of capturing PD-relevant levels of the FFM traits.

References

American Psychiatric Association (2013). *Diagnostic and statistical manual of mental disorders* (5th ed.). Washington, DC: Author.

Ashton, M. C., Jackson, D. N., Paunonen, S. V., Helmes, E., & Rothstein, M. G. (1995). The criterion validity of broad factor scales versus specific facet scales. *Journal of Research in Personality*, *29*(4), 432–442. https://doi.org/10.1006/jrpe.1995.1025.

Ashton, M. C., & Lee, K. (2001). A theoretical basis for the major dimensions of personality. *European Journal of Personality, 15*(5), 327–353. https://doi.org/10.1002/per.417.

Ashton, M. C., & Lee, K. (2005a). Honesty-humility, the big five, and the five-factor model. *Journal of Personality, 73*(5), 1321–1353. https://doi.org/10.1111/j.1467-6494.2005.00351.x.

Ashton, M. C., & Lee, K. (2005b). The lexical approach to the study of personality structure: toward the identification of cross-culturally replicable dimensions of personality variation. *Journal of Personality Disorders, 19*(3), 303–308. https://doi.org/10.1521/pedi.2005.19.3.303.

Ashton, M. C., & Lee, K. (2008). The prediction of Honesty-Humility-related criteria by the HEXACO and Five-Factor Models of personality. *Journal of Research in Personality, 42*(5), 1216–1228. https://doi.org/10.1016/j.jrp.2008.03.006.

Ashton, M. C., & Lee, K. (2009). The HEXACO-60: a short measure of the major dimensions of personality. *Journal of Personality Assessment, 91*(4), 340–345. https://doi.org/10.1080/00223890902935878.

Axelrod, S. R., Widiger, T. A., Trull, T. J., & Corbitt, E. M. (1997). Relations of five-factor model antagonism facets with personality disorder symptomatology. *Journal of Personality Assessment, 69*(2), 297–313. https://doi.org/10.1207/s15327752jpa6902_4.

Blais, M. A. (1997). Clinician ratings of the five-factor model of personality and the DSM-IV personality disorders. *Journal of Nervous and Mental Disease, 185*(6), 388–393. https://doi.org/10.1097/00005053-199706000-00005.

Boudreaux, M. J., Ozer, D. J., Oltmanns, T. F., & Wright, A. G. C. (2018). Development and validation of the Circumplex Scales of Interpersonal Problems. *Psychological Assessment, 30*(5), 594–609. https://doi.org/10.1037/pas0000505.

Bucher, M. A., & Samuel, D. B. (2018). Development of a short form of the Abridged Big Five-Dimensional Circumplex model to aid with the organization of personality traits. *Journal of Personality Assessment*, 1–9. https://doi.org/10.1080/00223891.2017.1413382.

Costa, P. T., Jr., & McCrae, R. R. (1992). The five-factor model of personality and its relevance to personality disorders. *Journal of Personality Disorders, 6*(4), 343–359.

Costa, P. T., Jr., & McCrae, R. R. (1995). Domains and facets - hierarchical personality- assessment using the revised neo personality-inventory. *Journal of Personality Assessment, 64*(1), 21–50. https://doi.org/10.1207/s15327752jpa6401_2.

Crego, C., Oltmanns, J. R., & Widiger, T. A. (2018). FFMPD scales: comparisons with the FFM, PID-5, and CAT-PD-SF. *Psychological Assessment, 30*(1), 62–73. https://doi.org/10.1037/pas0000495.

De Raad, B., & Perugini, M. (Eds.), (2002). *Big Five assessment*. Gottigen, Germany: Hogrefe & Huber.

DeYoung, C. G., Carey, B. E., Krueger, R. F., & Ross, S. R. (2016). Ten aspects of the Big Five in the Personality Inventory for DSM-5. *Personality Disorders-Theory Research and Treatment, 7*(2), 113–123. https://doi.org/10.1037/per0000170.

DeYoung, C. G., Quilty, L. C., & Peterson, J. B. (2007). Between facets and domains: 10 aspects of the big five. *Journal of Personality and Social Psychology, 93*(5), 880–896. https://doi.org/10.1037/0022-3514.93.5.880.

Digman, J. M. (1990). Personality structure - emergence of the 5-factor model. *Annual Review of Psychology, 41*, 417–440. https://doi.org/10.1146/annurev.psych.41.1.417.

Donnellan, M. B., Oswald, F. L., Baird, B. M., & Lucas, R. E. (2006). The mini-IPIP scales: tiny-yet-effective measures of the big five factors of personality. *Psychological Assessment, 18*(2), 192–203. https://doi.org/10.1037/1040-3590.18.2.192.

Goldberg, L. R. (1992). The development of markers for the Big-Five factor structure. *Psychological Assessment*, *4*, 26–42.

Goldberg, L. R. (1999). A broad-bandwidth, public domain, personality inventory measuring the lower-level facets of several five-factor models. I. Mervielde, I. Deary, F. De Fruyt, & F. Ostendorf (Eds.), *Vol. 7. Personality psychology in Europe* (pp. 7–28). Tilburg, The Netherlands: Tilburg University Press.

Goldberg, L. R., Johnson, J. A., Eber, H. W., Hogan, R., Ashton, M. C., Cloninger, C. R., et al. (2006). The international personality item pool and the future of public-domain personality measures. *Journal of Research in Personality*, *40*(1), 84–96. https://doi.org/10.1016/j.jrp.2005.08.007.

Gosling, S. D., Rentfrow, P. J., & Swann, W. B. (2003). A very brief measure of the Big-Five personality domains. *Journal of Research in Personality*, *37*(6), 504–528. https://doi.org/10.1016/S0092-6566(03)00046-1.

Haigler, E. D., & Widiger, T. A. (2001). Experimental manipulation of NEO-PI-R items. *Journal of Personality Assessment*, *77*(2), 339–358. https://doi.org/10.1207/S15327752jpa7702_14.

Harkness, A. R., Finn, J. A., McNulty, J. L., & Shields, S. M. (2012). The Personality Psychopathology-Five (PSY-5): recent constructive replication and assessment literature review. *Psychological Assessment*, *24*(2), 432–443. https://doi.org/10.1037/a0025830.

Harkness, A. R., & McNulty, J. L. (1994). The personality psychopathology five (PSY-5): issue from the pages of a diagnostic manual instead of a dictionary. In S. Strack & M. Lorr (Eds.), *Differentiating normal and abnormal personality*. New York: Springer.

Hofstee, W. K. B., Deraad, B., & Goldberg, L. R. (1992). Integration of the Big-5 and circumplex approaches to trait structure. *Journal of Personality and Social Psychology*, *63*(1), 146–163. https://doi.org/10.1037/0022-3514.63.1.146.

Hopwood, C. J., Ansell, E. B., Pincus, A. L., Wright, A. G. C., Lukowitsky, M. R., & Roche, M. J. (2011). The circumplex structure of interpersonal sensitivities. *Journal of Personality*, *79*(4), 707–739. https://doi.org/10.1111/j.1467-6494.2011.00696.x.

Hopwood, C. J., Thomas, K. M., Markon, K. E., Wright, A. G. C., & Krueger, R. F. (2012). DSM-5 personality traits and DSM-IV personality disorders. *Journal of Abnormal Psychology*, *121*(2), 424–432. https://doi.org/10.1037/A0026656.

Hopwood, C. J., Wright, A. G. C., Ansell, E. B., & Pincus, A. L. (2013). The interpersonal core of personality pathology. *Journal of Personality Disorders*, *27*(3), 270–295.

Horowitz, L. M., Alden, L. E., Wiggins, J. S., & Pincus, A. L. (2000). *Manual for the inventory of interpersonal problems*. San Antonio, TX: Psychological Corporation.

John, O. P., Donahue, E. M., & Kentle, R. L. (1991). *The big five inventory - Versions 4a and 54*. Berkeley, CA: University of California, Berkeley, Institute of Personality and Social Research.

John, O. P., Naumann, L. P., & Soto, C. J. (2008). Paradigm shift to the integrative Big Five trait taxonomy. In O. P. John, R. W. Robins, & L. A. Pervin (Eds.), *Handbook of personality* (pp. 114–158). (3rd ed.). New York: Guilford.

Johnson, J. A. (2005). *The good, the bad, and the ugly: The IPIP consultant's experiences recounted. Paper presented at the Association for Research in Personality, New Orleans, LA*.

Johnson, J. A. (2014). Measuring thirty facets of the Five Factor Model with a 120-item public domain inventory: development of the IPIP-NEO-120. *Journal of Research in Personality*, *51*, 78–89. https://doi.org/10.1016/j.jrp.2014.05.003.

Jones, S. E., Miller, J. D., & Lynam, D. R. (2011). Personality, antisocial behavior, and aggression: a meta-analytic review. *Journal of Criminal Justice*, *39*(4), 329–337. https://doi.org/10.1016/j.jcrimjus.2011.03.004.

Krueger, R. F., Derringer, J., Markon, K. E., Watson, D., & Skodol, A. E. (2012). Initial construction of a maladaptive personality trait model and inventory for DSM-5. *Psychological Medicine*, *42*(9), 1879–1890. https://doi.org/10.1017/S0033291711002674.

Krueger, R. F., & Markon, K. E. (2014). The role of the DSM-5 personality trait model in moving toward a quantitative and empirically based approach to classifying personality and psychopathology. *Annual Review of Clinical Psychology*, *10*, 477–501. https://doi.org/10.1146/annurev-clinpsy-032813-153732.

Leary, T. (1957). *Interpersonal diagnosis of personality; a functional theory and methodology for personality evaluation*. New York: Ronald Press Co..

Lee, K., & Ashton, M. C. (2004). Psychometric properties of the HEXACO personality inventory. *Multivariate Behavioral Research*, *39*(2), 329–358. https://doi.org/10.1207/s15327906mbr3902_8.

Lee, K., & Ashton, M. C. (2016). Psychometric properties of the HEXACO-100. *Assessment*. https://doi.org/10.1177/1073191116659134.

Lilienfeld, S. O., & Widows, M. (2005). *Professional manual for the Psychopathic Personality Inventory - Revised (PPI-R)*. Lutz, FL: PAR, Inc.

Locke, K. D. (2000). Circumplex scales of interpersonal values: reliability, validity, and applicability to interpersonal problems and personality disorders. *Journal of Personality Assessment*, *75*(2), 249–267. https://doi.org/10.1207/S15327752jpa7502_6.

Lynam, D. R., Sherman, E. D., Samuel, D., Miller, J. D., Few, L. R., & Widiger, T. A. (2013). Development of a short form of the elemental psychopathy assessment. *Assessment*, *20*(6), 659–669. https://doi.org/10.1177/1073191113502072.

Maples, J. L., Carter, N. T., Few, L. R., Crego, C., Gore, W. L., Samuel, D. B., et al. (2015). Testing whether the DSM-5 personality disorder trait model can be measured with a reduced set of items: an item response theory investigation of the Personality Inventory for DSM-5. *Psychological Assessment*, *27*(4), 1195–1210. https://doi.org/10.1037/pas0000120.

Maples, J. L., Guan, L., Carter, N. T., & Miller, J. D. (2014). A test of the International Personality Item Pool representation of the Revised NEO Personality Inventory and development of a 120-item IPIP-based measure of the five-factor model. *Psychological Assessment*, *26* (4), 1070–1084. https://doi.org/10.1037/pas0000004.

Maples-Keller, J. L., Williamson, R. L., Sleep, C. E., Carter, N. T., Campbell, W. K., & Miller, J. D. (2017). Using item response theory to develop a 60-item representation of the NEO PI-R using the international personality item Pool: development of the IPIP-NEO-60. *Journal of Personality Assessment*, 1–12. https://doi.org/10.1080/00223891.2017.1381968.

McCrae, R. R., & Costa, P. T., Jr. (2013). Introduction to the empirical and theoretical status of the five-factor model of personality traits. In T. A. Widiger & P. T. Costa, Jr., (Eds.), *Personality disorders and the Five-Factor Model of personality* (pp. 15–27). (3rd ed.). Washington, DC: American Psychological Association.

Miller, J. D., Gaughan, E. T., Maples, J., & Price, J. (2011). A comparison of agreeableness scores from the Big Five Inventory and the NEO PI-R: consequences for the study of narcissism and psychopathy. *Assessment*, *18*(3), 335–339. https://doi.org/10.1177/1073191111411671.

Miller, J. D., Gaughan, E. T., & Pryor, L. R. (2008). The Levenson Self-Report Psychopathy Scale: an examination of the personality traits and disorders associated with the LSRP factors. *Assessment*, *15*(4), 450–463. https://doi.org/10.1177/1073191108316888.

Morey, L. C. (1991). *Personality Assessment Inventory professional manual*. Odessa, FL: Psychological Assessment Resources.

Mullins-Sweatt, S. N., Jamerson, J. E., Samuel, D. B., Olson, D. R., & Widiger, T. A. (2006). Psychometric properties of an abbreviated instrument of the five-factor model. *Assessment, 13*(2), 119–137.

Pincus, A. L., Ansell, E. B., Pimentel, C. A., Cain, N. M., Wright, A. G. C., & Levy, K. N. (2009). Initial construction and validation of the Pathological Narcissism Inventory. *Psychological Assessment, 21*(3), 365–379. https://doi.org/10.1037/A0016530.

Pincus, A. L., & Hopwood, C. J. (2012). A contemporary interpersonal model of personality pathology and personality disorder. In T. A. Widiger (Ed.), *The Oxford handbook of personality disorders* (pp. 372–398). New York: Oxford University Press.

Reynolds, S. K., & Clark, L. A. (2001). Predicting dimensions of personality disorder from domains and facets of the Five-Factor Model. *Journal of Personality, 69*(2), 199–222. https://doi.org/10.1111/1467-6494.00142.

Rojas, S. L., & Widiger, T. A. (2014). Convergent and discriminant validity of the five factor form. *Assessment, 21*(2), 143–157. https://doi.org/10.1177/1073191113517260.

Samuel, D. B. (2013). Assessing the five-factor model of personality disorder. In T. A. Widiger (Ed.), *Personality disorders and the Five-Factor Model of personality* (pp. 221–232). (3rd ed.). Washington, DC: American Psychological Association.

Samuel, D. B., Mullins-Sweatt, S. N., & Widiger, T. A. (2013). An investigation of the factor structure and convergent and discriminant validity of the five-factor model rating form. *Assessment, 20*(1), 24–35. https://doi.org/10.1177/1073191112455455.

Samuel, D. B., & Widiger, T. A. (2008a). Convergence of narcissism measures from the perspective of general personality functioning. *Assessment, 15*(3), 364–374. https://doi.org/10.1177/1073191108314278.

Samuel, D. B., & Widiger, T. A. (2008b). A meta-analytic review of the relationships between the five-factor model and DSM-IV-TR personality disorders: a facet level analysis. *Clinical Psychology Review, 28*, 1326–1342. https://doi.org/10.1016/j.cpr.2008.07.002.

Saucier, G. (1994). Mini-markers - a brief version of Goldberg unipolar Big-5 markers. *Journal of Personality Assessment, 63*(3), 506–516. https://doi.org/10.1207/s15327752jpa6303_8.

Saucier, G., & Goldberg, L. R. (2002). Assessing the Big Five: applications of 10 psychometric criteria to the development of marker scales. In B. De Raad & M. Perugini (Eds.), *Big Five Assessment* (pp. 29–58). Bern, Switzerland: Hogrefe & Huber.

Saulsman, L. M., & Page, A. C. (2004). The five-factor model and personality disorder empirical literature: a meta-analytic review. *Clinical Psychology Review, 23*(8), 1055–1085. https://doi.org/10.1016/j.cpr.2002.09.001.

Sherman, E. D., Miller, J. D., Few, L. R., Campbell, W. K., Widiger, T. A., Crego, C., et al. (2015). Development of a short form of the Five-Factor Narcissism Inventory: the FFNI-SF. *Psychological Assessment*. https://doi.org/10.1037/pas0000100.

Simms, L. J., Goldberg, L. R., Roberts, J. E., Watson, D., Welte, J., & Rotterman, J. H. (2011). Computerized adaptive assessment of personality disorder: introducing the CAT-PD project. *Journal of Personality Assessment, 93*(4), 380–389. https://doi.org/10.1080/00223891.2011.577475.

Soto, C. J., & John, O. P. (2017a). The next Big Five Inventory (BFI-2): developing and assessing a hierarchical model with 15 facets to enhance bandwidth, fidelity, and predictive power (vol 113, pg 117, 2016). *Journal of Personality and Social Psychology, 113*(1), 143. https://doi.org/10.1037/pspp0000155.

Soto, C. J., & John, O. P. (2017b). Short and extra-short forms of the Big Five Inventory-2: the BFI-2-S and BFI-2-XS. *Journal of Research in Personality, 68*, 69–81. https://doi.org/10.1016/j.jrp.2017.02.004.

Suzuki, T., Griffin, S. A., & Samuel, D. B. (2017). Capturing the DSM-5 alternative personality disorder model traits in the Five-Factor Model's nomological net. *Journal of Personality*, *85*(2), 220–231.

Vize, C. E., Miller, J. D., & Lynam, D. R. (2018). FFM facets and their relations with different forms of antisocial behavior: an expanded meta-analysis. *Journal of Criminal Justice*, *57*, 67–75.

Widiger, T. A., Lynam, D. R., Miller, J. D., & Oltmanns, T. F. (2012). Measures to assess maladaptive variants of the Five-Factor Model. *Journal of Personality Assessment*, *94* (5), 450–455. https://doi.org/10.1080/00223891.2012.677887.

Widiger, T. A., & Simonsen, E. (2005). Alternative dimensional models of personality disorder: Finding a common ground. In *Journal of Personality Disorders: Vol. 19, Special Section: A Research Agenda for the Development of a Dimensional Classification of Personality Disorder* (pp. 110–130). https://doi.org/10.1521/pedi.19.2.110.62628 Part I.

Wiggins, J. S., Trapnell, P., & Phillips, N. (1988). Psychometric and geometric characteristics of the Revised Interpersonal Adjective Scales (IAS—R). *Multivariate Behavioral Research*, *23*(4), 517–530.

Williams, T. F., & Simms, L. J. (2016). Personality disorder models and their coverage of interpersonal problems. *Personality Disorders-Theory Research and Treatment*, *7*(1), 15–27. https://doi.org/10.1037/per0000140.

Wright, A. G. C., Pincus, A. L., Thomas, K. M., Hopwood, C. J., Markon, K. E., & Krueger, R. F. (2013). Conceptions of narcissism and the DSM-5 pathological personality traits. *Assessment*, *20*(3), 339–352. https://doi.org/10.1177/1073191113486692.

Wright, A. G. C., Scott, L. N., Stepp, S. D., Hallquist, M. N., & Pilkonis, P. A. (2015). Personality pathology and interpersonal problem stability. *Journal of Personality Disorders*, *29* (5), 684–706. https://doi.org/10.1521/pedi_2014_28_171.

Wright, A. G. C., & Simms, L. J. (2014). On the structure of personality disorder traits: conjoint analyses of the CAT-PD, PID-5, and NEO-PI-3 trait models. *Personality Disorders: Theory, Research, and Treatment*, *5*, 43–54. https://doi.org/10.1037/per0000037.

Biological correlates of antagonism

6

Julia McDonald, Edelyn Verona
Department of Psychology, University of South Florida, Tampa, FL, United States

Introduction and theoretical foundations

In 1848, Phineas Gage was working on a railroad when an explosion turned a railway spike into a projectile that impaled Gage through his skull. Gage survived; however, his personality was purportedly altered as a result of damage to his prefrontal cortex (Damasio, Grabowski, Frank, Galaburda, & Damasio, 1994). After the accident, "Gage was no longer Gage," showing behaviors described as "fitful, irreverent, and grossly profane, showing little deference for his fellows" (Harlow, 1868, pp. 13–14). And with that, the explosion of a metal rod ushered the field of neuroscience into the modern era.

While the idea that personality is inextricably linked to biology is by no means a new one, most contemporary theories of personality psychology, including the Five-Factor Model (FFM; Costa & McCrae, 1992), have not been mapped onto biological systems (Paris, 2000). This lack of data is unfortunate when considering that certain personality traits, such as antagonism (the low pole of FFM agreeableness), are key predictors of behaviors of particular concern for society, such as violence and crime (Skeem, Miller, Mulvey, Tiemann, & Monahan, 2005). A clearer understanding of the psychobiological processes associated with the antagonistic personality is essential to understanding etiology and maintenance factors.

High agreeableness is an obviously adaptive social strategy: empathy, straightforwardness, and cooperation are all related to increased social support, successful parenting, and conflict resolution (Nettle, 2006). Nonetheless, evolutionary theorists argue that the opposite pole, antagonism, is also an advantageous strategy for resource allocation and genetic reproduction (Buss, 1996). Studies have shown that aspects of antagonism are related to career success, successful short-term mating strategies, social dominance, and other traits that serve to protect and promote the interest of the person (Spurk, Keller, & Hirschi, 2016; Zeigler-Hill & Hobbs, 2017). As such, trait antagonism has persisted, as have the biological/genetic signatures associated with this trait dimension. Indeed, antagonistic traits are heritable, with estimates from twin studies ranging from 33% to 51% of the variance in antagonism accounted for by genes (for review see Bouchard & Loehlin, 2001).

Antagonism, as conceptualized within FFM, and measured by trait inventories like the NEO Personality Inventory—Revised (NEO-PI-R; Costa & McCrae, 1992), is comprised of separate but related facets of trust (versus distrust), straightforwardness

The Handbook of Antagonism. https://doi.org/10.1016/B978-0-12-814627-9.00006-2

(versus manipulation), altruism (versus self-centeredness), compliance (versus oppositionality), modesty (versus arrogance), and tender-mindedness (versus callousness). The individual facets are likely associated with distinct etiological factors and behavioral manifestations. For example, low physiological arousal allows antagonistic individuals to perform under high-stress situations (Hall & Benning, 2006), lack of responsiveness to the distress of others allows self-centered individuals to focus on their own needs before worrying about others (Shirtcliff et al., 2009), and hypervigilance to threat serves to protect distrustful individuals from being taken advantage of (Riedl & Javor, 2012). This chapter aims to provide an integrated review of the biological mechanisms associated with combinations of facets of antagonism. We aim to integrate findings from hormones, genes, peripheral physiology (e.g., bodily reactivity to emotional stimuli) as well as neurocircuitry (e.g., brain structures and systems) to identify common patterns characterizing a general tendency toward antagonism, as well as distinct biological processes across the facets.

Unconcern for others and low empathy (callousness, self-centeredness)

One of the defining features of antagonism includes *lower levels of caring or empathic concern for others*, captured by the antagonism facets of callousness and self-centeredness. Constructs associated with trait callousness include youth callous and unemotional (CU) traits (Frick & White, 2008); the affective traits of adult psychopathy (lack of emotional depth/empathy/remorse and shallow affect, as assessed by the Psychopathy Checklist-Revised; PCL-R, Hare, 2003); coldheartedness (Berg, Hecht, Latzman, & Lillienfeld, 2015); and the "meanness" dimension of the triarchic model of psychopathy (Patrick, Fowles, & Krueger, 2009). Self-centeredness overlaps conceptually with callousness in terms of its characteristic low level of concern for others, egocentricity, exploitiveness, and greedy behaviors. Self-centeredness is implicated in narcissistic personality disorder (Miller, Gentile, Wilson, & Campbell, 2013), Machiavellianism (Lynam et al., 2011), as well as several psychopathic traits (egocentrism, shallow affect, and reckless disregard for the safety of others; Hare, 2003).

Callous and egocentric traits show moderate to high heritability (Jang, Livesley, & Vernon, 1996; Jang, McCrae, Angleitner, Riemann, & Livesley, 1998). Results from a range of studies of youth CU traits and psychopathy have shown that callousness is linked to high levels of genetic (20%–71%) and nonshared environmental influence (54%–80%), without contribution from shared environment (Larsson et al., 2007; Viding, Jones, Frick, Moffitt, & Plomin, 2008). Callousness, as measured by the NEO-PI-R mirrors this research (Jang et al., 1996, 1998). Research on self-centeredness has repeatedly found a major influence of the nonshared environment (64%–80%; Jang et al., 1996, 1998), but less consistent estimates for the genetic and environmental influences (Bouchard & Loehlin, 2001). Together these studies suggest that while both self-centeredness and callousness are influenced by the nonshared environment, callousness is likely more heritable than self-centeredness.

Less is known about the individual genes involved in callousness and self-centeredness, although there is growing work in the area. For example, although the short allele of the serotonin linked polymorphic region of the serotonin transporter gene (5-HTTLPR) has been implicated in impulsivity and emotional excesses (Ficks & Waldman, 2014; Sadeh, Javdani, Jackson, & Reynolds, 2010), the long allele of 5-HTTLPR has received attention in regard to affective deficits in psychopathy (Sadeh et al., 2010; Sadeh, Verona, & Javdani, 2013). This double dissociation makes sense, given that the long allele of 5-HTTLPR has been linked to both reduced stress reactivity and emotional responding (Glenn, 2011), such as lower resting activation of the amygdala (Canli, Congdon, Gutknecht, Constable, & Lesch, 2005) and reduced stress system activity (Gotlib, Joormann, Minor, & Hallmayer, 2008) relative to the other variants of 5-HTTLPR.

The neurohormone oxytocin has been linked to attachment, pair bonding, social support, and prosocial behavior (Kumsta & Heinrichs, 2013), and thus deficits in oxytocin functioning are implicated in callousness and self-centeredness. In one study, intranasal administrations of oxytocin increased altruism (opposite pole of self-centeredness), with participants donating more money to charities with a social framing (i.e., helping people in need) than nature conservation (i.e., saving the rainforest; Marsh et al., 2015). Further, genetic variation in the oxytocin receptor (OXTR) gene, and related single-nucleotide polymorphisms on that gene (SNPs rs1042778, rs53576, and rs2254298; Thompson, Hurd, & Crespi, 2013), have been linked to empathy, social bonding, and social cue recognition (Gong et al., 2017), and more recently with the affective (callous) facet of psychopathy (Verona, Murphy, & Bresin, 2018). Furthermore, a recent epigenetics study found that high levels of both CU traits and OXTR methylation interacted to produce increased decoupling of amygdala and frontal regions (Aghajani et al., 2018). Functionally, this decoupling may affect processing involved in decoding and integrating socioaffective information. Together, this set of studies suggests reduced social sensitivity among persons high on callous/egocentric features of antagonism.

Consistent with this, studies across levels of analysis indicate that persons high on callous and self-centered traits show reduced stress reactivity, fear, and defensive responding. Studies of hormonal systems relevant to threat responsivity have found that CU traits and affective features of psychopathy are related to reduced levels of basal cortisol (Loney, Butler, Lima, Counts, & Eckel, 2006), as well as blunted cortisol reactivity (O'Leary, Loney, & Eckel, 2007). Further, affective features of psychopathy and CU traits are associated with reduced *reactivity* in skin conductance and heart rate to emotionally evocative conditions (Fung et al., 2005; Lorber, 2004), particularly unpleasant ones, as well as reduced *resting* heart rate and skin conductance (Lorber, 2004). Similarly, decades of research have shown that individuals high on psychopathic traits (particularly interpersonal and affective traits) and youth with CU traits do not show a normal startle reflex potentiation in response to aversive stimuli (Vaidyanathan, Hall, Patrick, & Bernat, 2011). These studies provide compelling evidence that behavioral manifestations relevant to callous/self-centered traits are associated with reduced defensive responding.

Findings of reduced stress reactivity are in line with research on the structure and function of the limbic system, with reduced volume and activity of the amygdala consistently linked to abnormal affective processing observed in psychopaths (Weber, Habel, Amunts, & Schneider, 2008). Neuroimaging studies have linked reduced amygdala functioning to psychopathy and CU traits (Blair, Jones, Clark, & Smith, 1997), callousness (Shirtcliff et al., 2009), and low empathy (Bernhardt & Singer, 2012). Notably, biological indicators of emotional responding such as the fear-potentiated startle (Angrilli et al., 1996) and hormone levels such as cortisol (van Stegeren et al., 2007), which show deficient levels in callousness, are modulated by amygdala reactivity.

At the level of larger brain networks, self-centeredness and callousness have been associated with dysfunction of the salience network (Shirtcliff et al., 2009). This network includes the anterior cingulate cortex (ACC) and the insula (Menon & Uddin, 2010) and has been implicated in generating physiological arousal and promoting attention in response to alerting stimuli. Individuals high in traits relevant to callousness and self-centeredness (e.g., affective traits of psychopathy) show reduced insula and ACC activation, including in response to signals of distress or pain experienced by others (Blair, 2013; Decety, Chen, Harenski, & Kiehl, 2013). However, narcissism (which is a behavioral manifestation relevant to self-centeredness, but also captured by arrogant/manipulative facets of antagonism, see later) has been associated with increased activation of the right anterior insula during evaluation of negative emotional images (Fan et al., 2011), a region often implicated in representations of the self. Thus, there is evidence of heightened salience network activation in narcissism-related self-centeredness, particularly in response to perceived threats to self (Jankowiak-Siuda & Zajkowski, 2013), which may distinguish it from other low empathy-related constructs.

In summary, the literature supports that callousness, and self-centeredness to a lesser extent, are manifestations of a particular underlying pattern of biology, which is heritable with mostly nonshared environmental influence. The physiological literature indicates a pattern of reduced sensitivity to social and emotional cues, which coincides with the "low fear" hypothesis (Lykken, 1995) of psychopathic/CU traits. This hypothesis characterizes callousness as the inability to properly process aversive or emotional stimuli, leading to the reduced subjective experience of fear and concomitant failures to avoid fear-provoking situations, recognize fear in others, and correct inappropriate behavior.

Hostile orientation toward others (oppositionality, distrust)

Another set of widely studied features of antagonism include oppositionality and distrustful traits—both reflecting a *general hostile orientation toward others.* Behavioral manifestations of oppositionality include lack of cooperation, combativeness, and willingness to fight back, with extreme manifestations represented in many of the disorders characterized by antisocial behavior and aggression

(Jones, Miller, & Lynam, 2011). Distrust represents tendencies toward feelings of persecution and viewing others in a hostile light, manifested in vulnerable narcissism (Miller et al., 2016) and paranoid personality disorder (Samuel & Widiger, 2008). While these behavioral manifestations are linked by a shared underlying association to trait antagonism, some are also thought to be influenced by lack of conscientiousness (Kotov et al., 2017) and/or neuroticism (Jones et al., 2011).

As with callousness, oppositionality and distrust seem to be moderately heritable (30%–52%; Hiraishi, Yamagata, Shikishima, & Ando, 2008; Jang et al., 1996; Rhee & Waldman, 2002; Tuvblad, Bezdjian, Raine, & Baker, 2014). Distrust, as measured by the NEO-PI-R, shows the largest environmental influences of all antagonism facets, with estimates of the amount of nonshared environmental influence highly consistent across studies (64%–70%; Jang et al., 1996; Jang, Livesley, Angleitner, Riemann, & Vernon, 2002). In contrast, shared environment only seems relevant to the expression of oppositionality (specifically, antisocial behavior; 14%–41% in boys; Larsson et al., 2007; Viding, Blair, Moffitt, & Plomin, 2005). Together, these studies suggest that oppositionality/distrust have heritable components but are highly influenced by the environment.

Candidate genes relevant to oppositionality have been most widely studied in relation to antisocial behavior. The low activity variant of monoamine oxidase A (MAOA) gene has been consistently linked to expressions of aggression, antisocial behavior, and violence across studies (Ficks & Waldman, 2014). Similarly, the short allele of the serotonin promoter variant 5-HTTLPR is related to increased antisocial behavior, aggression, and antisocial and impulsive facets psychopathy (Ficks & Waldman, 2014; Sadeh et al., 2010, 2013). The latter gene variant represents a possible etiological distinction between callousness and oppositionality: the long allele of 5-HTTLPR is related to blunted affect and decreased physiological reactivity (implicated in callousness), whereas the short allele of 5-HTTLPR is related to increased physiological reactivity in response to stressful or emotional stimuli (implicated in oppositionality, as reviewed later), respectively (Glenn, 2011). Although persons can be simultaneously high on both callousness and oppositionality, different etiological pathways (e.g., blunted affect or stress reactivity/dysregulation) can result in the same combined phenotype. In terms of environmental influences, more replicable findings show that the relationships between the MAOA or 5-HTTLPR gene variants and antisocial behavior or aggression are much stronger among persons with higher levels of childhood adversity or maltreatment (e.g., Kim-Cohen et al., 2006).

Hormone systems regulating testosterone, oxytocin, and cortisol have been jointly implicated in oppositionality and distrust. High levels of basal testosterone have been observed in persons high on oppositionality or distrust, especially in studies of oppositionality-related aggression traits (Geniole, Busseri, & McCormick, 2013). Testosterone may also promote distrust, with one study finding that the administration of the steroid hormone testosterone decreased perceptions of trust during a facial trustworthiness evaluation task (Bos, Terburg, & Van Honk, 2010). This result could be attributable to testosterone's inhibition of oxytocin (Huber, Veinante, & Stoop, 2005); indeed, distrust shows negative associations with oxytocin (Domes et al., 2007). Importantly, oxytocin release seems to suppress cortisol reactivity and amygdala activation, suggesting that enhanced stress reactivity underlies distrust tendencies, and combined with high testosterone, implicates higher threat sensitivity across oppositionality/distrust. Inconsistent with this conceptualization, however, low levels of basal cortisol (indicative of underarousal at rest) have been reported in persons with aggressive, oppositional, and antisocial behavior (Lopez-Duran, Olson, Hajal, Felt, & Vazquez, 2009; McBurnett, Lahey, & Rathouz, 2000), but the findings here have been somewhat mixed (Alink et al., 2008).

The idea of higher threat reactivity among those with antisocial/aggressive behaviors would also contradict evidence of blunted *resting* autonomic activity (Lorber, 2004; Portnoy & Farrington, 2015), especially electrodermal activity (Crider, 2008; Lorber, 2004). However, evidence from various literatures supports the idea that oppositionality (e.g., aggressive, violent, or antisocial behavior problems) is marked by threat sensitivity, including increased autonomic *reactivity*, especially in response to provocation (Pham, Philippot, & Rime, 2000) and increased processing of evocative stimuli (Lorber, 2004). Whereas callousness is characterized by both low baseline arousal and low stress reactivity (and blunted cortisol reactivity), oppositionality reflects low baseline arousal but *heightened* stress reactivity (and testosterone). This again illustrates that distinct developmental pathways may be involved in the manifestation of antagonism traits. This pattern of increased threat reactivity is also observed in neuroimaging work, with increased activation of the amygdala to evocative stimuli in oppositionality and distrust (Engell, Haxby, & Todorov, 2007), with some null findings (Matthys, Vanderchuren, & Schutter, 2013).

Other research indicates that enhanced emotional processing is combined with dysfunctions in cognitive control. That is, studies show deficits in structure and functioning of the prefrontal cortex among those with distrustful (Riedl & Javor, 2012) and oppositional traits (e.g., conduct and oppositional defiant disorder, psychopathy, antisocial/aggressive behavior; Matthys et al., 2013 Patrick, 2014). Studies using event-related potential techniques have consistently found that the P300 (the component thought to index cognitive control) is reduced among individuals with antisocial traits (Gao & Raine, 2009), and these cognitive control deficits are thought to uniquely characterize antisocial behavior, rather than the affective traits associated with callousness (Hicks et al., 2007).

Lastly, activation of the insula has been associated with abnormal expressions of interpersonal trust. For example, patients with focal damage to the insula were found to display continued trust for a dishonest stranger (Belfi, Koscik, & Tranel, 2015), and increased insula activation has been associated with heightened sensitivity toward betrayal (Aimone, Houser, & Weber, 2014). These studies suggest that heightened insula activation is related to distrust. In fact, distrust has been associated with both increased activation (Dimoka, 2010) and gray matter volume of the insula in non-clinical samples (Haas, Ishak, Anderson, & Filkowski, 2015). In the sense that the insula is part of the salience network, chronic activation can bias the cognitive and affective systems toward viewing many benign situations as indications of potential threats, subsequently resulting in increased likelihood for hostility and distrust (Verona & Bresin, 2015; Young et al., 2017).

Together, evidence suggests that oppositionality/distrust are characterized by a pattern of low baseline arousal but a chronically activated threat response system, coupled with difficulty downregulating impulses (reduced cognitive control). While this biobehavioral profile may be adaptive in dangerous environments, it also predisposes individuals toward hostility, aggression, and antisocial behaviors. The increased autonomic and amygdala reactivity and functioning of the insula represent a possible biological distinction between oppositionality/distrust and callousness/egocentricity. Whereas the former is undergirded by heightened sensitivity toward potential threat, the latter is insensitive to potential signs of threat.

Social dominance and deception (manipulation, arrogance)

The last major set of antagonism traits include manipulation and arrogance—both representing *strategies for deceiving and dominating others.* Antagonistic manipulation involves a duplicitous interpersonal style that utilizes flattery or deception to control others. This facet has been linked to Machiavellianism (O'Boyle, Forsyth, Banks, Story, & White, 2015); deceitfulness in antisocial personality disorder; and the interpersonal manipulation seen in psychopathy, narcissism, and borderline personality disorder (Lynam, 2012). Antagonistic arrogance is marked by apparent confidence, boastfulness, and belief of one's own superiority and is observed in grandiose features of psychopathy and grandiose narcissism (Miller et al., 2016), as well as histrionic personality disorder (Samuel & Widiger, 2008). These facets have less biological research, and behavioral manifestations of Machiavellianism and narcissism are also considerably driven by other FFM domains including high extraversion, high neuroticism, and low conscientiousness; therefore biological findings based on these phenotypes may be driven only partly by antagonism (O'Boyle et al., 2015).

The research on the heritability of these traits has suggested a typical combination of genetic and environmental influences. Heritability studies that have utilized the NEO-PI-R (Jang et al., 1996, 1998) have found that manipulation and arrogance are attributed mainly to the nonshared environment (53%–75%). However, whereas manipulation seems to be also driven by additive genetics (25%–47%), arrogance seems to be instead driven in part by shared family environment (26%–33%). These results are consistent with research on the Dark Triad (psychopathy, narcissism, and Machiavellianism), which reflect extremes in both arrogant and manipulative behaviors. Research suggests dark traits are driven mostly by genetic (31%–64%) and nonshared environmental factors (30%–41%), although Machiavellianism was also influenced by the shared environment (39%) (Vernon, Villani, Vickers, & Harris, 2008).

Like other facets of antagonism, arrogant/manipulative traits (at least as manifested in narcissism) have also been linked to hormones such as testosterone and cortisol. One study investigating the Dark Triad (measured using the Short Dark Triad measure; Jones & Paulhus, 2014) found that grandiose narcissism (but not Machiavellianism or psychopathy) was associated with increased basal levels of testosterone and cortisol, suggesting a link between these hormones and propensities toward social domination as well as a sensitivity toward social esteem and status (Pfattheicher, 2016). Grandiose narcissism, in particular, has been associated with increased cortisol reactivity in response to interpersonal stressors and perceived threats to the self (Edelstein, Yim, & Quas, 2010). This is consistent with the idea that social evaluation and status elicits a strong threat response for individuals with narcissism. Finally, testosterone levels have been found to underlie the relationship between grandiose narcissism and aggression (Lobbestael, Baumeister, Fiebig, & Eckel, 2014), suggesting that higher levels of basal testosterone may predispose narcissistic individuals toward aggressive behavior. However, others argue that the testosterone-cortisol ratio is most important, specifically low levels of cortisol combined with high levels of testosterone (Terburg, Morgan, & van Honk, 2009).

In a related vein, narcissism has been associated with heightened activation of the salience network, particularly increased right anterior insula activity, the region implicated in representation of the self (Fan et al., 2011). These data are consistent with theoretical interpretations of the narcissistic interpersonal style in regard to sensitivity to perceived threat to their ego, resulting in a variety of interpersonal strategies such as manipulation and arrogance as a means of self-protection (Baumeister, Smart, & Boden, 1996). Indeed, alterations in neural circuits related to the self are observed in narcissism, with evidence of weakened connectivity between the regions of the brain involved in processing of self-relevant stimuli (medial-prefrontal cortex) and reward (ventral-striatum) (Chester, Lynam, Powell, & DeWall, 2015). This physiological disconnect between representations of the self and reward would be consistent with self-regulatory theories of narcissism (Morf & Rhodewalt, 2001). Specifically, for narcissists, arrogance and external validation seeking serves as a regulatory strategy to compensate for deficits in deriving an intrinsic sense of self-worth.

While the arrogance associated with narcissism involves heightened reactivity and preoccupation with representations of the self, manipulative tendencies may relate to decreased sensitivity to the emotional consequences of deceiving others (e.g., anxiety, guilt, sympathy). For example, the brain has been shown to adapt to dishonesty, such that with continued lying, the amygdala response dampens to the negative feeling associated with preparing to tell a lie (Garrett, Lazzaro, Ariely, & Sharot, 2016). This suggests that habituation to deception may actually cause reduced amygdala activation, although more research is needed to determine the causal nature of the relationship. Further, the interpersonal-affective facet of psychopathy has been associated with lower activation of the amygdala and enhanced activation of the dorsolateral prefrontal cortex during an emotion-recognition task, suggesting that these individuals rely less on emotional centers of the brain for processing emotional information (Gordon, Baird, & End, 2004). Consistent with this, studies consistently find that intentionally deceiving someone in an experimental deception task is associated with increased activity in the prefrontal cortex among a nonclinical sample (Abe, Suzuki, Mori, Itoh, & Fujii, 2007). Studies have associated pathological lying (measured using the PCL-R) with increased prefrontal white matter (Yang et al., 2007) and Machiavellianism with increased prefrontal cortex gray matter volume (Verbeke et al., 2011).

Machiavellianism was also found to be associated with increased activation of the dorsolateral prefrontal cortex during a laboratory Trust game but only during conditions that required cooperation (Bereczkei et al., 2015). This suggests that for individuals with Machiavellian traits, cooperative social interactions require more cognitive effort, possibly because these interactions involve weighing the pros and cons of exploiting another person for personal gain. Collectively, these findings suggest that manipulation, in particular, relates to deficits in the emotional processing regions of the brain, in combination with increased prefrontal involvement in processing cues.

In summary, the arrogant and manipulative facets of antagonism have been less researched in the context of biological studies. These traits characterize individuals with an increased propensity toward social dominance and sensitivity toward social esteem/status, coupled with an ease with which to use deception and flattery to achieve one's goals. These tendencies are associated with at least two physiological profiles: the increased vigilance to threats to self (e.g., hyperactive salience network, increased basal testosterone and cortisol) observed in arrogance/narcissism, and the decreased reliance on emotional processing and more effortful control during deception. Whereas arrogance involves a biased preoccupation with the self, manipulation involves more calculated and cold processing of social cues to determine the most advantageous option for the self. The somewhat discordant biological findings across arrogance and manipulation may mirror the distinct social style differences observed between these traits (e.g., boastfulness versus deceit), but which all represent behavioral strategies for achieving/maintaining dominance over others.

Conclusions

The primary aim of this chapter was to summarize the existing literature on the biological correlates of trait antagonism. Few studies have directly investigated antagonism as measured by FFM inventories, so we have included relevant studies from various fields including psychopathology, personality/social psychology, behavioral economics, neuroscience, and criminology. The evidence suggests that antagonism is characterized by specific alterations in processes involved in bonding and attachment, social and emotional processing, and responding to threat cues. Importantly, our review suggests that different combinations of traits result in different manifestations at the behavioral level. We argue that the heterogeneity in antagonistic phenotypes is mirrored in their physiological manifestations, and the latter can help understand the social behavior in the former.

Antagonistic facets share tendencies toward lower social cooperation and decreased social bonding and a general insensitivity to social cues. This is substantiated biologically by reductions in oxytocin system activity observed across facets of antagonism (specifically, callousness, self-centeredness, distrust, and manipulation). While more research is needed to establish causality, it appears that deficits in levels of oxytocin may contribute to the decreased social bonding and affiliation associated with antagonism. When this generalized lower social bonding combines with mechanisms associated with specific facets, distinct biobehavioral manifestations of antagonism can be identified. As one example, the relative insensitivity to threat and distress cues and altered emotional processing shown by self-centered and callous persons can result in reduced empathy and reduced ability to recognize inappropriate behavior or avoid dangerous situations. There is evidence of a somewhat similar biological profile in persons showing deceit and manipulation, although the reduced processing of emotional information is combined with higher reliance on cognitive centers during interpersonal interactions. At the same time, arrogant narcissism is associated with heightened reactivity to threats to or representations of the self. This combined pattern makes it easier for individuals high on arrogance and manipulation to deceive and exploit others, especially when they detect threats to status. Relative to other antagonistic facets, the biological profile of oppositionality/distrust shows a fairly distinct pattern of heightened threat response and poor downregulation of impulses. These individuals are not reluctant to respond to frustrating or threatening situations with a hostile confrontation and have difficulty inhibiting these reactions in inappropriate circumstances. This tendency would result in frequent negative interpersonal interactions, which would then only serve to reinforce their continued mistrust and resentment of others.

This review serves to motivate future work in this area to improve our understanding of the neurobiology related to antagonism. First, future research should use the FFM to specifically study the biological correlates of antagonistic personality traits. This would reduce the ambiguity by addressing whether biological correlates are actually being driven by antagonism or by some other FFM domain. Second, as the literature on the biology of trait antagonism continues to grow, researchers should consider environmental and contextual factors that influence the expression of antagonistic traits (e.g., gender role). Third, mapping FFM antagonism traits to biobehavioral correlates can help inform treatment by identifying subtypes of individuals most amenable to certain intervention strategies. For instance, for individuals with primarily oppositional and mistrustful traits, treatment aimed at adjusting automatic negative reactions might be most useful; whereas for primarily callous or self-centered individuals, intervention might include learning to detect and understand the emotions of others.

Finally, there are a few caveats to note to avoid common misunderstandings that often accompany interpreting biological research. The study of biological factors does not rule out the importance of environmental influences. Rather, the ultimate cause of behavior is due to a complex interaction between both biology *and* environmental/social factors. Differences in brain and biology should not be taken to be fixed or innate; the environment has a powerful and lifelong influence on physiology. The goal of biological psychology is to gain a better understanding of how biological factors combine with environmental influences to promote behavior. As such, a truly biological perspective incorporates both nature and nurture and acknowledges that this dynamic interplay occurs throughout the lifetime.

References

Abe, N., Suzuki, M., Mori, E., Itoh, M., & Fujii, T. (2007). Deceiving others: distinct neural responses of the prefrontal cortex and amygdala in simple fabrication and deception with social interactions. *Journal of Cognitive Neuroscience*, *19*(2), 287–295.

Aghajani, M., Klapwijk, E. T., Colins, O. F., Ziegler, C., Domschke, K., Vermeiren, R. R., et al. (2018). Interactions between oxytocin receptor gene methylation and callous-unemotional traits impact socioaffective brain systems in conduct-disordered offenders. *Biological Psychiatry: Cognitive Neuroscience and Neuroimaging*, *3*(4), 379–391.

Aimone, J. A., Houser, D., & Weber, B. (2014). Neural signatures of betrayal aversion: an fMRI study of trust. *Proceedings of the Royal Society B*, *281*(1782), 20132127.

Alink, L. R. A., Van IJzendoorn, M. H., Bakermans-Kranenburg, M. J., Mesman, J., Juffer, F., & Koot, H. M. (2008). Cortisol and externalizing behavior in children and adolescents: mixed meta-analytic evidence for the inverse relation of basal cortisol and cortisol reactivity with externalizing behavior. *Developmental Psychobiology*, *50*(5), 427–450.

Angrilli, A., Mauri, A., Palomba, D., Flor, H., Birbaumer, N., Sartori, G., et al. (1996). Startle reflex and emotion modulation impairment after a right amygdala lesion. *Brain*, *119*(6), 1991–2004.

Baumeister, R. F., Smart, L., & Boden, J. M. (1996). Relation of threatened egotism to violence and aggression: the dark side of high self-esteem. *Psychological Review*, *103*(1), 5.

Belfi, A. M., Koscik, T. R., & Tranel, D. (2015). Damage to the insula is associated with abnormal interpersonal trust. *Neuropsychologia*, *71*, 165–172.

Bereczkei, T., Papp, P., Kincses, P., Bodrogi, B., Perlaki, G., Orsi, G., et al. (2015). The neural basis of the Machiavellians' decision making in fair and unfair situations. *Brain and Cognition*, *98*, 53–64.

Berg, J., Hecht, L. K., Latzman, R. D., & Lillienfeld, S. O. (2015). Examining the correlates of the coldheartedness factor of the psychopathic personality inventory–revised. *Psychological Assessment*, *27*(4), 1494–1499.

Bernhardt, B., & Singer, T. (2012). The neural basis of empathy. *Annual Review of Neuroscience*, *35*(1), 1–23.

Blair, R. J. R. (2013). The neurobiology of psychopathic traits in youths. *Nature Reviews Neuroscience*, *14*(11), 786.

Blair, R. J. R., Jones, L., Clark, F., & Smith, M. (1997). The psychopathic individual: a lack of responsiveness to distress cues. *Psychophysiology*, *34*(2), 192–198.

Bos, P. A., Terburg, D., & Van Honk, J. (2010). Testosterone decreases trust in socially naive humans. *Proceedings of the National Academy of Sciences*, *107*(22), 9991–9995.

Bouchard, T. J., Jr., & Loehlin, J. C. (2001). Genes, evolution, and personality. *Behavior Genetics*, *31*(3), 243–273.

Buss, D. M. (1996). Social adaptation and five major factors of personality. In J. S. Wiggins (Ed.), *The five factor model of personality: Theoretical perspectives* (pp. 180–207). New York, NY: Guilford.

Canli, T., Congdon, E., Gutknecht, L., Constable, R. T., & Lesch, K. P. (2005). Amygdala responsiveness is modulated by tryptophan hydroxylase-2 gene variation. *Journal of Neural Transmission*, *112*, 1479–1485.

Chester, D. S., Lynam, D. R., Powell, D. K., & DeWall, C. N. (2015). Narcissism is associated with weakened frontostriatal connectivity: a DTI study. *Social Cognitive and Affective Neuroscience*, *11*(7), 1036–1040.

Costa, P. T., Jr., & McCrae, R. R. (1992). *Revised NEO personality inventory (NEO-PI-R) and NEO five-factor inventory (NEO-FFI): Professional manual*. Odessa, FL: Psychological Assessment Resources.

Crider, A. (2008). Personality and electrodermal response lability: an interpretation. *Applied Psychophysiology and Biofeedback*, *33*(3), 141–148.

Damasio, H., Grabowski, T., Frank, R., Galaburda, A. M., & Damasio, A. (1994). The return of Phineas Gage: clues about the brain from the skull of a famous patient. *Science*, *264*(5162), 1102–1105.

Decety, J., Chen, C., Harenski, C., & Kiehl, K. A. (2013). An fMRI study of affective perspective taking in individuals with psychopathy: imagining another in pain does not evoke empathy. *Frontiers in Human Neuroscience*, *7*, 489.

Dimoka, A. (2010). What does the brain tell us about trust and distrust? Evidence from a functional neuroimaging study. *MIS Quarterly*, *34*(2), 373–396.

Domes, G., Heinrichs, M., Gläscher, J., Büchel, C., Braus, D. F., & Herpertz, S. C. (2007). Oxytocin attenuates amygdala responses to emotional faces regardless of valence. *Biological Psychiatry*, *62*(10), 1187–1190.

Edelstein, R. S., Yim, I. S., & Quas, J. A. (2010). Narcissism predicts heightened cortisol reactivity to a psychosocial stressor in men. *Journal of Research in Personality*, *44*(5), 565–572.

Engell, A. D., Haxby, J. V., & Todorov, A. (2007). Implicit trustworthiness decisions: automatic coding of face properties in the human amygdala. *Journal of Cognitive Neuroscience*, *19*(9), 1508–1519.

Fan, Y., Wonneberger, C., Enzi, B., De Greck, M., Ulrich, C., Tempelmann, C., et al. (2011). The narcissistic self and its psychological and neural correlates: an exploratory fMRI study. *Psychological Medicine*, *41*(8), 1641–1650.

Ficks, C., & Waldman, I. D. (2014). Candidate genes for aggression and antisocial behavior: a meta-analysis of association studies of the 5HTTLPR and MAOA-uVNTR. *Behavior Genetics*, *44*(5), 427–444.

Frick, P. J., & White, S. F. (2008). Research review: the importance of callous-unemotional traits for developmental models of aggressive and antisocial behavior. *Journal of Child Psychology and Psychiatry*, *49*(4), 359–375.

Fung, M. T., Raine, A., Loeber, R., Lynam, D. R., Steinhauer, S. R., Venables, P. H., et al. (2005). Reduced electrodermal activity in psychopathy-prone adolescents. *Journal of Abnormal Psychology*, *114*(2), 187–196.

Gao, Y., & Raine, A. (2009). P3 event-related potential impairments in antisocial and psychopathic individuals: a meta-analysis. *Biological Psychology*, *82*(3), 199–210.

Garrett, N., Lazzaro, S. C., Ariely, D., & Sharot, T. (2016). The brain adapts to dishonesty. *Nature Neuroscience*, *19*(12), 1727.

Geniole, S. N., Busseri, M. A., & McCormick, C. M. (2013). Testosterone dynamics and psychopathic personality traits independently predict antagonistic behavior towards the perceived loser of a competitive interaction. *Hormones and Behavior*, *64*(5), 790–798.

Glenn, A. L. (2011). The other allele: exploring the long allele of the serotonin transporter gene as a potential risk factor for psychopathy: a review of the parallels in findings. *Neuroscience and Biobehavioral Reviews*, *35*(3), 612–620.

Gong, P., Fan, H., Liu, J., Yang, X., Zhang, K., & Zhou, X. (2017). Revisiting the impact of OXTR rs53576 on empathy: a population-based study and a meta-analysis. *Psychoneuroendocrinology*, *80*(6).

Gordon, H. L., Baird, A. A., & End, A. (2004). Functional differences among those high and low on a trait measure of psychopathy. *Biological Psychiatry*, *56*(7), 516–521.

Gotlib, I. H., Joormann, J., Minor, K. L., & Hallmayer, J. (2008). HPA axis reactivity: a mechanism underlying the associations among 5-HTTLPR, stress, and depression. *Biological Psychiatry*, *63*(9), 847–851.

Haas, B. W., Ishak, A., Anderson, I. W., & Filkowski, M. M. (2015). The tendency to trust is reflected in human brain structure. *NeuroImage*, *107*, 175–181.

Hall, J. R., & Benning, S. D. (2006). The "successful" psychopath. In *Handbook of psychopathy* (pp. 459–478).

Hare, R. D. (2003). *Manual for the hare psychopathy checklist-revised.* Toronto: Multi-Health Systems.

Harlow, J. (1868). *Passage of an iron bar through the head*: (pp. 3–20).

Hicks, B. M., Bernat, E., Malone, S. M., Iacono, W. G., Patrick, C. J., Krueger, R. F., et al. (2007). Genes mediate the association between P3 amplitude and externalizing disorders. *Psychophysiology*, *44*(1), 98–105.

Hiraishi, K., Yamagata, S., Shikishima, C., & Ando, J. (2008). Maintenance of genetic variation in personality through control of mental mechanisms: a test of trust, extraversion, and agreeableness. *Evolution and Human Behavior*, *29*(2), 79–85.

Huber, D., Veinante, P., & Stoop, R. (2005). Vasopressin and oxytocin excite distinct neuronal populations in the central amygdala. *Science*, *308*(5719), 245–248.

Jang, K. L., Livesley, W. J., Angleitner, A., Riemann, R., & Vernon, P. A. (2002). Genetic and environmental influences on the covariance of facets defining the domains of the five-factor model of personality. *Personality and Individual Differences*, *33*(1), 83–101.

Jang, K. L., Livesley, W. J., & Vernon, P. A. (1996). Heritability of the big five personality dimensions and their facets: a twin study. *Journal of Personality*, *64*(3), 577–591.

Jang, K. L., McCrae, R. R., Angleitner, A., Riemann, R., & Livesley, W. J. (1998). Heritability of facet-level traits in a cross-cultural twin sample: support for a hierarchical model of personality. *Journal of Personality and Social Psychology*, *74*(6), 1556.

Jankowiak-Siuda, K., & Zajkowski, W. (2013). A neural model of mechanisms of empathy deficits in narcissism. *Medical Science Monitor: International Medical Journal of Experimental and Clinical Research*, *19*, 934.

Jones, S. E., Miller, J. D., & Lynam, D. R. (2011). Personality, antisocial behavior, and aggression: a meta-analytic review. *Journal of Criminal Justice*, *39*(4), 329–337.

Jones, D. N., & Paulhus, D. L. (2014). Introducing the short dark triad (SD3) a brief measure of dark personality traits. *Assessment*, *21*(1), 28–41.

Kim-Cohen, J., Caspi, A., Taylor, A., Williams, B., Newcombe, R., Craig, I. W., et al. (2006). MAOA, maltreatment, and gene–environment interaction predicting children's mental health: new evidence and a meta-analysis. *Molecular Psychiatry*, *11*, 903–913.

Kotov, R., Krueger, R. F., Watson, D., Achenbach, T. M., Althoff, R. R., Bagby, R. M., et al. (2017). The hierarchical taxonomy of psychopathology (HiTOP): a dimensional alternative to traditional nosologies. *Journal of Abnormal Psychology*, *126*(4), 454–477.

Kumsta, R., & Heinrichs, M. (2013). Oxytocin, stress and social behavior: neurogenetics of the human oxytocin system. *Current Opinion in Neurobiology*, *23*(1), 11–16.

Larsson, H., Tuvblad, C., Rijsdijk, F. V., Andershed, H., Grann, M., & Lichtenstein, P. (2007). A common genetic factor explains the association between psychopathic personality and antisocial behavior. *Psychological Medicine*, *37*(1), 15–26.

Lobbestael, J., Baumeister, R. F., Fiebig, T., & Eckel, L. A. (2014). The role of grandiose and vulnerable narcissism in self-reported and laboratory aggression and testosterone reactivity. *Personality and Individual Differences*, *69*, 22–27.

Loney, B. R., Butler, M. A., Lima, E. N., Counts, C. A., & Eckel, L. A. (2006). The relation between salivary cortisol, callous-unemotional traits, and conduct problems in an adolescent non-referred sample. *Journal of Child Psychology and Psychiatry*, *47*(1), 30–36.
Lopez-Duran, N. L., Olson, S. L., Hajal, N. J., Felt, B. T., & Vazquez, D. M. (2009). Hypothalamic pituitary adrenal axis functioning in reactive and proactive aggression in children. *Journal of Abnormal Child Psychology*, *37*(2), 169–182.
Lorber, M. F. (2004). Psychophysiology of aggression, psychopathy, and conduct problems: a meta-analysis. *Psychological Bulletin*, *130*(4), 531–552.
Lykken, D. T. (1995). *The antisocial personalities* (p. 259). Hillsdale, NJ: Lawrence Erlbaum Associates.
Lynam, D. R. (2012). Assessment of maladaptive variants of five-factor model traits. *Journal of Personality*, *80*(6), 1593–1613.
Lynam, D. R., Gaughan, E. T., Miller, J. D., Miller, D. J., Mullins-Sweatt, S., & Widiger, T. A. (2011). Assessing the basic traits associated with psychopathy: Development and validation of the Elemental Psychopathy Assessment. *Psychological Assessment*, *23*(1), 108.
Marsh, N., Scheele, D., Gerhardt, H., Strang, S., Enax, L., Weber, B., et al. (2015). The neuropeptide oxytocin induces a social altruism bias. *Journal of Neuroscience*, *35*(47), 15696–15701.
Matthys, W., Vanderchuren, L., & Schutter, D. J. L. G. (2013). The neurobiology of oppositional defiant disorder and conduct disorder: altered functioning in three mental domains. *Development and Psychopathology*, *25*(1), 193–207.
McBurnett, K., Lahey, B. B., & Rathouz, P. (2000). Low salivary cortisol and persistent aggression in boys referred for disruptive behavior. *Archives of General Psychiatry*, *57*(1), 38–43.
Menon, V., & Uddin, L. Q. (2010). Saliency, switching, attention and control: a network model of insula function. *Brain Structure and Function*, *214*(5–6), 655–667.
Miller, J. D., Gentile, B., Wilson, L., & Campbell, W. K. (2013). Grandiose and vulnerable narcissism and the DSM–5 pathological personality trait model. *Journal of Personality Assessment*, *95*(3), 284–290.
Miller, J. D., Lynam, D. R., McCain, J. L., Few, L. R., Crego, C., Widiger, T. A., et al. (2016). Thinking structurally about narcissism: an examination of the Five-Factor Narcissism Inventory and its components. *Journal of Personality Disorders*, *30*(1), 1–18.
Morf, C. C., & Rhodewalt, F. (2001). Unraveling the paradoxes of narcissism: a dynamic self-regulatory processing model. *Psychological Inquiry*, *12*(4), 177–196.
Nettle, D. (2006). The evolution of personality variation in humans and other animals. *The American Psychologist*, *61*(6), 622–631.
O'Leary, M. M., Loney, B. R., & Eckel, L. A. (2007). Gender differences in the association between psychopathic personality traits and cortisol response to induced stress. *Psychoneuroendocrinology*, *32*(2), 183–191.
O'Boyle, E. H., Forsyth, D. R., Banks, G. C., Story, P. A., & White, C. D. (2015). A meta-analytic test of redundancy and relative importance of the dark triad and five-factor model of personality. *Journal of Personality*, *83*(6), 644–664.
Paris, J. (2000). The classification of personality disorders should be rooted in biology. *Journal of Personality Disorders*, *14*(2), 127–136.
Patrick, C. J. (2014). Physiological correlates of psychopathy, antisocial personality disorder, habitual aggression, and violence. In *Vol. 21. Electrophysiology and psychophysiology in psychiatry and psychopharmacology* (pp. 197–227). Cham, Switzerland: Springer.
Patrick, C. J., Fowles, D. C., & Krueger, R. F. (2009). Triarchic conceptualization of psychopathy: Developmental origins of disinhibition, boldness, and meanness. *Development and Psychopathology*, *21*(3), 913–938.

Pfattheicher, S. (2016). Testosterone, cortisol and the Dark Triad: narcissism (but not Machiavellianism or psychopathy) is positively related to basal testosterone and cortisol. *Personality and Individual Differences*, *97*, 115–119.

Pham, T. H., Philippot, P., & Rime, B. (2000). Subjective and autonomic responses to emotion induction in psychopaths. *Encephale*, *26*, 45–51.

Portnoy, J., & Farrington, D. P. (2015). Resting heart rate and antisocial behavior: an updated systematic review and meta-analysis. *Aggression and Violent Behavior*, *22*, 33–45.

Rhee, S. H., & Waldman, I. D. (2002). Genetic and environmental influences on antisocial behavior: a meta-analysis of twin and adoption studies. *Psychological Bulletin*, *128*(3), 490.

Riedl, R., & Javor, A. (2012). The biology of trust: integrating evidence from genetics, endocrinology, and functional brain imaging. *Journal of Neuroscience, Psychology, and Economics*, *5*(2), 63.

Sadeh, N., Javdani, S., Jackson, J. J., & Reynolds, E. K. (2010). Serotonin transporter gene associations with psychopathic traits in youth vary as a function of socioeconomic resources. *Journal of Abnormal Psychology*, *119*(3), 604–609.

Sadeh, N., Verona, E., & Javdani, S. (2013). Analysis of monoaminergic genes, childhood abuse, and dimensions of psychopathy. *Journal of Abnormal Psychology*, *122*(1), 167–179.

Samuel, D. B., & Widiger, T. A. (2008). A meta-analytic review of the relationships between the five factor model and DSM-IV-TR personality disorders: a facet level analysis. *Clinical Psychology Review*, *28*(8), 1326–1342.

Shirtcliff, E. A., Vitacco, M. J., Graf, A. R., Gostisha, A. J., Merz, J. L., & Zahn-Waxler, C. (2009). Neurobiology of empathy and callousness: implications for the development of antisocial behavior. *Behavioral Sciences & the Law*, *27*(2), 131–171.

Skeem, J. L., Miller, J. D., Mulvey, E., Tiemann, J., & Monahan, J. (2005). Using a five-factor lens to explore the relation between personality traits and violence in psychiatric patients. *Journal of Consulting and Clinical Psychology*, *73*(3), 454–465.

Spurk, D., Keller, A., & Hirschi, A. (2016). Do bad guys get ahead or fall behind? Relationships of the dark triad of personality with objective and subjective career success. *Social Psychological and Personality Science*, *7*(2), 113–121.

Terburg, D., Morgan, B., & van Honk, J. (2009). The testosterone–cortisol ratio: a hormonal marker for proneness to social aggression. *International Journal of Law and Psychiatry*, *32*(4), 216–223.

Thompson, G. J., Hurd, P. L., & Crespi, B. J. (2013). Genes underlying altruism. *Biology Letters*, *9*(6), 20130395.

Tuvblad, C., Bezdjian, S., Raine, A., & Baker, L. A. (2014). The heritability of psychopathic personality in 14-to 15-year-old twins: A multirater, multimeasure approach. *Psychological Assessment*, *26*(3), 704.

Vaidyanathan, U., Hall, J. R., Patrick, C. J., & Bernat, E. (2011). Clarifying the role of defensive reactivity deficits in psychopathy and antisocial personality using startle reflex methodology. *Journal of Abnormal Psychology*, *120*(1), 253–258.

van Stegeren, A. H., Wolf, O. T., Everaerd, W., Scheltens, P., Barkhof, F., & Rombouts, S. A. (2007). Endogenous cortisol level interacts with noradrenergic activation in the human amygdala. *Neurobiology of Learning and Memory*, *87*(1), 57–66.

Verbeke, W. J., Rietdijk, W. J., van den Berg, W. E., Dietvorst, R. C., Worm, L., & Bagozzi, R. P. (2011). The making of the Machiavellian brain: a structural MRI analysis. *Journal of Neuroscience, Psychology, and Economics*, *4*(4), 205.

Vernon, P. A., Villani, V. C., Vickers, L. C., & Harris, J. A. (2008). A behavioral genetic investigation of the Dark Triad and the Big 5. *Personality and Individual Differences*, *44*(2), 445–452.

Verona, E., & Bresin, K. (2015). Aggression proneness: transdiagnostic processes involving negative valence and cognitive systems. *International Journal of Psychophysiology*, *98*, 321–329.

Verona, E., Murphy, B., & Bresin, K. (2018). Oxytocin-related single nucleotide polymorphisms, family environment, and psychopathic traits. *Personality Disorders: Theory, Research & Treatment*, *9*(6), 584–589.

Viding, E., Blair, R. J. R., Moffitt, T. E., & Plomin, R. (2005). Evidence for substantial genetic risk for psychopathy in 7-year-olds. *Journal of Child Psychology and Psychiatry*, *46*(6), 592–597.

Viding, E., Jones, A. P., Frick, P. J., Moffitt, T. E., & Plomin, R. (2008). Heritability of antisocial behaviour at 9: do callous-unemotional traits matter? *Developmental Science*, *11*(1), 17–22.

Weber, S., Habel, U., Amunts, K., & Schneider, F. (2008). Structural brain abnormalities in psychopaths—a review. *Behavioral Sciences & the Law*, *26*(1), 7–28.

Yang, Y., Raine, A., Narr, K. L., Lencz, T., LaCasse, L. O. R. I., Colletti, P., et al. (2007). Localisation of increased prefrontal white matter in pathological liars. *The British Journal of Psychiatry*, *190*(2), 174–175.

Young, C. B., Raz, G., Everaerd, D., Beckmann, C. F., Tendolkar, I., Hendler, T., et al. (2017). Dynamic shifts in large-scale brain network balance as a function of arousal. *Journal of Neuroscience*, *37*(2), 281–290.

Zeigler-Hill, V., & Hobbs, K. A. (2017). The darker aspects of motivation: pathological personality traits and the fundamental social motives. *Journal of Social and Clinical Psychology*, *36*(2), 87–107.

Agreeableness, antagonism, and mental health across cultures

7

Amber Gayle Thalmayer, Jérôme Rossier
Research Center in Vocational Psychology and Career Counseling, Institute of Psychology, University of Lausanne, Lausanne, Switzerland

Knowing whether a psychological phenomenon occurs across cultures is important for understanding the interplay between individuals and their cultural context. For example, learning that *bulimia nervosa* is specific to recent times and Western industrialized cultures (Keel & Klump, 2003), that the long-term prognosis for schizophrenia patients is worse in such cultures compared to developing nations (e.g., Leff, Sartorius, Jablensky, Korten, & Ernberg, 1992), or that *hikikomori* (extreme social withdrawal; Furlong, 2008) is a manifestation of anxiety specific to the Japanese cultural context lends insight to the challenges a culture may create. On the other hand, comparable syndromes of depression, bipolar disorder, and schizophrenia around the world inform us about universal vulnerabilities of the human psyche, although prevalence, symptoms, and beliefs about etiology can vary considerably, with important implications for locally relevant assessment and treatment (Tseng, 2001).

Posing questions about the culturally specific versus universal aspects of a psychological phenomenon is therefore important, but answering them can be complex. For one thing, simply importing personality measures or diagnostic criteria can preclude learning from the new culture. While such studies may provide evidence of replicable constructs, they cannot identify culture-specific ones, which may have better predictive and explanatory power (Cheung, van de Vijver, & Leong, 2011). Even when a construct has been deemed appropriate for import, measures and methods may need to be adapted to achieve equivalence in how they are perceived. Direct translation of terms such as proud or anxious, for example, can lead to different responses due to differing emotional/evaluative meanings (Thalmayer & Saucier, 2014). And when using a subjective scale such as degree of agreement about how "friendly" or "orderly" one is, one must compare oneself to well-known others, leading to potential reference group effects (Heine, Buchtel, & Norenzayan, 2008).

The core premise of personality psychology, that internal traits explain behavior, was developed in a Western context (Cross & Markus, 1999). While terms for personality differences are used universally across cultures (Saucier, Thalmayer, & Bel-Bahar, 2014), internal qualities may not be given the same causal significance everywhere. In some settings, roles, relationships, and obligations may be seen as larger influences on behavior (Cross & Markus, 1999). Relatedly, cultures differ on whether personality attributes are seen as fixed and enduring and the extent to which this is valued. In individualistic cultures, personality consistency is associated with social

The Handbook of Antagonism. https://doi.org/10.1016/B978-0-12-814627-9.00007-4

skills, well-being, and being well-liked (Suh, 2002). But in collectivistic cultures, behaving similarly regardless of context may be viewed as a lack of self-control, social skills, and maturity (Suh, 2002). In traditional cultures, many social contexts are largely scripted, demanding less variation and expression of individual psychological differences (Cross & Markus, 1999). The relative importance of personality in self-definition is therefore influenced by the cultural context. And in terms of mental disorders, Paris and Lis (2013) describe ways that culture and historical context can shape clinical presentation, for example, in terms of the locally understood symptoms and presentations, or "symptom bank," from which individuals subconsciously choose how to communicate their dysphoria to others, and in terms of local stressors or protective factors that can determine whether vulnerabilities become disorders.

The aim of this chapter, however, is to review and assess the best available evidence on the associations between Agreeableness/antagonism and mental health across cultures. Given contemporary migration flow and shifting demographics, it is important to consider whether our knowledge about these traits and conditions can be used with people and patients from backgrounds and contexts outside the mainstream of Western, industrialized cultures. Moreover, knowing if the traits and conditions in question are more timeless, universal vulnerabilities of the human psyche, or instead recent phenomenon specific to a cultural time and place is still an open question, which we will try to address in this chapter.

Agreeableness/antagonism across cultures

The personality dimension of Agreeableness, along with the rest of the Big Five, was defined by consistent patterns in personality inventories and models in use in the early part of the 20th century, by lexical studies of personality in English (Saucier & Goldberg, 2001), and by the Five-Factor Model of Costa and McCrae (1992). Models including an Agreeableness dimension were then replicated in many cultures in the 1990s and early 2000s (e.g., Saucier & Goldberg, 2001). Several large-scale studies have administered Big Five inventories across cultures. Peer ratings on the revised NEO Personality Inventory (NEO-PI-R; Costa & McCrae, 1992) were collected in 50 cultures (McCrae et al., 2005a) and mean profiles of self-ratings from 62 cultures were compared (Allik et al., 2017). Findings support the interpretability of this dimension and the model's structure, and differences between countries are consistently smaller than differences within countries. Although cross-cultural mean differences for Agreeableness are small and cannot yet be considered reliable (Church et al., 2011), many studies report slightly higher Agreeableness in collectivist societies (e.g., Rossier, Dahourou, & McCrae, 2005), though individualism appears to correlate more consistently with higher Extraversion than lower Agreeableness (McCrae et al., 2005b). Cross-cultural studies of personality inventories, however, have not yet been able to present evidence of scalar measurement invariance among cultures separated by large cultural distance, which would indicate reliability and validity for comparing mean scores across cultures (Church et al., 2011; Rossier, Ouedraogo, & Dahourou, 2017; Thalmayer & Saucier, 2014). This has been true for the Big Five Inventory

(BFI) in 56 nations (Schmitt, Allik, McCrae, & Benet-Martínez, 2007), and to a forager-farmer group in the Amazon (Gurven, Von Rueden, Massenkoff, Kaplan, & Lero Vie, 2013), and the closely related Big Six model using the Questionnaire Big Six (QB6) in 26 countries (Thalmayer & Saucier, 2014), as well as the NEO-PI-R. Thus it is not yet possible to trust that a person who receives a low score on Agreeableness on the inventory in Thai, for example, is really less Agreeable than someone with a high score in Swahili.

Indeed, a number of measurement issues must be considered. For example, reference group effects, as noted previously, may lead people to rate themselves against different standards. This would explain why Mexicans describe themselves as less sociable than North Americans, despite displaying more sociable behavior (Ramírez-Esparza, Mehl, Álvarez-Bermúdez, & Pennebaker, 2009). Students in schools with high standards achieve more, but have lower academic self-concepts than lower achieving students in less challenging contexts (Van de Gaer, Grisay, Schulz, & Gebhardt, 2012). Heine et al. (2008) found indicators of high national Conscientiousness (e.g., postal workers' speed, per capita GDP, life expectancy) to be positively correlated with perceptions of national character, but negatively with national mean Conscientiousness scores. Mõttus, Allik, and Realo (2010), on the other hand, show that such correlations become more intuitive when explored at the facet level and make a case for the future of national mean comparisons. The interplay between traits and sociocultural context, however, means that measurement issues are complex.

Studies using "emic" approaches, which build personality models from the ground up in a given locale, provide evidence for other relevant models and traits, information which can be obscured by reliance on an imported inventory. For example, Ashton et al. (2004) and Saucier (2009) showed that a six-factor model, including a factor related to honesty and moral character, better fit the cumulative results from a combined total of 14 indigenous lexical studies. These efforts have the advantage of building a culture-fair model, rather than simply testing replicability of a North American model. High Agreeableness in the Big Six focuses on conflict avoidance; low Agreeableness emphasizes reactive aggression, impatience, and hostility, whereas low Honesty/Propriety encompasses instrumental aggression, intentionally taking advantage of others (Thalmayer & Saucier, 2014). This distinction could be especially interesting regarding the externalizing syndromes of interest in this volume.

Other recent work continues to go further afield. Indigenous lexical studies in two of Africa's four main language groups, East African Maasai and West Africa Supyire-Senufo, led to a common four-dimensional structure, with factors tentatively labeled Anger, Laziness, Virtue, and Happiness; anger correlates moderately with Big Five and Six Agreeableness (Thalmayer, Saucier, Ole-Kotikash, Payne, & Carlson, 2018). The South African Personality Inventory (SAPI) project comprised extensive efforts to develop an indigenous inventory "culture fair" to the country's 4 ethnic and 11 language groups (Fetvadjiev, Meiring, van de Vijver, Nel, & Hill, 2015). The resulting inventory includes six dimensions, four of which overlap with Big Five domains, with the exception of Agreeableness—Social Relations-Positive, and -Negative seem conceptually related to Big Five Agreeableness, but are not highly correlated with it (.13 and .20; Fetvadjiev et al., 2015). A similar emic-etic approach used qualitative analyses of person descriptions to develop a personality questionnaire suited to spoken Arabic in the Levant (Zeinoun, Daouk-Öyry, Choueiri, & Van de Vijver, 2017). The resulting indigenous seven-factor model largely included the Big Five, including Agreeableness/Soft Heartedness (Zeinoun et al., 2017). Studies comparing emic and etic dimensions have shown that indigenous scales, for example, Interpersonal Relatedness in an emic Chinese personality inventory, can better predict life, work, and mental health outcomes than imported scales (Cheung, Cheung, & Fan, 2013; Sanchez-Burks, Nisbett, & Ybarra, 2000; Zeinoun et al., 2017).

As a starting point in exploring cross-cultural evidence for the relation of antagonism to mental health, we can conclude that a factor with the basic outlines of Agreeableness versus antagonism is measurable across cultures, and it arises in local emic studies in many cases. Findings from emic work, however, suggest that while an interpersonal domain may be universally relevant to personality conceptions, locally salient content may differ.

Gender and Agreeableness across cultures

Several etic studies report gender differences across cultures. In Western countries on both self- and peer-ratings, men consistently score higher than women on Assertiveness and lower on Agreeableness and Neuroticism (Costa, Terracciano, & McCrae, 2001; McCrae et al., 2005a; Schmitt, Realo, Voracek, & Allik, 2008). They also may score lower on Conscientiousness (Schmitt et al., 2008) and Openness to Feelings and higher on Openness to Ideas (Costa et al., 2001; McCrae et al., 2005a). These appear to be some of the most robust psychological differences between the sexes—while smaller than those for mate preferences, sexual behaviors, or physical strength, they appear larger and more consistent than differences in cognitive ability, attributional style, or self-esteem (Schmitt et al., 2008).

Sex differences on Agreeableness and Neuroticism are not surprising given gender stereotypes and the higher prevalence of mental disorders related to antagonism among men. More counterintuitive is the fact that they are consistently larger in Western, industrialized countries with higher gender equity; sex differences in Asia and Africa are consistently smaller, as is overall personality variation among men (Costa et al., 2001; McCrae et al., 2005b; Schmitt et al., 2008). This is contrary to patterns of sexual differentiation in other psychological variables, where sex differences are smaller in cultures with higher gender equity and standards of living (Schmitt et al., 2008).

Hypotheses explored by Schmitt et al. (2008) for this finding include social desirability biases, frames of reference, attribution processes, and measurement error, but they conclude that the evidence best supports the "evolutionary mismatch perspective." This posits that where contemporary environments differ more from the hunter-gatherer environments in which humans evolved, the development of psychological sex differences is attenuated. Sex-related differences are assumed to exist in domains where the sexes faced different adaptive problems during evolutionary history. If modern nation-states are psychologically closer to hunter-gatherer cultures, then such sex differences may be given fuller expression (Schmitt et al., 2008). While contrary to results for other psychological variables, this is analogous to sex differences in height and blood pressure, which are attenuated in less developed, agricultural-based societies; even within cultures, sex differences in height are larger for better-off groups, because boys grow taller. Indeed, in the same group of industrialized, egalitarian countries, men had higher blood pressure than women, whereas in less developed countries blood pressure was practically identical (Schmitt et al., 2008).

This interesting hypothesis, however, assumes homogeneity in early human societies. Work with ethnographic literature (e.g., Harpending & Draper, 1988) demonstrates an association between male aggressiveness and whether local conditions require long-term paternal investments. Individualistic, industrialized societies have conditions where cooperation is not essential to survival and more rewards may accrue to those who compete fiercely, leading to lower scores in Agreeableness for men. This may also be true among some traditional societies. And as discussed previously, in collectivistic cultures, behavior may be determined less by personality traits are more by social context (Rossier et al., 2005), which could explain smaller variation and lower gender differences in collectivistic cultures. Whatever their source, these differences are relevant to the question at hand, in part by indicating ways that personality dimensions are influenced by cultural setting. They also suggest that gender differences in the prevalence of mental health conditions related to low Agreeableness are likely to be larger in Western cultures, and that such conditions are likely to more prevalent here.

Change in Agreeableness over the lifespan across cultures

Cross sectional studies of Big Five traits consistently demonstrate higher scores on Agreeableness, Conscientious, and Emotional Stability, and sometimes lower scores on Extraversion and Openness for older adults compared to younger ones (e.g., Donnellan, Hill, & Roberts, 2015). A meta-analysis of longitudinal studies replicated these findings, showing that individuals increase in Conscientiousness, Emotional Stability, and social dominance (Extraversion) in young adulthood, then later increase in Agreeableness and decrease in social vitality (Extraversion) and Openness (Roberts, Walton, & Viechtbauer, 2006). Bleidorn et al. (2013) replicated these findings in 62 countries using the BFI. Across nations, Emotional Stability, Extraversion, Openness, Agreeableness, and Conscientiousness tended to increase from early to middle adulthood. Consistent with social investment theory, the team found that personality maturation occurred earlier in cultures with an earlier onset of adult-role responsibilities. Interestingly, the authors found that it was transition to the labor force, rather than family-role transitions such as marriage or parenthood, that predicted "maturation." They note that while this is contrary to some assumptions of social investment theory, it is consistent with lay beliefs. For example, Arnett (2001) found that American adolescents and adults considered becoming financially independent a stronger indicator of adult status than marriage or parenthood. These results suggest that opportunities for young people to integrate into meaningful social roles and economic independence can foster an increase in Agreeableness and presumably reduce disorders related to antagonism.

Agreeableness/antagonism relations to mental health

The mental disorders, symptoms, and behaviors known to correlate with antagonism in North America and other Western countries are reviewed later for cross-cultural evidence.

Childhood aggression and conduct disorder

Canino, Polanczyk, Bauermeister, Rohde, and Frick (2010) conducted a systematic review of cross-cultural evidence on conduct disorder (CD) and oppositional defiant disorder (ODD) to inform the American Psychiatric Association's Diagnostic and Statistical Manual of Mental Disorders, Fifth Edition (DSM-V) classifications. Cultural factors should play a role in the prevalence of these disorders due to their association with risk and protective factors like prenatal care, infant nutrition, neighborhood safety, and family environment, attachments, and supervision. Prevalence rates can also be impacted by cultural setting because symptoms may be differentially viewed as dysfunctional. The team, however, found similar prevalence rates for CD (3.2%) and ODD (3.3%) across 25 published studies using DSM criteria, primarily from North America and Europe. This indicates a reasonable basis for these conditions across Western societies, though they note that using DSM criteria likely increased homogeneity and that symptoms should be validated against external and clinical criteria (Canino et al., 2010).

More generally, parenting practices have been shown to relate to degree of aggression expressed by children, especially boys (e.g., Ekblad, 1988), for example, comparing American to Thai children (Weisz, Suwanlert, Chaiyasit, & Walter, 1987). Child Behavior Checklist scores in 16 regions indicated higher rates of internalizing and lower of externalizing syndromes in Asian compared to Western countries (Crijnen, Achenbach, & Verhulst, 1999). Children are certainly influenced by familial and cultural settings in the ways they express unhappiness and frustration, and whether these will include behaviors defined as aggressive, oppositional, or disordered.

Aggression

Cooke (1996) provided a review of aggressive behavior across cultures, citing evidence for substantial variation. Some groups, for example, the Inuit of the Artic, the Pygmies of Africa, and Mennonite and Amish communities in North America, rarely use violence, while others, for example, the Yanomami of the Upper Amazon, express physical and verbal aggression on a daily basis. Cultural socialization plays a significant role in whether and how aggression is expressed.

To expand psychologists' understanding of aggression beyond Western societies, Severance et al. (2013) used multidimensional scaling analyses of ratings on acts of aggression to explore perceptions between four cultures varying in "cultural logic" (Leung & Cohen, 2011). In Japan, a culture of face, self-worth stems from the views others hold, status in the hierarchy, and humility, modesty, and self-control. In this interdependent context, maintaining harmony with the group is central, and conflict is handled indirectly (Leung & Cohen, 2011). There is strong differentiation between direct and passive aggression, but because violence is rare, verbal aggression that can damage reputation is seen as direct; because aggressive acts can seriously damage someone's self-worth, such acts are viewed as extremely immoral and callous (Severance et al., 2013).

In Pakistan, a culture of honor, maintaining a reputation for strength is paramount. The collectivistic context means that shame for close others is experienced as highly personal. In the United States, the South has been shown to be a culture of honor, but the majority culture is one of dignity: Individuals are believed to have intrinsic worth which cannot easily be lost. Self-evaluations are most important, and the individualistic context means that close others are not strongly reflective on the self. Israel, a multicultural country combining Middle Eastern and European influences and value systems, embodies a mix of honor and dignity cultures (Leung & Cohen, 2011; Severance et al., 2013).

In Pakistan and Israel, being the object of an aggressive act is perceived as humiliating, a threat to honor and social status, indicating the danger of social exclusion in clan-based social systems. In Pakistan, verbal aggression is perceived as especially threatening, perhaps because in a culture of honor, verbal declarations become obligations. In the United States, other's aggression is less relevant to one's self-worth. Instead, infringements on material belongings or professional accomplishments, by extension on one's autonomy, are perceived as especially damaging. This is salient also in Israel, where gossip and public insults are also considered threatening to personal resources. Here more than elsewhere, verbal acts targeting one's family are perceived as direct threats (Severance et al., 2013). Relatedly, childhood maltreatment had a stronger impact on the development of later personality disorders (PDs) in Togo compared to France (Kounou et al., 2015). These cultural differences in how aggression and antagonism are communicated and perceived indicate the necessity of cultural knowledge when assessing individual behavior or traits.

Antisocial personality disorder, psychopathy, and criminal behavior

There is reason to believe that individuals with behavior patterns similar to psychopathy and antisocial personality disorder (ASPD) have existed across time and cultural settings. Murphy (1976) provides evidence for comparable syndromes among two nonindustrialized groups, *aranakan* among the Yoruba of Nigeria, and *kunlangeta* for Inuit Eskimos. Both syndromes describe persons who take advantage of others consistently and remorselessly, are unresponsive to social pressure or punishment, and are considered untreatable and unlikely to change. Sullivan and Kosson (2006) review historical examples, including a description of the Athenian general Alcibiades as a psychopath, and the reckless, cynical Trickster figures that appears across many cultures.

There are also reasons to expect prevalence to vary across cultures. Social norms and values may allow or even encourage behavior that ultimately fits a pattern of disorder. Individualistic societies are more likely than collectivistic ones to allow the development of ASPD symptoms, including irresponsibility, callousness, lack of remorse, glibness and superficiality, grandiosity, and promiscuity (Cooke, 1996; Cooke, Michie, Hart, & Clark, 2005). Harpending and Draper (1988) provide ethnographic evidence that aggressive and antisocial traits are more common in cultures where male competitiveness is high and parental effort low; where parental effort is high, such traits will be less common, as there are fewer rewards, and antisocial persons will be detected and ostracized. Indeed, rates of ASPD appear to be 10 times lower in Taiwan than in the United States (Compton et al., 1991).

The cross-cultural validity of psychopathy has been supported by studies importing the Psychopathy Checklist-Revised (PCL-R) to European countries (Cooke et al., 2005). Of the inventories three factors—deficient affective experience, arrogant and deceitful interpersonal style, impulsive and irresponsible behavioral style—the first appears to be the cross-cultural core of the construct, perhaps due to varying socialization across cultures, which may differentially interact with the core affective temperament to produce more or less pathological interpersonal and behavioral patterns (Cooke et al., 2005). In the same countries, Sullivan and Kosson (2006) report cross-Atlantic construct validity of psychopathy in terms of replicable positive associations with PD diagnoses, especially ASPD, secondarily with other Cluster B disorders; substance abuse; earlier initiation of criminal behavior; recidivism; rule infractions; and traits of impulsivity, aggression, and sensation seeking. North American prison populations typically have higher mean PCL-R scores, previously attributed to a lower prevalence of psychopathy in Europe due to cultural socialization. But another possibility is differences in criminal justice systems. In some nations, persons with psychopathic disorder are placed in mental hospitals rather than prisons. In others, incarceration rates are low. In Norway, the rate is 10 times lower than in the United States; only severe offenders are imprisoned, and nearly half the prison population meets criteria for psychopathy (Sullivan & Kosson, 2006). A recent study of incarcerated women in South Africa also found psychopathy to be particularly associated with Cluster B PDs (Botha, Louw, & Loots, 2017).

Borderline and other personality disorders

Although clinicians outside North America are less likely to make PD diagnoses, the constructs are comprehensible once imported (e.g., Paris & Lis, 2013). The Personality Disorder Questionnaire and Interview had acceptable psychometric properties in Chinese (Yang et al., 2000), and the International Personality Disorder Examination had acceptable interrater reliability and temporal stability in samples of clinical patients from cities across North America, Europe, Africa, and Asia (Loranger et al., 1994), a study that found Borderline Personality Disorder (BPD) especially prevalent. The inventory structure was also stable in a sample of French-speaking African countries, and when translated into Mooré, and administered by interview to villagers in Burkina Faso (Rossier, Ouedraogo, Dahourou, Verardi, & Meyer de Stadelhofen, 2013). Though thresholds for impairment may vary, there are surely individuals who "deviate markedly from the expectations of their culture" in every society (Tseng, 2001).

Paris and Lis (2013) argue that social risk factors, including modernity's disruptions to family structures, influence whether the traits that underlie PDs lead to disordered behavior—people with impulsivity and affective instability exist everywhere, but psychosocial risk or protective factors can determine whether their expression becomes pathological. Sociocultural factors are key to determining whether an individual's vulnerabilities create difficulties in meeting social expectations, a defining feature of PDs, and the "symptom bank" that will be drawn on. Specifically, patients in traditional societies are more likely to report internalizing problems than to exhibit self-harm and para-suicide, which are increasingly prevalent in the west, suggesting susceptibility to cultural factors (Paris & Lis, 2013). Miller (1996), however, argues that many culture-specific disorders define individuals who, like those with BPD, perceive themselves as unable to meet social expectations and who express their resulting distress in culturally relevant ways.

Substance use

In samples from Mexico, Germany, the Netherlands, Canada, and the United States including a sample of Mexican-Americans, Merikangas et al. (1998) report similar prevalence of disordered substance use and comorbidity with mood and anxiety disorders, CD, and ASPD. They conclude that a consistent relationship between number of comorbid disorders and substance use severity, especially for drugs, indicates a common link between psychopathology and substance disorders, despite cultural variation in substances available and normal usage. Bennett, Janca, Grant, and Sartorius (1993) conducted interviews with community members from cultures that traditionally include social drinking and those that do not, and document consistencies in perceptions of problem drinking, including drinking alone and in large quantities, despite differences in normal use.

Heath (2001) and Martin, Chung, and Langenbucher (2014) review substance use and abuse over time and across cultures. Substance use appears to be a human universal, with alcohol fermentation and use of psychoactive plants extending to distant history and nonhuman animals. Heath (2001) argues that the experience, behaviors, and dangers of addiction with a given substance are defined by goals—medical, ritual, social, self-development, or recreational—and expectations. Social disapproval, and thus the definition of disordered use, varies culturally in ways not always consistent with actual dangers. Social consequences are also inconsistent, for example, the disproportionate punishment of Black users of crack cocaine in the United States, despite more widespread use of powdered cocaine among White users in the same period (Heath, 2001). Martin et al. (2014) point out that while compulsive use coupled with dysfunctions in reward, motivation, and affective systems clearly constitutes dysfunction, the point at which this is considered harmful has not been well defined by

DSM criteria and varies across cultures. Thus while it appears likely that disordered substance use co-occurs with disorders related to antagonism across cultures, substance abuse can be hard to distinguish from use, especially without cultural knowledge, and thus may be a less dependable indicator.

Summary and conclusions

Agreeableness versus antagonism is a personality dimension that was defined first in North American cultures, but which corresponds to a reasonable degree with dimensions found in many other cultural settings. Studies translating Western measures into new languages have found that respondents in other cultural settings respond to Agreeableness items in similar ways, allowing a similar factor structure to emerge. There is not yet evidence for full measurement invariance of any personality measures in translation, thus there is not strong support for comparing mean scores across cultures, but such studies were reviewed. Of interest are findings that gender differences in Agreeableness, lower average scores for men, are more pronounced in industrialized nations with greater gender equity. Also of interest was the finding that Agreeableness appears to increase consistently across cultures with age, especially in the context of taking on financial responsibilities.

The disorders associated with antagonism also generally appear to exist across diverse cultural settings. A syndrome that matches psychopathy has been reported far back in time and across varied cultural settings. All human populations may include callous individuals who take advantage of others. Rates and types of aggressive behavior, however, vary considerably depending on local socialization processes, and thus associated disorders appear to be more common in the individualistic, industrialized west.

Future research of interest would include combined emic-etic studies of mental disorders in diverse cultures, in order to compare prevalence while also exploring local expressions of malaise. If the disorders described here are reliably less prevalent in more collectivistic, interdependent, and tight cultures, it would be useful to attempt to isolate cultural practices that could be imported to reduce antagonism. It would also be important to assess trade-offs in lower prevalence, for example, higher rates of internalizing syndromes. Similarly, if treatments vary in efficacy, the most effective could be tested for applicability to new contexts. Understanding that individualism, a dominant cultural value in Western cultures, likely increases antagonism, can help us understand the "shadow side" of the personal freedom and individualistic values we enjoy. Taking a fuller range of risks and benefits into account, we may find ways to temper the values we transmit to our children with appropriate concern for the feelings and the autonomy of others.

Acknowledgment

The contribution of Jérôme Rossier benefited from the support of the Swiss National Centre of Competence in Research LIVES—Overcoming vulnerability: Life course perspective, financed by the Swiss National Science.

References

Allik, J., Church, A. T., Ortiz, F. A., Rossier, J., Hřebı́čková, M., de Fruyt, F., et al. (2017). Mean profiles of the NEO personality inventory. *Journal of Cross-Cultural Psychology, 48*, 402–420. https://doi.org/10.1177/0022022117692100.

Arnett, J. J. (2001). Conceptions of the transition to adulthood: perspectives from adolescence through midlife. *Journal of Adult Development, 8*, 133–143. https://doi.org/10.1023/A:1026450103225.

Ashton, M. C., Lee, K., Perugini, M., Szarota, P., De Vries, R. E., Di Blas, L., et al. (2004). A six-factor structure of personality-descriptive adjectives: solutions from psycholexical studies in seven languages. *Journal of Personality and Social Psychology, 86*, 356–366. https://doi.org/10.1037/0022-3514.86.2.356.

Bennett, L. A., Janca, A., Grant, B. F., & Sartorius, N. (1993). Boundaries between normal and pathological drinking: a cross-cultural comparison. *Alcohol Research and Health, 17*(3), 190.

Bleidorn, W., Klimstra, T. A., Denissen, J. J., Rentfrow, P. J., Potter, J., & Gosling, S. D. (2013). Personality maturation around the world: a cross-cultural examination of social-investment theory. *Psychological Science, 24*, 2530–2540. https://doi.org/10.1177/0956797613498396.

Botha, R., Louw, D., & Loots, S. (2017). Psychopathy and its relation to personality psychopathology in a South African female forensic context. *South Africa Journal of Psychology* https://doi.org/10.1177/0081246317715351.

Canino, G., Polanczyk, G., Bauermeister, J. J., Rohde, L. A., & Frick, P. J. (2010). Does the prevalence of CD and ODD vary across cultures? *Social Psychiatry and Psychiatric Epidemiology, 45*, 695–704. https://doi.org/10.1007/s00127-010-0242-y.

Cheung, F. M., Cheung, S. F., & Fan, W. (2013). From Chinese to cross-cultural personality inventory: a combined emic–etic approach to the study of personality in culture. M. Gelfand, C. Y. Chiu, & Y. Y. Hong (Eds.), *Advances in culture and psychology* (pp. 117–180). Vol. 3(pp. 117–180). New York, NY: Oxford University Press. https://doi.org/10.1093/acprof:oso/9780199930449.003.0003.

Cheung, F. M., van de Vijver, F. J. R., & Leong, F. T. L. (2011). Toward a new approach to the study of personality in culture. *American Psychologist, 66*, 593–603. https://doi.org/10.1037/a0022389.

Church, A. T., Alvarez, J. M., Mai, N. T., French, B. F., Katigbak, M. S., & Ortiz, F. A. (2011). Are cross-cultural comparisons of personality profiles meaningful? Differential item and facet functioning in the Revised NEO Personality Inventory. *Journal of Personality and Social Psychology, 101*, 1068–1089. https://doi.org/10.1037/a0025290.

Compton, W. M., Helzer, J. E., Hwu, H. G., Yeh, E. K., McEvoy, L., Tipp, J. E., et al. (1991). New methods in cross-cultural psychiatry: psychiatric illness in Taiwan and the United States. *American Journal of Psychiatry, 148*, 1697–1704. https://doi.org/10.1176/ajp.148.12.1697.

Cooke, D. J. (1996). Psychopathic personality in different cultures. What do we know? What do we need to find out? *Journal of Personality Disorders, 10*, 23–40. https://doi.org/10.1521/pedi.1996.10.1.23.

Cooke, D. J., Michie, C., Hart, S. D., & Clark, D. (2005). Searching for the pan-cultural core of psychopathic personality disorder. *Personality and Individual Differences, 39*, 283–295. https://doi.org/10.1016/j.paid.2005.01.004.

Costa, P. T., Jr., & McCrae, R. R. (1992). *Revised NEO Personality Inventory (NEO-PI-R) and NEO Five-Factor Inventory (NEO-FFI) professional manual.* Odessa, FL: Psychological Assessment Resources.

Costa, P., Jr., Terracciano, A., & McCrae, R. R. (2001). Gender differences in personality traits across cultures: robust and surprising findings. *Journal of Personality and Social Psychology, 81*, 322–331. https://doi.org/10.1037/0022-3514.81.2.322.

Crijnen, A. A., Achenbach, T. M., & Verhulst, F. C. (1999). Problems reported by parents of children in multiple cultures: the Child Behavior Checklist syndrome constructs. *American Journal of Psychiatry, 156*(4), 569–574.

Cross, S. E., & Markus, H. R. (1999). The cultural constitution of personality. In L. A. Pervin & P. O. John (Eds.), *Handbook of personality* (pp. 378–396). New York: Guilford.

Donnellan, M. B., Hill, P. L., & Roberts, B. W. (2015). Personality development across the life span: current findings and future directions. M. Mikulincer, P. R. Shaver, M. L. Cooper, & R. J. Larsen (Eds.), *APA handbook of personality and social psychology* (pp. 107–126). *Personality processes and individual differences: Vol. 4*, (pp. 107–126). . https://doi.org/10.1037/14343-005.

Ekblad, S. (1988). Influence of child-rearing on aggressive behavior in a transcultural perspective. *Acta Psychiatrica Scandinavica, 78*, 133–139. https://doi.org/10.1111/j.1600-0447.1988.tb09012.x.

Fetvadjiev, V. H., Meiring, D., van de Vijver, F. J., Nel, J. A., & Hill, C. (2015). The South African Personality Inventory (SAPI): a culture-informed instrument for the country's main ethnocultural groups. *Psychological Assessment, 27*, 827–837. https://doi.org/10.1037/pas0000078.

Furlong, A. (2008). The Japanese Hikikomori phenomenon: acute social withdrawal among young people. *The Sociological Review, 56*, 309–325. https://doi.org/10.1111/j.1467-954X.2008.00790.x.

Gurven, M., Von Rueden, C., Massenkoff, M., Kaplan, H., & Lero Vie, M. (2013). How universal is the Big Five? Testing the five-factor model of personality variation among forager–farmers in the Bolivian Amazon. *Journal of Personality and Social Psychology, 104*, 354–370. https://doi.org/10.1037/a0030841.

Harpending, H., & Draper, P. (1988). Antisocial behavior and the other side of cultural evolution. In T. E. Moffitt & S. A. Mednick (Eds.), *Biological contributions to crime causation.* Boston, MA: Matinus Nijhoff.

Heath, D. B. (2001). Culture and substance abuse. *Psychiatric Clinics, 24*(3), 479–496. https://doi.org/10.1016/S0193-953X(05)70242-2.

Heine, S. J., Buchtel, E. E., & Norenzayan, A. (2008). What do cross-national comparisons of personality traits tell us? The case of conscientiousness. *Psychological Science, 19*, 309–313. https://doi.org/10.1016/S0193-953X(05)70242-2.

Keel, P. K., & Klump, K. L. (2003). Are eating disorders culture-bound syndromes? Implications for conceptualizing their etiology. *Psychological Bulletin, 129*, 747–769. https://doi.org/10.1037/0033-2909.129.5.747.

Kounou, K. B., Dogbe Foli, A. A., Djassoa, G., Amétépé, L. K., Rieu, J., Mathur, A., et al. (2015). Childhood maltreatment and personality disorders in patients with a major depressive disorder: a comparative study between France and Togo. *Transcultural Psychiatry, 52*, 681–699. https://doi.org/10.1177/1363461515572001.

Leff, J., Sartorius, N., Jablensky, A., Korten, A., & Ernberg, G. (1992). The International Pilot Study of Schizophrenia: five-year follow-up findings. *Psychological Medicine, 22*, 131–145.

Leung, A. K. Y., & Cohen, D. (2011). Within-and between-culture variation: individual differences and the cultural logics of honor, face, and dignity cultures. *Journal of Personality and Social Psychology, 100*, 507–526. https://doi.org/10.1037/a0022151.

Loranger, A. W., Sartorius, N., Andreoli, A., Berger, P., Buchheim, P., Channabasavanna, S. M., et al. (1994). The International Personality Disorder Examination: the World Health Organization/Alcohol, Drug Abuse, and Mental Health Administration international pilot study of personality disorders. *Archives of General Psychiatry*, *51*(3), 215–224.

Martin, C. S., Chung, T., & Langenbucher, J. W. (2014). Historical and cultural perspectives on substance use and substance use disorders. K. J. Sher (Ed.), *The Oxford handbook of substance use and substance use disorders* (pp. 29–49). Vol. 1(pp. 29–49). Oxford: Oxford University Press.

McCrae, R. R., Terracciano, A., & 78 Members of the Personality Profiles of Cultures Project (2005a). Universal features of personality traits from the observer's perspective: data from 50 cultures. *Journal of Personality and Social Psychology*, *88*, 547–561. https://doi.org/10.1037/0022-3514.88.3.547.

McCrae, R. R., Terracciano, A., & 79 Members of the Personality Profiles of Cultures Project (2005b). Personality profiles of cultures: aggregate personality traits. *Journal of Personality and Social Psychology*, *89*, 407–425. https://doi.org/10.1037/0022-3514.89.3.407.

Merikangas, K. R., Mehta, R. L., Molnar, B. E., Walters, E. E., Swendsen, J. D., Aguilar-Gaziola, S., et al. (1998). Comorbidity of substance use disorders with mood and anxiety disorders: results of the International Consortium in Psychiatric Epidemiology. *Addictive Behaviors*, *23*(6), 893–907. https://doi.org/10.1016/S0306-4603(98)00076-8.

Miller, S. G. (1996). Borderline personality disorder in cultural context: commentary on Paris. *Psychiatry*, *59*(2), 193–195.

Mõttus, R., Allik, J., & Realo, A. (2010). An attempt to validate national mean scores of Conscientiousness: no necessarily paradoxical findings. *Journal of Research in Personality*, *44*, 630–640. https://doi.org/10.1016/j.jrp.2010.08.005.

Murphy, J. M. (1976). Psychiatric labelling in cross-cultural perspective. *Science*, *191*(4231), 1019–1028.

Paris, J., & Lis, E. (2013). Can sociocultural and historical mechanisms influence the development of borderline personality disorder? *Transcultural Psychiatry*, *50*, 140–151. https://doi.org/10.1177/1363461512468105.

Ramírez-Esparza, N., Mehl, M. R., Álvarez-Bermúdez, J., & Pennebaker, J. W. (2009). Are Mexicans more or less sociable than Americans? Insights from a naturalistic observation study. *Journal of Research in Personality*, *43*(1), 1–7. https://doi.org/10.1016/j.jrp.2008.09.002.

Roberts, B. W., Walton, K. E., & Viechtbauer, W. (2006). Patterns of mean-level change in personality traits across the life course: a meta-analysis of longitudinal studies. *Psychological Bulletin*, *132*, 1–25. https://doi.org/10.1037/0033-2909.132.1.1.

Rossier, J., Dahourou, D., & McCrae, R. R. (2005). Structural and mean-level analyses of the five-factor model and locus of control: further evidence from Africa. *Journal of Cross-Cultural Psychology*, *36*, 227–246. https://doi.org/10.1177/0022022104272903.

Rossier, J., Ouedraogo, A., & Dahourou, D. (2017). Personality structure and assessment in French-speaking African cultures. T. Church (Ed.), *The Praeger handbook of personality across cultures* (pp. 73–104). *Trait psychology across cultures: Vol. 1*(pp. 73–104). Santa Barbara, CA: Praeger. Manuscript submitted for publication.

Rossier, J., Ouedraogo, A., Dahourou, D., Verardi, S., & Meyer de Stadelhofen, F. (2013). Personality and personality disorders in urban and rural Africa: results from a field trial in Burkina Faso. *Frontiers in Psychology*, *4*, 1–11. https://doi.org/10.3389/fpsyg.2013.00079.

Sanchez-Burks, J., Nisbett, R. E., & Ybarra, O. (2000). Cultural styles, relationship schemas, and prejudice against out-groups. *Journal of Personality and Social Psychology*, *79*, 174–189. https://doi.org/10.1037/0022-3514.79.2.174.

Saucier, G. (2009). Recurrent personality dimensions in inclusive lexical studies: indications for a Big Six structure. *Journal of Personality*, *77*, 1577–1614. https://doi.org/10.1111/j.1467-6494.2009.00593.x.

Saucier, G., & Goldberg, L. R. (2001). Lexical studies of indigenous personality factors: premises, products, and prospects. *Journal of Personality*, *69*, 847–888. https://doi.org/10.1111/1467-6494.696167.

Saucier, G., Thalmayer, A. G., & Bel-Bahar, T. (2014). Personality descriptors ubiquitous across 12 languages. *Journal of Personality and Social Psychology*, *107*, 199–216. https://doi.org/10.1037/a0036492.

Schmitt, D. P., Allik, J., McCrae, R. R., & Benet-Martínez, V. (2007). The geographic distribution of Big Five personality traits: patterns and profiles of human self-description across 56 nations. *Journal of Cross-Cultural Psychology*, *38*, 173–212. https://doi.org/10.1177/0022022106297299.

Schmitt, D. P., Realo, A., Voracek, M., & Allik, J. (2008). Why can't a man be more like a woman? Sex differences in Big Five personality traits across 55 cultures. *Journal of Personality and Social Psychology*, *94*, 168–182. https://doi.org/10.1037/0022-3514.94.1.168.

Severance, L., Bui-Wrzosinska, L., Gelfand, M. J., Lyons, S., Nowak, A., Borkowski, W., et al. (2013). The psychological structure of aggression across cultures. *Journal of Organizational Behavior*, *34*, 835–865. https://doi.org/10.1002/job.1873.

Suh, E. M. (2002). Culture, identity consistency, and subjective well-being. *Journal of Personality and Social Psychology*, *83*, 1378–1391. https://doi.org/10.1037/0022-3514.83.6.1378.

Sullivan, E. A., & Kosson, D. S. (2006). Ethnic and cultural variations in psychopathy. In C. J. Patrick (Ed.), *Handbook of psychopathy* (pp. 437–458). NY: Guilford.

Thalmayer, A. G., & Saucier, G. (2014). The Questionnaire Big Six (QB6) in 26 nations: developing cross-culturally applicable Big Six, Big Five, and Big Two inventories. *European Journal of Personality*, *28*, 482–496. https://doi.org/10.1002/per.1969.

Thalmayer, A. G., Saucier, G., Ole-Kotikash, L., Payne, D. L., & Carlson, R. (2018). *Indigenous personality structure in East and West Africa: Lexical studies of personality in Maa and Senoufo*. Manuscript submitted for publication.

Tseng, W.-S. (2001). *Handbook of cultural psychiatry*. San Diego, CA: Academic Press.

Van de Gaer, E., Grisay, A., Schulz, W., & Gebhardt, E. (2012). The reference group effect: an explanation of the paradoxical relationship between academic achievement and self-confidence across countries. *Journal of Cross-Cultural Psychology*, *43*, 1205–1228. https://doi.org/10.1177/0022022111428083.

Weisz, J. R., Suwanlert, S., Chaiyasit, W., & Walter, B. R. (1987). Over-and undercontrolled referral problems among children and adolescents from Thailand and the United States: the Wat and Wai of cultural differences. *Journal of Consulting and Clinical Psychology*, *55*, 719–726.

Yang, J., McCrae, R. R., Costa, P. T., Yao, S., Dai, X., Cai, T., et al. (2000). The cross-cultural generalizability of Axis-II constructs: an evaluation of two personality disorder assessment instruments in the People's Republic of China. *Journal of Personality Disorders*, *14*, 249–263. https://doi.org/10.1521/pedi.2000.14.3.249.

Zeinoun, P., Daouk-Öyry, L., Choueiri, L., & Van de Vijver, F. J. (2017). A mixed-methods study of personality conceptions in the Levant: Jordan, Lebanon, Syria, and the West Bank. *Journal of Personality and Social Psychology*, *113*(3), 453–465. https://doi.org/10.1037/pspp0000148.

Translational value of nonhuman primate models of antagonism

8

Isabella M. Palumbo, Robert D. Latzman
Department of Psychology, Georgia State University, Atlanta, GA, United States

In an attempt to elucidate the evolutionary and biological basis of personality, researchers have begun to examine dimensional variation in dispositional traits in nonhuman primates (NHPs), an effort that has important implications for understanding the processes underlying human mental health (Latzman, Green, & Fernandes, 2017). Generally, evolutionary psychologists have agreed that individual differences in personality are adaptive in nature, as dispositional variation may allow certain individuals to be suited for particular environments where others may not, leading to greater specialization, decreased competition, and various personality characteristics as optimal under different living and social conditions (see Figueredo et al., 2005 for a review).

However, it is important to acknowledge that specialized personality differences may constrain an individual's behavioral flexibility, potentially becoming maladaptive as it does not allow for an appropriate responsiveness inherent to different situations they might encounter. For example, with regard to agreeableness, specifically, whereas adaptive levels reflect an honest, trusting, giving, and empathic individual maintaining strong interpersonal relationships, extremely high levels can manifest as maladaptive traits, such as meekness, acquiescence, martyrdom, and naiveté. Evidence of such deleterious effects can be observed as low evolutionary success of submissive animals who accept food resources without protest or do not actively compete for mates (de Waal, 1986). Conversely, extremely low agreeableness, or antagonism, can characterize a combative, callous, greedy, and manipulative individual. However, antagonistic traits can be adaptive at a more modest level, characterizing a skeptical, cunning, and confident individual (Widiger & Mullins-Sweatt, 2005). Consequently, these modest-level traits may enable an individual to take advantage of various resources to thrive within the environment, whereas more severe antagonism often leads to aggression, interpersonal distress, and subsequent exclusion.

While it may be difficult or unethical to examine these outcomes in humans under tight experimental control, observational and naturalistic experimental animal studies allow for the opportunity to examine these complex interactions as it applies to human personality and behavior. NHP models are well poised to provide unique access to complex interactions among genes, neuroanatomy, and early developmental experiences in the explanation of stable personality traits and behaviors. Such advantages include close phylogeny and physiology to humans, and the similarity in brain structure and function, pharmacokinetics, and neurochemistry, which provide the basis for comparative analysis of the genetic and environmental factors underlying both

The Handbook of Antagonism. https://doi.org/10.1016/B978-0-12-814627-9.00008-6

normative and pathological outcomes in biobehavioral development. In addition, it is now widely accepted that human and NHPs share many emotional processes enabling more diverse neurobiological examinations of emotion, cognition, and behavior (LeDoux, 2012; Panksepp, 2007). Thus research with NHPs represents a particularly promising area of work from a translational value perspective (Latzman & Hopkins, 2016; Phillips et al., 2014).

The purpose of this chapter is to provide an overview, albeit brief, of the existing literature on personality, specifically antagonism, in NHPs and to suggest directions for future research. First, we provide a brief overview of the quantification and placement of dispositional antagonism within NHP models of personality that dovetail with existing human models. Second, we review neurobiological (i.e., neural and genetic) and environmental correlates of antagonism in NHPs with explicit links to the human literature. Third, we provide an example of a recently developed NHP model of personality pathology (i.e., psychopathy) in which antagonism plays an important role. Finally, we conclude with general recommendations for NHP research on antagonism.

Nonhuman primate models of antagonism

In both human and NHPs, quantitative models have revealed the existence of a bipolar dispositional trait dimension reflecting a general tendency toward antagonism on one pole and toward agreeableness on the opposing pole (e.g., Gosling, 2001). Although the ultimate number of factors found across NHP studies varies, factor-analytic research with chimpanzee samples has revealed the existence of a largely parallel five-factor structure, with one of these factors capturing agreeableness-related content (Freeman et al., 2013; Latzman, Freeman, Schapiro, & Hopkins, 2015). Similarly, a largely comparable structure has emerged in monkeys, with agreeableness generally reflecting sympathetic, helpful, and sensitive traits at the high pole and aggression, hostility, and poor cooperation capturing the low pole (Freeman & Gosling, 2010).

Two main methods of data collection have been employed with NHPs: behavioral coding and observer/caregiver trait ratings. Informant trait ratings involve individuals familiar with the animals providing a rating on a set of predefined traits or adjectives, accompanied by a relatively abstract definition (e.g., "apprehensive—seems to be anxious about everything"; King & Figueredo, 1997). Observational behavioral coding involves using standardized ethograms to behaviorally code individuals' discrete behaviors, typically across multiple observation sessions. Thus, much of the literature reviewed later describes findings with regard not only to informant ratings of antagonism, but also to associated behavioral manifestations (i.e., aggressive behavior).

One commonly used approach for operationalizing individual differences in NHPs involves trait ratings that are then used to form scale-level operationalizations of trait dimensions similar to psychometric questionnaires employed with humans (for a review see Gosling, 2001), which have been found to predict behavior in NHPs. For example, Pederson, King, and Landau (2005) demonstrated that, among chimpanzees, ratings of personality explained a range of social behaviors; specifically, among male but not female apes, low agreeableness evidenced a moderate-to-strong association with agonistic behaviors ($r = -0.42$). Further, in addition to lower levels of agreeableness, these individuals also evidenced increased levels of impulsivity-related traits suggesting a configuration of traits characterizing an impulsively aggressive individual.

Impulsively aggressive individuals are often socially isolated by their conspecifics. For example, Konečná et al. (2008) demonstrated in a sample of Hanuman langur males that low agreeableness was associated with increases in displacement and fewer affiliative behaviors, including less time spent grooming, and lower rates of initiated approach and number of received approaches. This is thought to reflect ostracism by group members, likely due to social deviancy rather than introversion or submission.

Neurobiological and environmental correlates of antagonism in NHPs

A large empirical literature demonstrates the heritability of personality in both humans (e.g., Bouchard, 2004) and NHPs (e.g., Brent et al., 2014; Latzman, Freeman,et al., 2015). Further, recent research on the neurobiological correlates of primate personality supports the evolutionary, ancestral basis of personality. For example, recent research with chimpanzees evidence similar genetic (e.g., Latzman, Hopkins, Keebaugh, & Young, 2014) and neuroanatomical (e.g.,Latzman, Hecht, Freeman, Schapiro, & Hopkins, 2015) contributions to individual differences in personality, similar to what has been demonstrated in the human literature (e.g., Bouchard, 2004; DeYoung, 2010, respectively). Specifically, estimates of the heritability (h^2) of agreeableness in humans have been found to range from 0.28 to 0.35 (McGue & Bouchard, 1998). Whereas agreeableness in chimpanzees has been found to evidence positive heritability estimates, these estimates have been modest and nonsignificant (e.g., Wilson et al., 2017; Latzman, Freeman, et al., 2015). In monkeys, however, antagonistic aggression has been found to be significantly genetically determined ($h^2 = 0.61$). Further, consistent with the conceptualization of antagonism reflecting an impulsive form of aggression, a strong genetic correlation has been found between social approach impulsivity and aggression (*RhoG* 0.78; Fairbanks et al., 2004).

Given strong evidence in support of the heritability of such dimensions of personality, researchers have begun to investigate specific potential neurobiological contributors in NHPs that might explain this heritability (e.g., Hong et al., 2011; Latzman et al., 2014). With regard to antagonism specifically, NHP studies have typically investigated genetic and neural effects on explicit, discrete behavior rather than aggregated personality trait dimensions. Thus the following section summarizes recent findings as they relate to antagonistic behavior with a specific focus on the serotonin system, the area that has garnered the lion's share of empirical attention.

Serotonergic system and antagonism

The existing literature suggests two forms of NHP aggression—competitive, goal-directed behaviors (nonviolent, socially dominant) and impulsive, unrestrained violence (antagonistic). Further underscoring the important differentiation of these phenotypes are findings suggesting different neurobiological systems underpinning each variation. In both human and NHPs, one of the most replicated findings in biological psychology and psychiatry is that low or impaired central nervous system (CNS) serotonin is correlated with impulse control deficits and impulsive aggression (Duke, Bègue, Bell, & Eisenlohr-Moul, 2013; Higley & Barr, 2008), whereas variation in testosterone levels has been found to predict competitive, dominant aggression (Terburg & van Honk, 2013). Therefore, as central serotonin functioning underlies stable personality traits, measured across time and between situations, interindividual stability should be observed in the serotonin system as well. Using small samples of cerebral spinal fluid (CSF), researchers are able to look for terminal products of neurotransmitters to assess which systems are activated under the experimental conditions of interest. One of those products, 5-HIAA, is the final metabolite of serotonin and is proportionate, such that high concentrations of 5-HIAA reflect high activity in the serotonin system.

In the last few decades, an increasing number of NHP studies have aimed at clarifying the genetic influence on differential expression of aggressive intent and action. For example, among male rhesus monkeys, the propensity to engage in antagonistic, unrestrained, and high-intensity aggression (as measured by the frequency of chases and physical fights), expressed as a proportion of all aggressive acts, has been found to covary inversely with individual differences in CSF 5-HIAA concentrations; that is, lower 5-HIAA concentrations are associated with increased aggression (Higley, Mehlman, et al., 1996; Mehlman et al., 1994). Importantly, however, displacements of other monkeys and threat gestures (low-intensity aggression as related to dominance), commonly used to establish and maintain social authority, do not correlate with CSF 5-HIAA levels; nor does the total number of aggressive acts. Interestingly, consistent with the notion that these two forms of aggression can be differentiated by variation in levels of testosterone and CSF 5-HIAA, CSF free testosterone in males has been found to associate only with the low-intensity aggression, and neither high-intensity nor overall number of aggressive acts. This high-intensity, aggressive fighting leads to more severe injuries and, in a 4-year longitudinal study, males who died due to injuries sustained during fights were found to have had lower concentrations of CSF 5-HIAA (Higley, Mehlman, et al., 1996).

Similarly, variation in central serotonin has also been observed in relation to aggression in female rhesus and pigtailed macaques. For example, Higley, Mehlman, et al. (1996) found that CSF 5-HIAA concentrations in individually housed females covaried inversely with spontaneous aggression (as indexed by chasing and physical fights) when animals were later housed together. These differential effects observed between CSF 5-HIAA and testosterone highlight the specificity of antagonism as it relates to impulsive aggression. Similar to monkeys low in agreeableness (Konečná et al., 2008), males with lower concentrations of CSF 5-HIAA are also seen to have fewer social companions, spend less time engaging in grooming behaviors with conspecifics and tend to emigrate from their natal groups at an earlier age. In addition, female monkeys with lower concentrations of CSF 5-HIAA are more likely to be removed from their social groups due to excessive aggression and treatment of wounds and less likely to hold socially dominant positions.

The consistency of findings between NHPs and humans is clear. Indeed, a meta-analysis of 16 human studies demonstrated a modest mean weighted effect size ($d = -0.45$) between levels of 5-HIAA and antisocial behavior and impulsive aggression (Moore, Scarpa, & Raine, 2002). Further, among criminal offenders, this effect is stronger in impulsive compared to nonimpulsive individuals, suggesting that reduced serotonergic activity is related to an inability to resist aggressive impulses (e.g., Berman, Tracy, & Coccaro, 1997). Similarly, conduct disorder and callous-unemotional traits are linked to aggression and difficulties in peer relationships (e.g., Waller, Hyde, Grabell, Alves, & Olson, 2015) and have recently been found to demonstrate an inverse relationship with serotonin levels (Moul, Dobson-Stone, Brennan, Hawes, & Dadds, 2013). Further underscoring the specificity of serotonin associations with impulsive aggression and antagonism, in an adolescent sample, high testosterone has been found to relate to antisocial behavior only in individuals low in agreeableness and conscientiousness (Reardon, 2014), and in adult men with reduced levels of serotonin (Kuepper et al., 2010).

Thus, a large reliable literature suggests that levels of testosterone and serotonin may have shared and unique contributions to expressions of aggressive behavior (e.g., Higley, King, et al., 1996; Moore et al., 2002): testosterone contributing to aggressive drive and purposeful motivation seen in competitive aggression, whereas serotonin regulates the threshold, intensity, and resulting frequency of violent, impulsive aggression. As such, those high in testosterone, with low to normative levels of serotonin, would be expected to display dominant forms of aggression, or assertiveness, in a variety of settings, but would rarely result in unrestrained violence. However, individuals with impaired serotonin functioning may exhibit compromised impulse control resulting in a low threshold for aggression and ultimately frequent engagement in violence, regardless of testosterone levels. Furthermore, as high testosterone increases aggressive drive and motivation, it would be expected that impairment in both systems would exacerbate the propensity to engage in aggressive behaviors as a result of difficulties in inhibiting aggressive behaviors before escalating to injury. All told, studies of both aggressively violent humans (Brown et al., 1982) and NHPs (McGuire, Raleigh, & Pollack, 1994; Raleigh et al., 1984) have shown that individuals high in social deviancy or low in competent social behaviors (Kruesi et al., 1990) have relatively low CSF 5-HIAA concentrations.

The contribution of the environment, uniquely and in interaction with genes

As it has been demonstrated that both personality and psychopathology result from a common etiology stemming from innate temperamental traits shaped by an individual's environment (Caspi et al., 2014; Clark, 2005), an extensive empirical literature highlights the influence of environment and early rearing experiences associated with emotional and cognitive outcomes in both humans (e.g., Kochanska, 2001; Oshino, Suzuki, Ishii, & Otani, 2007) and NHPs (e.g., Bennett & Pierre, 2010). Further, NHP models possess unique opportunities to investigate the complex interaction between genetic and environmental influences on personality and behavior, such as (1) accounting for every relationship in a pedigree, (2) fewer sociocultural influences accounting for variability, (3) less sensitivity to nonnormality, and (4) the ability to quantify different environmental components of variance, such as early social rearing experiences (Charmantier & Garant, 2005; Kruuk, 2004).

For example, the effects of early social rearing experiences on personality have been demonstrated in chimpanzees (Latzman, Freeman, et al., 2015); specifically, nursery-reared apes were found to exhibit higher levels of antagonism compared to their mother-reared peers. Similarly, peer-reared monkeys are more likely to necessitate removal from their social group for violent aggression and are more likely to act aggressively toward an infant who is not their own. Mother-reared monkeys, on the other hand, are likely to comfort and care for an infant in conditions in which they are required to "babysit" (Higley, Linnoila, & Suomi, 1994). Further, monkeys with fewer social experiences show high levels of impulsive aggression when confronted by other monkeys, despite size or rank of the stimulus monkey (Suomi, 1982). All told, it appears that early social rearing experiences not only confer an important direct influence on the development of antagonism, but also result in variation in the genetic contribution to the antagonism phenotype.

Indeed, even within rearing groups, not all NHPs are affected in the same way by more adverse early rearing experiences, suggesting a role for genetic influence. This interactive relationship of genetics and early life experiences is of great importance in investigations of individual variability in neurobiologically based processes, such as personality. For example, as noted previously, a broad temperament dimension reflecting the tendency toward undercontrolled, agonistic behavior was found to be heritable, albeit nonsignificantly, due to the relatively moderate sample size ($h^2 = 0.35$, $P = .07$), in a mother-reared sample of chimpanzees (Latzman, Freeman, et al., 2015). In another study, meanness, a construct analogous to antagonism described in more detail later, was heritable ($h^2 = 0.65$) in the mother- but not nursery-reared cohort (Latzman, Schapiro, & Hopkins, 2017). Consistent with the genetic correlation observed between social impulsivity and aggression in monkeys, within this chimpanzee sample, meanness and variation in an indicator of trait disinhibition/impulsivity evidenced a very high genetic correlation ($RhoG = 0.91$).

Similar to findings of genetic contributions varying by early social rearing experiences in apes, among macaques, monkeys reared without adults in peer-only groups show CNS serotonin impairments and have increased frequencies of serious, agonistic aggression (Higley, King, et al., 1996). Peer-reared juvenile monkeys with low CNS serotonin activity exhibit relatively high rates of aggressive behavior without provocation (Barr et al., 2003). These results suggest that serotonin activity may augment the influence of early maternal absence, resulting in increased frequency of aggressive behavior at a time early in psychosocial development. Although sample sizes for these studies are typically relatively small as compared to typical sample sizes employed in the human genetics literature, results are largely parallel with the human literature demonstrating the association between variations in serotonin function and disagreeableness (Greenberg et al., 2000; Mazzanti et al., 1998) as well as literature supporting both genetic and environmental roles in the etiology of impulsive aggressive disorders, such as antisocial personality disorder and conduct disorder (Brennan & Mednick, 1993; Caspi et al., 2002). As small sample sizes are susceptible to a restricted range of trait variation, thus potentially misrepresenting true associations, it is critical to study larger samples in future research.

Neural correlates of antagonism

Despite growing interest in comparative personality research among NHPs, investigations of the neuroanatomical basis for individual differences across these traits are still in its infancy. A recent study examining neuroanatomical correlates of personality in chimpanzees (Latzman, Hecht, et al., 2015) found low agreeableness to be negatively associated with frontal gray matter volume at the bivariate level. Additionally, Latzman, Boysen, and Schapiro (2018) found hippocampal volume to associate with a broad temperament dimension reflecting a tendency to behave in an undercontrolled and agonistic manner. Functional impairments of the prefrontal cortex and allied regions (i.e., hippocampus), particularly those governing affect regulation and inhibitory control of behavior, appear to confer liability for antagonistic manifestation of aggression. In rhesus monkeys, lesions of the amygdala have been shown to increase social aggression after the monkeys have been reintroduced back into their groups. Additionally, lesions of the orbital frontal cortex (OFC) are generally associated with reduced affiliative behaviors, such as grooming or approaches. However, aggression increases only in dominant males (Machado & Bachevalier, 2006) indicating that the OFC may be important for the interpretation of social cues and contributes to the appropriate response in complex social situations.

These results are consistent with the human neuroimaging literature confirming the role of various brain regions in explaining the neurobiology of personality and social behavior (Allen & DeYoung, 2017). Adaptive social interactions depend on accurate perception of social cues and emotional facial expressions of others, the appropriate selection and timing of behavioral responses, and adjustment of behavior in response to the subsequent reaction of others or changes in the environment. Emotional perception and expression within these social interactions are produced and modulated by a neural network that includes, but is not limited to: the amygdala, orbital frontal cortex, dorsolateral prefrontal cortex, and several temporal areas including the superior temporal sulcus and the fusiform gyrus (Adolphs, 2001; also see Bachevalier, 2000 for a review).

Chimpanzee model of psychopathic personality: An example translational model relevant to antagonism

Personality pathology can be conceptualized as a constellation of traits that differ in degree rather than kind and result in significant impairment to the individual or others. Leveraging NHP models to investigate the neurobiological and evolutionary foundations of personality helps to elucidate underlying processes associated with personality pathology (Latzman, Green, & Fernandes, 2017). One recent example of the utility of NHP models vis-à-vis personality pathology germane to dispositional antagonism is the recent development of a chimpanzee model of psychopathic personality (psychopathy) dimensions (Latzman, Drislane, et al., 2016).

Psychopathy encompasses a severe disturbance in behavioral control, interpersonal relationships, and emotional experience masked by an outward appearance of normalcy. Consistent with the conceptualization of psychopathy as a multifaceted construct, more recent theoretical and empirical work has aimed to more accurately define the component traits (e.g., Lynam et al., 2011; Marcus, Fulton, & Edens, 2013; Patrick, Fowles, & Krueger, 2009). Although there are various competing models of psychopathic personality, there is general consensus with regard to the inclusion of an antagonism-related dimension in the constellation of traits that make up psychopathy (Lilienfeld, Watts, Francis Smith, Berg, & Latzman, 2015; Miller & Lynam, 2015). Thus, NHP models of psychopathy are pertinent to those interested in antagonism.

The study of psychopathy has recently been extended to our closest living relatives, chimpanzees. Specifically, within the framework of the triarchic model (Patrick et al., 2009) which characterizes psychopathy as a configuration of three-dimensional trait constructs (*boldness*, *meanness*, *disinhibition*), Latzman, Drislane, et al. (2016) developed and initially validated a chimpanzee operationalization of such psychopathic personality dimensions. Within the triarchic model, antagonism is analogous to the construct of meanness, a dimension corresponding to the callous aggression subdimension of the externalizing spectrum encompassing traits such as deficient empathy, opposition to close attachments with others, and empowerment through cruelty (Krueger, Markon, Patrick, Benning, & Kramer, 2007).

Subsequently, the role of differential early rearing experiences (i.e., mother- vs. nonmother, nursery rearing) on genetic contributions to psychopathic tendencies was examined (Latzman, Patrick, Freeman, Schapiro, & Hopkins, 2017). Consistent with human studies, both genetic and environmental contributors emerged in the explanation of individual differences in subdimensions of psychopathy. Importantly, it was found that genetic contributions varied when examined separately by early rearing experiences—whereas psychopathy dimensions were heritable among mother-reared chimpanzees, heritability was not evident among nursery-reared apes. Further examination of genetic associations among the three dimensions within the mother-reared subsample revealed a substantial proportion of shared genetic variation in scores for meanness and disinhibition, likely reflecting their shared loading within the externalizing spectrum (Krueger et al., 2007).

All told, this line of research provides compelling evidence that psychopathic tendencies more broadly, and antagonism-related content (i.e., meanness) more specifically, are rooted in basic, evolutionarily meaningful dispositions. Further, in conjunction with research described previously, this work provides support for a primate-translational operationalization of antagonism-relevant constructs relevant both to psychopathy and to broader forms of psychopathology.

Conclusions and future directions

A number of considerations are important as translational NHP research moves forward. For example, it will be important for NHP researchers to begin to disentangle disinhibitory from antagonistic processes. In humans, quantitative structural results have repeatedly demonstrated that the broad externalizing spectrum of psychopathology is able to be differentiated into antagonistic externalizing, the subfactor most relevant to trait antagonism, and disinhibited externalizing (Kotov et al., 2017; Krueger et al., 2007). Differentiating these two subfactors is more difficult in NHPs given the reliance on observed behavior, which is most typically the phenotypic expression of a combination of both. Informant-report methodologies allow for quantitative modeling of these separable subfactors (e.g., Latzman, Freeman, et al., 2015; Latzman et al., 2018), but it will be important to develop methodologies that allow for the integration of standardized observational data into these models (e.g., Martin & Suarez, 2017).

Despite the clear relevance of NHP findings, human researchers are typically not well informed of this work. To most effectively advance the field, it is crucial for nonhuman animal researchers to properly disseminate their work and for both human and nonhuman researchers to keep abreast of recent findings from each respective literature.

The Research Domain Criteria (RDoC; Insel et al., 2010; Kozak & Cuthbert, 2016) initiative is one clear example of an attempt to foster exactly this sort of cross-talk. As efforts toward an empirical classification of psychopathology continue, a growing body of research with NHPs provide support for translational operationalizations of various RDoC domains and constructs. For example, consistent findings of a common quantitative structure of personality and psychopathology dimensions can dovetail basic research findings in nonhuman animals to human research on the underlying biobehavioral processes of psychopathology. Complementing this initiative, the Hierarchical Taxonomy of Psychopathology (HiTOP) consortium has developed a working model representing an attempt to organize the existing literature on empirical approaches to psychiatric classification (Kotov et al., 2017; Krueger et al., 2018). Paralleling quantitative findings with regard to the hierarchical structure of personality in NHPs (e.g., Latzman, Freeman, et al., 2015), the HiTOP model comprises higher order constructs summarizing tendencies for more fine-grained constructs (e.g., psychiatric disorders). Specifically, the broad externalizing dimension of psychopathology includes two spectra: antagonism and disinhibition. Thus NHP research on the underlying processes of dispositional antagonism has clear translational value within the HiTOP model, namely, with regard to antagonistic externalizing.

Taken together, human and NHP research complement one another. Increased cross-fertilization promises to provide invaluable insights and breakthroughs into the pathophysiology of antagonism-related forms of psychopathology specifically and mental illness more generally. Further, given the unparalleled nature of NHP animal models of dispositional constructs, along with the ability of researchers to implement experimental manipulations in ways not possible in humans, NHP research is well poised to investigate behavioral intervention approaches targeting general dispositional constructs such as antagonism.

References

Adolphs, R. (2001). The neurobiology of social cognition. *Current Opinion in Neurobiology, 11* (2), 231–239.

Allen, T. A., & DeYoung, C. G. (2017). Personality neuroscience and the Five Factor Model. In T. A. Widiger (Ed.), *Oxford handbook of the Five Factor Model* (pp. 319–352). New York, NY: Oxford University Press.

Bachevalier, J. (2000). The amygdala, social behavior, and autism. In J. Aggleton (Ed.), *The amygdala: A functional analysis* (pp. 509–544). New York, NY: Guilford Press.

Barr, C. S., Newman, T. K., Becker, M. L., Parker, C. C., Champoux, M., Lesch, K. P., et al. (2003). The utility of the non-human primate model for studying gene by environment interactions in behavioral research. *Genes, Brain and Behavior*, *2*, 336–340.

Bennett, A. J., & Pierre, P. J. (2010). Nonhuman primate research contributions to understanding genetic and environmental influences on phenotypic outcomes across development. In: K. E. Hood, C. T. Halpern, G. Greenberg, & R. M. Lerner (Eds.), *Handbook of developmental science, behavior, and genetics* (pp. 353–399). Oxford: John Wiley & Sons. https://doi.org/10.1002/9781444327632.ch12.

Berman, M. E., Tracy, J. I., & Coccaro, E. F. (1997). The serotonin hypothesis of aggression revisited. *Clinical Psychology Review*, *17*(6), 651–665.

Bouchard, T. J., Jr. (2004). Genetic influence on human psychological traits: a survey. *Current Directions in Psychological Science*, *13*(4), 148–151.

Brennan, P. A., & Mednick, S. A. (1993). Genetic perspectives on crime. *Acta Psychiatrica Scandinavica*, *87*(S370), 19–26.

Brent, L. J., Semple, S., MacLarnon, A., Ruiz-Lambides, A., Gonzalez-Martinez, J., & Platt, M. L. (2014). Personality traits in rhesus macaques (*Macaca mulatta*) are heritable but do not predict reproductive output. *International Journal of Primatology*, *35*(1), 188–209.

Brown, G. L., Ebert, M. H., Goyer, P. F., Jimersom, D. C., Klein, W. J., Bunney, W. E., Jr., et al. (1982). Aggression, suicide and serotonin (relationships to CSF amine metabolites). *The American Journal of Psychiatry*, *139*, 741–746.

Caspi, A., Houts, R. M., Belsky, D. W., Goldman-Mellor, S. J., Harrington, H., Israel, S., et al. (2014). The p factor: one general psychopathology factor in the structure of psychiatric disorders? *Clinical Psychological Science*, *2*(2), 119–137.

Caspi, A., McClay, J., Moffitt, T. E., Mill, J., Martin, J., Craig, I. W., et al. (2002). Role of genotype in the cycle of violence in maltreated children. *Science*, *297*(5582), 851–854.

Charmantier, A., & Garant, D. (2005). Environmental quality and evolutionary potential: lessons from wild populations. *Proceedings of the Royal Society of London B: Biological Sciences*, *272*(1571), 1415–1425.

Clark, L. A. (2005). Temperament as a unifying basis for personality and psychopathology. *Journal of Abnormal Psychology*, *114*(4), 505.

de Waal, F. B. (1986). The integration of dominance and social bonding in primates. *The Quarterly Review of Biology*, *61*(4), 459–479.

DeYoung, C. G. (2010). Personality neuroscience and the biology of traits. *Social and Personality Psychology Compass*, *4*(12), 1165–1180.

Duke, A. A., Bègue, L., Bell, R., & Eisenlohr-Moul, T. (2013). Revisiting the serotonin–aggression relation in humans: a meta-analysis. *Psychological Bulletin*, *139*(5), 1148.

Fairbanks, L. A., Newman, T. K., Bailey, J. N., Jorgensen, M. J., Breidenthal, S. E., Ophoff, R. A., et al. (2004). Genetic contributions to social impulsivity and aggressiveness in vervet monkeys. *Biological Psychiatry*, *55*(6), 642–647.

Figueredo, A. J., Sefcek, J. A., Vásquez, G., Brumbach, B. H., King, J. E., & Jacobs, W. J. (2005). Evolutionary personality psychology. In D. M. Buss (Ed.), *Handbook of evolutionary psychology* (pp. 851–877). Hoboken, NJ: Wiley.

Freeman, H. D., Brosnan, S. F., Hopper, L. M., Lambeth, S. P., Schapiro, S. J., & Gosling, S. D. (2013). Developing a comprehensive and comparative questionnaire for measuring personality in chimpanzees using a simultaneous top-down/bottom-up design. *American Journal of Primatology*, *75*(10), 1042–1053.

Freeman, H. D., & Gosling, S. D. (2010). Personality in nonhuman primates: a review and evaluation of past research. *American Journal of Primatology*, *72*(8), 653–671.

Gosling, S. D. (2001). From mice to men: what can we learn about personality from animal research? *Psychological Bulletin*, *127*(1), 45–86.

Greenberg, B. D., Li, Q., Lucas, F. R., Hu, S., Sirota, L. A., Benjamin, J., et al. (2000). Association between the serotonin transporter promoter polymorphism and personality traits in a primarily female population sample. *American Journal of Medical Genetics Part A*, *96* (2), 202–216.

Higley, J. D., & Barr, C. S. (2008). Neurochemistry and behavior. In T. M. Burbacher, G. P. Sackett, & K. S. Grant (Eds.), *Nonhuman primate models of children's health and developmental disabilities* (pp. 161–200). New York: Academic Press.

Higley, J. D., King, S. T., Jr., Hasert, M. F., Champoux, M., Suomi, S. J., & Linnoila, M. (1996). Stability of interindividual differences in serotonin function and its relationship to severe aggression and competent social behavior in rhesus macaque females. *Neuropsychopharmacology*, *14*(1), 67.

Higley, J. D., Linnoila, M., & Suomi, S. J. (1994). Ethological contributions: Experiential and genetic contributions to the expression and inhibition of aggression in primates. In M. Hersen, R. T. Ammerman, & L. Sisson (Eds.), *Handbook of aggressive and destructive behavior in psychiatric patients*. New York: Plenum Press.

Higley, J. D., Mehlman, P. T., Poland, R. E., Taub, D. M., Vickers, J., Suomi, S. J., et al. (1996). CSF testosterone and 5-HIAA correlate with different types of aggressive behaviors. *Biological Psychiatry*, *40*(11), 1067–1082.

Hong, K. W., Weiss, A., Morimura, N., Udono, T., Hayasaka, I., Humle, T., et al. (2011). Polymorphism of the tryptophan hydroxylase 2 (TPH2) gene is associated with chimpanzee neuroticism. *PLoS One*, *6*(7), e22144.

Insel, T., Cuthbert, B., Garvey, M., Heinssen, R., Kozak, M. J., Pine, D. S., et al. (2010). Research Domain Criteria (RDoC): Developing a valid diagnostic framework for research on mental disorders. *American Journal of Psychiatry*, *167*(7), 748–751.

King, J. E., & Figueredo, A. J. (1997). The five-factor model plus dominance in chimpanzee personality. *Journal of Research in Personality*, *31*(2), 257–271.

Kochanska, G. (2001). Emotional development in children with different attachment histories: the first three years. *Child Development*, *72*(2), 474–490.

Konečná, M., Lhota, S., Weiss, A., Urbánek, T., Adamová, T., & Pluháček, J. (2008). Personality in free-ranging Hanuman langur (*Semnopithecus entellus*) males: subjective ratings and recorded behavior. *Journal of Comparative Psychology*, *122*(4), 379.

Kotov, R., Krueger, R. F., Watson, D., Achenbach, T. M., Althoff, R. R., Bagby, R. M., et al. (2017). The Hierarchical Taxonomy of Psychopathology (HiTOP): a dimensional alternative to traditional nosologies. *Journal of Abnormal Psychology*, *126*(4), 454.

Kozak, M. J., & Cuthbert, B. N. (2016). The NIMH research domain criteria initiative: background, issues, and pragmatics. *Psychophysiology*, *53*(3), 286–297.

Krueger, R. F., Kotov, R., Watson, D., Forbes, M. K., Eaton, N. R., Ruggero, C. J., et al. (2018). Progress in achieving empirical classification of psychopathology. *World Psychiatry*, *17*, 282–293. https://doi.org/10.1002/wps.20566.

Krueger, R. F., Markon, K. E., Patrick, C. J., Benning, S. D., & Kramer, M. D. (2007). Linking antisocial behavior, substance use, and personality: an integrative quantitative model of the adult externalizing spectrum. *Journal of Abnormal Psychology*, *116*(4), 645.

Kruesi, M. J., Rapoport, J. L., Hamburger, S., Hibbs, E., Potter, W. Z., Lenane, M., et al. (1990). Cerebrospinal fluid monoamine metabolites, aggression, and impulsivity in disruptive behavior disorders of children and adolescents. *Archives of General Psychiatry*, *47*(5), 419–426.

Kruuk, L. E. (2004). Estimating genetic parameters in natural populations using the 'animal model'. *Philosophical Transactions of the Royal Society of London B: Biological Sciences*, *359*(1446), 873–890.

Kuepper, Y., Alexander, N., Osinsky, R., Mueller, E., Schmitz, A., Netter, P., et al. (2010). Aggression—interactions of serotonin and testosterone in healthy men and women. *Behavioural Brain Research*, *206*(1), 93–100.

Latzman, R. D., Boysen, S. T., & Schapiro, S. J. (2018). Neuroanatomical correlates of hierarchical personality traits in chimpanzees: associations with limbic structures. *Personality Neuroscience*. *1*, https://doi.org/10.1017/pen.2018.1 E4.

Latzman, R. D., Drislane, L. E., Hecht, L. K., Brislin, S. J., Patrick, C. J., Lilienfeld, S. O., et al. (2016). A chimpanzee (*Pan troglodytes*) model of triarchic psychopathy constructs: development and initial validation. *Clinical Psychological Science*, *4*(1), 50–66.

Latzman, R. D., Freeman, H. D., Schapiro, S. J., & Hopkins, W. D. (2015). The contribution of genetics and early rearing experiences to hierarchical personality dimensions in chimpanzees (*Pan troglodytes*). *Journal of Personality and Social Psychology*, *109*(5), 889.

Latzman, R. D., Green, L. M., & Fernandes, M. A. (2017). The importance of chimpanzee personality research to understanding processes associated with human mental health. *International Journal of Comparative Psychology*, 30.

Latzman, R. D., Hecht, L. K., Freeman, H. D., Schapiro, S. J., & Hopkins, W. D. (2015). Neuroanatomical correlates of personality in chimpanzees (*Pan troglodytes*): associations between personality and frontal cortex. *NeuroImage*, *123*, 63–71.

Latzman, R. D., & Hopkins, W. D. (2016). Letter to the Editor: Avoiding a lost opportunity for psychological medicine: importance of chimpanzee research to the National Institutes of Health portfolio. *Psychological Medicine*, *46*(11), 2445.

Latzman, R. D., Hopkins, W. D., Keebaugh, A. C., & Young, L. J. (2014). Personality in chimpanzees (*Pan troglodytes*): exploring the hierarchical structure and associations with the vasopressin V1A receptor gene. *PLoS One*, *9*(4), e95741.

Latzman, R. D., Patrick, C. J., Freeman, H. J., Schapiro, S. J., & Hopkins, W. D. (2017). Etiology of triarchic psychopathy dimensions in chimpanzees (Pan troglodytes). *Clinical Psychological Science*, *5*, 341–354. https://doi.org/10.1177/2167702616676582.

Latzman, R. D., Schapiro, S. J., & Hopkins, W. D. (2017). Triarchic psychopathy dimensions in chimpanzees (*Pan troglodytes*): investigating associations with genetic variation in the vasopressin receptor 1A gene. *Frontiers in Neuroscience*, *11*, 407.

LeDoux, J. (2012). Rethinking the emotional brain. *Neuron*, *73*(4), 653–676.

Lilienfeld, S. O., Watts, A. L., Francis Smith, S., Berg, J. M., & Latzman, R. D. (2015). Psychopathy deconstructed and reconstructed: identifying and assembling the personality building blocks of Cleckley's chimera. *Journal of Personality*, *83*(6), 593–610.

Lynam, D. R., Gaughan, E. T., Miller, J. D., Miller, D. J., Mullins-Sweatt, S., & Widiger, T. A. (2011). Assessing the basic traits associated with psychopathy: development and validation of the Elemental Psychopathy Assessment. *Psychological Assessment*, *23*(1), 108.

Machado, C. J., & Bachevalier, J. (2006). The impact of selective amygdala, orbital frontal cortex, or hippocampal formation lesions on established social relationships in rhesus monkeys (*Macaca mulatta*). *Behavioral Neuroscience*, *120*(4), 761.

Marcus, D. K., Fulton, J. J., & Edens, J. F. (2013). The two-factor model of psychopathic personality: evidence from the Psychopathic Personality Inventory. *Personality Disorders: Theory, Research, and Treatment*, *4*(1), 67.

Martin, J. S., & Suarez, S. A. (2017). Personality assessment and model comparison with behavioral data: a statistical framework and empirical demonstration with bonobos (*Pan paniscus*). *American Journal of Primatology*, *79*(8), e22670.

Mazzanti, C. M., Lappalainen, J., Long, J. C., Bengel, D., Naukkarinen, H., Eggert, M., et al. (1998). Role of the serotonin transporter promoter polymorphism in anxiety-related traits. *Archives of General Psychiatry*, *55*(10), 936–940.

McGue, M., & Bouchard, T. J., Jr. (1998). Genetic and environmental influences on human behavioral differences. *Annual Review of Neuroscience*, *21*(1), 1–24.

McGuire, M. T., Raleigh, M. J., & Pollack, D. B. (1994). Personality features in vervet monkeys: The effects of sex, age, social status, and group composition. *American Journal of Primatology*, *33*, 1–13. https://doi.org/10.1002/ajp.1350330102.

Mehlman, P. T., Higley, J. D., Faucher, I., Lilly, A. A., Taub, D. M., Vickers, J., et al. (1994). Low CSF 5-HIAA concentrations and severe aggression and impaired impulse control in nonhuman primates. *The American Journal of Psychiatry*, *151*(10), 1485.

Miller, J. D., & Lynam, D. R. (2015). Psychopathy and personality: advances and debates. *Journal of Personality*, *83*(6), 585–592.

Moore, T. M., Scarpa, A., & Raine, A. (2002). A meta-analysis of serotonin metabolite 5-HIAA and antisocial behavior. *Aggressive Behavior*, *28*(4), 299–316.

Moul, C., Dobson-Stone, C., Brennan, J., Hawes, D., & Dadds, M. (2013). An exploration of the serotonin system in antisocial boys with high levels of callous-unemotional traits. *PLoS One*, *8*(2), e56619.

Oshino, S., Suzuki, A., Ishii, G., & Otani, K. (2007). Influences of parental rearing on the personality traits of healthy Japanese. *Comprehensive Psychiatry*, *48*(5), 465–469.

Panksepp, J. (2007). Neurologizing the psychology of affects: how appraisal-based constructivism and basic emotion theory can coexist. *Perspectives on Psychological Science*, *2*(3), 281–296.

Patrick, C. J., Fowles, D. C., & Krueger, R. F. (2009). Triarchic conceptualization of psychopathy: developmental origins of disinhibition, boldness, and meanness. *Development and Psychopathology*, *21*(3), 913–938.

Pederson, A. K., King, J. E., & Landau, V. I. (2005). Chimpanzee (*Pan troglodytes*) personality predicts behavior. *Journal of Research in Personality*, *39*(5), 534–549.

Phillips, K. A., Bales, K. L., Capitanio, J. P., Conley, A., Czoty, P. W., 't Hart, B. A., et al. (2014). Why primate models matter. *American Journal of Primatology*, *76*(9), 801–827.

Raleigh, M. J., McGuire, M. T., Brammer, G. L., & Yuwiler, A. (1984). Social and environmental influences on blood serotonin concentrations in monkeys. *Archives of General Psychiatry*, *41*(4), 405–410.

Reardon, K. W. (2014). *Adolescent personality moderates the testosterone-externalizing association*. (Doctoral dissertation).

Suomi, S. J. (1982). Abnormal behavior and primate models of psychopathology. In L. J. Forbes & J. E. King (Eds.), *Primate behavior* (pp. 171–215). New York: Academic Press.

Terburg, D., & van Honk, J. (2013). Approach–avoidance versus dominance–submissiveness: a multilevel neural framework on how testosterone promotes social status. *Emotion Review*, *5*(3), 296–302.

Waller, R., Hyde, L. W., Grabell, A. S., Alves, M. L., & Olson, S. L. (2015). Differential associations of early callous-unemotional, oppositional, and ADHD behaviors: multiple domains within early-starting conduct problems? *Journal of Child Psychology and Psychiatry*, *56*(6), 657–666.

Widiger, T. A., & Mullins-Sweatt, S. N. (2005). Categorical and dimensional models of personality disorders. In J. M. Oldham, A. E. Skodol, & D. S. Bender (Eds.), *The American Psychiatric Publishing textbook of personality disorders* (pp. 35–53). Arlington, VA: American Psychiatric Publishing, Inc..

Wilson, V. A., Weiss, A., Humle, T., Morimura, N., Udono, T., Idani, G., et al. (2017). Chimpanzee personality and the arginine vasopressin receptor 1A genotype. *Behavior Genetics*, *47*, 215–226.

Theoretical conceptualizations of agreeableness and antagonism☆

9

William G. Graziano, Renée M. Tobin†*
*Department of Psychological Sciences, Purdue University, West Lafayette, IN, United States, †College of Education, Temple University, Philadelphia, PA, United States

Theoretical considerations of agreeableness and antagonism

For at least 3000 years, thoughtful people observed regularities in forms of antagonism, its control and regulation, and its links to personality. It helped them understand people and their social worlds. Through the eyes of modern personality psychology, we can look back on ancient texts and recognize familiar types of people and see modern dispositions that we would call extraversion/dominance, conscientiousness, neuroticism, and openness. Graziano and Tobin (2009, 2016, 2018) noted that one other set of characteristics appearing in many classical discussions (e.g., Aristotle's *Nicomachean Ethics*; Plutarch's *Lives of the Noble Greeks & Romans*) is best labeled as agreeableness, varying degrees of disposition-based motivation to establish and maintain positive relations with others. At one end of the continuum, some have many of these qualities (high agreeableness), whereas others at the other end of the continuum have very few (high antagonism).

Consensus is emerging (e.g., Crowe, Lynam, & Miller, 2017; Graziano & Tobin, 2009, 2018) that a coherent analysis of agreeableness will contain both structural and functional aspects. Regarding the structural aspect, agreeableness can be seen as a latent variable or hypothetical construct. It is an abstract, higher level summary label for hierarchical class relations among connected, lower level characteristics. As a domain, agreeableness describes individual differences in motives for communal aspects of human sociality and maintenance of social harmony. It is related to extraversion, but different from it in its expression. In lexical analyses of the low end of agreeableness, persons who were described by others as "antagonistic" were also likely to be described as "distrustful," "manipulative," and "arrogant," implicating a superordinate dimension that is enduring over time. Regarding the functional aspect, agreeableness does not suffer from a shortage of specific empirical correlates. Treated as a single, continuous individual difference variable, it is systematically related to a wide range of external criteria involving thoughts, feelings, and social behaviors. What integrates these seemingly diverse lower level individual differences

☆ We dedicate this chapter to the memory of John Digman who encouraged us to conduct focal research on agreeableness.

The Handbook of Antagonism. https://doi.org/10.1016/B978-0-12-814627-9.00009-8

functionally, and provides psychological processes mediating the link between dispositions and overt behavior, are motives.

In terms of overt behavioral correlates, several reliable connections have been established for agreeableness. For example, individuals low in agreeableness report less empathic concern in observing victims of misfortune relative to their peers (e.g., Habashi, Graziano, & Hoover, 2016). They also are less likely to volunteer to help victims (Graziano, Habashi, Sheese, & Tobin, 2007; Habashi et al., 2016), to engage in destructive tactics during interpersonal conflict (e.g., Gadke, Tobin, & Schneider, 2016; Graziano, Jensen-Campbell, & Hair, 1996), and to display more prejudice against out-group members (e.g., Graziano, Bruce, Sheese, & Tobin, 2007). Individuals low in agreeableness are more likely to be ostracized and excluded from peer groups than are individuals high in agreeableness (Hales, Kassner, Williams, & Graziano, 2016). Low agreeableness is related to frequency of hostile social cognition, and to latency to respond aggressively to provocation, needs for helping behavior, and cooperation.

These findings are not simply an artifact of one culture's norms or one language community. For example, Kohnstamm, Halverson, Mervielde, and Havill (1998) instructed parents from 11 different cultural groups to describe their own children in their native language. Across all languages and cultural groups, approximately half of the free descriptions involved agreeableness and extraversion. Cultures differed in the importance assigned to agreeableness, but all groups described it.

In one of the first comprehensive overviews of agreeableness as a single dimension of personality, Graziano and Eisenberg (1997) were forced to take positions on the nature of agreeableness with only limited empirical data. They cast agreeableness primarily in motivational terms. Specifically, agreeableness was described in terms of individual differences in motivation to maintain positive relations with others. Following this publication, we reviewed the conceptual and empirical literature on agreeableness in a succession of *Handbook* chapters (Graziano & Tobin, 2009, 2013, 2016, 2018). Each of these reviews had a different emphasis relative to the others. Most recently, Graziano and Tobin (2018) provided a three-level conceptual approach to agreeableness adapted from the literature on prosocial behavior (Penner, Dovidio, Piliavin, & Schroeder, 2005; Schroeder & Graziano, 2015). Here we build on our previous chapters, offering a theoretical analysis of agreeableness focusing specifically on antagonism, the negative pole of the agreeableness continuum.

In their review of the literature connecting the five dimensions of personality to psychopathy, Vachon, Lynam, Miller, and Krueger (2018) focus on the combination of low agreeableness and low conscientiousness in explaining disinhibition of negative, externalizing impulses. Interestingly, this focusing on this combination of agreeableness and conscientiousness maps onto Rothbart's theoretical work on effortful control. That is, Rothbart and colleagues noted theoretical connections between the early appearing temperamental process of effortful control, the ability to suppress a dominant response in favor of a subdominant one, and later adult personality (Ahadi & Rothbart, 1994; Rothbart & Bates, 2006; Rothbart & Posner, 1985). Specifically, Ahadi and Rothbart (1994) posited that effortful control serves as the foundation of agreeableness in the development of regulation of frustration in interpersonal interactions and the foundation of conscientiousness in efforts to regulate frustration in response to tasks.

Empirical work, particularly Jensen-Campbell's research, provides support for the theoretical connection between effortful control and these two dimensions of personality. Jensen-Campbell et al. (2002) found associations between both agreeableness and conscientiousness with two traditional measures of self-regulation (i.e., the Stroop Test and the Wisconsin Card Sorting Task). Cumberland-Li, Eisenberg, and Reiser (2004) also found that behavioral measures of effortful control predicted agreeableness, although they did not examine conscientiousness in their study. Jensen-Campbell and Graziano (2005) examined children's responses to clear and mixed messages about cheating in a study of resistance to temptation. They found that the "mixed message" situation (i.e., events during which performance standards are being assessed and there is reason to think that illicit means to the goal may be acceptable) activated both agreeableness and conscientiousness motives. Overall, they found that persons higher in agreeableness cheated less than persons lower in agreeableness did, but they also found that no evidence that agreeableness was related to cheating when conscientiousness levels were high. This pattern of results suggests again that agreeableness and conscientiousness may be linked by common control motivation and may even compensate for each other in temptation situations. Jensen-Campbell, Knack, Waldrip, and Campbell (2007) found a similar pattern of results in a multimethod study examining the links among agreeableness, conscientiousness, anger, and aggression. Linking to Vachon et al. (2018), the theoretical and empirical work supporting effortful control as an underlying substrate of agreeableness and conscientiousness suggests that deficits in effortful control early in development are the cornerstones to psychopathy in adulthood.

Brief overview of some empirical studies using personality facets

Graziano and Tobin (2016) reviewed the literature on agreeableness facets. A burgeoning literature examining multiple facet results, including meta-analytic reviews, links the agreeableness facets inversely to psychopathy and antisocial/aggressive behavior (e.g., Axelrod, Widiger, Trull, & Corbitt, 1997; De Cuyper, De Pauw, De Fruyt, De Bolle, & De Clercq, 2009; Jones, Miller, & Lynam, 2011) as early as adolescence (Salekin, Debus, & Barker, 2010). Similarly, Stead and Fekken (2014) found that agreeableness and its facets were inversely related to all three aspects of the Dark Triad (i.e., Machiavellianism, Narcissism, and Psychopathy). Across multiple studies, the six facets of agreeableness and the overall agreeableness dimension are inversely linked to psychopathy and/or antisocial/aggressive behavior, with the straightforwardness facet demonstrating the most frequent connection (De Cuyper et al., 2009; Jones et al., 2011).

These connections are also demonstrated in the significant inverse relations between the agreeableness domain and its facets and serious, planned destructive behaviors, including acts of violence, delinquency, and risky sexual behavior. For example, Heaven (1996) found significant inverse relations between agreeableness and interpersonal violence and vandalism/theft among 216 adolescents attending an Australian Catholic school. With a modest sample of 40 men, Madsen, Parsons, and Grubin (2006) found that convicted child molesters with personality disorders were lower in agreeableness, trust, straightforwardness, and compliance. Similarly, rape perpetrators had lower levels of agreeableness, tender-mindedness, and altruism relative to sexual assault perpetrators and nonperpetrators (Voller & Long, 2010). Bellah, Bellah, and Johnson (2003) found inverse relations between agreeableness facets and vengefulness, with low straightforwardness accounting for 27% of the variance. Finally, agreeableness and two of its facets were linked to risky sexual behavior (Miller et al., 2004) in a sample of 481 participants (mean age 21 years). None of these results are wildly counterintuitive.

The larger point here is that theoretical refinements leading to disaggregation of variables may be useful in unwrapping links among forms of antagonism-related (e.g., aggressive and antisocial) behaviors. Pearce and Amato (1980) noticed a grouping problem parallel to the one noted here in the literature on prosocial behavior and helping. Using multidimensional scaling, Pearce and Amato (1980) raised the possibility that noise and error of prediction could be reduced when helping situations were disaggregated and classified along three underlying dimensions: serious (vs. not serious), planned (vs. spontaneous), and direct (vs. indirect). These three dimensions may offer a useful model for classifying the expression of aggressive and antisocial behavior. How might we apply this system to our case? We might speculate, for example, that agreeableness would be more closely tied (inversely) to those forms of aggression and antisocial behavior that were serious, planned, and direct. That is, persons low in agreeableness would be more likely than person high in agreeableness to be aggressive and antisocial in situations involving serious forms of aggression, which required planning, and involved direct engagement with another person. Other settings or forms of aggression and antisocial behavior may not be well predicted from individual differences in agreeableness; they may be better predicted by main effects from situational contexts (e.g., frustration, provocation). Alternatively, it could be argued that if low agreeableness is driven largely by difficulties in self-regulation (e.g., Tobin, Graziano, Vanman, & Tassinary, 2000), then agreeableness becomes a good predictor of spontaneous, but not planned, aggressive and antisocial behavior. Ultimately, these conjectures could be wrong; these are empirical issues (see Gleason, Jensen-Campbell, & Richardson, 2004).

This issue is complicated further by the possibility that domain- and dimension level accounts may be painted with too broad a brush, being imprecise and even misleading (e.g., Crowe et al., 2017: Smith, McCarthy, & Zapolski, 2009; but maybe not: Gleason et al., 2004). We may be purchasing bandwidth from fidelity at a steep price. In theory, facet-level measures should provide greater fidelity for facet-specific content than do domain-level measures. It is probably fair to say that a positive definition implies that the domain and its corresponding components or facets form a positive manifold. Nevertheless, in theory a facet-level measure of altruism should predict external helping behavior better than either a facet-level measure of compliance or measures of the superordinate domain level of agreeableness. For the agreeableness domain, current evidence for this sort of improved precision is thin or at best indirect (Graziano & Tobin, 2016). It is still possible that aggressive or antisocial behavior is associated more closely with some facets (e.g., trust) than with others (e.g., altruism). This possibility does not create an insurmountable problem, but it does point to difficulties in generating convincing (much less air-tight) evidence of distinctive links among aggression/antisocial behavior, agreeableness-antagonism facets, and agreeableness-antagonism as a superordinate domain.

A third basic question is methodological. Moving from the conceptual to the operational level, variables like agreeableness need to be operationalized and measured. They are usually measured by self-report (e.g., Crowe et al., 2017; Graziano & Tobin, 2018). If both the predictor and the criterion are measured by verbal self-report only, then the mono-method bias makes evidence for a link between two constructs weaker than if at least one of the measures was observational or behavioral. In our search through the literature, a relatively small portion of agreeableness research included actual behavioral measures. There are a few noteworthy exceptions (e.g., Miller et al., 2009), but more to the point is that several critical gaps, both empirically and conceptually, remain.

Toward theoretical accounts

It is challenging to impose order on such a diverse set of empirical findings. One approach for imposing order is to remain close to issues of measurement (e.g., John & Benet-Martínez, 2014). Fig. 1 presents a simplified representation of the antagonism-agreeableness continuum from the perspective of a construct validity approach. As shown in Fig. 1, agreeableness ranges from extreme antisociality at one end of the continuum to extreme prosociality at the other end of this hypothetical construct. It reflects that individual differences in agreeableness predispose persons toward patterns of prosocial (positively) and antisocial (inversely) activities. Rather than using the standard facet structure for agreeableness, we offer something more general, better suited, we think, for work with antisociality and prosociality.

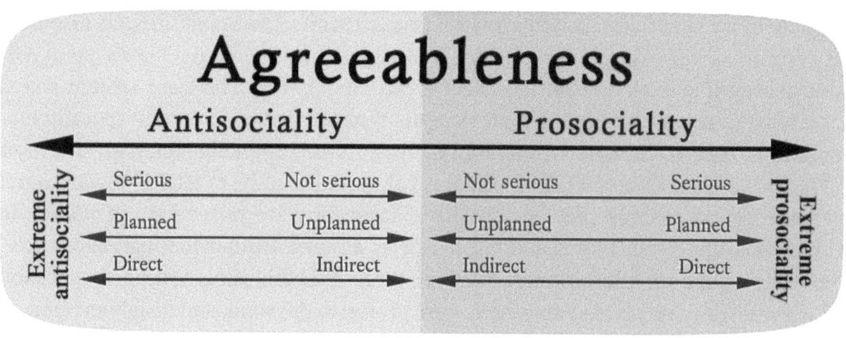

Fig. 1 Antagonism on the agreeableness continuum.

Pearce and Amato (1980) identified three aspects of prosociality on continua: Spontaneous-Planned, Not serious-Serious, and Indirect-Direct. These three aspects yield variation in expressions of observable prosociality ranging from mild (low on all three aspects of prosociality) to severe (high on all three aspects of prosociality).

Similarly, the low end of agreeableness (i.e., antagonism) can be broken down into the same three aspects, yielding variation in expressions of observable antagonism (e.g., aggressive and antisocial behavior) ranging from mild (low on all three aspects of antagonism) to severe (high on all three aspects of antagonism). Thus these abstract concepts can be rooted in the "soil of observation" (Feigl, 1970) such that these differences can be operationalized into observable measures. Operationally, if an observer were to watch a videotaped interaction, would they classify the act as premediated or spontaneous? A second aspect would involve the seriousness of the act. The third aspect deals with the directness of the act. Some (if not most) acts are ambiguous, but those that are not may be especially diagnostic and can be mapped onto theoretical accounts of agreeableness as we will discuss later in this chapter.

This theoretical approach is basic, but it does not add much explanatory power. It serves primarily as a means of organizing empirical outcomes. Graziano and Tobin (2013) proposed another way to conceptualize agreeableness based on seemingly unrelated work by Dijker and Koomen (2007), who focused on stigmatization and the evaluation of social "deviants." How do we explain the apparently inconsistent reaction of a person to one kind of deviant (e.g., drug addict), yet a caring reaction from the same person to another kind of deviant (e.g., homeless child)? At the descriptive level, this theoretical work seems to be tangential to our analysis here, but the mechanisms underlying the Dijker and Koomen can be adapted. For Dijker and Koomen, their system included two evolved, preverbal systems of motivation. Both of these motive systems reflect human evolutionary history. The first, older component is a Fight/Flight system that humans carry as part of our Paleo-reptilian heritage. Encounters with "unusual cases" ("deviance" in Dijker and Koomen) activate this system without conscious deliberation, priming a system that induces individuals to flee from danger, or to fight if forced to do so.

Archeological evidence suggests that humans evolved in small groups of genetically related individuals, so aggressive reactions to unusual cases had to be inhibited. Some of the unusual cases probably involved kin. In these cases, repair of deviance would be more beneficial than aggression or exclusion. As a result, there is also a second system, newer in evolutionary time that is part of the parental care system associated with kin selection (Hamilton, 1964; Trivers, 1972). The Care system has the capacity to suppress the Fight/Flight system. When exposed to certain specific environmental triggers, these two motivational systems can elicit characteristic emotions.

The Dijker and Koomen (2007) theoretical system can be extended toward agreeableness. Let us assume that personality dispositions are reflections of underlying mechanisms like Fight/Flight and Care. Let us assume further that agreeableness is the psychological manifestation of the Care system. If this is correct, then agreeableness may not only relate to sympathetic care giving to the weak and disadvantaged, but may also operate to suppress the responses associated with the more primitive Fight/Flight system. Some agreeableness phenomena may be fairly direct expressions of

Care, whereas others may be a product of Care-based suppression of Fight/Flight. Applied to our present analysis, most people may experience antagonistic reactions initially to a frustrating event, but as Care processes gradually come on line, that antagonism dissipates. For person low in agreeableness, the dissipation process may be slow or nonexistent. In the case of helping, most people may experience personal distress initially upon encountering a victim in need of help, but that distress will dissipate as the Care system comes on line. For persons high in agreeableness, the lag may be less or they may feel empathic concern directly for victims of misfortune (Graziano, Habashi, et al., 2007), but they may also suppress (perhaps effortfully) negative reactions to traditional targets of prejudice generated by their Fight/Flight system (Graziano, Bruce, et al., 2007).

Building on these assumptions, let us assume some connections between the Fight/Flight and Care systems of potential relevance to agreeableness. If we assume that both Fight/Flight and Care systems are present in almost all people (but at varying strengths) and that Fight/Flight occurs faster than Care upon exposure to an environmental oddity, then the two may operate in opposition to each other's preponderate responsive activation tendencies. If so, we can generate explanations for apparent paradoxes and anomalies. It is easier to describe in the case of prosocial behavior, but the general process should operate in contexts involving antagonism. Graziano and Tobin (2013) note that in the helping context, personal distress may inhibit prosocial acts because it is part of Fight/Flight, not Care. Empathic concern promotes helping because it is part of Care. Despite having opposite effects on helping, both personal distress and empathic concern are present in most people, explaining the usual positive correlation. Personal distress is the first response to a victim (or potential aggressor) because it is connected to the faster Fight/Flight system. If there is an opportunity for easy escape from the victim when personal distress is high, then the victim will not receive help. If escape cannot occur quickly, or if the observer must remain in proximity to the victim, then enough time may pass for the slower empathic concern system to become active. This activation would suppress the Fight/Flight system and increase the chances that the victim would receive help (or not become a target of aggression). This account explains why outcomes of research on Ease/Difficulty of Escape are unstable. The key variable—the time interval between exposure to the victim and the window of opportunity for escape—is unmeasured.

The system we describe resembles the opponent process model of motivation presented by Solomon and his colleagues (Solomon, 1980; Solomon & Corbit, 1974). In a search of the published literature, Graziano and Tobin (2013) found only two applications of the Solomon opponent process model to either prosocial or antagonism (Baumeister & Campbell, 1999; Piliavin, Callero, & Evanset, 1982). In both cases, the focus of attention was primarily on Solomon's opponent explanation for cycles of addictive behavior. The Graziano/Tobin version of the opponent approach is presented in Fig. 2. In keeping with Solomon, the first process activated is labeled State A. Its activation is virtually automatic, a kind of unconditioned response to the onset of an environmental stimulus. As in Solomon's model, it remains active while the evocative stimulus is present and ends when the stimulus is removed. The second process activated is an opponent, labeled State B. Its activation is slower, but it remains well after

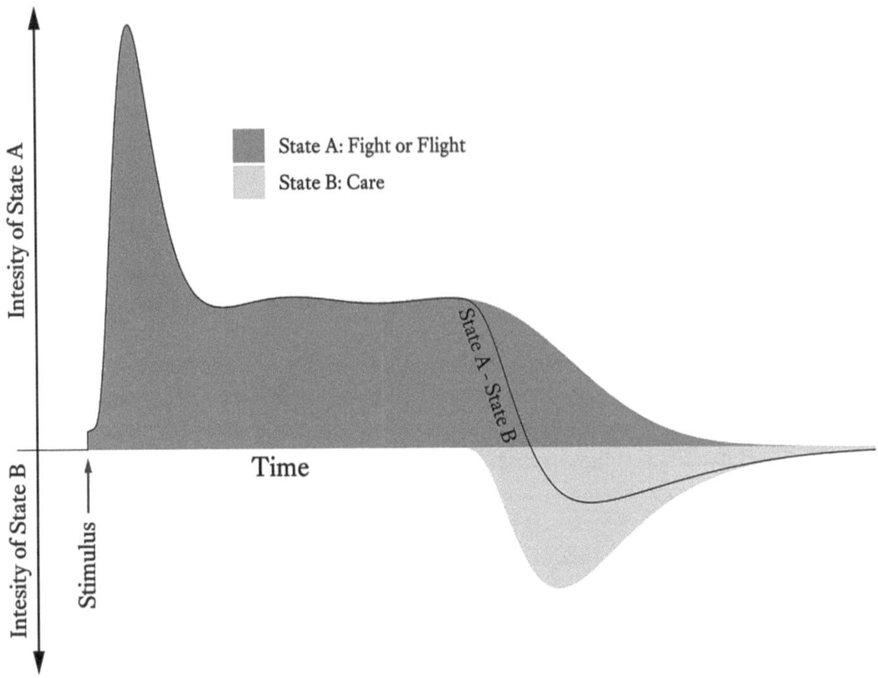

Fig. 2 Opponent process approach to agreeableness.

State A ends. A and B are opponents, but A occurs first and more quickly in response to an environmental event for some brief part of the sequence; State A operates in almost pure form (without an opponent) initially. Concretely, if State A is Personal Distress and State B is Empathic concern, then the first response to a victim or a frustrating event should be unopposed personal distress. If escape is possible in this interval, the victim will not receive help. By the same logic, initial reactions to unusual cases (e.g., victims of misfortune) as well as to members of out-groups would be personal distress and avoidance. With time, however, State B can be activated, opposing the processes of State A. These opponent processes map on well to the Pryor, Reeder, Yeadon, and Hesson-Mclnnis (2004) behavior correction findings. These researchers found that an individual's initial negative reaction to distance oneself from a person with a stigmatizing condition is adjusted over time.

Graziano and Tobin (2013) observed that Solomon's opponent process approach offers several additional insights relevant to agreeableness. Repeated exposure to the evocative (unconditioned) stimuli produces systematic changes in the relative strengths of State A and State B. State A becomes weaker, and State B becomes stronger. The prototype is drug addiction, in which repeated exposure to substances like cocaine creates smaller and shorter states of euphoria, and longer states of withdrawal. In the present application, repeated exposure to victims of misfortune should lead to smaller and shorter periods of personal distress and, at least in theory, to longer states of empathic concern. This connection might explain why there are individual differences, and why they appear in the form that they do. In most of these cases, the kinds of individual differences in motivation for helping reported by Oliner and Oliner (1988) and by others reflect the fact that the helpers had repeated exposure to various kinds of "unusual cases" of people earlier in their lives.

Graziano and Tobin (2013) also observed that Solomon's approach raises important questions about the conceptual status of large individual differences like agreeableness, the decomposition of molar behavior into constituent components, and the role of time in the expression of complex socially desirable and undesirable behavior. Regarding the first of these questions, at some level each individual is born prepared for a life trajectory by a set of inherited tendencies and motivation systems. Evolution may have left us with two powerful motive systems in Fight/Flight and Care (Dijker & Koomen, 2007), but there are probably individual differences in the relative strength of Fight/Flight and Care motivation. Observers might detect and label these socially important behavioral differences as neuroticism and agreeableness, respectively. At this point, we might be satisfied to build structural models or collect data showing intercorrelations among variables like Care, agreeableness, and some other disposition like, say, self-esteem. Such an approach would grossly underestimate the dynamic quality of the major dispositions and probably the range of influence of the individual difference under consideration. That being said, repeated exposure to certain kinds of environmental events could alter the basic parameters of the inherited dispositions and motives.

Turning to the second question, the expression of complex social behavior like helping or hurting another is almost certainly the outcome of several different but related systems. When these systems operate at the same time, one system may reduce the influence of another. In the opponent process approach, the influence of State A is much reduced once State B is activated. From observing a single episode of helping or hurting, a researcher might conclude that a single process is operative, but it is likely that the process is better studied only by observing the operation of the components over time.

The opponent process model linking agreeableness-antagonism to interpersonal behaviors and to more general self-regulatory processes (Graziano & Tobin, 2013; Tobin & Graziano, 2006) is novel, so many unanswered questions remain. Is agreeableness tied to the Care system only or to Fight/Flight as well? Is it tied to both personal distress and empathic concern, to both aggression/antisocial behavior and the suppression of such behavior, or to just one of these elements in each pair? We believe that the opponent process approach to agreeableness allows us to anticipate phenomena that cannot be found elsewhere. Here we offer a few preliminary thoughts.

To the best of our knowledge no empirical research has addressed the issue of delayed aggression in this framework (but see Penner, Fritzsche, Craiger, & Freifeld, 1995). In general, a common assumption is that the influence of a manipulation (e.g., partner provocation; frustration; victim need; mood state; or empathic concern) will dissipate for most or all people over time. That is, reactions (e.g., rates of helping; aggressive responding) are affected by the interval between provision of information and the opportunity to act on it. Note the analog to the correction of prejudicial behavior reported by Pryor et al. (2004). If the opponent process system operates roughly as described here, then some forms of aggression may be lessened after a short delay relative to when they are following an immediate request, but this reduction in the expression of antagonism may be less for persons low in agreeableness relative to persons high in agreeableness. The initial Fight/Flight reaction may come under the control of the opponent Care system. In the case of aggression, it may diffuse the tendency to aggress, but less so in person low in agreeableness (or high in antagonism). In the case of helping, the time lag diffuses the tendency to escape and not help. Undoubtedly, we would also see characteristic emotions. In the case of helping, it might be expressed as relief at finally having an opportunity to provide assistance. Based on the previous rationale, we would also expect persons high in agreeableness to offer more help, sooner and with less influence of delay, than persons low in agreeableness. In the case of aggression, persons low in agreeableness would aggress sooner, with shorter latencies than persons high in agreeableness, with a slower diminution when the Care state becomes active. At this point, such conjectures are speculative. Whatever outcomes do appear, it is clear that agreeableness and its associated motives for maintaining positive relationships with others will play a role in our deeper understanding of aggression/antisocial behavior and other interpersonal processes.

Acknowledgment

We thank W. Joel Schneider for his helpful suggestions and assistance in creating the figures in this chapter.

References

Ahadi, S. A., & Rothbart, M. K. (1994). Temperament, development, and the Big Five. In C. F. Halverson, Jr.,, G. A. Kohnstamm, & R. P. Martin (Eds.), *The developing structure of temperament and personality from infancy to adulthood* (pp. 189–207). Hillsdale, NJ: Erlbaum.

Axelrod, S. R., Widiger, T. A., Trull, T. J., & Corbitt, E. M. (1997). Relations of five-factor model antagonism facets with personality disorder symptomatology. *Journal of Personality Assessment*, *69*, 297–313.

Baumeister, R. F., & Campbell, W. K. (1999). The intrinsic appeal of evil: sadism, sensational thrills, and threatened egotism. *Personality and Social Psychology Review*, *3*, 210–221.

Bellah, C. G., Bellah, L. D., & Johnson, J. L. (2003). A look at dispositional vengefulness from the three and five-factor models of personality. *Individual Differences Research*, *1*, 6–16.

Crowe, M. L., Lynam, D. R., & Miller, J. D. (2017). Uncovering the structure of Agreeableness from self-report measures. *Journal of Personality*, *86*, 771–787. https://doi.org/10.1111/jopy.12358.

Cumberland-Li, A., Eisenberg, N., & Reiser, M. (2004). Relations of young children's agreeableness and resiliency to effortful control and impulsivity. *Social Development*, *13*, 193–212.

De Cuyper, M., De Pauw, S., De Fruyt, F., De Bolle, M., & De Clercq, B. J. (2009). A meta-analysis of psychopathy-, antisocial PD- and FFM associations. *European Journal of Personality*, *23*, 531–565.

Dijker, A. J. M., & Koomen, W. (2007). *Stigmatization, tolerance, and repair: An integrative psychological analysis of responses to deviance.* New York: Cambridge University Press.

Feigl, H. (1970). The "orthodox" view of theories: remarks in defense as well as critique. In M. Radner & S. Winokur (Eds.), *Minnesota studies in the philosophy of science: Analyses of theories & methods of physics & psychology* (pp. 3–16). Minneapolis, MN: University of Minnesota Press.

Gadke, D. L., Tobin, R. M., & Schneider, W. J. (2016). Agreeableness, conflict resolution tactics, and school behavior in second graders. *Journal of Individual Differences, 37*, 145–151. https://doi.org/10.1027/1614-0001/a000199.

Gleason, K. A., Jensen-Campbell, L. A., & Richardson, D. S. (2004). Agreeableness as a predictor of aggression in adolescence. *Aggressive Behavior, 30*, 43–61.

Graziano, W. G., Bruce, J. W., Sheese, B. E., & Tobin, R. M. (2007). Attraction, personality, and prejudice: liking none of the people most of the time. *Journal of Personality and Social Psychology, 93*, 565–582.

Graziano, W. G., & Eisenberg, N. (1997). Agreeableness: a dimension of personality. In R. Hogan, J. Johnson, & S. Briggs (Eds.), *Handbook of personality psychology* (pp. 795–824). San Diego, CA: Academic Press.

Graziano, W. G., Habashi, M. M., Sheese, B. E., & Tobin, R. M. (2007). Agreeableness, empathy, and helping: a person x situation perspective. *Journal of Personality and Social Psychology, 93*, 583–599.

Graziano, W. G., Jensen-Campbell, L. A., & Hair, E. C. (1996). Perceiving interpersonal conflict and reacting to it: the case for Agreeableness. *Journal of Personality and Social Psychology, 70*, 820–835.

Graziano, W. G., & Tobin, R. M. (2009). Agreeableness. In M. R. Leary & R. H. Hoyle (Eds.), *Handbook of individual differences in social behavior* (pp. 46–61). New York: Guilford.

Graziano, W. G., & Tobin, R. M. (2013). The cognitive and motivational foundations underlying agreeableness. In M. D. Robinson, E. Watkins, & E. Harmon-Jones (Eds.), *Handbook of cognition and emotion* (pp. 347–364). New York: Guilford.

Graziano, W. G., & Tobin, R. M. (2016). Agreeableness and the Five Factor Model. In T. A. Widiger (Ed.), *The Oxford handbook of the Five Factor Model* (pp. 105–132). Oxford: Oxford University Press. https://doi.org/10.1093/oxfordhb/9780199352487.013.17.

Graziano, W. G., & Tobin, R. M. (2018). Agreeableness: a three-level integration. In V. Zeigler-Hill & T. K. Shackelford (Eds.), *The SAGE handbook of personality and individual differences* (pp. 212–234). Thousand Oaks, CA: SAGE.

Habashi, M. M., Graziano, W. G., & Hoover, A. E. (2016). Searching for the prosocial personality: a big five approach to linking personality and prosocial behavior. *Personality and Social Psychology Bulletin, 42*, 1177–1192.

Hales, A., Kassner, M. P., Williams, K. D., & Graziano, W. G. (2016). Disagreeableness as a cause and consequence of ostracism. *Personality and Social Psychology Bulletin, 42*, 782–797.

Hamilton, W. D. (1964). The genetical evolution of social behaviour I and II. *Journal of Theoretical Biology, 7*, 1–32.

Heaven, P. C. L. (1996). Personality and self-reported delinquency: analysis of the "Big Five" personality dimensions. *Personality and Individual Differences, 20*, 47–54.

Jensen-Campbell, L. A., & Graziano, W. G. (2005). Two faces of temptation: differing motives for self-control. *Merrill-Palmer Quarterly, 51*, 287–324.

Jensen-Campbell, L. A., Knack, J. M., Waldrip, A. M., & Campbell, S. D. (2007). Do Big Five personality traits associated with self-control influence the regulation of anger and aggression? *Journal of Research in Personality, 41*, 403–424.

Jensen-Campbell, L. A., Rosselli, M., Workman, K. A., Santisi, M., Rios, J. D., & Bojan, D. (2002). Agreeableness, conscientiousness and effortful control processes. *Journal of Research in Personality, 36*, 476–489.

John, O. P., & Benet-Martínez, V. (2014). Measurement: reliability, construct validation, and scale construction. In H. T. Reis & C. M. Judd (Eds.), *Handbook of research methods in social and personality psychology* (pp. 473–503). New York: Cambridge University Press.

Jones, S. E., Miller, J. D., & Lynam, D. R. (2011). Personality, antisocial behavior, and aggression: a meta-analytic review. *Journal of Criminal Justice*, *39*, 329–337.

Kohnstamm, G. A., Halverson, C. F., Jr., Mervielde, I., & Havill, V. L. (1998). Analyzing parental free description of child personality. In G. A. Kohnstamm, C. F. Halverson, Jr.,, I. Mervielde, & V. L. Havill (Eds.), *Parental description of child personality: Developmental antecedents of the Big Five?* (pp. 1–19). Mahwah, NJ: Erlbaum.

Madsen, L., Parsons, S., & Grubin, D. (2006). The relationship between the five-factor model and DSM personality disorder in a sample of child molesters. *Personality and Individual Differences*, *40*, 227–236.

Miller, J. D., Campbell, W. K., Young, D. L., Lakey, C. E., Reidy, D. E., Zeichner, A., et al. (2009). Examining the relations among narcissism, impulsivity, and self-defeating behaviors. *Journal of Personality*, *77*, 761–794.

Miller, J. D., Lynam, D. R., Zimmerman, R. S., Logan, T. K., Leukefeld, C., & Clayton, R. (2004). The utility of the Five Factor Model in understanding risky sexual behavior. *Personality and Individual Differences*, *36*, 1611–1626.

Oliner, S. P., & Oliner, P. M. (1988). *The altruistic personality: Rescuers of Jews in Nazi Europe*. New York: Free Press.

Pearce, P., & Amato, P. R. (1980). A taxonomy of helping: a multidimensional scaling analysis. *Social Psychology Quarterly*, *43*, 363–371.

Penner, L. A., Dovidio, J., Piliavin, J. A., & Schroeder, D. A. (2005). Prosocial behavior: multilevel perspectives. *Annual Review of Psychology*, *56*, 356–392.

Penner, L. A., Fritzsche, B. A., Craiger, J. P., & Freifeld, T. S. (1995). Measuring the prosocial personality. In J. N. Butcher & C. D. Spielberger (Eds.), *Vol. 10. Advances in personality assessment* (pp. 147–163). Vol. 10(pp. 147–163). Hillsdale, NJ: Erlbaum.

Piliavin, J. A., Callero, P. L., & Evanset, D. E. (1982). Addiction to altruism? Opponent-process theory and habitual blood donation. *Journal of Personality and Social Psychology*, *43*, 1200–1213.

Pryor, J. B., Reeder, G. D., Yeadon, C., & Hesson-Mclnnis, M. (2004). A dual-process model of reactions to perceived stigma. *Journal of Personality and Social Psychology*, *87*, 436–452.

Rothbart, M. K., & Bates, J. E. (2006). Temperament. N. Eisenberg, W. Damon, & R. M. Lerner (Eds.), *Handbook of child psychology* (pp. 99–166). (6th ed.). *Social, emotional, and personality development: Vol. 3*(pp. 99–166). Hoboken, NJ: John Wiley & Sons Inc.

Rothbart, M. K., & Posner, M. I. (1985). Temperament and the development of self-regulation. In L. C. Hartlage & C. F. Telzrow (Eds.), *The neuropsychology of individual differences: A developmental perspective* (pp. 93–123). New York: Plenum.

Salekin, R. T., Debus, S. A., & Barker, E. D. (2010). Adolescent psychopathy and the five factor model: domain and facet analysis. *Journal of Psychopathology and Behavioral Assessment*, *32*, 501–514.

Schroeder, D. A., & Graziano, W. G. (2015). The field of prosocial behavior: an introduction and overview. In D. A. Schroeder & W. G. Graziano (Eds.), *The Oxford handbook of prosocial behavior* (pp. 3–34). New York: Oxford University Press.

Smith, G. T., McCarthy, D. M., & Zapolski, T. C. B. (2009). On the value of homogeneous constructs in construct validation, theory testing and the description of psychopathology. *Psychological Assessment*, *21*, 271–284.

Solomon, R. (1980). The opponent-process theory of acquired motivation: the costs of pleasure and the benefits of pain. *American Psychologist*, *35*, 691–712.

Solomon, R. L., & Corbit, J. D. (1974). An opponent-process theory of motivation: I. Temporal dynamics of affect. *Psychological Review*, *57*, 119–145.
Stead, R., & Fekken, G. C. (2014). Agreeableness at the core of the dark triad of personality. *Individual Differences Research*, *12*(4-A), 131–141.
Tobin, R. M., & Graziano, W. G. (2006). Development of regulatory processes through adolescence: A review of recent empirical studies. In D. Mroczek & T. Little (Eds.), *Handbook of personality development* (pp. 263–283). Mahwah, NJ: Erlbaum.
Tobin, R. M., Graziano, W. G., Vanman, E. J., & Tassinary, L. G. (2000). Personality, emotional experience, and efforts to control emotions. *Journal of Personality and Social Psychology*, *79*, 656–669.
Trivers, R. (1972). Parental investment and sexual selection. In B. Campbell (Ed.), *Sexual selections and the descent of man: 1871–1971* (pp. 136–179). Chicago, IL: Aldine.
Vachon, D. D., Lynam, D. R., Miller, J. D., & Krueger, R. F. (2018). Externalizing, psychopathology and antisocial personality disorder: a parsimonious trait-based approach. In V. Zeigler-Hill & T. K. Shackelford (Eds.), *SAGE handbook of personality & individual differences* (pp. 300–323). London: SAGE.
Voller, E. K., & Long, P. J. (2010). Sexual assault and rape perpetration by college men: the role of the Big Five personality traits. *Journal of Interpersonal Violence*, *25*, 457–480.

A social cognitive analysis of antagonism and reactive aggression

10

Michael D. Robinson, Benjamin M. Wilkowski†, Brian P. Meier‡*
*Department of Psychology, North Dakota State University, Fargo, ND, United States,
†Department of Psychology, University of Wyoming, Laramie, WY, United States,
‡Department of Psychology, Gettysburg College, Gettysburg, PA, United States

The Greeks recognized something like antagonism in the form of the choleric temperament. Whether due to an excess of bile or not, a sizeable minority of the population can be characterized as caustic, prickly, irritable, and sometimes just plain mean. Since that time, we have learned that traits such as these tend to co-occur in the person, but primarily in a way that defines a dimension of personality rather than a personality type. In addition to hostile and nonhostile people, that is, there are many people with moderate levels of hostility. The latter are sometimes prone to anger and aggression, but not with the frequency that characterizes particularly hostile people (Deffenbacher, 1992).

The dimension of antagonism can be located in several ways. People are antagonistic if they are low in the personality trait of agreeableness, a dimension of the Five-Factor Model (FFM) or Big 5 (John & Srivastava, 1999). Relatedly, Krueger and colleagues developed a version of the FFM that taps maladaptive variants of these traits, with antagonism as one of the scales. This DSM-5 version of antagonism correlates highly with the FFM trait of agreeableness, but has not yet been the focus of a great deal of research (McCabe, Vrabel, & Zeigler-Hill, 2017). Antagonism should also align itself with the hostility dimension of the interpersonal circumplex and arguably captures what is shared by the "dark triad" traits of narcissism, Machiavellianism, and psychopathy (Furnham, Richards, & Paulhus, 2013).

In addition, though, antagonism might be defined in terms of the trait of anger, a narrower trait, but one that captures the reactive, emotional tendencies emphasized in the aggression literature (Berkowitz, 1993). In favor of this idea, anger is strongly, and inversely, correlated with agreeableness (Zuckerman, Kuhlman, Joireman, Teta, & Kraft, 1993) and overlaps considerably with the construct of reactive aggression (Wilkowski & Robinson, 2008a). In point of fact, most of the research we review assesses antagonism in terms of trait anger or FFM agreeableness. For the sake of coherence, we will try to be consistent in translating these findings into the language of antagonism, with antagonism defined in terms of high levels of anger or low levels of agreeableness.

Regardless of measurement issues, there is considerable agreement about what antagonistic people are like. They have a more cynical view of the world and of other

The Handbook of Antagonism. https://doi.org/10.1016/B978-0-12-814627-9.00010-4

people. The world they inhabit is a darker one in which power plays, deceit, and exploitation are seen to occur with some frequency (Furnham et al., 2013). Perhaps not surprisingly, they tend to respond in turn. That is, antagonistic people are more manipulative and they are more callous, which can be defined in terms of lesser caring and compassion (Jones & Figueredo, 2013). Beyond these attitudinal components, there are behavioral components. Antagonistic people are more reactive to various forms of provocation and frustration (Bettencourt, Talley, Benjamin, & Valentine, 2006). And they react to such situations in a more approach-oriented, vengeful manner (Veenstra, Bushman, & Koole, 2018).

The preceding portrait can be fleshed out with some correlates. Among the Big 5 personality traits, antagonism seems to have the strongest correlations with aggressive behavior (Miller & Lynam, 2001). When anger is involved, the form of aggression can be termed emotional or reactive (Wilkowski & Robinson, 2008a). Antagonism is also a robust predictor of specific types of aggression that are consequential such as aggressive driving or domestic violence (Veenstra et al., 2018). Because antagonistic people seek and create conflict, and because they react to it more strongly, antagonistic traits predict cardiovascular outcomes such as blood pressure and heart disease (Smith, Glazer, Ruiz, & Gallo, 2004). Finally, antagonistic traits can be found in a number of personality disorders such as antisocial, narcissistic, and borderline (Axelrod, Widiger, Trull, & Corbitt, 1997).

Many of these correlates (e.g., cardiovascular responses) can be understood in terms of reactivity, whether to stressors or provocation. However, antagonism has broader correlates as well. Antagonistic people seem to be impulsive in a variety of ways. For example, they are more likely to use and abuse drugs like tobacco or alcohol (Veenstra et al., 2018). They are also prone to other "externalized" behaviors such as delinquency and criminality (Miller & Lynam, 2001). Some of these correlates could be understood in terms of the hostile attitudes that often accompany anger and reactive aggression (Wilkowski & Robinson, 2010). However, some of these correlates seem to implicate broader processes related to deficiencies in self-control. Although our analysis will primarily speak to reactive components of antagonism, and particularly those implicating hostility-related processes, we will also briefly touch on some wider questions about the relationship between antagonism and impulsivity.

A social cognitive analysis

In contrast to the global trait approach, the social cognitive approach to personality emphasizes situational factors and their role in how a person behaves. The social cognitive analysis is useful in the domain of reactive aggression because situational factors figure prominently in this form of aggression, relative to forms that are either proactive or unpredictable (Wilkowski & Robinson, 2010). Indeed, the role of situational factors would be hard to overemphasize. People who are prone to reactive aggression are not angry at all times. Rather, they are angry particularly when they think they have been provoked or are frustrated (Deffenbacher, 1992). Similarly, people who are prone to reactive aggression are not aggressive under all circumstances. Rather, they are aggressive particularly when—and, to some extent, only when—circumstances suggest provocation (Bettencourt et al., 2006).

Understanding reactive aggression, then, requires one to understand why people react very differently to cues of provocation or hostility. In other words, there is presumably something about these cues, and how they are processed, that might explain why reactivity varies across people. Alternatively, antagonistic people may have more favorable attitudes toward aggression or be less able to control such tendencies (Crick & Dodge, 1996). In either case, it makes sense to model the person-in-situation to better determine how behavior varies as a function of stimuli or situations. Social cognitive paradigms are designed to do this. Accordingly, and in speaking to questions of mechanism, we review lines of research that can allow us to probe the mechanisms involved in antagonism and how they may predispose people to outcomes such as anger, aggression, and externalizing behavior.

Attitudinal and interpersonal factors

A purely cognitive analysis might err in depicting antagonistic people as victims of their cognitive tendencies. For example, we might think of cognitive tendencies to select hostile over nonhostile cues as relatively low-level operations that have more to do with the visual system than with a person's goals or preferences. This viewpoint is probably mistaken, however, in that the cognitive biases that antagonistic people display are likely to follow from the goals they have, the attitudes they harbor, and their approach to interpersonal transactions (Crick & Dodge, 1996). Accordingly, it makes sense to touch on some of the attitudinal and interpersonal factors that set the stage for the cognitive analysis that follows.

Interpersonal goals. Agreeable people, or those low in antagonism, like other people and are motivated to be liked in return. Their interpersonal goals, therefore, favor mechanisms related to cooperation, respect, and nonretaliation (Hilbig, Zettler, Leist, & Heydasch, 2013). The goals that antagonistic people have are different. Antagonistic people are competitive and they often view others as tools to be used for their own ends (Figueredo & Jacobs, 2010). In the language of Hogan (2007), agreeable people want to get along with others whereas antagonistic people seem to place getting ahead in front of getting along. A greater degree of hostility and aggression would naturally follow from this interpersonal stance.

Attitudes toward aggression. At higher levels of antagonism, people view the possibility of aggressing against others (Crick & Dodge, 1996) and revenge (Stuckless & Goranson, 1992) more favorably. These attitudes are supported by a larger class of cognitions that favor aggression. For example, antagonistic people are more likely to believe that retribution is justified or that targets deserved their plight (Michel, Pace, Edun, Sawhney, & Thomas, 2014). Antagonistic people, furthermore, have greater self-efficacy for aggression and expect more favorable outcomes as a function of it (Crick & Dodge, 1994).

Situational selection. Through their actions, antagonistic people will tend to induce greater hostility in others (Smith et al., 2004). However, antagonistic people also gravitate toward more negative situations. Bresin and Robinson (2015) investigated processes of this type with a voluntary viewing task (Studies 1 and 2) and a media preference questionnaire (Study 3). In Studies 1 and 2, antagonistic people voluntarily viewed negative pictures for a longer period of time than positive pictures, whereas this was not the case for nonantagonistic people. In Study 3, antagonism predicted whether people preferred hostile and violent media (e.g., slasher movies) to gentler or more humorous options. Antagonistic people may also affiliate with antagonistic others (Lamkin, Maples-Keller, & Miller, 2018). In various ways, then, antagonistic people seem likely to inhabit environmental niches marked by greater hostility or negativity.

Interpretation, attribution, and appraisal. When we are slighted or mistreated, it can be unclear whether the other person intended to hurt us or not. Under these circumstances, antagonistic people tend to make hostile interpretations (e.g., a bump was intentional) whereas nonantagonistic people make more benign interpretations. Dodge (1980) first demonstrated this hostile attribution bias among aggressive children using scenarios in which hostile intent was almost certainly present, not present, or ambiguous. When intent was uncertain, children prone to aggression tended to make more hostile interpretations than nonaggressive children. Such attributional biases have been replicated many times since then (Crick & Dodge, 1994).

Children perceive their social interactions in somewhat simplistic ways and it might be uncertain whether the hostile attribution bias can be found among adults. This appears to be the case. Indeed, a number of studies have shown that aggressive or antagonistic adults are prone to hostile attributions under conditions of ambiguity (e.g., Dill, Anderson, & Deuser, 1997). This has been especially true to the extent that the relevant traits assess tendencies toward anger-motivated or reactive aggression relative to more calculated forms of aggression (Wilkowski & Robinson, 2008a). Indeed, anger mediates the relationship between the hostile attribution bias and aggression (Graham, Hudley, & Williams, 1992).

Hostile attributions are typically probed in explicit ways. That is, people are asked to make explicit judgments of intentionality (Wilkowski & Robinson, 2008a). Even so, the hostile attribution bias could operate in automatic ways as well. Evidence for this point comes from studies using reading comprehension and recall paradigms. Wingrove and Bond (2005) showed that angry, antagonistic people seem to make hostile interpretations even when attributional questions are not asked. Specifically, angry people were slower to read sentences that suggested a nonhostile interpretation of a previous ambiguous behavior, suggesting that the behavior had been interpreted in hostile terms. Similarly, Zelli, Cervone, and Huesmann (1996) showed that hostile cues facilitated the recall of ambiguously hostile sentences, again suggesting that these sentences had been interpreted—spontaneously—in hostility-related terms.

In the context of appraisal frameworks, the hostile attribution bias can be linked to a dimension termed other-blame. When people blame others for an aversive event, they are more likely to feel angry and act aggressively as a consequence (Smith & Lazarus, 1993). Antagonistic people seem prone to these appraisals, but they are also prone to other anger-eliciting appraisals as well. In this connection, Kuppens, Van Mechelen, and Rijmen (2008) presented scenarios suggestive of provocation and found that angry people tended toward higher frustration appraisals, higher other-blame appraisals, and higher unfairness appraisals. That is, angry people made multiple judgments that precipitate anger according to prominent theories. In summarizing these patterns, antagonistic people are more strongly displeased when their goals are blocked and "take things personally" under such circumstances (Kuppens & Tong, 2010).

Cognitive mechanisms and processing tendencies

Having discussed the goals, perceptions, and interests of antagonistic people, we are now ready to discuss the cognitive mechanisms that seem to support hostility among people possessing these traits. For the most part, these mechanisms relate to the manner in which hostile cues (e.g., angry expressions) are processed, but we also touch on wider mechanisms that may explain why antagonistic people are prone to impulsive behavior.

Selective attention. The world is full of objects that we could, in principle, attend to, but we can only process a small minority of them at any one time. There are some object properties (like movement) that capture attention in a bottom-up manner, but the bulk of attention selection seems to follow from the goals that people have or what they are trying to accomplish (Posner & Rothbart, 2007). Antagonistic people tend to have different goals than nonantagonistic people and their attention systems may prioritize hostile stimuli as a consequence.

Several studies are consistent with this idea. In the emotional Stroop task, people are asked to name the color of stimuli while ignoring meaning. A number of studies have shown that antagonistic people exhibit delayed latencies when hostility-related stimuli are involved (Wilkowski & Robinson, 2008a). This sort of bias has been found for both angry facial expressions and aggressive words, though there are concerns as to whether this task really assesses selective attention processes (Owen, 2011). Accordingly, investigators have used other tasks as well, such as visual search tasks or spatial cuing tasks. In these tasks, too (e.g., Smith & Waterman, 2003), angry, antagonistic people appear to prioritize hostile stimuli to a greater extent than nonantagonistic people.

There are questions about whether the relevant biases reflect orienting or disengagement processes, though (Owen, 2011). In this connection, the data of Wilkowski, Robinson, and Meier (2006) suggest that the second possibility may be true. In particular terms, Wilkowski et al. (2006) designed a task in which participants categorized hostile (e.g., provoke, torture) or helpful (e.g., foster, respect) words before responding to a spatial probe in the same area as the word versus on the opposite side of the screen. Antagonistic people displayed difficulties disengaging from hostile stimuli, whereas nonantagonistic people displayed difficulties disengaging from helpful stimuli, with a pattern akin to Fig. 1. As suggested by Wilkowski and

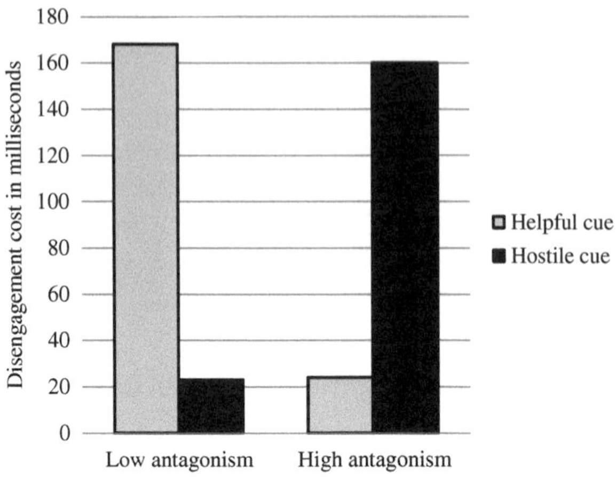

Fig. 1 Attention disengagement costs as a function of antagonism and cue type (helpful vs hostile).

Robinson (2008a), difficulties disengaging from hostile stimuli could support ruminative processes (which favor hostility and anger) at higher levels of antagonism.

When stimuli are isolated or unrelated, there is no larger context that can guide visual processing. When stimuli are related, however, the person may make an inference about what is happening in the situation, which can reverse selective attention biases. This effect is well known in the visual processing literature (Loftus & Mackworth, 1978). For example, once people infer that they are looking at a kitchen, they will then attend to objects that do not make sense within a kitchen (e.g., a live octopus). Something similar occurs when antagonistic people are presented with visual scenes that are ambiguous with respect to aggression. Under these circumstances, antagonistic people spend a longer period of time processing nonhostile cues, a pattern consistent with an early hostile interpretation of the scene (Wilkowski, Robinson, Gordon, & Troop-Gordon, 2007). Thus, in certain cases at least, the hostile interpretation bias seems to precede selective attention processes (Wilkowski & Robinson, 2010), with similar results occurring in reading comprehension paradigms (Wingrove & Bond, 2005).

Concept accessibility. Priming influences are thought to operate in terms of accessibility processes. Being primed with hostile words, for example, could lead people to interpret a social behavior as hostile because the concept of hostility was preactivated and ready to use. In fact, many situational influences on aggression—such as weapons exposure, social modeling, and violent media exposure—are thought to operate in in this way (Anderson & Bushman, 2002). Consistent with this idea, situational cues to aggression have been shown to both increase the accessibility of a person's hostile thoughts as well as the likelihood that the person will act aggressively (Anderson & Bushman, 2002). There are other influences on aggression, too, but accessible hostile thoughts figure prominently in several models (Berkowitz, 1993).

Independent of situational influences, people might also vary in the *chronic* accessibility of hostile concepts. That is, some people might be quick to assign hostile meaning to stimuli across a wide variety of circumstances; others, by contrast, may have difficulty applying hostility-related concepts to new events, precisely because they are not in the habit of doing so (Anderson & Bushman, 2002). It is intuitive to map these individual differences onto the dimension of antagonism. By this mapping, antagonistic people would have higher levels of activation for hostile thoughts relative to nonantagonistic people (Berkowitz, 1993). Despite the intuitive nature of this proposal, it does not seem to be supported by the data. Whether accessibility is measured in terms of production output, word fragment completions, or categorization speed, personality dimensions related to antagonism have rarely predicted cognitive performance in these tasks (e.g., Lindsay & Anderson, 2000; Meier, Robinson, & Wilkowski, 2007; see Wilkowski & Robinson, 2008a, for a review).

Consider the studies of Meier and Robinson (2004). In these studies, the investigators asked participants to categorize words as blameworthy (e.g., crime, murder) or not as quickly as possible because blame is a major elicitor of anger and aggression (Smith & Lazarus, 1993). Hostile thought accessibility was then quantified in terms of the speed with which these categorizations could be made. Personality differences in antagonism (agreeableness) did not correlate with performance in this task. On the other hand, hostile thought accessibility did matter. Specifically, people who were faster to categorize by blame tended to be angrier and more aggressive in their daily lives. Thus chronic accessibility for hostile thoughts could be considered an implicit, but not explicit, dimension of personality.

The self-regulation of hostile thoughts. The results of Meier and Robinson (2004) provide additional insights. Although antagonism and hostile thought accessibility both predicted daily anger and aggression, they also interacted with each other in a manner similar to Fig. 2. Among antagonistic people, anger and aggression varied straightforwardly with category accessibility: The higher the accessibility, the greater the anger and aggression. Among people low in antagonism, on the other hand, there was no relationship between hostile thought accessibility and the daily outcomes. Further, such interactions were conceptually replicated in a second study, which also included a priming manipulation of hostile thoughts: Such thoughts translated into

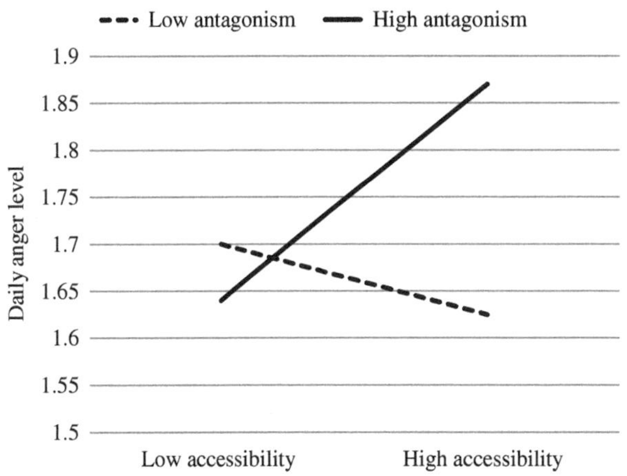

Fig. 2 Daily anger as a function of antagonism and hostile thought accessibility.

anger at high, but not low, levels of antagonism. Thus people low in antagonism seem capable of downregulating the influence of their hostile thoughts.

A weakness of the Meier and Robinson (2004) studies was that they did not capture self-regulatory tendencies in action. Meier, Robinson, and Wilkowski (2006) sought to do so in a sequential priming task in which the question was what would happen to the accessibility of prosocial thoughts (i.e., thoughts related to caring and helping) following hostile primes (e.g., words like *blame* or *criticize*). A straightforward prediction is that hostile primes would tend to undermine, or reduce, the accessibility of prosocial thoughts. This pattern was evident at high levels of antagonism. On the other hand, agreeable people (low antagonism) were *faster* to recognize prosocial targets following hostile primes, a pattern of performance suggestive of automatic forms of self-regulation. Conversely, antagonistic people should be more vulnerable to their hostile thoughts because they do not attempt to control them.

Related findings have been found in many paradigms. Robinson, Wilkowski, Meier, Moeller, and Fetterman (2012) found that low anger people, but not high anger or antagonistic people, paused following their negative evaluations in a manner suggestive of control. Wilkowski and Robinson (2007) examined similar control processes in a judgment task. Participants were primed with hostile thoughts and the question was whether they would react to the hostile primes by making more negative judgments subsequently. Antagonistic people always displayed this pattern of findings. Nonantagonistic people did not, however, if they were given sufficient time to make their ratings. Because time pressure mattered at low levels of antagonism, the suggestion was that nonantagonistic people use controlled processing resources to downregulate the influence of their hostile thoughts. Wilkowski and Robinson (2008b) found additional evidence for this point in a modified flanker task. Following hostile primes, nonantagonistic people displayed reduced flanker costs, indicating cognitive control recruitment in a hostile context. Antagonistic people did not exhibit this prime-contingent pattern.

Perhaps the best way of reinforcing these trends is to refer to the data of Bresin, Fetterman, and Robinson (2012). At the beginning of each trial, participants had to rehearse and memorize a word that was either neutral (e.g., *sweep*, *vacuum*) or hostility related (e.g., *argue*, *kill*). While rehearsing the trial-specific word, participants were asked to control their behavior as carefully as possible by holding a joystick over a presented visual target. The hostile thought primes had very different effects at low versus high levels of antagonism (agreeableness). Hostile primes undermined control at high levels of antagonism, consistent with a loss of control in hostile contexts. On the other hand, people low in antagonism actually displayed better control while rehearsing hostile actions, and the overall pattern was akin to that displayed in Fig. 3. As can be seen in the figure, antagonistic people displayed worse control both in general terms and in the context of their activated hostile thoughts. Both patterns make sense.

Motivational direction. There are several sources of data suggesting that antagonistic people tend to be more approach oriented than nonantagonistic people (Veenstra et al., 2018). This seems to be particularly true under conditions of stress, frustration, or provocation (Deffenbacher, 1992; Harmon-Jones, 2007). Under these

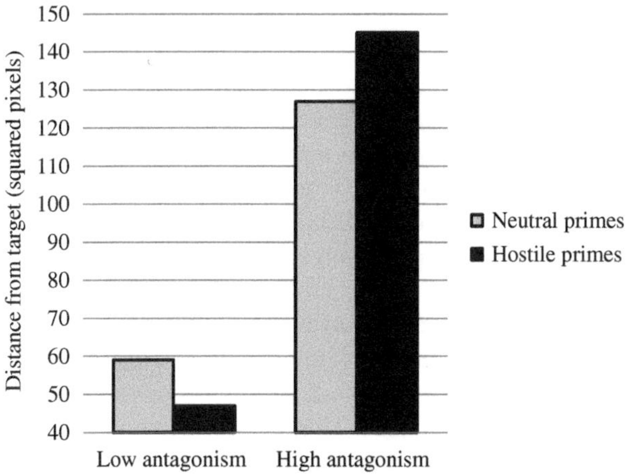

Fig. 3 Motor control as a function of antagonism and prime type (neutral vs hostile).

circumstances, the nonantagonistic person seems to be prone toward appeasement or withdrawal (Terburg & van Honk, 2013), whereas the antagonistic person becomes especially approach oriented (Veenstra et al., 2018), presumably in order to seek revenge or bolster social dominance (Terburg & van Honk, 2013).

Recently, several studies have demonstrated dynamics of this type. For example, Robinson, Boyd, and Persich (2016) created an approach-avoidance task based on Miller's (1944) theoretical analysis. Participants were asked to approach rewards and avoid threats in spatial-dynamic terms, using a joystick. On a minority of trials, there was an unsolvable approach-avoidance conflict created by placing both the words "reward" and "threat" in the same location of the computer screen. People should approach such locations only when approach motivation is stronger than avoidance motivation (Miller, 1944). Robinson et al. (2016) found that angry, antagonistic people tended to resolve these conflicts in an approach-related direction, but only when they had been provoked by noise blasts. These same noise blasts reduced tendencies toward approach among nonantagonistic people.

Similar results have been reported by others. Using a joystick task, Lobbestael, Cousijn, Brugman, and Wiers (2016) found that participants high (vs low) in reactive aggression displayed enhanced tendencies toward approach in the context of physical attack stimuli. This same bias was not evident as a function of proactive aggression levels. Similarly, Wilkowski and Meier (2010) found that angry, antagonistic people were faster to make approach movements when they saw pictures of angry others staring at them and this was particularly true when the approach behaviors served to dismiss the apparent provocateurs.

As a final point, studies have shown that processes related to motivational direction can be used to reduce levels of anger or aggression. Along these lines, several studies have shown that the relationship between trait anger and state anger is weaker under conditions thought to inhibit approach motivation (e.g., darkness, a backward lean, as reported in Veenstra et al., 2018). And training people to make avoidance movements in response to angry facial pictures seems to reduce levels of anger and aggression as well (Veenstra, Schneider, & Koole, 2017).

Summary and conclusions

We presented a social cognitive analysis of antagonistic personality traits, with a particular focus on reactive aggression. According to this analysis, individual differences in anger and reactive aggression can be understood in terms of more particular tendencies with respect to how people attend to, appraise, or respond to hostile situational cues. Indeed, even the emotion of anger might follow from, rather than precede, more basic processes with respect to attention, interpretation, and the like (Wilkowski & Robinson, 2008a).

This sort of analysis has been a productive one. Antagonistic people seem quick to make hostile inferences, even when hostile intent is ambiguous and there are no instructions to make dispositional inferences (Wingrove & Bond, 2005). Antagonistic people also selectively attend to hostile stimuli, and such processes can both contribute to, as well as follow from, the hostile attributions that they make (Wilkowski & Robinson, 2008a). Antagonistic people do not like being provoked or slighted, yet they gravitate toward situational contexts that create such events (Bresin & Robinson, 2015). Finally, antagonistic people do not back down from provocation, but rather appear approach oriented under such circumstances (Terburg & van Honk, 2013).

Although antagonistic people are notable in important ways, nonantagonistic people are equally remarkable. These nice, agreeable people have learned to disattend to hostile stimuli despite their attention-grabbing nature (Wilkowski et al., 2006). Even when these people have hostile thoughts, though, they seem capable of disarming them in relatively expert ways (Meier & Robinson, 2004). And nonantagonistic people recruit cognitive control in the precise circumstances that could trigger tendencies toward interpersonal conflict or reactive aggression (Wilkowski & Robinson, 2008b). In sum, a collection of self-regulatory skills can play a major role in understanding variability in hostile cue or thought reactivity.

An advantage of a cognitive analysis is that the relevant mechanisms can be changed, potentially reducing aggressive tendencies in return. Several lines of research have successfully pursued this direction. It is possible to mitigate the hostile attribution bias and manipulations of this type seem to reduce anger and aggression among predisposed children (Hudley & Graham, 1993). Working with an agreeableness model of self-regulation, Meier, Wilkowski, and Robinson (2008) showed that training people to recruit prosocial thoughts following hostile primes reduces subsequent levels of laboratory aggression. And Veenstra et al. (2017) have shown that training people to make avoidance movements in response to angry facial expressions can decrease anger and aggression as well. More generally, we agree with Owen (2011) that the sort of data we reviewed can serve as a basis for new developments in the cognitive-behavioral treatment of anger-related problems.

There are limitations to our analysis, however, and they can guide future research. The scales used to assess antagonistic traits have varied across studies and it would be useful to anchor more of this research in the DSM-5 tradition, which explicitly focuses on antagonistic traits (Gore & Widiger, 2013). The bulk of our analysis has focused on anger-motivated or reactive aggression and different mechanisms may be needed to explain tendencies toward proactive aggression (Wilkowski & Robinson, 2010). Also, our analysis has been relatively silent on the broader tendencies toward impulsive behavior that seem to characterize antagonistic people (Miller & Lynam, 2001). To understand these outcomes, one could build on the cognitive analysis of Bresin and Robinson (2013) or Young et al. (2009).

References

Anderson, C. A., & Bushman, B. J. (2002). Human aggression. *Annual Review of Psychology*, *53*, 27–51.

Axelrod, S. R., Widiger, T. A., Trull, T. J., & Corbitt, E. M. (1997). Relations of Five-Factor Model antagonism facets with personality disorder symptomology. *Journal of Personality Assessment*, *69*, 297–313.

Berkowitz, L. (1993). *Aggression: Its causes, consequences, and control*. New York, NY: Mcgraw-Hill Book Company.

Bettencourt, B. A., Talley, A., Benjamin, A. J., & Valentine, J. (2006). Personality and aggressive behavior under provoking and neutral conditions: a meta-analytic review. *Psychological Bulletin*, *132*, 751–777.

Bresin, K., Fetterman, A. K., & Robinson, M. D. (2012). Motor control accuracy: a consequential probe of individual differences in emotion regulation. *Emotion*, *12*, 479–486.

Bresin, K., & Robinson, M. D. (2013). Losing control, literally: relations between anger control, trait anger, and motor control. *Cognition and Emotion*, *27*, 995–1012.

Bresin, K., & Robinson, M. D. (2015). You are what you see and choose: agreeableness and situation selection. *Journal of Personality*, *83*, 452–463.

Crick, N. R., & Dodge, K. A. (1994). A review and reformulation of social information-processing mechanisms in children's social adjustment. *Psychological Bulletin*, *115*, 74–101.

Crick, N. R., & Dodge, K. A. (1996). Social information-processing mechanisms in reactive and proactive aggression. *Child Development*, *67*, 993–1002.

Deffenbacher, J. L. (1992). Trait anger: theory, findings, and implications. In C. D. Spielberger & J. N. Butcher (Eds.), *Vol. 9. Advances in personality assessment* (pp. 177–201). Hillsdale, NJ: Lawrence Erlbaum Associates.

Dill, K. E., Anderson, C. A., & Deuser, W. E. (1997). Effects of aggressive personality on social expectations and social perceptions. *Journal of Research in Personality*, *31*, 272–292.

Dodge, K. A. (1980). Social cognition and children's aggressive behavior. *Child Development*, *51*, 162–170.

Figueredo, A. J., & Jacobs, W. J. (2010). Aggression, risk-taking, and alternative life history strategies: the behavioral ecology of social deviance. In M. Frias-Armenta & V. Corral-Verdugo (Eds.), *Bio-psycho-social perspectives on interpersonal violence* (pp. 3–27). Hauppauge, NY: Nova Science Publishers.

Furnham, A., Richards, S. C., & Paulhus, D. L. (2013). The dark triad of personality: a 10 year review. *Social and Personality Psychology Compass*, *7*, 199–216.

Gore, W. L., & Widiger, T. A. (2013). The DSM-5 dimensional trait model and five-factor models of general personality. *Journal of Abnormal Psychology*, *122*, 816–821.

Graham, S., Hudley, C., & Williams, E. (1992). Attributional and emotional determinants of aggression among African-American and Latino young adolescents. *Developmental Psychology*, *28*, 731–740.

Harmon-Jones, E. (2007). Trait anger predicts relative left frontal cortical activation to anger-inducing stimuli. *International Journal of Psychophysiology*, *66*, 154–160.

Hilbig, B. E., Zettler, I., Leist, F., & Heydasch, T. (2013). It takes two: honesty-humility and agreeableness differentially predict active versus reactive cooperation. *Personality and Individual Differences*, *54*, 598–603.

Hogan, R. (2007). *Personality and the fate of organizations*. Mahwah, NJ: Lawrence Erlbaum Associates.

Hudley, C., & Graham, S. (1993). An attributional intervention to reduce peer-directed aggression among African-American boys. *Child Development*, *64*, 124–138.

John, O. P., & Srivastava, S. (1999). The Big Five trait taxonomy: history, measurement, and theoretical perspectives. In L. Pervin & O. P. John (Eds.), *Handbook of personality: Theory and research* (2nd ed., pp. 102–138). New York, NY: Guilford Press.

Jones, D. N., & Figueredo, A. J. (2013). The core of darkness: uncovering the heart of the Dark Triad. *European Journal of Personality*, *27*, 521–531.

Kuppens, P., & Tong, E. M. W. (2010). An appraisal account of individual differences in emotional experience. *Social and Personality Psychology Compass*, *4*, 1138–1150.

Kuppens, P., Van Mechelen, I., & Rijmen, F. (2008). Toward disentangling sources of individual differences in appraisal and anger. *Journal of Personality*, *76*, 969–1000.

Lamkin, J., Maples-Keller, J. L., & Miller, J. D. (2018). How likable are personality disorder and general personality traits to those who possess them? *Journal of Personality*, *86*, 173–185.

Lindsay, J. J., & Anderson, C. A. (2000). From antecedent conditions to violent actions: a general affective aggression model. *Personality and Social Psychology Bulletin*, *26*, 533–547.

Lobbestael, J., Cousijn, J., Brugman, S., & Wiers, R. W. (2016). Approach and avoidance towards aggressive stimuli and its relation to reactive and proactive aggression. *Psychiatry Research*, *240*, 196–201.

Loftus, G., & Mackworth, N. H. (1978). Cognitive determinants of fixation location during picture viewing. *Journal of Experimental Psychology: Human Perception and Performance*, *4*, 565–572.

McCabe, G. A., Vrabel, J. K., & Zeigler-Hill, V. (2017). The connections between pathological personality traits and interpersonal behavior. *Psihologijske Teme*, *26*, 163–178.

Meier, B. P., & Robinson, M. D. (2004). Does quick to blame mean quick to anger? The role of agreeableness in dissociating blame and anger. *Personality and Social Psychology Bulletin*, *30*, 856–867.

Meier, B. P., Robinson, M. D., & Wilkowski, B. M. (2006). Turning the other cheek: agreeableness and the regulation of aggression-related primes. *Psychological Science*, *17*, 136–142.

Meier, B. P., Robinson, M. D., & Wilkowski, B. M. (2007). Aggressive primes activate hostile information in memory: who is most susceptible? *Basic and Applied Social Psychology*, *29*, 23–34.

Meier, B. P., Wilkowski, B. M., & Robinson, M. D. (2008). Bringing out the agreeableness in everyone: using a cognitive self-regulation model to reduce aggression. *Journal of Experimental Social Psychology*, *44*, 1383–1387.

Michel, J. S., Pace, V. L., Edun, A., Sawhney, E., & Thomas, J. (2014). Development and validation of an explicit aggressive beliefs and attitudes scale. *Journal of Personality Assessment*, *96*, 327–338.

Miller, N. E. (1944). Experimental studies of conflict. In J. M. V. Hunt (Ed.), *Personality and the behavior disorders* (pp. 431–465). Oxford, England: Ronald Press.

Miller, J. D., & Lynam, D. (2001). Structural models of personality and their relation to antisocial behavior: a meta-analytic review. *Criminology*, *39*, 765–798.

Owen, J. M. (2011). Transdiagnostic cognitive processes in high trait anger. *Clinical Psychology Review*, *31*, 193–202.

Posner, M. I., & Rothbart, M. K. (2007). Research on attention networks as a model for the integration of psychological science. *Annual Review of Psychology*, *58*, 1–23.

Robinson, M. D., Boyd, R. L., & Persich, M. R. (2016). Dispositional anger and the resolution of the approach-avoidance conflict. *Emotion*, *16*, 838–849.

Robinson, M. D., Wilkowski, B. M., Meier, B. P., Moeller, S. K., & Fetterman, A. K. (2012). Counting to ten milliseconds: low-anger, but not high-anger, individuals pause following negative evaluations. *Cognition and Emotion*, *26*, 261–281.

Smith, T. W., Glazer, K., Ruiz, J. M., & Gallo, L. C. (2004). Hostility, anger, aggressiveness, and coronary heart disease: an interpersonal perspective on personality, emotion, and health. *Journal of Personality*, *72*, 1217–1270.

Smith, C. A., & Lazarus, R. S. (1993). Appraisal components, core relational themes, and the emotions. *Cognition and Emotion*, *7*, 233–269.

Smith, P., & Waterman, M. (2003). Processing bias for aggression words in forensic and nonforensic samples. *Cognition and Emotion*, *17*, 681–701.

Stuckless, N., & Goranson, R. (1992). The Vengeance Scale: development of a measure of attitudes toward revenge. *Journal of Social Behavior and Personality*, *7*, 25–42.

Terburg, D., & van Honk, J. (2013). Approach-avoidance versus dominance-submissiveness: a multilevel neural framework on how testosterone promotes social status. *Emotion Review*, *5*, 296–302.

Veenstra, L., Bushman, B. J., & Koole, S. L. (2018). The facts on the furious: a brief review of the psychology of trait anger. *Current Opinion in Psychology*, *19*, 98–103.

Veenstra, L., Schneider, I. K., & Koole, S. L. (2017). The effects of motivational training on state anger and aggressive impulses among people varying in trait anger. *Motivation Science*, *3*, 354–368.

Wilkowski, B. M., & Meier, B. P. (2010). Bring it on: angry facial expressions potentiate approach-motivated motor behavior. *Journal of Personality and Social Psychology*, *98*, 201–210.

Wilkowski, B. M., & Robinson, M. D. (2007). Keeping one's cool: trait anger, hostile thoughts, and the recruitment of limited capacity control. *Personality and Social Psychology Bulletin*, *33*, 1201–1213.

Wilkowski, B. M., & Robinson, M. D. (2008a). The cognitive basis of trait anger and reactive aggression: an integrative analysis. *Personality and Social Psychology Review*, *12*, 3–21.

Wilkowski, B. M., & Robinson, M. D. (2008b). Guarding against hostile thoughts: trait anger and the recruitment of cognitive control. *Emotion*, *8*, 578–583.

Wilkowski, B. M., & Robinson, M. D. (2010). The anatomy of anger: an integrative cognitive model of trait anger and reactive aggression. *Journal of Personality*, *78*, 9–38.

Wilkowski, B. M., Robinson, M. D., Gordon, R. D., & Troop-Gordon, W. (2007). Tracking the evil eye: trait anger and selective attention within ambiguously hostile scenes. *Journal of Research in Personality*, *41*, 650–666.

Wilkowski, B. M., Robinson, M. D., & Meier, B. P. (2006). Agreeableness and the prolonged spatial processing of antisocial and prosocial information. *Journal of Research in Personality*, *40*, 1152–1168.

Wingrove, J., & Bond, A. J. (2005). Correlation between trait hostility and faster reading times for sentences describing angry reactions to ambiguous situations. *Cognition and Emotion, 19*, 463–472.

Young, S. E., Friedman, N. P., Miyake, A., Willcutt, E. G., Corley, R. P., Haberstick, B. C., et al. (2009). Behavioral disinhibition: liability for externalizing spectrum disorders and its genetic and environmental relation to response inhibition across adolescence. *Journal of Abnormal Psychology, 118*, 117–130.

Zelli, A., Cervone, D., & Huesmann, L. R. (1996). Behavioral experience and social inference: individual differences in aggressive experience and spontaneous versus deliberate trait inference. *Social Cognition, 14*, 165–190.

Zuckerman, M., Kuhlman, D. M., Joireman, J., Teta, P., & Kraft, M. (1993). A comparison of three structural models for personality: the Big Three, the Big Five, and the Alternative Five. *Journal of Personality and Social Psychology, 65*, 757–768.

Antagonism from the perspective of interpersonal theory

11

Aidan G.C. Wright
Department of Psychology, University of Pittsburgh, Pittsburgh, PA, United States

Antagonism is a broad maladaptive personality domain encompassing a range of lower order facets that place one at odds with others. As a disposition, or in its specific manifestations in thoughts, feelings, and behavior, antagonism is rooted in interpersonal or social processes. Interpersonal theorists (e.g., Leary, 1957; Pincus & Ansell, 2013; Sullivan, 1953a) conceptualize personality as "the relatively enduring pattern of recurrent interpersonal situations that characterize a human life" (Sullivan, 1953a, pp. 110–111). From this perspective, the most important adaptive and maladaptive expressions of personality occur in social interactions. Contemporary integrative interpersonal theory (CIIT; Pincus & Ansell, 2013) would therefore seem to have much to offer the field's understanding of antagonism and antagonistic behavior. In this chapter, the specific assumptions of CIIT regarding personality structure and process are covered, followed by a review of empirical findings relevant to antagonism.

Contemporary integrative interpersonal theory

CIIT is an evidenced-based model of personality that links an empirically derived structure with dynamic social-cognitive, affective, and behavioral processes that offer a scientifically grounded framework to generate testable hypotheses regarding individual differences and situational behavior. CIIT uses a two-dimensional model called the interpersonal circumplex (IPC; see Fig. 1) to describe and measure interpersonal functioning (Horowitz, 2004). The major dimensions of the IPC are dominance versus submissiveness on the vertical axis, and affiliation versus disaffiliation on the horizontal axis. Interpersonal theory asserts that, "all forms of social behavior can in turn be viewed as combinations of the four poles" (Fournier, Moskowitz, & Zuroff, 2011, p. 58). The IPC has long served as a "key conceptual map" (Kiesler, 1996, p. 172) in personality and clinical psychology for the identification of dispositional interpersonal styles among diverse populations (Pincus & Wright, 2011). Moreover, it serves as an integrative framework, uniting models of traits, motives, cognition, behavior, and psychopathology (Hopwood, Wright, Ansell, & Pincus, 2013; Locke, 2011).

The IPC organizes not only the *static* relations among the interpersonal variables (i.e., the ordering around the circle), but also the *dynamic* processes of transactions based on the interpersonal bids and pulls between individuals in interpersonal situations (Horowitz, 2004; Pincus & Ansell, 2013). Sullivan (1953a, 1953b) argued that as a social species, humans are motivated to come together (i.e., interpersonally) in the

The Handbook of Antagonism. https://doi.org/10.1016/B978-0-12-814627-9.00011-6

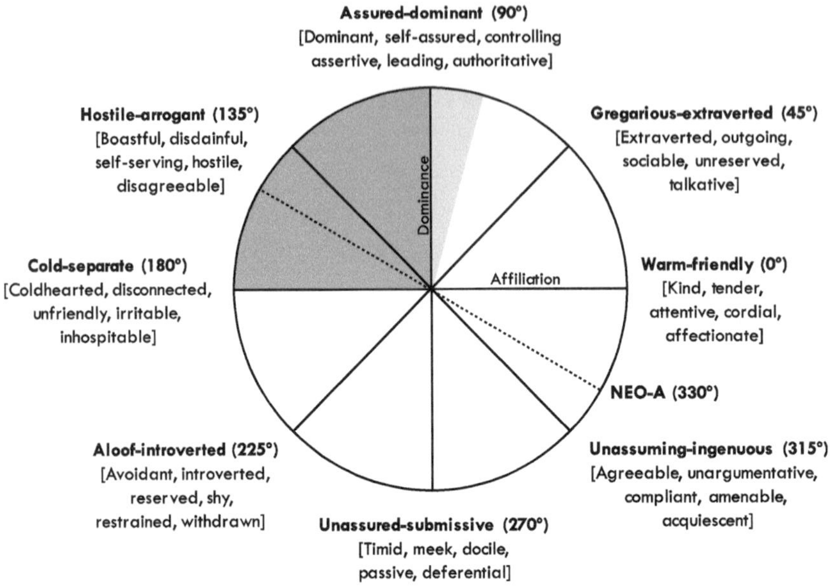

Fig. 1 The interpersonal circumplex. *Shading* represents the area of interpersonal functioning reflective of antagonism.

pursuit of satisfactions (generally a large class of biologically grounded needs), security (i.e., anxiety-free functioning), and self-esteem. Importantly, in CIIT the term interpersonal does not exclusively refer to overt behaviors that occur between people, but also what occurs inside people's minds via the capacity for mental representation of self and others. As such, an important component of the interpersonal situation is an individual's perception of the others' behavior as well as expectations for the outcomes or responses to one's own behavior. Both the outward and internal aspects of interpersonal situations reflect an individual's relational strategies, regulatory functioning, and self-concept. Therefore dynamic interpersonal processes involve the patterns of perceiving, interpreting, feeling, and behaving over time and across situations.

Fig. 2 is designed to depict the important features of interpersonal situations (Hopwood, Harrison, et al., in press; Hopwood, Pincus, & Wright, in press; Pincus, Hopwood, & Wright, in press). Naturally, a static diagram struggles to capture the dynamic nature of real interpersonal situations. So, Fig. 2 is perhaps best understood as a time-lapse image of a situation. As a distilled representation, Fig. 2 includes two vertical rectangles to represent two individuals, within each rectangle are circles that represent an individual's self-construal (here the broader terms agency and communion are used instead of the more behavioral dominance and affiliation) and affect, and arrows link the two rectangles and circles within the rectangles. The first set of arrows (marked with bold A) represent overt behavior between interacting partners, the second set (B) reflect perceptions, both one's perception of the other (those going between rectangles) and one's own self-monitoring (curved arrows), the third set

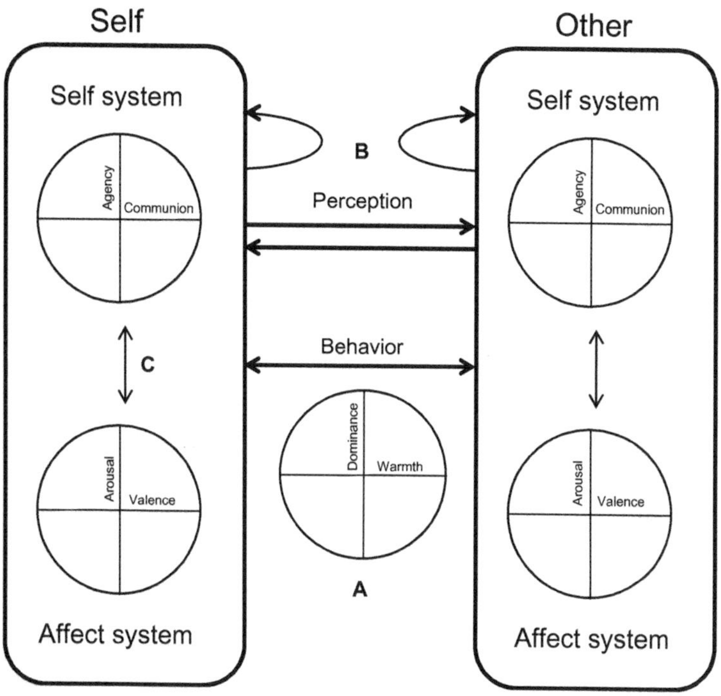

Fig. 2 The interpersonal situation.

(C) link self-construal and affect. These paths in Fig. 2, along with the major components they link (behavior, perception, self-construal, affect) can be used identify the patterns of interpersonal functioning that give rise to what we understand as personality. For instance, an individual who has a characteristic self-construal as agentic and communal, accompanied with a positive and high arousal affective set point, a tendency to perceive others as interested, and consistently behaves in a dominant and warm manner might be understood as extraverted. However, it is also important to note that when confronted with the variety of situations that are representative of daily life, the extraverted individual will likely need to shift in behavior and affect based on the perceived situational demands, and the path values would thus shift dynamically across situations to some degree.

Although the interpersonal situation can be flexibly used to chart any specific patterning of interpersonal functioning, CIIT has established probabilistic patterns of social transaction termed *interpersonal complementarity* (Carson, 1969; Kiesler, 1983). Complementarity refers to the match or mismatch of individuals' interpersonal needs in an interpersonal situation and the tendency to adjust behaviors in response to others' behavior (Horowitz et al., 2006). Specifically, complementarity has often been defined behaviorally as similarity on the affiliation dimension and opposite on the dominance dimension (Carson, 1969; Sadler, Ethier, & Woody, 2011). That is, one person's affiliation pulls for another person's affiliation (and vice versa), and one person's dominance invites the other's submissiveness (and vice versa; Carson, 1969; Kiesler, 1983; Sadler et al., 2011). Complementarity is not intended to be a universal law of interaction, although empirical studies consistently find support for its probabilistic predictions (Sadler et al., 2011). As such, it is best understood as a common baseline for the reciprocal influence of interpersonal behavior associated with healthy socialization, and deviations from complementary interpersonal patterns are more likely to be costly to an individual or those around them. Chronic deviations from normative social processes may reflect impairments in: (1) grasping common expectations of interpersonal situations, (2) appreciating and/or accepting the needs of others and the goals of their behavior, and (3) adaptively pursuing one's own needs and motives. Each of these reduces the likelihood that the interpersonal needs of both persons will be satisfied in the interpersonal situation (Hopwood et al., 2013; Horowitz et al., 2006). Maladaptive expressions of personality, including antagonism, can be understood in terms of these kinds of impairments (Hopwood et al., 2013; Pincus & Wright, 2011).

Empirical findings

This review of empirical findings is necessarily selective, and it subordinates early descriptive findings and privileges, for in-depth discussion, recent work that targets behavior across and within interpersonal situations. Chapters rarely report new empirical results. However, the published data that inform the relationship between antagonism and dynamic interpersonal processes are relatively sparse. To enrich this discussion of how antagonism manifests in interpersonal functioning across and within situations, new data and results from four samples of ecological momentary assessment (EMA) data of interpersonal behavior and/or perception are presented. Three were collected from undergraduate volunteers who participated, in return for course credit, in a baseline assessment and EMA studies for 7–8 days. Detailed information on participants and procedures for samples 1 and 2 can be found in Edershile et al. (2018) and Himmelstein, Woods, and Wright (2018), respectively. Sample 3 is not previously published, but the procedures mirrored Sample 1. In each study, participants completed up to 6 ratings per day of interpersonal interactions lasting at least 5 minutes using an application loaded on their personal smartphones. Participants rated how they perceived the other person to behave and how they behaved on two bipolar visual analog items for dominance (*assured/dominant/controlling* to *accommodating/submissive/timid*) and affiliation (*cold/distant/hostile* to *warm/friendly/caring*; Woods et al., 2018). Each sample provided one measure of trait antagonism (Sample 1, Comprehensive Assessment of Traits for Personality Disorder [CAT-PD; see e.g., Wright & Simms, 2014] antagonism domain score; Sample 2, the Big-Five Inventory-2 [Soto & John, 2017] reversed agreeableness score; Sample 3, Personality Disorder for DSM-5 [PID-5; Krueger, Derringer, Markon, Watson, & Skodol, 2012] brief [5-item] antagonism domain). In addition, Sample 1 provided ratings on interpersonal problems using the IIP-SC (Soldz, Budman, Demby, & Merry, 1995), interpersonal values using the Circumplex Scales for Interpersonal Values (Locke, 2000), and interpersonal sensitivities (Hopwood et al., 2011).

The fourth sample was a daily diary study of participants diagnosed with personality disorders. Methodological details can be found in Wright and Simms (2016) and Wright, Hopwood, and Simms (2015). Interpersonal behavior was measured using daily ratings of 8 interpersonal adjectives scored for dominance and affiliation. Trait antagonism was measured using the average of the PID-5 antagonism facets (*Callousness*, *Manipulativeness*, *Grandiosity*, *Attention Seeking*, *Deceitfulness*, and *Hostility*) and as the reverse score of the NEO-FFI agreeableness scale (Costa & McCrae, 1992). Daily antagonism was measured as the mean of daily ratings on *hostility*, *exhibitionism*, and *manipulativeness* as described in Wright and Simms (2016). Relevant results from these four samples are included in the review of empirical findings that follow.

Cross-sectional dispositional research

A circumplex is a formal geometric model, and multiscale inventories developed to fit this structure can be used to make precise and testable predictions for evaluating the associations among constructs. Leveraging the circumplex structure of many inventories of dispositional interpersonal functioning (e.g., traits, problems), Gurtman (1992) developed the structural summary method, which offers a way to reduce multiscale profiles to several key parameters and to test theoretically prescribed patterns in the data. Technical information is offered elsewhere (Wright, Pincus, Conroy, & Hilsenroth, 2009; Zimmermann & Wright, 2017), but briefly the structural summary method can be used to test whether a pattern of means or correlations with circumplex scales conforms to a circular pattern, and then reduces this profile into three parameters: elevation (average value), amplitude (how differentiated is the pattern), and angular location (where in the IPC the profile peaks).[1] This can be used, for instance, to evaluate the pattern of correlations from a measure of interest (e.g., antagonism scale) with interpersonal problem scales. An elevated profile would suggest antagonism is associated with interpersonal distress, a high amplitude would suggest antagonism has a specific interpersonal style, and the angular location would reveal what that style is. Noninterpersonal variables are unlikely to have this sort of pattern. Thus the structure of the IPC serves as a nomological net for evaluating external constructs (e.g., antagonism).

Early dispositional work examined the location of NEO-PI agreeableness in interpersonal trait space, locating it at approximately 330 degrees (see dotted line in Fig. 1; e.g., McCrae & Costa Jr, 1989; Pincus, 2002). If antagonism is defined as the inverse pole of agreeableness, then it would have been located at approximately 150 degrees in IPC space, in the *Hostile-Arrogant* octant shifted toward *Cold-Separate*. Ansell and Pincus (2004) found that vignettes describing individuals low in agreeableness were rated as falling almost exactly in this location (155–160 degrees) by naïve raters.

[1]Readers interested in implementing this analytic approach are directed to a shiny web application "fullcircle" developed by Jeffrey Girard (http:/r.jmgirard.com/shiny/fullcircle/) for an easy-to-use graphical user interface.

As such, from a trait perspective, FFM agreeableness, and by extension antagonism, can be largely construed as a rotational variant of the IPC's affiliation axis.

At around the same time of this basic work integrating the trait systems, Wiggins and Pincus (Wiggins and Pincus, 1989; Pincus & Wiggins, 1990) examined the associations between personality disorders and interpersonal traits and problems. Several of the personality disorders, most notably narcissistic, antisocial, but also paranoid and borderline, have shown marked associations with antagonism (Samuel & Widiger, 2008). Wiggins and Pincus found that narcissistic and antisocial personality disorder scales were located within the upper left quadrant of the IPC (90–180 degrees) across both trait and problem surfaces (see dark shading in Fig. 1). Exact locations varied somewhat across scales, although narcissism tended to fall mostly within the *Assured-Dominant* octant, whereas antisocial fell within the *Hostile-Arrogant* octant. Results for borderline and paranoid in these early studies were equivocal. More recently, however, Wilson, Stroud, and Durbin (2017) meta-analyzed associations between personality disorders and interpersonal problems, finding that narcissistic (110 degrees), antisocial (114 degrees) paranoid (141 degrees), and borderline (128 degrees) all fell within the upper-left quadrant of the problems circumplex, all with highly differentiated (amplitude range = .22–.38) and elevated (elevation range = .19–.37) profiles. Thus each of these personality disorder constructs fall within the typical range of antagonism, with clear interpersonal themes despite elevated general distress.

Contemporary conceptualizations of personality pathology favor a hierarchical dimensional maladaptive trait model over discrete disorders (Wright, Thomas, et al., 2012). A trait model of this sort was ultimately included in the alternative personality disorder model in the DSM-5 and includes a domain devoted to antagonism. Indeed, accumulating evidence suggests that much of psychopathology might be accommodated within a similar model (Kotov et al., 2017). For instance, Wright and Simms (2015) factor analyzed major mental disorders, including clinical syndromes and personality disorders, and the PID-5 showing that they could be organized within a shared structure. Wright, Pincus et al. (2012) found that the DSM-5's antagonism dimension had an elevated and distinct problem profile that peaked in the *Assured-Dominant* octant. Interestingly, antagonism in the DSM-5 model also incorporates constructs such as attention seeking that are traditionally the hallmark of histrionic personality disorder, the interpersonal profile for which generally peaks in the Gregarious-Extraverted octant (Pincus & Wiggins, 1990; Wiggins & Pincus, 1989; Wilson et al., 2017). Thus when this content is incorporated into the conceptualization of antagonism, it shifts its interpersonal profile toward dominance and away from cold dominance (see light shaded area in Fig. 1). For instance, in a recent study, Girard et al. (2017) found that narcissistic, paranoid, and histrionic served as indicators for a single factor, which had an elevated and moderately differentiated interpersonal problem profile that peaked in the *Assured-Dominant* octant.

To extend these findings to other interpersonal surfaces using a contemporary measure of antagonism per se, Sample 1 was used to examine antagonism's interpersonal profile of problems, values, and sensitivities using the structural summary method with bootstrapped confidence intervals (Zimmermann & Wright, 2017) (see

Table 1 Structural summary of CAT-PD antagonism and interpersonal problems, values, and sensitivities

	Structural summary parameters					
	Elevation	**Dominance**	**Affiliation**	**Amplitude**	**Angle**	R^2
Problems	.24 (.18, .31)	.28 (.24, .33)	−.12 (−.16, −.07)	.31 (.26, .35)	112° (104°, 121°)	.91
Values	.25 (.18, .31)	.12 (.08, .16)	−.27 (−.32, −.22)	.30 (.25, .35)	156° (148°, 164°)	.90
Sensitivities	.19 (.12, .25)	−.15 (−.20, −.10)	.05 (.00, .10)	.16 (.11, .21)	288° (270°, 307°)	.91

Note. Point estimates and 95% confidence intervals *(in parentheses)* based on 2000 bootstrapped samples using R package SSM (Zimmermann & Wright, 2017) as implemented in http:/r.jmgirard.com/shiny/fullcircle/ Problems = Inventory of Interpersonal Problems – Short Circumplex (Soldz et al., 1995); Values = Circumplex Scales of Interpersonal Values (Locke, 2000); Sensitivities = Interpersonal Sensitivities Circumplex Scales. R^2 = Goodness of fit to predicted sine pattern.

Table 1 for results). Consistent with prior results, we found that antagonism's problem profile was elevated, but also had a very clearly differentiated peak falling at the border between the *Assured-Dominant* and *Hostile-Arrogant* octants (i.e., 112 degrees). Similarly, the values profile was elevated and differentiated, but peaked at the border of the *Hostile-Arrogant* and *Cold-Separate* octants (156 degrees). Conversely, the sensitivities profile peaked in the *Unassured-Submissive* octant (288 degrees), although it was also differentiated and elevated. Together these results suggest that individuals high in antagonism value appearing forceful, having the upper hand, avenging insults, and appearing cool and detached, while at the same time they struggle with being too domineering in the service of these goals. They also are generally misanthropic, being bothered by most forms of interpersonal behavior, but particularly submissive and obsequious behavior.

These novel results align with recent work that has examined antagonism-related constructs (e.g., Dark Triad) across multiple interpersonal surfaces, both in the general location of the scales and the consistency across surfaces (excepting sensitivities which are reflected across the IPC; Dowgwillo & Pincus, 2017). Accordingly, these findings suggest normative consistency across different surfaces, rather than discrepancies as Leary (1957) hypothesized and as others have indicated as useful when working individually with patients (e.g., Dawood & Pincus, 2016; Pincus et al., 2014). However, future work should specifically test whether discrepancies between surfaces (e.g., mismatch between values and problems) increment the prediction of antagonism and other maladaptive dispositions using appropriate methods like response surface analysis (see Barranti, Carlson, & Côté, 2017; cf. Wright & Pincus, 2010).

In sum, dispositional research suggests that antagonism in its various forms is well situated within the various dispositional representations of interpersonal functioning (traits, problems, motivations, etc.). However, variation in the conceptualization of antagonism and scales used to measure it results in somewhat different interpersonal locations within the IPC, largely clustered around the upper left quadrant. In fact, as mentioned earlier, the broader antagonism domain encompasses diverse facets (e.g., manipulativeness, callousness, hostility) and each of these exhibits some variability in its location in interpersonal space. A full cataloging of these facets' interpersonal profiles goes well beyond the scope of this chapter, but the interested reader is referred to several publications that include facet-level information (e.g., Pincus, 2002; Williams & Simms, 2016; Wright, Pincus, et al., 2012).

Cross-situational research

Moving beyond basic dispositional associations between antagonism and interpersonal functioning, it is important to examine how antagonism manifests in and across situations in perceptions and behavior. To study interpersonal behavior across situations, interpersonal researchers have made good use of ambulatory assessment techniques like EMA. Various assessment tools have been developed that measure one's own behavior as well as perceptions of others in situations intensively and repeatedly in naturalistic settings (Moskowitz, 1994; Moskowitz & Zuroff, 2005; Woods et al., 2018). This approach has been used to study key components of the interpersonal situation as depicted in Fig. 2, as well as within-person variability across situations.

As noted previously, this is an area with relatively few published findings, so the results of de novo ambulatory assessment studies are presented. An initial, and very basic question, is whether dispositional antagonism scales predict individual differences in average reported perceptions of others' behavior and one's own behavior across situations. Across three EMA studies (see Table 2), the consistent finding was that antagonism, operationalized in different ways across studies, predicted perceptions of lower affiliation and lower affiliation in one's own behavior across situations, although there was some variability in effect size. No association was observed with dominance for either perceptions or one's own behavior. The findings from dispositional antagonism predicting average daily ratings of behavior were largely consistent. Therefore it appears that the strongest effect of antagonism on interpersonal behavior is on lower affiliation and perceptions thereof. Although it would be tempting to interpret the perception findings as "bias," (e.g., Miller, Lynam, & Jones, 2008) the results remain ambiguous. That individuals who are antagonistic tend to view others as less affiliative, and by extension prompting their own quarrelsome behavior, is one possibility. However, it is also possible that they select in to less affiliative encounters or evoke lower affiliation from others (e.g., Lamkin, Clifton, Campbell, & Miller, 2014). Each is an interesting possibility, and they need not be mutually exclusive, but each would have different implications for understanding and possibly intervening with antagonism. Future research should focus on disambiguating this finding.

Results for daily antagonism deviated somewhat from these findings, in that at both the daily and person levels significant but modest effects were observed for dominance. That is, on days when individuals report more antagonistic behavior, they also report being more dominant. The same is true for individual who report more daily antagonism on average (i.e., trait level as assessed by daily diary), they also report being more dominant. In contrast, effects for affiliation were negative, but very small. Although these results are presented for completeness, it is not clear whether the measure or the assessment approach is responsible for these discrepancies. Regardless, the pattern falls well within the area of the IPC described previously. That the strongest

Table 2 Associations between measures of antagonism and daily and momentary interpersonal behavior and perceptions

	Dominance			Affiliation		
	β	95% CI	*P*	*β*	95% CI	*P*
Daily Diary Study						
NEO-FFI agreeableness (reversed)	.07	(−11, .26)	.439	**−.38**	**(−.56, −.20)**	**<.001**
PID-5 antagonism	.17	(−.03, .38)	.095	−.16	(−.35, .03)	.097
Daily antagonism						
Within-person	**.24**	**(.19, .29)**	**<.001**	**−.08**	**(−.13, −.03)**	**.002**
Between-person	**.27**	**(.10, .44)**	**.002**	−.17	(−.38, .04)	.119
EMA Sample 1						
CAT-PD antagonism						
Perception of other behavior	.09	(−.02, .19)	.118	**−.25**	**(−.36, −.14)**	**<.001**
Self-rated behavior	**.16**	**(.05, .26)**	**.003**	**−.33**	**(−.43, −.22)**	**<.001**
EMA Sample 2						
BFI-2 agreeableness (reversed)						
Perception of other behavior	−.09	(.06, .24)	.248	**−.24**	**(.12, .36)**	**<.001**
Self-rated behavior	.11	(.24, −.02)	.097	**−.30**	**(−.18, .42)**	**<.001**
EMA Sample 3						
Brief PID-5 antagonism						
Perception of other behavior	−.15	(−.31, .01)	.069	**−.16**	**(−.30, −.01)**	**.038**
Self-rated behavior	.05	(−.14, .24)	.591	**−.17**	**(−.31, −.02)**	**.022**

Note. Bolded values for $P < .05$; Sample sizes for studies (persons/observations): Daily Diary Study = 101/8631; ecological momentary assessment (EMA) Sample 1 = 396/4956; EMA Sample 2 = 288/6905; EMA Sample 3 = 206/3606. NEO-FFI = NEO-Five Factor Inventory; PID-5 = Personality Inventory for DSM-5; Daily Antagonism = Sum of items from Exhibitionism, Hostility, and Manipulativeness scales from Wright and Simms (2016); CAT-PD = Comprehensive Assessment of Traits for Personality Disorders; BFI-2 = Big-Five Inventory-2.

association with momentary behavior is with low affiliation, sometimes conceptualized as quarrelsomeness in the interpersonal EMA literature, suggests that Moskowitz' (2010) review of quarrelsomeness in daily life is relevant as well. The interested reader is directed to her review.

Expanding on these links between dispositional and daily antagonism and interpersonal perceptions and behavior, researchers have also examined how dispositional variables related to antagonism impact the perceptual, affective, and behavioral processes that comprise an interpersonal situation (Fig. 2). Two studies in particular illustrate how the processes that lead to the expression of antagonistic behavior differ across contexts depending on the nature of their psychopathology. These studies also highlight general processes likely shared by most individuals regardless of pathology. In the first, Sadikaj, Moskowitz, Russell, Zuroff, and Paris (2013) compared participants diagnosed with borderline personality disorder and community controls on their perceptions of others, negative affect, and interpersonal behavior following interactions over 21 days. Recall that borderline personality disorder is consistently associated with dispositional ratings of antagonism (Wilson et al., 2017; see also Samuel & Widiger, 2008). The authors examined differences in the within-person links between perceptions of quarrelsomeness, negative affect, and quarrelsome behavior across situations. They found that the borderline group had stronger links between perceptions of quarrelsomeness and one's own quarrelsome behavior, as well as perceptions and negative affect. For participants diagnosed with borderline personality disorder, more of their own antagonistic behavior could be explained by situational features. That is to say, for these individuals who are sensitive to others pulling away and being at odds with them, they are more likely to experience negative affect and attack in response than the average community member. Also of note is that the link between negative affect and quarrelsomeness did not differ between groups, suggesting this is a general process; experiencing negative emotions is associated with behaving in a more hostile manner.

In similar approach, Wright et al. (2017) examined the impact of narcissistic personality disorder criteria on the links between perceptions of others' behavior, negative affect, and one's own behavior. In a comparable manner, narcissistic pathology amplified the link between perceptions of others' behavior and negative affect during an interpersonal situation. However, in contrast to the prior study, the perceptions that lead to amplified negative affect for those high in narcissism were different. Narcissism did not amplify the link between perceptions of other's quarrelsomeness and negative affect, but rather amplified the link between perceptions of others dominance and negative affect. Accordingly, the context that "triggered" negative affect and ultimately quarrelsomeness was interacting with someone who the individual high in narcissism perceived as being dominant. Similar to Sadikaj et al.'s (2013) study, narcissism had little effect on the relationship between negative affect and one's own quarrelsomeness ($P = .044$), again suggesting this pathway is general. Combined, the results of these two studies illustrate that dispositional associations between psychopathology and antagonism may belie contextual differences in the dynamic processes that give rise to antagonistic behavior.

Within situation research

Recently, methods have been developed to continuously assess and record the momentary interpersonal dynamics within situations (Girard & Wright,2018; Sadler, Ethier, Gunn, Duong, & Woody, 2009). Sadler et al. (2009) showed that a joystick could be used to reliably and validly track an individual's behavior continuously, recording a location on the IPC with fine granularity (e.g., every half second). This can be used to code videos of, for example, in-lab dyadic interactions to study cooperative behavior or conflict in romantic dyads. This method places the dynamic microprocesses that occur between individuals as they transact within a situation within a researcher's grasp. Software is available for easy implementation on most contemporary computers (Girard & Wright, 2018).

Relatively little research has examined dispositional influences, including trait antagonism, on within-situation interpersonal processes. There are, however, two recent studies that provide relevant information about how antagonistic behavior manifests within situations. Hopwood, Harrison, et al. (in press) and Hopwood, Pincus, and Wright (in press) compared continuous ratings of interpersonal behavior during conflict and cooperative interactions across several laboratory studies. They found that mean ratings of behavior were lower in affiliation and higher in dominance for conflictual relative to cooperative interactions. Although these results are highly consistent with the dispositional results, they do not reflect individual differences, but rather average situational effects on behavior. When we find ourselves at odds with each other, we tend to behave as if we are someone who lives their lives at odds with others. Note that the mean of affiliation was not negative, just greatly reduced from the average in cooperative situations. Conflictual situations (relative to cooperative situations) were also characterized by lower affiliative correspondence, but stronger dominance reciprocity. Thus the effect of conflict on interpersonal complementarity seems to erode normative affiliative matching, but amplifies dominance processes.

A second study, conducted by Ross et al. (2017), examined associations between momentary ratings using the *Specific Affect Rating System* (SPAFF; Gottman & Krokoff, 1989) and interpersonal behavior of both the self (actor effects) and other (partner effects). Many results emerged as predicted (e.g., *affection* and *validation* SPAFF codes were associated with higher self and other affiliative behavior in the moment), and in general complementarity patterns were strong. However, although SPAFF codes that would be considered antagonistic (*defensiveness*, *contempt*, *criticism*, *domineering*, and *stonewalling*) were largely associated with lower affiliative behavior, as predicted, an unexpected pattern emerged for dominant behavior. Ross and colleagues found that *defensiveness*, *contempt*, *criticism*, and *domineering* were negatively associated with one's own dominance (i.e., more submissive behavior), but positively associated with a partner's dominance. In other words, these presumably antagonistic behaviors were characterized by cold-submissiveness in the context of a partner being cold and dominant, not the other way around as might be suggested by the dispositional and cross-situational study findings. One possibility worth considering is that antagonistic behavior is enacted not when the person is in the dominant position, but when the individual feels the need to claim or regain the dominant position or undercut someone else's dominant position. This would be in line with the interpretation of Wright et al. (2017) on the impact of narcissism on cross-situational interpersonal behavior and affect. Taken together, these results may provide a glimpse into the motivations underlying the manifestation of antagonistic behaviors. At the same time, several caveats are warranted. For one, *stonewalling* did not follow this pattern, although behavior coded as such was exceedingly rare, raising questions about reliability of the finding. Further, these results generally should be replicated and examined in a wider group of samples and contexts (i.e., the SPAFF and interpersonal behaviors were coded during a conflict task, participants were psychiatric patients and their partners).

Conclusion and future directions

Interpersonal theory offers a framework for moving beyond static and dispositional understanding of antagonism to reveal the processes and possibly the mechanisms by which it manifests and is maintained. With the data that exists, it can be concluded that dispositional antagonism is well represented by low affiliation and high dominance across various levels of interpersonal functioning (goals, traits, problems, strengths, etc.). Admixtures of dominance and low affiliation vary as a function of definition and operationalization of antagonism. When assessed using ratings of behavior in and across situations, a similar pattern emerges, although low affiliation is the stronger signal. The same can be said for perceptions of others' behavior, although it remains unclear what accounts for this effect. Emerging research suggests that antagonism as manifested in quarrelsome behavior may be in the service of addressing certain goals or in response to certain triggers that may differ across individuals.

Why do antagonistic people behave the way they do? What are they hoping to achieve? There is ample room for more research in this domain. Indeed, one thing this review highlights is that there is more left to learn about the processes underlying antagonism than we currently know. The diagram of the interpersonal situation presented in Fig. 2 can be used to identify targets for future inquiry. Yet it is difficult for any one study to capture all potentially interesting components, and therefore researchers will likely need to prioritize subsets of pathways. There is also a clear need for more sophisticated assessment of motivations as they might vary across time, especially using methods that can disentangle them from behavior. There are good theoretical reasons for prioritizing interpersonal motivations when understanding an individuals' behavior and the outcome of situations (e.g., Horowitz et al., 2006). Finally, more research is needed on the development of interpersonal dispositions and patterns, especially as reinforcement processes might lead to increases or decreases of antagonism over time (e.g., Baumert et al., 2017; Wright, Pincus, et al., 2012).

Acknowledgment

Aidan Wright's effort on this project was supported by the National Institute of Mental Health (L30 MH101760). The opinions expressed are solely those of the authors and not those of the funding source.

References

Ansell, E. B., & Pincus, A. L. (2004). Interpersonal perceptions of the five-factor model of personality: an examination using the structural summary method for circumplex data. *Multivariate Behavioral Research*, *39*(2), 167–201.

Barranti, M., Carlson, E. N., & Côté, S. (2017). How to test questions about similarity in personality and social psychology research: description and empirical demonstration of response surface analysis. *Social Psychological and Personality Science*, *8*(4), 465–475.

Baumert, A., Schmitt, M., Perugini, M., Johnson, W., Blum, G., Borkenau, P., et al. (2017). Integrating personality structure, personality process, and personality development. *European Journal of Personality*, *31*(5), 503–528.

Carson, R. C. (1969). *Interaction concepts of personality*. Chicago, IL: Aldine.

Costa, P. T., & McCrae, R. R. (1992). *NEO PI-R: Revised NEO Personality Inventory and NEO Five-factor Inventory (NEO FFI): Professional Manual*. Psychological Assessment Resources.

Dawood, S., & Pincus, A. L. (2016). Multisurface interpersonal assessment in a cognitive-behavioral therapy context. *Journal of Personality Assessment*, *98*(5), 449–460.

Dowgwillo, E. A., & Pincus, A. L. (2017). Differentiating dark triad traits within and across interpersonal circumplex surfaces. *Assessment*, *24*(1), 24–44.

Edershile, E. A., Woods, W. C., Sharpe, B. M., Crowe, M. L., Miller, J. D., & Wright, A. G. C. (2018). A day in the life of narcissus: measuring narcissistic grandiosity and vulnerability in daily life (manuscript submitted for publication).

Fournier, M. A., Moskowitz, D. S., & Zuroff, D. C. (2011). Origins and applications of the interpersonal circumplex. In L. M. Horowitz & S. Strack (Eds.), *Handbook of interpersonal psychology: Theory, research, assessment, and therapeutic interventions* (pp. 57–73). Hoboken, NJ: Wiley & Sons Publishers.

Girard, J. M., & Wright, A. G. C. (2018). DARMA: Dual axis review and media annotation. *Behavioral Research Methods*, *50*, 902–909.

Girard, J. M., Wright, A. G. C., Beeney, J. E., Lazarus, S., Scott, L. N., Stepp, S. D., et al. (2017). Interpersonal problems across levels of the psychopathology hierarchy. *Comprehensive Psychiatry*, *79*, 53–69.

Gottman, J. M., & Krokoff, L. J. (1989). Marital interaction and satisfaction: a longitudinal view. *Journal of Consulting and Clinical Psychology*, *57*, 47–52.

Gurtman, M. B. (1992). Construct validity of interpersonal personality measures: the interpersonal circumplex as a nomological net. *Journal of Personality and Social Psychology*, *63*, 105–118.

Himmelstein, P. H., Woods, W. C., & Wright, A. G. C. (2018). A comparison of signal- and event-contingent ambulatory (manuscript submitted for publication).

Hopwood, C. J., Ansell, E. B., Pincus, A. L., Wright, A. G. C., Lukowitsky, M. R., & Roche, M. J. (2011). The circumplex structure of interpersonal sensitivities. *Journal of Personality*, *79*, 708–740.

Hopwood, C. J., Harrison, A. L., Amole, M., Girard, J. M., Wright, A. G. C., Thomas, K. M., et al. (in press). Properties of the continuous assessment of interpersonal dynamics across sex, level of familiarity, and interpersonal conflict. *Assessment*.

Hopwood, C. J., Pincus, A. L., & Wright, A. G. C. (in press). The interpersonal situation: Integrating clinical assessment, formulation, and intervention. In D. Samuel & D. Lynam (Eds.), Using basic personality research to inform the personality disorders. New York: Oxford.

Hopwood, C. J., Wright, A. G. C., Ansell, E. B., & Pincus, A. L. (2013). The interpersonal core of personality pathology. *Journal of Personality Disorders*, *27*, 270–295.

Horowitz, L. M. (2004). *Interpersonal foundations of psychopathology*. Washington, DC: American Psychological Association.

Horowitz, L. M., Wilson, K. R., Turan, B., Zolotsev, P., Constantino, M. J., & Henderson, L. (2006). How interpersonal motives clarify the meaning of interpersonal behavior: a revised circumplex model. *Personality and Social Psychology Review*, *10*, 67–86.

Kiesler, D. J. (1983). The 1982 interpersonal circle: a taxonomy for complementarity in human transactions. *Psychological Review*, *90*, 185–214.

Kiesler, D. J. (1996). *Contemporary interpersonal theory and research: Personality, psychopathology, and psychotherapy*. Hoboken, NJ: Wiley.

Kotov, R., Krueger, R. F., Watson, D., Achenbach, T. M., Althoff, R. R., Bagby, M., et al. (2017). The Hierarchical Taxonomy of Psychopathology (HiTOP): a dimensional alternative to traditional nosologies. *Journal of Abnormal Psychology*, *126*(4), 454–477.

Krueger, R. F., Derringer, J., Markon, K. E., Watson, D., & Skodol, A. E. (2012). Initial construction of a maladaptive personality trait model and inventory for DSM-5. *Psychological Medicine*, *42*(9), 1879–1890.

Lamkin, J., Clifton, A., Campbell, W. K., & Miller, J. D. (2014). An examination of the perceptions of social network characteristics associated with grandiose and vulnerable narcissism. *Personality Disorders*, *5*(2), 137–145.

Leary, T. (1957). *Interpersonal diagnosis of personality*. New York, NY: Ronald Press.

Locke, K. D. (2000). Circumplex scales of interpersonal values: reliability, validity, and applicability to interpersonal problems and personality disorders. *Journal of Personality Assessment*, *75*, 249–267.

Locke, K. D. (2011). Circumplex measures of interpersonal constructs. In L. M. Horowitz & S. Strack (Eds.), *Handbook of interpersonal psychology* (pp. 313–324). Hoboken, NJ: Wiley.

McCrae, R. R., & Costa, P. T., Jr. (1989). The structure of interpersonal traits: Wiggins's Circumplex and the Five-Factor Model. *Journal of Personality and Social Psychology*, *56*(4), 586–595.

Miller, J. D., Lynam, D. R., & Jones, S. (2008). Externalizing behavior through the lens of the five-factor model: a focus on agreeableness and conscientiousness. *Journal of Personality Assessment*, *90*(2), 158–164.

Moskowitz, D. S. (1994). Cross-situational generality and the interpersonal circumplex. *Journal of Personality and Social Psychology*, *66*, 921–933.

Moskowitz, D. S. (2010). Quarrelsomeness in daily life. *Journal of Personality*, *78*(1), 39–66.

Moskowitz, D. S., & Zuroff, D. C. (2005). Assessing interpersonal perceptions using the interpersonal grid. *Psychological Assessment*, *17*(2), 218–230.

Pincus, A. L. (2002). Constellations of dependency within the five-factor model of personality. In P. T. Costa & T. A. Widiger (Eds.), *Personality disorders and the five-factor model of personality* (pp. 203–214). (2nd ed.). Washington, DC: American Psychological Association.

Pincus, A. L., & Ansell, E. B. (2013). Interpersonal theory of personality. J. Suls & H. Tennen (Eds.), *Handbook of psychology* (pp. 141–159). (2nd ed.). *Personality and social psychology: Vol. 5*(pp. 141–159). Hoboken, NJ: Wiley.

Pincus, A. L., Hopwood, C. J., & Wright, A. G. C. (in press). The interpersonal situation: an integrative framework for the study of personality, psychopathology, and psychotherapy. In D. Funder, J.F. Rauthmann, & R. Sherman (Eds), *Oxford handbook of psychological situations*. New York: Oxford.

Pincus, A. L., Sadler, P., Woody, E., Roche, M. J., Thomas, K. M., & Wright, A. G. C. (2014). Assessing interpersonal dynamics. In C. J. Hopwood & R. F. Bornstein (Eds.), *Multimethod clinical assessment* (pp. 51–91). New York, NY: Guilford Press.
Pincus, A. L., & Wiggins, J. S. (1990). Interpersonal problems and conceptions of personality disorders. *Journal of Personality Disorders, 4*(4), 342–352.
Pincus, A. L., & Wright, A. G. C. (2011). Interpersonal diagnosis of psychopathology. In L. M. Horowitz & S. Strack (Eds.), *Handbook of interpersonal psychology* (pp. 359–381). Hoboken, NJ: Wiley.
Ross, J. M., Girard, J. M., Wright, A. G. C., Beeney, J. E., Scott, L. N., Hallquist, M. N., et al. (2017). Momentary patterns of covariation between specific affects and interpersonal behavior: linking relationship science and personality assessment. *Psychological Assessment, 29*(2), 123–134.
Sadikaj, G., Moskowitz, D. S., Russell, J. J., Zuroff, D. C., & Paris, J. (2013). Quarrelsome behavior in borderline personality disorder: influence of behavioral and affective reactivity to perceptions of others. *Journal of Abnormal Psychology, 122*, 195–207.
Sadler, P., Ethier, N., Gunn, G. R., Duong, D., & Woody, E. (2009). Are we on the same wavelength? Interpersonal complementarity as shared cyclical patterns during interactions. *Journal of Personality and Social Psychology, 97*, 1005–1020.
Sadler, P., Ethier, N., & Woody, E. (2011). Interpersonal complementarity. In L. M. Horowitz & S. Strack (Eds.), *Handbook of interpersonal psychology* (pp. 123–142). Hoboken, NJ: Wiley.
Samuel, D. B., & Widiger, T. A. (2008). A meta-analytic review of the relationships between the five-factor model and DSM-IV-TR personality disorders: a facet level analysis. *Clinical Psychology Review, 28*(8), 1326–1342.
Soldz, S., Budman, S., Demby, A., & Merry, J. (1995). A short form of the Inventory of Interpersonal Problems Circumplex scales. *Assessment, 2*, 53–63.
Soto, C. J., & John, O. P. (2017). The Next Big Five Inventory (BFI-2): developing and assessing a hierarchical model with 15 facets to enhance bandwidth, fidelity, and predictive power. *Journal of Personality and Social Psychology, 113*(1), 117–143.
Sullivan, H. S. (1953a). *Conceptions of modern psychiatry*. New York, NY: Norton.
Sullivan, H. S. (1953b). *The interpersonal theory of psychiatry*. New York, NY: Norton.
Wiggins, J. S., & Pincus, A. L. (1989). Conceptions of personality disorders and dimensions of personality. *Psychological Assessment, 1*(4), 305–316.
Williams, T. F., & Simms, L. J. (2016). Personality disorder models and their coverage of interpersonal problems. *Personality Disorders, 7*(1), 15–27.
Wilson, S., Stroud, C. B., & Durbin, C. E. (2017). Interpersonal dysfunction in personality disorders: a meta-analytic review. *Psychological Bulletin, 143*(7), 677–734.
Woods, W. C., Himmelstein, P. H., Edershile, E. A., Sharpe, B. M., Creswell, D., Pincus, A. L., et al. (2018). Using visual analogue scales for ambulatory assessment of interpersonal behavior (manuscript submitted for publication).
Wright, A. G. C., Hopwood, C. J., & Simms, L. J. (2015). Daily interpersonal and affective dynamics in personality disorder. *Journal of Personality Disorders, 29*(4), 503–525.
Wright, A. G. C., & Pincus, A. L. (2010, June). Cross-sectional intraindividual variability in interpersonal functioning. In *Paper presented at the 13th annual meeting of the Society for Interpersonal Theory and Research, Philadelphia, PA.*
Wright, A. G. C., Pincus, A. L., Conroy, D. E., & Hilsenroth, M. J. (2009). Integrating methods to optimize circumplex description and comparison of groups. *Journal of Personality Assessment, 91*(4), 311–322.

Wright, A. G. C., Pincus, A. L., Hopwood, C. J., Thomas, K. M., Markon, K. E., & Krueger, R. F. (2012). An interpersonal analysis of pathological personality traits in DSM-5. *Assessment*, *19*(3), 263–275.

Wright, A. G. C., & Simms, L. J. (2014). On the structure of personality disorder traits: conjoint analyses of the CAT-PD, PID-5, and NEO-PI-3 trait models. *Personality Disorders: Theory, Research, and Treatment*, *5*, 43–54.

Wright, A. G. C., & Simms, L. J. (2015). A metastructural model of mental disorders and pathological personality traits. *Psychological Medicine*, *45*(11), 2309–2319.

Wright, A. G. C., & Simms, L. J. (2016). Stability and fluctuation of personality disorder features in daily life. *Journal of Abnormal Psychology*, *125*(5), 641–656.

Wright, A. G. C., Stepp, S. D., Scott, L. N., Hallquist, M. N., Beeney, J. E., Lazarus, S., et al. (2017). The effect of pathological narcissism on interpersonal and affective processes in social interactions. *Journal of Abnormal Psychology*, *126*(7), 898–910.

Wright, A. G. C., Thomas, K. M., Hopwood, C. J., Markon, K. E., Pincus, A. L., & Krueger, R. F. (2012). The hierarchical structure of DSM-5 pathological personality traits. *Journal of Abnormal Psychology*, *121*(4), 951–957.

Zimmermann, J., & Wright, A. G. C. (2017). Beyond description in interpersonal construct validation: methodological advances in the circumplex structural summary approach. *Assessment*, *24*(1), 3–23.

Antagonism's place in psychiatric nosology

12

Martin Sellbom
Department of Psychology, University of Otago, Dunedin, New Zealand

The main goal of this chapter is to elaborate on the general location and representation of antagonism in the broader structure of psychopathology. The permeating assumption is that psychopathology constructs are generally dimensional, like personality traits, and can be arranged in a hierarchical fashion (e.g., Kotov et al., 2017). This chapter will review the general scientific base for the placement of antagonism within this broader structure, propose that antagonism is a spectrum, and that this spectrum explains variance in certain underlying disorders. Although subsequent chapters will provide detailed accounts of the links between antagonism and specific disorders, the current chapter will offer a general overview of which disorders at least in part represent the broader antagonism psychopathology spectrum.

Hierarchical and dimensional structure of psychopathology

There is ample evidence to support the notion that psychopathology is dimensional in nature (e.g., Haslam, Holland, & Kuppens, 2012) and that mental health symptoms and maladaptive personality traits generally conform to a hierarchical structure (e.g., Kotov et al., 2017). Categorical syndromes evince problems with arbitrary thresholds, poor diagnostic reliability, excessive heterogeneity in symptom manifestation (and thus multiple potential underlying mechanisms), problematic comorbidity levels, and insufficient coverage of all distressed or impaired patients (see, e.g., Kotov et al., 2017, for a review), whereas dimensional, individual differences representations of psychopathology and personality constructs overcome these issues. More specifically, no arbitrary thresholds or cut points are needed, symptom dimension covariation is represented in higher order spectra, and all patients can be captured in terms of symptom manifestation and severity (Kotov, 2016).

The Hierarchical Taxonomy of Psychopathology (HiTOP; Kotov et al., 2017) is a recent and arguably the most ambitious attempt at organizing psychopathology dimensions in a hierarchical fashion by relying on an extensive literature that provides evidence for the structure of various mental disorders. HiTOP postulates six broad spectra (somatoform, internalizing, thought disorder, disinhibited externalizing, antagonistic externalizing, and detachment) of psychopathology with underlying subfactors (e.g., distress, fear for the internalizing spectrum) at the subsequent lower order level and individual disorders symptoms (e.g., depression under distress; panic disorder under fear) at the observed syndromal level. HiTOP is very much a start for a

The Handbook of Antagonism. https://doi.org/10.1016/B978-0-12-814627-9.00012-8

comprehensive reorganization of psychopathology, but much work is necessary to fully elucidate this structure. For now, it is a helpful framework within which antagonism can be viewed in a broader psychiatric nosology.

Indeed, antagonism is represented in this structure as the "antagonistic externalizing" spectrum, but the nature of this spectrum and how antagonism clearly fit into it from a psychiatric nosology perspective is not fully clear. This chapter aims to further clarify this role via a careful review of the literature. But first, it is worth discussing the broader externalizing superspectrum (Kotov et al., 2017) from which antagonistic externalizing is an outgrowth, and a major reason why antagonism and disinhibition are less distinct from one another relative to the other four spectra in the HiTOP model.

Structural models of externalizing spectrum of psychopathology

The earliest psychopathology structure research broadly detailed the emergence of a domain that was labeled externalizing (e.g., Achenbach, 1966; Krueger, Caspi, Moffitt, & Silva, 1998). The underlying disorders, which include antisocial personality disorder, conduct disorder, and alcohol and substance use disorders (and sometimes also attention-deficit hyperactivity disorder [e.g., Young, Stallings, Corley, Krauter, & Hewitt, 2000]), are treated as conceptually distinct, and placed in different sections of the *DSM-5*, but a plethora of studies have observed high levels of comorbidity (see Krueger & South, 2009, for a review). This research indicated the potential presence of a higher order latent factor.

Indeed, research studies using factor analysis of common mental disorders have revealed that externalizing psychopathology is separate from an internalizing psychopathology (i.e., unipolar mood and anxiety disorders) factor in studies using both youth (i.e., child and adolescent) and adult samples (see Krueger & Markon, 2006, for a meta-analysis). Research has further demonstrated that over 80% of the shared externalizing variance can be attributed to genetic effects, whereas most of the unique variances associated with individual disorders have been more strongly linked to nonshared environmental effects (Kendler, Prescott, Myers, & Neale, 2003; Krueger et al., 2002; Young et al., 2000), indicating the possibility for shared biological mechanisms. In addition, Krueger, Markon, Patrick, and Iacono (2005) found that general externalizing represented a dimensional (rather than discontinuous) vulnerability factor for the individual mental disorders.

Krueger, Markon, Patrick, Benning, and Kramer (2007) elaborated on a more comprehensive model of the externalizing liability using narrow-band aspects of antisocial behaviors/personality, substance use disorders, and disinhibited personality traits that were viewed as elements of an externalizing spectrum. They measured 23 different personality and behavior constructs that served as indicators in a series of competing structural models in large samples of university students and prison inmates. The optimal model conformed to a hierarchical bifactor structure, meaning that all measured variables in the model loaded onto a *general externalizing factor*, whereas only specific subsets of the manifest variables loaded onto separate respective *callous-aggression* and *substance misuse* factors that were orthogonal from the general factor. More specifically, the general externalizing liability factor was related to all of the examined behaviors/symptoms, but was most strongly related to measures of irresponsibility and problematic impulsivity. The callous-aggression liability factor was primarily comprised of a range of aggressive and unempathetic behaviors and attitudes, much akin to antagonism (e.g., Krueger, Derringer, Markon, Watson, & Skodol, 2012), and suggesting the potential for distinct (from general externalizing) underlying liability factors for such traits (Patrick, Foell, Venables, & Worthy, 2016). These findings have been replicated by Sellbom (2016) in correctional, forensic, and community samples. However, neither of these studies provides much insight into antagonism as a separate spectrum of psychopathology from general or "disinhibited" externalizing or much evidence for how such a domain emerges in broader psychopathology context.

Markon (2010) modeled the externalizing spectrum in the broader context of other mental disorders using data from the British Office for National Statistics Survey of Psychiatric Morbidity study ($n = 8405$). Psychiatric symptoms were assessed via various clinical interviews or self-report questionnaires (depending on the construct). Markon estimated a second-order latent factor model, which comprised an externalizing factor in addition to internalizing, thought disorder, and pathological introversion factors. A closer examination of the first-order latent factors loading on the externalizing higher order factor reveals noteworthy results. Two first-order factors in particular, hostility and attention seeking (which accounted for a combined set of histrionic and narcissistic PD symptoms) had substantially smaller factor loadings (.30 and .49, respectively) on the externalizing higher order factor than the remaining first-order factors (e.g., antisocial, alcohol problems, drug problems; loadings >.65). Markon's (2010) findings indicated that these symptom domains were less representative of general externalizing than were the more disinhibitory symptoms, and indeed suggested the possibility that, in the context of additional indicators, an antagonism factor could break off from a more disinhibited externalizing factor.

Research on antagonism and structure of psychopathology

The research on antagonism with the broader framework of psychopathology has not been extensive and is generally limited to factor analytic studies that contain a sufficient number of indicators to form a viable factor on its own. Also, the adult and youth literatures have not produced consistent findings and will be reviewed separately.

Adult research

In the first published study that identified antagonism in the context of a broader examination of psychopathology structure, Kotov et al. (2011) used Rhode Island Methods to Improve Diagnostic Assessment and Services (MIDAS) project data, which consisted of 2900 consecutive outpatients. They had all been administered the Structured Clinical Interview for DSM-IV Axis I Disorders (SCID-I; First, Spitzer, Gibbon, & Williams, 1995) and Structured Interview for DSM-IV Personality Disorders (SIDP-IV; Pfohl, Blum, & Zimmerman, 1997) from which 25 lifetime diagnoses were derived with sufficient prevalence rates for analyses. A series of confirmatory factor analyses yielded a factor labeled antagonism (on which antisocial, histrionic, narcissistic, borderline, and paranoid PDs loaded prominently) in addition to factors representing traditional externalizing (substance use disorders, antisocial PD, and conduct problems), internalizing, thought disorder, and somatoform disorder.

In the same year, Røysamb et al. (2011) published a study on 2974 twins from the Norwegian Institute of Public Health Twin Panel. They were administered the Composite International Diagnostic Interview (CIDI; Wittchen & Pfister, 1997) for (former) Axis I disorders and the SIDP-IV for personality disorders. They split the twins into two samples and conducted and exploratory factor analysis (EFA) in the first sample and a confirmatory factor analysis (CFA) on the preferred solution from sample 1 in the second sample. Røysamb et al.'s preferred structure was a four-factor solution, which included traditional externalizing (antisocial PD, conduct disorder, substance use disorders) and a factor they labeled "cognitive-relational disturbance" (paranoid, schizotypal, narcissistic, histrionic, and obsessive-compulsive PDs, and to a lesser degree, borderline PD). The latter factor was similar to the personality disorder factor that Kotov et al. labeled antagonism. A major drawback with Røysamb et al.'s study was that due to very low prevalence rates for personality disorders, they used dimensional counts for PD variables but categorical diagnostic estimates for the Axis I disorders, which might have introduced a method artifact into their factor analyses.

Kendler et al. (2011) used the same Norwegian twin dataset and variables, but estimated separate genetic and environmental polychoric correlation matrices that they subjected to EFA. The genetic analysis revealed a four-factor structure quite similar to that of Røysamb et al., with an "Axis II externalizing" factor that included the same PDs as the cognitive-relational disturbance factor, except schizotypal PD which loaded preferentially on an "Axis II Internalizing" (better characterized as detachment) factor. The environmental EFA resulted in a three-factor structure among which all 10 PDs loaded on the same factor, suggesting (despite the authors' claim to otherwise) a clear method factor.

In a study focused on the Minnesota Multiphasic Personality Inventory-2-Restructured Form (MMPI-2-RF; Ben-Porath & Tellegen, 2008), McNulty and Overstreet (2014) examined the structure of its 42 substantive scales (corrected for item overlap) in two large outpatient ($n = 1219$) and inpatient ($n = 1024$) samples. In a series of EFAs, separated by gender, they consistently observed six factors. Five corresponded to the Personality Psychopathy Five structure (aggressiveness, psychoticism, disconstraint, negative emotionality, and introversion) as well as sixth somatization factor. The "aggressiveness" factor is similar to antagonism and consisted of psychopathology and personality scales reflective of instrumental aggression, grandiosity, and dominance. The disconstraint factor, which was more akin to the traditional externalizing factor observed in previous studies, explained variance in scales measuring antisocial behavior, poor impulse control, aggressive behavior, sensation seeking, and substance abuse.

A subsequent study combined both DSM-5 clinical (formerly Axis I) and personality disorder symptom counts with maladaptive personality traits measures for a structural analysis (Wright & Simms, 2015). A total of 628 outpatients were assessed via the Mini International Neuropsychiatric Inventory (MINI; Sheehan & LeCrubier, 2010), Structured Clinical Interview for DSM-IV Axis II Disorders-Personality Questionnaire (SCID-II-PD; First, Gibbon, Spitzer, Williams, & Benjamin, 1997), and Personality Inventory for DSM-5 (PID-5; Krueger et al., 2012). Using exploratory structural equation modeling in which method factors for instrumentation were specified, Wright and Simms concluded that a five-factor model was the best representation of their data. These factors were labeled internalizing, antagonism, disinhibition, detachment, and psychoticism, and mirrored that of McNulty and Overstreet (2014) as well as the DSM-5 Alternative Model for Personality Disorders (American Psychiatric Association, 2013) to a substantial degree. More specifically, the most prominent loadings on the antagonism factor were narcissistic PD, PID-5 grandiosity, deceitfulness, manipulativeness, callousness, and attention seeking. Histrionic PD also loaded on this factor, but more so on detachment (negatively). Paranoid PD, PID-5 suspiciousness, hostility, and rigid perfectionism also loaded on antagonism, but more strongly on internalizing.

In sum, these studies have generally observed factors that include personality disorders as being reflective of antagonism. Across these studies, narcissistic, histrionic, and paranoid PDs have consistently loaded on this factor, borderline PD to a much lesser degree (and always loading more strongly on internalizing factors) and antisocial PD (but always loading more strongly on a disinhibition/traditional externalizing factor). Findings appear to be clearer in studies where nondiagnostic variables such as symptom or trait scales are included (McNulty & Overstreet, 2014; Wright & Simms, 2015) and method variance is controlled for (Wright & Simms, 2015). In Wright and Simms's study, Borderline PD was (appropriately) aligned with internalizing disorders and Histrionic and Paranoid PD also exhibited larger cross-loadings on other conceptually relevant factors. Unfortunately, none of these structural studies have included measures of psychopathy, which is arguably more saturated with antagonism from a personality perspective than any other disorder (e.g., Lynam & Miller, 2015). Its inclusion would likely have influenced the findings of several of these studies.

Youth studies

The attempts at modeling multiple factors of externalizing in the child and adolescent literature have yielded somewhat inconsistent and ambiguous findings, at least in terms of the presence of an antagonism factor. Ivanova, Achenbach, Dumenci, et al. (2007) and Ivanova, Achenbach, Rescorla, et al. (2007) examined the factor structure of the Child Behavior Checklist (CBLC; Achenbach & Rescorla, 2001) and the Youth Self-Report (YSR; Achenbach & Rescorla, 2001) using samples from 30 and 23 countries, respectively. They reported consistent factor structures for both the CBCL and YSR items, with both measures indicating a higher order structure of "rule breaking" (e.g., lying, stealing, truancy, running away, bad friends) and "aggressive" (e.g., poor temper, tantrums, vandalism, assaults).

Farmer, Seeley, Kosty, and Lewinsohn (2009) used data from 816 adolescents from the longitudinal Oregon Adolescent Depression Project; these participants had been administered the Schedule for Affective Disorders and Schizophrenia for School-Age Children (K-SADS; Kaufman et al., 1997) and Longitudinal Interval Follow-up Evaluation (LIFE; Keller et al., 1987) at multiple time points. Farmer and colleagues restricted their examination to externalizing disorders. They tested a variety of competing longitudinal CFA models and observed that a correlated two-factor model representing oppositional behavior (oppositional defiant disorder [ODD], attention deficit hyperactivity disorder [ADHD]) and social norm-violating disorders (conduct disorder, adult antisocial behavior, and substance use disorders) best fit the available data. In a follow-up study, Farmer, Seeley, Kosty, Olino, and Lewinsohn (2013) extended their analyses to age 30 and also included markers of internalizing disorders. They tested a series of longitudinal EFA bass-ackwards models (Goldberg, 2006), which provides for a hierarchical representation starting with a one-factor model and breaking down into two, three, four, and five factors, with factors from two adjacent levels being correlated. An externalizing factor emerged at the second level of the hierarchy and the same oppositional behavior and norm-violating factors emerged at the third level as a direct outgrowth of externalizing.

Verona, Javdani, and Sprague (2011) recruited 223 treatment and nontreatment referred community-dwelling youths (aged 10–17) for a larger study on risk factors for youth psychopathology and antisocial behavior. These youths were administered the K-SADS, CBLC, and Alcohol Use Disorders Identification Test (AUDIT; Saunders, Aasland, Babor, de la Fuente, & Grant, 1993). They observed a best-fitting CFA model that included internalizing, externalizing, and substance use disorder factors. The externalizing factor accounted for the common variance in conduct disorder, ODD, ADHD, and CBCL externalizing symptom counts and scores.

Castellanos-Ryan et al. (2014) examined 1778 adolescents in a longitudinal study at age 14 and later at age 16. At the earlier age, they were all administered various self-report and parent-rated measures of externalizing behaviors. They specified a bifactor model analogous to Krueger et al. (2007) with a general externalizing factor and two group factors that indicated ADHD/conduct problems and substance misuse. The overall model showed that some indicators like bullying behavior, self-reported conduct problems, and likelihood of conduct disorder diagnosis did not loan meaningfully on its group factor, whereas none of the substance use disorder indicators loaded substantively (<.40) on the general factor. Although not formally tested, these findings suggest the potential for a correlated two-factor model of mostly ADHD vs substance misuse.

Finally, Blanco et al. (2015) used a large representative sample of adolescents from the National Comorbidity Survey Adolescent Supplement (NCS-A). They were all administered the CIDI which assesses for 12-month prevalence of mental disorders. They reported on a final, hierarchical CFA model with general psychopathology factor on top, two internalizing and externalizing second-order factors, and underlying the externalizing factor, behavioral disorder (conduct disorder, ODD, and ADHD) and substance use disorder first-order factors.

In sum, the youth literature has not clearly identified an antagonism factor in any study that included a variety of externalizing indicators. The various factor structures are also rather inconsistent. In the majority of studies, substance use disorder is clearly distinct from a general externalizing factor (Blanco et al., 2015; Castellanos-Ryan et al., 2014; Ivanova, Achenbach, Dumenci, et al., 2007; Ivanova, Achenbach, Rescorla, et al., 2007; Verona et al., 2011). The general externalizing factor includes markers of both antagonism and disinhibition. Two studies with a sufficient number of indicators (Ivanova, Achenbach, Dumenci, et al., 2007; Ivanova, Achenbach, Rescorla, et al., 2007) separate aggression from rule-breaking factors. While the aggression factor to some degree could be indicative of antagonism, the rule-breaking factor actually included items such as lying and lack of guilt, which are also markers of the antagonism personality domain. Farmer and colleagues' studies modeled ADHD and ODD as a separate oppositional factor from norm violating, which makes the former a candidate for antagonistic personality, but it is far from pure since ADHD symptoms are mostly indicative of disinhibition. Unfortunately, as is the case with the adult literature, none of these studies included measurement of callous-unemotional traits (or, limited prosocial emotions in DSM-5; APA, 2013), which are arguably the best childhood disorder equivalent of antagonistic personality traits. Indeed, in the youth psychopathy literature, callous-unemotional traits frequently form their own separate factor from other disinhibitory personality traits (e.g., Poythress, Dembo, Wareham, & Greenbaum, 2006).

In-depth examination of the antagonism factor and its associated disorders

In the psychiatric nosology literature, the antagonism factor has mostly arisen from various personality disorder factors and has not otherwise emerged in these larger studies when such indicators (with the exception of antisocial PD) have not been included. Kotov et al.'s (2017) interpretation of this literature, from the HiTOP perspective, is that the antagonistic-externalizing spectrum accounts for the shared variance in four personality disorders (narcissistic, paranoid, histrionic, and borderline) and, together with the disinhibited-externalizing spectrum, the shared variation in antisocial PD, conduct disorder, ODD, and ADHD. Disinhibited externalizing, on the other hand, accounts for the shared variance in substance use disorders. Absent from this consideration is psychopathy, though this construct is formally represented as antisocial PD in the DSM-5 (albeit a highly inadequate operationalization). Next, the degree to which these various disorders are truly markers or psychiatric representations of antagonism is discussed[1]; and because the antagonism factor has emerged more distinctly in the adult literature, only such disorders will be on focus in this section.

[1]The reader is directed to other chapters in this volume for a more detailed discussion of how antagonism aligns with psychopathy (Chapter 15), narcissistic PD (Chapter 16), and borderline PD (Chapter 18). Only a cursory review to make specific points about antagonism's place in psychiatric nosology is provided here.

Psychopathy/antisocial PD. Psychopathy is a multifaceted and severe personality disorder that involves deficiencies in affective and interpersonal functioning (e.g., callousness, lack of empathy, remorse, and emotional depth, fearlessness, superficial charm, grandiosity, and deceitfulness) as well as regulation of behavior (e.g., impulsivity, irresponsibility, anger proneness, aggression) (e.g., Cooke, Hart, Logan, & Michie, 2012; Skeem, Polaschek, Patrick, & Lilienfeld, 2011). It is operationalized as antisocial PD in the DSM-5 (American Psychiatric Association, 2013), which emphasizes the behavioral deficiencies to a far greater degree than the affective/interpersonal aspects. This issue is not trivial because it likely has implications for the degree to which the disorder is associated with antagonism as opposed to its closest trait domain relative, disinhibition.

A plethora of research studies has clearly linked psychopathy to the trait domain of antagonism. Lynam and Miller (2015) argued that antagonism represents the core of psychopathic personality in light of impressive evidence from a range of sources. Specifically, they noted that total scores for the most common psychopathy measures were all more strongly correlated with (low) agreeableness trait facets than those from any other FFM domain; that expert ratings of a prototypical psychopath (Miller, Lyman, Widiger, & Leukefeld, 2001) indicated very low ratings on all agreeableness facets; and when the Psychopathy Checklist—Revised (Hare, 1991) was translated into FFM language (see Widiger & Lynam, 1998), the PCL-R items were most strongly linked to (low) agreeableness. Furthermore, recent meta-analyses of FFM traits and PD associations (Samuel & Widiger, 2008; Saulsman & Page, 2004) indicate that antisocial PD is moderately and negatively correlated with agreeableness, and weakly to moderately negatively correlated with conscientiousness.

In sum, the multifaceted psychopathic personality disorder construct has antagonism as a major core and should be considered a severe psychiatric manifestation of this trait domain. Its DSM-5 operationalization of antisocial PD is substantially linked to this domain as well, but its relative proportion of disinhibition/low conscientiousness variance is larger, which likely explains why antisocial PD (and also conduct disorder) often loads more strongly (or even exclusively) on disinhibition rather than antagonism domains in some studies. Future research on the structure of psychiatric symptoms would be better informed if psychopathy (in adult studies) and limited prosocial emotion (in youth studies) indicators were included.

Narcissistic PD. Narcissistic PD is clearly a psychiatric representation of antagonism. Such indicators in the various latent structural models reviewed preferentially and distinctly load on factors that are interpreted to represent antagonism. In addition, meta-analyses (Samuel & Widiger, 2008; Saulsman & Page, 2004) indicate that narcissistic PD is moderately and negatively correlated with FFM agreeableness, but no other FFM domains. Furthermore, Miller et al. (2016) observed that virtually all types of narcissism measures (DSM-based, grandiose, vulnerable) exhibited large correlations with antagonism, but associations with other maladaptive FFM domains were dependent on the manifestation (grandiose vs vulnerable) of narcissism. Thus, in sum, the personality trait core of Narcissistic PD is clearly antagonism.

Paranoid PD. Paranoid PD is the third personality disorder with a substantial antagonism relation. It is complex from a trait perspective, with major sources of personality variance coming from paranoid ideation/mistrust, alienation, and anger/hostility, which are facets that load on different broader personality domains depending on the model considered (e.g., DSM-5 AMPD, FFM, PSY-5). From an FFM perspective, these traits fall under the neuroticism and (low) agreeableness domains, which is consistent with the two major meta-analyses (Samuel & Widiger, 2008; Saulsman & Page, 2004) on FFM traits and PDs. More specifically, paranoid PD is moderately and positively associated with neuroticism, whereas it is moderately and negatively associated with agreeableness. Some studies have also linked paranoid PD to a psychoticism domain (e.g., Bagby, Sellbom, Costa, & Widiger, 2008; Finn, Arbisi, Erbes, Polusny, & Thuras, 2014; Hopwood, Thomas, Markon, Wright, & Krueger, 2012) in non-FFM models, and structurally, Kotov et al. (2011) observed a cross-loading on a thought disorder factor in addition to the antagonism. In sum, paranoid PD is clearly antagonism related, but multifaceted from a personality perspective with clear influences from neuroticism (e.g., anger/hostility, alienation) and psychoticism (e.g., unusual beliefs) as well.

Histrionic PD. This PD is arguably more questionable as a psychiatric representation of antagonism. Although it loads on the antagonism factor in structural studies, the FFM literature (Samuel & Widiger, 2008; Saulsman & Page, 2004) indicates that it is more relevant to the extraversion domain (mean weighted r's = .33 and .42) than the agreeableness domain (mean weighted r's = −.11 and −.06). In Wright and Simms (2015), histrionic PD loaded more strongly (and negatively) on a detachment/introversion factor than antagonism. However, in other models where the definitional trait of attention seeking loads exclusively on antagonism (e.g., Krueger et al., 2012) and where antagonism is also linked to extraversion (e.g., PSY-5 Aggressiveness; Harkness & McNulty, 1994), histrionic PD is clearly associated with antagonism as well if not most strongly so (Bagby et al., 2008; Finn et al., 2014; Hopwood et al., 2012; Wright & Simms, 2015). In sum, the personality science of histrionic PD, a disorder that some contend should not even exist (e.g., Blashfield, Reynolds, & Stennett, 2012), is equivocal at best. It is clearly a disorder highly influenced by extraversion, but its relation to antagonism is inconsistent and tends to depend on what personality trait model is being considered. At this point, it is difficult to proffer this PD as a major psychiatric marker of antagonism.

Borderline PD. Borderline PD is a very heterogeneous disorder from a personality (and symptom) perspective. Its position as a psychiatric marker of antagonism is highly questionable and potentially misleading. Many scholars have argued that emotional dysregulation is the core of this disorder (e.g., Glenn & Klonsky, 2009; Gratz, 2003; Linehan, 1993), which means that borderline PD is more clearly a disorder of neuroticism/negative affectivity than antagonism. Both Samuel and Widiger (2008) and Saulsman and Page (2004) reported weak average weighted correlations between FFM domains and borderline PD, whereas the average associations with neuroticism were of large magnitude. In addition, studies from the DSM-5 AMPD trait perspective that indicate that borderline PD has its smallest association with antagonism (and, as expected, largest with negative affectivity), and when such traits are entered into a regression model to predict latent borderline PD variance, no antagonism facets augment this prediction (e.g., Sellbom, Sansone, Songer, & Anderson, 2014). Furthermore, structural evidence is highly inconsistent with respect to borderline PD loading on antagonism factors, and when dimensional traits are considered in addition to psychiatric diagnoses, this PD loads clearly on internalizing (Wright & Simms, 2015).

Thus, in sum, it is difficult to make an argument for borderline PD serving as a major psychiatric representation for antagonism. It is related to antagonism in terms of anger/hostility and aggression, but these manifestations are likely more directly mediated through high levels of neuroticism.

Summary and conclusion

The representation of antagonism in psychiatric nosology is not straightforward, which is likely a reflection of the heterogeneous and to some extent arbitrary nature of current psychiatric syndromes more so than of this personality domain itself. Research that has examined the hierarchical structure of adult psychopathology, and identified a latent factor that identified by loadings of various PDs (most commonly antisocial, narcissistic, paranoid, histrionic, but sometimes also borderline PD), has typically characterized it as antagonism (even if other labels have been used). This factor has also emerged as robust in the context of dimensional personality traits (Wright & Simms, 2015). This literature led Kotov et al. (2017) to propose an antagonistic-externalizing spectrum of psychopathology, which accounts for all of the PDs just mentioned (in addition to conduct problems, ODD, and ADHD in childhood). But a careful examination of these individual "antagonism" disorders suggests that they definitely vary in the degree to which they are psychiatric presentations of this personality construct. Narcissistic PD is definitely such a representation; antisocial and paranoid PDs can be viewed as such representations, but also signify disinhibition and neuroticism, respectively. Histrionic PD is more likely a psychiatric reflection of pathological levels of extraversion more so than antagonism, whereas borderline PD is predominately a representation of extreme neuroticism. Indeed, this latter diagnosis should not be listed at all under antagonistic externalizing in the HiTOP model.

The youth literature is far more ambiguous and one might even conclude that antagonism might not be developmentally important in a psychopathology context, at least from a structural perspective. But such a conclusion would be problematic as it is tied to the limitations of factor analysis, which is solely dependent on what indicators are included. Unlike the adult literature, there are no diagnoses or symptom measures of callous-unemotional traits, narcissism, paranoia/suspiciousness, or even attention seeking/exhibitionism included, which makes it virtually impossible for a similar factor to emerge in the youth literature. Furthermore, the personality traits to disorders links are also not as established in the youth literature, making an analysis from this perspective less straightforward. Future research is definitely needed to obtain a clearer picture of psychiatric representations of antagonism in youth, especially beyond what are typically referred to as callous-unemotional traits.

Finally, it is this author's opinion that future research needs to move beyond locating antagonism in traditional psychiatric disorders and consider severe and impairing manifestations of this construct in its own right. As evident from several other chapters in this volume, antagonism is a stable and robust personality domain that is distinct from other higher order personality domains. It does not suffer from the "comorbidity" problems its psychiatric representations do; it will capture all severity levels from interpersonal difficulties to extreme impairment in functioning; and it has robust correlates. Future research can determine if a disorder of antagonism confers greater validity and utility than the traditional and often fallible diagnostic categories that currently appear in the DSM-5.

References

Achenbach, T. M. (1966). The classification of children's psychiatric symptoms: a factor analytic study. *Psychological Monographs*, *80*, 1–37.

Achenbach, T. M., & Rescorla, L. A. (2001). *Manual for the ASEBA school-age forms and profiles*. Burlington, VA: University of Vermont Research Center for Children, Youth, and Families.

American Psychiatric Association. (2013). *Diagnostic and statistical manual of mental disorders* (5th ed.). Washington, DC: Author.

Bagby, R. M., Sellbom, M., Costa, P. T., & Widiger, T. A. (2008). Predicting Diagnostic and Statistical Manual of Mental Disorders-IV personality disorders with the five-factor model of personality and the personality psychopathology five. *Personality and Mental Health*, *2*(2), 55–69.

Ben-Porath, Y. S., & Tellegen, A. (2008). *MMPI-2-RF, Minnesota Multiphasic Personality Inventory-2 Restructured Form: Manual for Administration, Scoring and Interpretation*. University of Minnesota Press.

Blanco, C., Wall, M. M., He, J. P., Krueger, R. F., Olfson, M., Jin, C. J., et al. (2015). The space of common psychiatric disorders in adolescents: comorbidity structure and individual latent liabilities. *Journal of the American Academy of Child & Adolescent Psychiatry*, *54*, 45–52.

Blashfield, R. K., Reynolds, S. M., & Stennett, B. (2012). The death of histrionic personality disorder. In T. A. Widiger (Ed.), *The Oxford handbook of personality disorders* (pp. 603–627). New York: Oxford University Press.

Castellanos-Ryan, N., Struve, M., Whelan, R., Banaschewski, T., Barker, G. J., Bokde, A. L., et al. (2014). Neural and cognitive correlates of the common and specific variance across externalizing problems in young adolescence. *American Journal of Psychiatry*, *171*, 1310–1319.

Cooke, D. J., Hart, S. D., Logan, C., & Michie, C. (2012). Explicating the construct of psychopathy: development and validation of a conceptual model, the Comprehensive Assessment of Psychopathic Personality (CAPP). *International Journal of Forensic Mental Health*, *11*(4), 242–252.

Farmer, R. F., Seeley, J. R., Kosty, D. B., & Lewinsohn, P. M. (2009). Refinements in the hierarchical structure of externalizing psychiatric disorders: patterns of lifetime liability from mid-adolescence through early adulthood. *Journal of Abnormal Psychology*, *118*, 699–710.

Farmer, R. F., Seeley, J. R., Kosty, D. B., Olino, T. M., & Lewinsohn, P. M. (2013). Hierarchical organization of axis I psychiatric disorder comorbidity through age 30. *Comprehensive Psychiatry*, *54*, 523–532.

Finn, J. A., Arbisi, P. A., Erbes, C. R., Polusny, M. A., & Thuras, P. (2014). The MMPI–2 restructured form personality psychopathology five scales: Bridging DSM–5 section 2 personality disorders and DSM–5 section 3 personality trait dimensions. *Journal of Personality Assessment*, *96*(2), 173–184.

First, M. B., Gibbon, M., Spitzer, R. L., Williams, J. B. W., & Benjamin, L. S. (1997). *Structured Clinical Interview for DSM–IV Axis II personality disorders (SCID–II)*. Washington, DC: American Psychiatric Press.

First, M. B., Spitzer, R. L., Gibbon, M. W. J. B., & Williams, J. B. (1995). *Structured clinical interview for DSM-IV axis I disorders*. New York: New York State Psychiatric Institute.

Glenn, C. R., & Klonsky, E. D. (2009). Emotion dysregulation as a core feature of borderline personality disorder. *Journal of Personality Disorders*, *23*(1), 20–28.

Goldberg, L. R. (2006). Doing it all bass-ackwards: the development of hierarchical factor structures from the top down. *Journal of Research in Personality*, *40*(4), 347–358.

Gratz, K. L. (2003). Risk factors for and functions of deliberate self-harm: an empirical and conceptual review. *Clinical Psychology: Science and Practice*, *10*(2), 192–205.

Hare, R. D. (1991). *The Hare psychopathy checklist-revised: Manual*. Toronto: Multi-Health Systems.

Harkness, A. R., & McNulty, J. L. (1994). The Personality Psychopathology Five (PSY-5): issue from the pages of a diagnostic manual instead of a dictionary. In S. Strack & M. Lorr (Eds.), *Differentiating normal and abnormal personality* (pp. 291–315). New York, NY: Springer.

Haslam, N., Holland, E., & Kuppens, P. (2012). Categories versus dimensions in personality and psychopathology: a quantitative review of taxometric research. *Psychological Medicine*, *42*, 903–920.

Hopwood, C. J., Thomas, K. M., Markon, K. E., Wright, A. G., & Krueger, R. F. (2012). DSM–5 personality traits and DSM–IV personality disorders. *Journal of Abnormal Psychology*, *121*, 424–432.

Ivanova, M. Y., Achenbach, T. M., Dumenci, L., Rescorla, L. A., Almqvist, F., Weintraub, S., et al. (2007). Testing the 8-syndrome structure of the child behavior checklist in 30 societies. *Journal of Clinical Child and Adolescent Psychology*, *36*, 405–417.

Ivanova, M. Y., Achenbach, T. M., Rescorla, L. A., Dumenci, L., Almqvist, F., Bilenberg, N., et al. (2007). The generalizability of the Youth Self-Report syndrome structure in 23 societies. *Journal of Consulting and Clinical Psychology*, *75*, 729–738.

Kaufman, J., Birmaher, B., Brent, D., Rao, U. M. A., Flynn, C., Moreci, P., et al. (1997). Schedule for affective disorders and schizophrenia for school-age children-presentand lifetime version (K-SADS-PL): initial reliability and validity data. *Journal of the American Academy of Child & Adolescent Psychiatry*, *36*(7), 980–988.

Keller, M. B., Lavori, P. W., Friedman, B., Nielsen, E., Endicott, J., & McDonald-Scott, P. A. (1987). The Longitudinal Interval Follow-up Evaluation: a comprehensive method for assessing outcome in prospective longitudinal studies. *Archives of General Psychiatry*, *44*, 540–548.

Kendler, K. S., Aggen, S. H., Knudsen, G. P., Røysamb, E., Neale, M. C., & Reichborn-Kjeennerud, T. (2011). The structure of genetic and environmental risk factors for syndromal and subsyndromal common DSM-IV Axis I and Axis II disorders. *American Journal of Psychiatry*, *168*, 29–39.

Kendler, K. S., Prescott, C. A., Myers, J. M., & Neale, M. C. (2003). The structure of genetic and environmental risk factors for common psychiatric and substance use disorders in men and women. *Archives of General Psychiatry*, *60*, 929–937.

Kotov, R. (2016). The quantitative classification of mental illness: emerging solution to boundary problems. In E. Bromet (Ed.), *Long-term outcomes in psychopathology research: Rethinking the scientific agenda* (pp. 140–157). New York, NY: Oxford University Press.

Kotov, R., Krueger, R. F., Watson, D., Achenbach, T. M., Althoff, R. R., Bagby, R. M., et al. (2017). The Hierarchical Taxonomy of Psychopathology (HiTOP): a dimensional alternative to traditional nosologies. *Journal of Abnormal Psychology*, *126*(4), 454–477.

Kotov, R., Ruggero, C. J., Krueger, R. F., Watson, D., Yuan, Q., & Zimmerman, M. (2011). New dimensions in the quantitative classification of mental illness. *Archives of General Psychiatry*, *68*, 1003–1011.

Krueger, R. F., Caspi, A., Moffitt, T. E., & Silva, P. A. (1998). The structure and stability of common mental disorders (DSM-III-R): a longitudinal-epidemiological study. *Journal of Abnormal Psychology*, *107*, 216–227.

Krueger, R. F., Derringer, J., Markon, K. E., Watson, D., & Skodol, A. E. (2012). Initial construction of a maladptive personality trait model and inventory for DSM-5. *Psychological Medicine*, *42*, 1879–1890.

Krueger, R. F., Hicks, B. M., Patrick, C. J., Carlson, S. R., Iacono, W. G., & McGue, M. (2002). Etiologic connections among substance dependence, antisocial behavior and personality: modeling the externalizing spectrum. *Journal of Abnormal Psychology*, *111*, 411–424.

Krueger, R. F., & Markon, K. E. (2006). Reinterpreting comorbidity: a model-based approach to understanding and classifying psychopathology. *Annual Review of Clinical Psychology*, *2*, 111–133.

Krueger, R. F., Markon, K. E., Patrick, C. J., Benning, S. D., & Kramer, M. D. (2007). Linking antisocial behavior, substance use, and personality: an integrative quantitative model of the adult externalizing spectrum. *Journal of Abnormal Psychology*, *116*, 645–666.

Krueger, R. F., Markon, K. E., Patrick, C. J., & Iacono, W. G. (2005). Externalizing psychopathology in adulthood: a dimensional-spectrum conceptualization and its implications for DSM-V. *Journal of Abnormal Psychology*, *114*(4), 537–550.

Krueger, R. F., & South, S. C. (2009). Externalizing disorders: cluster 5 of the proposed metastructure for DSM-V and ICD-11. *Psychological Medicine*, *39*, 2061–2070.

Linehan, M. (1993). *Cognitive-behavioral treatment of borderline personality disorder*. New York: Guilford press.

Lynam, D. R., & Miller, J. D. (2015). Psychopathy from a basic trait perspective: the utility of a five-factor model approach. *Journal of Personality*, *83*(6), 611–626.

Markon, K. E. (2010). Modeling psychopathology structure: a symptom-level analysis of Axis I and II disorders. *Psychological Medicine*, *40*, 273–288.

McNulty, J. L., & Overstreet, S. R. (2014). Viewing the MMPI–2–RF structure through the Personality Psychopathology Five (PSY–5) lens. *Journal of Personality Assessment*, *96*, 151–157.

Miller, J. D., Lyman, D. R., Widiger, T. A., & Leukefeld, C. (2001). Personality disorders as extreme variants of common personality dimensions: can the five factor model adequately represent psychopathy? *Journal of Personality*, *69*(2), 253–276.

Miller, J. D., Lynam, D. R., McCain, J. L., Few, L. R., Crego, C., Widiger, T. A., et al. (2016). Thinking structurally about narcissism: an examination of the Five-Factor Narcissism Inventory and its components. *Journal of Personality Disorders*, *30*, 1–18.

Patrick, C. J., Foell, J., Venables, N. C., & Worthy, D. A. (2016). Substance use disorders as externalizing outcomes. In T. P. Beauchaine & S. P. Hinshaw (Eds.), *The Oxford handbook of externalizing spectrum disorders* (pp. 38–60). Oxford, England: Oxford University Press.

Pfohl, B., Blum, N., & Zimmerman, M. (1997). *Structured Interview for DSM–IV Personality (SIDP–IV)*. Washington, DC: American Psychiatric Press.

Poythress, N. G., Dembo, R., Wareham, J., & Greenbaum, P. E. (2006). Construct validity of the Youth Psychopathic Traits Inventory (YPI) and the Antisocial Process Screening Device (APSD) with justice-involved adolescents. *Criminal Justice and Behavior*, *33*, 26–55.

Røysamb, E., Kendler, K. S., Tambs, K., Orstavik, R. E., Neale, M. C., Aggen, S. H., et al. (2011). The joint structure of DSM-IV Axis I and Axis II disorders. *Journal of Abnormal Psychology*, *120*, 198–209.

Samuel, D. B., & Widiger, T. A. (2008). A meta-analytic review of the relationships between the five-factor model and DSM-IV-TR personality disorders: a facet level analysis. *Clinical Psychology Review*, *28*, 1326–1342.

Saulsman, L. M., & Page, A. C. (2004). The five-factor model and personality disorder empirical literature: a meta-analytic review. *Clinical Psychology Review*, *23*, 1055–1085.

Saunders, J. B., Aasland, O. G., Babor, T. F., De la Fuente, J. R., & Grant, M. (1993). Development of the alcohol use disorders identification test (AUDIT): WHO collaborative project on early detection of persons with harmful alcohol consumption-II. *Addiction*, *88*(6), 791–804.

Sellbom, M. (2016). Elucidating the validity of the externalizing spectrum of psychopathology in correctional, forensic, and community samples. *Journal of Abnormal Psychology*, *125*(8), 1027–1038.

Sellbom, M., Sansone, R. A., Songer, D. A., & Anderson, J. L. (2014). Convergence between DSM-5 Section II and Section III diagnostic criteria for borderline personality disorder. *The Australian and New Zealand Journal of Psychiatry*, *48*(4), 325–332.

Sheehan, D. V., & LeCrubier, Y. (2010). *The Mini International Neuropsychiatric Interview version 6.0 (MINI 6.0)*. Jacksonville, FL: Medical Outcomes System Inc.

Skeem, J. L., Polaschek, D. L., Patrick, C. J., & Lilienfeld, S. O. (2011). Psychopathic personality: bridging the gap between scientific evidence and public policy. *Psychological Science in the Public Interest*, *12*(3), 95–162.

Verona, E., Javdani, S., & Sprague, J. (2011). Comparing factor structures of adolescent psychopathology. *Psychological Assessment*, *23*, 545–551.

Widiger, T. A., & Lynam, D. R. (1998). Psychopathy and the five-factor model of personality. In T. Millon, E. Simonsen, M. Birket-Smith, & R. D. David (Eds.), *Psychopathy: Antisocial, criminal, and violent behavior* (pp. 171–187). New York: Guilford Press.

Wittchen, H. U., & Pfister, H. (1997). *DIA–X interviews (M–CIDI)*. Frankfurt, Germany: Swets & Zeitlinger.

Wright, A. G. C., & Simms, L. J. (2015). A metastructural model of mental disorders and pathological personality traits. *Psychological Medicine*, *45*, 2309–2319.

Young, S. E., Stallings, M. C., Corley, R. P., Krauter, K. S., & Hewitt, J. K. (2000). Genetic and environmental influences on behavioral disinhibition. *American Journal of Medical Genetics*, *96*, 684–695.

Antagonism and the DSM-5 alternative model of personality disorders

13

Nicole Cosentino, R. Michael Bagby†*
*Department of Psychology, University of Toronto Scarborough, Toronto, ON, Canada,
†Departments of Psychology and Psychiatry, University of Toronto, Toronto, ON, Canada

When preparations were made to revise the fourth, text-revised edition of the *Diagnostic and Statistical Manual for Mental Disorders* (4th ed., text rev.; *DSM-IV-TR*; American Psychiatric Association, 2000), long-standing debates about the *DSM*'s overall organization and the validity of its categorical diagnostic model for personality disorders (PDs) reemerged. The *DSM-IV-TR* maintained a multiaxial diagnostic system, which clustered those mental disorders thought to be most distressing and impairing (i.e., mood disorders, anxiety disorders, etc.) in Axis I, relegating personality disorders (PDs) to Axis II, and medical conditions and neurological disorders to Axis III. The final two axes, Axis IV and V, accounted for psychosocial factors and assessed global functioning, respectively. Overall, the multiaxial system of *DSM-IV-TR* was designed to measure all domains of well-being, a system which, some argued, could provide a more comprehensive, clinical picture of clients than any previously developed diagnostic system. When assessing the strengths and limitations of *DSM-IV-TR*, the utility and the structural validity of this multiaxial system was disputed and it was ultimately dispelled in the fifth edition of the *DSM* (5th ed.; *DSM-5*; American Psychiatric Association, 2013; Krueger, 2002). Rather than clustering disorders in distinct axes, all diagnoses were included along a single axis, thus removing artificial boundaries between types of psychopathology and reemphasizing that PDs were not qualitatively distinct from other mental health concerns.

In addition to determining where the PD section would appear in the *DSM*-5, a second key consideration was the validity of the categorical diagnostic system that was employed in *DSM-IV-TR* and considered for continued use in the fifth edition. Though this categorical system was in place for all mental disorders in the *DSM*, its continued use for the assessment and diagnosis of PDs was especially contentious. In *DSM-IV-TR*, 10 PDs were included in Axis II and separated into three clusters based on minimal empirical evidence (Cluster A—odd, bizarre, eccentric PDs; Cluster B—dramatic, erratic PDs; Cluster C—anxious, fearful PDs), much like the somewhat arbitrary clustering of disorders along axes in *DSM-IV* and *DSM-IV-TR* (Widiger, Simonsen, Krueger, Livesley, & Verheul, 2005). In *DSM-IV-TR*, each PD had its own set of diagnostic criteria and corresponding, polythetic clinical thresholds (American Psychiatric Association, 2000). Thus a client needed to endorse a subset

The Handbook of Antagonism. https://doi.org/10.1016/B978-0-12-814627-9.00013-X

of the total symptoms listed for a given PD to warrant diagnosis. Several criticisms of the categorical system were made since the introduction of *DSM-IV* (Clark, Livesley, & Morey, 1997; Cloninger, 2000; Tyrer, 2001; Widiger & Trull, 2007). There was limited empirical evidence to suggest that PDs did indeed represent distinct, latent categories nor was there sufficient research to demonstrate the validity of the clinical thresholds that had been identified for diagnosis (Krueger et al., 2011; Widiger et al., 2005). Furthermore, the diagnostic criteria for PDs exclusively captured maladaptive behaviors characteristic of each disorder, failing to assess the underlying personality factors that could be leading to these dysfunctional patterns. From an assessment perspective, the result was an incomplete diagnostic picture of each PD, a lack of discriminant validity between diagnoses, and extremely high rates of comorbidity, all of which made case conceptualization and treatment recommendation very difficult (Widiger & Trull, 2007).

In December 2004, the *DSM* planning committee hosted the "Dimensional Models of Personality Disorder: Etiology, Pathology, Phenomenology, and Treatment" conference discussing the merits of shifting from a categorical to a dimensional diagnostic system for PDs (Widiger et al., 2005). Before planning for *DSM-5* commenced, the implementation of a dimensional diagnostic system that could capture pathological features common across disorders in Axes I and II was discussed, a system that would once again emphasize that PDs were not unique from other forms of mental illness (Widiger & Simonsen, 2005). However, in December 2004, overwhelming support was shown for the construction and validation of a dimensional diagnostic model that was specific to PDs alone (Widiger et al., 2005). Initial efforts to develop a dimensional diagnostic system subsequently began in 2007 (Widiger et al., 2005). The hybrid categorical–dimensional diagnostic system for PDs that was eventually proposed for inclusion in *DSM-5* stipulated that diagnoses would be formulated based on (1) the assessment of self- and personality-functioning and (2) the measurement of pathological personality traits which, essentially, represent maladaptive poles of the five-factor model (FFM) of personality (Widiger & Simonsen, 2005).

One of the five personality domains proposed for inclusion in the alternative diagnostic model was antagonism, conceptualized as the low end of agreeableness and defined as, "behaviours that put the individual at odds with other people, including an exaggerated sense of self-importance and a concomitant expectation of special treatment, as well as a callous antipathy toward others, encompassing both an unawareness of others' needs and feelings and a readiness to use others in service of self-enhancement" (American Psychiatric Association, 2013, p. 780). This higher order domain is comprised of six underlying facets: manipulativeness, deceitfulness, grandiosity, attention-seeking, callousness, and hostility. In the proposed alternative diagnostic model, antagonism is implicated in the diagnosis of those PDs that formerly belonged to Cluster B: borderline personality disorder (BPD), narcissistic personality disorder (NPD), and antisocial personality disorder (ASPD). Elevated scores in antagonism, or in its select underlying facets, comprise the pathological personality profile for all three of these PDs. As such, antagonism represents an integral component of PDs that are primarily characterized by problems with emotion regulation, impulse control, and communal interpersonal problems (American Psychiatric Association, 2013; Wright, Scott, Stepp, Hallquist, & Pilkonis, 2015). Indeed, BPD, NPD, and ASPD are all associated with severe interpersonal deficits that result in marked impairment in relationships and daily functioning (Wright et al., 2015). Given the deleterious nature of these three PDs, they have become some of the most widely researched mental disorders to date. Antagonism consequently represents one of the most important of the five proposed personality domains in the alternative hybrid categorical–dimensional diagnostic model for PDs. The current chapter will provide a review of the development of the alternative personality model for *DSM-5* and will specifically focus on (1) the measurement of antagonism, and (2) the construct validity of antagonism.

Development of the dimensional diagnostic model for PDs in *DSM-5*

Proposed structures for the dimensional diagnostic model for PDs in DSM-5

While there was overwhelming support for the implementation of a dimensional diagnostic model for PDs during the planning stages of *DSM-5*, the actual dimensional model that was formally proposed and eventually published in *DSM-5*'s Section III: "Emerging Measures and Models" had not yet been decided upon. Indeed, several proposals for an alternative diagnostic model had been made long before the *DSM* planning committee's initial conference on the topic in December 2004. In a comprehensive review of the alternative models that had been proposed in the literature, Widiger and Simonsen (2005) noted 18 unique models published from 1987 (i.e., Eysenck, 1987) to 2004 (i.e., Shedler & Westen, 2004), demonstrating that efforts to produce an alternative diagnostic model had stretched across the course of nearly two decades. Though a variety of models had been produced, Widiger and Simonsen (2005) identified three common organizational structures specific to the models proposed for the PD section of *DSM-5*. The following section will provide a brief overview of each proposed structure.

Hybrid categorical–dimensional structure. The first structure identified by Widiger and Simonsen (2005) was essentially a hybrid categorical–dimensional model, much like the one that was eventually published in Section III of *DSM-5*. These proposed models (i.e., Oldham & Skodol, 2000; Tyrer & Johnson, 1996; Westen & Shedler, 2000) maintained the existing, latent PD categories found in Axis II of the *DSM-IV-TR* but replaced each PD's polythetic diagnostic criteria with dimensional criteria instead. Though this proposed structure bared a striking resemblance to that of *DSM-IV-TR*, maintenance of the PD diagnostic categories was considered beneficial rather than restrictive as retaining these categories would arguably bridge the gap between *DSM-IV-TR* and *DSM-5*, ensuring some degree of continuity between the two systems. This continuity could bolster the new dimensional system's clinical utility, as it was anticipated that clinicians would be less hesitant to adopt a new diagnostic system if it had some amount of overlap with the previous one. Despite its strengths, the hybrid categorical–dimensional structure was criticized for its failure to capture the underlying reasons for the high rates of comorbidity observed across PDs, a critical issue with the latent PD categories in *DSM-IV-TR*.

Maladaptive personality dimensions. Widiger and Simonsen (2005) hypothesized that PDs commonly occur together because they share common maladaptive personality features. The second structure identified by Widiger and Simonsen (2005) captured this underlying reason for high rates of comorbidity. These models eliminated the discrete diagnostic PD categories and instead advocated that individuals should be assessed along a series of maladaptive personality dimensions (i.e., Clark, 1993; Harkness & McNulty, 1994; Livesley, 2003; Shedler & Westen, 2004). The aim would be to establish a sense of coherence across PDs as well as to capture their shared features.

Adaptive and maladaptive personality trait dimensions. Though maladaptive personality functioning is inherent to PDs, individuals in the community can exhibit or experience PD symptomatology without meeting clinical threshold for a PD diagnosis (Livesley, 2003; Widiger & Sanderson, 1995). As such, one should be able to observe subclinical endorsement of maladaptive personality traits in the general population, just as one would be able to observe normal personality features as well. The third proposed structure attempted to capture this variability in pathological personality features. Four of the models identified by Widiger and Simonsen (2005) proposed dimensional diagnostic systems in which the personality dimensions integrated both adaptive and maladaptive personality features. These bipolar dimensions would include an adaptive pole, representing normal personality, and a maladaptive pole, representing pathological personality, and thus capturing both the strengths and weaknesses within a client (Cloninger, 2000; Costa & McCrae, 1992; Eysenck, 1987; Millon et al., 1996; Tellegen & Waller, 1987; Tyrer, 2000; Wiggins, 2003). The advantage to this structure is that it could capture normal variance in human personality. Additionally, for those who do demonstrate evidence of a PD, notation of their strengths could potentially buffer against internalized stigma.

Summary. As planning for *DSM-5* commenced, a survey of proposed dimensional models for the revised PD section was undertaken. In the literature, the three most commonly described models were (1) a hybrid categorical–dimensional model, (2) a purely dimensional model that would only involve measuring maladaptive personality features, and (3) a purely dimensional model that would assess adaptive and maladaptive personality features along bipolar dimensions. While varied models had indeed been suggested, all three of the structures noted by Widiger and Simonsen (2005) proposed the use of dimensional personality assessment to aid in diagnosis and generally converged on use of either the five-factor model of personality (FFM; Costa & McCrae, 1992) or a model of personality that had been derived from the FFM, for example, the Personality Psychopathology Five (PSY-5; Harkness & McNulty, 1994). The following section will provide a brief overview of the FFM, its relationship to PDs, and the development of the alternative personality model for eventual inclusion in the PD section of *DSM-5*.

The alternative personality model for DSM-5

The five-factor model of personality and its role in PDs

The FFM is a hierarchical personality model comprised of five higher order personality domains (neuroticism, extraversion, agreeableness, conscientiousness, and openness to experience), each of which have six lower order facets (Costa & McCrae, 1992). With the exception of neuroticism and its underlying facets, the domain and facet names of the FFM reflect adaptive qualities. Indeed, the FFM is intended to serve as a model of normative personality. However, FFM traits can be observed across both clinical and nonclinical samples, suggesting that personality is not qualitatively different in the presence or absence of pathology (O'Connor, 2002). Each of the five personality dimensions is bipolar indicating both a desirable and undesirable degree to which any one of the traits can be endorsed. For example, someone who endorses very high levels of agreeableness may be overly accommodating, to the point that he or she fails to consider his or her own needs, or is easily manipulated by other people. In comparison, someone who endorses very low levels of agreeableness is likely to show little concern for others, demonstrate antagonistic tendencies, and experience interpersonal dysfunction as a result. So, while agreeableness conceptually appears to be a wholly adaptive trait, the possibility for dysfunction becomes strikingly apparent when considering the consequences of its high or low endorsement. As such, it has been argued that pathology can be modeled in terms of excesses and/or deficits in these five core personality domains even though they were developed to capture normative personality features (see e.g., O'Connor & Dyce, 2001).

To provide a comprehensive summary of the extensive research examining the relationship between the FFM and PDs, Saulsman and Page (2004) performed a meta-analysis of 12 studies conducted with both clinical and nonclinical samples that included measures of the five factors and measures of PD symptomatology. Results indicated that all FFM domains were significantly associated with PDs, apart from openness to experience. Additionally, each PD maintained a distinct FFM profile, meaning there were predictable sets of trait endorsements observed for each of the diagnoses which could, potentially, aid in assessment and case conceptualization. While four of the five domains were associated with PDs, neuroticism, extraversion, and agreeableness had the most number of significant correlations across the PDs and the largest weighted mean effect sizes. As such, these three domains seemingly represent the core personality characteristics implicated in personality pathology. Neuroticism was positively associated with PDs characterized by emotional distress (i.e., BPD) while agreeableness was negatively associated with those PDs characterized by severe interpersonal deficits (i.e., paranoid PD, ASPD, BPD, NPD). Unlike neuroticism and agreeableness, which both showed very consistent directionality in their correlations, extraversion demonstrated bidirectionality. Positive associations with extraversion were observed among those PDs characterized by charm and charisma (i.e., NPD, histrionic PD) and negative associations were observed among PDs characterized by introversion or social apathy (i.e., schizoid PD, schizotypal PD). Samuel and Widiger (2008) performed a meta-analysis of 16 studies whose results not only replicated the associations observed by Saulsman and Page (2004) but also demonstrated significant relationships between the facets of these four personality domains and the PD diagnostic categories. Several important clinical implications can be drawn from these two meta-analyses. First, each PD has a unique set of associated personality traits, which speaks to the utility of potentially retaining the categorical PD labels but using dimensional personality profiles for diagnosis instead of behavioral checklists. Second, the number of correlations between PDs and neuroticism, agreeableness, and extraversion as well as the relatively consistent direction of these effects highlights common features of personality pathology that could be important targets of psychotherapy in the future (Saulsman & Page, 2004). Third, the suspected role of agreeableness, or lack thereof, in many of the PDs suggested antagonism's importance in any dimensional model to be developed for *DSM-5*.

Development of the Personality Inventory for DSM-5 (PID-5; Krueger, Derringer, Markon, Watson, & Skodol, 2012)

In their comprehensive literature review, Widiger and Simonsen (2005) identified a common set of bipolar trait dimensions observed in the proposed PD models for *DSM-5* that were loosely based on the FFM: (1) extroversion versus introversion, (2) antagonism versus compliance, (3) constraint versus impulsivity, and (4) negative affect versus emotional stability. A fifth possible dimension that approximated openness to experience, and which Widiger and Simonsen (2005) termed unconventionality versus closedness to experience, was also noted, though less consistently observed across the models. When Krueger et al. (2012) developed the alternative personality model for *DSM-5* and its accompanying measure, the *Personality Inventory for DSM-5* (PID-5), the a priori personality domains identified by the authors were based on those domains noted by Widiger and Simonsen (2005). To develop the PID-5, an initial set of 296 personality items were written by the *DSM-5* Personality and PD Work Group to describe 37 facets that had been generated based on models of maladaptive personality found in the literature. These 37 facets measured by 296 items were culled to 25 facets measured by 220 items based on results from item-level, within-domain exploratory factor analyses. These items demonstrated good fit with a five-factor model that seemed to capture maladaptive personality. The five factors included negative affect, detachment, antagonism, disinhibition, and psychoticism. While the PID-5 domains are very similar to the FFM in content, in terms of valence, they are closer to Harkness and McNulty's (1994) Personality Psychopathology Five (PSY-5), another five-factor model of pathological personality. The PID-5 has been validated in undergraduate and clinical adult samples and is intended to measure personality dimensionally for the diagnosis of the seven PDs retained in the alternative hybrid categorical–dimensional model in *DSM-5* Section III (Hopwood, Thomas, Markon, Wright, & Krueger, 2012; Quilty, Ayearst, Chmieleski, Pollock, & Bagby, 2013).

Antagonism in the alternative personality model for DSM-5

During development of the PID-5, the initial facets that were selected for antagonism prior to the first round of data collection included manipulativeness, deceitfulness, grandiosity, attention-seeking, and callousness, all of which are measured by the PID-5 and all of which are listed as facets of antagonism in *DSM-5* Section III (Krueger et al., 2012). During the development of the PID-5, aggression was included as a facet of antagonism rather than hostility as hostility was initially considered to be a facet of negative affectivity alone. After analyzing the second round of data and observing its poor fit, aggression was dropped as a personality facet altogether and hostility replaced it within the antagonism domain. As such, hostility is included as a facet of both the negative affectivity and antagonism domains, indicating some degree of conceptual overlap between these two domains of personality.

Krueger et al. (2012) assessed the fit of items to each facet using item response theory (IRT). Test information curves (TICs) from the final 25 facets indicated adequate reliability of all five antagonism facets. The items loading on each facet retained a single factor structure and the facets within antagonism were moderately intercorrelated, indicating good construct validity. However, some facets of antagonism showed a greater number of strong within-domain intercorrelations ($r \geq .50$) compared to the others across three rounds of data analysis. Deceitfulness, callousness, and attention-seeking had the greatest number of strong within-domain intercorrelations. Not only were deceitfulness and callousness strongly correlated with one another, but they showed a strong relationship with two of the same facets of antagonism—grandiosity and hostility—leading one to potentially question whether the PID-5 items for deceitfulness and callousness are possibly measuring the same construct despite the conceptual differences between the two personality traits. Deceitfulness and callousness also demonstrated strong, positive correlations with many other facets across the other four domains of the alternative personality model for DSM-5. They maintained 8 and 11 strong correlations, respectively, with facets outside of antagonism. Hostility also maintained 9 strong correlations with facets outside of the domain and, beyond that, no strong correlations with the other facets of antagonism. Moreover, these correlated facets had no clear theoretical relationship to one another. Overall, this pattern of correlational findings strongly suggested that deceitfulness and callousness are at the core of antagonism however hostility, which is shared with negative affectivity, may be less associated with this construct.

Though the development of the PID-5 represented a substantial step toward the implementation of a dimensional diagnostic system, Krueger et al. (2012) recognized that further validation was required before this measure could be administered in clinical settings. Quilty et al. (2013) tested the factor structure and validity of the PID-5 in a sample of 201 outpatients who had participated in the *DSM-5* Field Trial and who had completed the PID-5 as part of their clinical assessment. To evaluate the PID-5's factor structure, parallel and MAP analyses were run. Parallel analyses supported a one-factor solution for all facet scales of antagonism. This finding was replicated with MAP tests for all facets but hostility. Despite this inconsistency between parallel and

MAP analyses, the authors conclude that each facet of antagonism represents a distinct factor, thus confirming the conclusion drawn in Krueger et al.'s (2012) initial development paper. Unlike in Krueger et al. (2012)'s study, Quilty et al. (2013) found that the antagonism facets were all strongly intercorrelated. The antagonism facets were also significantly correlated across domains and so, while one could interpret this as poor discriminant validity, the authors attributed this finding to the shared contribution of each domain to personality pathology and distress in general.

Summary. Initial efforts to develop and validate the PID-5, undertaken by Krueger et al. (2012) and Quilty et al. (2013), produced evidence to suggest that antagonism represents its own distinct personality construct that is also implicated in diffuse pathological processes given its strong associations with the other four personality domains of the PID-5. The following section will provide an overview of the convergent and discriminant validity of antagonism.

Convergent and discriminant validity of PID-5 antagonism

Normative personality and PID-5 antagonism

Revised NEO Personality Inventory (NEO-PI-R; Costa & McCrae, 1992**).** Quilty et al. (2013) investigated the convergent validity of antagonism and the other PID-5 domains by evaluating associations between the domains and facets of the PID-5 and the domains of the Revised NEO Personality Inventory (NEO-PI-R; Costa & McCrae, 1992), a self-report measure of the FFM. As expected, antagonism was negatively correlated with agreeableness. This finding was replicated at the facet level of antagonism as well. The facets also showed significant correlations with many other FFM domains that were not theoretically connected. Callousness, deceitfulness, hostility, and attention-seeking were positively correlated with neuroticism. Extraversion was negatively associated with callousness and hostility but positively associated with attention-seeking. Finally, conscientiousness was negatively associated with callousness, deceitfulness, attention-seeking, and manipulativeness. Overall, the authors argue that these findings cast some doubt on the discriminant validity of antagonism and the other PID-5 domains. The diffuse intercorrelation of facets across domains is consistent with Saulsman and Page's (2004) observation that agreeableness is negatively correlated with a number of PDs and, as such, is an underlying factor in personality pathology and accompanying distress generally, rather than involved in specific pathogenic processes.

Pathological personality and PID-5 antagonism

Personality Psychopathology-Five (PSY-5; Harkness & McNulty, 1994, 2007**).** The PSY-5 is frequently described as a pathological variant of the FFM. Much like the FFM, it encompasses both adaptive and maladaptive personality traits and is comprised of five domains of personality measured using the Minnesota Multi-Phasic Personality Inventory (MMPI-2-RF; Ben-Porath & Tellegen, 2008), one of the most widely used and comprehensive clinical screening measures available. These domains include negative emotionality/neuroticism (NEGE), introversion/low positive emotionality (INTR), aggressiveness (AGGR), disconstraint (DISC), and psychoticism (PSYC) (Harkness & McNulty, 1994, 2007). The PID-5 and PSY-5 are very similar insofar as both capture aspects of personality pathology. Moreover, the domains of the PID-5 quite clearly parallel the domains of the PSY-5 in terms of content as both are derived from the FFM. Indeed, the PID-5's antagonism domain is very similar, conceptually, to the PSY-5's aggressiveness domain (Anderson et al., 2012). Much like antagonism, aggressiveness captures grandiosity, callousness, and some elements of manipulativeness (Anderson et al., 2012; Harkness & McNulty, 1994). However, unlike antagonism, aggressiveness emphasizes overall interpersonal dominance, which the PID-5's antagonism domain implies but neither clearly nor explicitly captures (Anderson et al., 2012; Harkness & McNulty, 1994). Despite similarity in content across the PID-5 and PSY-5 domains, until recently there has been limited empirical evidence to demonstrate convergence across the two measures. Anderson et al. (2012) administered the PID-5 and the MMPI-2-RF to a sample of undergraduates and assessed the convergent and discriminant validity between the two measures. As expected, antagonism domain and facet subscale scores were both highly correlated with scores on the aggression (AGG-r) scale of the MMPI-2-RF. However, unexpectedly, antagonism domain and facet subscale scores were also highly correlated with scores on the disconstraint (DISC-r) scale, a domain which captures impulsivity and sensation-seeking and more closely matches the PID-5's disinhibition domain. Indeed, PID-5 disinhibition and DISC-r are highly correlated. Manipulativeness and grandiosity exhibited the strongest correlations with AGG-r while deceitfulness, callousness, and attention-seeking demonstrated the strongest correlations with the DISC-r scores. Regression analyses further demonstrated that AGG-r and DISC-r accounted for equal amounts of variance in antagonism scores. Overall, Anderson et al. (2012) argue that antagonism likely encompasses elements of disinhibition as well as aggression. This finding either indicates that antagonism, as a construct, needs to be expanded within the DSM's current dimensional framework to include relevant aspects of disinhibition or, alternatively, that the five factors of the PID-5 and PSY-5 do not perfectly map on to one another but may instead maintain a higher order factor structure instead relevant to personality pathology generally.

Personality Assessment Inventory (PAI; Morey, 1991). The PAI is another omnibus measure of personality that is commonly administered as an alternative to the MMPI-2-RF during clinical assessment. In addition to scales that assess interpersonal functioning, pathology, and treatment outcome predictors, the PAI also indexes normal personality using three higher order domains: internalizing, externalizing, and social dominance scales. To examine the convergent validity between the PID-5 and PAI scales, Hopwood et al. (2012) administered the PID-5 and PAI to a sample of undergraduates and found a diffuse number of correlations among the facets of antagonism and those of the PAI. Manipulativeness and deceitfulness were most strongly correlated with egocentricity, one of the facets of the PAI's antisocial features scale. In comparison, hostility was most strongly correlated with affective instability, a facet of the PAI's borderline features scale. Callousness maintained diffuse and strong correlations with the facets from both the antisocial features and aggression scales, demonstrating the strongest relationship with the physical aggression subscale. However, while manipulativeness, deceitfulness, hostility, and callousness demonstrated convergent validity, grandiosity and attention-seeking maintained only weak relationships to the PAI's facet subscales, with the exception of one strong correlation shared with the PAI's grandiosity subscale. Overall, correlational results suggest the overall convergence between PID-5 antagonism and theoretically relevant personality domains and pathogenic processes as measured by the PAI. Unlike comparisons to the PSY-5, the role of disinhibition processes appears to be less pronounced.

Hopwood et al. (2013) additionally ran a conjoint factor analysis using the subscales from both the PAI and PID-5 and found support for a seven-factor structure. For the purposes of this chapter, only those factors relevant to antagonism will be discussed. Within this model of personality and psychopathology, the antagonism subscales generally loaded on to a single factor, which also included the PAI's manic grandiosity subscale. This factor was appropriately labeled "antagonism." PID-5 risk-taking and impulsiveness as well as the PAI scales of self-harm and sensation-seeking all loaded on to a single factor labeled "impulsivity." That facets of antagonism did not load on this impulsivity factor provides further evidence to disconfirm Anderson et al.'s (2012) finding that disinhibition accounts for half of the variance in antagonism scores. Scales from both the PID-5 and the PAI related to hostility and aggression loaded on to a single factor that was labeled "aggression." Finally, PID-5 rigid perfectionism loaded on to the same factor as PAI aggression, dominance, and mania resulting in a factor labeled "assertiveness" and which was thought to reflect a desire for interpersonal dominance. Hopwood et al. (2013) argue that this seven-factor structure indicates that normative personality and pathological personality features can have clinical utility when integrated.

Conclusion

Despite addressing many of the reported shortcomings of the categorical diagnostic model for PDs in *DSM-IV-TR*, the alternative diagnostic model was thought to require further validity research before it could replace the existing categorical system. As such, it was not implemented in *DSM-5* but rather published in *DSM-5*'s Section III: "Emerging Measures and Models" as a means of promoting further research that could legitimize the model and lead to its implementation in future editions of the *DSM*. With this effort to validate the overall system, comes the need to clearly establish the construct validity of each identified personality domain, with antagonism having special importance given its clear relationship to so many of the PDs retained in Section III. Antagonism generally showed a strong pattern of within-domain intercorrelations across studies indicating strong construct validity. Convergence was also observed with the NEO-PI-R, the PSY-5, and the PAI (Anderson et al., 2012; Hopwood et al., 2013; Quilty et al., 2013). Antagonism, along with the other domains of the PID-5, has been shown to covary with normal personality. For instance, Hopwood et al. (2013) demonstrated that normal and abnormal personality traits together form a higher order personality structure. So, while the new proposed dimensional personality model of *DSM-5* wholly focuses on the pathological poles of personality, revisions may involve reworking the structure of the model to account for this covariation between normal and abnormal personality features.

References

American Psychiatric Association. (2000). *Diagnostic and statistical manual of mental disorders: DSM-IV-TR*. Washington, DC: American Psychiatric Association.

American Psychiatric Association. (2013). *Diagnostic and statistical manual of mental disorders* (5th ed.). Washington, DC: American Psychiatric Association.

Anderson, J. L., Sellbom, M., Bagby, R. M., Quilty, L. C., Veltri, C. O. C., Markon, K. E., et al. (2012). On the convergence between PSY-5 domains and PID-5 domains and facets: implications for assessment of *DSM-5* personality traits. *Assessment*, *20*(3), 286–294. https://doi.org/10.1177/1073191112471141.

Ben-Porath, Y. S., & Tellegen, A. (2008). *Minnesota Multiphasic Personality Inventory-2 Restructured Form: Manual for administration, scoring, and interpretation*. Minneapolis: University of Minnesota Press.

Clark, L. A. (1993). *Schedule for Nonadaptive and Adaptive Personality (SNAP-2)*. Minneapolis, MN: University of Minnesota Press.

Clark, L. A., Livesley, W. J., & Morey, L. (1997). Personality disorder assessment: the challenge of construct validity. *Journal of Personality Disorders*, *11*, 205–231.

Cloninger, C. R. (2000). A practical way to diagnosis personality disorders: a proposal. *Journal of Personality Disorders*, *14*, 99–108.

Costa, P. T., & McCrae, R. R. (1992). *Revised NEO Personality Inventory (NEO-PI-R) and NEO Five-Factor Inventory (NEO-FFI) professional manual*. Odessa, FL: Psychological Assessment Resources.

Eysenck, H. J. (1987). The definition of personality disorders and the criteria appropriate for their description. *Journal of Personality Disorders*, *1*, 211–219.

Harkness, A. R., & McNulty, J. L. (1994). The personality psychopathology five (PSY-5): Issue from the pages of a diagnostic manual instead of a dictionary. In S. Strack & M. Lorr (Eds.), *Differentiating normal and abnormal personality* (pp. 291–315). New York: Springer.

Harkness, A. R., & McNulty, J. L. (2007). Restructured versions of the MMPI-2 Personality Psychopathology Five (PSY-5) Scales. *Paper presented at the meeting of the*. San Francisco, CA: American Psychological Association.

Hopwood, C. J., Thomas, K. M., Markon, K. E., Wright, A. G. C., & Krueger, R. F. (2012). *DSM-5* personality traits and *DSM-IV* personality disorders. *Journal of Abnormal Psychology*, *121*(2), 424–432. https://doi.org/10.1037/a0026656.

Hopwood, C. J., Wright, A. G. C., Krueger, R. F., Schade, N., Markon, K. E., & Morey, L. C. (2013). *DSM-5* pathological personality traits and the personality assessment inventory. *Assessment*, *20*(3), 269–285. https://doi.org/10.1177/1073191113486286.

Krueger, R. F. (2002). Psychometric perspectives on comorbidity. In J. E. Helzer & J. J. Hudziak (Eds.), *Defining psychopathology in the 21st century: DSM-V and beyond* (pp. 41–54). Washington, DC: American Psychiatric Publishing.

Krueger, R. F., Derringer, J., Markon, K. E., Watson, D., & Skodol, A. E. (2012). Initial construction of a maladaptive personality trait model and inventory for *DSM-5*. *Psychological Medicine*, *42*, 1879–1890. https://doi.org/10.1017/S0033291711002674.

Krueger, R. F., Eaton, N. R., Clark, L. A., Watson, D., Markon, K. E., Derringer, J., et al. (2011). Deriving an empirical structure of personality pathology for *DSM-5*. *Journal of Personality Disorders*, *25*(2), 170–191.

Livesley, W. J. (2003). Diagnostic dilemmas in classifying personality disorder. In K. A. Phillips, M. B. First, & H. A. Pincus (Eds.), *Advancing DSM: Dilemmas in psychiatric diagnosis* (pp. 153–190). Washington, DC: American Psychiatric Association.

Millon, T., Davis, R. D., Millon, C. M., Wenger, A. W., Van Zuilen, M. H., Fuchs, M., et al. (1996). *Disorders of personality. DSM-V and beyond.* New York: John Wiley & Sons.

Morey, L. C. (1991). *Personality Assessment Inventory professional manual.* Odessa, FL: Psychological Assessment Resources.

O'Connor, B. P. (2002). The search for dimensional structure differences between normality and abnormality: A statistical review of published data on personality and psychopathology. *Journal of Personality and Social Psychology*, *83*(4), 962–982.

O'Connor, B. P., & Dyce, J. A. (2001). Rigid and extreme: A geometric representation of personality disorders in five-factor model space. *Journal of Personality and Social Psychology*, *81*(6), 1119–1130.

Oldham, J. M., & Skodol, A. E. (2000). Charting the future of Axis II. *Journal of Personality Disorders*, *14*, 17–29.

Quilty, L. C., Ayearst, L., Chmieleski, M., Pollock, B. G., & Bagby, R. M. (2013). The psychometric properties of the Personality Inventory for *DSM-5* in an APA *DSM-5* field trial sample. *Assessment*, *20*(3), 362–369. https://doi.org/10.1177/1073191113486183.

Samuel, D. B., & Widiger, T. A. (2008). A meta-analytic review of the relationships between the five-factor model and *DSM-IV-TR* personality disorders: a facet level analysis. *Clinical Psychology Review*, *28*, 1326–1342. https://doi.org/10.1016/j.cpr.2008.07.002.

Saulsman, L. M., & Page, A. C. (2004). The five-factor model and personality disorder empirical literature: a meta-analytic review. *Clinical Psychology Review*, *23*, 1055–1085.

Shedler, J., & Westen, D. (2004). Refining *DSM-IV* personality disorder diagnosis: integrating science and practice. *American Journal of Psychiatry*, *148*, 1647–1658.

Tellegen, A., & Waller, N. G. (1987). *Exploring personality through test construction: Development of the Multidimensional Personality Questionnaire.* Minneapolis, MN. Unpublished manuscript.

Tyrer, P. (Ed.), (2000). *Personality disorder: Diagnosis, management, and course.* (2nd ed.). London: Arnold.

Tyrer, P. (2001). Personality disorder. *British Journal of Psychiatry*, *179*, 81–84.

Tyrer, P., & Johnson, T. (1996). Establishing the severity of personality disorder. *American Journal of Psychiatry*, *153*, 1593–1597.

Westen, D., & Shedler, J. (2000). A prototype matching approach to diagnosing personality disorders: toward *DSM-V*. *Journal of Personality Disorders*, *14*, 109–126.

Widiger, T. A., & Sanderson, C. J. (1995). Towards a dimensional model of personality disorders in DSM-IV and DSM-V. In W. J. Livesley (Ed.), *The DSM-IV personality disorders* (pp. 433–458). New York: Guilford Press.

Widiger, T. A., & Simonsen, E. (2005). Alternative dimensional models of personality disorder: finding a common ground. *Journal of Personality Disorders*, *19*(2), 110–130.

Widiger, T. A., Simonsen, E., Krueger, R., Livesley, J., & Verheul, R. (2005). Personality disorder research agenda for DSM-V. *Journal of Personality Disorders*, *19*(3), 315–338. https://doi.org/10.1521/pedi.2005.19.3.315.

Widiger, T. A., & Trull, T. J. (2007). Plate tectonics in the classification of personality disorder: shifting to a dimensional model. *American Psychologist*, *62*(2), 71–83. https://doi.org/10.1037/0003-066X.62.2.71.

Wiggins, J. S. (2003). *Paradigms of personality assessment*. New York: Guilford Press.
Wright, A. G. C., Scott, L. N., Stepp, S. D., Hallquist, M. N., & Pilkonis, P. A. (2015). Personality pathology and interpersonal problem stability. *Journal of Personality Disorders*, *29* (5), 684–706.

Antagonism in psychopathy

14

David D. Vachon
Department of Psychology, McGill University, Montreal, QC, Canada

Despite long-standing and vigorous debate regarding the "core" components of psychopathy, every model and measure of psychopathy is replete with antagonism. In this chapter, I demonstrate the centrality and near sufficiency of antagonism in capturing psychopathy using seven lines of evidence. First, I demonstrate the conceptual importance of antagonism using classic descriptions of psychopathy (**description evidence**). Second, I present evidence from criterion-translation approaches, which convert individual psychopathy criteria into the language of the Five-Factor Model (FFM) of personality (**translation evidence**). Third, I show that meta-analytic correlations between antagonism and psychopathy are larger than those between antagonism and all other personality disorders, and larger than those between psychopathy and all other basic traits (**empirical evidence**). Fourth, I present expert consensus data regarding the importance of antagonism in psychopathy (**consensus evidence**). Fifth, I show that the full trait profile of antagonism—including its primary and secondary loadings on facet traits from other FFM domains—is more similar to the empirical and consensus trait profiles of psychopathy than to those of other prototypical personality disorders (**similarity evidence**). Sixth, I present factor analytic evidence showing that antagonism is a central factor extracted from various measures of psychopathy (**factor evidence**). And seventh, I show that antagonism and psychopathy have a similar pattern of external correlates, and that antagonism is nearly sufficient to capture these correlates (**nomological evidence**). Before presenting these seven lines of evidence, however, I describe and differentiate two major models of psychopathy that diverge in their conception, referred to here as *antisocial psychopathy* and *bold psychopathy*.

Two conceptions of psychopathy

Antisocial psychopathy

Antisocial psychopathy is what most measures of psychopathy capture and what most of the psychopathy literature reflects. The standardized measurement of this construct began with Hare's Psychopathy Checklist (PCL; Hare & Frazelle, 1980), a preliminary research rating scale developed for the assessment of psychopathy in criminal populations. The PCL was largely influenced by the clinical observations of Hervey Cleckley, who described the features of psychopathy in his book, *The Mask of Sanity* (Cleckley, 1941). Although psychopathy had been assessed via clinical judgment for decades before the development of the PCL, the PCL was developed because no

The Handbook of Antagonism. https://doi.org/10.1016/B978-0-12-814627-9.00014-1

reliable and valid measure to assess psychopathy existed at the time, because clinical decisions were being made with little to no consideration for personality and behavioral traits, and because research assessment scales of psychopathy were not explicitly connected to the clinical construct (Brazil & Forth, 2018).

The PCL was later replaced by the widely used Psychopathy Checklist—Revised (PCL-R; Hare, 1991, 2003), which spawned a family of measures, including a screening version (Psychopathy Checklist: Screening Version, PCL:SV; Hart, Cox, & Hare, 1995), a youth version (Psychopathy Checklist: Youth Version, PCL:YV; Forth, Kosson, & Hare, 2003), and self-report versions for use in adults (Self-Report Psychopathy Scale, SRP-III; Paulhus, Neumann, & Hare, in press) and youth (Antisocial Process Screening Device, APSD; Frick & Hare, 2001). Outside the PCL family of measures, other scales were also created to measure antisocial psychopathy in adults and youth, including the Levenson Self-Report Psychopathy Scale (LSRP; Levenson, Kiehl, & Fitzpatrick, 1995), Psychopathy Resemblance Index (PRI; Miller, Lynam, Widiger, & Leukefeld, 2001), Elemental Psychopathy Assessment (EPA; Lynam et al., 2011), Child Psychopathy Scale (CPS; Lynam, 1997), and Youth Psychopathic Traits Inventory (YPI; Andershed, Kerr, Stattin, & Levander, 2002).

Numerous factor analyses of these antisocial psychopathy measures yield two related factors, including an interpersonal-affective factor (Factor 1, or F1) and an impulsive-antisocial factor (Factor 2 or F2; Hare et al., 1990). Subsequent analyses further divide each factor into two facets (e.g., Hare & Neumann, 2008), with F1 splitting into an Interpersonal facet (deception, manipulation, and superficial charm) and an Affective facet (low empathy and lack of remorse), and F2 splitting into a Lifestyle facet (recklessness and impulsivity), and an Antisocial facet (overt antisociality and disobedience).

The similarities between antisocial psychopathy and another personality disorder, Antisocial Personality Disorder (APD), are strong. For example, in the Diagnostic and Statistical Manual of Mental Disorders (DSM-5; American Psychiatric Association, 2013), APD is overtly linked to psychopathy, "The essential feature of APD is a pervasive pattern of disregard, and violation of, the rights of others…This pattern has also been referred to as psychopathy." Additionally, the explicit diagnostic criterion set for APD represents all four facets of antisocial psychopathy: the Interpersonal facet is represented by APD criterion A2 (lying, deception, and manipulation); the Affective facet is represented by APD criterion A7 (lack of remorse); the Lifestyle facet is represented by APD criterion A5 (reckless disregard for safety) and criterion A3 (impulsivity); and the Antisocial facet is represented by APD criterion A1 (failure to obey laws and norms, performing acts that are grounds for arrest), criterion A6 (consistent irresponsibility), and criterion C (conduct disorder present before age 15). Although psychopathic traits such as low empathy and superficial charm are missing from the APD criteria, the DSM-5 text description for APD includes these criteria, "Individuals with APD frequently lack empathy…and may display a glib, superficial charm" (p. 660).

Instantiating these additional characteristics directly into the criteria for APD would make it virtually indistinguishable from antisocial psychopathy; arguments for their continued divergence would be difficult to justify empirically. In fact, some have already called for their amalgamation, arguing that psychopathy and APD are versions of the same disorder that only grew apart due to historical reasons (Lynam & Vachon, 2012). For a fleeting moment, during an early iteration of the DSM-5, the members of the personality disorder committee did just that, renaming APD as "APD/psychopathy." However, this merger was ultimately abandoned, presumably because this conception disregarded bold psychopathy traits and invalidated models and measures that include them.

In any case, even without harmonized criteria between antisocial psychopathy and APD, their FFM profiles are remarkably similar across the domains and facets of the Revised NEO Personality Inventory (NEO PI-R; Costa & McCrae, 1992). Fig. 1 displays the domain and facet trait profile for meta-psychopathy and meta-APD (Decuyper, De Pauw, De Fruyt, De Bolle, & De Clercq, 2009). At the domain level (top panel), meta-psychopathy and meta-APD profiles are highly correlated (double-entry ICC = 0.92), with meta-psychopathy showing stronger correlations with antagonism. At the facet level (bottom panel), both meta-profiles remain highly correlated (double-entry ICC = 0.92), and meta-psychopathy remains more strongly related to each of the antagonism facets than meta-APD. Because meta-psychopathy is derived from a range of studies, 20% of which use measures of bold psychopathy, excluding these studies increases the correspondence between antisocial psychopathy and APD even further (double-entry ICC increases from 0.92 to 0.97).

Bold psychopathy

Bold psychopathy models broaden the conceptualization of psychopathy to include other constructs, such as fearlessness (Lilienfeld & Andrews, 1996), interpersonal dominance (Patrick, Fowles, & Krueger, 2009), and emotional invulnerability (Lynam et al., 2011). This new conception of bold psychopathy is clearly different from antisocial psychopathy and APD. If the goal is to differentiate psychopathy and APD rather than unify them, then the addition of bold traits to psychopathy is useful. Moreover, if psychopathy is characterized as the absence of internal controls, then the addition of bold traits is attractive because it includes features such as low fear and low social inhibition. A recent example of this approach comes from the Triarchic Model of Personality, which proposes that psychopathy encompasses three constructs, labeled *meanness*, *disinhibition*, and *boldness* (Patrick et al., 2009). Although meanness and disinhibition are well aligned with models of antisocial psychopathy, boldness diverges markedly and represents a proclivity toward confidence, social assertiveness, emotional resiliency, and adventurousness.

Proponents of the Triarchic model argue that the boldness aspect of their model reemphasizes a lost feature of psychopathy that was originally a part of Cleckley's seminal conception (i.e., ostensible charm and social poise, absence of nervousness, and low suicide risk). They also cite other key referents for boldness, including theories of low fear and anxiety (e.g., Fowles & Dindo, 2009; Lykken, 1995), the Fearless Dominance factor of the PPI (Lilienfeld & Andrews, 1996), and various links to neurobiology (Patrick & Drislane, 2014). Critics, however, have used meta-analytic

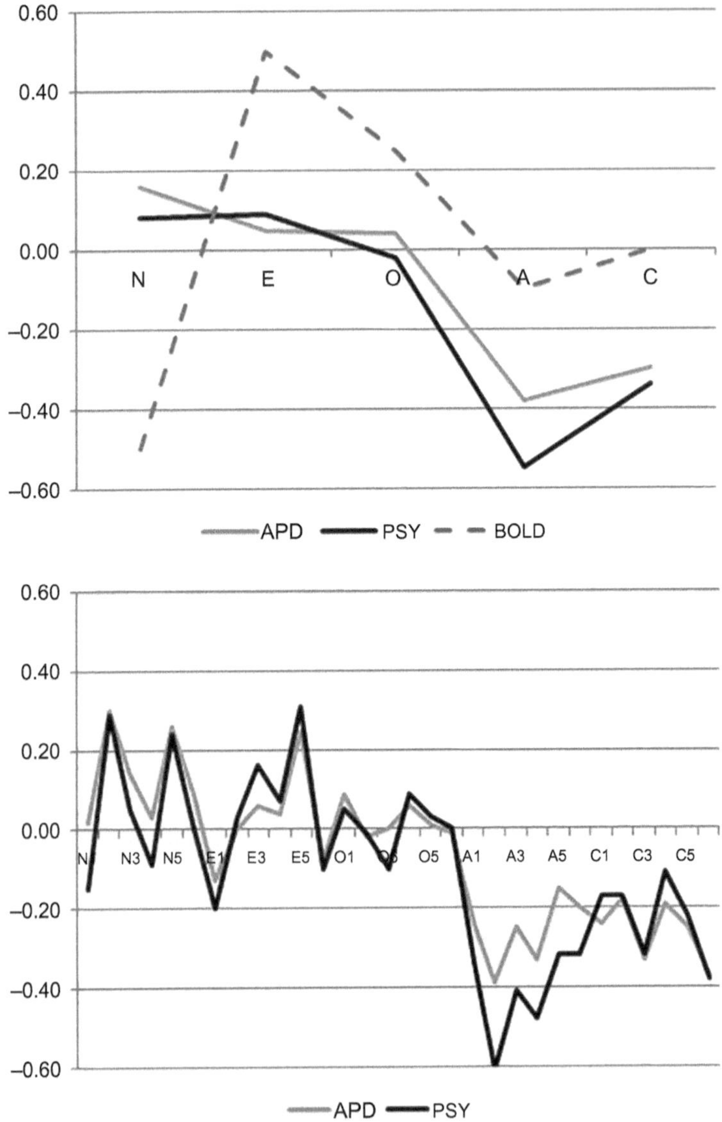

Fig. 1 FFM domain- and facet-level profiles for meta-psychology and meta-APD. *APD*, antisocial personality disorder; *PSY*, psychopathy (80% of studies in the meta-analysis measured antisocial psychopathy, 20% of studies measured bold psychopathy). Reproduced with permission from Vachon, D. D., Lynam, D. R., Miller, J.D., & Krueger, R.F. (2018). Externalizing, psychopathy, and antisocial personality disorder: A parsimonious, trait-based approach. In V. Zeigler-Hill, & T. K. Shackelford (Eds.), The SAGE handbook of personality and individual differences. SAGE Publications. Meta-trait profiles for APD and PSY from Decuyper, M., De Pauw, S., De Fruyt, F., De Bolle, M., & De Clercq, B. J. (2009). A meta-analysis of psychopathy-, antisocial PD- and FFM-associations. European Journal of Personality, 23, 531–565

evidence to show that boldness is uncorrelated with other aspects of psychopathy (mean $r = .05$), that it better represents psychological health and adjustment, and that it carries no risk for psychopathy or any other form of psychopathology—if anything, it acts as a protective factor (Miller & Lynam, 2012). From this perspective, boldness is better construed as stable extraversion, an adaptive factor that is empirically and conceptually unrelated to all other aspects of psychopathy. Importantly, the trait profile of boldness diverges significantly from other measures of psychopathy (double-entry ICC = .08) and APD (double-entry ICC = −.03) and is only weakly correlated with antagonism (meta-$r = -.10$; see Fig. 1).

Antagonism as the foundation of antisocial psychopathy—7 lines of evidence

Setting aside bold psychopathy—which includes a boldness factor virtually unrelated to antagonism and other psychopathy scales—here I present seven lines of evidence suggesting that antagonism is the foundation of antisocial psychopathy, including description, translation, empirical, consensus, similarity, factor, and nomological evidence.

Description evidence

Antagonism is the most frequently represented FFM domain in classical accounts of psychopathy, including conceptualizations advanced by Cleckley (1941/1988), McCord and McCord (1964), Hare (1991, 2003), and Karpman (1941, 1948). For a description of these accounts, see Miller and Lynam (2015). After antagonism, the next most frequently represented domain is low conscientiousness, followed by a mix of high and low facets from neuroticism (e.g., high angry hostility, low depression) and extraversion (e.g., high excitement-seeking, low warmth). However, as described elsewhere (c.f., Vachon, Lynam, Miller, & Krueger, 2018), these aspects of conscientiousness, neuroticism, and extraversion have strong cross-loadings on antagonism: individuals with high antagonism will also tend to have low conscientiousness, high anger, low depression, high excitement-seeking, low warmth, and so on. This pattern of traits—high antagonism accompanied by secondary, "passenger" traits from other domains—may create the impression that psychopathy is complex and multifaceted when it can actually be parsimoniously captured by antagonism alone (an idea I return to in the conclusion of this chapter). In any case, text analyses of these classic accounts of psychopathy, such as the one provided by Miller and Lynam (2015), unambiguously highlight the centrality of antagonism (see Table 1).

Translation evidence

A translation of each PCL-R criterion into the language of the FFM also highlights antagonism and, to a lesser degree, low conscientiousness and aspects of neuroticism and extraversion (Widiger & Lynam, 1998). Beginning with narrative descriptions of

Table 1 Classical descriptions of psychopathy using the FFM

	Hare	Cleckley	McCords	Karpman	Total
Neuroticism					**−9**
Anxiety	Average	Very low	Very low	Low	−5
Angry hostility	High	High	Very high	Average	+4
Depression	Low	Very low	Low	Low	−5
Self-consciousness	Average	Very low	Very low	Very low	−6
Impulsiveness	High	Very high	Very high	Very high	+7
Vulnerability	Average	Very low	Low	Low	−4
Extraversion					**+2**
Warmth	Low	Very low	Very low	Very low	−7
Gregariousness	Average	High	Average	Average	+1
Assertiveness	Average	Very high	High	Average	+3
Activity	Average	High	Average	High	+2
Excitement seeking	High	Very high	Very high	Very high	+7
Positive emotions	Low	Low	Low	Low	−4
Openness					**+2**
Fantasy	Average	Average	Average	Average	0
Aesthetics	Average	Low	Average	Average	−1
Feelings	Average	Low	Low	Low	−3
Actions	Average	Very high	High	High	+4
Ideas	Average	High	Average	Average	+1
Values	Average	Average	High	Average	+1
Agreeableness					**−47**
Trust	Very low	Very low	Very low	Low	−7
Straightforwardness	Very low	Very low	Very low	Very low	−8
Altruism	Very low	Very low	Very low	Very low	−8
Compliance	Very low	Very low	Very low	Very low	−8
Modesty	Very low	Very low	Very low	Very low	−8
Tender-mindedness	Very low	Very low	Very low	Very low	−8
Conscientiousness					**−24**
Competence	Average	Very high	Low	Low	0
Order	Average	Average	Average	Average	0
Dutifulness	Very low	Very low	Very low	Very low	−8
Achievement striving	Very low	Average	Average	Low	−2
Self-discipline	Very low	Low	Very low	Very low	−7
Deliberation	Very low	Very low	Very low	Low	−7

Note. The "Total" column was added; here, scores represent the sum of expert descriptions (where −2 = very low, −1 = low, 0 = average, +1 = high, +2 = very high). *Bolded* totals for each domain represent the sum of the facet totals. Modified with permission from Miller, J. D., & Lynam, D. R. (2015). Understanding psychopathy using the basic elements of personality. *Social and Personality Psychology Compass*, *9*, 223–237.

Table 2 Two factors of the PCL-R from the perspective of the FFM

Factor 1: Antagonism
2. Grandiose sense of self-worth (antagonism)
4. Pathological lying (antagonism)
5. Conning/manipulative (antagonism)
6. Lack of remorse or guilt (antagonism)
8. Callousness/lack of empathy (antagonism)
16. Failure to accept responsibility (antagonism)
1. Glib and superficial charm (low neuroticism)
7. Shallow affect (antagonism and introversion)
Factor 2: Low conscientiousness and antagonism
15. Irresponsibility (low conscientiousness)
13. Lack of realistic, long-term goals (low conscientiousness)
9. Parasitic lifestyle (antagonism and low conscientiousness)
12. Early behavior problems (antagonism and low conscientiousness)
18. Juvenile delinquency (antagonism and low conscientiousness)
19. Revocation of conditional release (antagonism and low conscientiousness)
14. Impulsivity (low conscientiousness and high neuroticism)
3. Need for stimulation/proneness to boredom (extraversion)
10. Poor behavioral controls (antagonism, low conscientiousness, high neuroticism)

Note. Items 11 (promiscuity), 17 (many short-term marriages), and 20 (criminal versatility) from the PCL-R (Hare, 1991) are not included.
Reproduced with permission from Widiger, T. A., & Lynam, D. R. (1998). Psychopathy and the five-factor model of personality. In T. Millon, E. Simonsen, M. Birket-Smith, & R. D. Davis (Eds.), *Psychopathy: Antisocial, criminal, and violent behavior* (pp. 171–187). New York: Guilford Press.

the 20 PCL-R items, Widiger and Lynam identified FFM domains that they believe captured the content of the PCL-R items. Table 2 provides a summary of their translation, including a characterization of the two PCL-R factors, where F1 (interpersonal/affective factor) is characterized by antagonism and F2 (impulsive-antisocial factor) is characterized by a blend of antagonism and low conscientiousness—a theme which recurs across multiple lines of evidence.

Empirical evidence

A third way of establishing the centrality of antagonism in psychopathy is to ask a two-sided question: is psychopathy more strongly related to antagonism than to any other trait, and is antagonism more strongly related to psychopathy than to any other personality disorder? The answer to both sides of this question is a resounding, yes. Displayed in Tables 3 and 4 are the meta-analytic FFM domain and facet trait profiles for psychopathy (from Decuyper et al., 2009) and the 10 main-text DSM personality disorders (from Samuel & Widiger, 2008). As seen in the psychopathy column of Tables 3 and 4, psychopathy is more strongly correlated with antagonism at the domain level ($r = .08, .09, -.02, -.55, -.34$ for N, E, O, A, C domains, respectively), as well as the facet level (mean absolute facet $r = .14, .15, .05, .41, .23$ for N, E, O, A, C facets, respectively; means given in absolute values because positive and negative

Table 3 Meta-analytic correlations between FFM domains and personality disorders

FFM domain	PAR	SZD	SZT	ASL	BDL	HIS	NAR	AVD	DEP	OC	PSY
N	0.40	0.22	0.38	0.18	0.54	0.10	0.11	0.52	0.44	0.18	0.08
E	−0.21	−0.46	−0.28	0.04	−0.12	0.33	0.09	−0.49	−0.15	−0.12	0.09
O	−0.04	−0.11	0.09	0.08	0.10	0.15	0.07	−0.08	−0.03	−0.04	−0.02
A	−0.34	−0.16	−0.17	−0.36	−0.24	−0.11	−0.37	−0.07	0.08	−0.05	−0.55
C	−0.11	−0.10	−0.14	−0.33	−0.29	−0.11	−0.10	−0.16	−0.20	0.24	−0.34

Note. Personality disorders: *ASL*, antisocial; *AVD*, avoidant; *BDL*, borderline; *DEP*, dependent; *HIS*, histrionic; *NAR*, narcissistic; *OC*, obsessive compulsive; *PAR*, paranoid; *PSY*, psychopathy; *SZD*, schizoid; *SZT*, schizotypal. FFM traits: *A*, agreeableness; *C*, conscientiousness; *E*, extraversion; *N*, neuroticism; *O*, openness.
Modified with permission from Decuyper, M., De Pauw, S., De Fruyt, F., De Bolle, M., & De Clercq, B. J. (2009). A meta-analysis of psychopathy-, antisocial PD- and FFM-associations. *European Journal of Personality*, *23*, 531–565 and Samuel, D.B., & Widiger, T.A. (2008). A meta-analytic review of the relationships between the Five-Factor Model and DSM-IV-TR personality disorders: a facet-level analysis. *Clinical Psychology Review*, *28*, 1326–1342.

Table 4 FFM meta-analytic correlations with psychopathy and other personality disorders

FFM domain	FFM facet	PAR	SZD	SZT	ASL	BDL	HIS	NAR	AVD	DEP	OC	PSY
N	Anxiousness	0.27	0.13	0.27	0.00	0.38	0.00	0.02	0.41	0.39	0.16	−0.15
	Angry hostility	0.41	0.19	0.29	0.27	0.48	0.08	0.23	0.29	0.18	0.10	0.29
	Depressiveness	0.35	0.28	0.39	0.12	0.50	−0.06	0.03	0.53	0.41	0.09	0.05
	Self-consciousness	0.29	0.23	0.32	0.02	0.35	−0.11	−0.03	0.56	0.42	0.13	−0.09
	Impulsiveness	0.15	0.00	0.17	0.27	0.34	0.17	0.14	0.14	0.17	−0.07	0.24
	Vulnerability	0.22	0.14	0.25	0.04	0.39	0.01	−0.01	0.40	0.43	0.03	0.00
E	Warmth	−0.28	−0.42	−0.28	−0.13	−0.20	0.26	−0.07	−0.35	−0.03	−0.07	−0.20
	Gregariousness	−0.20	−0.48	−0.25	0.02	−0.12	0.35	0.04	−0.42	−0.03	−0.16	0.03
	Assertiveness	−0.08	−0.22	−0.13	0.06	−0.09	0.27	0.19	−0.39	−0.21	−0.01	0.16
	Activity	−0.08	−0.25	−0.13	0.02	−0.10	0.25	0.09	−0.29	−0.12	0.03	0.07
	Excitement seeking	−0.01	−0.21	−0.04	0.25	0.06	0.27	0.16	−0.23	−0.06	−0.12	0.31
	Positive emotions	−0.27	−0.38	−0.26	−0.09	−0.26	0.23	−0.02	−0.39	−0.15	−0.09	−0.10
O	Fantasy	0.00	−0.05	0.14	0.10	0.13	0.16	0.11	0.00	0.05	−0.09	0.05
	Aesthetics	−0.05	−0.06	0.07	0.00	0.05	0.10	0.04	−0.03	0.01	0.01	−0.01
	Feelings	−0.02	−0.17	0.03	−0.02	0.09	0.18	0.05	−0.04	0.05	0.01	−0.10
	Actions	−0.10	−0.13	−0.06	0.10	−0.03	0.12	0.04	−0.20	−0.13	−0.12	0.09
	Ideas	−0.03	0.00	0.09	0.04	−0.01	0.04	0.07	−0.05	−0.12	0.03	0.03
	Values	−0.05	−0.05	0.01	0.08	0.05	0.04	−0.01	−0.05	−0.04	−0.09	0.00
A	Trust	−0.45	−0.28	−0.31	−0.22	−0.29	0.05	−0.20	−0.29	−0.07	−0.08	−0.34
	Straightforwardness	−0.24	−0.09	−0.16	−0.37	−0.21	−0.10	−0.31	−0.06	0.00	0.04	−0.61
	Altruism	−0.21	−0.19	−0.15	−0.24	−0.18	0.02	−0.20	−0.12	0.03	0.04	−0.41
	Compliance	−0.27	−0.08	−0.13	−0.32	−0.27	−0.12	−0.26	−0.02	0.10	0.01	−0.48
	Modesty	−0.06	0.08	0.05	−0.17	0.03	−0.16	−0.37	0.20	0.16	0.02	−0.32
	Tender-mindedness	−0.18	−0.11	−0.05	−0.19	−0.09	0.02	−0.17	−0.02	0.09	0.00	−0.31

Continued

Table 4 Continued

FFM domain	FFM facet	PAR	SZD	SZT	ASL	BDL	HIS	NAR	AVD	DEP	OC	PSY
C	Competence	−0.13	−0.13	−0.18	−0.21	−0.29	−0.01	0.01	−0.23	−0.25	0.19	−0.17
	Order	0.00	−0.02	−0.06	−0.18	−0.10	−0.05	−0.03	−0.03	−0.06	0.25	−0.17
	Dutifulness	−0.10	−0.08	−0.10	−0.29	−0.22	−0.08	−0.10	−0.09	−0.08	0.25	−0.32
	Achieve. striving	−0.07	−0.13	−0.13	−0.19	−0.19	0.04	0.02	−0.19	−0.16	0.25	−0.11
	Self-discipline	−0.14	−0.12	−0.18	−0.25	−0.29	−0.04	−0.09	−0.22	−0.23	0.21	−0.22
	Deliberation	−0.09	−0.02	−0.10	−0.38	−0.27	−0.16	−0.13	−0.01	−0.06	0.24	−0.38
	Mean A facet	−0.24	−0.11	−0.13	−0.25	−0.17	−0.05	−0.25	−0.05	0.05	0.01	−0.41

Note. *ASL*, antisocial; *AVD*, avoidant; *BDL*, borderline; *DEP*, dependent; *HIS*, histrionic; *NAR*, narcissistic; *OC*, obsessive compulsive; *PAR*, paranoid; *PSY*, psychopathy; *SZD*, schizoid; *SZT*, schizotypal. FFM traits: *A*, agreeableness; *C*, conscientiousness; *E*, extraversion; *N*, neuroticism; *O*, openness.
Modified with permission from Decuyper, M., De Pauw, S., De Fruyt, F., De Bolle, M., & De Clercq, B. J. (2009). A meta-analysis of psychopathy-, antisocial PD- and FFM-associations. *European Journal of Personality*, *23*, 531–565 and Samuel, D. B., & Widiger, T. A. (2008). A meta-analytic review of the relationships between the Five-Factor Model and DSM-IV-TR personality disorders: a facet-level analysis. *Clinical Psychology Review*, *28*, 1326–1342.

facet correlations would wash out using standard mean values). Similarly, the antagonism rows of Tables 3 and 4 show that antagonism is more strongly related to psychopathy (A domain $r = -.55$, mean A facet $r = -.41$), than to any other personality disorder, including narcissistic (A domain $r = -.37$, mean A facet $r = -.25$), antisocial (A domain $r = -.36$, mean A facet $r = -.25$), paranoid (A domain $r = -.34$, mean A facet $r = -.24$), borderline (A domain $r = -.24$, mean A facet $r = -.17$), and so on down to dependent personality disorder (A domain $r = .08$, mean A facet $r = .05$).

Consensus evidence

Yet another approach to place psychopathy within the framework of the FFM is to invite psychopathy experts to describe the personalities of the prototypical psychopath using the language of the FFM. This expert consensus approach improves on the translation approach because it does not rely on a single conception of psychopathy; instead, it aggregates ratings across a range of conceptions, emphasizing areas of agreement and blunting idiosyncratic differences. Table 5 displays the result of this approach, used to develop expert prototypes for psychopathy (Miller et al., 2001) and the 10 DSM personality disorders (Lynam & Widiger, 2001). One can again ask the two-sided question: are experts' conceptions of psychopathy more strongly related to antagonism than to any other trait, and is antagonism more strongly related to expert conceptions of psychopathy than those of other personality disorders? And again, the answer to both sides of this question is yes. Expert ratings, which range from 1 (very low) to 5 (very high), show that psychopathy is more strongly characterized by antagonism than other traits (average facet ratings were 2.30, 3.47, 2.98, 1.30, 2.42 for N, E, O, A, C, respectively; in terms of deviations from the neutral value of 3, average facet deviations were −0.70, 0.47, −0.02, −1.70, −0.58 for N, E, O, A, C, respectively). Antagonism is also more strongly related to psychopathy (average A facet = 1.30) than to any other personality disorder, including narcissistic (1.40), antisocial (1.50), paranoid (1.75), and so on down to dependent personality disorder (4.03).

Similarity evidence

Earlier I made the point that antagonism has substantial cross-loadings on the facets from other FFM domains, including conscientiousness, neuroticism, and extraversion. One way of examining the similarity between antagonism and psychopathy is to compare the full loading profile of antagonism to the trait profiles of psychopathy derived using various methods. For example, displayed in Table 6 is the factor loading profile for antagonism (i.e., reverse-scored factor loadings for agreeableness from the NEO manual, Costa & McCrae, 1992) and the diverse psychopathy profiles described previously, including the description, translation, empirical, and consensus profiles. At the bottom of Table 6 are the similarity indices between antagonism and the psychopathy profiles. Remarkably, the factor loading profile of antagonism is just as strongly related to the psychopathy profiles as they are to one another: the average similarity between antagonism and the four psychopathy profiles is $r = .82$, whereas the average

Table 5 FFM expert consensus prototype scores for psychopathy and other personality disorders

FFM domain	FFM facet	PAR	SZD	SZT	ASL	BDL	HIS	NAR	AVD	DEP	OC	PSY
N	Anxiousness	3.60	2.23	4.25	1.82	4.04	3.42	2.33	4.76	4.32	4.00	1.47
	Angry hostility	4.00	2.54	3.08	4.14	4.75	3.42	4.08	2.81	2.42	3.00	3.87
	Depressiveness	3.30	3.15	3.58	2.45	4.17	2.68	2.42	3.95	3.63	3.18	1.40
	Self-consciousness	3.30	3.31	4.00	1.36	3.17	2.00	1.50	4.67	4.16	3.29	1.07
	Impulsiveness	2.90	2.08	3.17	4.73	4.79	4.32	3.17	1.62	2.32	1.53	4.53
	Vulnerability	3.60	3.31	3.75	2.27	4.17	3.95	2.92	4.52	4.32	3.12	1.47
E	Warmth	1.30	1.08	1.58	2.14	3.21	3.89	1.42	2.33	3.84	2.06	1.73
	Gregariousness	1.70	1.00	1.58	3.32	2.92	4.74	3.83	1.29	3.26	2.18	3.67
	Assertiveness	2.90	1.54	2.17	4.23	3.17	3.84	4.67	1.19	1.32	3.00	4.47
	Activity	2.90	1.92	2.25	4.00	3.29	4.16	3.67	2.05	2.26	3.35	3.67
	Excitement seeking	2.20	1.38	2.17	4.64	3.88	4.47	4.17	1.24	2.26	1.59	4.73
	Positive emotions	2.20	1.23	1.92	2.86	2.63	4.16	3.33	1.67	2.53	2.41	2.53
O	Fantasy	2.90	3.23	3.83	2.82	3.29	4.37	3.75	3.14	3.05	2.06	3.07
	Aesthetics	2.20	2.77	3.17	2.36	2.96	3.53	3.25	3.05	2.89	2.59	2.33
	Feelings	2.40	1.31	2.17	2.27	4.00	4.16	1.92	3.43	3.74	1.82	1.80
	Actions	2.00	1.62	2.42	4.23	4.00	4.21	4.08	2.00	2.21	1.53	4.27
	Ideas	3.50	3.38	4.33	2.91	3.21	3.11	2.92	3.19	2.84	1.76	3.53
	Values	1.90	2.31	2.42	3.00	2.88	3.63	2.67	2.57	2.89	1.76	2.87
A	Trust	1.00	2.38	2.08	1.45	2.21	4.00	1.42	2.24	4.26	2.65	1.73
	Straightforwardness	2.00	2.77	3.00	1.41	2.08	2.32	1.83	2.90	3.11	3.47	1.13
	Altruism	1.90	2.38	2.75	1.41	2.46	2.21	1.00	2.90	3.95	2.76	1.33
	Compliance	1.40	3.00	2.50	1.77	2.00	2.53	1.58	3.52	4.68	3.18	1.33
	Modesty	2.40	3.31	3.08	1.68	2.83	2.32	1.08	4.33	4.26	3.06	1.00
	Tender-mindedness	1.80	2.38	3.00	1.27	2.79	3.05	1.50	3.43	3.89	2.82	1.27

C	Competence	3.30	2.85	2.33	2.09	2.71	2.37	3.25	3.05	2.58	4.53	4.20
	Order	3.70	3.08	2.00	2.41	2.38	2.10	2.92	3.43	2.89	4.76	2.60
	Dutifulness	3.40	3.00	2.50	1.41	2.29	2.10	2.42	3.29	3.79	4.76	1.20
	Achieve. striving	3.00	2.38	2.25	2.09	2.50	2.68	3.92	2.67	2.47	4.29	3.07
	Self-discipline	3.50	3.15	2.67	1.81	2.33	1.79	2.08	3.05	2.84	4.53	1.87
	Deliberation	3.80	3.23	2.67	1.64	1.88	1.74	2.25	3.43	3.00	4.59	1.60
	Mean A facet	1.75	2.70	2.74	1.50	2.40	2.74	1.40	3.22	4.03	2.99	1.30

Note. Expert consensus prototype ratings range from 1 (very low) to 5 (very high). Personality disorders: *ASL*, antisocial; *AVD*, avoidant; *BDL*, borderline; *DEP*, dependent; *HIS*, histrionic; *NAR*, narcissistic; *OC*, obsessive compulsive; *PAR*, paranoid; *PSY*, psychopathy; *SZD*, schizoid; SZT, schizotypal. FFM traits: *A*, agreeableness; *C*, conscientiousness; *E*, extraversion; *N*, neuroticism; *O*, openness.

Modified with permission from Lynam, D. R., & Widiger, T. A. (2001). Using the five-factor model to represent the DSM-IV personality disorders: an expert consensus approach. *Journal of Abnormal Psychology*, *110*, 401–412.

Table 6 Comparing the antagonism factor loading profile versus various psychopathy profiles

FFM domain	FFM facet	Antagonism factor loadings	PSY—description	PSY—translation	PSY—empirical	PSY—consensus
N	Anxiousness	0.00	−5.00	0.00	−0.15	1.47
	Angry hostility	0.45	4.00	1.00	0.29	3.87
	Depressiveness	0.02	−5.00	−1.00	0.05	1.40
	Self-consciousness	−0.07	−6.00	0.00	−0.09	1.07
	Impulsiveness	0.17	7.00	1.00	0.24	4.53
	Vulnerability	0.04	−4.00	0.00	0.00	1.47
E	Warmth	−0.29	−7.00	−1.00	−0.20	1.73
	Gregariousness	−0.01	1.00	0.00	0.03	3.67
	Assertiveness	0.30	3.00	0.00	0.16	4.47
	Activity	0.17	2.00	0.00	0.07	3.67
	Excitement seeking	0.31	7.00	1.00	0.31	4.73
	Positive emotions	−0.15	−4.00	−1.00	−0.10	2.53
O	Fantasy	0.14	0.00	0.00	0.05	3.07
	Aesthetics	−0.11	−1.00	0.00	−0.01	2.33
	Feelings	0.01	−3.00	0.00	−0.10	1.80
	Actions	−0.02	4.00	0.00	0.09	4.27
	Ideas	0.07	1.00	0.00	0.03	3.53
	Values	0.04	1.00	0.00	0.00	2.87
A	Trust	−0.44	−7.00	−2.00	−0.34	1.73
	Straightforwardness	−0.63	−8.00	−2.00	−0.61	1.13
	Altruism	−0.57	−8.00	−2.00	−0.41	1.33
	Compliance	−0.69	−8.00	−2.00	−0.48	1.33
	Modesty	−0.50	−8.00	−2.00	−0.32	1.00
	Tender-mindedness	−0.52	−8.00	−2.00	−0.31	1.27

C	Competence	−0.09	0.00	0.00	−0.17	4.20
	Order	−0.03	0.00	0.00	−0.17	2.60
	Dutifulness	−0.24	−8.00	−2.00	−0.32	1.20
	Achieve. striving	0.07	−2.00	−2.00	−0.11	3.07
	Self-discipline	−0.12	−7.00	−2.00	−0.22	1.87
	Deliberation	−0.22	−7.00	−2.00	−0.38	1.60

	Similarity indices				
	Antagonism factor loadings	**PSY—description**	**PSY—translation**	**PSY—empirical**	**PSY—consensus**
Antagonism factor loadings	1.00				
PSY—description	0.82	1.00			
PSY—translation	0.81	0.85	1.00		
PSY—empirical	0.92	0.88	0.86	1.00	
PSY—consensus	0.77	0.94	0.69	0.77	1.00

Note. Antagonism Factor Loadings column obtained from the NEO PI-R manual, Costa and McCrae (1992). PSY—description column obtained from Table 1. PSY—translation column obtained from Widiger and Lynam (1998). PSY—empirical column obtained from Table 4. PSY—consensus column obtained from Table 5. *A*, agreeableness; *C*, conscientiousness; *E*, extraversion; *N*, neuroticism; *O*, openness; *PSY*, psychopathy.

similarity among the four psychopathy profiles is $r = .83$. Furthermore, the four psychopathy profiles are much more similar to the factor loading profile of antagonism ($r = .82$) than those of conscientiousness ($r = -.22$), extraversion ($r = .21$), neuroticism ($r = .16$), or openness ($r = .02$). The antagonism factor loading profile is also more similar to psychopathy than to other personality disorders. For example, correlating the antagonism loading profile from Table 6 with the empirical personality disorder profiles from Table 4, antagonism is more strongly correlated with psychopathy ($r = .92$) than with narcissistic ($r = .85$), antisocial ($r = .80$), paranoid ($r = .61$), borderline ($r = .52$), and so on down to dependent personality disorder ($r = -.24$).

Factor evidence

Another way to determine the centrality of antagonism in psychopathy is to conduct an exploratory factor analysis on multiple psychopathy measures and then use the FFM to assay the factors that are extracted. For example, Lynam and Miller (2014) conducted an exploratory factor analysis on a variety of antisocial psychopathy and bold psychopathy scales, including the 13 subscales of the SRP, LSRP, YPI, and DSM-5 APD and its psychopathy specifier. Using principal axis factoring with a direct oblimin rotation, the analysis yielded three factors that accounted for 93% of the total variance. As seen in Table 7, one of these factors (Factor 2) only loaded on the two psychopathy subscales representing boldness (PPI Fearless Dominance and the DSM-5 psychopathy specifier); this factor was weakly correlated with antagonism (mean A facet $r = .16$) and weakly negatively correlated with the other two extracted factors ($rs = -.15$ and $-.11$, Factors 1 and 3, respectively). The other two factors were strongly correlated with one another ($r = .56$), with Factor 1 characterized by antagonism and low conscientiousness (mean facet $rs = .20, -.03, .01, -.32, -.39$ for N, E, O, A, C, respectively), and Factor 3 characterized by antagonism (mean facet $rs = .00, -.11, -.10, -.43, -.15$ for N, E, O, A, C, respectively).

Thus, while the second extracted factor represents bold psychopathy, the first factor aligns closely with traditional "F2" descriptions of psychopathy (impulsive-antisocial factor) in that it correlates with both antagonism and low conscientiousness and comprises F2-related subscales (i.e., YPI Impulsive/Irresponsible, SRP Erratic Lifestyle, SRP Antisocial Behavior, DSM APD, PPI Self-Centered Impulsivity, and LSRP F2). Similarly, the third extracted factor aligns closely with "F1" descriptions of psychopathy (interpersonal-affective factor) in that it correlates with antagonism and comprises F1-related subscales (i.e., YPI Callous/Unemotional, SRP Callous Affect, LSRP F1, YPI Grandiose/Manipulative, and SRP Interpersonal Manipulation.

Nomological evidence

The seventh way of revealing the centrality of antagonism in psychopathy is to compare their nomological nets. Three questions can be asked: (A) How comparable are measures of antagonism and psychopathy? (B) Do measures of antagonism and psychopathy predict the same things? (C) Is antagonism sufficient in describing

Table 7 Correlations between NEO PI-R facets and psychopathy subscales, organized by three factors extracted from an EFA

FFM domain	FFM facet	Factor 1: Antagonism (low A) and disinhibition (low C)						Factor 2: Fearless Dominance		Factor 3: Antagonism (low A)				
		YPI	**SRP**	**SRP**	***DSM***	**PPI**	**LSRP**	**PPI**	***DSM***	**YPI**	**SRP**	**LSRP**	**YPI**	**SRP**
		I/I	**ELS**	**ASB**	**APD**	**SCI**	**F2**	**FD**	**PS**	**C/U**	**CA**	**F1**	**G/M**	**IPM**
N	N1: Anxiety	−0.10	−0.25	−0.10	0.22	0.10	0.11	**−0.62**	**−0.65**	**−0.32**	−0.22	−0.13	−0.12	−0.07
	N2: Angry hostility	0.26	0.17	0.22	**0.56**	**0.49**	**0.53**	−0.29	−0.29	0.17	0.21	0.32	0.27	**0.35**
	N3: Depression	0.07	0.10	0.15	0.29	**0.39**	**0.37**	**−0.39**	**−0.60**	−0.09	0.00	0.02	−0.02	0.14
	N4: Self-consciousness	−0.11	−0.21	0.02	0.19	0.18	0.27	**−0.55**	**−0.61**	−0.16	−0.14	0.04	−0.14	−0.04
	N5: Impulsiveness	**0.33**	**0.36**	0.15	**0.52**	**0.33**	0.28	−0.13	−0.08	−0.11	−0.02	0.02	0.10	0.21
	N6: Vulnerability	0.24	−0.02	0.10	**0.37**	0.28	**0.47**	**−0.59**	**−0.56**	−0.06	−0.21	0.11	0.05	−0.05
E	E1: Warmth	−0.09	−0.03	−0.17	−0.22	−0.43	−0.31	**0.31**	**0.73**	**−0.46**	**−0.36**	**−0.44**	−0.27	−0.23
	E2: Gregariousness	0.19	0.19	−0.02	−0.06	−0.13	−0.06	**0.36**	**0.71**	−0.23	−0.16	−0.14	0.01	−0.03
	E3: Assertiveness	0.05	0.15	−0.03	0.10	0.01	−0.12	**0.51**	**0.61**	0.08	0.07	0.03	0.21	0.09
	E4: Activity	0.01	0.10	−0.10	0.01	−0.14	−0.12	**0.32**	**0.55**	−0.12	0.00	−0.14	0.08	−0.03
	E5: Excitement seeking	0.19	**0.42**	0.04	0.43	0.01	0.07	**0.44**	0.26	−0.09	0.14	0.06	0.06	0.18
	E6: Positive emotions	−0.08	−0.03	−0.17	−0.14	**−0.34**	**−0.40**	0.24	**0.69**	**−0.46**	**−0.35**	**−0.39**	−0.23	−0.23
O	O1: Fantasy	0.06	0.25	0.09	0.15	−0.01	−0.12	0.07	0.04	−0.19	−0.02	−0.19	−0.01	0.15
	O2: Aesthetics	−0.01	0.07	0.10	0.01	−0.03	−0.09	0.13	0.23	−0.16	−0.25	−0.24	−0.03	−0.09
	O3: Feelings	−0.04	0.03	−0.09	0.00	−0.21	−0.26	−0.02	0.27	**−0.47**	**−0.32**	**−0.39**	−0.22	−0.07
	O4: Actions	0.19	0.31	0.11	−0.03	0.06	0.12	**0.34**	**0.41**	−0.02	0.04	−0.03	0.05	−0.02
	O5: Ideas	−0.09	0.23	0.16	−0.04	−0.13	−0.25	0.19	0.16	−0.07	0.12	−0.20	−0.02	0.15
	O6: Values	−0.02	0.12	0.11	−0.09	−0.11	−0.15	0.09	0.04	−0.19	−0.11	−0.20	−0.20	0.07

Continued

Table 7 Continued

FFM domain	FFM facet	Factor 1: Antagonism (low A) and disinhibition (low C)						Factor 2: Fearless Dominance		Factor 3: Antagonism (low A)				
		YPI	SRP	SRP	*DSM*	PPI	LSRP	PPI	*DSM*	YPI	SRP	LSRP	YPI	SRP
		I/I	ELS	ASB	APD	SCI	F2	FD	PS	C/U	CA	F1	G/M	IPM
A	A1: Trust	−0.20	−0.15	−0.19	**−0.37**	**−0.34**	**−0.42**	0.22	**0.53**	**−0.35**	**−0.38**	**−0.43**	**−0.33**	**−0.47**
	A2: Straightforwardness	**−0.39**	**−0.44**	**−0.38**	**−0.68**	**−0.54**	**−0.35**	−0.15	0.04	**−0.44**	**−0.42**	**−0.64**	**−0.62**	**−0.72**
	A3: Altruism	−0.27	−0.29	−0.28	**−0.48**	**−0.61**	**−0.51**	0.18	0.25	**−0.55**	**−0.50**	**−0.57**	**−0.44**	**−0.41**
	A4: Compliance	**−0.31**	**−0.31**	−0.09	**−0.53**	**−0.37**	**−0.45**	−0.11	0.01	**−0.30**	**−0.33**	**−0.42**	**−0.36**	**−0.44**
	A5: Modesty	−0.29	−0.19	−0.15	−0.28	**−0.32**	−0.15	−0.13	**−0.30**	**−0.35**	−0.18	**−0.47**	**−0.51**	−0.29
	A6: Tender-mindedness	−0.18	−0.22	−0.20	−0.11	−0.29	**−0.33**	−0.07	0.17	**−0.36**	**−0.51**	**−0.56**	−0.28	**−0.31**
C	C1: Competence	**−0.35**	**−0.37**	**−0.35**	**−0.46**	**−0.50**	**−0.55**	0.24	**0.30**	−0.16	−0.06	−0.28	−0.13	−0.17
	C2: Order	**−0.34**	−0.29	−0.20	−0.17	−0.29	**−0.41**	−0.01	0.09	−0.03	−0.11	−0.13	−0.07	−0.15
	C3: Dutifulness	**−0.48**	**−0.31**	−0.29	**−0.46**	**−0.49**	**−0.49**	0.20	0.10	−0.24	−0.02	−0.36	−0.27	−0.23
	C4: Achieve. striving	−0.29	−0.23	−0.21	−0.17	**−0.39**	**−0.47**	0.21	**0.33**	−0.13	−0.02	−0.22	−0.04	−0.10
	C5: Self-discipline	**−0.40**	−0.26	−0.23	**−0.33**	**−0.47**	**−0.59**	0.20	0.24	−0.10	0.00	−0.20	−0.11	−0.16
	C6: Deliberation	**−0.51**	**−0.66**	**−0.30**	**−0.67**	**−0.52**	**−0.45**	−0.22	−0.07	−0.15	−0.11	−0.24	−0.28	−0.23

Note. Correlations >.30 were *bolded* to reflect characteristic traits. *N*s = 288 for LSRP correlations, 304 for PPI correlations, 188 for SRP correlations; 376 for YPI correlations; 106 for *DSM-5* correlations. *A*, agreeableness; *C*, conscientiousness; *DSM APD*, *DSM-5* Section III antisocial personality disorder; *DSM PS*, *DSM-5* Section III Psychopathy Specifier; *E*, extraversion; *LSRP F1*, Factor 1 from LSRP; *LSRP F2*, Factor 2 from LSRP; *N*, neuroticism; *O*, openness to experience; *PPI FD*, Fearless Dominance from PPI; *PPI SCI*, Self-Centered Impulsivity from PPI; *SRP ASB*, antisocial behavior from SRP; *SRP CA*, callous affect from SRP; *SRP ELS*, erratic lifestyle from SRP; *SRP IPM*, interpersonal manipulation from SRP; *YPI C/U*, callous unemotional from YPI; *YPI G/M*, grandiose/manipulative from YPI; *YPI I/I*, impulsive/irresponsible from YPI.
Modified with permission from Lynam, D.R., & Miller, J.D. (2014). Psychopathy from a basic trait perspective: the utility of a Five-Factor Model approach. Journal of Personality, 83, 611–626.

psychopathy, or are other traits needed? I provide preliminary answers to each of these following questions using data from a sample of 787 undergraduates surveyed in the United States (82% Caucasian, 53% female, mean age = 19.33 years, SD = 2.19 years).

(A) How comparable are measures of antagonism and psychopathy? The upper half of Table 8 shows the correlations between an FFM antagonism scale (from the NEO Five-Factor Inventory, NEO FFI; Costa & McCrae, 1992) and several measures of antisocial psychopathy (the SRP-III, LSRP, and EPA). The average correlation between FFM antagonism and the psychopathy measures ($r = .72$) was extremely high and comparable to the average correlation among psychopathy measures ($r = .75$).

(B) Do measures of antagonism and psychopathy predict the same things? The lower half of Table 8 examines the nomological net surrounding psychopathy; it includes variables commonly associated with psychopathy, such as substance use, antisocial behavior, interpersonal violence, gambling behaviors, narcissism, and Machiavellianism. The average correlation between antagonism and these external variables (mean $r = .25$) was nearly as strong as between psychopathy and the external variables (mean rs = .30, .26, .34 for the SRP-III, LSRP, EPA, respectively). Furthermore, as seen at the bottom of Table 8, the average similarity index between antagonism and the psychopathy scales ($r = .88$)

Table 8 Correlating and comparing antagonism and psychopathy

	Antagonism	Psychopathy		
	NEO-FFI	**SRP-III**	**LSRP**	**EPA**
Psychopathy				
SRP-III total	0.70			
LSRP total	0.74	0.71		
EPA total	0.72	0.79	0.75	
External correlates				
CAB substance use	0.25	0.36	0.24	0.33
CAB antisocial behavior	0.28	0.41	0.29	0.40
CAB interpersonal violence	0.13	0.09	0.13	0.15
CAB gambling behaviors	0.23	0.35	0.26	0.39
DD narcissism	0.21	0.23	0.24	0.27
DD machiavellianism	0.41	0.38	0.40	0.47
	Similarity indices for external correlates			
Psychopathy				
SRP-III total	0.77			
LSRP total	0.98	0.79		
EPA total	0.90	0.93	0.94	

Note. CAB, Crimes and Analogous Behavior Scale; *DD*, Dirty Dozen; *EPA*, Elemental Psychopathy Scale; *LSRP*, Levenson Self-Report Psychopathy Scale; *NEO-FFI*, NEO Five-Factor Inventory; *SRP*, Self-Report Psychopathy Scale.

was extremely high and comparable to the average similarity index among the psychopathy scales ($r = .89$). The average similarity between the other FFM domains and the psychopathy scales was much lower: C ($r = .24$), N ($r = .10$), E ($r = .09$), and O ($r = .02$).

(C) **Is antagonism sufficient to describe psychopathy or are other traits needed?** Based on the earlier evidence, antagonism seems nearly sufficient in characterizing psychopathy—perhaps missing a dash of low conscientiousness. The success of antagonism is partly due to the fact that it has strong cross-loadings on several facet traits from other domains relevant to psychopathy. To empirically test whether the addition of other traits brings antagonism even closer to psychopathy, I ran a set of hierarchical regressions that predict psychopathy scores using antagonism (Step 1); the other FFM domain traits—N, E, O, and C (Step 2); and a measure of boldness—PPI Fearless Dominance (Step 3). The results of this approach suggest that other traits have something to add, but not much. In predicting SRP psychopathy, changes in R^2 were as follows: Step 1 = 49%, Step 2 = 5%, Step 3 = 7%. In predicting LSRP psychopathy, changes in R^2 were as follows: Step 1 = 54%, Step 2 = 5%, Step 3 = 1%. And in predicting EPA psychopathy, changes in R^2 were as follows: Step 1 = 51%, Step 2 = 14%, Step 3 = 8%. Thus, on average, antagonism predicted 51% of the variance in psychopathy, the other FFM traits combined added 8%, and boldness added a further 5%.

Conclusion

This mix—antagonism plus a bit of low conscientiousness—is a consistent finding yielded by multiple approaches. Descriptive evidence across classical accounts of psychopathy highlights the central role of antagonism and the lesser role of low conscientiousness (Table 1). Translation evidence exposes each PCL-R criterion as a manifestation of antagonism, conscientiousness, or a facet with substantial cross-loadings on antagonism (Table 2). Empirical and expert consensus evidence shows the same pattern (Tables 3–5). Similarity evidence demonstrates how the full antagonism facet loading profile matches descriptive, translational, empirical, and consensus accounts of psychopathy (Table 6). Factor analytic techniques extract the typical F1/F2 factors seen in other accounts, where F1 is characterized by antagonism and F2 by a blend of antagonism and low conscientiousness (Table 7). Finally, nomological evidence shows that measures of antagonism and psychopathy are highly related and comparable in terms of their nomological networks. And, in contrast to other lines of evidence, conscientiousness and other FFM traits have little to add to antagonism in a direct test of incremental prediction. Other FFM traits and boldness slightly improve the prediction of psychopathy, but this increase was modest. In capturing psychopathy, antagonism may not be sufficient, but it is very, very close.

References

American Psychiatric Association (2013). *Diagnostic and statistical manual of mental disorders* (5th ed.). Arlington, VA: American Psychiatric Publishing.

Andershed, H., Kerr, M., Stattin, H., & Levander, S. (2002). Psychopathic traits in non-referred youths: initial test of a new assessment tool. In E. Blaauw & L. Sheridan (Eds.), *Psychopaths: Current international perspectives* (pp. 131–158). The Hague, The Netherlands: Elsevier.

Brazil, K. J., & Forth, A. E. (2018). Hare psychopathy checklist (PCL). In V. Ziegler-Hill & T. K. Shackelford (Eds.), *Encyclopedia of personality and individual differences*. Springer International Publishing.

Cleckley, H. M. (1941/1988). *The mask of sanity*. St. Louis, MO: Mosby.

Costa, P. T., & McCrae, R. R. (1992). *Revised NEO Personality Inventory (NEO PI-R) and the NEO Five-Factor Inventory (NEO-FFI) professional manual*. Odessa, FL: Psychological Assessment Resources.

Decuyper, M., De Pauw, S., De Fruyt, F., De Bolle, M., & De Clercq, B. J. (2009). A meta-analysis of psychopathy-, antisocial PD- and FFM-associations. *European Journal of Personality*, *23*, 531–565.

Forth, A. E., Kosson, D. S., & Hare, R. D. (2003). *The Hare Psychopathy Checklist: Youth version*. Toronto: Multi-Health Systems.

Fowles, D. C., & Dindo, L. (2009). Temperament and psychopathy: a dual-pathway model. *Current Directions in Psychological Science*, *18*, 179–183.

Frick, P. J., & Hare, R. (2001). *Antisocial process screening device*. Toronto, Canada: Multi-Health Systems.

Hare, R. D. (1991). *The Hare Psychopathy Checklist—Revised*. Toronto: Multi-Health Systems.

Hare, R. D. (2003). *The Hare Psychopathy Checklist—Revised* (2nd ed.). Toronto: Multi-Health Systems.

Hare, R. D., & Frazelle, J. L. (1980). *Some preliminary notes on the use of a research scale for the assessment of psychopathy in criminal populations*. Vancouver: University of British Columbia Unpublished manuscript.

Hare, R. D., Harpur, T. J., Hakstian, A. R., Forth, A. E., Hart, S. D., & Newman, J. P. (1990). The Revised Psychopathy Checklist: reliability and factor structure. *Psychological Assessment*, *2*, 338–341.

Hare, R. D., & Neumann, C. S. (2008). Psychopathy as a clinical and empirical construct. *Annual Review of Clinical Psychology*, *4*, 217–246.

Hart, S. D., Cox, D. N., & Hare, R. D. (1995). *The Hare Psychopathy Checklist: Screening version*. Toronto, Ontario, Canada: Multi-Health Systems.

Karpman, B. (1941). On the need of separating psychopathy into two distinct clinical types: the symptomatic and the idiopathic. *Journal of Criminal Psychopathology*, *3*, 112–137.

Karpman, B. (1948). The myth of the psychopathic personality. *American Journal of Psychiatry*, *104*, 523–534.

Levenson, M. R., Kiehl, K. A., & Fitzpatrick, C. M. (1995). Assessing psychopathic attributes in a noninstitutionalized population. *Journal of Personality and Social Psychology*, *68*, 151–158.

Lilienfeld, S. O., & Andrews, B. P. (1996). Development and preliminary validation of a self-report measure of psychopathic personality traits in noncriminal populations. *Journal of Personality Assessment*, *66*, 488–524.

Lykken, D. T. (1995). *The antisocial personalities*. Hillsdale, NJ: Erlbaum.

Lynam, D. R. (1997). Pursuing the psychopath: capturing the fledgling psychopath in a nomological net. *Journal of Abnormal Psychology*, *106*, 425–438.

Lynam, D. R., Gaughan, E. T., Miller, J. D., Miller, D. J., Mullins-Sweatt, S., & Widiger, T. A. (2011). Assessing the basic traits associated with psychopathy: development and validation of the Elemental Psychopathy Assessment. *Psychological Assessment*, *23*, 108–124.

Lynam, D. R., & Miller, J. D. (2014). Psychopathy from a basic trait perspective: the utility of a Five-Factor Model approach. *Journal of Personality*, *83*, 611–626.

Lynam, D. R., & Vachon, D. D. (2012). Antisocial personality disorder in DSM-5: missteps and missed opportunities. *Personality Disorders: Theory, Research, and Treatment*, *3*, 483–495.

Lynam, D. R., & Widiger, T. A. (2001). Using the five-factor model to represent the DSM-IV personality disorders: an expert consensus approach. *Journal of Abnormal Psychology, 110*, 401–412.

McCord, W., & McCord, J. (1964). *The psychopath: An essay on the criminal mind.* Princeton, NJ: Van Nostrand.

Miller, J. D., & Lynam, D. R. (2012). An examination of the psychopathic personality inventory's nomological network: a meta-analytic review. *Personality Disorders: Theory, Research, and Treatment, 3*, 305–326.

Miller, J. D., & Lynam, D. R. (2015). Understanding psychopathy using the basic elements of personality. *Social and Personality Psychology Compass, 9*, 223–237.

Miller, J. D., Lynam, D. R., Widiger, T. A., & Leukefeld, C. (2001). Personality disorders as extreme variants of common personality dimensions: can the Five-Factor Model adequately represent psychopathy? *Journal of Personality, 69*, 253–276.

Patrick, C., & Drislane, L. E. (2014). Antisocial personality disorder and psychopathy. In P. Blaney, R. Krueger, & T. Millon (Eds.), *Oxford textbook of psychopathology* (pp. 681–706). New York, NY: Oxford.

Patrick, C. J., Fowles, D. C., & Krueger, R. F. (2009). Triarchic conceptualization of psychopathy: developmental origins of disinhibition, boldness, and meanness. *Development and Psychopathology, 21*, 913–938.

Paulhus, D. L., Neumann, C. S., & Hare, R. D. (in press). Manual for the Hare Self-Report Psychopathy scale. Toronto, Ontario, Canada: Multi-Health Systems.

Samuel, D. B., & Widiger, T. A. (2008). A meta-analytic review of the relationships between the Five-Factor Model and DSM-IV-TR personality disorders: a facet-level analysis. *Clinical Psychology Review, 28*, 1326–1342.

Vachon, D. D., Lynam, D. R., Miller, J. D., & Krueger, R. F. (2018). Externalizing, psychopathy, and antisocial personality disorder: a parsimonious, trait-based approach. In V. Zeigler-Hill & T. K. Shackelford (Eds.), *The SAGE handbook of personality and individual differences.* SAGE Publications.

Widiger, T. A., & Lynam, D. R. (1998). Psychopathy and the five-factor model of personality. In T. Millon, E. Simonsen, M. Birket-Smith, & R. D. Davis (Eds.), *Psychopathy: Antisocial, criminal, and violent behavior* (pp. 171–187). New York: Guilford Press.

A Trifurcated Model of Narcissism: On the pivotal role of trait Antagonism

15

Brandon Weiss, W. Keith Campbell*, Donald R. Lynam†, Joshua D. Miller**
*Department of Psychology, University of Georgia, Athens, GA, United States, †Department of Psychological Sciences, Purdue University, West Lafayette, IN, United States

Across the myriad instantiations of narcissism (i.e., Greek myth, psychoanalytic conceptualization, scientific models), antagonistic traits, defined by grandiosity, callousness, hostility, manipulativeness, and oppositionality, are omnipresent. According to Greek myth (Ovid & Miller, 1946), Narcissus showed vanity and disdain for others, remorselessly leaving beautiful and besotted suitors nursing their own narcissistic wounds. Psychoanalytic scholars have characterized pathological narcissism by aggressive behavior and narcissistic rage, thought to often emanate from defensive functions of the grandiose self in response to emotional injury (Kernberg, 1974; Kohut, 1972). In the modern era, empirical examinations of narcissistic traits have resulted in several widely used and validated models where antagonistic traits are a central focus. In the present chapter, we answer two questions concerning Antagonism in the context of narcissism: (a) Is Antagonism the core trait of narcissism? and (b) Is the Antagonism of Grandiose narcissism the same as the Antagonism of Vulnerable narcissism?

In answering both questions, we use the Trifurcated Model of Narcissism (Miller et al., 2016; Miller, Lynam, Hyatt, & Campbell, 2017) to examine which aspects of narcissism bear the most meaningful associations with constructs central to psychological functioning (i.e., love styles, interpersonal styles, pathological traits). Most research on narcissism has examined narcissism at two primary levels of organization, namely, the single-factor model (e.g., NPD, PNI total score) and the two-factor model (i.e., Grandiose narcissism, Vulnerable narcissism). In the current study, we focus on a three-factor model of narcissism that further delineates narcissism into Agentic Extraversion, Antagonism, and Neuroticism (see Miller et al., 2016, 2017; see also Krizan & Herlache, 2018). To quantify the role that Antagonism plays in narcissism, we compare its empirical correlates to those generated by factors across narcissism's three levels of organization (i.e., single factor; Grandiose and Vulnerable; Agentic Extraversion, Antagonism, and Neuroticism) using intraclass correlations (ICCs) that assess absolute similarity between correlate profiles.

To answer the second question, we examine how levels of specific antagonistic traits vary across narcissism constructs at different levels of organization (i.e., NPD, Grandiose narcissism, Vulnerable narcissism, trifurcated factors). To do so,

The Handbook of Antagonism. https://doi.org/10.1016/B978-0-12-814627-9.00015-3

we use the framework of the most prominent general and pathological personality trait model—the Five-Factor Model (FFM; e.g., APA, 2013; Costa & McCrae, 1992). Accordingly, antagonistic traits will be examined using facets of FFM Agreeableness.

Narcissism as one, two, or three factors

At the single-factor level, narcissism measures combine content across Antagonism, Agentic Extraversion, and Neuroticism (e.g., NPD, FFNI Total score), albeit to varying degrees. Although NPD symptoms as described in the DSM-5 criteria primarily (Fossati et al., 2005; Miller, Hoffman, Campbell, & Pilkonis, 2008) resemble Grandiose narcissism, the full DSM-5 description of NPD makes it clear that vulnerability is thought to be involved as well: "vulnerability in self-esteem makes individuals with narcissistic personality disorder very sensitive to 'injury' from criticism or defeat. Although they may not show it outwardly, criticism may haunt these individuals and may leave them feeling humiliated, degraded, hollow, and empty" (APA, 2013, p. 671).

At the two-factor level, one finds the commonly described and studied dimensions of Grandiose and Vulnerable narcissism (Cain, Pincus, & Ansell, 2008; Miller & Campbell, 2008; Wink, 1991), both of which include antagonistic traits. In general, *Grandiose narcissism* is associated with immodesty, interpersonal dominance, self-absorption, callousness, and manipulativeness, whereas *Vulnerable narcissism* is associated with psychological distress, negative affectivity (e.g., anxiety, shame), low self-esteem, distrustfulness, egocentrism, reactive anger, and hostility. These two narcissism dimensions have been discussed using a variety of titles with Grandiose narcissism also referred to as manipulative, phallic, overt, egotistical, oblivious, exhibitionistic, psychopathic; and Vulnerable narcissism also referred to as craving, contact-shunning, thin-skinned, hypervigilant, and shy (Cain et al., 2008).

At the three-factor level of narcissism, we conceptualize narcissism as being divisible into agentic aspects of trait Extraversion, Antagonism (or low Agreeableness), and Neuroticism. The approach appears to be part of an emerging consensus with respect to (a) conceptualizing narcissism involving three dimensions and (b) an understanding of the biological and personality bases underlying phenotypic manifestations of narcissism. The trifurcated model is instantiated in the Five-Factor Narcissism Inventory (FFNI; Glover, Miller, Lynam, Crego, & Widiger, 2012), a measure of narcissism based on the framework of general personality, which includes at the subordinate (and most parsimonious) level of its organization three dimensions: Antagonism, Agentic Extraversion, and Neuroticism (Miller et al., 2016, 2017). Like our own trifurcated model (Fig. 1), Krizan and Herlache's (2018) Narcissism Spectrum Model characterizes narcissistic individuals by two main dimensions involving a common elevation in Entitled Self-importance, and fairly distinct functional qualities involving either an approach-oriented Boldness or an avoidance-oriented Reactivity. This model is similar to our conceptualization in which we see Antagonism (akin to their Entitled Self-importance) as the core feature with the other two dimensions (Neuroticism/Reactivity vs Agentic Extraversion/Reactivity) as diagnostic

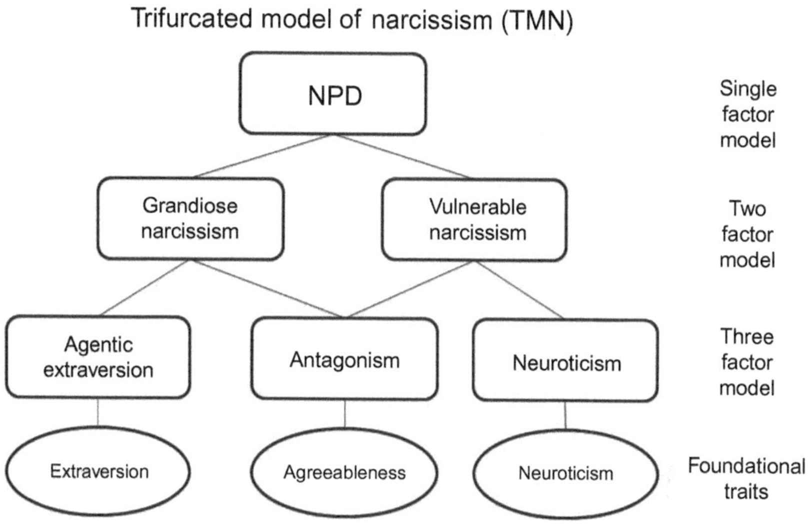

Fig. 1 Trifurcated model of narcissism (TMN). *NPD,* Narcissistic Personality Disorder. *From* OSF.IO/2UA35 under CC0 1.0 Universal.

specifiers (Miller et al., 2017).[1] Although other expressions of narcissism are possible (e.g., high Antagonism, Agentic Extraversion, and Neuroticism akin to narcissistic personality disorder), a negative association between the latter two traits makes this presentation less likely to occur. Table 1 delineates how contemporary models/measures fit into this integrated model of narcissism.

FFM facet-level profile and correlates of individual functioning at narcissism's three levels of organization

In the following sections, we illustrate how Antagonism contributes to functioning, and examine FFM facet-level correlates of narcissism at three levels of organization (i.e., single-factor; two-factor: Grandiose vs Vulnerable; three-factor: Antagonism, Agentic Extraversion, and Neuroticism) to highlight the role of Antagonism across levels. To accomplish these goals, we combined results from five datasets that included the FFNI. Where measures were identical across datasets, we combined the data before conducting analyses; where outcome measures were similar across datasets, but not identical, we conducted correlational analyses separately for each dataset and averaged across the two sets of correlational values using Fisher z conversion and sample size weighting.

[1] Of note, the Antagonism of the FFNI model is broader than the entitlement and self-importance in the NSM of Krizan and Herlache (2018).

Table 1 Instantiations of the three-factor model across measures/models of narcissism

Five-Factor Model traits	Extraversion	(Low) Agreeableness	Neuroticism
Trifurcated Model of Narcissism	Agentic Extraversion	Antagonism	Neuroticism
Narcissism Spectrum Model	Boldness	Entitled Self-Importance	Reactivity
Five-factor Narcissism Inventory	Agentic Extraversion	Antagonism	Neuroticism
Pathological Narcissism Inventory	– Grandiose narcissism		Vulnerable narcissism
Wink (1992)	Autonomy	Willfulness	Hypersensitivity
Russ, Shedler, Bradley, and Westen (2008)	High-functioning/Exhibitionistic	Grandiose/Malignant	Fragile
NARQ	Admiration	Rivalry	–
Narcissistic Personality Inventory	Leadership/Authority Grandiose Exhibitionism	Leadership/Authority Grandiose Exhibitionism Entitlement/Exploitativeness	–
Narcissistic Grandiosity Scale	Narcissistic Grandiosity		–
PID-5 NPD	Antagonism		–
Narcissistic Vulnerability Scale	–	Narcissistic Vulnerability	
Hypersensitive Narcissism Scale	–	Hypersensitive Narcissism	
Psychological Entitlement Scale	–	Entitlement	–
Interpersonal Exploitativeness Scale	–	Interpersonal Exploitativeness	–

Note. Narcissism Spectrum Model = Krizan and Herlache (2018); Five-factor Narcissism Inventory = Glover et al. (2012); Pathological Narcissism Inventory = Pincus et al. (2009); NARQ = Narcissistic Admiration and Rivalry Questionnaire = Back et al. (2013); Narcissistic Personality Inventory = Raskin and Terry (1988); Narcissistic Grandiosity Scale = Rosenthal, Hooley, and Steshenko (2007); Narcissistic Vulnerability Scale = Crowe et al. (2018); PID-5 = Personality Inventory for DSM-5 = Krueger, Derringer, Markon, Watson, and Skodol (2012); Hypersensitive Narcissism Scale = Hendin and Cheek (1997); Psychological Entitlement Scale = Campbell, Bonacci, Shelton, Exline, and Bushman (2004); Interpersonal Exploitativeness Scale = Brunell et al. (2013).

From OSF.IO/2UA35 under CC0 1.0 Universal.

Table 2 Psychopathological markers in relation to narcissism

	Single-factor model	Two-factor model		Three-factor model			
	FFNI total	**FFNI G**	**FFNI V**	**FFNI A**	**FFNI E**	**FFNI N**	***n***
DSM-5 traits							
Negative affectivity	**.33***	**–.07**	**.84***	.44*	**–.28***	**.74***	~95
Detachment	**.17**	**–.18**	**.70***	.38*	**–.49***	.55*	~95
Psychoticism	**.37***	**.20**	.42*	.48*	**–.13**	.25	~95
Disinhibition	.42*	.36*	**.20**	.49*	**.08**	**.16**	~95
Antagonism	**.73***	**.53***	**.54***	.80*	**.18**	.31*	~95
Manipulative	.68*	.61*	**.29***	.67*	**.36***	**.15**	~95
Deceitfulness	**.59***	**.38***	.53*	.70*	**.02**	**.40***	~95
Grandiosity	.61*	.57*	**.22**	.62*	**.30***	**.01**	~95
Attention seeking	.56*	.51*	**.23**	.47*	.44*	**.14**	~95
Callousness	**.50***	**.37***	**.36***	.67*	**–.05**	**.15**	~95
Hostility	**.46***	**.17**	.64*	.56*	**–.07**	.41*	~95
Internalizing							
Anger	.33*	**.10**	.53*	.40*	**–.10**	.38*	~95
Anxiety^{m}	.17	**–.09**	**.64**	.14	**–.08**	**.54**	~690
Depression^{m}	.13	**–.13**	**.64**	.15	**–.17**	**.55**	~690
Self-esteem^{m}	–.13	**.10**	**–.58**	–.14	**.18**	**–.56**	~1070

Note. G = Grandiose; V = Vulnerable; A = Antagonism; E = Agentic Extraversion; N = Neuroticism; m superscript indicates where inferential statistical results are not presented given correlation values were combined across multiple datasets; bold indicates where FFNI A correlation values significantly differ from FFNI total, FFNI G, FFNI V, FFNI E, and FFNI N; $P < .01$.

Correlates of individual functioning at three levels of organization

In this section, we examine correlates of functioning/impairment across three levels of organization. We selected three important areas: psychopathology (Table 2); externalizing behaviors, aggression, and psychopathy (Table 3); and interpersonal and attachment styles (Table 4). To determine if correlates differ significantly between FFNI Antagonism and other narcissism factors, the correlations for FFNI Antagonism were tested against the correlations for the other factors using tests of dependent *r*s ($P \leq .01$).

Psychopathological markers. To examine the relations between factors of narcissism and psychopathology, we examined psychopathological correlates including DSM-5 pathological personality traits, internalizing symptoms of anger, anxiety, and depression, and self-esteem (Table 2). We first examined correlates at the single-factor level; FFNI Total narcissism was substantively associated with all

Table 3 Externalizing behaviors, aggression, and psychopathy in relation to narcissism

	Single-factor model	Two-factor model		Three-factor model			
	FFNI total	FFNI G	FFNI V	FFNI A	FFNI E	FFNI N	*n*
Externalizing behaviors							
Substance use^m	.12	.11	.07	.12	**.03**	**–.02**	~1070
Antisocial behavior^m	.20	.19	**.11**	.22	**.09**	**–.03**	~1070
Aggression							
Proactive	**.36***	**.34***	**.19***	.44*	**.15***	–.02	~790
Reactive	.33*	**.21***	**.43***	.33*	**.16***	**.19***	~790
Psychopathy	**.69***	**.63***	**.39***	.80*	**.07**	**.05**	~370

Note. G = Grandiose; V = Vulnerable; A = Antagonism; E = Agentic Extraversion; N = Neuroticism; m superscript indicates where inferential statistical results are not presented given correlation values were combined across multiple datasets; bold indicates where FFNI A correlation values significantly differ from FFNI total, FFNI G, FFNI V, FFNI E, and FFNI N; $P < .01$.

Table 4 Interpersonal styles in relation to narcissism

	Single-factor model	Two-factor model		Three-factor model			
	FFNI total	FFNI G	FFNI V	FFNI A	FFNI E	FFNI N	*n*
Interpersonal circumplex^m							
Assured dominant	**.30**	**.41**	**–.11**	.19	**.48**	**–.28**	~475
Arrogant calculating	.57	.61	**.19**	.57	**.26**	**–.10**	~475
Cold-hearted	**.54**	**.51**	**.31**	.66	**–.07**	**–.03**	~475
Aloof introverted	**.37**	**.26**	**.42**	.52	**–.29**	**.18**	~475
Unassured submissive	**.02**	**–.12**	**.31**	.11	**–.38**	**.30**	~475
Unassuming ingenuous	**–.22**	**–.28**	**.04**	–.15	**–.34**	**.10**	~475
Warm agreeable	**–.38**	**–.36**	**–.22**	–.53	**.15**	**.02**	~475
Gregarious extraverted	**–.21**	**–.09**	–.36	–.39	**.38**	**–.21**	~475
Dominant	**.08**	**.24**	**–.29**	–.07	**.54**	**–.30**	~475
Love	**–.56**	**–.51**	**–.37**	–.70	**.11**	**–.03**	~475

Table 4 Continued

Attachment style							
Anxious	.32*	**.14**	**.53***	.35*	**−.08**	.43*	~285
Avoidant	**.32***	**.27***	**.26***	.44*	**−.18***	**.04**	~285
Love styles^m							
Eros	**−.03**	**.02**	−.15	−.11	**.15**	−.10	~705
Ludus	**.32**	**.27**	**.25**	.39	**.08**	**.13**	~705
Storge	−.08	−.04	−.14	−.09	.01	−.10	~705
Pragma	**.24**	.22	.14	.19	.24	.09	~705
Mania	.31	**.17**	**.43**	.29	**.11**	.32	~705
Agape	**−.02**	−.05	**.04**	−.08	**.04**	**.08**	~705

Note. G = Grandiose; V = Vulnerable; A = Antagonism; E = Agentic Extraversion; N = Neuroticism; m superscript indicates where inferential statistical results are not presented given correlation values were combined across multiple datasets; bold indicates where FFNI A correlation values significantly differ from FFNI total, FFNI G, FFNI V, FFNI E, and FFNI N; $P < .01$.

PID-5 Antagonism facets, as well as the domains of Disinhibition, Psychoticism, and Negative Affectivity. The total narcissism score was also related to problems with anger and unrelated to self-esteem. Next, we examined correlates at the two-factor level, which reflect levels of psychopathology across the main two dimensions of narcissism. Grandiose narcissism exhibited moderate to strong associations with DSM-5 Disinhibition and Antagonism, with particularly high elevations for facets of Manipulativeness, Grandiosity, and Attention Seeking. Vulnerable narcissism exhibited strong associations with Anger, as well as DSM-5 Negative Affectivity, Detachment, and Antagonism (highest facet-level elevations on deceitfulness and hostility), and evinced strong associations with all internalizing domains including anxiety, depression, and self-esteem (negative relation). The general lack of discriminant validity found for Vulnerable narcissism, compared to Grandiose narcissism, is consistent with previous work (e.g., Miller et al., 2011) and the fact that this construct is primarily composed of trait Neuroticism (Miller, Lynam, Viz et al., 2018)—a robust risk factor for psychopathology (e.g., Lahey, 2009).

Next, we examined correlates at the three-factor level to understand the degree to which Antagonism, versus Agentic Extraversion and Neuroticism, is responsible for psychopathology outcomes across Grandiose and Vulnerable dimensions. With respect to Grandiose narcissism, Antagonism, relative to Agentic Extraversion, appears primarily responsible for the association between Grandiose narcissism and PID-5 Psychoticism, Disinhibition, and Antagonism. Interestingly, although Agentic Extraversion is equally related to psychopathological traits involving Grandiosity, Attention Seeking, and Manipulativeness, it appears to *mute* the effect of Antagonism on trait Negative Affectivity and Detachment. With respect to Vulnerable narcissism, Antagonism appears primarily responsible for the association between Vulnerable narcissism and DSM-5 domains of Psychoticism and Antagonism. Conversely, FFNI Neuroticism appears primarily responsible for associations between Vulnerable narcissism and internalizing forms of psychopathology.

Externalizing behaviors, aggression, and psychopathy. To examine the relations between factors of narcissism and externalizing behaviors, aggression, and psychopathy, we examined relevant correlates including counts of substance use and antisocial behavior, reactive and proactive aggression, and psychopathy (Table 3). We first examined correlates at the single-factor level and two-factor level in order to understand narcissism's general association with externalizing, aggression, and psychopathy. FFNI Total and Grandiose narcissism were both positively correlated with reactive and proactive aggression, as well as psychopathic traits. Our pattern of results was consistent with previous research suggesting that Grandiose and Vulnerable narcissism are differentially related to proactive and reactive aggression (Vize et al., 2017). Next, we examined the degree to which Antagonism may drive the association between Grandiose and Vulnerable narcissism and outcomes. Antagonism appears primarily responsible for the association between both narcissism dimensions and antisocial behavior, aggression, and psychopathy, showing a weak to moderate correlation with antisocial behavior ($r=.22$), moderate correlations with proactive and reactive aggression ($rs=.44$, .33, respectively), and a strong correlation with psychopathy ($r=.80$). The effect sizes for Antagonism exceeded those for Agentic Extraversion and Neuroticism across all outcomes.

Interpersonal correlates. We next examined the relations between factors of narcissism and interpersonal, attachment, and romantic correlates (Table 4). We first examined correlates at the single- and two-factor levels in order to understand narcissism's general association with interpersonal circumplex (IPC) correlates. The FFNI Total narcissism score manifested a strong negative correlation with IPC love but was unrelated to dominance, manifested moderate associations with attachment difficulties, and moderate positive relations with several love styles including a game playing approach (i.e., ludus). As expected, Grandiose and Vulnerable narcissism manifested similarly negative correlations with IPC love but differed with respect to IPC dominance (Grandiose: positive; Vulnerable: negative) and Vulnerable narcissism demonstrated more pervasive attachment difficulties, as expected (Dickinson & Pincus, 2003; Miller et al., 2010, 2011). Both Grandiose and Vulnerable narcissism were related to ludus and mania love styles. Ludus is described as a "game-playing" love, whereas mania is described as a "possessive, dependent love" (Hendrick & Hendrick, 1986, p. 393).

Next, we examined the degree to which Antagonism, relative to Agentic Extraversion and Neuroticism, is responsible for the association between Grandiose and Vulnerable narcissism and interpersonal correlates. Antagonism appears primarily responsible for the association between both narcissism dimensions and styles related to IPC love (negative), avoidant attachment styles, as well as a tendency toward a ludus-related love style, which is consistent with previous work (e.g., Miller et al., 2011; White, Hendrick, & Hendrick, 2004). Notably, Agentic Extraversion and Neuroticism appear to disproportionately influence each narcissistic dimension's interpersonal style related to dominance (Grandiose: positive; Vulnerable; negative), which is broadly consistent with Krizan and Herlache's (2018) argument regarding these constructs relations with approach versus avoidance-orientation.

FFM facet-level profile at three levels of organization

Our primary source of data for examining the FFM trait profiles of narcissism at the one-, two-, and three-factor levels of organization involved a meta-analytically combined dataset containing data from the FFNI and two measures of FFM personality, namely, the NEO Personality Inventory-Revised (NEO PI R; Costa & McCrae, 1992) and IPIP-NEO 120 (Maples, Guan, Carter, & Miller, 2014). To determine if correlates differed significantly between FFNI Antagonism and other narcissism factors, tests of dependent *r*s were conducted using a *P*-value equal to or less than .01 (see Table 5).

Single-factor level. The FFNI Total score exhibited weak to strong relations across all Agreeableness facets (Table 5) with correlations ranging from −.24 (Trust) to −.57 (Straightforwardness) with a median of −.35. These findings are roughly consistent with correlates related to NPD (Samuel & Widiger, 2008).

Two-factor level. FFNI Grandiose narcissism manifested its largest correlations with facets of Straightforwardness (−.53) and Modesty (−.58) with smaller relations for Trust (−.06) and Altruism (−.18). Conversely, FFNI Vulnerable narcissism manifested its strongest relations with Trust (−.46) and Compliance (−.33) with no relation to Modesty (.06). These findings are largely consistent with discussions regarding how Antagonism may be expressed differently across Grandiose and Vulnerable dimensions. Krizan and Herlache (2018) posit that Agentic Extraversion and Neuroticism may be key dimensions in influencing the types of antagonistic traits that people exhibit. For example, research suggests that vulnerably narcissistic individuals with an avoidance-orientation are more distrustful and are more likely than Grandiose individuals to read malevolent intent in the actions of others. Grandiosely narcissistic individuals with an approach-orientation are more likely to exhibit immodest behavior, possibly linked to motives involving self-enhancement and status-acquisition as well as early life parental overvaluation (Brummelman et al., 2015).

Three-factor level. We next examined the facet-level profile of Antagonism, Agentic Extraversion, and Neuroticism in our meta-analytically combined dataset (Table 5). As expected, given its development, FFNI Antagonism shows moderate to strong negative correlations across FFM Antagonism facets with correlations ranging from −.32 (Trust) to −.63 (Straightforwardness). Conversely, FFNI Agentic Extraversion (range −.45 [Modesty] to .15 [Altruism]) and FFNI Neuroticism (range −.12 [Trust] to .21 [Modesty]) manifested a mixture of positive and negative relations.

Similarity of correlates across narcissism

We next examined the similarity of relations to functioning and FFM facets across our three levels of organization (Table 6). Similarity was calculated using intraclass correlations that take into account absolute similarity of the correlational profiles. FFNI Antagonism closely maps onto the single-factor score (i.e., FFNI Total; $ICC = .97$), exceeding both Grandiose narcissism and Vulnerable narcissism in its convergence. The same is not true of either the Agentic Extraversion ($ICC = .17$) or Neuroticism

Table 5 Five-Factor Model agreeableness facets in relation to narcissism

FFM	Single-factor model				Two-factor model		Three-factor model		
	Academic ratings (NPD)	**Clinician ratings (NPD)**	**Lay ratings (narcissism)**	**FFNI total**	**FFNI G**	**FFNI V**	**FFNI A**	**FFNI E**	**FFNI N**
Trust	1.42	1.86	2.09	**–.24**	**–.06**	**–.46**	–.32	**.08**	**–.12**
Straightforwardness	1.83	1.91	1.98	**–.57**	**–.53**	**–.28**	–.63	**–.27**	**–.10**
Altruism	1.00	1.73	1.77	**–.25**	**–.18**	**–.23**	–.42	**.15**	**–.05**
Compliance	1.58	1.77	1.98	**–.44**	**–.36**	**–.33**	–.51	**–.17**	**–.08**
Modesty	1.08	1.23	1.55	–.48	**–.58**	**.06**	–.48	–.45	**.21**
Tendermindedness	1.5	1.77	2.00	**–.25**	**–.25**	**–.10**	–.39	**.02**	**.08**
n				~857	~857	~857	~857	~857	~857
Profile similarity (second order rs)									
FFNI total	–.43	.21	.27						
FFNI G	–.18	.51	.54						
FFNI V	–.30	–.62	–.55						

Note. G = Grandiose; V = Vulnerable; A = Antagonism; E = Agentic Extraversion; N = Neuroticism; Academician ratings = Lynam and Widiger (2001); Clinician ratings = Samuel and Widiger (2004); Lay ratings = Miller, Lynam, Siedor et al. (2018); Inferential statistical results are not presented given correlation values were combined across multiple datasets; bold indicates where FFNI A correlation values significantly differ from FFNI total, FFNI G, FFNI V, FFNI E, and FFNI N; $P < .01$.

Table 6 Profile similarities for all FFM traits and correlates across narcissism

	FFNI Total	FFNI G	FFNI V	FFNI A	FFNI E
FFNI G	.90	–			
FFNI V	.70	.36	–		
FFNI A	.97	.82	.75	–	
FFNI E	.17	.46	−.37	.02	–
FFNI N	.31	−.04	.82	.35	−.54

Note. A, Antagonism; *E*, Agentic Extraversion; *G*, Grandiose; *N*, Neuroticism; *V*, Vulnerable; $P < .01$.

(*ICC* = .31) factors, which both show a much weaker match with the FFNI total score' empirical profile. At the two-factor level, Antagonism shows strong overlap with both Grandiose narcissism (*ICC* = .82), and Vulnerable narcissism (*ICC* = .75), whereas Agentic Extraversion and Neuroticism are related differentially to Grandiose (Agentic Extraversion: *ICC* = .46; Neuroticism: −.04) and Vulnerable narcissism (Agentic Extraversion: *ICC* = −.37; Neuroticism: .82). At the three-factor level, Antagonism appears to converge moderately with Neuroticism (*ICC* = .35), while showing no convergence with Agentic Extraversion (*ICC* = .02). These results are consistent with the notion that Antagonism represents the core of narcissism, whether studied at a single- or two-factor (Grandiose vs Vulnerable) level of the hierarchy and that narcissistic aspects of Extraversion and Neuroticism play key roles in describing the Grandiose versus Vulnerable dimensions.

Antagonism in narcissism: A summary

We begin with the first question: Can Antagonism be considered the core trait of narcissism? Historically, researchers have identified Antagonism as narcissism's core by virtue of its structural presence in narcissism's two main dimensions (i.e., Grandiose, Vulnerable). Our results reflect Antagonism's structural relevance to narcissism across single- and two-factor models, as well as Antagonism's functional relevance within narcissism's nomological network. First, FFM Antagonism trait correlates overlap substantially with the single- and two-factor models of narcissism. Grandiose narcissism is most strongly characterized by a lack of modesty and straightforwardness whereas Vulnerable narcissism reflects Antagonism in the form of distrust and oppositionality. Furthermore, both Grandiose and Vulnerable narcissism reflect almost exclusively negative associations with FFM Agreeableness facets, suggesting a common core of Antagonism.

Second, examinations of external correlates with dimensions of the trifurcated model indicate that, overall, Antagonism seems primarily responsible for the externalizing behaviors associated with pathological and Grandiose narcissism (e.g., aggressive; manipulative, grandiose, angry, noncommunal, game playing), as well as its overlap with its "near neighbor," psychopathy. There are notable exceptions however, where other trifurcated dimensions besides Antagonism appear to explain equally well certain behaviors. For Grandiose narcissism, Agentic Extraversion counteracts

Antagonism's negative association with altruism, while contributing to greater immodesty. For Vulnerable narcissism, Neuroticism may counteract Antagonism's positive association with immodesty and may in part explain the limited amount of grandiosity expressed in Vulnerable narcissism.

With respect to our second question (i.e., is the Antagonism of Grandiose narcissism the same as the Antagonism of Vulnerable narcissism?), although Antagonism may be the core of both primary narcissistic presentations, this core is itself multifaceted, consisting of multiple antagonistic traits that appear differentially related to each. Vulnerable narcissism demonstrates its weakest relations with Modesty and Tender-mindedness and highest relations with Trust, whereas Grandiose narcissism shows an inverse pattern.

Implications for a syncretic model of narcissism

We believe that the time has come to clarify and consolidate varied yet overlapping conceptualizations/models of narcissism, especially since many of them converge in important ways. We offer four propositions to this end: First, narcissism can be conceptualized as existing at multiple hierarchical levels. The decision regarding at which level to work (e.g., 1, 2, 3) depends on the aims and the constraints of the researcher. Second, numerous measures contain information relevant to one of the three factors of narcissism outlined here, but most of these do not provide coverage across all of them (e.g., HSNS, NARQ, PES). Thus there is a need for researchers to use (a) measurement "stacks," such as the NPI and HSNS, or NGS and PNI, or (b) a combined measure like the FFNI, if they want to examine all aspects of narcissism. Third, the antagonistic component of Grandiose and Vulnerable narcissism may largely share negative relations with traits related to straightforwardness, altruism, and compliance, yet fail to share relations with traits related to modesty, trust, and tender-mindedness. These patterns of relations have important implications for future assessment of narcissistic presentations. Rather than use a nonoverlapping set of antagonistic traits to characterize Grandiose and Vulnerable narcissism, an approach that assesses all antagonistic traits would comprehensively capture both antagonistic traits held in common across different presentations. Fourth, the alternative model of NPD in Section III of DSM-5 (i.e., Alternative DSM-5 Model for Personality Disorders) may not adequately assess the antagonistic features characteristic of narcissism (e.g., Miller et al., 2017). It is our contention that the core of narcissism/NPD is made of traits related to Antagonism and that traits from this domain should form the bedrock of NPD's assessment in DSM. Indeed, the present findings illustrate that both Grandiose and Vulnerable narcissism show a pattern of meaningful associations with all Criterion B facets of Antagonism. Regrettably, the use of only two traits to assess NPD as part of Criterion B (i.e., Grandiosity, Attention Seeking) may provide inadequate coverage of the NPD construct, especially Vulnerable narcissism (Miller, Gentile, & Campbell, 2013).

We propose that the traits used to assess NPD should be expanded to include other relevant traits beyond Grandiosity and Attention Seeking, including Manipulativeness, Deceitfulness, Callousness, and Hostility, which are consistent with traits emphasized by other expert-based characterizations (e.g., manipulativeness, callousness, entitlement; Ackerman, Hands, Donnellan, Hopwood, & Witt, 2016; Lynam & Widiger, 2001; Samuel, Lynam, Widiger, & Ball, 2012), We believe that the overall construct validity of NPD's diagnosis must be prioritized over discriminant validity-related concerns, even if the inclusion of these additional traits increases its overlap with near neighbor disorders like antisocial PD (Miller et al., 2017).

Future directions

The Trifurcated Model of Narcissism represents an important step beyond the Grandiose versus Vulnerable distinction that has been the focus of research for the past decade (and which itself was a major step forward in understanding narcissism). While the Grandiose versus Vulnerable distinction remains indispensable, the three-factor model (a) provides an avenue for richer explanatory models of narcissism and (b) can be used to assess an individual's presentation with high granularity.

References

Ackerman, R. A., Hands, A. J., Donnellan, M. B., Hopwood, C. J., & Witt, E. A. (2016). Experts' views regarding the conceptualization of narcissism. *Journal of Personality Disorders*, *31*, 1–16.

American Psychiatric Association. (2013). *Diagnostic and statistical manual of mental disorders* (5th ed.). Washington, DC: American Psychiatric Association.

Back, M. D., Küfner, A. P., Dufner, M., Gerlach, T. M., Rauthmann, J. F., & Denissen, J. A. (2013). Narcissistic admiration and rivalry: disentangling the bright and dark sides of narcissism. *Journal of Personality and Social Psychology*, *105*, 1013–1037.

Brummelman, E., Thomaes, S., Nelemans, S. A., de Castro, B. O., Overbeek, G., & Bushman, B. J. (2015). Origins of narcissism in children. *Proceedings of the National Academy of Sciences of the United States of America*, *112*, 3659–3662.

Brunell, A. B., Davis, M. S., Scheley, D. R., Eng, A. L., Dulmen, M. H. M., Wester, K. L., et al. (2013). A new measure of interpersonal exploitativeness. *Frontiers in Psychology*, *4*, 1–9.

Cain, N. M., Pincus, A. L., & Ansell, E. B. (2008). Narcissism at the crossroads: phenotypic description of pathological narcissism across clinical theory, social/personality psychology, and psychiatric diagnosis. *Clinical Psychology Review*, *28*, 638–656.

Campbell, W. K., Bonacci, A. M., Shelton, J., Exline, J. J., & Bushman, B. J. (2004). Psychological entitlement: interpersonal consequences and validation of a self-report measure. *Journal of Personality Assessment*, *83*(1), 29–45.

Costa, P. T., & McCrae, R. R. (1992). *Revised NEO personality inventory (NEO PI-R) and NEO five-factor inventory (NEO-FFI) professional manual*. Lutz, FL: PAR.

Crowe, M., Edershile, E. A., Wright, A. G. C., Keith Campbell, W., Lynam, D. R., & Miller, J. D. (2018). Development and validation of the Narcissistic Vulnerability Scale: an adjective rating scale. *Psychological Assessment*, *30*, 978–983.

Dickinson, K. A., & Pincus, A. L. (2003). Interpersonal analysis of grandiose and vulnerable narcissism. *Journal of Personality Disorders*, *17*, 188–207.

Fossati, A., Beauchaine, T. P., Grazioli, F., Carretta, I., Cortinovis, F., & Maffei, C. (2005). A latent structure analysis of Diagnostic and Statistical Manual of Mental Disorders, Narcissistic Personality Disorder criteria. *Comprehensive Psychiatry*, *46*, 361–367.

Glover, N., Miller, J. D., Lynam, D. R., Crego, C., & Widiger, T. A. (2012). The Five-Factor Narcissism Inventory: a five-factor measure of narcissistic personality traits. *Journal of Personality Assessment*, *94*, 500–512.

Hendin, H. M., & Cheek, J. M. (1997). Assessing hypersensitive narcissism: a reexamination of Murray's Narcissism Scale. *Journal of Research in Personality*, *31*, 588–599.

Hendrick, C., & Hendrick, S. S. (1986). A theory and method of love. *Journal of Personality and Social Psychology*, *50*, 392–402.

Kernberg, O. F. (1974). Contrasting viewpoints regarding the nature and psychoanalytic treatment of narcissistic personalities. *Journal of the American Psychoanalytic Association*, *22*, 255–267.

Kohut, H. (1972). Thoughts on narcissism and narcissistic rage. *Psychoanalytic Study of the Child*, *27*, 360–400.

Krizan, Z., & Herlache, A. D. (2018). The narcissism spectrum model: a synthetic view of narcissistic personality. *Personality and Social Psychology Review*, *22*, 3–31.

Krueger, R. F., Derringer, J., Markon, K. E., Watson, D., & Skodol, A. E. (2012). Initial construction of a maladaptive personality trait model and inventory for DSM-5. *Psychological Medicine*, *42*, 1879–1890.

Lahey, B. B. (2009). Public health significance of neuroticism. *American Psychologist*, *64*, 241–256.

Lynam, D. R., & Widiger, T. A. (2001). Using the five-factor model to represent the DSM-IV personality disorders: an expert consensus approach. *Journal of Abnormal Psychology*, *110*, 401.

Maples, J. L., Guan, L., Carter, N. T., & Miller, J. D. (2014). A test of the International Personality Item Pool representation of the Revised NEO Personality Inventory and development of a 120-item IPIP-based measure of the five-factor model. *Psychological Assessment*, *26*, 1070–1084.

Miller, J. D., & Campbell, W. K. (2008). Comparing clinical and social-personality conceptualizations of narcissism. *Journal of Personality*, *76*, 449–476.

Miller, J. D., Dir, A., Gentile, B., Wilson, L., Pryor, L. R., & Campbell, W. K. (2010). Searching for a vulnerable dark triad: comparing factor 2 psychopathy, vulnerable narcissism, and borderline personality disorder. *Journal of Personality*, *78*, 1529–1564.

Miller, J. D., Gaughan, E. T., Maples, J., Gentile, B., Lynam, D. R., & Widiger, T. A. (2011). Examining the construct validity of the Elemental Psychopathy Assessment. *Assessment*, *18*, 106–114.

Miller, J. D., Gentile, B., & Campbell, W. K. (2013). A test of the construct validity of the Five-Factor Narcissism Inventory. *Journal of Personality Assessment*, *95*, 377–387.

Miller, J. D., Hoffman, B. J., Campbell, W. K., & Pilkonis, P. A. (2008). An examination of the factor structure of Diagnostic and Statistical Manual of Mental Disorders, narcissistic personality disorder criteria: one or two factors? *Comprehensive Psychiatry*, *49*, 141–145.

Miller, J. D., Lynam, D. R., Hyatt, C. S., & Campbell, W. K. (2017). Controversies in narcissism. *Annual Review of Clinical Psychology*, *13*, 1–25.

Miller, J. D., Lynam, D. R., McCain, J. L., Few, L. R., Crego, C., Widiger, T. A., et al. (2016). Thinking structurally about narcissism: an examination of the five-factor narcissism inventory and its components. *Journal of Personality Disorders*, *30*, 1–18.

Miller, J. D., Lynam, D. R., Siedor, L., Crowe, M., & Campbell, W. K. (2018). Consensual lay profiles of narcissism and their connection to the Five-Factor Narcissism Inventory. *Psychological Assessment*, *30*, 10–18.

Miller, J. D., Lynam, D. R., Vize, C., Crowe, M., Sleep, C., Maples-Keller, J. L., et al. (2018). Vulnerable narcissism is (mostly) a disorder of neuroticism. *Journal of Personality*, *86*, 186–199.

Ovid, & Miller, F. J. (1946). *Ovid: Metamorphoses*: (p. 1946). Cambridge/London: Harvard University Press/Heinemann.

Pincus, A. L., Ansell, E. B., Pimentel, C. A., Cain, N. M., Wright, A. G., & Levy, K. N. (2009). Initial construction and validation of the Pathological Narcissism Inventory. *Psychological Assessment*, *21*, 365–379.

Raskin, R., & Terry, H. (1988). A principal-components analysis of the Narcissistic Personality Inventory and further evidence of its construct validity. *Journal of Personality and Social Psychology*, *54*, 890–902.

Rosenthal, S. A., Hooley, J. M., & Steshenko, Y. (2007). *Distinguishing grandiosity from self-esteem: Development of the Narcissistic Grandiosity Scale*. Unpublished manuscript.

Samuel, D. B., Lynam, D. R., Widiger, T. A., & Ball, S. A. (2012). An expert consensus approach to relating the proposed DSM-5 types and traits. *Personality Disorders: Theory, Research, and Treatment*, *3*, 1–16.

Samuel, D. B., & Widiger, T. A. (2004). Clinicians' personality descriptions of prototypic personality disorders. *Journal of Personality Disorders*, *18*, 286–308.

Samuel, D. B., & Widiger, T. A. (2008). A meta-analytic review of the relationships between the five-factor model and DSM-IV-TR personality disorders: a facet level analysis. *Clinical Psychology Review*, *28*, 1326–1342.

Vize, C. E., Collison, K. L., Crowe, M. L., Campbell, W. K., Miller, J. D., & Lynam, D. R. (2017). Using dominance analysis to decompose narcissism and its relation to aggression and externalizing outcomes. *Assessment*, 1–11.

White, J. K., Hendrick, S. S., & Hendrick, C. (2004). Big five personality variables and relationship constructs. *Personality and Individual Differences*, *37*, 1519–1530.

Wink, P. (1991). Two faces of narcissism. *Journal of Personality and Social Psychology*, *61*, 590–597.

Antagonism and borderline personality disorder

16

Neil A. Meyer, Jiwon Min, Stephanie N. Mullins-Sweatt
Department of Psychology, Oklahoma State University, Stillwater, OK, United States

As described throughout this book, the five-factor model (FFM) of personality is a well-validated model of general personality that describes adaptive and maladaptive personality functioning. The FFM has been used to examine personality disorders in over 100 research studies (Widiger, Gore, Crego, Rojas, & Oltmanns, 2017). A number of these studies have specifically examined the relationship of the FFM with borderline personality disorder (BPD), one of the most commonly researched personality disorders in the *Diagnostic and Statistical Manual of Mental Disorders* (5th ed., DSM-5; American Psychiatric Association, 2013). This chapter will review how antagonism relates to the BPD diagnosis as well as to the individual symptoms and associated correlates of BPD. Next, this chapter will examine existing literature that has compared the FFM with self-report measures of BPD and transdiagnostic characteristics of BPD (e.g., emotion dysregulation). Finally, the clinical utility and implications of antagonism's relationship with BPD will be explored.

Antagonism and BPD defined

BPD is a highly debilitating disorder characterized by interpersonal dysfunction, unstable identity, emotion dysregulation, and behavioral impulsivity (see Table 1; American Psychiatric Association, 2013). The median estimate of BPD's prevalence in the general population is between 1.6% (Lenzenweger, Lane, Loranger, & Kessler, 2007) and 5.9% (Grant et al., 2008). Research has indicated that these symptoms are experienced more intensely earlier in the lifespan (Distel et al., 2008), with approximately 75% of treatment-receiving individuals no longer meeting diagnostic criteria 15 years after their initial diagnosis (Paris, Brown, & Nowlis, 1987). Zanarini, Frankenburg, Hennen, and Silk (2003) found that nearly 70% of patients with BPD were in remission at 6-year follow-up. BPD is also highly heritable, even after controlling for environmental effects (Torgersen, 1984; Torgersen et al., 2000). Recently, Distel et al. (2008) demonstrated that biological factors account for 42% of the variance in BPD symptom severity within 5496 monozygotic and dizygotic twins (using samples from The Netherlands, Belgium, and Australia).

Within the last 25 years, a number of studies have examined the relationship of BPD with the FFM. BPD is characterized by high scores on the neuroticism domain and all six facets of neuroticism (Samuel & Widiger, 2008). However, given that a

The Handbook of Antagonism. https://doi.org/10.1016/B978-0-12-814627-9.00016-5

Table 1 DSM-5 diagnostic criteria for borderline personality disorder.

A pervasive pattern of instability of interpersonal relationships, self-image, and affects, and marked impulsivity beginning by early adulthood and present in a variety of contexts, as indicated by five (or more) of the following:
1. Frantic efforts to avoid real or imagined abandonment
2. A pattern of unstable and intense interpersonal relationships characterized by alternating between extremes of idealization and devaluation
3. Identity disturbance: notably and persistently unstable self-image or sense of self
4. Impulsivity in at least two areas that are potentially self-damaging (e.g., spending, sex, substance misuse, reckless driving, binge eating)
5. Recurrent suicidal gestures, or threats or self-mutilating behavior
6. Affective instability caused by a distinct reactivity of mood (e.g., intense episodic dysphoria, irritability, or anxiety usually lasting a few hours and only rarely more than a few days)
7. Chronic feelings of emptiness
8. Inappropriate intense anger or difficulty controlling anger (e.g., frequent displays of temper, constant anger, recurrent physical fights)
9. Transient, stress-related paranoid ideation or severe dissociative symptoms

number of PDs are characterized by high neuroticism (e.g., avoidant, dependent, schizotypal; Samuel & Widiger, 2008), antagonism is an important trait that distinguishes BPD from these disorders. Recent efforts have compared each of the nine DSM-5 BPD symptoms with the domains of the FFM by comparing the mean differences in NEO-PI-R domain scores in those who did and did not meet criteria for a given BPD symptom (Säämänen et al., 2016). Using the Structured Clinical Interview for DSM-IV Axis II Personality Questionnaire (SCID-II-PQ; First, Benjamin, Gibbon, Spitzer, & Williams, 1997) in a sample of 43 psychiatric inpatients, antagonism related most strongly to the "inappropriate anger" symptom ($r=0.68$). Antagonism also was related to "affective instability" ($r=0.64$) and "impulsivity" ($r=0.64$; Säämänen et al., 2016). Notably, neuroticism related to nearly all symptoms, with the exception of "chronic feelings of emptiness" and "unstable relationships," while extraversion related to "impulsivity" and "affective instability." While antagonism was not significantly related to the total number of BPD symptoms, it was significantly related to the total number of questions endorsed in SCID-II-PQ BPD ($r=0.39$). The authors report that their results support previous studies that indicate a relationship between antagonism, neuroticism, and BPD, though the associations between BPD and antagonism found in their study may not generalize outside of an inpatient sample (Säämänen et al., 2016). Within the antagonism domain, several of its facets are related to symptoms of BPD. Analyses of BPD symptoms suggest that four symptoms (i.e., frantic efforts to avoid real or imagined abandonment, pattern of unstable relationship, suicidality, and identity disturbances) were positively related to antagonism using DSM-III criteria (Clarkin, Hull, & Hurt, 1993).

FFM conceptualization of BPD

As implied before, while a categorical diagnosis of BPD remains in DSM-5, an emerging body of research suggests that BPD also can be conceptualized as maladaptive variants of the FFM (Madsen, Parsons, & Grubin, 2006; Miller, Reynolds, & Pilkonis, 2004; Nestadt et al., 2008; Rolland & De Fruyt, 2003). Lynam and Widiger (2001) surveyed 24 BPD experts to develop a consensus profile of BPD. Using a 1 to 5 point scale (with 1 being "very low" and 5 being "very high"), the mean consensus profile indicated that BPD was described as high neuroticism, low agreeableness, and low conscientiousness. At the facet level, agreeableness traits were generally rated between "low" and "neither high nor low." Trust, deception, altruism, and compliance were described as relatively "low." Samuel and Widiger (2004) expanded this research by recruiting 154 private practitioners to develop a clinician-based FFM consensus of BPD. Using the same Likert scale, Samuel and Widiger's (2004) results were congruent with those of Lynam and Widiger (2001). For example, trust, straightforwardness, altruism, compliance, modesty, and tender-mindedness all ranged between "extremely low" and "neither high nor low." Additionally, all but one facet of neuroticism (self-consciousness) was characteristic of BPD, as was one facet from extraversion (excitement seeking) and openness to experience (fantasy) (Table 2).

Following these hypothesis-driven ratings among experts and clinicians, a growing body of empirical work enabled Saulsman and Page (2004) to examine how the FFM relates to BPD and other personality disorders by conducting a meta-analysis. The authors compared 12 studies and found that BPD was positively related to neuroticism and antagonism and negatively related to conscientiousness. Samuel and Widiger (2008) furthered this research by conducting a meta-analysis on 16 studies to provide facet-level data on these relationships. This research found that BPD was characterized by high neuroticism, high antagonism, and low conscientiousness. At the facet level, 27 of 30 facets were significantly related to BPD, including 3 antagonism facets (mistrust, deception, and oppositionality) were related (Samuel & Widiger, 2008). More recently, Samuel, Lynam, Widiger, and Ball (2012) solicited expert ratings utilizing the DSM-5 Alternative Model of Personality Disorder. Experts described a prototypic case or narrative description of PD in terms of the 37 traits proposed for inclusion in DSM-5. Experts who described a prototypic case of BPD indicated high levels of negative emotionality as well as the DSM-5 antagonism facets of hostility and aggression. Taken together, these results suggest that while high neuroticism seems to be most characteristic of BPD, antagonism distinguishes BPD from other personality disorders that are high in neuroticism (Samuel & Widiger, 2008).

Antagonism and self-report measures of BPD

The measures used to assess BPD have a direct influence on which facets of antagonism relate to the disorder. Costa and McCrae (1992a, 1992b) initially proposed two facets of antagonism as conceptually and theoretically related to BPD: oppositionality—which they believed was related to the DSM-III-R description of BPD, and deception—which

Table 2 Theoretical and empirical traits of borderline personality disorder.

	Lynam and Widiger (2001)	Saulsman and Page (2004)	Samuel and Widiger (2008)	Widiger, Costa, Gore, and Crego (2012)
Neuroticism	*4.12*	*0.49*	*0.54*	
Anxiety	4.04	–	0.38	High
Hostility	4.75	–	0.48	High
Depression	4.17	–	0.50	High
Self-consciousness	3.17	–	0.35	High
Impulsiveness	4.79	–	0.34	High
Vulnerability	4.17	–	0.39	High
Extraversion	*3.18*	*−0.09*	*−0.12*	
Warmth	3.21	–	−0.20	
Gregariousness	2.92	–	−0.12	
Assertiveness	3.17	–	−0.09	
Activity	3.29	–	−0.10	
Excitement-seeking	3.88	–	0.06	
Positive emotions	2.63	–	−0.26	
Openness to experience	*3.39*	*−0.02*	*0.10*	
Fantasy	3.29	–	0.13	High
Aesthetics	2.96	–	0.05	
Feelings	4.00	–	0.09	
Actions	4.00	–	−0.03	
Ideas	3.21	–	−0.01	
Values	2.88	–	0.05	
Agreeableness	*2.40*	*−0.23*	*−0.24*	
Trust	2.21	–	−0.29	Low
Straightforwardness	2.08	–	−0.21	Low
Altruism	2.46	–	−0.18	
Compliance	2.00	–	−0.27	Low
Modesty	2.83	–	0.03	
Tender-mindedness	2.79	–	−0.09	
Conscientiousness	*2.35*	*−0.23*	*−0.29*	
Competence	2.71	–	−0.29	
Order	2.38	–	−0.10	
Dutifulness	2.29	–	−0.22	
Achievement striving	2.50	–	−0.19	
Self-discipline	2.33	–	−0.29	
Deliberation	1.88	–	−0.27	Low

they posited in response to their experience of the literature and their clinical work. Their conceptual analysis also included the six facets of neuroticism, three from extraversion and one from conscientiousness. Widiger and Costa (1994) reviewed literature to examine how the FFM related to measures of BPD. In 11 of the studies outlined, antagonism was significantly related (small to medium effect sizes) to DSM-III measures of BPD in all but two of the studies.

A number of studies demonstrate that antagonism consistently relates to BPD, even utilizing different measures of personality pathology. For example, Mullins-Sweatt, Jamerson, Samuel, Olson, and Widiger (2006) evaluated the psychometric properties of the FFM Rating Form (FFMRF), correlating it with domains and facets of BPD. They constructed BPD scale scores using the average coefficients of three measures of personality pathology (the OMNI, PDQ-4, and SNAP), collected over four different studies. The three facets of antagonism were significantly correlated (small effect sizes) with the average of those BPD scales: oppositionality, arrogance, and tough-mindedness. Mistrust, deception, and exploitation were not significantly related.

While previous studies demonstrate variance in the way that individual measures of BPD relate with the FFM, Mullins-Sweatt et al. (2012) developed a measure of BPD specifically from the perspective of the FFM. The Five-Factor Borderline Inventory (FFBI) contains one total scale score and 12 subscales. Seven subscales assess the six facets of neuroticism (the vulnerability facet is split into Affective Dysregulation and Fragility), one subscale assesses openness (Dissociative Tendencies), three subscales assess facets of antagonism (Distrust, Manipulativeness, Oppositional), and one subscale assesses conscientiousness (Rashness). Mullins-Sweatt et al. (2012) provided initial validation data for the measure within two samples (an undergraduate sample and a female residential substance abuse facility). A study seeking to further test the construct validity of the FFBI (DeShong, Lengel, Sauer-Zavala, O'Meara, & Mullins-Sweatt, 2015) correlated the FFBI with their parent facets of agreeableness from the NEO-PI-R (Distrust, Manipulativeness, Oppositional) and the IPIP-NEO (Distrust, Manipulativeness, Oppositional), demonstrating strong relationships with both FFM measures. Notably, the FFBI facet scales also strongly correlated with their parent facets in neuroticism, openness to experience, and conscientiousness. An abbreviated version of the measure was subsequently developed by DeShong et al. (2015). The short form was moderately to strongly correlated with antagonism in three of five samples. Neuroticism and conscientiousness also were correlated with the FFBI (openness to experience was the least consistently correlated domain in only one of five samples).

Antagonism and underlying theoretical components of BPD

Borderline personality's etymological origins are in early psychoanalytic theory (Kernberg, 1967; Stern, 1938). Kernberg's (1967) theory of borderline personality organization posited that individuals with this personality organization lie on the delineating line (or "border line") between neurosis and psychosis. Linehan's (1993) theoretical model of BPD sought to integrate these clinical observations and descriptions within an empirically based cognitive-behavioral framework. Linehan's biosocial theory of BPD states that individuals with BPD (1) have a biological vulnerability (or proclivity) to experience negative emotions, (2) have experienced chronic environmental invalidation, and (3) have difficulty regulating their emotions.

This results in a vulnerability to a combination of unhelpful (or lack of) coping strategies used to regulate emotion, a heightened sensitivity to emotions, and difficulty physiologically returning to baseline after experiencing a negative emotion (Linehan, 1993). It would make sense that individuals who are more sensitive to emotional information and respond more intensely would self-report antagonistic personality traits. For example, Linehan (1993) describes problematic behavioral patterns of "shutting down, blocking, and avoiding" (p. 263) that may put pressures on an individual's social support system, leading an individual to resort to deceptive or exploitative behaviors in order to maintain that support. In the long-term, those behaviors may then further exacerbate underlying impairment while supporting the belief that others cannot be counted on, and that all people will inevitably abandon them. Similarly, the perpetuation of the belief that others will inevitably abandon them may also lead them to believe that others cannot be trusted.

Chronic environmental invalidation references the discrepancy between how one internally labels and experiences an emotion and how others label, judge, or diminish that emotional experience (Linehan, 1993). The chronic parental invalidation in childhood and individual experiences may be linked to antagonism. DeShong et al. (2015) correlated the FFBI with a measure of childhood invalidation, finding that the FFBI Oppositional subscale significantly associated with maternal and paternal invalidation.

As emotion dysregulation is believed to be a core component of BPD, research examining the strategies one uses to regulate their emotions has evolved into an area of increasing focus within the clinical psychology literature. Given that as many as 75% of all DSM-5 clinical disorders are associated with emotion dysregulation, this research interest is needed (Werner & Gross, 2010). Gratz and Roemer's (2004) theoretical model of emotion regulation was developed in the context of BPD and in response to Gross and John's (2003) cognitively based theoretical model. According to Gratz and Roemer (2004), Gross and John's (2003) model relies heavily on cognition and does not account for important other components (e.g., emotional acceptance). Gratz and Roemer's (2004) theoretical model contains six domains: nonacceptance of emotional responses, difficulties engaging in goal-directed behavior, impulse control difficulties, lack of emotional awareness, limited access to emotion regulation strategies, and lack of emotional clarity. Some research has related these constructs with the FFM; for example, a three-part study conducted by Stanton, Rozek, Stasik-O'Brien, Ellickson-Larew, and Watson (2016) sought to examine how FFM domains relate with the Difficulties in Emotion Regulation Scale (DERS; Gratz & Roemer, 2004) in a community sample ($n=299$). Factor analyses indicated a two-factor solution for the DERS. The first factor, Problematic Responses, consists of DERS subscales that measure how one responds to strong negative emotion (i.e., limited access to emotion regulation strategies, nonacceptance of emotional responses, difficulties engaging in goal-directed behavior, and impulse control difficulties). The second factor, Poor Recognition, contains subscales related to insight or awareness of emotional experiences (i.e., lack of emotional awareness and lack of emotional clarity). Both factors were moderately correlated with antagonism (Problematic Responses, $r=0.41$; Poor Recognition, $r=0.38$), strongly correlated with neuroticism, and negatively correlated with conscientiousness. These results suggest that antagonism and neuroticism are meaningful personality variables that further establish a connection between emotion dysregulation and BPD. An important caveat to the results of this study is that participants completed the DERS an average of 306.5 days after completing measures of general personality, though the authors attempted to address this by comparing correlations of similar measures across the time points.

DeShong et al. (2015) also examined the DERS within an FFM framework by correlating the FFBI subscales with each subscale of the DERS. While facet subscales related to neuroticism were clearly most strongly and consistently correlated, FFBI Distrust correlated with five of the six DERS subscales (i.e., nonacceptance of emotional responses, difficulties engaging in goal-directed behavior, impulse control difficulties, limited access to emotion regulation strategies, and lack of emotional clarity).

Natural changes in antagonism and BPD over time

There are a number of studies that suggest some personality trait change over the course of one's lifetime (e.g., Neyer & Asendorpf, 2001; Robins, Fraley, Roberts, & Trzesniewski, 2001; Srivastava, John, Gosling, & Potter, 2003). Meta-analysis of longitudinal studies (Roberts, Walton, & Viechtbauer, 2006) found that facets of extraversion (social dominance), conscientiousness, and emotional stability significantly increased across the lifespan, especially in early adulthood. Roberts et al. (2006) showed that antagonism decreases over the lifespan, though this decrease was statistically significant for only one age period (i.e., from 50 to 60). Soto, John, Gosling, and Potter (2011) found that antagonism and neuroticism tend to decrease in adulthood, while conscientiousness tends to increase. Given that antagonism, neuroticism, and conscientiousness are frequently associated with BPD, it is perhaps unsurprising that previously reviewed studies suggest that symptoms of BPD decrease over time (Distel et al., 2008; Zanarini et al., 2003). In a longitudinal study following patients with personality disorders, Gunderson et al. (2011) found that the number of criteria met for BPD decreased steadily for 10 years in the sample. Only 9% of the patients with BPD met diagnostic criteria for BPD after 10 years. Also, the percentage prevalence of each criterion decreased steadily, suggesting that all three phenotypes of BPD (affective, behavioral, and interpersonal) show similar pattern of stability. Wright, Hopwood, and Zanarini (2015) furthered this research by examining the underlying assumption that BPD symptoms and FFM traits change over time in tandem with each other. They found that reductions in BPD symptoms are strongly associated with reductions in neuroticism and antagonism, increases in conscientiousness, and are moderately associated with increases in extraversion. Given that individuals are less likely to meet criteria for BPD as they age, there appears to be a direct relationship with how personality traits and BPD symptoms change over time.

Antagonism's role in describing disorders comorbid with BPD

There appears to be a direct relationship with antagonism and interpersonal dysfunction across psychopathology, including in BPD. An examination of antagonism's function in other psychological disorders may demonstrate similar mechanisms of impairment (e.g., interpersonal dysfunction). A high percentage of individuals with BPD meet criteria for other disorders (Zanarini, Frankenburg, Hennen, Reich, & Silk, 2004). These comorbid diagnoses may impede treatment. The most common comorbidities cited include mood disorders (48%–54%) and substance use disorders (SUD) (14%–56%). Zanarini et al. (2004) examined comorbidity rates in 6 years of prospective follow-up in individuals with BPD. These results suggested that while comorbidity rates declined, at the 6-year follow-up, 75% of patients with BPD met criteria for a mood disorder, 60% for an anxiety disorder, 34% for an eating disorder, and 19% for a SUD. Interestingly, the strongest predictor of remission from BPD was the absence of a SUD. Although speculative, it is possible that shared traits with antagonism might explain this relationship. Interpersonal antagonism has been implicated in the initiation of substance use, the development of substance use, and the maintenance of substance dependence (Ball, 2005).

Trull and Sher (1994) examined how Axis I disorders (e.g., substance use, substance dependence, posttraumatic stress disorder, social phobia, agoraphobia, simple phobia, major depression) related to domains of the FFM. Using a series of regression analyses, antagonism significantly predicted Substance Use Disorder and Alcohol Dependence, but did not significantly predict other Axis I psychopathology. Substance use's relationship with antagonism was also implicated in a series of meta-analyses examining the FFM's relationship with a broad range of psychopathology in 175 studies (Kotov, Gamez, Schmidt, & Watson, 2010). They found significant relationships between antagonism and two specifiers of SUD, specifically drugs and mixed substances. Unsurprisingly, neuroticism related to all of the evaluated disorders (e.g., Major Depressive Disorder (MDD), Generalized Anxiety Disorder (GAD), Posttraumatic Stress Disorder (PTSD), Obsessive-Compulsive Disorder (OCD), Panic Disorder, Agoraphobia, Social Anxiety Disorder, SUD) and conscientiousness related to all disorders except Specific Phobia. In order to statistically control for neuroticism, the average effect size estimates were converted into Pearson correlation coefficients. Before controlling for neuroticism, they found that SUD, SUD Mixed Substances, and SUD Drugs were significantly related to antagonism. After controlling for neuroticism, Agoraphobia and Specific Phobia, and the two previously noted subtypes of SUD were significantly related with antagonism (SUD Mixed Substances; SUD Drugs), while SUD failed to reach statistical significance. Kotov et al. (2010) provide strong evidence to support the unique role of antagonism in the etiology of SUD, Agoraphobia, and Specific Phobia, when statistically isolated from neuroticism.

Studies also suggest positive associations of BPD symptoms with interpersonal aggression (e.g.,Newhill, Eack, & Mulvey, 2012; Sansone & Sansone, 2012; Scott et al., 2017; Stepp, Smith, Morse, Hallquist, & Pilkonis, 2012; Zanarini et al., 2017). Stepp et al. (2012) demonstrated the role of interpersonal functioning in BPD symptoms and three types of aggression (physical, interpersonal, psychological). Researchers found that individuals with BPD symptoms who were higher in interpersonal sensitivity were significantly less likely to experience physical aggression. Similarly, individuals with BPD symptoms higher in interpersonal aggression were more likely to be on the receiving end of physical aggression and more likely physically and psychologically aggressive with others. Further reinforcing the notion that antagonism's function in BPD is a maladaptive one, Miller, Zeichner, and Wilson (2012) correlated facets of the FFM with another three types of aggression: relational aggression, reactive aggression, and proactive aggression. They found that each type of aggression positively correlated with neuroticism and antagonism, and negatively correlated with conscientiousness. Additionally, using a series of regression equations to account for any shared variance among the three types of aggression, Miller et al. (2012) found that antagonism has a central role in each type of aggression.

Comorbidity of BPD with other "Cluster B" personality disorders also may be due to antagonism. A meta-analysis of personality disorders and the FFM revealed that BPD, antisocial personality disorder, and narcissistic personality disorder were positively related to antagonism (Saulsman & Page, 2004). Samuel and Widiger (2008) also replicated these findings, reporting that BPD, Antisocial Personality Disorder (ASPD), and Narcissistic Personality Disorder (NPD) were associated with high antagonism. Specifically, BPD, ASPD, and NPD were associated with several facets of antagonism, such as mistrust, deception, and oppositionality.

Antagonism has also been associated with traits of the Dark Triad. The Dark Triad (Paulhus & Williams, 2002) refers to the common co-occurrence of traits in narcissism, psychopathy, and Machiavellianism. Each component of the Dark Triad has been associated with antagonism (Paulhus & Williams, 2002). Miller et al. (2011) hypothesized a second (or alternate) model of the Dark Triad (known as the vulnerable dark triad; VDT), which consists of BPD, vulnerable narcissism, and factor 2 psychopathy (i.e., "social deviance"; Hare, 2003; Miller et al., 2011). They created composite scales of each of the VDT constructs, using a variety of existing measures. Specifically, the BPD composite scale was moderately correlated with antagonism and its four facets: mistrust, deception, exploitation, and oppositionality. The results of this study indicate that the VDT is comprised of antagonistic interpersonal style and emotional vulnerability (Miller et al., 2011), suggesting that antagonism has an important function in the VDT and in BPD.

Miller et al.'s (2011) exploration of the VDT is helpful in elucidating BPD's relationship with psychopathy. BPD appears to have some behavioral overlap with psychopathy (Kraus & Reynolds, 2001). In fact, BPD and BPD traits appear to be highly common among prison populations, with Black et al. (2007) reporting that nearly 30% of inmates newly entering the prison system met diagnostic criteria for BPD and 93.2% endorse at least one BPD symptom. Conn et al. (2010) found similar prevalence rates, with nearly 45% of inmate participants scoring above clinical threshold on the Personality Assessment Inventory (PAI) (i.e., T scores greater than 65). This is likely due to the antagonism and disinhibition that characterizes BPD and psychopathy.

Antagonism and treatment planning

Antagonism has significant implications in treatment settings. Widiger and Presnall (2013) suggest that clients high in antagonism are more likely to resist therapists' efforts to establish rapport and to oppose therapists' decisions. Further, they are more likely to be dishonest and to blame others for their own problems. While the use of this information could potentially result in biased action taken toward a client, informing therapists may enable them to take steps that benefit the therapeutic alliance. Indeed, antagonism is related to difficulties in social situations (Hopwood et al., 2009; Ozer & Benet-Martinez, 2006), and that those who are high in antagonism are also unlikely to have healthy relationships (Widiger & Presnall, 2013) and report less satisfaction in their relationships (Malouff, Thorsteinsson, Schutte, Bhullar, & Rooke, 2010). For example, individuals who are high in antagonism could be dishonest and manipulative in treatment settings as an extension of these problematic relationships. Widiger and Presnall (2013) stated that in these cases, clinicians should consciously avoid engaging in power struggles and defensiveness when challenged. Additionally, those who are particularly antagonistic may not be suitable for group therapy. Additionally, in marital-family therapy or group therapy settings, antagonism may be useful in anticipating certain conflicts and problems among group members. For those with BPD, this may be an important consideration, as a significant portion of Dialectical Behavior Therapy includes skills groups.

Targeting antagonism in treatment

Researchers have also investigated associations between personality traits and psychological treatment. Bagby et al. (2008) conducted randomized controlled trial comparing personality traits to outcomes (i.e., depression severity) following cognitive behavioral therapy (CBT) and pharmacotherapy. Their results indicated that individuals high in tough-mindedness were more likely to respond to CBT over pharmacotherapy, while those who were high in mistrust and deception had less depression severity following pharmacotherapy than CBT. Glinski and Page (2010) found that group CBT for a group of participants with social anxiety disorder reduced neuroticism and the antagonism facet of mistrust. Additionally, all five domains of the FFM changed significantly following a 6-week drug rehabilitation program. Specifically, antagonism and neuroticism significantly decreased, while conscientiousness significantly increased. These changes held when assessed at 15-month follow-up. On a related note, group member disengagement also may be associated with antagonism (Krueger & Eaton, 2010; Widiger & Mullins-Sweatt, 2009).

Significant changes in personality traits also have also been observed in treatment studies targeting BPD. Davenport, Bore, and Campbell (2010) examined personality differences between individuals with a primary diagnosis of BPD who had not completed Dialectical Behavior Therapy (DBT) to those who had successfully completed DBT. They found that the pretreatment group reported higher antagonism and lower conscientiousness than the posttreatment group. In fact, posttreatment scores in antagonism, extraversion, conscientiousness, and openness to experience were comparable to previously established norms for the NEO-PI-R. It is possible that these personality trait scores changed due to DBT; however, it is unclear if these changes are due to the treatment or due to inherent differences among those who successfully completed treatment.

Some studies show promise for the prospect of feasibly targeting individual personality traits; however, no known treatments have been developed or evaluated to do this specifically. Additionally, while a body of research suggests that personality assessment can be an important and valuable step in aiding a clinician's treatment decisions (Lengel, Helle, DeShong, Meyer, & Mullins-Sweatt, 2016), it is not entirely clear how such a treatment would differ from other therapies. Conversely, it may be that the empirical literature has failed to adequately test this idea in extant psychotherapies, such that perhaps some therapy modules of manualized treatments already target personality change, albeit inadvertently. In DBT, for example, the Interpersonal Effectiveness may unintentionally target antagonism by guiding clients to a more balanced perspective on interpersonal exchanges. While some research suggests these changes may occur in response to completed treatment (Davenport et al., 2010), future studies may provide valuable information regarding change at the module or session level.

Conclusions

This chapter sought to review how antagonism relates to BPD, its transdiagnostic characteristics, and its implications for treating BPD. The continued inclusion of FFM measures in studies of BPD will provide valuable information furthering the understanding of how antagonism functions in the context of BPD. Such knowledge might inform assessment and intervention efforts.

References

American Psychiatric Association. (2013). *Diagnostic and statistical manual of mental disorders (DSM-5)*. Washington, DC: American Psychiatric Press.

Bagby, R. M., Quilty, L. C., Segal, Z. V., McBride, C. C., Kennedy, S. H., & Costa, P. T., Jr. (2008). Personality and differential treatment response in major depression: a randomized controlled trial comparing cognitive-behavioural therapy and pharmacotherapy. *The Canadian Journal of Psychiatry*, *53*(6), 361–370.

Ball, S. A. (2005). Personality traits, problems, and disorders: clinical applications to substance use disorders. *Journal of Research in Personality*, *39*(1), 84–102.

Black, D. W., Gunter, T., Allen, J., Blum, N., Arndt, S., Wenman, G., et al. (2007). Borderline personality disorder in male and female offenders newly committed to prison. *Comprehensive Psychiatry*, *48*(5), 400–405.

Clarkin, J. F., Hull, J. W., & Hurt, S. W. (1993). Factor structure of borderline personality disorder criteria. *Journal of Personality Disorders*, *7*(2), 137–143.

Conn, C., Warden, R., Stuewig, J., Kim, E. H., Harty, L., Hastings, M., et al. (2010). Borderline personality disorder among jail inmates: how common and how distinct? *Corrections Compendium*, *35*(4), 6.

Costa, P. T., & McCrae, R. R. (1992a). Four ways five factors are basic. *Personality and Individual Differences*, *13*(6), 653–665.

Costa, P. T., & McCrae, R. R. (1992b). Normal personality assessment in clinical practice: the NEO Personality Inventory. *Psychological Assessment*, *4*(1), 5.

Davenport, J., Bore, M., & Campbell, J. (2010). Changes in personality in pre- and post-dialectical behaviour therapy borderline personality disorder groups: a question of self-control. *Australian Psychologist*, *45*(1), 59–66.

DeShong, H. L., Lengel, G. J., Sauer-Zavala, S. E., O'Meara, M., & Mullins-Sweatt, S. N. (2015). Construct validity of the five factor borderline inventory. *Assessment*, *22*(3), 319–331.

Distel, M. A., Trull, T. J., Derom, C. A., Thiery, E. W., Grimmer, M. A., Martin, N. G., et al. (2008). Heritability of borderline personality disorder features is similar across three countries. *Psychological Medicine*, *38*(9), 1219–1229.

First, M. B., Benjamin, L. S., Gibbon, M., Spitzer, R. L., & Williams, J. B. (1997). *Structured clinical interview for DSM-IV axis II personality disorders.* American Psychiatric Press.

Glinski, K., & Page, A. C. (2010). Modifiability of neuroticism, extraversion, and agreeableness by group cognitive behaviour therapy for social anxiety disorder. *Behaviour Change*, *27*(1), 42–52.

Grant, B. F., Chou, S. P., Goldstein, R. B., Huang, B., Stinson, F. S., Saha, T. D., et al. (2008). Prevalence, correlates, disability, and comorbidity of DSM-IV borderline personality disorder: results from the Wave 2 National Epidemiologic Survey on Alcohol and Related Conditions. *The Journal of Clinical Psychiatry*, *69*(4), 533.

Gratz, K. L., & Roemer, L. (2004). Multidimensional assessment of emotion regulation and dysregulation: development, factor structure, and initial validation of the difficulties in emotion regulation scale. *Journal of Psychopathology and Behavioral Assessment*, *26*(1), 41–54.

Gross, J. J., & John, O. P. (2003). Individual differences in two emotion regulation processes: implications for affect, relationships, and well-being. *Journal of Personality and Social Psychology*, *85*(2), 348.

Gunderson, J. G., Stout, R. L., McGlashan, T. H., Shea, M. T., Morey, L. C., Grilo, C. M., et al. (2011). Ten-year course of borderline personality disorder: psychopathology and function from the Collaborative Longitudinal Personality Disorders study. *Archives of General Psychiatry*, *68*(8), 827–837.

Hare, R. D. (2003). *The psychopathy checklist–revised.* Toronto, ON: Multi-Health Systems.

Hopwood, C. J., Morey, L. C., Ansell, E. B., Grilo, C. M., Sanislow, C. A., McGlashan, T. H., et al. (2009). The convergent and discriminant validity of five-factor traits: current and prospective social, work, and recreational dysfunction. *Journal of Personality Disorders*, *23*(5), 466–476.

Kernberg, O. (1967). Borderline personality organization. *Journal of the American Psychoanalytic Association*, *15*(3), 641–685.

Kotov, R., Gamez, W., Schmidt, F., & Watson, D. (2010). Linking "big" personality traits to anxiety, depressive, and substance use disorders: a meta-analysis. *Psychological Bulletin*, *136*(5), 768.

Kraus, G., & Reynolds, D. J. (2001). The "A-BC's" of the Cluster B's: identifying, understanding, and treating Cluster B personality disorders. *Clinical Psychology Review*, *3*(21), 345–373.

Krueger, R. F., & Eaton, N. R. (2010). Personality traits and the classification of mental disorders: toward a more complete integration in DSM–5 and an empirical model of psychopathology. *Personality Disorders: Theory, Research, and Treatment*, *1*(2), 97.

Lengel, G. J., Helle, A. C., DeShong, H. L., Meyer, N. A., & Mullins-Sweatt, S. N. (2016). Translational applications of personality science for the conceptualization and treatment of psychopathology. *Clinical Psychology: Science and Practice*, *23*(3), 288–308.

Lenzenweger, M. F., Lane, M. C., Loranger, A. W., & Kessler, R. C. (2007). DSM-IV personality disorders in the National Comorbidity Survey Replication. *Biological Psychiatry*, *62*(6), 553–564.

Linehan, M. M. (1993). *Cognitive behavioral therapy of borderline personality disorder. Vol. 51*. New York: Guilford Press.

Lynam, D. R., & Widiger, T. A. (2001). Using the five-factor model to represent the DSM-IV-TR personality disorders: an expert consensus approach. *Journal of Abnormal Psychology*, *110*(3), 401–412.

Madsen, L., Parsons, S., & Grubin, D. (2006). The relationship between the five-factor model and DSM personality disorder in a sample of child molesters. *Personality and Individual Differences*, *40*(2), 227–236.

Malouff, J. M., Thorsteinsson, E. B., Schutte, N. S., Bhullar, N., & Rooke, S. E. (2010). The five-factor model of personality and relationship satisfaction of intimate partners: a meta-analysis. *Journal of Research in Personality*, *44*(1), 124–127.

Miller, J. D., Hoffman, B. J., Gaughan, E. T., Gentile, B., Maples, J., & Keith Campbell, W. (2011). Grandiose and vulnerable narcissism: a nomological network analysis. *Journal of Personality*, *79*(5), 1013–1042.

Miller, J. D., Reynolds, S. K., & Pilkonis, P. A. (2004). The validity of the five-factor model prototypes for personality disorders in two clinical samples. *Psychological Assessment*, *16*(3), 310.

Miller, J. D., Zeichner, A., & Wilson, L. F. (2012). Personality correlates of aggression: evidence from measures of the five-factor model, UPPS model of impulsivity, and BIS/BAS. *Journal of Interpersonal Violence*, *27*(14), 2903–2919.

Mullins-Sweatt, S. N., Edmundson, M., Sauer-Zavala, S., Lynam, D. R., Miller, J. D., & Widiger, T. A. (2012). Five-factor measure of borderline personality traits. *Journal of Personality Assessment*, *94*(5), 475–487.

Mullins-Sweatt, S. N., Jamerson, J. E., Samuel, D. B., Olson, D. R., & Widiger, T. A. (2006). Psychometric properties of an abbreviated instrument of the five-factor model. *Assessment*, *13*(2), 119–137.

Nestadt, G., Costa, P. T., Hsu, F. C., Samuels, J., Bienvenu, O. J., & Eaton, W. W. (2008). The relationship between the five-factor model and latent Diagnostic and Statistical Manual of Mental Disorders, personality disorder dimensions. *Comprehensive Psychiatry*, *49*(1), 98–105.

Newhill, C. E., Eack, S. M., & Mulvey, E. P. (2012). A growth curve analysis of emotion dysregulation as a mediator for violence in individuals with and without borderline personality disorder. *Journal of Personality Disorders*, *26*(3), 452–467.

Neyer, F. J., & Asendorpf, J. B. (2001). Personality–relationship transaction in young adulthood. *Journal of Personality and Social Psychology*, *81*, 1190–1204.

Ozer, D. J., & Benet-Martinez, V. (2006). Personality and the prediction of consequential outcomes. *Annual Review of Psychology*, *57*, 401–421.

Paris, J., Brown, R., & Nowlis, D. (1987). Long-term follow-up of borderline patients in a general hospital. *Comprehensive Psychiatry*, *28*(6), 530–535.

Paulhus, D. L., & Williams, K. M. (2002). The dark triad of personality: narcissism, Machiavellianism, and psychopathy. *Journal of Research in Personality*, *36*(6), 556–563.

Roberts, B. W., Walton, K. E., & Viechtbauer, W. (2006). Patterns of mean-level change in personality traits across the life course: a meta-analysis of longitudinal studies. *Psychological Bulletin*, *132*, 1–25.

Robins, R. W., Fraley, R. C., Roberts, B. W., & Trzesniewski, K. H. (2001). A longitudinal study of personality change in young adulthood. *Journal of Personality, 69*, 617–640.

Rolland, J. P., & De Fruyt, F. (2003). The validity of FFM personality dimensions and maladaptive traits to predict negative affects at work: a six month prospective study in a military sample. *European Journal of Personality, 17*(S1), S101–S121.

Säämänen, T. S., Voutilainen, J., Lahti, J. M. T., Isometsä, E. T., Heikkinen, M., & Lahti, M. (2016). The associations of borderline personality disorder symptoms, five-factor model personality dimensions, and personality fragmentation among depressed inpatients. *Journal of Psychiatry, 19*(3), 1–8.

Samuel, D. B., Lynam, D. R., Widiger, T. A., & Ball, S. A. (2012). An expert consensus approach to relating the proposed DSM-5 types and traits. *Personality Disorders: Theory, Research, and Treatment, 3*, 1–16.

Samuel, D. B., & Widiger, T. A. (2004). Clinicians' personality descriptions of prototypic personality disorders. *Journal of Personality Disorders, 18*(3), 286–308.

Samuel, D. B., & Widiger, T. A. (2008). A meta-analytic review of the relationships between the five-factor model and DSM-IV-TR personality disorders: a facet level analysis. *Clinical Psychology Review, 28*(8), 1326–1342.

Sansone, R. A., & Sansone, L. A. (2012). Borderline personality and externalized aggression. *Innovations in Clinical Neuroscience, 9*(3), 23.

Saulsman, L. M., & Page, A. C. (2004). The five-factor model and personality disorder empirical literature: a meta-analytic review. *Clinical Psychology Review, 23*(8), 1055–1085.

Scott, L. N., Wright, A. G., Beeney, J. E., Lazarus, S. A., Pilkonis, P. A., & Stepp, S. D. (2017). Borderline personality disorder symptoms and aggression: a within-person process model. *Journal of Abnormal Psychology, 126*(4), 429.

Soto, C. J., John, O. P., Gosling, S. D., & Potter, J. (2011). Age differences in personality traits from 10 to 65: Big Five domains and facets in a large cross-sectional sample. *Journal of Personality and Social Psychology, 100*, 330–348.

Srivastava, S., John, O. P., Gosling, S. D., & Potter, J. (2003). Development of personality in early and middle adulthood: set like plaster or persistent change? *Journal of Personality and Social Psychology, 84*(5), 1041–1053.

Stanton, K., Rozek, D. C., Stasik-O'Brien, S. M., Ellickson-Larew, S., & Watson, D. (2016). A transdiagnostic approach to examining the incremental predictive power of emotion regulation and basic personality dimensions. *Journal of Abnormal Psychology, 125*(7), 960.

Stepp, S. D., Smith, T. D., Morse, J. Q., Hallquist, M. N., & Pilkonis, P. A. (2012). Prospective associations among borderline personality disorder symptoms, interpersonal problems, and aggressive behaviors. *Journal of Interpersonal Violence, 27*(1), 103–124.

Stern, A. (1938). Psychoanalytic investigation of and therapy in the border line group of neuroses. *The Psychoanalytic Quarterly, 7*(4), 467–489.

Torgersen, S. (1984). Genetic and nosological aspects of schizotypal and borderline personality disorders: a twin study. *Archives of General Psychiatry, 41*(6), 546–554.

Torgersen, S., Lygren, S., Øien, P. A., Skre, I., Onstad, S., Edvardsen, J., et al. (2000). A twin study of personality disorders. *Comprehensive Psychiatry, 41*(6), 416–425.

Trull, T. J., & Sher, K. J. (1994). Relationship between the five-factor model of personality and Axis I disorders in a nonclinical sample. *Journal of Abnormal Psychology, 103*(2), 350–360.

Werner, K., & Gross, J. J. (2010). Emotion regulation and psychopathology: a conceptual framework. In A. M. Kring & D. M. Sloan (Eds.), *Emotion regulation and psychopathology: A transdiagnostic approach to etiology and treatment* (pp. 13–37). New York: Guilford Press.

Widiger, T. A., & Costa, P. T., Jr. (1994). Personality and personality disorders. *Journal of Abnormal Psychology*, *103*(1), 78.

Widiger, T. A., Costa, P. T., Gore, W. L., & Crego, C. (2012). Five-factor model personality disorder research. In T. A. Widiger & P. T. Costa, Jr., (Eds.), *Personality disorders and the five-factor model of personality*. (3rd ed.). American Psychological Association.

Widiger, T. A., Gore, W. L., Crego, C., Rojas, S. L., & Oltmanns, J. R. (2017). Five Factor Model and personality disorder. In *The Oxford handbook of the Five Factor Model* (p. 449). Oxford, UK: Oxford University Press.

Widiger, T. A., & Mullins-Sweatt, S. N. (2009). Five-factor model of personality disorder: a proposal for DSM-V. *Annual Review of Clinical Psychology*, *5*, 197–220.

Widiger, T. A., & Presnall, J. R. (2013). Clinical application of the Five Factor Model. *Journal of Personality*, *81*(6), 515–527.

Wright, A. G., Hopwood, C. J., & Zanarini, M. C. (2015). Associations between changes in normal personality traits and borderline personality disorder symptoms over 16 years. *Journal of Personality Disorders*, *6*(1), 1–11.

Zanarini, M. C., Frankenburg, F. R., Hennen, J., Reich, D. B., & Silk, K. R. (2004). Axis I comorbidity in patients with borderline personality disorder: 6-year follow-up and prediction of time to remission. *American Journal of Psychiatry*, *161*, 2108–2114.

Zanarini, M. C., Frankenburg, F. R., Hennen, J., & Silk, K. R. (2003). The longitudinal course of borderline psychopathology: 6-year prospective follow-up of the phenomenology of borderline personality disorder. *American Journal of Psychiatry*, *160*(2), 274–283.

Zanarini, M. C., Temes, C. M., Ivey, A. M., Cohn, D. M., Conkey, L. C., Frankenburg, F. R., et al. (2017). The 10-year course of adult aggression toward others in patients with borderline personality disorder and axis II comparison subjects. *Psychiatry Research*, *252*, 134–138.

Antagonism in the Dark Triad

17

Colin E. Vize, Joshua D. Miller†, Donald R. Lynam**
*Department of Psychological Sciences, Purdue University, West Lafayette, IN, United States, †Department of Psychology, University of Georgia, Athens, GA, United States

The Dark Triad (DT) is a collection of three interrelated, malevolent personality constructs: narcissism, psychopathy, and Machiavellianism (Paulhus & Williams, 2002).[1] Though DT research focuses on the simultaneous assessment of the DT constructs, each DT construct has its own independent literature base. Narcissism has a robust literature in both social and clinical research domains and is represented by Narcissistic Personality Disorder (NPD) within the American Psychiatric Association's Diagnostic and Statistical Manual of Mental Disorders (DSM-5; APA, 2013). Research on narcissism has identified two dimensions: grandiose and vulnerable (Miller, Hoffman, et al., 2011; Pincus & Lukowitsky, 2010). Nearly all of DT research on narcissism has focused on the grandiose dimension, though different DT measures of narcissism contain differing amounts of grandiose and vulnerable content (e.g., Maples, Lamkin, & Miller, 2014). Grandiosely narcissistic individuals are characterized by exhibitionism, lack of humility/modesty, and interpersonal dominance, whereas vulnerably narcissistic individuals are characterized by negative affect, distrust, selfishness, and a need for attention and recognition (Dickinson & Pincus, 2003; Miller, Price, Gentile, Lynam, & Campbell, 2012).

Research on psychopathy has been conducted primarily within forensic and clinical psychology due to its robust links with crime and antisocial behavior (Lynam, Miller, Vachon, Loeber, & Stouthamer-Loeber, 2009; Neumann, Hare, & Pardini, 2015). Similar to narcissism, psychopathy is characterized by antagonistic personality traits (e.g., callousness, lack of empathy, and meanness) but differs from narcissism in its relations with disinhibition, which features prominently in nearly all conceptions of psychopathy (e.g., Cleckley, 1941; Hare, 1980; see Miller & Lynam, 2015 for a review). Of the DT constructs, psychopathy is typically considered to be more malevolent and problematic than the other two DT constructs (Paulhus & Williams, 2002) due to its relations with more extreme and frequent antisocial behavior.

Empirical research on Machiavellianism began with Christie and Geis' (Christie & Geis, 1970) development of the MACH-IV, a 20-item self-report instrument whose items were created by Christie through the selection and adaptation of portions of Niccolo Machiavelli's writings from the 16th century. Machiavellian individuals are thought to be strategic, skilled manipulators and callous and ambitious pragmatists

[1]Other researchers have also argued for the inclusion of sadism, whose inclusion leads to what has been termed the Dark Tetrad of personality (Buckels, Jones, & Paulhus, 2013; Paulhus, 2014). However, the current chapter will focus solely on the Dark Triad, given that the vast majority of research has tended to exclude the assessment of sadism.

The Handbook of Antagonism. https://doi.org/10.1016/B978-0-12-814627-9.00017-7

who strive for long-term success. Although Christie initially developed the measure to examine traits involved in authoritarianism and other sociopolitical outcomes, research on Machiavellianism has become popular in both social psychology and industrial/organizational (I/O) psychology. Machiavellianism became a focus in I/O psychology (e.g., Gemmill & Heisler, 1972; Siegel, 1973) because it was thought that some characteristics of the construct might be adaptive in particular workplace contexts and/or implicated in white-collar antisocial behavior (Deshong, Grant, & Mullins-Sweatt, 2015; Jonason, Slomski, & Partyka, 2012).

Within much of the literature, the DT constructs are often mistakenly referred to as "traits" and frequently discussed as unidimensional constructs. However, the independent literatures for each DT construct are consistent in highlighting that the DT constructs are best understood as multidimensional composites of multiple, more basic traits (DeShong, Helle, Lengel, Meyer, & Mullins-Sweatt, 2017; Lynam et al., 2011; Miller et al., 2016). Failure to account for the multidimensionality and to examine these subdimensions can have important implications for subsequent results (e.g., Miller et al., 2010; Watts, Waldman, Smith, Poore, & Lilienfeld, 2017). Thus we refer to the DT elements as constructs rather than traits in the present chapter to appropriately reflect their composite nature.

Paulhus and Williams (2002) were the first to assess the three constructs simultaneously in an effort to elucidate the similarities and differences among them. Since the introduction of the DT, research has been broadly concerned with two overarching questions: how are the DT constructs similar to one another? and how are they different? The investigation of these two questions has produced a large literature surrounding the DT, with researchers examining the relations between the DT and a wide array of outcomes ranging from short-term mating behaviors (e.g., Jonason, Li, & Webster, 2009) to internet trolling (e.g., Buckels, Trapnell, & Paulhus, 2014).

In terms of the first question (i.e., what makes the DT constructs similar to one another), researchers have searched the "core" of the DT. Typically, "core" in these contexts refers to the shared traits and/or behaviors that explain the conceptual and empirical overlap of the DT constructs. A variety of traits and behaviors have been offered as contenders for the core of the DT including low agreeableness (e.g., Paulhus & Williams, 2002), more specific traits related to callousness and manipulation (Jones & Figueredo, 2013), an exploitative, fast life history strategy (Jonason, Kaufman, Webster, & Geher, 2013), and traits related to the Honesty-Humility factor of the HEXACO personality model (Ashton, Lee, & De Vries, 2014; Book et al., 2016). The present chapter aims to summarize the available literature on which traits/behaviors make up the core of the DT, highlight important methodological considerations that will likely affect interpretations of what constitutes this core, and future directions for further examining this issue.

Research on the core of the Dark Triad

Numerous articles have explicitly addressed the question of the common core of the DT, while many other studies have offered indirect insights into the overlap among the DT. Of the proposed candidates for the core of the DT, many fall under the umbrella of

Agreeableness-Antagonism—a fundamental personality domain within the Big Five (Goldberg, 1993) and Five-Factor Models (McCrae & John, 1992) that describes individual differences in motivation to maintain positive social relations with others. Agreeableness is generally seen as being firmly grounded in an interpersonal context (Graziano & Eisenberg, 1997; Graziano & Tobin, 2017). From this perspective, individuals high in agreeableness are likely to be consistently motivated to maintain harmonious relations across many interpersonal contexts and likely to be described as kind, altruistic, selfless, and value honesty. At the opposite pole of high Agreeableness is Antagonism, an interpersonal style characterized by combativeness, callousness, and manipulation (e.g., Crowe, Lynam, & Miller, 2018). Given the prominence of such characteristics in descriptions of narcissism, psychopathy, and Machiavellianism, Antagonism is an obvious candidate for the core of the DT. However, Jonason and colleagues (e.g., Jonason, Koenig, & Tost, 2010) have offered a slightly different explanation. These researchers have argued that the DT constructs share a common tendency to employ fast life history strategies, which include preferences for short-term, exploitative mating strategies as well as a more general preference for short- versus long-term gains. This body of research has also incorporated evolutionary theory into understanding the DT constructs (e.g., Jonason, Li, & Czarna, 2013; Jonason, Luevano, & Adams, 2012; Jonason, Valentine, Li, & Harbeson, 2011). However, there appear to be three primary issues with understanding the core of the DT as being based in life history strategies.

First, meta-analytic evidence suggests that the DT constructs are more weakly linked to indicators reflecting fast life strategies (e.g., short-term mating behaviors, impulsivity, sensation seeking; meta-analytic r range = .20 to .35) than they are to indicators of Agreeableness (meta-analytic r range = −.22 to −.46; Vize, Collison, Miller, & Lynam, 2018). Other meta-analytic data found even stronger negative relations when examining specific features of Agreeableness related traits, like the honesty-humility factor of the HEXACO-PI-R (r range = −.41 to −.61; Muris, Merckelbach, Otgaar, & Meijer, 2017).

Second, fast life history strategies do not fully map onto the theoretical profiles of each DT component. Though there are clear links between psychopathy and fast life strategies, the links are less clear for narcissism and Machiavellianism. Indeed, the theoretical underpinnings of Machiavellianism emphasize traits that run counter to a fast life strategy (e.g., being planful, calculating, strategic, etc.). Though Machiavellianism has tended to show positive relations with outcomes related to fast life strategies, like psychopathy, this has been highlighted as a problem with extant measures of Machiavellianism as they do not assess the theoretical construct of Machiavellianism but rather function as secondary measures of psychopathy (McHoskey, Worzel, & Szyarto, 1998; Miller, Hyatt, Maples-Keller, Carter, & Lynam, 2017; Vize, Lynam, Collison, & Miller, 2018).

Third, it is unlikely that fast life strategies and the other contenders for the core of the DT (i.e., antagonism related traits) are independent. Agreeableness tends to show a moderate positive relation with traits and behaviors related to slow life strategies (e.g., Gladden, Figueredo, & Jacobs, 2009) and given Agreeableness' positive relations with inhibitory control in early development (e.g., Cumberland-li, Eisenberg, & Reiser,

2004; Jensen-Campbell et al., 2002), it seems likely that Agreeableness-related traits are developmental precursors for the eventual deployment of fast life strategies.

The remaining hypotheses regarding the core of the DT all have more direct links with Antagonism, though they vary in specificity. In their seminal article, Paulhus and Williams (2002) first suggested that, "members of the Dark Triad share a common core of disagreeableness." (p. 561). Paulhus and Williams based their initial judgment on their analysis of the DT correlations with the Big Five domains, as measured by the Big Five Inventory (BFI; Goldberg, 1999). The results showed that the only domain with consistent relations across the DT constructs was agreeableness; each DT component showed moderate negative relations with the domain (*r*s ranging from −.25 to −.47). Later work that also suggested (low) agreeableness was the core of the DT found large negative relations with NEO-PI-R agreeableness (*r* range = −.45 to −.66; Stead & Fekken, 2014), a measure with substantially more content related to immodesty and dishonesty (Miller, Gaughan, Maples, & Price, 2011).

Other work has examined specific aspects of antagonism, namely, callousness and manipulativeness as assessed by the Self-report Psychopathy scale (SRP; Williams, Paulhus, & Hare, 2007). In the initial study examining callousness and manipulativeness as the core of the DT, Jones and Figueredo (2013) made use of structural equation modeling (SEM) to extract a DT latent factor derived from subscales of commonly used DT measures: the SRP, the Narcissistic Personality Inventory (NPI; Raskin & Hall, 1979), and the MACH-IV (Christie & Geis, 1970). They then examined whether the variance in the latent factor could be best accounted for by specific subscale combinations (i.e., Interpersonal Manipulation and Callousness subscales from the SRP; Grandiosity and Entitlement subscales from the NPI, etc.). The results showed that the combination of Callousness and Interpersonal Manipulation accounted for the largest amount of variance in the latent DT factor ($R^2 = .79$, average R^2 of all other subscale combinations = .55). However, the Interpersonal Manipulation subscale was a stronger predictor of the latent factor compared to the Callousness subscale. Jones and Figueredo (2013) also found that these two SRP subscales outperformed BFI-Agreeableness in accounting for variance in the latent DT factor.

Using the same measures (the NPI, SRP, and MACH-IV), Marcus, Preszler, and Zeigler-Hill (2018) used the subscales of the DT measures (along with a measure of spite) in a series of network analyses in two large samples. Similar to the results of Jones and Figueredo (2013), Marcus et al. (2018) found that in both samples, the Callousness and Interpersonal Manipulation subscales of the SRP were the most central components in the DT subscale network. These SRP subscales were the only two DT subscales to achieve above-average values on metrics of centrality (i.e., strength, closeness, and betweenness; Costantini et al., 2015). Notably, the SRP subscales were strongly related to one another across the four samples in Jones and Figueredo (2013) and Marcus et al. (2018) (*r* range = .59 to .68) and the Interpersonal Manipulation and Callousness subscales tend to be strongly related to one another more generally (e.g., Gordts, Uzieblo, Neumann, Van den Bussche, & Rossi, 2017). Thus there may be some redundancy in using both subscales to represent the core of the DT, though little research has specifically focused on the overlap between the SRP subscales while examining hypotheses regarding the core of the

DT. Both of these subscales demonstrate substantial overlap with all facets of FFM Agreeableness (Gaughan, Miller, Pryor, & Lynam, 2009), which many believe undergirds psychopathic traits (e.g., Miller, Lynam, Widiger, & Leukefeld, 2001; Sherman, Lynam, & Heyde, 2014).

Other work has focused on features of honesty and humility as the core of the DT, with these traits typically being assessed by the honesty-humility (H/H) factor of the HEXACO-PI-R (Lee & Ashton, 2004). Using canonical correlations across two samples, Book, Visser, and Volk (2015) found that the HEXACO model accounted for a significantly larger amount of variance in the DT measures than both a BFI-based big five model and a fast life history model. Furthermore, adding the Callousness subscale of the SRP into the model with the HEXACO did not improve performance. Using the same methodological approach in a separate study, a similar pattern of findings emerged (i.e., the HEXACO model outperformed all other models) when including sadism with the other DT members (Book et al., 2016).

In a separate study, Hodson et al. (2018) used meta-analytic data to examine the degree of overlap between latent DT and H/H factors across four samples (total $N=1402$) that had completed measures of the DT (all samples used the Short Dark Triad [SD3]; Jones & Paulhus, 2014) and the facet scales of H/H (Sincerity, Fairness, Greed Avoidance, and Modesty). The results show strong evidence that H/H accounted for the shared variance across the SD3 DT scales—the DT and H/H latent factors were nearly perfectly negatively correlated ($r=-.95$). Furthermore, the near perfect inverse relation between the latent H/H and DT factors was also observed in two smaller samples that relied on peer reports. Hodson et al. (2018) took this as evidence that the covariance of the DT constructs can be entirely explained by their shared core of low H/H.

In sum, research that has aimed at exploring what constitutes the core of the DT has been consistent in highlighting that antagonism-related traits lie at the core of the DT. The centrality of antagonism-related traits is underscored by the fact that these traits consistently emerge as the strongest predictors of the DT core across a variety of analytical approaches. Moreover, there is good evidence that more specific features of antagonism, such as (low) modesty and (low) honesty may lie at the core of the DT, rather than a more general antagonistic core. These findings have important implications for research on the DT and also highlight important methodological considerations in regard to assessment approaches of the DT.

Assessment and methodological considerations

Explorations of the core of the DT have highlighted that assessments of agreeableness that contain content related to modesty/humility and straightforwardness/honesty, like the HEXACO-PI-R and NEO-PI-R (Costa & McCrae, 1992), should be preferred over other assessment instruments that lack such content (i.e., the BFI; Miller, Gaughan, et al., 2011). In fact, in the research highlighted previously that has pitted hypotheses regarding the core of the DT against one another, BFI-Agreeableness has typically been the construct used to represent the "(low) agreeableness as the core of the

DT" hypothesis. Unfortunately, little research to date has used NEO-Agreeableness to represent the hypotheses that low agreeableness is at the core of the DT (cf., Sleep, Lynam, Hyatt, & Miller, 2017—NEO Agreeableness manifested correlations with the DT that ranged from −.50 to −.80). Ultimately, the low agreeableness hypothesis was doomed to fail given that BFI-A has been criticized as a measure of agreeableness that leaves out important agreeableness-related content (Crowe et al., 2018; Miller, Gaughan, et al., 2011).

For example, in an examination of the degree of overlap between the DT constructs that can be explained by agreeableness, we made use of meta-analytic structural equation modeling (MASEM; Cheung, 2014) to explore whether different agreeableness measures resulted in different conclusions regarding the importance of agreeableness in accounting for DT overlap.[2] A total of six SEM path models were estimated, with each DT component serving as the predicted outcome. At the first step, the meta-analytic zero-order correlation between two of the DT constructs was estimated to examine the degree of shared variance between them. At step 2, agreeableness was added as a predictor in the SEM model, and its overlap with the DT predictor was accounted for. In other words, the relation between the two DT constructs at step 2 is equivalent to a squared semipartial correlation (sr^2). In turn, the degree of reduction in the sr^2 moving from step 1 to step 2 highlights the amount of overlap between the DT constructs that can be accounted for by agreeableness.

Table 1 shows the meta-analytic results for all agreeableness measures while Tables 2 and 3 display results for BFI-Agreeableness and NEO-HEXACO Agreeableness, respectively.[3] Table 1 shows that there is a modest degree of reduction in sr^2 across the DT constructs once agreeableness is included in the SEM path model (Variance reduction range = 18%–50%). However, Tables 2 and 3 show that the modest degree of overlap explained by agreeableness is largely due to BFI-Agreeableness accounting for significantly less overlap among the DT constructs (Variance reduction range = 0%–38%) when compared to NEO/HEXACO-Agreeableness (Variance reduction range = 38%–58%).

The results in Table 2 show that BFI-Agreeableness does not account for any of the overlap between narcissism, psychopathy, and Machiavellianism when narcissism serves as the predicted outcome. However, when psychopathy and Machiavellianism serve as the predicted outcomes, BFI-Agreeableness does account for more substantive amounts of variance. However, the amount of variance accounted for suggests that there remains significant variance left unexplained in regard to DT overlap. Furthermore, the results highlight that BFI-Agreeableness does not sufficiently capture the core of the DT. The results in Table 3 also highlight that there is substantial overlap between DT constructs left unexplained by agreeableness,

[2]These data come from previous meta-analytic work on the DT (Vize, Collison, et al., 2018). Descriptions of MASEM techniques and meta-analytic procedures (i.e., data collection, exclusion criteria, etc.) are outlined in Vize, Collison, et al. (2018). All data and study information are available online at https:/osf.io/he8s7/.

[3]For the purposes of the meta-analysis, HEXACO Agreeableness was calculated by averaging the two correlations between a DT component and the HEXACO Agreeableness and H/H domains.

Table 1 Meta-analytic relations among DT constructs while controlling for agreeableness

	sr^2	sr^2 reduction
Narcissism		
Step 1		
Psychopathy	.11	–
Step 2		
Psychopathy	.09	18%
Agreeableness	.01	
Step 1		
Machiavellianism	.12	–
Step 2		
Machiavellianism	.10	16%
Agreeableness	.01	
Psychopathy		
Step 1		
Narcissism	.11	–
Step 2		
Narcissism	.06	45%
Agreeableness	.16	
Step 1		
Machiavellianism	.26	–
Step 2		
Machiavellianism	.14	46%
Agreeableness	.09	
Machiavellianism		
Step 1		
Narcissism	.12	–
Step 2		
Narcissism	.06	50%
Agreeableness	.16	
Step 1		
Psychopathy	.26	–
Step 2		
Psychopathy	.16	38%
Agreeableness	.06	

Note: $N=19{,}858$; $sr=$ semipartial correlation; the sr^2 reduction represents the percentage decrease in variance accounted for in the original sr^2 at step 1, after Agreeableness has been included in the model.

but less so when compared to the BFI results in Table 2. A potential reason for the notable amount of remaining variance is that the previous work using the H/H factor made use of facet scales. The additional specificity provided by the facets of H/H may in turn account for more overlap among the DT constructs. Previous research has shown that inclusion of facet scales typically leads to incremental variance being accounted for in study outcomes above and beyond the domain (Costa & McCrae, 1995).

Table 2 Meta-analytic relations among DT constructs while controlling for BFI agreeableness

	sr^2	sr^2 reduction
Narcissism		
Step 1 Psychopathy	.10	–
Step 2 Psychopathy Agreeableness	.11 .00[a]	0%
Step 1 Machiavellianism	.11	–
Step 2 Machiavellianism Agreeableness	.12 .00[a]	0%
Psychopathy		
Step 1 Narcissism	.10	–
Step 2 Narcissism Agreeableness	.07 .17	30%
Step 1 Machiavellianism	.24	–
Step 2 Machiavellianism Agreeableness	.15 .09	38%
Machiavellianism		
Step 1 Narcissism	.11	–
Step 2 Narcissism Agreeableness	.09 .12	18%
Step 1 Psychopathy	.24	–
Step 2 Psychopathy Agreeableness	.17 .04	29%

Note: $N = 8883$; $sr =$ semipartial correlation; the sr^2 reduction represents the percentage decrease in variance accounted for in the original sr^2 at step 1, after Agreeableness has been included in the model.
[a]Narcissism was positively related to Agreeableness after taking into account psychopathy and Machiavellianism's relations with Agreeableness.

Table 3 Meta-analytic relations among DT constructs while controlling for NEO/HEXACO agreeableness

	sr^2	sr^2 reduction
Narcissism		
Step 1		
Psychopathy	.13	–
Step 2		
Psychopathy	.08	38%
Agreeableness	.03	
Step 1		
Machiavellianism	.12	–
Step 2		
Machiavellianism	.07	42%
Agreeableness	.03	
Psychopathy		
Step 1		
Narcissism	.13	–
Step 2		
Narcissism	.06	54%
Agreeableness	.16	
Step 1		
Machiavellianism	.27	–
Step 2		
Machiavellianism	.14	48%
Agreeableness	.09	
Machiavellianism		
Step 1		
Narcissism	.12	–
Step 2		
Narcissism	.05	58%
Agreeableness	.16	
Step 1		
Psychopathy	.27	–
Step 2		
Psychopathy	.15	44%
Agreeableness	.08	

Note: $N=7511$; $sr=$ semipartial correlation; the sr^2 reduction represents the percentage decrease in variance accounted for in the original sr^2 at step 1, after Agreeableness has been included in the model.

Implications for Dark Triad research

The present review highlights a number of important insights into research on the core of the DT. First, for researchers who explicitly want to focus on the core of the DT, available data suggest that BFI-Agreeableness does not sufficiently capture the overlap among the DT constructs. Measures of agreeableness/antagonism that include sufficient content related to the DT core (i.e., content related to honesty, straightforwardness, and modesty) include the H/H factor of the HEXACO-PI-R and the Interpersonal Manipulation and Callousness subscales of the SRP. Fewer data are available to determine the extent to which NEO-Agreeableness also sufficiently captures the core of the DT. The data that are available suggest that NEO-Agreeableness compares favorably to H/H or SRP Interpersonal Manipulation and Callousness in accounting for the core of the DT, given that NEO-Agreeableness tends to show as strong relations with the DT constructs as the H/H and the SRP subscales do (e.g., Miller, Gaughan, et al., 2011, Miller et al., 2017; O'Boyle, Forsyth, Banks, Story, & White, 2015; Stead & Fekken, 2014). Nonetheless, explicit testing of these hypotheses is required before one can be sure of the comparability of the candidates for the core of the DT.

A second important insight derived from research on the core of the DT is that the independent research on H/H and SRP Manipulation and Callousness (i.e., conducted without explicitly mentioning the DT) can be understood as research on the core of the DT. In regard to H/H, it simply represents the inverse of the DT core (Hodson et al., 2018). Thus DT researchers may benefit from incorporating results from the literatures that surround H/H and the SRP. Incorporating the results from the separate literatures around H/H and the SRP can help inform researchers' expectations about the nomological networks that surround the DT constructs themselves.

A third implication of this research suggests that explicating the core of the DT may better allow researchers to understand what the residualized DT constructs represent once the core has been statistically partialed out. Importantly, because research on the core of the DT has tended to show that specific features of antagonism underlie the DT constructs, it is unlikely that all antagonism related traits will be partialed out of each DT component. As an example, research has found that narcissism is unrelated or positively related to agreeableness once its overlap with the other DT constructs has been taken into account (Vize, Collison, et al., 2018). However, the same is not true of psychopathy and Machiavellianism—both of these constructs still showed moderate negative relations with agreeableness after partialing (*r*s of −.33 and −.25, respectively). This finding suggests that a greater degree of antagonism is included within measures of psychopathy and Machiavellianism compared to narcissism (O'Boyle et al., 2015), and partialing may have different consequences for each of the DT constructs. After partialing, traits that may still be well represented in the residualized DT psychopathy and Machiavellianism include callousness/cold-heartedness, distrust of others, and combativeness, while such content may be completely absent in residualized narcissism (although immodesty remains; Sleep et al., 2017). Therefore it is more likely that residualized narcissism may represent unique characteristics of narcissism mostly unrelated to antagonism (i.e., extraversion related traits), but the same is unlikely to be true of psychopathy and Machiavellianism. This is an important concern, given that researchers have argued that residualized psychopathy and Machiavellianism represent constraint and impulse control after partialing antagonism-related traits (e.g., Paulhus, 2014). Ultimately, careful consideration of what the residualized variables represent is recommended (Lynam, Hoyle, & Newman, 2006; Sleep et al., 2017;

Vize, Collison, et al., 2018), and research on the core of the DT can aid such interpretations.

Last, the final implication of research on the core of the DT is that the available data suggest that the DT constructs can primarily be classified as disorders of antagonism. Though DT research was not designed to assess clinical levels of these constructs, much of the data have shown that the DT constructs show relations with a variety of maladaptive outcomes (e.g., Muris et al., 2017; O'Boyle, Forsyth, Banks, & McDaniel, 2012; Vize, Lynam, et al., 2018). Our position is that the DT constructs show relations to many of these maladaptive outcomes because each construct possesses high levels of antagonistic content.

Future directions

There has been noticeable progress in explicating the core of the DT. Yet, additional research is needed in order to directly test the current leading proposals against one another. Specifically, work is needed to examine whether the HEXACO-H/H, SRP-Callousness and SRP-Interpersonal Manipulation, and NEO-Agreeableness hypotheses emerge as either a superior or equivalent to one another. Research that has shown Agreeableness to be a relatively poorer candidate for the core of the DT has used the BFI to assess Agreeableness, which we believe is an inadequate test of the Agreeableness hypothesis. In addition, more focus can be given to whether the SRP subscales of Interpersonal Manipulation and Callousness are redundant in accounting for the core of the DT. It is encouraging to note that testing the competing hypotheses against one another can be done in a straightforward manner through the use of various multivariate techniques. Examples include relative importance analysis (Tonidandel & Lebreton, 2011), dominance analysis (Azen & Budescu, 2003), or the use of model comparison techniques among competing SEM models. These more stringent tests of the candidate hypotheses can shed further light onto what truly lies at the core of the DT.

References

American Psychiatric Association (2013). *Diagnostic and statistical manual for mental disorders* (5th ed.). Washington, DC: American Psychiatric Association.

Ashton, M. C., Lee, K., & De Vries, R. E. (2014). The HEXACO Honesty-Humility, Agreeableness, and Emotionality factors: a review of research and theory. *Personality and Social Psychology Review*, *18*, 139–152. https://doi.org/10.1177/1088868314523838.

Azen, R., & Budescu, D. V. (2003). The dominance analysis approach for comparing predictors in multiple regression. *Psychological Methods*, *8*, 129–148. https://doi.org/10.1037/1082-989X.8.2.129.

Book, A., Visser, B. A., Blais, J., Hosker-Field, A., Methot-Jones, T., Gauthier, N. Y., et al. (2016). Unpacking more "evil": what is at the core of the dark tetrad? *Personality and Individual Differences*, *90*, 269–272. https://doi.org/10.1016/j.paid.2015.11.009.

Book, A., Visser, B. A., & Volk, A. A. (2015). Unpacking "evil": claiming the core of the Dark Triad. *Personality and Individual Differences*, *73*, 29–38. https://doi.org/10.1016/j.paid.2014.09.016.

Buckels, E. E., Jones, D. N., & Paulhus, D. L. (2013). Behavioral confirmation of everyday sadism. *Psychological Science*, *24*, 2201–2209. https://doi.org/10.1177/0956797613490749.

Buckels, E. E., Trapnell, P. D., & Paulhus, D. L. (2014). Trolls just want to have fun. *Personality and Individual Differences*, *67*, 97–102. https://doi.org/10.1016/j.paid.2014.01.016.

Cheung, M. W.-L. (2014). Fixed- and random-effects meta-analytic structural equation modeling: examples and analyses in R. *Behavior Research Methods*, *46*, 29–40. https://doi.org/10.3758/s13428-013-0361-y.

Christie, R., & Geis, F. (1970). *Studies in Machiavellianism*. New York, NY: Academic Press, Inc.

Cleckley, H. (1941). *The mask of sanity*. St. Louis, MO: Mosbyhttps://doi.org/10.1037/h0050245.

Costa, P. T., & McCrae, R. R. (1992). *NEO PI-R professional manual*. Odessa, FL: Psychological Assessment Resources.

Costa, P. T., & Mccrae, R. R. (1995). Domains and facets: hierarchical personality assessment using the revised NEO Personality Inventory. *Journal of Personality Assessment*, *64*, 21–50. Retrieved from https://pdfs.semanticscholar.org/c2d3/dabde2e40e2985ddc7f211975aed820307e3.pdf.

Costantini, G., Epskamp, S., Borsboom, D., Perugini, M., Mõttus, R., Waldorp, L. J., et al. (2015). State of the aRt personality research: a tutorial on network analysis of personality data in R. *Journal of Research in Personality*, *54*, 13–29. https://doi.org/10.1016/j.jrp.2014.07.003.

Crowe, M. L., Lynam, D. R., & Miller, J. D. (2018). Uncovering the structure of agreeableness from self-report measures. *Journal of Personality*, *86*, 771–787. https://doi.org/10.1111/jopy.12358.

Cumberland-li, A., Eisenberg, N., & Reiser, M. (2004). Relations of young children's agreeableness and resiliency to effortful control and impulsivity. *Social Development*, *13*, 193–212.

Deshong, H. L., Grant, D. M., & Mullins-sweatt, S. N. (2015). Comparing models of counterproductive workplace behaviors: the Five-Factor Model and the Dark Triad. *Personality and Individual Differences*, *74*, 55–60. https://doi.org/10.1016/j.paid.2014.10.001.

DeShong, H. L., Helle, A. C., Lengel, G. J., Meyer, N., & Mullins-Sweatt, S. N. (2017). Facets of the Dark Triad: utilizing the Five-Factor Model to describe Machiavellianism. *Personality and Individual Differences*, *105*, 218–223. https://doi.org/10.1016/j.paid.2016.09.053.

Dickinson, K. A., & Pincus, A. L. (2003). Interpersonal analysis of grandiose and vulnerable narcissism. *Journal of Personality Disorders*, *17*, 188–207. https://doi.org/10.1521/pedi.17.3.188.22146.

Gaughan, E. T., Miller, J. D., Pryor, L. R., & Lynam, D. R. (2009). Comparing two alternative measures of general personality in the assessment of psychopathy: a test of the NEO PI-R and the MPQ. *Journal of Personality*, *77*, 965–996.

Gemmill, G. R., & Heisler, W. J. (1972). Machiavellianism as a factor in managerial job strain, job satisfaction, and upward mobility. *Personnel Psychology*, *25*, 241–250. https://doi.org/10.1111/j.1744-6570.1972.tb01101.x.

Gladden, P. R., Figueredo, A. J., & Jacobs, W. J. (2009). Life history strategy, psychopathic attitudes, personality, and general intelligence. *Personality and Individual Differences*, *46*, 270–275. https://doi.org/10.1016/j.paid.2008.10.010.

Goldberg, L. R. (1993). The structure of phenotypic personality traits. *The American Psychologist*, *48*, 26–34. https://doi.org/10.1037/0003-066X.48.12.1302.

Goldberg, L. R. (1999). A broad-bandwidth, public domain, personality inventory measuring the lower-level facets of several five-factor models. In Vol. 7. *Personality psychology in Europe* (pp. 7–28). Tilburg, The Netherlands: Tilburg University Press.

Gordts, S., Uzieblo, K., Neumann, C., Van den Bussche, E., & Rossi, G. (2017). Validity of the Self-Report Psychopathy Scales (SRP-III full and short versions) in a community sample. *Assessment, 24*, 308–325. https://doi.org/10.1177/1073191115606205.

Graziano, W. G., & Eisenberg, N. (1997). Agreeableness: a dimension of personality. In R. Hogan, J. Johnson, & S. Briggs (Eds.), *Handbook of personality psychology* (pp. 795–824). San Diego, CA: Academic Press.

Graziano, W. G., & Tobin, M. (2017). Agreeableness and the Five-Factor Model. In T. A. Widiger (Ed.), *The Oxford handbook of the Five Factor Model* (pp. 105–132). Oxford University Press.

Hare, R. D. (1980). A research scale for the assessment of psychopathy in criminal populations. *Personality and Individual Differences, 1*, 111–119.

Hodson, G., Book, A., Visser, B. A., Volk, A. A., Ashton, M. C., & Lee, K. (2018). Is the Dark Triad common factor distinct from low honesty-humility? *Journal of Research in Personality, 73*, 123–129. https://doi.org/10.1016/J.JRP.2017.11.012.

Jensen-campbell, L. A., Rosselli, M., Workman, K. A., Santisi, M., Rios, J. D., & Bojan, D. (2002). Agreeableness, conscientiousness, and effortful control processes. *Journal of Research in Personality, 36*, 476–489.

Jonason, P. K., Kaufman, S. B., Webster, G. D., & Geher, G. (2013). What lies beneath the Dark Triad Dirty Dozen: varied relations with the Big Five. *Individual Differences Research, 11*, 81–90.

Jonason, P. K., Koenig, B. L., & Tost, J. (2010). Living a fast life: the Dark Triad and life history theory. *Human Nature, 21*, 428–442. https://doi.org/10.1007/s12110-010-9102-4.

Jonason, P. K., Li, N. P., & Czarna, A. Z. (2013). Quick and dirty: some psychosocial costs associated with the dark triad in three countries. *Evolutionary Psychology, 11*, 172–185.

Jonason, P. K., Li, N. P., & Webster, G. D. (2009). The Dark Triad: facilitating a short-term mating in men. *European Journal of Personality, 23*, 5–18.

Jonason, P. K., Luevano, V. X., & Adams, H. M. (2012). How the Dark Triad traits predict relationship choices. *Personality and Individual Differences, 53*, 180–184. https://doi.org/10.1016/j.paid.2012.03.007.

Jonason, P. K., Slomski, S., & Partyka, J. (2012). The Dark Triad at work: how toxic employees get their way. *Personality and Individual Differences, 52*, 449–453. https://doi.org/10.1016/j.paid.2011.11.008.

Jonason, P. K., Valentine, K. A., Li, N. P., & Harbeson, C. L. (2011). Mate-selection and the Dark Triad: facilitating a short-term mating strategy and creating a volatile environment. *Personality and Individual Differences, 51*, 759–763. https://doi.org/10.1016/j.paid.2011.06.025.

Jones, D. N., & Figueredo, A. J. (2013). The core of darkness: uncovering the heart of the Dark Triad. *European Journal of Personality, 27*, 521–531. https://doi.org/10.1002/per.1893.

Jones, D. N., & Paulhus, D. L. (2014). Introducing the short Dark Triad (SD3): a brief measure of dark personality traits. *Assessment, 21*, 28–41. https://doi.org/10.1177/1073191113514105.

Lee, K., & Ashton, M. C. (2004). Psychometric properties of the HEXACO Personality Inventory. *Multivariate Behavioral Research, 39*, 329–358. https://doi.org/10.1207/s15327906mbr3902.

Lynam, D. R., Gaughan, E. T., Miller, J. D., Miller, D. J., Mullins-Sweatt, S., & Widiger, T. a. (2011). Assessing the basic traits associated with psychopathy: development and validation of the Elemental Psychopathy Assessment. *Psychological Assessment, 23*, 108–124. https://doi.org/10.1037/a0021146.

Lynam, D. R., Hoyle, R. H., & Newman, J. P. (2006). The perils of partialling: cautionary tales from aggression and psychopathy. *Assessment, 13*, 328–341. https://doi.org/10.1177/1073191106290562.

Lynam, D. R., Miller, D. J., Vachon, D., Loeber, R., & Stouthamer-Loeber, M. (2009). Psychopathy in adolescence predicts official reports of offending in adulthood. *Youth Violence and Juvenile Justice*, *7*, 189–207. https://doi.org/10.1177/1541204009333797.

Maples, J. L., Lamkin, J., & Miller, J. D. (2014). A test of two brief measures of the dark triad: the dirty dozen and short dark triad. *Psychological Assessment*, *26*, 326–331. https://doi.org/10.1037/a0035084.

Marcus, D. K., Preszler, J., & Zeigler-Hill, V. (2018). A network of dark personality traits: what lies at the heart of darkness? *Journal of Research in Personality*, *73*, 56–62. https://doi.org/10.1016/J.JRP.2017.11.003.

McCrae, R. R., & John, O. P. (1992). An introduction to the five-factor model and its applications. *Journal of Personality*, *60*, 175–215. https://doi.org/10.1111/j.1467-6494.1992.tb00970.x.

McHoskey, J. W., Worzel, W., & Szyarto, C. (1998). Machiavellianism and psychopathy. *Journal of Personality and Social Psychology*, *74*, 192–210. https://doi.org/10.1037/0022-3514.74.1.192.

Miller, J. D., Dir, A., Gentile, B., Wilson, L., Pryor, L. R., & Campbell, W. K. (2010). Searching for a vulnerable Dark Triad: comparing factor 2 psychopathy, vulnerable narcissism, and borderline personality disorder. *Journal of Personality*, *78*, 1529–1564. https://doi.org/10.1111/j.1467-6494.2010.00660.x.

Miller, J. D., Gaughan, E. T., Maples, J., & Price, J. (2011). A comparison of agreeableness scores from the Big Five Inventory and the NEO PI-R: consequences for the study of narcissism and psychopathy. *Assessment*, *18*, 335–339. https://doi.org/10.1177/1073191111411671.

Miller, J. D., Hoffman, B. J., Gaughan, E. T., Gentile, B., Maples, J., & Keith Campbell, W. (2011). Grandiose and vulnerable narcissism: a nomological network analysis. *Journal of Personality*, *79*, 1013–1042. https://doi.org/10.1111/j.1467-6494.2010.00711.x.

Miller, J. D., Hyatt, C. S., Maples-Keller, J. L., Carter, N. T., & Lynam, D. R. (2017). Psychopathy and Machiavellianism: a distinction without a difference? *Journal of Personality*, *85*, 439–453. https://doi.org/10.1111/jopy.12251.

Miller, J. D., & Lynam, D. R. (2015). Understanding psychopathy using the basic elements of personality. *Social and Personality Psychology Compass*, *9*, 223–237. https://doi.org/10.1111/spc3.12170.

Miller, J. D., Lynam, D. R., McCain, J. L., Few, L. R., Crego, C., Widiger, T. A., et al. (2016). Thinking structurally about narcissism: an examination of the Five-Factor Narcissism Inventory and its components. *Journal of Personality Disorders*, *29*, 1–18. https://doi.org/10.1521/pedi_2015_29_177.

Miller, J. D., Lynam, D. R., Widiger, T. A., & Leukefeld, C. (2001). Personality disorders as extreme variants of common personality dimensions: can the Five-Factor Model adequately represent psychopathy? *Journal of Personality*, *69*, 253–276. https://doi.org/10.1111/1467-6494.00144.

Miller, J. D., Price, J., Gentile, B., Lynam, D. R., & Campbell, W. K. (2012). Grandiose and vulnerable narcissism from the perspective of the interpersonal circumplex. *Personality and Individual Differences*, *53*, 507–512. https://doi.org/10.1016/j.paid.2012.04.026.

Muris, P., Merckelbach, H., Otgaar, H., & Meijer, E. (2017). The malevolent side of human nature: a meta-analysis and critical review of the literature on the Dark Triad (narcissism, Machiavellianism, and pscyhopathy). *Perspectives on Psychological Science*, *12*, 183–204. https://doi.org/10.1177/1745691616666070.

Neumann, C. S., Hare, R. D., & Pardini, D. A. (2015). Antisociality and the construct of psychopathy: data from across the globe. *Journal of Personality*, *83*, 678–692. https://doi.org/10.1111/jopy.12127.

O'Boyle, E. H., Forsyth, D. R., Banks, G. C., & McDaniel, M. A. (2012). A meta-analysis of the Dark Triad and work behavior: a social exchange perspective. *Journal of Applied Psychology, 97*, 557–579. https://doi.org/10.1037/a0025679.

O'Boyle, E. H., Forsyth, D. R., Banks, G. C., Story, P. A., & White, C. D. (2015). A meta-analytic test of redundancy and relative importance of the dark triad and five-factor model of personality. *Journal of Personality, 83*, 644–664. https://doi.org/10.1111/jopy.12126.

Paulhus, D. L. (2014). Toward a taxonomy of dark personalities. *Current Directions in Psychological Science, 23*, 421–426. https://doi.org/10.1177/0963721414547737.

Paulhus, D. L., & Williams, K. M. (2002). The Dark Triad of personality: narcissism, Machiavellianism, and psychopathy. *Journal of Research in Personality, 36*, 556–563.

Pincus, A. L., & Lukowitsky, M. R. (2010). Pathological narcissism and narcissistic personality disorder. *Annual Review of Clinical Psychology, 6*, 421–446. https://doi.org/10.1146/annurev.clinpsy.121208.131215.

Raskin, R. N., & Hall, C. S. (1979). A narcissistic personality inventory. *Psychological Reports, 45*, 590. https://doi.org/10.2466/pr0.1979.45.2.590.

Sherman, E. D., Lynam, D. R., & Heyde, B. (2014). Agreeableness accounts for the factor structure of the youth psychopathic traits inventory. *Journal of Personality Disorders, 28*, 262–280. https://doi.org/10.1521/pedi_2013_27_124.

Siegel, J. P. (1973). Machiavellianism, MBA's and managers: leadership correlates and socialization effects. *Academy of Management Journal, 16*, 404–411. https://doi.org/10.2307/255001.

Sleep, C. E., Lynam, D. R., Hyatt, C. S., & Miller, J. D. (2017). Perils of partialing redux: the case of the Dark Triad. *Journal of Abnormal Psychology, 126*, 939.

Stead, R., & Fekken, G. C. (2014). Agreeableness at the core of the Dark Triad of personality. *Individual Differences Research, 12*, 131–141.

Tonidandel, S., & Lebreton, J. M. (2011). Relative importance analysis: a useful supplement to regression. *Journal of Business and Psychology, 26*, 1–9.

Vize, C. E., Collison, K. L., Miller, J. D., & Lynam, D. R. (2018). Examining the effects of controlling for shared variance among the dark triad using meta-analytic structural equation modelling. *European Journal of Personality, 61*, 46–61. https://doi.org/10.1002/per.2137.

Vize, C. E., Lynam, D. R., Collison, K. L., & Miller, J. D. (2018). Differences among Dark Triad components: a meta-analytic investigation. *Personality Disorders: Theory, Research, and Treatment, 9*, 101–111. https://doi.org/10.1037/per0000222.

Watts, A. L., Waldman, I. D., Smith, S. F., Poore, H. E., & Lilienfeld, S. O. (2017). The nature and correlates of the dark triad: The answers depend on the questions. *Journal of Abnormal Psychology, 126*, 951–968.

Williams, K. M., Paulhus, D. L., & Hare, R. D. (2007). Capturing the four-factor structure of psychopathy in college students via selfreport. *Journal of Personality Assessment, 88*, 205–219.

Antagonism and romantic relationships

18

Joanna Lamkin[*,†], *Justin A. Lavner*[‡]
[*]VA HSR&D Houston Center of Excellence, VA South Central MIRECC, Houston, TX, United States, [†]Baylor College of Medicine, Houston, TX, United States, [‡]Department of Psychology, University of Georgia, Athens, GA, United States

Introduction

"Antagonistic" and "disagreeable" are not words you often find in dating profiles, or overhear when someone is describing the qualities of their ideal mate. To the contrary, research spanning three decades indicates that men and women both rank "kind and understanding" as their most preferred trait in a potential partner, above characteristics such as "exciting personality," "intelligent," and "physically attractive" (Buss et al., 1990; Buss & Barnes, 1986; Watson, Beer, & McDade-Montez, 2014). Even individuals who rate themselves as disagreeable do not view antagonism in a potential romantic partner positively (Sleep, Lavner, & Miller, 2017).

Given the fairly uniform preference for agreeableness in romantic partners, it's reasonable to wonder: What's the big deal? How problematic are low levels of agreeableness/high levels of antagonism in romantic relationships? Of the Big 5 personality traits, neuroticism has often been the focus of research on personality and romantic relationships (e.g., Karney & Bradbury, 1997; McNulty, 2008), with meta-analyses indicating that it has the strongest associations with marital satisfaction and stability over time (Karney & Bradbury, 1995). Agreeableness has not received as much attention, despite its prominence in relationship preferences as described previously. Here we address this gap by examining the association between antagonism and relationship outcomes (satisfaction and dissolution) and identifying the interpersonal and intrapersonal processes that may explain these links. We conclude by discussing limitations of this work as well as future directions.

Antagonism and relationship outcomes

The vast majority of work on romantic relationships examines the role of various characteristics in predicting relationship satisfaction/quality and in predicting relationship dissolution. There is robust meta-analytic evidence for a negative association between antagonism and relationship quality: In marital and nonmarital relationships, individuals who rate themselves lower in agreeableness report lower levels of relationship satisfaction (Heller, Watson, & Ilies, 2004), as do their romantic partners (Malouff, Thorsteinsson, Schutte, Bhullar, & Rooke, 2010). Importantly, these appear to be

The Handbook of Antagonism. https://doi.org/10.1016/B978-0-12-814627-9.00018-9

independent effects, such that partner disagreeableness negatively predicts self-rated relationship quality, above and beyond the effects of one's own disagreeableness (Solomon & Jackson, 2014; Weidmann, Ledermann, & Grob, 2017). Additionally, perceptions of partner antagonism have been associated with relationship functioning, such that individuals who perceive their partner to be less agreeable and who are perceived by their partner as being less agreeable have lower levels of satisfaction (Furler, Gomez, & Grob, 2014).

These conclusions, though robust, have primarily been based on cross-sectional research. There has been relatively little longitudinal research examining how antagonism predicts the trajectory of marital quality over time, including whether it is associated with initial levels of marital quality (intercepts) and/or changes in marital quality (slopes). The limited research available suggests that antagonism is associated with initial levels but not associated with slopes (Lavner, Weiss, Miller, & Karney, 2018; Solomon & Jackson, 2014), indicating that the marriages of individuals low in agreeableness start off less satisfying and remain that way over time, rather than starting off at similarly positive levels and declining at a more rapid pace. When comparing satisfaction at different relationship stages, agreeableness was related more strongly to satisfaction in dating than in marriage, again suggesting that any negative effects from agreeableness are likely to be apparent very early in relationships rather than emerging over time (Watson, Hubbard, & Wiese, 2000).

Despite robust associations between antagonism and relationship quality, evidence for an association between agreeableness and relationship dissolution is limited. Assessing this question well necessitates longitudinal data, which are more difficult to collect, thereby resulting in relatively few studies examining these associations. A meta-analysis examining predictors of *nonmarital* romantic relationship dissolution included 137 studies over a period of 33 years, but only four of these examined agreeableness (Le, Dove, Agnew, Korn, & Mutso, 2010). Among these studies, there was no significant overall association between agreeableness and relationship dissolution. A meta-analysis of the association between agreeableness and *marital* dissolution ($n = 4$ studies for wives and 3 studies for husband) found small, but significant, effects for husbands' and wives' agreeableness on marital stability (Karney & Bradbury, 1995). However, more recent evidence has been weaker. Specifically, recent research using large, nationally representative samples from Germany (Lundberg, 2010) and Britain (Boertien, von Scheve, & Park, 2017) found no significant associations between agreeableness and divorce. A 4-year longitudinal study using nationally representative data from Australia found a significant association between antagonism and divorce, but this effect was no longer significant after controlling for the other Big Five traits and for demographic variables (Solomon & Jackson, 2014). This last set of findings underscores the importance of considering agreeableness alongside other characteristics to ensure that effects are unique to this trait.

Together, these findings indicate that the relationships of antagonistic individuals are less satisfying for themselves and for their romantic partners compared to the relationships of less antagonistic individuals, but they are not more vulnerable to dissolution. These findings raise important questions about *why* these relationships prove less satisfying, a question to which we devote the remainder of this review.

Antagonism and relationship processes

The processes that have been investigated regarding antagonism in a romantic relationship context can be categorized into two domains. The first is *interpersonal* processes, which include negative behaviors such as costly relationship tactics, intimate partner violence, aggression (psychological and physical), hostility, and infidelity. For example, as we describe in more detail later, antagonistic individuals choose and use strategies that are upsetting and hurtful to their partner. The second domain, which holds the potential to explain these behaviors, is *intrapersonal* processes. These processes include (negative) perceptions of one's partner, beliefs and expectations about what they anticipate their partner to do, and (poor) insight. Throughout this section, we also explore the role of gender in romantic relationships as it pertains to antagonism.

Of note, most of the findings about these processes come from college students in dating relationships and young married couples, often exclude nonheterosexual couples, and are cross-sectional. It will be important for future studies to include a more diverse representation of couples as well as establish a stronger understanding of longitudinal patterns. Longitudinal studies also will offer the ability to make stronger claims regarding the linkages between intrapersonal processes, interpersonal processes, and ultimately, relationship quality and dissolution among antagonistic individuals.

Antagonism and interpersonal processes

Communication and relationship behaviors. Broadly, in romantic relationships, antagonistic individuals are more likely to behave in ways that are hurtful and upsetting to their partner. In a study of over 100 married couples, both husbands and wives who had low agreeableness were more likely to engage in actions that upset their spouses in the past year (Buss, 1991). Similarly, when asked to track real-life interactions with their romantic partner in a diary study, disagreeable people reported more negative exchanges (Tov, Nai, & Lee, 2016). These patterns have been replicated using observational data from the lab as well: Married men and women reporting lower levels of agreeableness displayed more negative behaviors during a 25-minute interaction during which they discussed the history of their relationship, the current status of their relationship, areas of agreement and disagreement in their relationship, and their future plans together (Donnellan, Conger, & Bryant, 2004). These negative behaviors included higher levels of angry coercion, antisocial behavior, and hostility, and lower levels of responsiveness, prosocial behavior, and warmth.

Some patterns of antagonistic behavior in romantic relationships are more likely when certain conditions are met. In a series of studies, disagreeable individuals were more likely to engage in behaviors that they expected to upset or hurt their partner (e.g., flirting with others, spending excessively, using substances) when they perceived their partner to be *more* forgiving in general (McNulty & Russell, 2016). The hypothesized motivation for this behavior was that low agreeable people engaged in transgressions because they thought they would get away with it, not because it was the right thing to do. That is, they expected that their forgiving partners would not become angry. Conversely, high agreeable people were less likely to engage in transgressions when they perceived their partner to be forgiving.

Beyond general interactions, antagonistic individuals are especially likely to engage in hurtful behaviors in response to conflict. In romantic and other types of relationships, even though all participants rated power assertion as the least ideal tactic in response to conflict, individuals with lower agreeableness rated power assertion tactics as a better option than participants with high agreeableness (Graziano, Jensen-Campbell, & Hair, 1996). Furthermore, those with higher antagonism may *automatically* opt for more destructive responses during a conflict with their partner. For example, individuals in a dating relationship were presented with a hypothetical conflict wherein their partner said something argumentative and then asked to choose between a prosocial and nonprosocial response (Perunovic & Holmes, 2008). Overall, those with low agreeableness were more likely to select the nonprosocial response. Under time pressure, selecting this type of option was even more pronounced—and this pattern persisted regardless of self-reported relationship quality (satisfaction, closeness, and commitment) or length.

Antagonistic individuals are also more likely to use tactics that are detrimental to the relationship when working toward a particular goal. When asked to report tactics used to manipulate one's spouse into doing something, those with low agreeableness endorsed using coercion (e.g., demanding, criticizing, and yelling) and the silent treatment (e.g., ignoring until the spouse performs the desired behavior; Buss, 1992). Mate retention strategies (i.e., things people do to keep their romantic partners in the relationship) employed by antagonistic individuals are more costly than beneficial to their partners—a strategy that seems contradictory to its goal. For example, those with high antagonism were more willing to manipulate, deceive, or exploit in order to retain their mate (Holden, Roof, McCabe, & Zeigler-Hill, 2015). Individuals with low agreeableness were more likely to report using cost-inducing tactics toward their partner *and* perceived rivals (de Miguel & Buss, 2011).

Given our understanding of antagonism as a general personality trait, behaviors that engender and exacerbate conflict rather than keep the peace are not necessarily surprising. However, the frequency and automaticity of the behaviors seems to be particularly salient in the context of romantic relationships. For example, when asked to rate what bothers them in face-to-face interactions, young adults rated antagonism as more of a problem in romantic relationships than in friendships or acquaintanceships (Hopwood et al., 2011). This pattern was especially prominent if the rater was low on antagonism, suggesting that antagonism is particularly aversive in romantic relationships when the other partner is more agreeable.

Aggression and intimate partner violence. Associations between antagonism and negative relationship behaviors extend into more severe behaviors such as aggression and intimate partner violence as well. Studies of intimate partner violence and personality typically focus on specific personality disorders that involve antagonism and other traits, especially antisocial and borderline PDs. While informative, these findings are difficult to apply to nonclinical populations where antagonism may still have significant consequences. Only recently have researchers attempted to characterize these patterns more broadly by using general personality trait measures as well as pathological personality measures such as the PID-5 (Krueger, Derringer, Markon, Watson, & Skodol, 2012).

Antagonism has been consistently linked to intimate partner violence in undergraduate samples (e.g., Dowgwillo, Ménard, Krueger, & Pincus, 2016). Low agreeableness was the second strongest predictor (after male gender) of self-reported sexual harassment behaviors in college students (Ménard, Shoss, & Pincus, 2010). However, these patterns appear to have gender-specific effects within the context of relationships, such that women with low agreeableness are more likely to perpetrate and/or receive aggression. In a large sample of college students, women with higher antagonism reported greater perpetration of relationship violence (Dowgwillo et al., 2016). In college students currently in a relationship (Hines & Saudino, 2008), women with low agreeableness reported perpetrating more physical and psychological aggression. These women also reported receiving more physical, psychological, and sexual aggression from their partner, suggesting that their relationships may be marked by a higher level of reciprocated aggression between partners.

As with the other reviewed relationship behaviors, the likelihood of antagonistic individuals engaging in these aggressive behaviors may be shaped by context. For example, perceived risk or threat to the relationship has a seemingly counterintuitive effect for antagonism. It appears to be a combination of low agreeableness and *low* perceived risk of partner infidelity that leads to partner-directed violence in men (Kaighobadi et al., 2009). In other words, when antagonistic men think that their partner is unlikely to cheat on them, they are more likely to use violence. Again, we see a pattern of engaging in hurtful behaviors when antagonistic individuals believe they can get away with it. Given that stronger linkages have been shown between antagonism and intimate partner violence among women, additional research is needed to clarify the circumstances under which these behaviors are most likely to occur.

Infidelity. In addition to engaging in more negative and/or aggressive behaviors in their relationships, antagonistic individuals are likely to engage in other types of behaviors that prove damaging to their relationships as well. Most notably, antagonistic individuals are more likely to be unfaithful to their romantic partner. Cross-cultural studies including thousands of individuals from dozens of countries indicate that low levels of agreeableness are associated with higher levels of relationship infidelity and higher levels of sexual promiscuity (Schmitt, 2004), as well as increased interest in short-term mating, more attempts at trying to attract someone else's partner (i.e., mate poaching), greater likelihood of having succumbed to others' poaching attempts, and a lower overall level of relationship exclusivity (Schmitt & Buss, 2001; Schmitt & Shackelford, 2008). In another study, individuals with low agreeableness were more likely not only to engage in infidelity but to attempt to conceal the infidelity (Weiser & Weigel, 2015).

Positive interpersonal processes. Lastly, although most of the research on antagonism's association with interpersonal processes in romantic relationships has focused on negative interpersonal processes, there has been some work showing that antagonism is associated with lower levels of positive interpersonal processes as well. For example, women with lower levels of agreeableness were less likely to express forgiveness toward their husbands in response to hypothetical marital transgressions (e.g., the partner snapping at them; McNulty, 2011). Individuals lower in agreeableness are also less likely to engage in support seeking in response to stressors and engage in lower levels of empathic responding—but higher levels of confrontive coping—in response to marital conflict (DeLongis & Holtzman, 2005).

Antagonism and intrapersonal processes

As reviewed previously, the interpersonal behaviors associated with antagonism in romantic relationships are well established, and these behaviors are costly to partners and the relationship itself. Until recently, there has been little attention to the motivations and levels of insight that may drive these behaviors. Here we briefly review the early findings in this domain, which is underdeveloped and in need of further study.

When social motives are considered, antagonistic individuals demonstrate several approaches to social behavior that are likely to create difficulties in their romantic relationships. Those with low agreeableness place less value on mate retention, yet have more concerns about relationship breakups, a pattern that relates to greater unfaithfulness as well as an orientation toward short-term relationships instead of long-term relationships (Neel, Kenrick, White, & Neuberg, 2016). Other work similarly indicates that individuals with high antagonism report stronger motives related to mate seeking and breakup concerns, but lower valuing of mate retention (Zeigler-Hill & Hobbs, 2017). Lower levels of agreeableness among young adults in dating relationships were also associated with desiring less closeness in those relationships (Goodboy & Booth-Butterfield, 2009).

Antagonism also relates to perceptions of and expectations about others' behavior. Wives with low agreeableness reported multiple upsetting behaviors by their husbands (note: husbands with low agreeableness did not report these behaviors in their wives; Buss, 1991), raising interesting questions about whether these women were more likely to simply *perceive* negative behaviors in their husbands or whether they were actually more likely to *experience* these behaviors (perhaps in response to their own negative behaviors, as described previously). Women with low agreeableness were also more likely to expect that their husbands were susceptible to engaging in a wide range of unfaithful behaviors, from one night stands to brief affairs to serious affairs (Buss & Shackelford, 1997). Understandably, expecting one's partner to engage in affairs, even if there is no history or evidence of such behavior, could have detrimental effects on relationship quality over time.

Although we focus primarily on adult romantic relationships here, one study connecting teenage disagreeableness to romantic relationships in young adulthood is worth mentioning. In a study assessing long-term consequences of disagreeableness (Hafen, Allen, Schad, & Hessel, 2015), teens (aged 14–15) who had low agreeableness did not report relationship difficulties at age 21. Yet, their romantic partners reported that their relationship was low in quality. The authors term this "relationship blindness," reflecting the notion that the oppositional style of antagonistic young adults may function to limit insight (or willingness to report) problems in relationships. Poor insight may help to explain why the negative interpersonal strategies and tactics used by antagonistic in romantic relationships sometimes seem counterintuitive to their purported goals (e.g., mate retention, concerns about breakups). These concerns are likely to be compounded by the limited degree of perspective-taking in romantic relationships (e.g., trying to understand what the partner may be thinking) that is characteristic of antagonistic individuals (Vater & Schröder-Abé, 2015).

Summary and future directions

Together, these findings generally indicate that antagonism is associated with more negative relationship functioning, with significant impairments seen in multiple aspects of relationships. Centrally, antagonism is associated with engaging in behaviors that are hurtful and upsetting to the partner. These behaviors range from hostile tactics to intimate partner violence to infidelity, alongside lower levels of positive behaviors such as forgiveness and empathic responding. These robust associations certainly explain why antagonism is associated with less satisfying relationships for the partners of antagonistic individuals, but do less to explain why antagonism is associated with lower levels of one's own relationship quality. Internal processes, such as perceptions, values, and insight, may help to explain this missing piece, but these data are limited.

The existing data suggest that intimate relationships—particularly longer term relationships—reflect a range of competing urges for antagonistic individuals. They have heightened concerns about relationship dissolution, despite having less interest in intimacy, more interest in short-term relationships, and less concern about retaining their partner. They are more likely to think their partners will be unfaithful, yet are more likely to engage in infidelity themselves. And in general, these individuals have limited understanding—or willingness to acknowledge—how their behavior affects their partner, which is likely to be problematic given their propensity to engage in negative behaviors toward their partner. Given these associations, some of the connections between individuals' own antagonism and their self-reported relationship quality may reflect primarily intrapersonal processes such as inherently finding relationships less rewarding and/or more difficult. It is also likely, given the dyadic nature of relationships, that the association between individuals' own antagonism and relationship quality may reflect the consequences of their interpersonal behavior. In this hypothesized feedback loop, one's own negative behavior leads the partner to behave negatively, which in turn creates a less satisfying relationship for the antagonistic individual (who is likely to respond with more negative behavior). Future research examining these types of dynamic processes would be valuable.

Another important missing piece in the literature is an explanation for why antagonistic traits are not associated with greater likelihood of relationship dissolution, despite being consistently associated with poorer relationship quality and negative relationship processes. Again, these data are limited, necessitating some caution in interpretation, but the inconsistent (and largely nonsignificant) associations call for some attempt to explain these less satisfying, but stable relationships. One possibility is that individuals and their partners learn to manage these difficult traits—not necessarily in a way that makes them less bothersome but by containing the behaviors so that they do not create worsening tensions. This view is supported by the longitudinal findings reviewed earlier indicating that antagonism is associated with levels, but not slopes, of marital satisfaction over time (Lavner et al., 2018; Solomon & Jackson, 2014). It is also possible that antagonistic individuals become less antagonistic over time due to contingencies shaped by the relationship (Roberts, Wood, & Smith, 2005), such that initial levels of antagonism do not accurately reflect individuals' standing on this trait later in the relationship. Accordingly, it may be the case that initial antagonism does not predict dissolution, but later antagonism (and its changes over time) might. The relationship literature generally does not treat personality as a dynamic predictor of relationship functioning: Antagonism is typically assessed only once, and this is generally at the beginning of the relationship (or of the study). Yet, recent findings call attention to how personality is likely to change in the context of intimate relationships and the benefits of considering changes as well as initial levels when assessing relationship quality over time (Bleidorn, Hopwood, & Lucas, 2018; Lavner et al.,2018). Future research examining these questions among other longitudinal samples—particularly samples focused on populations other than newlywed couples—would help clarify the workings of antagonism in relationships over time.

In addition to addressing these significant gaps in the literature, future work on antagonism in romantic relationships should move beyond the prevailing univariate approach that examines its effects in isolation. It goes without saying that individuals are not solely disagreeable (or neurotic, or extraverted), but most of the research in this area has failed to consider how the association between antagonism and various relationship outcomes may be moderated by other traits. This research should include other personality traits as well as other relationship characteristics. For example, one study found that the association between antagonism and observed hostility was moderated by commitment (Lemay & Dobush, 2015). Specifically, for antagonistic individuals, believing oneself to be *less* committed than one's partner may promote expression (instead of inhibition) of hostility during conflict. In behavioral tasks, individuals with low agreeableness and similar characteristics were more likely to engage in hostile behavior toward their partner when they considered themselves to be less committed to the relationship. Hostility did not manifest for committed, disagreeable people or for noncommitted, agreeable people. The authors suggested that perceptions of asymmetrical commitment may relate to perceptions of power, another potential motivator for antagonistic individuals. The more general point is that the associations between antagonism and various outcomes are likely to differ based on a whole host of factors, but these types of complex associations have generally been overlooked.

Similarly, more attention needs to be given to the moderating effects of partner traits. As one example of the promise of this type of approach, longitudinal data from couples over the transition to parenthood indicated that one's own neuroticism interacted with the partner's agreeableness to predict depressive symptoms, such that individuals high in neuroticism partnered with someone low in agreeableness experienced higher levels of depressive symptoms (Marshall, Simpson, & Rholes, 2015). These associations were even stronger if the couple had poor problem-solving communication and/or higher levels of aggression prior to the birth of the child. These findings underscore the importance of considering additional traits of the individual and of the partner that may moderate the association between antagonism and relationship functioning in order to clarify the contexts under which antagonistic traits prove especially problematic.

Finally, future research must reflect the realities of modern relationships. For example, at a time when dating apps and websites are increasingly used to meet potential mates (e.g., Finkel, Eastwick, Karney, Reis, & Sprecher, 2012), it is increasingly important to consider how personality traits are associated with various relationship behaviors "online." One study found that individuals low in agreeableness were more likely to misrepresent aspects of themselves online in order to get a date, including their personal assets (e.g., income, education), relationship goals (e.g., interest in a serious relationship), personal interests, personal attributes (e.g., politeness), and information about their past relationships (Hall, Park, Song, & Cody, 2010). Whether—and how—these early deceptions affect the subsequent development of relationships is an open question. More broadly, social and cultural forces have led to increases in cohabitation, declines in the marriage rate, increases in the average age at marriage, and increases in the number of children born to unmarried couples (Lavner & Bradbury, in press). These trends point to the importance of considering associations between antagonistic traits and relationship outcomes in samples with these demographic profiles, in addition to samples that are more racially, ethnically, and economically diverse than those that have typically been the focus of research to date. We note also the lack of research on same-sex couples, which could allow for interesting tests of the gendered nature of several of the findings reviewed here (e.g., whether antagonistic traits prove especially problematic for women or whether they are only problematic when women with these traits are partnered with men). Increasing the diversity of our samples—and of the types of relationships these samples include—will ultimately allow for stronger conclusions about *how* and *why* antagonism proves problematic in romantic relationships.

References

Bleidorn, W., Hopwood, C. J., & Lucas, R. E. (2018). Life events and personality trait change. *Journal of Personality*, *86*, 83–96.

Boertien, D., von Scheve, C., & Park, M. (2017). Can personality explain the educational gradient in divorce? Evidence from a nationally representative panel survey. *Journal of Family Issues*, *38*, 1339–1362.

Buss, D. M. (1991). Conflict in married couples: personality predictors of anger and upset. *Journal of Personality*, *59*, 663–703.

Buss, D. M. (1992). Manipulation in close relationships: five personality factors in interactional context. *Journal of Personality*, *60*, 477–499.

Buss, D. M., Abbott, M., Angleitner, A., Asherian, A., Biaggio, A., Blanco-Villasenor, A., et al. (1990). International preferences in selecting mates: a study of 37 cultures. *Journal of Cross-Cultural Psychology*, *21*, 5–47.

Buss, D. M., & Barnes, M. (1986). Preferences in human mate selection. *Journal of Personality and Social Psychology*, *50*, 559–570.

Buss, D. M., & Shackelford, T. K. (1997). Susceptibility to infidelity in the first year of marriage. *Journal of Research in Personality, 31*, 193–221.

de Miguel, A., & Buss, D. M. (2011). Mate retention tactics in Spain: personality, sex differences, and relationship status. *Journal of Personality, 79*(3), 563–586.

DeLongis, A., & Holtzman, S. (2005). Coping in context: the role of stress, social support, and personality in coping. *Journal of Personality, 73*, 1633–1656.

Donnellan, M. B., Conger, R. D., & Bryant, C. M. (2004). The Big Five and enduring marriages. *Journal of Research in Personality, 38*, 481–504.

Dowgwillo, E. A., Ménard, K. S., Krueger, R. F., & Pincus, A. L. (2016). DSM-5 pathological personality traits and intimate partner violence among male and female college students. *Violence and Victims, 31*(3), 416–437.

Finkel, E. J., Eastwick, P. W., Karney, B. R., Reis, H. T., & Sprecher, S. (2012). Online dating: a critical analysis from the perspective of psychological science. *Psychological Science in the Public Interest, 13*, 3–66.

Furler, K., Gomez, V., & Grob, A. (2014). Personality perceptions and relationship satisfaction in couples. *Journal of Research in Personality, 50*, 33–41.

Goodboy, A. K., & Booth-Butterfield, M. (2009). Individual differences in romantic partners' desire for less closeness. *North American Journal of Psychology, 11*, 209–218.

Graziano, W. G., Jensen-Campbell, L. A., & Hair, E. C. (1996). Perceiving interpersonal conflict and reacting to it: the case for agreeableness. *Journal of Personality and Social Psychology, 70*, 820–835.

Hafen, C. A., Allen, J. P., Schad, M. M., & Hessel, E. T. (2015). Conflict with friends, relationship blindness, and the pathway to adult disagreeableness. *Personality and Individual Differences, 81*, 7–12.

Hall, J. A., Park, N., Song, H., & Cody, M. J. (2010). Strategic misrepresentation in online dating: the effects of gender, self-monitoring, and personality traits. *Journal of Social and Personal Relationships, 27*, 117–135.

Heller, D., Watson, D., & Ilies, R. (2004). The role of person versus situation in life satisfaction: a critical examination. *Psychological Bulletin, 130*, 574–600.

Hines, D. A., & Saudino, K. J. (2008). Personality and intimate partner aggression in dating relationships: the role of the "Big Five" *Aggressive Behavior, 34*, 593–604.

Holden, C. J., Roof, C. H., McCabe, G., & Zeigler-Hill, V. (2015). Detached and antagonistic: pathological personality features and mate retention behaviors. *Personality and Individual Differences, 83*, 77–84.

Hopwood, C. J., Ansell, E. B., Pincus, A. L., Wright, A. C., Lukowitsky, M. R., & Roche, M. J. (2011). The circumplex structure of interpersonal sensitivities. *Journal of Personality, 79*(4), 707–740. https://doi.org/10.1111/j.1467-6494.2011.00696.x.

Kaighobadi, F., Shackelford, T. K., Popp, D., Moyer, R. M., Bates, V. M., & Liddle, J. R. (2009). Perceived risk of female infidelity moderates the relationship between men's personality and partner-directed violence. *Journal of Research in Personality, 43*, 1033–1039.

Karney, B. R., & Bradbury, T. N. (1995). The longitudinal course of marital quality and stability: a review of theory, method, and research. *Psychological Bulletin, 118*, 3–34.

Karney, B. R., & Bradbury, T. N. (1997). Neuroticism, marital interaction, and the trajectory of marital satisfaction. *Journal of Personality and Social Psychology, 72*, 1075–1092.

Krueger, R. F., Derringer, J., Markon, K. E., Watson, D., & Skodol, A. E. (2012). Initial construction of a maladaptive personality trait model and inventory for DSM-5. *Psychological Medicine, 42*, 1879–1890.

Lavner, J. A., & Bradbury, T. N. (in press). Marriage and committed partnerships. In B. Fiese (Ed.), APA handbook of contemporary family psychology Washington, DC: American Psychological Association.

Lavner, J. A., Weiss, B., Miller, J. D., & Karney, B. R. (2018). Personality change among newlyweds: Patterns, predictors, and associations with marital satisfaction over time. *Developmental Psychology*, *54*, 1172–1185.

Le, B., Dove, N. L., Agnew, C. R., Korn, M. S., & Mutso, A. A. (2010). Predicting nonmarital romantic relationship dissolution: a meta-analytic synthesis. *Personal Relationships*, *17*, 377–390.

Lemay, E. J., & Dobush, S. (2015). When do personality and emotion predict destructive behavior during relationship conflict? The role of perceived commitment asymmetry. *Journal of Personality*, *83*, 523–534.

Lundberg, S. (2010). *Personality and marital surplus.* (IZA discussion paper no. 4945). Retrieved from http://ftp.iza.org/dp4945.pdf.

Malouff, J. M., Thorsteinsson, E. B., Schutte, N. S., Bhullar, N., & Rooke, S. E. (2010). The five-factor model of personality and relationship satisfaction of intimate partners: a meta-analysis. *Journal of Research in Personality*, *44*, 124–127.

Marshall, E. M., Simpson, J. A., & Rholes, W. S. (2015). Personality, communication, and depressive symptoms across the transition to parenthood: a dyadic longitudinal investigation. *European Journal of Personality*, *29*, 216–234.

McNulty, J. K. (2008). Neuroticism and interpersonal negativity: the independent contributions of perceptions and behaviors. *Personality and Social Psychology Bulletin*, *34*, 1439–1450.

McNulty, J. K. (2011). The dark side of forgiveness: the tendency to forgive predicts continued psychological and physical aggression in marriage. *Personality and Social Psychology Bulletin*, *37*, 770–783.

McNulty, J. K., & Russell, V. M. (2016). Forgive and forget, or forgive and regret? Whether forgiveness leads to less or more offending depends on offender agreeableness. *Personality and Social Psychology Bulletin*, *42*, 616–631.

Ménard, K. S., Shoss, N. E., & Pincus, A. L. (2010). Attachment and personality predicts engagement in sexual harassment by male and female college students. *Violence and Victims*, *25*, 770–786.

Neel, R., Kenrick, D. T., White, A. E., & Neuberg, S. L. (2016). Individual differences in fundamental social motives. *Journal of Personality and Social Psychology*, *110*, 887–907.

Perunovic, M., & Holmes, J. G. (2008). Automatic accommodation: the role of personality. *Personal Relationships*, *15*, 57–70.

Roberts, B. W., Wood, D., & Smith, J. L. (2005). Evaluating five factor theory and social investment perspectives on personality trait development. *Journal of Research in Personality*, *39*, 166–184.

Schmitt, D. P. (2004). The big five related to risky sexual behaviour across 10 world regions: differential personality associations of sexual promiscuity and relationship infidelity. *European Journal of Personality*, *18*, 301–319.

Schmitt, D. P., & Buss, D. M. (2001). Human mate poaching: tactics and temptations for infiltrating existing mateships. *Journal of Personality and Social Psychology*, *80*, 894–917.

Schmitt, D. P., & Shackelford, T. K. (2008). Big Five traits related to short-term mating: from personality to promiscuity across 46 nations. *Evolutionary Psychology*, *6*, 246–282.

Sleep, C. E., Lavner, J. A., & Miller, J. D. (2017). Do individuals with maladaptive personality traits find these same traits desirable in potential romantic partners? *Personality and Individual Differences*, *119*, 317–322.

Solomon, B. C., & Jackson, J. J. (2014). Why do personality traits predict divorce? Multiple pathways through satisfaction. *Journal of Personality and Social Psychology*, *106*, 978–996.
Tov, W., Nai, Z. L., & Lee, H. W. (2016). Extraversion and agreeableness: divergent routes to daily satisfaction with social relationships. *Journal of Personality*, *84*, 121–134.
Vater, A., & Schröder-Abé, M. (2015). Explaining the link between personality and relationship satisfaction: Emotion regulation and interpersonal behaviour in conflict discussions. *European Journal of Personality*, *29*, 201–215.
Watson, D., Beer, A., & McDade-Montez, E. (2014). The role of active assortment in spousal similarity. *Journal of Personality*, *82*, 116–129.
Watson, D., Hubbard, B., & Wiese, D. (2000). General traits of personality and affectivity as predictors of satisfaction in intimate relationships: evidence from self- and partner-ratings. *Journal of Personality*, *68*, 413–449.
Weidmann, R., Ledermann, T., & Grob, A. (2017). Big Five traits and relationship satisfaction: the mediating role of self-esteem. *Journal of Research in Personality*, *69*, 102–109.
Weiser, D. A., & Weigel, D. J. (2015). Investigating experiences of the infidelity partner: who is the "other man/woman"? *Personality and Individual Differences*, *85*, 176–181.
Zeigler-Hill, V., & Hobbs, K. A. (2017). The darker aspects of motivation: pathological personality traits and the fundamental social motives. *Journal of Social and Clinical Psychology*, *36*, 87–107.

Antagonism and work outcomes: Implicit and explicit considerations

19

Levi K. Shiverdecker, James M. LeBreton
Department of Psychology, Pennsylvania State University, University Park, PA, United States

Antagonism in the workplace

Explicit Antagonism

Within work contexts, the study of antagonism has generally followed one of two distinct research traditions. The first (and more popular) tradition has defined and treated antagonism as part of the explicit personality. This approach essentially focuses on those aspects of antagonism that are consciously accessible and amenable to measurement via self-report surveys. Within the organizational sciences, trait antagonism has most frequently been studied via the Five-Factor Model of personality. Specifically, antagonism has been conceptualized as the low end of the agreeableness trait. Individuals who are low in agreeableness or high in antagonism are often described as untrustworthy, deceptive, selfish, uncooperative, lacking empathy, and arrogant. In this chapter, we will refer to trait antagonism as being directly operationalized and measured via the agreeableness dimension of the FFM. Thus, when appropriate, we have reversed the direction of effect sizes to be consistent with defining this trait in terms of antagonism, rather than agreeableness.

Although the majority of organizational research has focused on directly assessing trait antagonism, some research has *indirectly* investigated links between workplace outcomes and antagonism by studying a cluster of personality traits known as the Dark Triad (DT). The DT traits are comprised of Machiavellianism, narcissism, and psychopathy which, at their core, all include the common trait of antagonism (Book, Visser, & Volk, 2015; Paulhus & Williams, 2002). Although antagonism is a central component underlying each of the DT traits, in theory, the traits differ in the way that antagonism manifests. For instance, Machiavellians are characterized by behaviors related to deception and manipulation; narcissists are more likely to use displays of dominance and self-promotion tactics; and psychopaths are cold, callous, and impulsive.

These different manifestations are also reflected in how the DT traits relate to the traits of the FFM. For example, O'Boyle, Forsyth, Banks, Story, and White's (2015) meta-analytic review found that Machiavellianism was negatively correlated with conscientiousness ($r = -.21$), but essentially uncorrelated with extraversion ($r = -.01$), neuroticism ($r = .09$), and openness ($r = -.04$). In contrast, narcissism

The Handbook of Antagonism. https://doi.org/10.1016/B978-0-12-814627-9.00019-0

was essentially uncorrelated with conscientiousness ($r = .09$), but positively correlated with extraversion ($r = .40$) and openness ($r = .20$) while being negatively correlated with neuroticism ($r = -.16$). Finally, psychopathy demonstrated a strong negative correlation with conscientiousness ($r = -.31$) but was uncorrelated with the traits of extraversion ($r = .04$), neuroticism ($r = .05$), and openness ($r = .04$). Results were largely consistent when examining the facets underlying the global traits of the FFM, but some notable exceptions emerged. For example, while narcissism was negatively correlated with overall levels of neuroticism, it was positively correlated with facets related to hostility ($r = .25$) and impulsivity ($r = .13$). Similarly, while psychopathy was generally unrelated to neuroticism and extraversion, several significant correlations emerged at the facet level including hostility ($r = .28$), impulsivity ($r = .28$), and the excitement-seeking aspects of extraversion ($r = .20$).

Finally, an additional caveat regarding the operationalization of the DT traits must be addressed before continuing. The DT traits of narcissism and psychopathy have roots in clinical psychology and thus may be linked back to personality disorders such as antisocial personality disorder and narcissistic personality disorder); however, researchers studying the DT in the workplace typically focus on measuring the subclinical aspects of these traits (Wu & LeBreton, 2011).

Implicit Antagonism

The second, and smaller, tradition has defined and treated antagonism as part of the implicit personality. The implicit personality focuses on those aspects of personality that largely operate outside of conscious awareness (e.g., latent motives, implicit biases, defense mechanisms) and thus must be indirectly measured. Within the organizational sciences, the implicit aspects of antagonism have been studied under the rubric of implicit motives—most notably the implicit motive to aggress (James & LeBreton, 2010, 2012).

Because the explicit tradition has dominated organizational research, it is the primary focus of our chapter. However, we conclude our chapter with a brief review of the work in the implicit tradition, emphasizing how the implicit and explicit traditions may be integrated with one another to improve our understanding of how antagonism is related to work outcomes. Thus our chapter begins with a review of how explicit antagonism measured directly (via FFM) and indirectly (via the antagonistic core of the DT) is related to the most commonly studied outcomes in organizational psychology. Specifically, we review how explicit (trait) antagonism is related to:

1. Job performance (including core task performance, counterproductive workplace behaviors, and organizational citizenship behaviors),
2. Job attitudes (including job satisfaction and organizational commitment), and
3. Leadership (including leader effectiveness and leader emergence).

Then, we review the more limited literature linking implicit antagonism to work outcomes. Finally, we summarize research demonstrating that implicit and explicit conceptualizations of antagonism often work in complementary ways and conclude that future work would benefit from the systematic integration of implicit and explicit antagonism.

Antagonism and job performance

Over the last 100 years, job performance has served as the primary criterion of interest for organizational psychologists. Performance is typically conceptualized as spanning three broad domains—task performance, counterproductive workplace behaviors (CWB), and organizational citizenship behaviors (OCB). Task performance represents an evaluation of behaviors performed by an employee as part of their job description (i.e., in-role behaviors; Borman & Motowidlo, 1997); CWBs refer to deviant behaviors (i.e., theft) that have harmful consequences for the organization or individuals belonging to the organization (Robinson & Bennett, 1995); OCBs represent prosocial behaviors (i.e., helping) performed by employees which span beyond the scope of behaviors outlined in an individual's job description (Bateman & Organ, 1983).

Task performance

Trait antagonism. Several meta-analytic reviews have found that, on average, the relationship between antagonism and task performance is relatively modest. For example, Judge, Rodell, Klinger, Simon, and Crawford (2013) found a small, but significant, negative relationship between trait antagonism and task performance (sample weighted mean $r = -.08$, 95% CI [−.14, −.06]. This finding resonates with an earlier meta-analytic investigation conducted by Hurtz and Donovan (2000), who found a similarly small negative relationship (sample weighted mean $r = -.07$). These two meta-analytic investigations provide evidence suggesting that, on average, there is a small negative association between trait antagonism and task performance. However, the findings presented by Judge et al. (2013) suggest that a nuanced inspection of the subfacets of antagonism may be more appropriate than using a single broad dimension. Their results exposed that the confidence intervals for only two of the six subfacets of antagonism (e.g., compliance and trust) did not contain zero. Additionally, the slight change between the mean correlation from the beginning of the new millennium to the findings presented 13 years later by Judge et al. (2013) may underscore the need for organizational researchers to investigate how this link may evolve with the changing nature of work. For example, how will trait antagonism affect task performance as tasks become more interdependent and collaborative?

Antagonistic core of DT. Although antagonism is at the core of the DT, the links between the DT and task performance are not entirely consistent with one another. For instance, O'Boyle, Forsyth, Banks, and McDaniel (2012) reported small significant negative relationships between Machiavellianism and task performance (sample weighted mean $r = -.06$, 95% CI [−.09, −.02]) as well as psychopathy and task performance (sample weighted mean $r = -.08$, 95% CI [−.11, −.05]). These findings are consistent with those linking trait antagonism and task performance. Interestingly, narcissism was not significantly related to task performance (sample weighted mean $r = -.02$, 95% CI [−.06, .02]). Although the correlation between narcissism and task performance was also in the negative direction, subtle construct differences between the traits, or differences in the way antagonism manifests behaviorally, may account for the lack of significance found for narcissism. Looking ahead, additional research examining how specific subtraits or facets of the DT differentially relate to task performance may provide greater insights into the relationship between the antagonistic core of the DT and task performance.

Conclusion. In sum, meta-analytic evidence suggests that there is a small negative relationship between antagonistic personality and task performance and this relationship is relatively consistent across the primary ways antagonism has been studied within the organizational sciences (i.e., FFM and DT). But, there is ample room for expanding investigation on the topic to develop a more nuanced understanding that may provide insight into the impact that slight variation in the subfacets of the four constructs may have on task performance.

Counterproductive Workplace Behaviors

Counterproductive workplace behaviors (CWBs) are the most relevant job performance criteria to consider when linking trait antagonism to organizational outcomes. CWBs, sometimes studied under the guise of workplace deviance or workplace aggression, refer to extra-role behaviors that are harmful to others in one's work environment (e.g., coworker, boss, support staff, etc.) or to the organization as a whole (Robinson & Bennett, 1995). These behaviors can be directly targeted and purposeful (e.g., theft) or may be unconsciously performed behaviors that still hold negative consequences for the target of the behavior (e.g., incivility). The interpersonal nature of these maladaptive behaviors is consistent with theory describing the way in which antagonistic personality may manifest behaviorally.

Trait antagonism. Berry, Ones, and Sackett's (2007) meta-analytic review distinguished between two facets of CWBs—those behaviors that are directed at other individuals in the workplace (CWB-I) and those directed more generally at the organization (CWB-O). They found that antagonism had a larger sample weighted mean correlation with CWB-Is ($r = .36$, 90% CV [.33, .58]) compared to CWB-Os ($r = .25$, 90% CV [.21, .42]). The estimated correlation between antagonism and an overall measure of CWB was larger, especially after correcting for sampling error and measurement error ($\rho = .44$). Additional tests of moderation indicated that the relationship between antagonism and CWB-overall was weaker when CWBs were measured by self-report methodologies (corrected correlation of $\rho = .44$; correcting for sampling and measurement error) versus studies not using self-report measurements of CWBs (corrected correlation of $\rho = .57$; correcting for sampling and measurement error).

These findings offer strong evidence suggesting that antagonism is likely to be manifested at work and take the form of CWBs. It is particularly interesting to note the stronger association to CWBs targeted at *individuals* rather than at the organization as a whole. One avenue for understanding this phenomenon may be found by investigating the differences through a construal-level theoretical lens (Liberman, Trope, & Stephan, 2007). For instance, targeting an individual may provide a more concrete and temporally proximal outlet for one's antagonistic behaviors. Additionally, the stronger link to CWBs that are not measured through self-report methods may indicate that some of these behaviors manifest out of conscious awareness of the perpetrator or that antagonistic perpetrators are more inclined to engage in impression management/faking when completing self-assessments of CWBs.

Antagonistic core of DT. The interpersonally maladaptive behaviors associated with the DT personality traits also provide a compelling theoretical rationale for how antagonistic traits may be related to CWBs. Consequently, researchers interested in the DT traits have amassed a substantial body of empirical efforts investigating the topic. O'Boyle et al. (2012) meta-analytic review linked each of the DT traits to CWBs. This meta-analysis specifically included studies using CWB-specific scales and various CWB behaviors to create an overall CWB variable (CWB-overall). The findings indicated that each of the DT traits had a significant positive association with CWB-overall. However, the magnitude of the relationship varied substantially across each of the three DT traits. Narcissism was found to have the strongest relationship (sample weighted mean $r=.35$, 95% CI [.18, .51]), followed by Machiavellianism (sample weighted mean $r=.20$, 95% CI [.12, .29]), and then by psychopathy (sample weighted mean $r=.06$, 95% CI [.01, .11]). Once again, the variation in the strength of association across the three traits may be attributable to the subtle differences between the constructs that fall outside of the core antagonistic construct space shared by the three. For example, the stronger relationship observed for narcissism may be a reflection of the propensity of highly narcissistic individuals to retaliate when their grandiose self-image is threatened; however, highly Machiavellian individuals may engage in CWBs, but with less frequency or intensity because they are less likely to experience such intense ego threat.

The weak relationship between psychopathy and CWBs was surprising, but a closer examination of the primary studies revealed three interesting findings. First, 20 of the 23 psychopathy-CWB effect sizes were obtained from samples comprised of police officers/cadets, corrections officers, and military personnel. Second, psychopathy in these samples tended to be measured using the Minnesota Multiphasic Personality Inventory—Psychopathic Deviate scale. This scale is designed to identify clinical, not subclinical, levels of psychopathy; contains diverse content related to frank antisocial behavior, familial discord, authority problems, and alienation; and is rarely, if ever, used as a stand-alone measure of psychopathy in the mainstream psychopathy literature. Finally, given the use of a clinical screening inventory that includes assessment of antisocial behavior in highly restricted samples of military and police personnel, it is not surprising to learn that psychopathy was the only trait that was judged to be range restricted. Thus, looking ahead, future research should explore how antagonistic tendencies imbedded within the DT may be related to CWBs in nonpolice/military samples using nonclinical tests of psychopathy. Additionally, future research should examine how antagonistic tendencies within the DT may be differentially related to CWBs directed toward individuals and CWBs directed toward the organization.

Organizational Citizenship Behaviors

Unlike the intuitive appeal linking maladaptive traits (i.e., antagonism & DT traits) to maladaptive workplace outcomes (i.e., CWBs), linking such traits to prosocial outcomes is a more counterintuitive endeavor. OCBs are defined as extra-role behaviors that can be directed toward individuals or toward the organization and are beneficial to the target of the behavior. Most organizational researchers interested in linking personality to OCBs have studied the relationship using the FFM. Consequently, much of the available OCB-related research is based on pure measures of antagonism/agreeableness.

Trait antagonism. Chiaburu, Oh, Berry, Li, and Gardner's (2011) meta-analytic review included effect sizes linking antagonism with OCBs directed toward individuals (OCB-I), OCBS directed toward the organization (OCB-O), and an overall composite measure of OCB (OCB-overall). Results indicated there were, on average, small negative relationships between antagonism and OCBs with sample weighted mean correlations of $r = -.11$, $r = -.13$, and $r = -.12$ (for OCB-overall, OCB-I, and OCB-O, respectively). Confidence intervals were provided for the correlation estimates after first correcting those estimates for measurement unreliability and indicated that the relationships for OCB-overall ($\rho = -.14$, 95% CI [−.18, −.11]), OCB-I ($\rho = -.18$, 95% CI [−.22, −.15]), and OCB-O ($\rho = -.17$, 95% CI [−.24, −.10]) were each significantly different than zero. In addition, the authors noted significant variability across effect sizes, suggesting the presence of potential moderator variables. They tested for two methodological moderators (e.g., publication bias; form of OCBs), but neither was significant. Overall, it appears that antagonism may be related to OCBs, but the precise mechanisms that give rise to, or attenuate the relationships between antagonism and OCBs remain unclear.

Antagonistic core of DT. Although there have not been any large-scale meta-analytic summaries linking the DT to OCBs, there have been a number of interesting studies in the area over the last few years. For example, Liu (2008) tested the willingness of individuals high in Machiavellianism to share knowledge with coworkers. Consistent with theory characterizing Machiavellians as individuals who are willing to participate in social tactics that will ensure an advantage over others, the study found that those higher in Machiavellianism were less likely to share knowledge with others. Also investigating the link between Machiavellianism to OCBs, Becker and Dan O'Hair (2007) found that there is a stronger negative link between Machiavellianism and OCBs when the behavior is targeted toward the organization versus toward an individual. Future research may look to investigate why this difference in association across OCB target has been observed. Consistent with the research linking Machiavellianism to OCBs, Boddy, Ladyshewsky, and Galvin (2010) found a negative relationship between CEO psychopathy and corporate social responsibility. Although there have only been a limited number of primary investigations on the topic, there does appear to be an overall negative association between DT traits and OCBs. These findings, which are consistent with the underlying antagonistic core shared between the DT traits, provide researchers with a foundation to build upon in future investigations.

Conclusion. The research linking antagonism to OCBs reveals a relatively consistent negative relationship between them. The strength of this relationship has also been meta-analytically shown to be contingent upon the target of the OCBs (i.e., individual vs organization). Future work is needed to clarify what variables may mediate or moderate the antagonism-OCB relationship.

Job and workplace attitudes

Although linking personality to various job performance criteria has been a priority for most organizational scientists, there has also been a long-standing interest in linking personality to employee attitudes, especially the attitudes of job satisfaction and organizational commitment. Typically, these attitudinal variables have been studied as outcome variables and to a lesser degree as mediating or moderating variables.

Job satisfaction

Trait antagonism. Costa, McCrae, and Dye (1991) argued that agreeableness should be positively related to life satisfaction because individuals partially derive a sense of happiness through the positive interpersonal interactions throughout one's life. Similarly, Judge, Heller, and Mount (2002) suggested that positive interpersonal relationships within the workplace will promote satisfaction and happiness. Antagonistic individuals are likely to struggle with developing such positive relationships making them more likely to experience lower levels of job satisfaction. Consistent with these predictions, Judge et al. (2002) found a small, but statistically significant, negative relationship between antagonism and job satisfaction (sample weighted mean $r = -.13$, 90% CI [−.22, −.12]). A subsequent meta-analysis by Bruk-Lee, Khoury, Nixon, Goh, and Spector (2009) reached a similar conclusion—reporting a sample weighted mean $r = -.13$, 95% CI [−.15, −.10]) between antagonism and job satisfaction.

Antagonistic core of DT. Bruk-Lee et al. (2009) also investigated the potential links between job satisfaction with both Machiavellianism and narcissism. Psychopathy was not included in this particular meta-analysis. Machiavellianism was found to have a significant negative relationship with job satisfaction (sample weighted mean $r = -.19$, 95% CI [−.25, −.14]). In contrast, the relationship between narcissism and job satisfaction, while negative, was not judged to be statistically significant (sample weighted mean $r = -.07$, 95% CI [−.14, .00]).

Once again, the observed difference between the correlations may reflect the subtle differences between the constructs that extend beyond their antagonistic core. These findings suggest that the nature of the relationship between DT traits and job satisfaction is complex and future research should look to provided theoretical and empirical insight into the mediators and moderators that could be contributing to these differences.

Organizational commitment

Trait antagonism. Organizational commitment is defined as the connectedness, or bond, that an individual has toward the organization by whom they are employed. This connection with one's organization can take several forms including an emotional attachment (i.e., affective commitment), a feeling of obligation to stay (i.e., normative commitment), or a need to stay based on the potential costs of leaving (i.e., continuance commitment). Theoretically, one would anticipate a negative relationship between antagonism and commitment, especially affective commitment which is based on building positive affective bonds with the organization. Indeed, a recent meta-analysis by Choi, Oh, and Colbert (2015) provided evidence consistent with this basic hypothesis. They found that antagonism had a small-to-moderate negative relationship with measure of overall organizational commitment (sample weighted mean $r = -.20$ ($\rho = -.24$), 95% CI [−.30, −.18]). Additional analyses were performed after partitioning the overall commitment variable into affective, normative, and continuance forms of commitment. In line with expectations, antagonism had the strongest negative association to affective commitment (sample weighted mean $r = -.24$ ($\rho = -.31$), 95% CI [−.48, −.13]) and normative commitment (sample weighted mean $r = -.20$ ($\rho = -.26$), 95% CI [−.35, −.17]). However, antagonism was not significantly related to continuance commitment (sample weighted mean $r = -.05$ ($\rho = -.06$), 95% CI [−.02, .14]). These findings suggest that antagonism has the greatest impact on affective and normative commitment which can be theoretically explained by the trait's maladaptive interpersonal qualities restricting the growth of relationships that are critical to these more interdependent types of commitment. On the other hand, continuance commitment is based on self-oriented cost/benefit analysis and was not significantly impacted by antagonistic tendencies.

Antagonistic core of DT. In our current review of the literature, only one study was found directly linking the DT to organizational commitment. In their investigation of the link between Machiavellianism and organizational commitment, Zettler, Friedrich, and Hilbig (2011) found a significant negative correlation between the two. Unfortunately, no other primary investigations on the topic were found. However, we encourage researchers interested in the topic to help fill this gap in the literature through the development of theory linking the DT traits to organizational commitment and/or adding empirical evidence on the subject.

Leadership

Two frequently evaluated leadership criteria are leader effectiveness and leader emergence. Leader effectiveness provides an evaluation of leader performance, whereas leader emergence refers to the extent to which an individual is identified by others as a leader. Trait theories of leadership have been a prominent framework for understanding leader effectiveness and leader emergence in the organizational sciences for over half a century. More recently, organizational researchers have shown increased interest in linking trait antagonism to leader effectiveness and emergence using both FFM conceptualizations of antagonism, as well as more indirect conceptualizations based on DT traits.

Trait antagonism. Theory would suggest that antagonistic individuals would be ineffective in leadership positions given their toxic interpersonal tendencies. Similarly, these antagonistic individuals are unlikely to be viewed favorably by others during initial interactions, thus making it less likely that antagonistic individuals will organically emerge as group leaders. A meta-analysis conducted by Judge, Bono, Ilies, and Gerhardt (2002) yielded results consistent with these expectations. Specifically, these authors found that antagonism had a significant negative relationship with leader effectiveness ($\rho = -.21$). But, no significant relationship was found between antagonism and leader emergence ($\rho = -.05$). The lack of relationship found between antagonism and leader emergence may be due to the way in which the trait manifests behaviorally in these initial interactions. The unwavering, aggressive, and noncompliant behaviors related to trait antagonism may be seen as inappropriate leader behaviors to some but may be viewed as exemplary leader behaviors by others. So, it may be necessary to investigate the interplay between individual differences characterizing the individuals evaluating the behaviors. Additionally, the context (e.g., military vs retail industry) and the temporal dynamics (e.g., short vs long interaction) may be useful for disentangling these unintuitive findings.

Judge et al. (2002) also evaluated the relationship between antagonism and an overall leadership criterion. This overall leadership criterion was created by pooling across the leadership effectiveness and emergence criteria. They found a small, but significant, negative relationship between antagonism and their pooled measure of leadership (sample weighted mean $r = -.06$ ($\rho = -.06$), 95% CI [−.13, −.02]). In addition, the authors noted that the relationship appeared to vary across settings, providing preliminary evidence for the moderating role that work context may have on this relationship. For instance, studies conducted in business and government/military settings concluded there was a positive (although nonsignificant) correlation between antagonism and overall leadership (sample weighted mean $r = .04$). On the other hand, using studies conducted with student samples found a significant negative relationship between antagonism and leadership (sample weighted mean $r = -.18$). These findings suggest that researchers should be careful when extrapolating findings from student samples to organizational contexts, at least when the outcome variables are related to leadership.

Antagonistic core of DT. Grijalva, Harms, Newman, Gaddis, and Fraley (2015) provided a meta-analytic review of the relationships that narcissism has with leader effectiveness and leader emergence. Unlike the relationship seen with trait antagonism, narcissism was shown to have a nonsignificant relationship with leader effectiveness. However, narcissism had a significant positive relationship with leader emergence (sample weighted mean $r = .12$ ($\rho = .16$), 95% CI [.08, .15]). The authors examined an interesting moderator of the antagonism-emergence relationship—acquaintance time. They found that narcissism had a stronger relationship to leader emergence in short-term interactions versus longer acquaintance times (sample weighted mean correlations of $r = .13$ ($\rho = .18$), 95% CI [.09, .18], and $r = .07$ ($\rho = .09$), 95% CI [.002, .14] respectively). These findings suggest that narcissistic individuals may have behavioral characteristics that facilitate their initial emergence as group leaders, but that this emergence is not always associated with higher levels of leader effectiveness (see also Paulhus, 1998).

Looking ahead: Models combining explicit and implicit antagonism

As noted at the start of our chapter, the vast majority of research within organizational psychology has focused on studying antagonism either directly as a component of the FFM or indirectly as a common aspect underlying all three of the DT traits. Both of these approaches are consistent with the dominant tradition for conceptualizing and assessing personality, which emphasizes the explicit components of personality. The focal constructs in models of explicit personality are traits, which are defined as patterns of thinking, feeling, and behaving that are introspectively accessible to individuals; therefore the traits can be measured via self-report survey (James & LeBreton, 2012; LeBreton & Schoen, 2017). In contrast, there is a much smaller (but growing) tradition in organizational psychology that focuses on defining and measuring the implicit aspects of personality. The focal constructs in models of implicit personality are often latent or unconscious motives, which, by definition, are not available/accessible via introspection. Instead, the implicit aspects of personality must be measured indirectly. There is now substantial evidence (across all areas of psychology) that many personality dispositions have both implicit and explicit components (see Chapter 1; James & LeBreton, 2012 for a review) and that optimal prediction of behavior is frequently a function of integrating or combining measures of both implicit and explicit personality (see Chapters 4 and 5; James & LeBreton, 2012 for reviews).

Measuring implicit antagonism via conditional reasoning. Within organizational psychology, the implicit aspects of antagonism have been conceptualized and measured under the rubric of the implicit motive to aggress (James & LeBreton, 2010, 2012). This motive is operationalized as a desire or intent to "overcome opposition forcefully, to fight, to revenge an injury, to attack another with intent to injure or kill, and to oppose forcefully or punish another" (James & LeBreton, 2012, p. 25). Within organizational psychology, implicit antagonism has most commonly been assessed using the conditional reasoning test for aggression (CRT-A). As James and LeBreton (2010) explained, "Conditional reasoning is the name given to [a] new system for assessing personality. This system is based on the principle that people with a strong desire to engage in a behavior will develop biased ways of reasoning that make the behavior seem rational and sensible as opposed to irrational and foolish. These biases are referred to as justification mechanisms to indicate that they serve to enhance the rational appeal of behaviors that express a desire" (p. 30).

LeBreton, Barksdale, Robin, and James (2007) explained that justification mechanisms enhance the logical appeal of antagonistic behavior by influencing social information processing and reasoning strategies. As an example, consider a person whose social interactions and reasoning processes are influenced by the justification mechanism of *hostile attribution bias*. As LeBreton et al. (2007) noted, "Such an individual might selectively attend to information that indicates others should not be trusted. Furthermore, he or she may engage in reasoning strategies that seek to confirm this initial impression and thus justify aggressive behavior against this untrustworthy person. In other words, the individual may overemphasize irrelevant information supporting his or her perception and discount salient information that might disconfirm this perception" (p. 2). Reasoning is said to be conditional, because the likelihood that an individual will infer that a particular course of action is acceptable/appropriate depends on the extent to which his or her thinking is shaped by justification mechanisms.

The CRT-A measures antagonism-related justification mechanisms (e.g., hostile attribution bias, retribution bias, derogation of target bias) by asking respondents to solve a new type of inductive reasoning problem. Each problem consists of three parts: (1) an item stem containing a set of premises, (2) an inference task for the respondent (e.g., what answer is most reasonable; what answer weakens or strengthens the arguments in the item stem), and (3) a set of solutions to the inference task. Fig. 1 contains an illustrative item designed to measure the hostile attribution bias. Whereas traditional reasoning problems consists of a single "correct" answer and multiple "incorrect" answers, conditional reasoning problems contain two inductively "correct" answers. In this example problem, response option "b" is designed to be more logically appealing to antagonistic individuals, especially those with a strong hostile attribution bias. In contrast, option "c" is designed to be more logically appealing to nonantagonistic individuals. For additional information about conditional reasoning problems, the interested reader is directed to James and LeBreton (2010, 2012) and LeBreton et al. (2007).

Implicit antagonism and work outcomes. There is a small, but growing literature linking implicit antagonism measured via the CRT-A to various work outcomes. For example, several meta-analytic reviews have linked scores on the CRT-A to counterproductive workplace behaviors and job performance. The reviews generally reached similar conclusions, but some differences emerged as a function of the subjective judgment calls that guided the inclusion and coding of studies. Nevertheless, scores on the CRT-A appear to be positively related to CWBs with sample weighted mean effect sizes ranging from $r = .16$ (Berry, Sackett, & Tobares, 2010) to $r = .27$ (James & LeBreton, 2012). The results linking implicit antagonism to task

---

A large number of business partnerships break up. One reason for the large number of breakups is that dissolving a partnership is quick and easy. If the partners can agree on how to split the assets of the partnership fairly, then they can break up simply by filling out the appropriate forms. They do not need to engage lawyers.

Which of the following is the most reasonable conclusion based on the above?

(a) The longer a partnership has existed, the less likely it is to break up.
(b) If one's partner hires a lawyer, then he/she is not planning to play fair.
(c) Partners might resolve their differences if breaking up was harder and took longer.
(d) The younger partner is more likely to initiate the break up.

Fig. 1 Illustrative conditional reasoning problem.

performance are more complex. Berry et al. (2010) reported a positive relationship between antagonism and task performance with a sample weighted mean effect size of $r = .14$ ($k = 4$; $n = 583$). In contrast, James and LeBreton reported a negative relationship with a sample weighted mean effect size of $r = -.18$ ($k = 6$; $n = 969$). The difference between these two effect sizes largely stems from differences in inclusion criteria and the fact that both effect sizes are based on a questionably small number of studies. Thus future work should continue to examine how implicit antagonism may (or may not) be related to task performance. Finally, James and LeBreton (2012) also reported a small negative relationship between implicit antagonism and organizational citizenship behaviors with a sample weighted mean effect size of $r = -.08$.

Several studies have sought to link implicit antagonism to other work outcomes. For example, Harris and Reiter-Palmon (2015) found that implicit antagonism predicted malevolent forms of creativity ($r = .35$, $p < .001$). Here, the authors defined malevolent creativity as a solution to a problem that "results in harmful or undesirable outcomes for one or more parties" (p. 58). For another example, this time at the team level, Baysinger, Scherer, and LeBreton (2014) examined how average levels of implicit antagonism were related to a variety of team-level variables including average levels of team member task participation ($r = -.17$, $p < .05$), team-level displays of negative socioemotional behaviors ($r = .19$, $p < .05$), group commitment ($r = -.20, p < .05$), and group cohesion ($r = -.24, p < .01$). Finally, in a recent study using a Croatian translation of the CRT-A, Galic, Ruzojcic, Jerneic, and Grabovac (in press) found that implicit antagonism was positively related to CWBs ($r = .31$, $p < .01$) and employee perceptions of organizational cynicism ($r = .22, p < .01$) while also being negatively related to attitudes such as job satisfaction ($r = -.16, p < .01$) and organizational justice ($r = -.25$, $p < .01$).

Integrating implicit and explicit antagonism. As noted earlier, there is growing awareness that many dispositional constructs have both implicit and explicit components and that these components are relatively uncorrelated. For example, James and LeBreton (2012) reported a set of 10 correlations between the CRT-A and various self-report measures of antagonism with values ranging from $-.18$ to $.26$ (sample weighted mean $r = .10$). In addition, researchers now recognize that it is often possible to improve our prediction of important outcomes (both work and nonwork outcomes) by integrating or combining information about the explicit personality with information about the implicit personality. Models that combine both aspects of personality are often described as channeling models (James & LeBreton, 2010; Winter, John, Stewart, Klohnen, & Duncan, 1998). These models are predicated on the assumption that aspects of implicit personality (e.g., implicit motives) are often channeled (i.e., expressed behaviorally) through aspects of explicit personality (e.g., explicit traits). Such channeling models presume that there will be a statistical interaction between measures of implicit and explicit personality in the prediction of different outcomes.

Building on Winter et al.'s (1998) classic test of channeling models, two studies have explored channeling models of antagonism. Using a sample of intramural basketball players, Frost, Ko, and James (2007) concluded that both implicit and explicit antagonism were useful predictors of both overt (e.g., physical) and covert (e.g., passive; obstructionism) forms of aggression. However, the interaction between implicit and explicit was significant and consistent with a priori hypotheses. Specifically, individuals with high levels of implicit antagonism and high levels of explicit antagonism were most likely to express antagonism in very overt, often physical, ways (e.g., intentional fouls, technical fouls, starting physical fights). In contrast, high implicit antagonism was channeled differently into behavior for individuals with low levels of explicit antagonism. Specifically, these individuals were more likely to behaviorally express antagonism in more covert, often passive, ways (e.g., not giving the ball up after scoring; blocking). Bing et al. (2007) also tested channeling models of implicit and explicit antagonism in a sample of hospital employees. Consistent with expectations, high levels of implicit antagonism were channeled into different types of behavior, conditional on the employees' level of explicit antagonism. For example, high implicit antagonism was more likely to be channeled into overt forms of CWBs (e.g., active forms of organizational deviance) for individuals who also had higher levels of explicit antagonism. In contrast, high implicit antagonism tended to be channeled into more covert and subtle behaviors (e.g., filing grievances) for individuals with lower levels of explicit antagonism. Similarly, implicit antagonism was differentially related to organizational citizenship behaviors, conditional on the levels of explicit antagonism.

Conclusion

Antagonism has been studied under different auspices for many years by organizational psychologists. In this chapter, we sought to provide a bird's eye view of the antagonism forest. We focused our attention on antagonism as studied directly through the FFM and more indirectly through the DT. We concluded with a brief introduction to how antagonism has also been conceptualized as having implicit components. We provided some preliminary evidence from two published studies indicating that prediction of important behavioral outcomes is enhanced by integrating information about implicit antagonism with information about explicit antagonism. Thus, to have the most complete account of how dispositional antagonism is related to important outcomes, we encourage psychologists to routinely consider how measures of implicit and explicit antagonism may provide unique, incremental and complementary information about individuals. Finally, given space limitations, we elected to restrict our review of antagonism and work outcomes to those criteria that have historically dominated organizational research—job performance, job attitudes, and leadership. We recognize that this decision undoubtedly omitted other relevant research linking antagonism to work outcomes such as mentoring, interpersonal negotiations, occupational health, and work-family conflict (just to name a few). We hope that our chapter serves as a useful review of existing research and serves to catalyze additional research linking antagonism to important work outcomes.

References

Becker, J. A., & Dan O'Hair, H. (2007). Machiavellians' motives in organizational citizenship behavior. *Journal of Applied Communication Research, 35*(3), 246–267.

Bateman, T. S., & Organ, D. W. (1983). Job satisfaction and the good soldier: the relationship between affect and employee "citizenship" *Academy of Management Journal, 26*(4), 587–595.

Baysinger, M. A., Scherer, K. T., & LeBreton, J. M. (2014). Exploring the disruptive effects of psychopathy and aggression on group processes and group effectiveness. *Journal of Applied Psychology, 99*(1), 48–65.

Berry, C. M., Ones, D. S., & Sackett, P. R. (2007). Interpersonal deviance, organizational deviance, and their common correlates: A review and meta-analysis. *Journal of applied psychology, 92*(2), 410.

Berry, C. M., Sackett, P. R., & Tobares, V. (2010). A meta-analysis of conditional reasoning tests of aggression. *Personnel Psychology, 63*, 361–384.

Bing, M. N., Stewart, S. M., Davison, H. K., Green, P. D., McIntyre, M. D., & James, L. R. (2007). An integrative typology of personality assessment for aggression: implications for predicting counterproductive workplace behavior. *Journal of Applied Psychology, 92*, 722–744.

Boddy, C. R., Ladyshewsky, R. K., & Galvin, P. (2010). The influence of corporate psychopaths on corporate social responsibility and organizational commitment to employees. *Journal of Business Ethics, 97*(1), 1–19.

Book, A., Visser, B. A., & Volk, A. A. (2015). Unpacking "evil": claiming the core of the Dark Triad. *Personality and Individual Differences, 73*, 29–38.

Borman, W. C., & Motowidlo, S. J. (1997). Task performance and contextual performance: the meaning for personnel selection research. *Human Performance, 10*(2), 99–109.

Bruk-Lee, V., Khoury, H. A., Nixon, A. E., Goh, A., & Spector, P. E. (2009). Replicating and extending past personality/job satisfaction meta-analyses. *Human Performance, 22*(2), 156–189.

Chiaburu, D. S., Oh, I. S., Berry, C. M., Li, N., & Gardner, R. G. (2011). The five-factor model of personality traits and organizational citizenship behaviors: A meta-analysis. *Journal of Applied Psychology, 96*(6), 1140.

Choi, D., Oh, I. S., & Colbert, A. E. (2015). Understanding organizational commitment: A meta-analytic examination of the roles of the five-factor model of personality and culture. *Journal of Applied Psychology, 100*(5), 1542.

Costa, P. T., Jr., McCrae, R. R., & Dye, D. A. (1991). Facet scales for agreeableness and conscientiousness: A revision of the NEO Personality Inventory. *Personality and individual Differences, 12*(9), 887–898.

Frost, B. C., Ko, C. E., & James, L. R. (2007). Implicit and explicit personality: a test of a channeling hypothesis for aggressive behavior. *Journal of Applied Psychology, 92*, 1299–1319.

Galic, Z., Ruzojcic, M., Jerneic, Z. & Grabovac, M.T. (in press). Disentangling the relationship between implicit aggressiveness and counterproductive work behaviors: the role of job attitudes. Human Performance. https://doi.org/10.1080/08959285.2018.1455686.

Grijalva, E., Harms, P. D., Newman, D. A., Gaddis, B. H., & Fraley, R. C. (2015). Narcissism and leadership: A meta-analytic review of linear and nonlinear relationships. *Personnel Psychology, 68*(1), 1–47.

Harris, D. J., & Reiter-Palmon, R. (2015). Fast and furious: the influence of implicit aggression, premeditation, and provoking situations on malevolent creativity. *Psychology of Aesthetics, Creativity, and the Arts*, *9*(1), 54–64.

Hurtz, G. M., & Donovan, J. J. (2000). Personality and job performance: the Big Five revisited. *Journal of Applied Psychology*, *85*(6), 869.

James, L. R., & LeBreton, J. M. (2010). Assessing aggression using conditional reasoning. *Current Directions in Psychological Science*, *19*(1), 30–35.

James, L. R., & LeBreton, J. M. (2012). *Assessing the implicit personality through conditional reasoning*. Washington, DC: American Psychological Association.

Judge, T. A., Bono, J. E., Ilies, R., & Gerhardt, M. W. (2002). Personality and leadership: a qualitative and quantitative review. *Journal of Applied Psychology*, *87*(4), 765.

Judge, T. A., Heller, D., & Mount, M. K. (2002). Five-factor model of personality and job satisfaction: A meta-analysis. *Journal of Applied Psychology*, *87*(3), 530.

Judge, T. A., Rodell, J. B., Klinger, R. L., Simon, L. S., & Crawford, E. R. (2013). Hierarchical representations of the five-factor model of personality in predicting job performance: integrating three organizing frameworks with two theoretical perspectives. *Journal of Applied Psychology*, *98*(6), 875.

LeBreton, J. M., Barksdale, C. D., Robin, J., & James, L. R. (2007). Measurement issues associated with conditional reasoning tests: indirect measurement and test faking. *Journal of Applied Psychology*, *92*(1), 1–16.

LeBreton, J. M., & Schoen, J. B. (2017). Conditional reasoning. In S. G. Rogelberg (Ed.), *The SAGE encyclopedia of industrial and organizational psychology* (pp. 208–210). (2nd ed.). Thousand Oaks, CA: SAGE Publications.

Liberman, N., Trope, Y., & Stephan, E. (2007). Psychological distance. A. W. Kruglanski & E. T. Higgins (Eds.), *Social psychology:* Vol. 2. *Handbook of basic principles* (pp. 353–383). New York, NY: Guilford Press.

Liu, C. C. (2008). The relationship between Machiavellianism and knowledge sharing willingness. *Journal of Business and Psychology*, *22*(3), 233–240.

O'Boyle, E. H., Forsyth, D. R., Banks, G. C., & McDaniel, M. A. (2012). A meta-analysis of the Dark Triad and work behavior: A social exchange perspective. *Journal of Applied Psychology*, *97*(3), 557.

O'Boyle, E. H., Forsyth, D. R., Banks, G. C., Story, P. A., & White, C. D. (2015). A meta-analytic test of redundancy and relative importance of the dark triad and five-factor model of personality. *Journal of Personality*, *83*(6), 644–664.

Paulhus, D. L. (1998). Interpersonal and intrapsychic adaptiveness of trait self-enhancement: a mixed blessing? *Journal of Personality and Social Psychology*, *74*(5), 1197–1208.

Paulhus, D. L., & Williams, K. M. (2002). The dark triad of personality: narcissism, Machiavellianism, and psychopathy. *Journal of Research in Personality*, *36*(6), 556–563.

Robinson, S. L., & Bennett, R. J. (1995). A typology of deviant workplace behaviors: a multidimensional scaling study. *Academy of Management Journal*, *38*(2), 555–572.

Winter, D. G., John, O. P., Stewart, A. J., Klohnen, E. C., & Duncan, L. E. (1998). Traits and motives: toward an integration of two traditions in personality research. *Psychological Review*, *105*, 230–250.

Wu, J., & LeBreton, J. M. (2011). Reconsidering the dispositional basis of counterproductive work behavior: the role of aberrant personality traits. *Personnel Psychology*, *64*, 593–626.

Zettler, I., Friedrich, N., & Hilbig, B. E. (2011). Dissecting work commitment: the role of Machiavellianism. *Career Development International*, *16*(1), 20–35.

Antagonism and crime

20

Matt DeLisi
Department of Sociology, Iowa State University, Ames, IA, United States

Introduction

For 5 years, the current author worked as a pretrial services officer at a large urban jail in the western United States. Pretrial service officers interview criminal defendants after they have been arrested and booked into jail. The interview involves gathering of information relating to the defendant's current criminal justice system status, self-reported and official criminal history, residency and social history, employment history, psychiatric history, and substance use history for the purposes of bond setting. This was a unique job in that it was a judicial position that involved interfacing with approximately 15 law enforcement agencies and was located in the booking area of the jail. Because many active correctional clients continue to get arrested, the job also facilitated interaction with probation and parole agents and occasionally practitioners within the federal criminal justice system. In other words, the job encompassed the three grand players of the criminal justice system: police, courts, and corrections.

During this work experience, the current author interviewed several thousand criminal defendants and interacted with thousands more. The criminal defendants spanned the vast expanse of criminality ranging from mostly normatively behaving individuals who were arrested for benign charges, usually traffic offenses, to offenders who had hundreds of arrests on their official record and who had engaged in the most grievous crimes, including murder, rape, kidnapping, child molestation, armed robbery, armed burglary, and many others. The variance in criminality and criminal history was vividly apparent.

There was also tremendous variance in the style and ease with which the criminal defendants would behave during the interview. Admittedly, the bond interview is a stressful experience. It is a formal legal proceeding in which the defendant is sworn in and thus placed under oath. It occurs closely after one has been arrested and brought to a jail—protean emotional experiences to be sure. Defendants usually have many questions about their charges, about how the arrest will impact their family, employment status, and citizenship, whether they will be able to be released, and many others. Despite these travails, most defendants were trusting, earnest and straightforward, compliant, and humble. It was common for defendants to cry and exhibit considerable distress during the interview. Yet, most defendants had the basic Agreeableness to get through it.

It was also in the best interests of the defendant to participate in and complete the interview. Naturally depending on the nature of their criminal charges, for those who had little to no criminal history, little to no history of missing court appearance, and

The Handbook of Antagonism. https://doi.org/10.1016/B978-0-12-814627-9.00020-7

basic adequacy in their social functioning (e.g., they had a residence and were not transient), it was common for them to be released on their own recognizance without having to pay any money. A defendant could not be released on their own recognizance without a fully completed bond interview.

Other defendants took a very different tack. These defendants were deeply suspicious of my role as a criminal justice practitioner and expressed that like the police officer who had arrested them, it was likely that I had hidden motives. If they participated in the interview, these offenders were evasive, minimizing, and manipulative in their exchange (and withholding) of information. These defendants were indifferent to other defendants and any victims in their crimes, and instead focused entirely on themselves. Their noncompliance ranged from unwillingness to answer certain questions to refusing to sign their bond interview to reluctance in providing basic information. Some of these defendants yelled profanities directly to my face, and a small number of defendants became physically uncooperative and had to be removed from my office by force.

Many factors can explain the stark behavioral and dispositional differences that unfolded in my prior work. The current chapter focuses on one of those, the personality feature of Agreeableness and particularly those who are very low scoring on Agreeableness and are thus Antagonistic.[1] Herein, the empirical associations between Agreeableness/Antagonism and various manifestations of antisocial behavior and crime are reviewed. Since my practitioner experiences are not unique, the chapter also examines the multitudinous ways that criminal offenders who are highly Antagonistic run afoul of the criminal justice system during the course of their interaction with law enforcement, with judicial personnel, and with correctional staff. In this way, Antagonism is an important and largely underresearched area for criminologists to consider when studying differential ways that offenders respond to criminal justice practitioners and adjust to criminal justice sanctions.

Agreeableness and Antagonism

Agreeableness is a foundational component of the human personality. In the influential Five-Factor Model (Costa & McCrae, 1992; Costa & Widiger, 1994; Digman, 1990; Goldberg, 1990), Agreeableness is comprised of six facets. Trust is the belief that others have good intentions. Straightforwardness relates to directness when performing tasks or dealing with others. Altruism reflects concern and care about others. Compliance is tendency to follow commands and respond to conflict without confrontation. Modesty is humility or concern about others before oneself. Tender-mindedness is feeling compassion for others and being dictated by soft emotion. Agreeableness like all personality dimensions exists on a distribution. Those who are high scoring can be considered agreeable or demonstrating Agreeableness. Those who are low scoring can be considered antagonistic or demonstrating Antagonism. Agreeableness and Antagonism thus exist in polarity to the other.

[1]For a general overview of Agreeableness, readers can consult Graziano and Eisenberg (1997).

In the *Diagnostic and Statistical Manual of Mental Disorders, fifth edition (DSM-5)*, Antagonism versus Agreeableness is one of five personality disorder trait domains included in the Alternative Model of Personality Disorder found in Section III (American Psychiatric Association, 2013). Specifically, Antagonism is described as behaviors that put an individual at odds with other people, including an exaggerated sense of self-importance and a concomitant expectation of special treatment, as well as a callous antipathy toward others, encompassing both an awareness of others' needs and feelings and a readiness to use others in the service of self-enhancement (Krueger & Markon, 2014, p. 487). Consistent with its colloquial meaning, Antagonism is effectively a simile for an antisocial disposition.[2]

Evidence that Antagonism is equivalent to an antisocial disposition can be seen in psychopathy research. Antagonism is a core feature of psychopathic personality. Across centuries of research, several theorists have described the psychopath's basic nature as one comprised of selfishness, disregard, meanness, coldness, detachment from emotional life, and limited emotional connections to others (for an overview, see DeLisi, 2016). In terms of raw personality functioning within the Five-Factor Model, Lynam and Widiger's (2007) translation of psychopathy into a structural personality model context included extremely high interpersonal Antagonism or extremely low Agreeableness as a core feature.

Using this approach, research has shown that psychopathic individuals with their requisite Antagonism are significantly more involved in diverse criminal and antisocial behaviors including aggression, delinquency, substance use, deviant sexual behaviors, and other externalizing features (Lynam & Miller, 2015; Miller, Lyman, Widiger, & Leukefeld, 2001; Miller & Lynam, 2003). Beyond structural personality models, Antagonism in many forms, including meanness, is a core feature of psychopathy theorizing (e.g., Brislin, Drislane, Smith, Edens, & Patrick, 2015; Lilienfeld, Watts, Francis Smith, Berg, & Latzman, 2015; Lynam et al., 2005; Miller & Lynam, 2015; Reidy, Zeichner, Miller, & Martinez, 2007; Seibert, Miller, Few, Zeichner, & Lynam, 2011; Sherman, Lynam, & Heyde, 2014). A metaanalysis of 26 independent samples containing 6913 participants reported significant personality associations for psychopathy using the Five-Factor Model (Decuyper, De Pauw, De Fruyt, De Bolle, & De Clercq, 2009). The metaanalysis confirms the strongly negative personality disposition of those who are low on Agreeableness and are instead significantly untrusting, devious, selfish, noncompliant, arrogant, and harsh.

Given its relevance to psychopathy theory, Antagonism is also a focal area for measurement. For instance, in the Elemental Psychopathy Assessment Super-Short Form (Collison, Miller, Gaughan, Widiger, & Lynam, 2016), Antagonism is one of three

[2]It is important to acknowledge the low self-control construct from the influential general theory in criminology (Gottfredson & Hirschi, 1990). Their self-control construct was characterized as having a bad temper, being impulsive, being self-centered and indifferent to others, having low gratification delay, and other aversive features. Although they explicitly eschewed personality psychology in their work, the individual with low self-control is clearly consistent with having low Agreeableness. The empirical support of self-control theory is formidable (De Ridder, Lensvelt-Mulders, Finkenauer, Stok, & Baumeister, 2012; Hay & Meldrum, 2015; Vazsonyi, Mikuška, & Kelley, 2017).

factors of psychopathic personality (along with Disinhibition and Emotional Stability) and it contains eight subscales. These include Arrogance (e.g., "I deserve special treatment"), Coldness (e.g., "I care a lot about my relationships with others" reverse scored), Callousness (e.g., "Feeling sorry for others is a sign of weakness"), Distrust (e.g., "When someone does something nice for me, I wonder what they want from me"), Disobliged (e.g., "People would say I am a reliable and dependable person" reverse scored), Impersistence (e.g., "I quit things pretty easily"), Manipulative (e.g., "I could make a living as a con artist"), and Self-Centered (e.g., "I have more important things to worry about than other people's feelings").

In short, deficits in Agreeableness are associated with a range of conduct problems and cognate behaviors. When Agreeableness is thoroughly lacking, the individual is antagonistic and the antagonistic profile is consistent with psychopathic personality.

Agreeableness, Antagonism, and antisocial behavior

Several metaanalyses revealed that Agreeableness is robustly and inversely associated with diverse forms of antisocial conduct (Heaven, 1996; Jones, Miller, & Lynam, 2011; Miller & Lynam, 2001). In their review of 53 studies, Jones et al. (2011) found that Agreeableness had the strongest associations with antisocial conduct among the components of the Five-Factor Model. Specifically, the weighted average effect size for the association between Agreeableness and antisocial behavior was −0.308 and the weighted average effect size for the association between Agreeableness and aggression was −0.327. Moreover, Jones and colleagues found that the relationship between Agreeableness and antisocial conduct permeated all facets of the personality dimension. Specifically, the mean effect sizes for antisocial behavior and aggression, respectively, by facet included Trust ($r = -0.174$ and $r = -0.181$), Straightforwardness ($r = -0.297$ and $r = -0.246$), Altruism ($r = -0.210$ and $r = -0.256$), Compliance ($r = -0.268$ and $r = -0.264$), Modesty ($r = -0.170$ and $r = -0.162$), and Tender-mindedness ($r = -0.113$ and $r = -0.171$). Empirically, there is no question that Agreeableness matters for the study of antisocial conduct.

Curiously, for most of its history, academic criminology went to great lengths to deny the association between personality functioning, criminality, and criminal behavior even when their own data rejected such a thesis (cf., Andrews & Wormith, 1989; Hindelang, 1972; Schuessler & Cressey, 1950; Tennenbaum, 1977; Waldo & Dinitz, 1967). This denial was even more curious in that systematic reviews of personality differences between offenders and nonoffenders routinely showed significant differences particularly for Agreeableness and Conscientiousness. In this way, criminology was overtly antagonistic to personality. It has been suggested (Wright & DeLisi, 2015) that since American criminology was a subdiscipline of sociology, researchers rejected the psychological focus on personality in favor of macro, sociological constructs, or social processes (e.g., labeling, peer effects) that were "preferred" ways to conceptualize the criminal offender.

The general associations between Antagonism and deviance are also seen among specific forms of criminal behavior. To illustrate, Mitsopoulou and Giovazolias

(2015) reviewed 27 studies and found that Agreeableness was the strongest personality correlate of bullying with an effect size of $r = -0.24$. However, Agreeableness was negatively but not significantly associated with criminal victimization. In their study using data from nearly 1700 high school students, van Geel, Goemans, Toprak, and Vedder (2017) found that Agreeableness was significantly inversely correlated with traditional bullying, cyberbullying, Machiavellianism, narcissism, psychopathy, and sadism. In multivariate models, Agreeableness was significantly predictive of both traditional bullying and cyberbullying even when controlling for other personality dimensions and powerful psychological constructs, such as psychopathy.

Lower Agreeableness has also been reported for a variety of other offender classifications including risky driving/traffic offenders (Brown et al., 2017), general delinquency and victimization (Wilcox, Sullivan, Jones, & Van Gelder, 2014), interpersonal violators (McNulty & Russell, 2016), animal abusers (Parfitt & Alleyne, 2018), homicide offenders (Khalili et al., 2017), sexual offenders (Challinor & Duff, 2017), and violent offenders (Kolla, Meyer, Bagby, & Brijmohan, 2017). Agreeableness is also inversely associated with subclinical behaviors, such as plagiarism (Wilks, Cruz, & Sousa, 2016), externalizing symptoms (Miller, Lynam, & Jones, 2008), being influenced by media (Meier, Robinson, & Wilkowski, 2006), confrontation (Kammrath, McCarthy, Cortes, & Friesen, 2015), and fear of crime (Ellis & Renouf, 2018).

In forensic samples that include the most pathological types of offenders, such as those who perpetrate sexual homicide and multiple homicide, the offender personality style is not only Antagonistic, but also often malevolent and sadistic (Chan & Heide, 2016; Geberth & Turco, 1997; Meloy, 2000; Myers & Monaco, 2000). These offenders are chillingly cold and callous, and their grandiose and self-centered needs are so pathological that they feel entitled to sexually assault and murder victims. Sexual homicide and multiple homicide offenders, such as those that perpetrate mass murders, often feel tremendous estrangement from others and from society at large and thus experience little altruism or warm. Often part and parcel of these personality features are feelings of persecution and the belief that the offender is morally above or better than others. Indeed, an antagonistic notion that other people do not matter facilitates their ability to indiscriminately kill.

Agreeableness, Antagonism, and criminal justice system involvement

Across the offending continuum, Agreeableness and Antagonism are associated with deviant acts, thus it is expected that these individuals will engage in conduct that places them at odds with the legal system. A diverse body of research has shown that arrestees, prisoners, probationers, parolees, and other criminal justice system clients generally have significantly lower Agreeableness than those in the general population (DeLisi et al., 2010; DeLisi & Berg, 2006; Eriksson, Masche-No, & Dåderman, 2017; Falk et al., 2017; Hepper, Hart, Meek, Cisek, & Sedikides, 2014; Hosie, Gilbert,

Simpson, & Daffern, 2014).[3] Consider the following assessment by DeLisi and Berg (2006, p. 159, italics added):

> Persons with low self-control are short-tempered and generally unlikable, and it is possible that practitioners across criminal justice agencies are generally responding to this *disagreeable, negative trait*. This might explain continuity in criminal justice experiences for various types of offenders. For example, offenders with exceedingly low self-control might consistently *antagonize* police, court officers, and correctional staff.

There are multiple explanations for greater Antagonism among offender populations than the general population including greater prevalence and exposure to adverse childhood experiences (Hengartner et al., 2015), heritability of difficult dispositions (Baardstu, Karevold, & von Soest, 2017), neuropsychological factors (Brown et al., 2016), different cognitive styles (Zeigler-Hill, Mandracchia, Dahlen, Shango, & Vrabel, 2017), and dysfunctional parenting (Jin, Cheng, Liu, Zhou, & Wang, 2016).

Agreeableness is an effective sorting mechanism for understanding why some individuals are more likely to be contacted by police. To illustrate, O'Riordan and O'Connell (2014) analyzed data from 7205 adult participants who were involved in the National Child Development Study which is a longitudinal study of all 17,634 people born in 1 week in March 1958 in England, Scotland, and Wales. In their data, just 14% of the sample had received a police warning, a police caution, had been arrested, or had been found guilty in criminal court between the ages of 33 and 42 years. Agreeableness was significantly inversely associated with criminal justice system contact and withstood confounding effects of other personality features, gender, school problems, birth weight, paternal social class, family size, occupational status at age 33, and academic achievement.

The salience of Agreeableness to the criminal justice system is not limited to law enforcement but also has correctional implications. For instance, Međedović (2017) surveyed 256 male offenders who were serving time in penitentiaries in Serbia to examine whether their personality functioning was associated with reports of antisocial conduct. Agreeableness was strongly and negatively correlated with self-reported antisocial behavior, official rating of antisocial behavior, misconduct as indicated by prison files, and a cumulative crime measure. In multivariate models, Agreeableness was similarly predictive of all four antisocial outcomes. A related study found that Agreeableness was the only personality feature that significantly predicted recidivism among former prisoners (Međedović, Kujačić, & Knežević, 2012). In their study of prison inmates, Collison et al. (2016) reported strong and significant correlations between Antagonism and total self-reported psychopathic traits, interpersonal manipulation, callous affect, erratic lifestyle, self-reported antisocial behavior, alcohol use, and official antisocial behaviors.

[3] Some of this research does not include personality measures and thus does not focus on Agreeableness per se. Instead, criminological studies focus on disputatiousness or a generalized sense of noncompliance that serious offenders frequently exhibit during their criminal careers (see Baron, Forde, & Kennedy, 2007; DeLisi, 2001; DeLisi, Hochstetler, Higgins, Beaver, & Graeve, 2008; Langton, 2006; Sherman, 1993).

Although Antagonism is a broadband risk factor for noncompliance with criminal justice system personnel, it also likely confers some protective capacity. As alluded to in the anecdotes at the beginning of this chapter, highly antagonistic offenders are significantly less likely to cooperate with law enforcement, judicial, and correctional staff in a variety of contexts. While this does not endear them to justice practitioners, it also minimizes their potential exposure for further sanctioning. For example, when an offender invokes their Miranda rights and refuses to talk with police, it substantively weakens the investigative process. Experimental research supports the paradoxical advantages of Antagonism. A study of university students and their compliance in an interrogation setting found that students who were more Agreeable were more likely to falsely confess to a criminal or academic offense/violation (Larmour, Bergstrøm, Gillen, & Forth, 2015).

As indicated earlier, criminology has sought to minimize the importance of personality traits for understanding variance in antisocial behavior. For example, in their general theory of crime, Gottfredson and Hirschi (1990, p. 109) suggested, "Contrary to the psychological view, the evidence for personality differences between offenders and nonoffenders beyond self-control is, at best, unimpressive." Clearly, this statement misses the mark when considering the numerous ways that Agreeableness distinguishes offenders from nonoffenders and also the ways that Agreeableness explains the collateral deficits in social behavior that offenders exhibit. For example, in the Pittsburgh Youth Study, a well-known criminological dataset, Agreeableness explained significant variance in total years of schooling completed, whether a youth was expelled or dropped out of high school, whether a youth was employed, whether a youth maintained a committed relationship, whether a youth was a teenage father, and whether a youth was arrested and the number of convictions (Kern et al., 2013). From this perspective, Agreeableness can be understood as a master status variable upon which to understand an individual's development, social achievement, and behavioral functioning.

There are many important research hypotheses that criminologists should explore using a personality framework with specific attention to Agreeableness. In the policing realm, there are numerous interactional points between criminal suspects and officers. These include whether to consent to a search of the suspect's vehicle, whether to participate in field sobriety tests, and whether to invoke Miranda rights and thus not participate in police interrogations. It is likely that more antagonistic individuals will also elect more deviant behavioral responses to officers including eluding, initiating police chases, using an alias, resisting arrest, resisting arrest with force, and using physical or attempted lethal force on an officer. In the event that a highly antagonistic person does converse with an officer, he or she would be more inclined to provide false information to sabotage the investigation. Criminologists commonly use mere demographic characteristics, such as sex, age, and race to examine differential criminal justice outcomes; however, the effects of demographics are miniscule compared to legal factors based on behaviors, such as criminal history, current criminal justice system status, and seriousness of charges (Beaver et al., 2013; Blumstein, 1982; Caudill, Morris, Sayed, Yun, & DeLisi, 2013; Klein, Petersilia, & Turner, 1990; Wilbanks, 1987). The current author contends that personality variables would be extremely valuable in articulating why some criminal defendants repeatedly have adverse and problematic interactions with law enforcement.

In the judicial sphere, there are also many hypotheses to explore. The bond interviews described at the beginning of this chapter are one example where more antagonistic offenders face negative consequences by refusing to cooperate with judicial personnel. But there are many others. Is Agreeableness inversely associated with refusing to cooperate with counsel, with rejecting plea offers from counsel, and with defying legal advice such as whether to take the stand in one's defense? A criminal defendant's demeanor and presentation of self also—rightfully or wrongfully—sends messages to all courtroom participations, including jurors, bailiffs, witnesses, counsel, the judge, and spectators. To illustrate, some criminal defendants are so enraged and bellicose in court that they have to be restrained or kept in an isolation cell for court proceedings. Such extreme, obdurate behavior is certainly consistent with a purely Antagonistic personality profile and is also consistent with the behavioral repertoire of psychopathic offenders.

In the correctional domain, there are similarly many interactional points between offenders and staff. At the pretrial phase during jail confinement, inmates must interact with diagnostic and classification staff, medical staff, and jailers. What are the associations between Agreeableness and malingering, between Agreeableness and reporting of accurate symptoms to medical staff, and between Agreeableness and the ability to get along with other inmates without discord and violence? At the post-adjudication phase during prison confinement, variations in Agreeableness are also likely associated with willingness to participate in educational and vocational programs, with mental health and substance abuse treatment, and with cognitive-behavioral programs. It is hypothesized that prisoners who are acutely Antagonistic are more likely to manufacture, possess, and use deadly weapons; to be involved in security threat groups; to refuse to obey basic prison rules and regulations; and to engage in an assortment of acts of misconduct including rioting, assaults on staff, assaults on inmates, sexual misconduct, drug misconduct, and others. Penological research has consistently shown that prior criminal history measures are among the most robust predictors of maladjustment to prison and diverse manifestations of misconduct. Using Agreeableness would allow for investigations within variations in criminal history to articulate which offenders are the most recalcitrant and difficult to manage.

There are also many research opportunities for investigating how offender personality functioning interacts with criminal justice practitioner personality functioning. Rather diverse findings have been produced about the association between Agreeableness/Antagonism among criminal justice practitioners and job performance and ability to interact with offenders (Miller, Mire, & Kim, 2009; Philliber, 1987; Sanders, 2008; Schuerger, Kochevar, & Reinwald, 1982). On one hand, practitioners who are high on Agreeableness are able to build rapport with offenders and handle disputes with them in a courteous, professional manner whereas those who are low on Agreeableness can engage in battle of wills with offenders and escalate situational dynamics. On the other hand, more Antagonistic and dominant officers are able to promulgate a sense of power and control over offenders that serves a deterrent function. Thus there are likely curvilinear effects of Agreeableness/Antagonism on interactional outcomes between practitioners and offenders. There are also potentially threshold effects whereby an offender can be so antisocial and Antagonistic that he or she will produce a negative interaction with correctional staff regardless of that officer's personality functioning.

Conclusion

Irrespective of the antipathy with which criminology has held toward personality, the evidence is clear that personality features have profound effects on an individual's subjective wellbeing, mental health, physical health, educational and socioeconomic achievement and functioning, relationship status, and conduct (Jensen-Campbell, Knack, & Gomez, 2010; Roberts, Kuncel, Shiner, Caspi, & Goldberg, 2007). Whether one is generally agreeable or generally disagreeable has nontrivial implications for their behavioral functioning and overall quality of life. Indeed, the successful bond interviews from my past could safely be sorted into the Agreeable bin while the grossly unsuccessful, confrontational, and occasionally violent ones could safely by sorted into the Antagonism bin. The criminological study of Agreeableness is woefully understudied, which is unfortunate given the salience of the personality feature to conduct problems and behaviors that are the exact purview of the criminal justice system.

References

American Psychiatric Association (2013). *Diagnostic and statistical manual of mental disorders (DSM-5®)*. Arlington, VA: American Psychiatric Publishing.

Andrews, D. A., & Wormith, J. S. (1989). Personality and crime: knowledge destruction and construction in criminology. *Justice Quarterly*, *6*(3), 289–309.

Baardstu, S., Karevold, E. B., & von Soest, T. (2017). Childhood antecedents of Agreeableness: a longitudinal study from preschool to late adolescence. *Journal of Research in Personality*, *67*, 202–214.

Baron, S. W., Forde, D. R., & Kennedy, L. W. (2007). Disputatiousness, aggressiveness, and victimization among street youths. *Youth Violence and Juvenile Justice*, *5*(4), 411–425.

Beaver, K. M., DeLisi, M., Wright, J. P., Boutwell, B. B., Barnes, J. C., & Vaughn, M. G. (2013). No evidence of racial discrimination in criminal justice processing: results from the National Longitudinal Study of Adolescent Health. *Personality and Individual Differences*, *55*(1), 29–34.

Blumstein, A. (1982). On the racial disproportionality of United States' prison populations. *Journal of Criminal Law & Criminology*, *73*, 1259–1281.

Brislin, S. J., Drislane, L. E., Smith, S. T., Edens, J. F., & Patrick, C. J. (2015). Development and validation of triarchic psychopathy scales from the Multidimensional Personality Questionnaire. *Psychological Assessment*, *27*(3), 838–851.

Brown, T. G., Ouimet, M. C., Eldeb, M., Tremblay, J., Vingilis, E., Nadeau, L., et al. (2016). Personality, executive control, and neurobiological characteristics associated with different forms of risky driving. *PLoS ONE*, *11*(2), e0150227.

Brown, T. G., Ouimet, M. C., Eldeb, M., Tremblay, J., Vingilis, E., Nadeau, L., et al. (2017). The effect of age on the personality and cognitive characteristics of three distinct risky driving offender groups. *Personality and Individual Differences*, *113*, 48–56.

Caudill, J. W., Morris, R. G., Sayed, S. E., Yun, M., & DeLisi, M. (2013). Pathways through the juvenile justice system: predictors of formal disposition. *Youth Violence and Juvenile Justice*, *11*(3), 183–195.

Challinor, L. E., & Duff, S. (2017). Sexual offending hierarchies, personality attributions, and the clinical implications. *Journal of Forensic Practice*, *19*(3), 190–197.

Chan, H. C. O., & Heide, K. M. (2016). Sexual homicide offenders distinguished from non-homicidal sexual offenders: a review of the literature. *Aggression and Violent Behavior*, *31*, 147–156.

Collison, K. L., Miller, J. D., Gaughan, E. T., Widiger, T. A., & Lynam, D. R. (2016). Development and validation of the super-short form of the Elemental Psychopathy Assessment. *Journal of Criminal Justice*, *47*, 143–150.

Costa, P. T., Jr., & McCrae, R. R. (1992). Four ways five factors are basic. *Personality and Individual Differences*, *13*(6), 653–665.

Costa, P. T., Jr., & Widiger, T. A. (1994). *Personality disorders and the five-factor model of personality*. Washington, DC: American Psychological Association.

De Ridder, D. T., Lensvelt-Mulders, G., Finkenauer, C., Stok, F. M., & Baumeister, R. F. (2012). Taking stock of self-control: a meta-analysis of how trait self-control relates to a wide range of behaviors. *Personality and Social Psychology Review*, *16*(1), 76–99.

Decuyper, M., De Pauw, S., De Fruyt, F., De Bolle, M., & De Clercq, B. J. (2009). A meta-analysis of psychopathy-, antisocial PD-and FFM associations. *European Journal of Personality*, *23*(7), 531–565.

DeLisi, M. (2001). Designed to fail: self-control and involvement in the criminal justice system. *American Journal of Criminal Justice*, *26*(1), 131–148.

DeLisi, M. (2016). *Psychopathy as general theory of crime*. New York, NY: Palgrave Macmillan.

DeLisi, M., Beaver, K. M., Vaughn, M. G., Trulson, C. R., Kosloski, A. E., Drury, A. J., et al. (2010). Personality, gender, and self-control theory revisited: results from a sample of institutionalized juvenile delinquents. *Applied Psychology in Criminal Justice*, *6*(1), 31–46.

DeLisi, M., & Berg, M. T. (2006). Exploring theoretical linkages between self-control theory and criminal justice system processing. *Journal of Criminal Justice*, *34*(2), 153–163.

DeLisi, M., Hochstetler, A., Higgins, G. E., Beaver, K. M., & Graeve, C. M. (2008). Toward a general theory of criminal justice: low self-control and offender noncompliance. *Criminal Justice Review*, *33*(2), 141–158.

Digman, J. M. (1990). Personality structure: emergence of the five-factor model. *Annual Review of Psychology*, *41*(1), 417–440.

Ellis, D. A., & Renouf, K. J. (2018). Predicting fear of crime: personality outperforms prior victimisation. *The Journal of Forensic Psychiatry & Psychology*, *29*(3), 403–418.

Eriksson, T. G., Masche-No, J. G., & Dåderman, A. M. (2017). Personality traits of prisoners as compared to general populations: signs of adjustment to the situation? *Personality and Individual Differences*, *107*, 237–245.

Falk, Ö., Sfendla, A., Brändström, S., Anckarsäter, H., Nilsson, T., & Kerekes, N. (2017). Personality and trait aggression profiles of male and female prison inmates. *Psychiatry Research*, *250*, 302–309.

Geberth, V. J., & Turco, R. N. (1997). Antisocial personality disorder, sexual sadism, malignant narcissism, and serial murder. *Journal of Forensic Science*, *42*(1), 49–60.

Goldberg, L. R. (1990). An alternative "description of personality": the big-five factor structure. *Journal of Personality and Social Psychology*, *59*(6), 1216–1229.
Gottfredson, M. R., & Hirschi, T. (1990). *A general theory of crime*. Stanford, CA: Stanford University Press.
Graziano, W. G., & Eisenberg, N. (1997). Agreeableness: a dimension of personality. In R. Hogan, J. A. Johnson, & S. R. Briggs (Eds.), *Handbook of personality psychology* (pp. 795–824). Boston, MA: Elsevier/Academic Press.
Hay, C., & Meldrum, R. (2015). *Self-control and crime over the life course*. Thousand Oaks, CA: Sage.
Heaven, P. C. (1996). Personality and self-reported delinquency: analysis of the "Big Five" personality dimensions. *Personality and Individual Differences*, *20*(1), 47–54.
Hengartner, M. P., Cohen, L. J., Rodgers, S., Müller, M., Rössler, W., & Ajdacic-Gross, V. (2015). Association between childhood maltreatment and normal adult personality traits: exploration of an understudied field. *Journal of Personality Disorders*, *29*(1), 1–14.
Hepper, E. G., Hart, C. M., Meek, R., Cisek, S., & Sedikides, C. (2014). Narcissism and empathy in young offenders and non-offenders. *European Journal of Personality*, *28*(2), 201–210.
Hindelang, M. J. (1972). The relationship of self-reported delinquency to scales of the CPI and MMPI. *The Journal of Criminal Law, Criminology, and Police Science*, *63*(1), 75–81.
Hosie, J., Gilbert, F., Simpson, K., & Daffern, M. (2014). An examination of the relationship between personality and aggression using the general aggression and five factor models. *Aggressive Behavior*, *40*(2), 189–196.
Jensen-Campbell, L. A., Knack, J. M., & Gomez, H. L. (2010). The psychology of nice people. *Social and Personality Psychology Compass*, *4*(11), 1042–1056.
Jin, F., Cheng, Z., Liu, X., Zhou, X., & Wang, G. (2016). The roles of family environment, parental rearing styles and personality traits in the development of delinquency in Chinese youth. *Med One*, *1*, 1–5.
Jones, S. E., Miller, J. D., & Lynam, D. R. (2011). Personality, antisocial behavior, and aggression: a meta-analytic review. *Journal of Criminal Justice*, *39*(4), 329–337.
Kammrath, L. K., McCarthy, M. H., Cortes, K., & Friesen, C. (2015). Picking one's battles: how assertiveness and unassertiveness abilities are associated with extraversion and agreeableness. *Social Psychological and Personality Science*, *6*(6), 622–629.
Kern, M. L., Duckworth, A. L., Urzúa, S. S., Loeber, R., Stouthamer-Loeber, M., & Lynam, D. R. (2013). Do as you're told! Facets of agreeableness and early adult outcomes for inner-city boys. *Journal of Research in Personality*, *47*(6), 795–799.
Khalili, M., Ranggar, B., Ahmadi, A., Ismaieli, I., Mousavi, F., & Saberi, S. M. (2017). Personality traits of mentally disordered males who committed homicide. *International Journal of Medical Toxicology and Forensic Medicine*, *7*(2), 89–97.
Klein, S., Petersilia, J., & Turner, S. (1990). Race and imprisonment decisions in California. *Science*, *247*(4944), 812–816.
Kolla, N. J., Meyer, J. H., Bagby, R. M., & Brijmohan, A. (2017). Trait anger, physical aggression, and violent offending in antisocial and borderline personality disorders. *Journal of Forensic Sciences*, *62*(1), 137–141.
Krueger, R. F., & Markon, K. E. (2014). The role of the DSM-5 personality trait model in moving toward a quantitative and empirically based approach to classifying personality and psychopathology. *Annual Review of Clinical Psychology*, *10*, 477–501.
Langton, L. (2006). Low self-control and parole failure: an assessment of risk from a theoretical perspective. *Journal of Criminal Justice*, *34*(5), 469–478.
Larmour, S. R., Bergstrøm, H., Gillen, C. T., & Forth, A. E. (2015). Behind the confession: relating false confession, interrogative compliance, personality traits, and psychopathy. *Journal of Police and Criminal Psychology*, *30*(2), 94–102.

Lilienfeld, S. O., Watts, A. L., Francis Smith, S., Berg, J. M., & Latzman, R. D. (2015). Psychopathy deconstructed and reconstructed: identifying and assembling the personality building blocks of Cleckley's chimera. *Journal of Personality*, *83*(6), 593–610.

Lynam, D. R., Caspi, A., Moffitt, T. E., Raine, A., Loeber, R., & Stouthamer-Loeber, M. (2005). Adolescent psychopathy and the Big Five: results from two samples. *Journal of Abnormal Child Psychology*, *33*(4), 431–443.

Lynam, D. R., & Miller, J. D. (2015). Psychopathy from a basic trait perspective: the utility of a five-factor model approach. *Journal of Personality*, *83*(6), 611–626.

Lynam, D. R., & Widiger, T. A. (2007). Using a general model of personality to identify the basic elements of psychopathy. *Journal of Personality Disorders*, *21*(1), 160–178.

McNulty, J. K., & Russell, V. M. (2016). Forgive and forget, or forgive and regret? Whether forgiveness leads to less or more offending depends on offender agreeableness. *Personality and Social Psychology Bulletin*, *42*(5), 616–631.

Međedović, J. (2017). The profile of a criminal offender depicted by HEXACO personality traits. *Personality and Individual Differences*, *107*, 159–163.

Međedović, J., Kujačić, D., & Knežević, G. (2012). Personality-related determinants of criminal recidivism. *Psihologija*, *45*(3), 277–294.

Meier, B. P., Robinson, M. D., & Wilkowski, B. M. (2006). Turning the other cheek: agreeableness and the regulation of aggression-related primes. *Psychological Science*, *17*(2), 136–142.

Meloy, J. R. (2000). The nature and dynamics of sexual homicide: an integrative review. *Aggression and Violent Behavior*, *5*(1), 1–22.

Miller, J. D., Lyman, D. R., Widiger, T. A., & Leukefeld, C. (2001). Personality disorders as extreme variants of common personality dimensions: can the Five Factor Model adequately represent psychopathy? *Journal of Personality*, *69*(2), 253–276.

Miller, J. D., & Lynam, D. (2001). Structural models of personality and their relation to antisocial behavior: a meta-analytic review. *Criminology*, *39*(4), 765–798.

Miller, J. D., & Lynam, D. R. (2003). Psychopathy and the five-factor model of personality: a replication and extension. *Journal of Personality Assessment*, *81*(2), 168–178.

Miller, J. D., & Lynam, D. R. (2015). Psychopathy and personality: advances and debates. *Journal of Personality*, *83*(6), 585–592.

Miller, J. D., Lynam, D. R., & Jones, S. (2008). Externalizing behavior through the lens of the five-factor model: a focus on agreeableness and conscientiousness. *Journal of Personality Assessment*, *90*(2), 158–164.

Miller, H. A., Mire, S., & Kim, B. (2009). Predictors of job satisfaction among police officers: does personality matter? *Journal of Criminal Justice*, *37*(5), 419–426.

Mitsopoulou, E., & Giovazolias, T. (2015). Personality traits, empathy and bullying behavior: a meta-analytic approach. *Aggression and Violent Behavior*, *21*, 61–72.

Myers, W. C., & Monaco, L. (2000). Anger experience, styles of anger expression, sadistic personality disorder, and psychopathy in juvenile sexual homicide offenders. *Journal of Forensic Science*, *45*(3), 698–701.

O'Riordan, C., & O'Connell, M. (2014). Predicting adult involvement in crime: personality measures are significant, socio-economic measures are not. *Personality and Individual Differences*, *68*, 98–101.

Parfitt, C. H., & Alleyne, E. (2018). Animal abuse proclivity: behavioral, personality and regulatory factors associated with varying levels of severity. *Psychology, Crime & Law*, *24*(5), 538–557.

Philliber, S. (1987). Thy brother's keeper: a review of the literature on correctional officers. *Justice Quarterly*, *4*(1), 9–37.

Reidy, D. E., Zeichner, A., Miller, J. D., & Martinez, M. A. (2007). Psychopathy and aggression: examining the role of psychopathy factors in predicting laboratory aggression under hostile and instrumental conditions. *Journal of Research in Personality, 41*(6), 1244–1251.

Roberts, B. W., Kuncel, N. R., Shiner, R., Caspi, A., & Goldberg, L. R. (2007). The power of personality: the comparative validity of personality traits, socioeconomic status, and cognitive ability for predicting important life outcomes. *Perspectives on Psychological Science, 2*(4), 313–345.

Sanders, B. A. (2008). Using personality traits to predict police officer performance. *Policing: An International Journal of Police Strategies & Management, 31*(1), 129–147.

Schuerger, J. M., Kochevar, K. F., & Reinwald, J. E. (1982). Male and female corrections officers: personality and rated performance. *Psychological Reports, 51*(1), 223–228.

Schuessler, K. F., & Cressey, D. R. (1950). Personality characteristics of criminals. *American Journal of Sociology, 55*(5), 476–484.

Seibert, L. A., Miller, J. D., Few, L. R., Zeichner, A., & Lynam, D. R. (2011). An examination of the structure of self-report psychopathy measures and their relations with general traits and externalizing behaviors. *Personality Disorders: Theory, Research, and Treatment, 2*(3), 193–208.

Sherman, L. W. (1993). Defiance, deterrence, and irrelevance: a theory of the criminal sanction. *Journal of Research in Crime and Delinquency, 30*(4), 445–473.

Sherman, E. D., Lynam, D. R., & Heyde, B. (2014). Agreeableness accounts for the factor structure of the Youth Psychopathic Traits Inventory. *Journal of Personality Disorders, 28*(2), 262–280.

Tennenbaum, D. J. (1977). Personality and criminality a summary and implications of the literature. *Journal of Criminal Justice, 5*(3), 225–235.

van Geel, M., Goemans, A., Toprak, F., & Vedder, P. (2017). Which personality traits are related to traditional bullying and cyberbullying? A study with the Big Five, Dark Triad and sadism. *Personality and Individual Differences, 106*, 231–235.

Vazsonyi, A. T., Mikuška, J., & Kelley, E. L. (2017). It's time: a meta-analysis on the self-control-deviance link. *Journal of Criminal Justice, 48*, 48–63.

Waldo, G. P., & Dinitz, S. (1967). Personality attributes of the criminal: an analysis of research studies, 1950-65. *Journal of Research in Crime and Delinquency, 4*(2), 185–202.

Wilbanks, W. (1987). *The myth of a racist criminal justice system.* Monterey, CA: Brooks/Cole.

Wilcox, P., Sullivan, C. J., Jones, S., & Van Gelder, J. L. (2014). Personality and opportunity: an integrated approach to offending and victimization. *Criminal Justice and Behavior, 41*(7), 880–901.

Wilks, D. C., Cruz, J. N., & Sousa, P. (2016). Personality traits and plagiarism: an empirical study with Portuguese undergraduate students. *Journal of Academic Ethics, 14*(3), 231–241.

Wright, J., & DeLisi, M. (2015). *Conservative criminology: A call to restore balance to the social sciences.* New York, NY: Routledge.

Zeigler-Hill, V., Mandracchia, J. T., Dahlen, E. R., Shango, R., & Vrabel, J. K. (2017). Pathological personality traits and criminogenic thinking styles. *Personality and Individual Differences, 110*, 41–48.

Stability and change in antagonism over the lifespan

21

Patrick L. Hill, Patrick J. Cruitt, Joshua J. Jackson, Thomas F. Oltmanns
Department of Psychological and Brain Sciences, Washington University St. Louis, St. Louis, MO, United States

Self-help and business manuals frequently reference the 16th-century Scottish theologian John Knox, who reportedly stated, "You cannot antagonize and influence at the same time" (e.g., Maxwell, 2011). Though these manuals are focused on helping individuals become better leaders, this quote also implicitly speaks to one reason why the world is not full of antagonistic people, namely, that antagonism runs counter to prevailing societal and social norms. With a few notable exceptions, when individuals focus on getting ahead and getting along in today's society, agreeableness rather than antagonism often proves more valuable.

Accordingly, it is worth considering whether and how antagonistic individuals may change their ways. A valuable first step on this front is to consider the evidence for stability and change in antagonism across the lifespan, to understand whether changes are possible, and if they may occur naturally without intervention. The current chapter explores these topics, focusing on three central research questions to guide future research. First, how do personality psychologists define stability and change, and what are the different metrics involved in the discussion? Second, what are the lifespan trajectories for antagonism and are there theoretical frameworks that can help us understand why these trajectories occur? Third, what are some of the missing pieces in the story of stability and change in antagonism? In this final section, we consider the need for additional work with adolescent samples, as well as for research on whether the story for stability and change differs based on the approach taken for measuring and conceptualizing antagonism.

While this last section will consider alternative perspectives, for most of this discussion, we focus on antagonism as framed within the Big Five taxonomy of traits (John, Naumann, & Soto, 2008), which characterizes antagonism as the opposite pole of agreeableness. Personality inventories from a Big Five approach measure agreeableness as a constellation of lower order facets that include a proclivity toward being trusting, straightforward, altruistic, cooperative or compliant, modest, and sympathetic or tender-minded (Costa & McCrae, 1992; Goldberg, 1999). Research has suggested that each of these facets negatively load onto an antagonism factor from a clinical perspective (Wright & Simms, 2014), though that work points to straightforwardness, altruism, and compliance as the strongest loadings. Put differently, though these three facets appear most closely aligned with clinical antagonism from the DSM-5, all facets of agreeableness from a Big Five perspective appear associated

The Handbook of Antagonism. https://doi.org/10.1016/B978-0-12-814627-9.00021-9

with antagonism in other frameworks. Accordingly, we focus below on change and stability in agreeableness as a broad domain, given that most of the literature has failed to consider trait change at the facet level.

Defining personality trait stability and change

In literatures such as genetics, the term "trait" has been employed to refer to variables perceived to be largely unmalleable and stable over time, such as one's height or eye color. Though this viewpoint was similarly espoused in the past personality psychology literature (e.g., Costa & McCrae, 1992), contemporary views have focused on how personality traits reflect relatively enduring tendencies to act in a given fashion when the situation presents (Roberts, 2009; Roberts & Jackson, 2008). Sociogenomic models of traits (e.g., Roberts, Hill, & Davis, 2017; Roberts & Jackson, 2008) emphasize that personality traits may influence how a given individual acts, feels, and thinks in a given setting or environment, but one should not expect personality traits to be associated with a perfectly consistent pattern of behaviors, feelings, and cognitions across situations. Accordingly, personality traits should not be viewed as absolutely stable over time or as a representation of absolute behavioral consistency.

That said, the terms "stability" and "change" can reflect very different concepts, depending on the researcher's interest. The first thing that may come to mind is whether individuals' levels on a given trait change over time, typically referred to as *mean-level change* or *stability*. Questions of mean-level change may focus on whether individuals change their personality trait levels from pre- to postintervention, or across a developmental transition. Typical analyses on this front include comparing means for the same sample on a trait over multiple assessments; for instance, with more than two assessments, researchers using latent growth models may consider the mean for the latent slope parameter.

Another common metric to consider is rank-order stability. Rank-order stability focuses on how individuals score *relative to* others in the given sample. Stability in this sense reflects whether an individual who has a higher score relative to the sample on a trait at time 1 also scores relatively higher at time 2, irrespective of whether that individual actually increased, decreased, or stayed the same on the trait. Alternatively, if the individuals who were more antagonistic at time 1 were those more agreeable at time 2, it would reflect large changes in rank order. Questions of rank-order stability are typically answered through correlational analyses, examining the extent to which time 1 scores are associated with time 2 scores.

Finally, increasing attention has been paid to the question of whether individuals differ in their patterns of change on a given trait. In other words, if a researcher finds that a sample on average declines on antagonism over time, is it true that all individuals experience similar levels of decline, or might some individuals decline more, stay relatively the same, or even increase on antagonism? Within a latent change or growth framework, researchers may examine whether there is significant variance in the slope parameter, typically described as interindividual variability in intraindividual trajectories of change. Establishing evidence for this variability typically serves as the first step before identifying potential predictors of change patterns; if there is no variability in patterns of change, then everyone exhibits similar trajectories for the trait. Though certainly related conceptually to rank-order stability, it is possible for researchers to find evidence for high rank-order stability and still see differential patterns of change in a sample, and vice versa. For instance, consider a case where the top and bottom scorers on antagonism at T1 remain the highest and lowest scorers at T2, but participants in "the middle" differ with respect to whether they increase, decrease, or show no change on the trait. In this case, one might evidence moderate to high rank-order stability paired with evidence for interindividual differences in intraindividual change. With these definitions of change in place, we consider two theoretical frameworks that provide a foundation on which to consider why changes in antagonism may occur.

Theoretical frameworks for understanding change in antagonism

With regard to how personality traits "normatively" change over time, a series of related models have focused on social role adoption (or failure to adopt) and dissolution as catalysts for personality change, falling within a category broadly described as "social investment" theories (Roberts, Wood, & Caspi, 2008; Roberts, Wood, & Smith, 2005). The central tenet guiding this set of theories is that individuals should be likely to develop or entrench those traits that promote the successful adoption and future engagement within the roles valued by society. Most individuals begin to adopt these roles, including marriage, employment, and community engagement, as they enter adulthood. Greater success in these adult roles typically comes to those individuals who are more conscientious, emotionally stable, and agreeable, three traits viewed as characteristics of a "mature" individual (Hogan & Roberts, 2004).

As noted in other chapters from this volume (e.g., Chapter 1), research has consistently demonstrated that antagonistic individuals face greater difficulties with securing, entering, and succeeding in adult roles. In line with expectations following an Invest-and-Accrue framework of trait change (Hill & Jackson, 2016), experiencing these "failures" should encourage individuals to desire greater agreeableness over antagonism. This framework suggests that individuals should be motivated to become more agreeable over time, as a result of observing accrued personal benefits of being agreeable, or from observing how agreeable others tend to experience such benefits. The Invest-and-Accrue model was developed initially for describing changes specific to conscientiousness, and although it largely can be applied to agreeableness in the same manner, the case of antagonism presents some interesting challenges. Counter to the case of conscientiousness, a trait broadly associated with positive benefits across adult roles (e.g., Hill & Jackson, 2016; Hill, Nickel, & Roberts, 2014; Roberts, Kuncel, Shiner, Caspi, & Goldberg, 2007), there is some evidence that lower agreeableness may be adaptive when it comes to occupation-related outcomes. Specifically, agreeableness can be a negative predictor of income and net worth over time (Hill, Turiano, Mroczek, & Burrow, 2016; Judge, Livingston, & Hurst, 2012), which has been suggested to result from the potential for more antagonistic individuals to benefit in some workplace situations, such as contract negotiations and efforts to obtain promotions. Accordingly, though social investment frameworks would predict consistent normative increases for conscientiousness during adulthood, there may be reason to believe the trends may be less clear for agreeableness.

Mean-level trajectories for antagonism during adulthood

To consider how antagonism changes over time, it is valuable to consider the literature compiled with respect to how the Big Five traits change across the lifespan; in so doing, we again consider antagonism as the opposite end of agreeableness. A meta-analytic review of the literature examined mean-level change in agreeableness, and the other Big Five traits, from adolescence to older adulthood (Roberts, Walton, & Viechtbauer, 2006). Counter to estimates for traits like conscientiousness and emotional stability, this review found that while estimates of mean-level change in agreeableness were positive in direction (i.e., less antagonism) across all age ranges investigated, the estimated increases only reached significance for individuals in their 50s and 60s. This finding has been supported by cross-sectional evidence from across the world, as older adults tend to score higher on agreeableness than their younger counterparts (Bleidorn et al., 2013). Another way of representing this change is to consider the estimate of cumulative change on the trait across an individual's life; in other words, what is the total amount of change on a trait one should expect by the time individuals reach their 20s, 30s, 40s, and so on? When considering this metric, the average individual only increases about one-third of a standard deviation on agreeableness between ages 10 and 50 (Roberts & Mroczek, 2008). In comparison, the normative cumulative change on emotional stability and conscientiousness, two other traits indicative of maturity, is over double that amount.

More recent evidence casts further doubt on the notion that people generally become more agreeable with age. Large longitudinal studies with German samples similarly find that adults reported comparable levels of agreeableness from late adolescence until middle-to-older adulthood, with an uptick in mean levels thereafter (Lucas & Donnellan, 2011; Specht, Egloff, & Schmukle, 2011). This work also charted how individuals changed on their personality traits over the next 2 years following the first assessment. First, this work provides clear evidence that interindividual variability does exist across the adult years for changes in antagonism. Second, these studies provide some of the most comprehensive investigations into the rank-order stability of the Big Five traits. Across the entire sample, moderate to strong rank-order stability was evidenced for agreeableness over the 2 years. Third, regarding the mean-level change on agreeableness over the 2 years, the average individual in the study increased on *antagonism* (decreased on agreeableness) over that span, and more marked increases were shown for older than younger adults (Specht et al., 2011). This latter finding may be, in part, an artifact of the fact that older adults had lower "starting points" on antagonism to start. More broadly, this work provides further support that one should not expect people to naturally become less antagonistic with time.

So why might one expect greater normative stability than change in antagonism, at least prior to middle-to-older adulthood? One reason comes from the point made earlier regarding the applicability of the Invest-and-Accrue model; namely, there are situations and contexts in which agreeableness may not be preferable. For an example, it is valuable to consider the work on how being dispositionally forgiving may not always be adaptive (Luchies, Finkel, McNulty, & Kumashiro, 2010; McNulty & Fincham, 2012), given that dispositional forgiveness is a strong correlate of agreeableness (Steiner, Allemand, & McCullough, 2012), and Big Five inventories sometimes ask about willingness to forgive when assessing agreeableness (John & Srivastava, 1999). That literature shows that if individuals always forgive another person who frequently transgresses against them, without any consideration, this could lead to the "doormat effect" (Luchies et al., 2010) wherein the forgiver begins to lose self-esteem and self-worth. Moreover, when abusive partners are consistently forgiven without amends, it may actually lead to continued incidence of abuse in the future (McNulty, 2010). These examples along with the work on income show that higher agreeableness may not always lead to benefits; in turn, based on the Invest-and-Accrue model (Hill & Jackson, 2016), it may be less immediately clear whether individuals should consistently "invest" in becoming less antagonistic and more agreeable, at least when considering antagonism within the "normal range" of personality traits. Indeed, several workplace environments may leave individuals wondering whether antagonism is actually appropriate, if their coworkers tend to be more competitive rather than cooperative.

Changing antagonism by focusing at the state level

The clear conclusion from this research then is that one cannot expect individuals to simply "age out" of their antagonistic tendencies. It may take more effort to convince individuals to become more agreeable relative to other societally preferred traits, such as conscientiousness, if the benefits are not as consistently apparent. Accordingly, alternative frameworks may be necessary for considering interventions to change trait antagonism. Toward this end, it is worth returning to the definition of trait in contemporary personality psychology. Specifically, personality traits are viewed as relatively enduring tendencies toward certain states of cognitions, affect, and behaviors (Roberts, 2009; Roberts & Jackson, 2008). For instance, individuals higher on trait antagonism may have a greater propensity to enact antisocial behaviors in a given situation (see Chapter 20), though it is not the case that antagonistic individuals will behave that way in all contexts or relationships.

Though attempting to change "traits" may seem a daunting challenge, focusing on the state level provides new opportunities for personality intervention. Researchers have espoused the value of following a "sociogenomic" approach to personality trait interventions (e.g., Roberts et al., 2017), which captures how personality dispositions have genetic, behavioral, cognitive, and emotional signatures. Rather than focusing on the genetic level, for obvious reasons, the primary focus of these interventions then typically is to enact change at the behavioral or cognitive level. For instance, efforts to change conscientiousness may attempt to encourage individuals to set goals and maintain a schedule that allows them to engage in those activities they value and find meaningful (Roberts et al., 2017). In this way, it is similar to cognitive-behavioral therapy approaches such as behavioral activation, insofar that the intervention strives to change that individual's typical cognitions and behaviors (Magidson, Roberts, Collado-Rodriguez, & Lejuez, 2014).

With respect to changing antagonism, it may be important first to begin by having participants monitor and report their social behavior across weeks, forcing participants to see the extent to which they often act in a disagreeable manner. Given that studies suggest that adults desire to become more agreeable across age groups (Hudson & Fraley, 2016), it is likely that this self-monitoring will provide a valuable first step toward getting the individual to want to change their antagonistic tendencies. The next steps will include teaching participants strategies for cooperation and trust exercises. Changing these state behaviors over time then would be expected to hold downstream effects in the form of changing the broader personality trait in the long-term. Though couching them within a sociogenomic trait intervention framework may be novel, these ideas certainly are not novel. Indeed, they have been discussed as central tenets for a wide range of interventions including clinical efforts to treat antagonism (see Chapters 24–27, this volume) and social cognition approaches to reduce antisocial behavior among youth (Dodge, Godwin, & Conduct Problems Prevention Research Group, 2013; Conduct Problems Prevention Research Group, 2011). With these frameworks for considering why changes in antagonism occur in mind, we proceed to next steps for research to further our understanding of stability and change in antagonism, starting with the need for work with younger samples.

Next steps: Antagonism in adolescence

A frequent focus for psychology-based interventions has been to reduce delinquent and antisocial behavior among adolescents (see Hill, Roberts, Grogger, Guryan, & Sixkiller, 2011 for a review). Common to these interventions is an intent to change the youth's dispositional behavioral and cognitive tendencies with the hope that intervention participants will act and interpret social situations in a more adaptive fashion in the long-term. For example, one well-known effort has focused on changing patterns of social information processing among adolescents, wherein youth are taught (a) how to identify when others are and are not hostile, (b) to reduce their tendencies to provoke or challenge others, and (c) to produce socially adaptive responses when in group settings (Dodge et al., 2013; Conduct Problems Prevention Research Group, 2011). Clearly, the goal of increasing these capabilities is in line with efforts to produce a less antagonistic individual, which is a desired outcome for helping individuals transition to adulthood.

Given the long-term benefits of reducing antagonism prior to adulthood, and the frequent intervention efforts in the literature, there is a clear need for understanding the development of antagonism during childhood and adolescence (see Chapter 3). This developmental period is absent from the discussion of stability and change in the studies described earlier, as much of the literature focuses on personality change during adulthood. One reason for the paucity of work was the previous lack of validated personality self-reports for use with child and adolescent samples, an issue that has been rectified (see Shiner, 2010 for a review). Another reason is that a handful of studies recently conducted on trajectories for antagonism/agreeableness among youth have led to an unclear picture.

For instance, one study investigated the Big Five personality traits among German youth followed students from fifth-grade through eighth-grade (Göllner et al., 2017). Unique to this study was the incorporation of both child- and parent-reports of the youth's personality during this span of time. First, for both child- and parent-reports, there were markedly high levels of rank-order stability across the waves; indeed, parent-reports suggested near perfect rank-order stability over time. Second, regarding mean-level change, results for the child self-reports suggested that agreeableness was largely stable until a slight decline at the final assessment (eighth-grade). However, parents reported consistent mean-level declines in their children's agreeableness over time, perhaps reflecting the tendency for youth to become more argumentative with parents as they enter adolescence. Third, the stories differed again with respect to interindividual differences in patterns of intraindividual change. Though significant variability occurred in the change patterns when looking at child-reports, no variability was found for the parent-reports. In summary, this study presents a multifaceted and complex picture for change in antagonism during early adolescence. From the child's perspective, the trait demonstrated little to no mean-level change over the years, but with significant individual differences in how children changed on the trait. From the parent's perspective, antagonism levels increased consistently during early adolescence, with little individual-level variability in those patterns of change. Accordingly, this study not only demonstrates the difficulty with coming to a consistent story regarding changes in antagonism during adolescence, but also points to the value of moving beyond a sole focus on self-reports in the study of antagonism (see Chapter 6 for further discussion).

Similarly, inconsistent findings have been found when considering other studies conducted during the adolescent years. Counter to the earlier German study, research with Dutch samples has suggested that agreeableness actually shows mean-level increases during adolescence (Klimstra, Hale III, Raaijmakers, Branje, & Meeus, 2009), though perhaps only for girls (Branje, van Lieshout, & Gerris, 2007). Another study with Swiss youth found no mean-level change across two assessments a year apart (Hill et al., 2013). Though these samples come from different contexts, all three countries hold similar expectations for the timeline for the adoption of societally prescribed adult roles (Bleidorn et al., 2013). Accordingly, it is less likely that the discrepancies in findings reflect sampling differences, and rather reflect how difficult it is to identify "normative" mean-level trends in antagonism during the adolescent years. That said, these studies have provided further evidence for interindividual variability in these change patterns with self-reported personality, suggesting the capacity for both identifying potential predictors of increases or decreases in antagonism, such as experiences or intervention.

Accordingly, one clear future research need is to add to the evidentiary base for understanding normative change in antagonism during adolescence, in hopes of understanding why these discrepant findings occur. Following these additional studies on describing stability and change, the next step is to understand the predictors of individual differences in change patterns. A recent review of the adolescent personality literature has suggested that, in addition to adult role adoption, two change catalysts worth considering are identity development processes and academic experiences (Hill & Edmonds, 2017). First, with respect to identity, youth who believe that others have inconsistent expectations for them (e.g., parents versus teachers, friends, etc.) tend to become more antagonistic with time (Hill et al., 2013). Though this association may hold over the lifespan, the processes of identity development occur in earnest during adolescence (e.g., Erikson, 1959, 1968), and thus may be more influential for personality trait change during this period. As such, interventions may wish to focus on providing youth with clear and consistent expectations for their behavior across different life domains and social relationships. Second, educational contexts provide important social contexts during adolescence, and work with university students shows that nonnormative social experiences may also influence change in agreeableness; for instance, one study found that university students who studied abroad were more likely to increase on agreeableness (Lüdtke, Roberts, Trautwein, & Nagy, 2011), presumably because that experience provided new opportunities for perspective-taking and to cooperate with diverse others. It may prove valuable then to introduce youth into novel social situations that require greater cooperation. Couching future investigations within the well-developed literatures on adolescent identity development and educational experiences during adolescence should prove fruitful for future research into why antagonism may change prior to the adult years.

Next steps: Stability and change across antagonism facets

As noted earlier, the conceptualization used thus far focuses primarily on "normal range" manifestations of antagonism, in reference to one of the poles of agreeableness within the Big Five taxonomy. However, with the advent of the *DSM-5*, Alternative Model for Personality Disorders, there is increasing attention to antagonism as a clinical dimension (see Chapters 12 and 13). Building from this framework, researchers emphasize a different set of lower order facets including attention seeking, grandiosity, callousness, deceitfulness, and manipulativeness (e.g., Wright et al., 2015). Several of these are conceptually similar (though in the negative direction) to the facets listed earlier for agreeableness; for instance, an altruistic, straightforward, and compliant individual should score low on trait grandiosity, manipulativeness, and deceitfulness. It thus may be unsurprising that, as noted earlier, these three agreeableness facets may hold the strongest loadings onto antagonism from a more "clinical" perspective (Wright & Simms, 2014).

A common thread across literatures is that questions of stability and change are rarely addressed at this facet level. Though this issue is a concern for research across several personality traits, a handful of studies have provided initial insights into (a) patterns of mean-level change at the facet level and (b) whether life events differentially impact change on the facets. Regarding the first point, a large cross-sectional study of over a million participants, aged 10–65, investigated cross-sectional age differences on the Big Five and their facets (Soto, John, Gosling, & Potter, 2011). In this study, the researchers were able to capture the facets of compliance and altruism across ages, and results suggested that the change patterns for these traits were roughly similar to one another. In line with the earlier meta-analysis (Roberts et al., 2006), both facets showed modest to no change from late teens into middle adulthood, with an uptick thereafter. Though not longitudinal in nature, these findings at least show some evidence that patterns of mean-level change may be fairly consistent across facets.

Additional work has investigated how facets change in response to divorce, a major life event one might anticipate would influence antagonism. However, studies on this front have tended to find no evidence of change in agreeableness or its facets (Allemand, Hill, & Lehmann, 2015; Costa, Herbst, McCrae, & Siegler, 2000). For instance, one study followed participants over 12 years in middle adulthood, and the findings suggest marked rank-order and mean-level stability in participants' non-antagonistic orientation and prosocial orientation (Allemand et al., 2015). Moreover, the experience of a divorce and, if so, the time duration since that divorce did not significantly predict change in these traits over the 12 years. Accordingly, the evidence thus far is limited regarding whether major life events play a role on changes in facet-level antagonism, though it is worth noting that evidence was found for interindividual variability in intraindividual change for both facets across the 12 years.

A central direction for future research then is to continue investigations into patterns of stability and change on the facets of antagonism across the lifespan. In addition, if this work continues to demonstrate evidence of interindividual variability in patterns of change, then research is needed to understand whether the predictors of change differ across the facets. Accruing research suggests that romantic life events like divorce or widowhood may hold limited effect on trait change for agreeableness (Bleidorn, Hopwood, & Lucas, 2018), though some recent work suggests that recently married individuals may actually increase in antagonism over time (Lavner, Weiss, Miller, & Karney, 2018). Accordingly, it may be important to focus on events that are conceptually tied to the structure of antagonism, such as military service (Jackson, Thoemmes, Jonkmann, Lüdtke, & Trautwein, 2012). For instance, one might expect life achievements (or at least, perceived achievements) to potentially encourage grandiosity, while experiencing obstacles to achievement may be more associated with attention seeking and manipulativeness. Though certainly speculative, if evidence was found for these predictions, it would provide evidence for a more nuanced picture of changes in antagonism over the lifespan, given that investing in certain antagonism facets may "pay off" more than others.

Conclusions and future directions

Antagonism presents an interesting case for researchers of personality development. Despite its obvious negative connotation, there is limited evidence that individuals will naturally decrease on antagonism during the transition to adulthood, and with the adoption of societally prescribed roles. Indeed, the strongest evidence for normative increases in agreeableness does not come until middle-to-later adulthood. Moreover, the adolescent years present a further challenge insofar that studies are markedly mixed regarding whether any mean-level trends can be identified for the trait during this developmental period. Accordingly, it proves difficult to explain patterns of stability and change in antagonism using frameworks commonly employed for other traits, such as conscientiousness and emotional stability, particularly given that increasing on agreeableness may not entail uniform benefits for the individual.

The next steps for research then include the need for further attention regarding changes during adolescence and at the facet level. As described earlier (Göllner et al., 2017), it may be the case that the story for change differs based on the reporter (self- versus observer-report). Discrepancies may be even more important to consider given the facets of antagonism lend to self-report biases, as people may be less willing to report their tendency to be manipulative or deceitful. In addition, it may be particularly valuable to gather observer-reports to understand whether observers may provide a different appraisal of whether the target participant is really trusting of others. Given the limited information available at the facet level even with self-reports, a clear direction for future work is to investigate not only whether facets differ in their patterns of change but also whether reporter type influences these findings.

Moreover, given the salience of antagonism within the new *DSM-5*, Alternative Model for Personality Disorders, research is needed to understand whether the patterns of change described previously, with respect to the Big Five taxonomy, hold when discussing the trait as a clinical manifestation. Put differently, do findings for trait stability and change differ depending on how antagonism is conceptualized and measured? As part of these investigations, researchers should investigate whether measures of antagonism across perspectives evidence measurement invariance, or if the inventories used to examine antagonism may mean something different across the lifespan. In other words, the presentation of antagonism may differ across the lifespan, which may obscure or complicate the interpretation of mean-level change. Addressing these questions are important for then considering whether the trait holds differential effects across the lifespan. For instance, higher levels of grandiosity may be more preferable at certain points of the lifespan, as evidenced in work showing differential associations between that trait and life satisfaction with age (Hill & Roberts, 2012). Similarly, it may be the case that changes in antagonism hold differential effects across the lifespan, or operate on health well-being through distinctive mechanisms, underscoring the importance of developing lifespan models to understand the potential positive and ill effects of the personality trait.

In sum, though there is a large literature on stability and change in antagonism, at least from certain theoretical perspectives, the gestalt from this work is largely that there are more questions remaining for personality development research in the years ahead. The story is complicated by the lack of evidence for a coherent story, wherein the maturation process or transition to adulthood cleanly leads individuals toward being less antagonistic, as one might expect for reductions in similar traits like disinhibition. In other words, though it may be difficult to antagonize and influence others at the same time, work is still needed to understand why changes in the adoption of leadership roles may hold modest associations with changes in antagonism, at least until middle adulthood.

References

Allemand, M., Hill, P. L., & Lehmann, R. (2015). Divorce and personality development across middle adulthood. *Personal Relationships*, *22*(1), 122–137.

Bleidorn, W., Hopwood, C. J., & Lucas, R. E. (2018). Life events and personality trait change. *Journal of Personality*, *86*(1), 83–96.

Bleidorn, W., Klimstra, T. A., Denissen, J. J., Rentfrow, P. J., Potter, J., & Gosling, S. D. (2013). Personality maturation around the world: a cross-cultural examination of social-investment theory. *Psychological Science*, *24*(12), 2530–2540.

Branje, S. J., Van Lieshout, C. F., & Gerris, J. R. (2007). Big Five personality development in adolescence and adulthood. *European Journal of Personality*, *21*(1), 45–62.

Conduct Problems Prevention Research Group (2011). The effects of the Fast Track preventive intervention on the development of conduct disorder across childhood. *Child Development*, *82*(1), 331–345.

Costa, P. T., Jr., Herbst, J. H., McCrae, R. R., & Siegler, I. C. (2000). Personality at midlife: stability, intrinsic maturation, and response to life events. *Assessment*, *7*(4), 365–378.

Costa, P. T., Jr., & McCrae, R. R. (1992). Four ways five factors are basic. *Personality and Individual Differences*, *13*(6), 653–665.

Dodge, K. A., Godwin, J., & Conduct Problems Prevention Research Group (2013). Social-information-processing patterns mediate the impact of preventive intervention on adolescent antisocial behavior. *Psychological Science*, *24*(4), 456–465.

Erikson, E. H. (1959). *Identity and the life cycle.* New York: International Universities Press.

Erikson, E. H. (1968). *Identity: Youth and crisis.* New York: Norton.

Goldberg, L. R. (1999). A broad-bandwidth, public domain, personality inventory measuring the lower-level facets of several five-factor models. I. Mervielde, I. J. Deary, F. De Fruyt, & F. Ostendorf (Eds.), Vol. 7, *Personality psychology in Europe* (pp. 7–28). Tilburg: Tilburg University Press.

Göllner, R., Roberts, B. W., Damian, R. I., Lüdtke, O., Jonkmann, K., & Trautwein, U. (2017). Whose "storm and stress" is it? Parent and child reports of personality development in the transition to early adolescence. *Journal of Personality*, *85*(3), 376–387.

Hill, P. L., Allemand, M., Grob, S. Z., Peng, A., Morgenthaler, C., & Käppler, C. (2013). Longitudinal relations between personality traits and aspects of identity formation during adolescence. *Journal of Adolescence*, *36*(2), 413–421.

Hill, P. L., & Edmonds, G. W. (2017). Personality development in adolescence. In J. Specht (Ed.), *Personality development across the lifespan* (pp. 25–38). London: Academic Press.

Hill, P. L., & Jackson, J. J. (2016). The invest-and-accrue model of conscientiousness. *Review of General Psychology*, *20*(2), 141–154.

Hill, P. L., Nickel, L. B., & Roberts, B. W. (2014). Are you in a healthy relationship? Linking conscientiousness to health via implementing and immunizing behaviors. *Journal of Personality*, *82*(6), 485–492.

Hill, P. L., & Roberts, B. W. (2012). Narcissism, well-being, and observer-rated personality across the lifespan. *Social Psychological and Personality Science*, *3*(2), 216–223.

Hill, P. L., Roberts, B. W., Grogger, J. T., Guryan, J., & Sixkiller, K. (2011). *Decreasing delinquency, criminal behavior, and recidivism by intervening on psychological factors other*

than cognitive ability: A review of the intervention literature (No. w16698). National Bureau of Economic Research.
Hill, P. L., Turiano, N. A., Mroczek, D. K., & Burrow, A. L. (2016). The value of a purposeful life: sense of purpose predicts greater income and net worth. *Journal of Research in Personality, 65*, 38–42.
Hogan, R., & Roberts, B. W. (2004). A socioanalytic model of maturity. *Journal of Career Assessment, 12*(2), 207–217.
Hudson, N. W., & Fraley, R. C. (2016). Do people's desires to change their personality traits vary with age? An examination of trait change goals across adulthood. *Social Psychological and Personality Science, 7*(8), 847–856.
Jackson, J. J., Thoemmes, F., Jonkmann, K., Lüdtke, O., & Trautwein, U. (2012). Military training and personality trait development: does the military make the man, or does the man make the military? *Psychological Science, 23*(3), 270–277.
John, O. P., Naumann, L. P., & Soto, C. J. (2008). Paradigm shift to the integrative big five trait taxonomy. In O. P. John, R. W. Robins, & L. A. Pervin (Eds.), *Handbook of personality: Theory and research* (pp. 114–158). (3rd ed.). New York: Guilford Press.
John, O. P., & Srivastava, S. (1999). The Big Five trait taxonomy: history, measurement, and theoretical perspectives. In L. A. Pervin & O. P. John (Eds.), *Handbook of personality: Theory and research* (pp. 102–138). (2nd ed.). New York: Guilford Press.
Judge, T. A., Livingston, B. A., & Hurst, C. (2012). Do nice guys—and gals—really finish last? The joint effects of sex and agreeableness on income. *Journal of Personality and Social Psychology, 102*(2), 390–407.
Klimstra, T. A., Hale, W. W., III, Raaijmakers, Q. A., Branje, S. J., & Meeus, W. H. (2009). Maturation of personality in adolescence. *Journal of Personality and Social Psychology, 96*(4), 898–912.
Lavner, J. A., Weiss, B., Miller, J. D., & Karney, B. R. (2018). Personality change among newlyweds: patterns, predictors, and associations with marital satisfaction over time. *Developmental Psychology, 54*, 1172–1185.
Lucas, R. E., & Donnellan, M. B. (2011). Personality development across the life span: longitudinal analyses with a national sample from Germany. *Journal of Personality and Social Psychology, 101*(4), 847–861.
Luchies, L. B., Finkel, E. J., McNulty, J. K., & Kumashiro, M. (2010). The doormat effect: when forgiving erodes self-respect and self-concept clarity. *Journal of Personality and Social Psychology, 98*(5), 734–749.
Lüdtke, O., Roberts, B. W., Trautwein, U., & Nagy, G. (2011). A random walk down university avenue: life paths, life events, and personality trait change at the transition to university life. *Journal of Personality and Social Psychology, 101*(3), 620–637.
Magidson, J. F., Roberts, B. W., Collado-Rodriguez, A., & Lejuez, C. W. (2014). Theory-driven intervention for changing personality: expectancy value theory, behavioral activation, and conscientiousness. *Developmental Psychology, 50*(5), 1442–1450.
Maxwell, J. C. (2011). *The 5 levels of leadership: Proven steps to maximize your potential.* New York: Center Street.
McNulty, J. K. (2010). Forgiveness increases the likelihood of subsequent partner transgressions in marriage. *Journal of Family Psychology, 24*(6), 787–790.
McNulty, J. K., & Fincham, F. D. (2012). Beyond positive psychology? Toward a contextual view of psychological processes and well-being. *American Psychologist, 67*(2), 101–110.
Roberts, B. W. (2009). Back to the future: personality and assessment and personality development. *Journal of Research in Personality, 43*(2), 137–145.

Roberts, B. W., Hill, P. L., & Davis, J. P. (2017). How to change conscientiousness: the sociogenomic trait intervention model. *Personality Disorders: Theory, Research, and Treatment*, *8*(3), 199–205.

Roberts, B. W., & Jackson, J. J. (2008). Sociogenomic personality psychology. *Journal of Personality*, *76*(6), 1523–1544.

Roberts, B. W., Kuncel, N. R., Shiner, R., Caspi, A., & Goldberg, L. R. (2007). The power of personality: the comparative validity of personality traits, socioeconomic status, and cognitive ability for predicting important life outcomes. *Perspectives on Psychological Science*, *2*(4), 313–345.

Roberts, B. W., & Mroczek, D. (2008). Personality trait change in adulthood. *Current Directions in Psychological Science*, *17*(1), 31–35.

Roberts, B. W., Walton, K. E., & Viechtbauer, W. (2006). Patterns of mean-level change in personality traits across the life course: a meta-analysis of longitudinal studies. *Psychological Bulletin*, *132*(1), 1–25.

Roberts, B. W., Wood, D., & Caspi, A. (2008). The development of personality traits in adulthood. In O. P. John, R. W. Robins, & L. A. Pervin (Eds.), *Handbook of personality: Theory and research* (pp. 375–398). (3rd ed.). New York: Guilford Press.

Roberts, B. W., Wood, D., & Smith, J. L. (2005). Evaluating five factor theory and social investment perspectives on personality trait development. *Journal of Research in Personality*, *39*(1), 166–184.

Shiner, R. L. (2010). Mapping the landscape of personality in childhood and adolescence. *Social and Personality Psychology Compass*, *4*(11), 1084–1097.

Soto, C. J., John, O. P., Gosling, S. D., & Potter, J. (2011). Age differences in personality traits from 10 to 65: Big Five domains and facets in a large cross-sectional sample. *Journal of Personality and Social Psychology*, *100*(2), 330–348.

Specht, J., Egloff, B., & Schmukle, S. C. (2011). Stability and change of personality across the life course: the impact of age and major life events on mean-level and rank-order stability of the Big Five. *Journal of Personality and Social Psychology*, *101*(4), 862–882.

Steiner, M., Allemand, M., & McCullough, M. E. (2012). Do agreeableness and neuroticism explain age differences in the tendency to forgive others? *Personality and Social Psychology Bulletin*, *38*(4), 441–453.

Wright, A. G., Calabrese, W. R., Rudick, M. M., Yam, W. H., Zelazny, K., Williams, T. F., et al. (2015). Stability of the DSM-5 Section III pathological personality traits and their longitudinal associations with psychosocial functioning in personality disordered individuals. *Journal of Abnormal Psychology*, *124*(1), 199–207.

Wright, A. G., & Simms, L. J. (2014). On the structure of personality disorder traits: conjoint analyses of the CAT-PD, PID-5, and NEO-PI-3 trait models. *Personality Disorders: Theory, Research, and Treatment*, *5*(1), 43–54.

Treatment of antagonism: Motivational Interviewing

22

Megan Wrona, Brian Burke
Department of Psychology, Fort Lewis College, Durango, CO, United States

Case study

Franklin ("Frank") Jackson is a 46-year-old male who was referred to therapy by the Human Resources Department at the company that employs him. He initially presented with an imposing presence, with a tall, muscular build, a well-pressed suit and a tie, and a large brief case, which he forcefully placed directly between himself and the therapist. Frank reportedly has a history of negative, confrontational interactions with his colleagues and supervisors in his work as a regional sales manager for a manufacturing company. Whereas Frank can present as charming and engaging with his clients, ensuring that his sales numbers are regularly among the highest in the company, he has had increasing conflict with the employees he supervises as well as other regional sales managers. Frank's confrontational style has typically been overlooked due to his high performance but a series of outbursts and threats over the past 6 months led to the current action plan. In his most recent outburst, Frank exploded during a staff meeting and shoved another manager before abruptly leaving the meeting, slamming the door behind him. As this was his third significant outburst, Frank's employer has required at least 6 sessions of "anger management" with a therapist.

When Frank initially came to therapy, he made his disinterest quite clear. He explained that he went to therapy as an adolescent after he was expelled from school. He also shared that he went to one couples therapy session at the request of his wife. He noted that both of these experiences were "worthless," "stupid," and "a complete waste of time." He explained that he expects a similar outcome this time. Frank noted that he planned to be compliant with attendance to meet his employer's requirement but denied having any problems that needed to be addressed so "this will be easy work for you." He explained that he was only joking in the meeting and that everyone made a big deal out of absolutely nothing. Frank jokingly described psychology as a "sham of a profession" and provided mostly factual background information during the first session.

Outside of work, Frank denied that any significant problematic issues exist. He has been married for 20 years and has two children, a 14-year-old son and 16-year-old daughter. However, in speaking with his wife with Frank's permission, she painted a very different picture. She shared a history of significant marital issues that began to

The Handbook of Antagonism. https://doi.org/10.1016/B978-0-12-814627-9.00022-0

worsen when their children were born. Shortly after the birth of their son, she requested that Frank accompany her to couples therapy because the arguing between them had become so constant and unbearable. She acknowledged this was not helpful as Frank only attended one session with her and refused to return because of the "inadequacies" of the therapist. Since then, their relationship has continued to struggle and she perceives that problems have escalated. She shared that Frank is typically disengaged from the family, unless one of their children gets in trouble. When that occurs, he responds quickly and harshly. She noted that after particularly heavy periods of drinking, Frank often becomes physical with her. She denied significant physical altercations but acknowledged that he does shove her and grab her tightly when he is drunk. She generally responds to this with her own anger and threatens to leave him and/or kick him out of the house. Typically, after her anger reaches that tipping point, a large, heated argument ensues. Frank usually stops drinking for a few days after the argument and they reconcile. His wife admitted this is a poor pattern but described she has learned to cope with it because she does not expect that Frank will change as he has frequently blamed her for his high level of drinking and the conflict in their marriage.

Motivational Interviewing with antagonistic clients

Motivational Interviewing (MI) is a client-centered yet directive counseling style designed to help people make behavioral changes (Miller & Rollnick, 1991, 2002, 2013). MI is a way of structuring conversations so that people enhance their internal motivation to make a specific change by themselves presenting arguments for why and how they will do so. Advances have been made toward "looking under the hood" of MI to understand the underlying mechanisms by which it affects behavior change (Miller & Rose, 2009). Notably, one theory of MI emphasizes two specific active components: a relational component focused on empathy and the interpersonal spirit of MI, and a technical component involving the differential evocation and reinforcement of client change talk, or arguments that a client makes about a particular behavioral change (Miller & Rose, 2009). Another model of MI (Miller & Rollnick, 2013) puts forth four overlapping processes as follows: (1) engaging, wherein client and therapist establish a helpful working relationship; (2) focusing, the development of a specific direction or target behavior in the conversation about change; (3) evoking, eliciting change talk or the client's own motivation for changing the behavior; and (4) planning, the phase in which client and therapist collaborate to form and commit to a concrete action plan to change the target behavior. Throughout this chapter, we employ these four processes of MI in the case of Frank above as we demonstrate how this model might approach the treatment of his antagonism.

Hundreds of controlled research studies of MI have illustrated its efficacy for a wide variety of problems ranging from substance use (alcohol, marijuana, tobacco use) to reducing risky behaviors (unsafe sex, needle sharing) and increasing healthy behaviors (e.g., medication adherence, diet, and exercise; Lundahl, Kunz, Brownell, Tollefson, & Burke, 2010). MI is significantly more effective than no treatment and at least as effective as other viable treatments, with a dose effect such that more sessions tend to produce more behavioral change (Burke, Arkowitz, & Menchola, 2003), yet MI typically operates as a brief treatment with higher cost effectiveness than the alternatives (Lundahl & Burke, 2009). MI works for clients regardless of problem severity, age, or gender, with outcomes appearing durable up to 1 year posttreatment (Lundahl et al., 2010). Finally, MI is learnable by practitioners of diverse professions (Lundahl et al., 2013), optimally via a 9–16 h interactive workshop (Madson, Loignon, & Lane, 2009) followed by three or four feedback/coaching sessions over a 6-month period (Schwalbe, Oh, & Zweben, 2014).

One of the largest psychotherapy outcome studies ever conducted, Project Match, involved MI. Clients were randomly assigned to one of three 12-week, manual-guided, individual treatments for problem drinking: Cognitive Behavioral Coping Skills Therapy (CBT), Motivational Enhancement Therapy (MET, a modified version of MI), or Twelve-Step Facilitation Therapy (TSF). Two parallel but independent randomized clinical trials were conducted: One with 952 outpatients and another with 774 aftercare clients. Participants were monitored over 15 months including a 1-year posttreatment period for days abstinent and drinks per drinking day. Only two (of many) a priori contrasts demonstrated significant posttreatment attribute by treatment interactions, including the finding that outpatient clients who were high in anger and treated in MET had lower posttreatment drinking than those in CBT (Project MATCH Research Group, 1997). Thus an MI-based treatment showed specific value for problem drinkers high in antagonism. In fact, MI's consistently demonstrated efficacy in the realm of substance use and related problems (Lundahl et al., 2010), which often involve clients high in anger or antagonism (Terracciano, Löckenhoff, Crum, Bienvenu, & Costa, 2008) like the case of Frank outlined at the beginning of this chapter, suggest that it may be a promising initial approach to treat these types of clients. In fact, MI and MI-inspired treatments have been shown to be effective for people who are mandated to treatment even when the individual did not initially want to work on the change in the first place (i.e., LaChance, Feldstein Ewing, Bryan, & Hutchinson, 2009; Nirenberg, Baird, Longabaugh, & Mello, 2012). MI-inspired treatments (such as MET described previously) have been shown to be effective even within treatment for perpetrators of intimate partner violence, a population that is likely to be antagonistic within therapy and other interpersonal interactions (Woodin, 2015). We will discuss how MI may be implemented with an antagonistic client such as Frank through each of its four key overlapping phases/processes.

Engaging: The relational foundation

Like any successful therapy intervention, MI begins with the establishment of rapport and engagement within the therapeutic relationship. The establishment of a good therapeutic relationship and other common factors in psychotherapy cannot be underestimated and may account for more change than specific types or models of therapy, with estimates ranging from 30% to 70% (Imel & Wampold, 2008). Building a strong therapeutic relationship and engaging a client in MI is founded on the notion of expressing true empathy and compassion to help build a collaborative relationship in which a client can consider the possibility of changing their behavior (Miller & Arkowitz, 2015). In this dynamic, the therapist aims to position the client as the "expert" who holds the solutions to their own problems. A number of specific strategies used within this phase of treatment can be particularly helpful for individuals who exhibit resistance to treatment and may not want to change a problem behavior—both traits that are likely to be displayed by someone who is high on antagonism. MI, with its open style to exploring ambivalence, is well suited to help someone who is high on antagonism to consider making changes and engage in their therapy. Additionally, MI can be used by a therapist to help motivate a client before jumping into another treatment intervention such as CBT (see later chapters in this volume).

To help build a strong, collaborative relationship, MI uses specific techniques to help foster the relationship. Whereas these techniques are used throughout the different phases of MI, they are especially important as the relationship is developing. The techniques, described with the acronym OARS, include open-ended questions, affirmations, reflection, and summarization. To begin with, *open-ended questions* are used to gather information and gain information about the client's own perspective. By keeping questions open, the client begins to share what is most important for them rather than the therapist asking directly for specific information. The MI therapist follows the direction the client wishes to pursue and shapes open questions around that direction.

Next, *affirming statements* are used to help identify strengths or progress, even very small bits of progress, that the client may not see themselves. Rather than giving vague positive praise (e.g., "Good job!"), affirmations in MI are clear, specific, and authentic (e.g., "Even though you haven't stopped smoking yet, your persistence to succeed by trying to stop smoking again is evident" or "I appreciate you making time to be here, even though you aren't sure that therapy will be helpful"). Affirmations aim to improve client self-efficacy and highlight positive growth.

Reflections are critical to utilize during the engagement phase. Using reflections helps to develop trust that the therapist can understand the client and allows a client to feel heard, free of judgment. Reflections can range from repeating a particularly poignant word or phrase used by the client to recognizing and reflecting the emotional experiences that underlie what the client is sharing. With the latter reflections, therapists help the client identify feelings, ideas, or thoughts of which they might not yet be aware. Good reflections help deepen the client's understanding of themselves and often move the session forward without using too many questions (Miller & Arkowitz, 2015).

Finally, *summarization* is a skill that helps consolidate larger chunks of information or insight. With a summary, the therapist aims to provide an overview of what has been shared, including insights and feelings. Summaries serve a number of purposes including demonstrating that the therapist is listening and engaged, highlighting the value of what the client is sharing, and providing the client with time to reflect internally on the bigger picture. Additionally, summaries can help the therapist check for understanding and let the client correct any inaccuracies, as in the case of Frank excerpt that follows.

Therapist: Thanks for making the decision to meet with me today. I got the paperwork your boss sent regarding us meeting, which has some background information but certainly not the full picture of what is going on. What is your view of why you are here? [**Open Ended Question**]

Frank: Let me start by being clear: I didn't "make the decision" to be here, my boss did. She seems to think I need therapy for my "anger problems," which I don't have. Everything has been blown way out of proportion.

Therapist: You really don't want to be here and feel misunderstood by your boss. **[Reflection]**

Frank: Absolutely. She totally misunderstood the situation and always sides with other employees over me. I am in the middle of a major sale and don't have time for this right now. Can you tell me what I need to do to get this over with?

Therapist: Well, it sounds like your boss wants you to attend at least six sessions here. Being here is not a priority for you, which I understand since you don't see your anger as a problem and this is crunch time for you at work. You have many things you are juggling right now. However, you also made the time to be here today and didn't ignore your boss's request completely. **[Summary]**

Frank: Yeah, sometimes it feels easier to just get things over with than fight them. I want to do whatever I can to check this box and move on to other more important things are work.

Therapist: You are committed to your job and focused on your priorities at work. Coming here to meet a requirement, even if you don't think it will be valuable, says a lot about what you are willing to do to be successful at your job. **[Affirmation]**

Frank: Yeah, it is important to me to do the best I can at work.

Therapist: Tell me about what that means, "to do the best I can?" **[Open Ended Question]**

Focusing: The strategic direction

At some point, in order for therapy to be productive, it is essential to help the client develop a focus, a specific problem behavior that they wish to change. With clients high in antagonism such as Frank, however, they may come to view their problems as caused primarily by other people (i.e., externalize blame) and/or the unfair treatment they perceive from those around them. Frank believes his wife is oversensitive and his supervisees are "soft." The pursuit of any change goal that the client does not currently espouse necessarily involves interventions designed to enable the client to adopt and accept the shared goal (Miller & Rollnick, 2013). This process may comprise the major part of the treatment in antagonism, that is, how to identify and work with the client on specific behavior changes that only they have the ability to make.

Yalom's (2017) 99% rule for responsibility assumption may be valuable in this regard. The notion is that, even if most (or 99%) of the negative events that happen to us are indeed someone else's fault, psychotherapy can only target a client's own behaviors. The goal therefore is to get the client to frame each of their frustrating issues with the outside world as behaviors that they may be able to change. For example, instead of believing that "people treat me badly," the opportunity for change in that respect could be something like "I will react differently when I feel I am being wronged." The following Frank's session transcript illustrates this approach.

Frank: My work is so frustrating—the people under me are lazy and unmotivated so all the pressure falls on me.

Therapist: I can understand how challenging it can be to work with others who may not share your work ethic. **[Reflective Listening]**

Frank: Yes, it certainly is. That's why I get so mad sometimes. It's their fault.

Therapist: Maybe it *is* their fault. But, unfortunately, in our work together, we can only work on changing your behavior, not theirs. What might you be able to do differently in those frustrating situations? [**99% rule—assuming responsibility by asking an Open Ended Question**]

Frank: I guess I could wait until the meeting is over before I get angry and yell at people.

Therapist: Excellent idea—that might be something for us to work on together. [**Affirmation and possible focus**]

Murphy (2008) provides another suitable strategy for focusing in MI. In his work with combat veterans (who also may be high on antagonistic traits), Murphy explains that they frequently have a general externalizing coping style that interferes with their ability to problem-solve and acknowledge their own role in the challenges that they face in life. Murphy's suggestion is to give clients a Problem Identification Worksheet (2008, p. 81) on which they write down their possible problems in four separate columns: *Problems I Definitely Have, Problems I Might Have, Problems Other People Told Me I Have, and Problems I Definitely Do Not Have*. This list can be done collaboratively in session or by the client for homework between sessions and then utilized as a starting point for a focusing discussion as in the example of Frank as follows.

Frank: I have that sheet you asked me to fill out for homework.

Therapist: Great—let's look at it together. Ah, I noticed your list of *Problems I Definitely Have* are mainly what you talked about earlier, that other people are hard to work and live with. [**Using** Murphy's, 2008 **strategy to find a behavioral focus; Summarization/Reflections**]

Frank: Yes.

Therapist: And for *Problems I Definitely Do Not Have*, you wrote that you are neither an alcoholic nor an asshole. That's good!

Frank: Right.

Therapist: So let's examine what you put for *Problems I Might Have* and for *Problems Other People Told Me I Have*. You believe that you have overly high expectations at times and that you are judgmental. And other people tell you that you argue and yell too much, that you are rude or dismissive at times, and that you drink too much alcohol. What do you make of that? [**Using the list as Feedback and ending with an Open Ended Question**]

Frank: Well, I don't think I drink too much but it does make me angrier than I want to be sometimes...

Therapist: Can you give me an example? [**Eliciting more change talk regarding drinking by asking for elaboration via an Open Ended Question**]

Another strategy that can be employed during the focusing phase of MI, especially if the client is unable or unwilling to generate a suitable problem list using Murphy's (2008) approach, is to give the client honest feedback about what you as the therapist have observed in their behavior. This is optimally accomplished via what MI terms Elicit-Provide-Elicit (EPE; Miller & Rollnick, 2013, p. 139), in which the therapist first asks for permission to discuss a topic further or what the client knows about a topic before then providing tailored information or feedback and closing by asking the client what they think. This is what the use of EPE might look like with Frank if he had not come up with anything useful via Murphy's (2008) list.

Frank: I did not do the list you gave me for homework—it seemed pretty stupid.

Therapist: That's okay, Frank. But would it be alright if I gave you some feedback about what I have noticed about you in the time we have spent together so far? **[Elicit #1: Asking Permission]**

Frank: Sure, I guess so.

Therapist: You seem really strong and smart and I think we could do some really good work together. But you put me and our work down sometimes, like just before when you called the homework "stupid." It gets in our way of what could be a valuable collaboration. What do you think about what I said? **[Providing Feedback and then eliciting client's understanding]**

Frank: You're not the first person to tell me that.

Therapist: Can you give me an example of where you heard the feedback before? **[Eliciting more focusing talk by asking for elaboration]**

Evoking: Preparing for change

One of the keys to successful MI is recognizing how motivated a client is for change and, subsequently, tailoring interventions based on that level of motivation. Prochaska and DiClemente's (1982) Transtheoretical Model of Change provides a guide for therapists to identify the level of motivation for change. The Transtheoretical Model includes six different phases of change: precontemplation, contemplation, preparation, action, maintenance, and relapse. In precontemplation, a client does not recognize that a problem exists and does not see any reasons to make changes. In contemplation, a client sees that a problem exists but remains ambivalent about whether they wish to change the problem behavior. Both precontemplation and contemplation are stages where the impact of MI can be particularly high. During the preparation phase, the client and therapist collaborate on planning to make the change and then implement the change during the action phase. Finally, because changing entrenched behaviors is very difficult, relapse is a stage many encounter as they fall back on previous patterns of behavior. Relapse does not mean failure and the goal of the MI therapist is to help a client return to the planned behavior change as quickly and easily as possible.

MI can be optimally beneficial for clients in the precontemplation and contemplation stages of change. During these stages, the therapist still relies on OARS but open-ended questions are designed to elicit and evoke change talk more specifically. The goal is to help the client begin to explore their own motivation for change and how change might help them. To succeed in this, the therapist must be willing to entertain all options and goals, even if the therapist does not view the goals as positive in the long run. Often, antagonistic individuals may not initially see any reason to change and are likely to see many positives related to not changing a behavior. For example, if a client is trying to stop using substances, it is important for the therapist to validate that there are positives associated with using substances such as stress reduction or personal enjoyment. Using a decisional balance, in which a client explores the pros and cons of changing a behavior as well as the pros and cons of NOT changing that behavior, is one way to help clients identify possible reasons for change without ignoring the other side. Similarly, one might explore the pros and cons of changing antagonistic traits such as grandiosity (e.g., pros: people may like the client more; cons: people won't know about accomplishments if one doesn't inform others of them).

Additionally, scaling questions help clients talk about a possible change while also helping to increase their own self-efficacy, motivation, and confidence. In these questions, the therapist asks the client to rate a concept (i.e., importance or confidence) on a scale of 0–10, where 0 is the lowest level (i.e., the change is not important at all) and 10 is the highest level (i.e., the change is as important as can be). Once the client provides a rating, the therapist then chooses a number below that rating and asks why the rating was not lower. For example, "why did you rate your importance of reducing your drinking as a 4 rather than a 2?" Whereas this might seem counterintuitive at first, this type of question invites the client to begin to argue for change, rather than the therapist (or other family members) suggesting why the change might be useful. When the therapist or others in the client's life are telling the client why they must change, the natural tendency of the client (and most people!) is to defend what they are already doing and minimize the severity of the problem. Scaling questions help reverse this dynamic and highlight the client's view on why the change might be helpful.

Beyond scaling, MI therapists listen carefully for any indication of possible change talk and use specific questions or reflections to elicit more change talk. By highlighting the changes clients are already talking about, clients begin to notice more reasons within themselves to change. MI therapists want to support and affirm any movement toward the targeted behavior, even if the action is small. The therapist then strives to strengthen client motivation and move toward planning and action to make changes. In working with individuals who exhibit counterproductive levels of antagonism, identifying their role in making change is especially important as they tend to place blame on those around them rather than themselves and may be more likely to be ambivalent to changing. Here is how evoking and amplifying change talk went with Frank.

Therapist: From what we have discussed so far, Frank, you have identified that those around you tend to think you argue and yell a lot and you shared that sometimes when you drink that anger intensifies. Would it be okay if we talked a little more about the connection you made between alcohol and anger? [**Asking Permission**]

Frank: I guess so, but I'm not sure it is that related.

Therapist: It may not be, but you noted that your anger worsens when you drink.

Frank: I guess that's true—especially with my wife. She tells me that all the time. I have tried to drink less around her because she's always nagging me about it. **[Client identifying history of trying to change]**

Therapist: Sounds like she would like you to cut back. And that you have tried to minimize drinking around her, which demonstrates your commitment to her and is great way of trying to meet her halfway [**Affirmation**]. What made you decide to do that? **[Open Ended Question, Evoking change talk]**

Frank: Well, I can see some of her reasons behind it and I don't want her to leave me.

Therapist: So, even though you don't think it is a major problem, you have tried to reduce your drinking to help her and your relationship. On a scale of 0 to 10, how important is it to you personally to reduce your drinking? **[Scaling question]**

Frank: Maybe, somewhere around 3. It's not that big of a deal to me.

Therapist: It definitely doesn't seem like a high priority right now, compared to other things you are working on. But, I am curious. If it isn't a priority at all, why did you chose 3 instead of a 1 or a 0? **[Scaling follow-up question].**

Frank: Well, I think, I guess there is some benefit.

Therapist: Like what? **[Evoking change talk about possible benefits]**

Frank: I wouldn't have to listen to the nagging as much... And, maybe it would help reduce some fighting and lessen the chance of her wanting to separate.

Therapist: What would it be like to have less fighting and nagging? **[Evoking change talk]**

Evoking change talk can take many directions in MI as the therapist follows the client. Whereas the earlier transcript shows some possible questions to use, there are many other specific questions that could help Frank build motivation for change, including the following:

"Regarding the importance of reducing drinking, what would it take to move from a 3 to a 5?"

"What might you give up if you reduced your drinking? What might you gain?"

"When you reduced your drinking around your wife before, what benefits did you notice for yourself?"

"What made you successful the last time you worked on reducing your drinking?"

"How do drinking and arguing with your wife fit with your overall goal of success in your life?"

Planning: The bridge to change

In some cases, MI ends after evoking change talk and the plan is quite simply for the client to engage in other models of psychotherapeutic treatment, as the next three chapters in this book will discuss. In other words, MI may have a chief role to play as a prelude to other treatments. In fact, previous research found that MI's efficacy was higher when it was employed as a first step to subsequent non-MI treatment (Burke et al., 2003). MI was initially designed to prepare clients for change in a small number of sessions, with further sessions using other models to follow if needed to help clients to initiate and maintain the change.

Nevertheless, it may be fruitful to enter the planning stage with a client using MI if they are ready to do so, especially since work on volitional personality change suggests that specific plans for change are necessary for subsequent change (Hudson & Fraley, 2015). In order to know when it is time to begin crafting a change plan with your client, it is essential to look to them for cues. For instance, signs such as increased change talk, taking steps, and questions about change could all serve as harbingers of readiness to plan. To find out whether the client is ready to move into the planning phase, the therapist has two choices: Ask them directly ("What do you think about making a specific plan to change how you react in those meetings at work?"), or proceed as in Frank's session as follows to explore a change plan as the session unfolds.

Therapist: You have mentioned so many important things so far. **[Affirmation]** You're not an alcoholic or, more importantly, an asshole. But you can be judgmental and yell at people on occasion, especially when you get angry, and you sometimes lose control when you drink too much. You know that you cannot change other people's behavior that makes you frustrated with them, but you been wondering about changing the way you react, especially in office meetings. So where does all this leave you? [**Summary and Key Question**]

Frank: I'm not sure. Maybe I could start by changing what I do when I get angry.

Therapist: That sounds like a strong idea, Frank. How about if we discuss the details of what that change might look like? [**Affirmation and Open Ended Question to move into planning**]

If Frank indicates that he is ready and willing to discuss a change plan, the therapist's job is to maintain the spirit of MI, that is, not launching into advice-giving or telling the client how to change. Instead, an MI therapist would use OARS again (open-ended question, affirmations, reflections, and summaries) to help guide the client through a specific and realistic change plan.

Therapist: What first steps could you take to reach your goal of reacting better when you get angry in work meetings? [**Open Ended Question to begin a specific change plan**]

Frank: I suppose I could just wait until the meeting is over to get mad in private in my office.

Therapist: Good idea. What other options could you try? [**Open Ended Question to gather more change plan ideas before narrowing down**]

Frank: I don't know.

Therapist: I have another idea if you want to hear it. [**EPE as in focusing phase above**]

Frank: Yes.

Therapist: You could tell yourself that your coworkers are not making you mad on purpose. And take a deep breath. What do you think of that? [**EPE; Note that this particular idea borrows from CBT, which is discussed at length in the next chapter in this volume**]

Frank: I could try that.

[Next the therapist would help Frank narrow down to specific ideas that he wants to try, who could help with his plan, and when Frank will implement the plan. Then:]

Therapist: What might get in your way? **[Troubleshooting the change plan]**

Frank: I'm not sure. But sometimes I get so angry in the moment that I feel like I am going to explode.

Therapist: How would you deal with these obstacles? **[Troubleshooting the change plan]**

The therapist would then summarize Frank's change plan and ask a scaling question such as:

"How committed are you on a scale of 0–10 to this plan, Frank?"

Conclusion

Motivational Interviewing is a promising intervention for those who exhibit a high level of antagonistic traits. Whereas limited research has looked at MI's efficacy with antagonism specifically, MI has already been shown to be effective for many individuals who *may* demonstrate antagonistic traits, such as individuals with substance use problems or those with a history of perpetrating violence. The style of MI can be especially useful as the therapist is nonconfrontational and explores a range of outcomes along with the client's ambivalence related to changing or not changing their antagonistic behavior. This style may help to disarm individuals with high antagonism who may have previously felt pushed or trapped in to changing their behavior, which often results in disengagement or discontinuation of therapy. In doing so, MI serves to promote change in individuals who may be particularly antagonistic, difficult to engage, or resistant to change.

References

Burke, B. L., Arkowitz, H., & Menchola, M. (2003). The efficacy of motivational interviewing: a meta-analysis of controlled clinical trials. *Journal of Consulting and Clinical Psychology*, *71*(5), 843–861. https://doi.org/10.1037/0022-006X.71.5.843.

Imel, Z. E., & Wampold, B. E. (2008). Treatment and the science of common factors in psychotherapy. In S. D. Brown & R. W. Lent (Eds.), *Handbook of counseling psychology* (4th ed., pp. 249–266). Hoboken, NJ: John Wiley and Sons, Inc.

Hudson, N. W., & Fraley, R. C. (2015). Volitional personality trait change: Can people choose to change their personality traits? *Journal of Personality and Social Psychology*, *109*(3), 490–507. https://doi.org/10.1037/pspp0000021.

LaChance, H., Feldstein Ewing, S. W., Bryan, A. D., & Hutchinson, K. E. (2009). What makes group MET work? A randomized controlled trial of college student drinkers in mandated alcohol diversion. *Psychology of Addictive Behaviors*, *23*(4), 598–612. https://doi.org/10.1037/a0016633.

Lundahl, B. W., & Burke, B. L. (2009). The effectiveness and applicability of motivational interviewing: a practice-friendly review of four meta-analyses. *Journal of Clinical Psychology*, *65*(11), 1232–1245. https://doi.org/10.1002/jclp.20638.

Lundahl, B. W., Kunz, C., Brownell, C., Tollefson, D., & Burke, B. L. (2010). A meta-analysis of motivational interviewing: twenty-five years of empirical studies. *Research on Social Work Practice*, *20*(2), 137–160. https://doi.org/10.1177/1049731509347850.

Lundahl, B., Moleni, T., Burke, B. L., Butters, R., Tollefson, D., Butler, C., et al. (2013). Motivational interviewing in medical care settings: a systematic review and meta-analysis of randomized controlled trials. *Patient Education and Counseling, 93*(2), 157–168. https://doi.org/10.1016/j.pec.2013.07.012.

Madson, M. B., Loignon, A. C., & Lane, C. (2009). Training in motivational interviewing: A systematic review. *Journal of Substance Abuse Treatment, 36*(1), 101–109. https://doi.org/10.1016/j.jsat.2008.05.005.

Miller, W. R., & Arkowitz, H. (2015). Learning, applying and extending motivational interviewing. In H. Arkowitz, W. R. Miller, & S. Rollnick (Eds.), *Motivational interviewing in the treatment of psychological problems* (pp. 1–32). New York: The Guilford Press.

Miller, W. R., & Rollnick, S. (1991). *Motivational interviewing: Preparing people to change addictive behavior*. New York: Guilford Press.

Miller, W. R., & Rollnick, S. (2002). *Motivational interviewing: Preparing people for change* (2nd ed.). New York: Guilford Press.

Miller, W. R., & Rollnick, S. (2013). *Motivational interviewing: Helping people change* (3rd ed.). New York: Guilford Press.

Miller, W. R., & Rose, G. S. (2009). Toward a theory of motivational interviewing. *American Psychologist, 64*(6), 527–537. https://doi.org/10.1037/a0016830.

Murphy, R. T. (2008). Enhancing combat veterans' motivation to change posttraumatic stress disorder symptoms and other problem behaviors. In H. Arkowitz, H. A. Westra, W. R. Miller, S. Rollnick, H. Arkowitz, & H. A. Westra et al. (Eds.) *Motivational interviewing in the treatment of psychological problems* (pp. 57–84). New York: Guilford Press.

Nirenberg, T., Baird, J., Longabaugh, & Mello, M. J. (2012). Motivational counseling reduces future police charges in court-referred youth. *Accident Analysis and Prevention, 55*, 89–99. https://doi.org/10.1016/j.aap.2013.01.006.

Prochaska, J. O., & DiClemente, C. C. (1982). Transtheoretical therapy: toward a more integrative model of change. *Psychotherapy, 19*(3), 276–288. https://doi.org/10.1037/h0088437.

Project MATCH Research Group. (1997). Project MATCH secondary a priori hypotheses. *Addiction, 92*(12), 1671–1698.

Schwalbe, C. S., Oh, H. Y., & Zweben, A. (2014). Sustaining motivational interviewing: A meta-analysis of training studies. *Addiction, 109*(8), 1287–1294. https://doi.org/10.1111/add.12558.

Terracciano, A., Löckenhoff, C. E., Crum, R. M., Bienvenu, O. J., & Costa, P. T. (2008). Five-Factor Model personality profiles of drug users. *BMC Psychiatry, 8*, 22. https://doi.org/10.1186/1471-244X-8-22.

Woodin, E. M. (2015). Motivational interviewing for intimate partner violence. In H. Arkowitz, W. R. Miller, & S. Rollnick (Eds.), *Motivational interviewing in the treatment of psychological problems* (pp. 320–343). New York: The Guilford Press.

Yalom, I. D. (2017). *The gift of therapy: An open letter to a new generation of therapists and their patients*. New York: Harper Perennial.

Psychodynamic approaches to treating antagonism

23

Christopher J. Hopwood, Robert F. Bornstein†*
*Department of Psychology, University of California, Davis, CA, United States, †School of Psychology, Adelphi University, Garden City, NY, United States

Although trait and psychodynamic approaches to personality have taken adversarial positions at times (e.g., McWilliams, 2012), we see them as complementary (Wiggins, 2003). Trait psychology supplements complex psychodynamic theories with an evidence-based model of individual differences that can be used to generate reliable assessment methods useful for testing dynamic hypotheses about personality, psychopathology, and psychotherapy. Psychodynamic theories enrich descriptive trait approaches, enhance their clinical utility, provide a coherent framework for interpreting multimethod assessment data, and generate testable hypotheses about mechanisms underlying personality processes (see Hopwood & Bornstein, 2014; Hopwood, Zimmermann, Pincus, & Krueger, 2015). In this chapter we take a step toward integrating these complementary theoretical perspectives with respect to assessing and treating *antagonism*. We first describe similarities and differences between trait and psychodynamic conceptualizations of antagonism, with a focus on the specific features of the psychodynamic perspective that can augment a trait perspective. We then illustrate these features in describing principles of psychodynamic psychotherapy for antagonism.

Trait and psychodynamic models of personality

The primary method for discerning the organization of different elements of personality from a trait perspective has involved some form of *covariance analysis* (e.g., factor analysis). This method assumes that there are linear relations among different attributes that can be parsimoniously summarized in terms of associations with relatively broad concepts. For instance, a relative consensus has emerged among personality psychologists that personality traits can be summarized, at a broad level of abstraction, in terms of five factors (John & Srivastava, 1999). Antagonism can be regarded as one pole of one of those five factors (the other pole being Agreeableness). The large body of literature showing similar structural models based on other types of data and analytic methods (Harkness, Reynolds, & Lilienfeld, 2014) supports the use of covariance modeling to identify and organize personality units into a coherent structure.

In these sorts of models traits such as antagonism are regarded as *dimensional*, in the sense that individuals do not "have" (or "not have") particular traits, but rather all

The Handbook of Antagonism. https://doi.org/10.1016/B978-0-12-814627-9.00023-2

individuals can be ranked according to their standing on a given trait dimension. Maladaptive functioning is generally albeit imperfectly associated with extreme levels of these traits, as when, for example, too much—or too little—extraversion leads to interpersonal difficulties (see Williams & Simms, 2018). Evidence in favor of the dimensionality principle comes from the finding that no personality trait or disorder has been found to be purely categorical in direct tests (Arntz et al., 2009) and that conceptualizing personality traits dimensionally increases their assessment reliability and validity (Markon, Chmielewski, & Miller, 2011).

Covariance analyses of normal and maladaptive personality dimensions yields a *hierarchical* model with broad traits at the top and increasingly narrow traits at the bottom. Antagonism is a relatively broad trait that can be split into aspects involving the behavioral predispositions of rudeness and callousness (DeYoung, Quilty, & Peterson, 2007). These aspects can be further divided into more specific trait facets like immodesty, impoliteness, cruelty, and dishonesty. Conceptualizing traits hierarchically has two principal advantages. First, this allows for the empirical synthesis and integration of disparate trait models into an integrative whole. Second, hierarchies are clinically useful in that they provide a framework for clinicians to conceptualize patients' personalities in terms of a level of specificity that suits the situation (Kotov et al., 2017).

Although covariance analysis has played a less important role in the development of psychodynamic models of personality, there is nothing inherently incompatible between these approaches and psychodynamic thinking. There are also major dimensions of functioning in psychodynamic models of personality structure. For example, Kernberg (1984) suggested that individuals with PDs vary according to how organized their personality is and how extraverted they are. Within these broad dimensions are more specific features, like the defenses and object relational configurations that distinguish patients with better or poorer personality organization, or who are more or less extraverted. Although antagonism has not been posited as a major organizing dimension in psychodynamic models, it plays a role in the underlying dynamics of many PD subtypes and can be integrated with psychodynamic thinking relatively easily. For instance, dependency and histrionic personality configurations typically involve low antagonism whereas psychopathic and narcissistic personality configurations involve relatively high antagonism. This is not to say that these configurations can be understood merely as low or high levels of this—or any—trait; psychodynamic theory has a lot to say about the dynamics of PDs beyond trait dispositions (see Lingiardi & McWilliams, 2017). Differences in emphasis notwithstanding, trait and psychodynamic models do share the assumption that a trait like antagonism is descriptive of such personalities at a relatively broad level of abstraction. Psychodynamic theory further assumes that underlying—often hidden—elements of a broad trait like antagonism will help distinguish individuals in a way that is empirically sound and clinically useful (e.g., reliance on more malignant vs higher level defenses). In this respect psychodynamic frameworks implicitly adopt a hierarchical model for conceptualizing people.

This convergence provides a basis for integrating trait and psychodynamic models of antagonistic behavior. From both perspectives, people can be organized in terms of the general and specific features associated with antagonism, and this will have important prognostic and therapeutic implications. However, there are also some important ways in which psychodynamic theory differs from, and can enhance, a trait perspective on antagonism.

Dynamics

A wide range of psychodynamic conceptualizations of personality exist, and though all share an emphasis on unconscious processes and defensive self-deception, these models often have substantially different assumptions about origins, taxonomy, and treatment (Bornstein, 2003; Greenberg & Mitchell, 1983; Pine, 1990). Across different psychodynamic models, behavior is presumed to be *determined* in the sense that people are assumed to be perpetually trying to achieve something of which might not be fully—or even partially—aware (Schafer, 1976). Whatever people are trying to do is always in reference to some *object*—people try to do something to, for, or with some other thing. That thing is typically another person, a representation of another person (real or imagined), or a nonperson which nevertheless has some person-like qualities (e.g., can be loved or hated). Thus personality from a psychodynamic perspective is understood in terms of dynamic patterns of *self in relation to other* (Kernberg, 1995; Luyten & Blatt, 2013). This connection between self and other is invariably colored by some affective experience. From a psychodynamic perspective, both self and other can have antagonistic qualities, but those qualities are understood in terms of what a person is trying to achieve with respect to some other (as opposed to a description of a general behavioral tendency).

Interactions with important early caregivers provide a template for how future relationships may be expected to develop in terms of relatively stable configurations of self-other-affect. These *internal working models* (or *scripts*) help individuals navigate their social worlds and are thus generally helpful. Consistencies in such patterns reflect a general personality configuration, and symptoms arise when this configuration does not work in some manner (e.g., when the configuration leads to interpersonal conflict or intrapsychic distress).

Fig. 1 depicts four configurations that eventuate in different expressions of Antagonism, to illustrate how individual differences in personality configuration can be integrated with a trait perspective. The first is a sadistic prototype, in which the other is experienced as neglectful, which makes the person angry, who is cruel in response. This person differs from the prototypical psychopath, for whom others' neglect represents an opportunity for poised manipulation. In contrast, the narcissistic prototype describes a person provoked by other's expressions of dominance, who reacts with immodest behavior. Finally, the passive-aggressive person will tend to interpret others' domineering behavior as both reflecting and reinforcing their own powerlessness, and react by subtly undermining the other's authority. In both trait and psychodynamic models, these different personality prototypes can be distinguished by underlying dispositions, but whereas in trait models the dispositions refer to broad and narrow behavioral tendencies, in psychodynamic models they refer to configurations of self in relation to other.

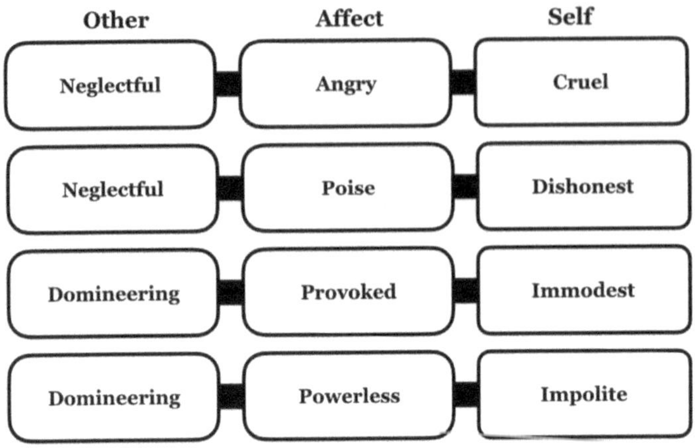

Fig. 1 Individual differences in object relations configurations.

Thematic connections across situations are central to both trait and psychodynamic models of personality (see McWilliams, 2012). However, in a psychodynamic model the thematic connections tend to specifically focus on configurations across different types of relationship (e.g., Luborsky & Crits-Christoph, 1998; Strupp & Binder, 1984). Three such relationships are particularly important in psychodynamic psychotherapy. The first is the here-and-now relationship between clinician and patient. This is the entry point to understanding how the patient relates to others, because it is the only relationship to which the therapist has direct access. The second set of important relationships are those in other areas of the patient's life. Typically, the patient will present for treatment because something is going awry in one or more of these relationships. The third set of key relationships are those from the patient's past—developmentally important relationships with caregivers. Psychodynamic clinicians generally assume that (1) the origins of thematic personality patterns can be found in early caregiving dynamics (though these dynamics may be shaped by nature, nurture, or a combination of the two) and (2) understanding these early patterns can help free patients to choose different paths in current and future relationships.

Fig. 2 gives an example of a similar personality configuration across these three types of relationships for an antagonistic patient, who we will call Dennis. Dennis presents because of problems with his girlfriend. In listening to his initial presentation, Dennis's therapist, Sheila, discerns a general pattern in which Dennis perceives his girlfriend as not being sufficiently attentive, which makes him angry, to which he responds with threats to leave the relationship. Upon reflection Dennis recognizes that there have been times when his perceptions were not accurate, and his anger was not justified; with this new understanding he acknowledges that he doesn't actually want to leave his girlfriend, but makes these threats under stress. Dennis and Sheila agree to focus on this dynamic in therapy, and in exploring the therapeutic relationship they realize that its turbulent moments often have the same structure: Dennis thinks Sheila

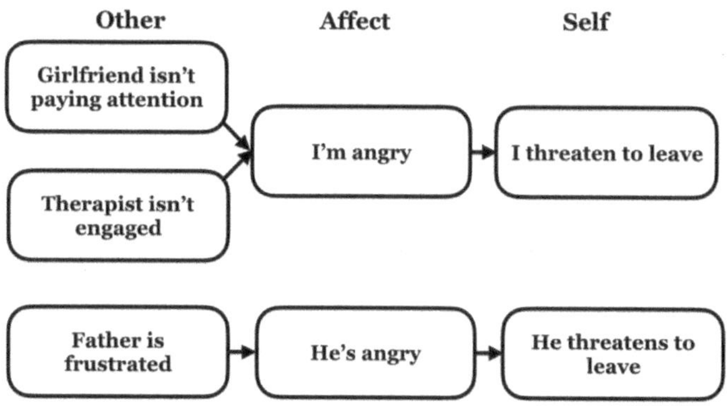

Fig. 2 Thematic connections between object relations configurations in past, current, and therapeutic relationships.

is not listening to him, becomes angry, and threatens to discontinue therapy, but never follows through on these threats. In exploring Dennis's early life, Dennis comes to realize that he is acting the way he experienced his father as being: becoming angry for reasons Dennis did not understand, "blowing up," and threatening to leave (but always returning).

Reportability

The origin of trait psychology is typically credited to Allport and Odbert (1936), who reasoned that important features of human personality could be found in the dictionary, since one of the main functions of language is to allow humans to communicate about themselves and one another (Goldberg, 1993). Based on this assumption, dictionary adjectives were distilled into a range of questionnaires to be completed by research participants, providing raw data for studying the nature of personality. A corollary of the lexical hypothesis is that these participants could basically answer questions about themselves in a reasonably accurate manner. That is, trait psychology assumes that personality is *reportable*. Correlations between questionnaires and a variety of important life outcomes (Ozer & Benet-Martinez, 2006; Roberts, Kuncel, Shiner, Caspi, & Goldberg, 2007) support trait theorists' assumptions regarding the reportability of personality traits.

In contrast, perhaps the signature feature of a psychodynamic model of personality is its assumption that individuals are unaware of many important aspects of their personality. This assumption contrasts with the trait principle of reportability, giving rise to a rather different approach to conceptualization and assessment (Bornstein, 2012; although, see Vazire, 2010). With regard to assessment, this assumption creates some skepticism regarding the veridicality of self-report questionnaires and impels the clinician to use other methods, such as narratives (Westen, 1991), stimulus-attribution approaches (Bornstein, 2010; Bornstein & Masling, 2005), or the therapeutic

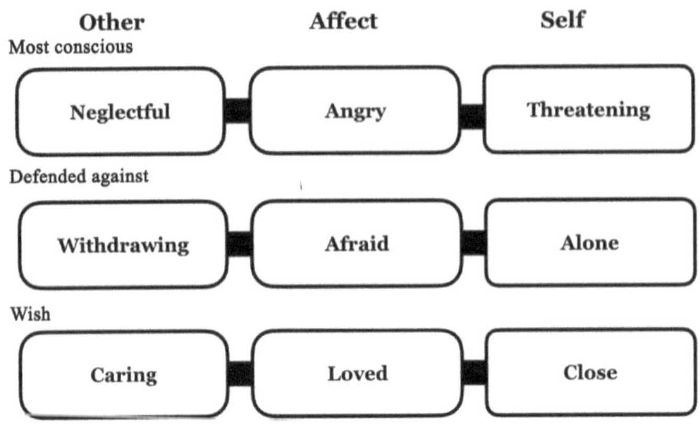

Fig. 3 Object relations configurations across levels of awareness.

relationship itself (Hopwood, 2010; Strupp & Binder, 1984) to complement self-reports and draw more nuanced inferences about personality. A major focus of therapy, from this perspective, is using the therapeutic relationship to help patients become more aware of what they are doing and why, so they can make more mindful choices and have the freedom to change long-standing life patterns.

Fig. 3 distinguishes three aspects of Dennis's core dynamic across different levels of awareness. The most conscious representation is what we have already described: the other is experienced as neglectful, so Dennis becomes angry and threatens to leave. In exploring the moments when this dynamic plays out, though, Sheila and Dennis observe a different dynamic, which is not prominent in Dennis's mind during the heat of the moment but which he can acknowledge with Sheila's encouragement. Without fully realizing it Dennis is afraid that the other will withdraw, and he will be alone. This is a more vulnerable position than self-righteous anger, so Dennis defends against this fear by adopting a pretense of autonomy. But his true intent is revealed by the fact that he never carries through on his threat to leave. By threatening to leave Dennis actually seeks to actualize the opposite: He would like to be cared for by the other, to feel love, and to be close.

Summary

Antagonism can be understood as a broad quantitative dimension (from a trait perspective) which represents an organizing construct for self and other, which are always in some dynamic relationship (from a psychodynamic perspective). Trait psychology can augment psychodynamic theory by articulating an evidence-based measurement model for the potential attributes that structure self, other, and affect (Hopwood et al., 2015). Psychodynamic theory can augment trait psychology by providing a coherent model of personality dynamics, which are of central importance in psychotherapy. In the next section, we illustrate the importance of dynamic concepts in psychodynamic psychotherapy for antagonism.

From behavior to process: Treating antagonism from a psychodynamic perspective

A number of psychodynamic treatment approaches have been summarized in manuals that can be used clinically and in treatment research (e.g., Bateman & Fonagy, 2006; Clarkin, Yeomans, & Kernberg, 2007; Strupp & Binder, 1984). Research comparing these treatments to other forms of psychotherapy suggests that psychodynamic treatment is about as effective as other approaches that have been designed to work for problems related to personality, mood, and interpersonal functioning (Leichsenring, Luyten, Hilsenroth, et al., 2015; Messer & Wampold, 2002), though some reviews suggest that psychodynamic methods may be particularly effective for certain types of problems and particular types of patients (see Leichsenring & Rabiung, 2008; Weiner & Bornstein, 2009). Conceptual and empirical limitations in the primary methods that have historically been used to compare treatments, including randomized controlled trials (Cartwright & Deaton, 2016; Westen, Novotny, & Thompson-Brenner, 2004) and meta-analyses (Braver, Thoemmes, & Rosenthal, 2014), complicate interpretations of this literature. With these limitations in mind, the transition among treatment researchers to examining specific trans-theoretical factors that help account for therapeutic gains (Ackerman & Hilsenroth, 2003; Levy et al., 2006) is a productive development. In this spirit, we summarize some of the techniques common to different psychodynamic approaches (Blagys & Hilsenroth, 2000) as they apply to antagonism.

Generally speaking, psychodynamic psychotherapy has three goals (Weiner & Bornstein, 2009). The first is to relieve the patient's distress. The second is to help him solve his specific presenting problems. The third is to help him modify his personality so he can function better in the future. Psychodynamic psychotherapy proceeds in three phases, during which different techniques are used to achieve these goals. In what follows we describe psychodynamic techniques in the initial, middle, and termination phases of psychotherapy with a specific focus on antagonism.

Initial phase

The goals of the initial phase are to assess the patient, develop a case formulation and treatment plan, agree to a treatment contract, and establish the process by which therapy will occur. From a psychodynamic perspective a key goal to set the stage for successful psychotherapy is to assess the patient's level of personality organization (Lingiardi & McWilliams, 2017). This information will inform prognosis, duration, the importance of supportive (vs uncovering) techniques, and the risks of problematic transference and countertransference dynamics that threaten the therapeutic alliance (Hopwood, 2018). Personality disorganization comes in a variety of forms that can be described in general terms using traits, and antagonistic people can have more or less organized personalities. For instance, a person who has learned to sublimate her antagonism by identifying occupational and social networks in which it is a strength (see Wiggins, 2003) may have a better organized personality than a person whose antagonism manifests as blatantly antisocial behavior.

Beyond level of personality organization, an important aim of the initial formulation is to understand predominant themes in the self-other-affect configuration present in past, current, and therapeutic relationships that are functionally related to the patient's symptoms. This aspect of the case formulation tells the therapist what to expect and where to focus, although it is modifiable as the treatment progresses and new insights are achieved (e.g., through analysis of transference; see Bornstein, 2018).

A treatment contract supports the next phase of psychotherapy by establishing the expectations, roles, goals, and boundaries of treatment. Contracts vary with respect to parameters such as fees, time, place, and frequency (Weiner & Bornstein, 2009); the key is that the contract be collaborative to the degree possible, explicit, adhered to strictly by the therapist, and discussed when agreements in the contract are not upheld by the patient. In general, the therapist's role is to be available, to try her best to be helpful, and to be professional. The patient's role is to show up at mutually agreed-upon times, pay the fee, and be open to discussing the nature of and reasons for his difficulties. Ideally the goals of treatment are articulated by the patient with the help of the clinician, shaped by findings from assessment data, and involve a shared understanding of the presenting problem.

Establishing the therapeutic process is as much a matter of how the therapist behaves as what she says or does. In psychodynamic therapy, the therapist will tend to listen more than talk, to focus on here and now dynamics related to the self-other-affect configuration in the therapeutic relationship, as well as in past and other current relationships, and to comment primarily on the patient's goals, frustrations, and defenses as they manifest within and outside therapy (Ackerman & Hilsenroth, 2003). The therapeutic posture is generally warm, empathic, genuine, and neutral, with neutrality being the aspect of this posture that is most unique to the psychodynamic approach. Neutrality means that the therapist is careful not to take a side regarding what the patient should want, do, or behave. The technical rationale for this stance is that when the therapist is neutral, any patterns that emerge in the therapeutic relationship reflect the dynamics of the patient rather than those of the therapist. For instance, rather than asserting that antagonistic behavior is maladaptive and should be reduced, the psychodynamic therapist would try to help the patient understand the meaning of her antagonistic behavior so she may decide for herself whether—and if so how—she would like it to change.

Middle phase

During the middle phase of therapy, the clinician applies therapeutic techniques designed to foster and maintain a strong alliance (Hammond & Nichols, 2008; Levy et al., 2006) and ultimately help the patient achieve his goals based on the initial formulation and plan, in a manner consistent with the treatment contract. These techniques center on the interpretation (including clarification and, on occasion, confrontation) of here-and-now interpersonal dynamics in the therapeutic relationship (Hilsenroth & Cromer, 2007) and encouragement of the patient to reflect on the meaning of his behavior (Beitman & Soth, 2006) within that context. The dynamics of particular focus for the therapist can be grouped into three categories: transference, countertransference, and patient resistance (Weiner & Bornstein, 2009).

Transference is the displacement of a developmental self-other-affect configuration onto the current interpersonal situation (see Andersen & Przybylinski, 2014, for a discussion of the dynamics that underlie this process). A gap between the reality of the situation (the therapist and patient have agreed to pursue certain therapeutic goals in a professional context) and the patient's relational experience (the therapist may judge or otherwise hurt me) invariably develops, and this gap can be explored to help the patient learn about how her unconscious desires and interpersonal schema interfere with her functioning in present-day relationships.

Because of its central role in therapeutic progress, the development of transference should be encouraged via technical neutrality and processed via interpretation. At the same time, extreme and unexamined transference responses can threaten the working alliance, so there is a careful balance between techniques that deepen awareness and promote change but threaten the alliance (e.g., interpretation) and techniques that support the alliance (e.g., warmth and empathy). The difficulties related to unexamined transference patterns do not invariably arise from the patient, but from the therapist as well, often in the form of countertransference responses that undermine empathic connectedness and compromise therapeutic neutrality (see, e.g., Eagle, 2000).

Effective transference interpretations typically contrast the transferred and actual self-other-affect configuration as it is occurring in the therapeutic relationship, then link the transferred configuration to some other important relationship. For instance, Sheila might say to Dennis:

> *You have been talking about your arguments with your girlfriend, in which she is dismissive of you and you become angry and sometimes even threaten to leave. It sounds like you also love her and are worried that you may lose her but resent that she is not really listening to what you say. Now, in here, you talk about how this plays out, and I do not respond, perhaps making you feel as though I am dismissive just like she is. It makes you angry, and you threaten to leave.*

In this interpretation, the therapist describes the self (antagonistic), other (dismissive), and affect (anger) that has been transferred from the patient's relationship with his girlfriend to his relationship with the therapist. Depending on the therapist's assessment of the patient's overall personality organization, and the patient's level of stress (and distress) at that moment, she may also move toward the more vulnerable, less conscious wish:

> *But I wonder if, both with your girlfriend and in here, part of you also wants to stay and work on things?*

Reference might also be made to the relevant developmental pattern

> *This reminds me of how you talk about your father, who would sometimes 'blow up' and 'storm off', seeming to leave you and your mom in the lurch. You must have felt angry with him for leaving but also sad about being left, and it is difficult and even overwhelming to put both of those feelings together. I wonder if that is how you feel now, a little overwhelmed?*

The timing and concatenation of each of these comments is crucial: Effective interpretations depend on the clinician's assessment of the patient's readiness to make use of them, taking into account the patient's overall level of functioning, defensive style, and other factors. These considerations notwithstanding, transference interpretation almost invariably directs the patient's focus to the affective experience of this interpersonal situation, as the therapist warmly and gently balances the goals of maintaining a strong alliance via support with pushing the patient toward productive discomfort and increased motivation for change.

Countertransference occurs when the therapist has feelings, motives thoughts, and behaviors about the patient that are related to their real human relationship, as opposed to their professional working relationship. Like transference, it is important to be as aware as possible of countertransference, in part because it can threaten the therapy, and also because understanding it may provide important information about the patient, her effect on others, and their likely reactions (see Eagle, 2000). Although traditionally countertransference was regarded as an impediment to treatment, contemporary psychodynamic frameworks regard this process as potentially illuminating. Thus, as with transference, countertransference should be allowed to develop, analyzed empathically, and used to inform the treatment. It is sometimes important to share countertransference reactions with patients, if it is thought that this will help them understand themselves better. For instance:

> *You know, I understand that you get angry with me, but sometimes when you say that you feel like I am not listening and threaten to quit therapy, I feel a little hurt and defensive. Part of me wants to say, 'well go ahead then!'. Of course, I am committed to helping you as we agreed, but I wonder if this feeling can't help us. I mean, your girlfriend might feel the same way when you threaten her, and this might be important to understand, because it can help us see the impact you could have on other people you care about.*

Resistance occurs when the patient defends against making the use of the therapeutic relationship to effect personality change. This should be a primary focus for the therapist. Left unexplored resistance inevitably interferes with treatment. Moreover, understanding the pattern of resistance often sheds light on the patient's characteristic ways of coping with challenge and discomfort. As psychodynamic therapy is relatively unstructured, resistance takes many forms. So, for example, histrionic patients often use seduction as a means of transforming the therapeutic relationship from a neutral one to a romantic one, thereby undermining treatment. Another common form of resistance—especially for more obsessional patients—is to focus on trivial topics. This behavior can be understood as a resistance to therapeutic work, and interpreting it can be an entry point into a deeper therapeutic dialogue. For example:

> *Last time we discussed how some of the ways you feel about me are similar to some of the ways you felt about your father. That was probably a little uncomfortable to talk about, but it also seemed like it led you to understand some important things about how and why you get angry with your girlfriend. So it is notable that today you have started the session by talking about your work schedule instead of picking up on that theme. Do you think it is possible that you are ambivalent about discussing your anger in relation to me, your father, and your girlfriend because it is uncomfortable?*

Interpretive comments should be relatively infrequent and must be well timed (Hilsenroth & Cromer, 2007). As a general rule, the psychodynamic therapist should have an explicit and well-reasoned justification for saying something. Missed opportunities are made rare by the tendency for important relational dynamics to recur; interpretive errors can be extremely costly in that they diminish the patient's engagement in the therapeutic process and trust in the therapist. Thus, the predominant focus for the therapist is to listen carefully, using the self-other-affect configuration across different important relationships as a rubric, and interpret occasionally. Through this process, the patient gradually becomes more aware of how these patterns impact his functioning and better able to explore different, more adaptive patterns with the therapist—and ultimately in important relationships outside of therapy.

Final phase

A different emphasis characterizes the final, *termination* phase of therapy because of the pain and loss associated with the end of treatment. Because the therapeutic relationship can be understood as a metaphoric reenactment of earlier relationships with caregivers (Bornstein & Becker-Matero, 2011), termination of therapy can be extremely difficult for some patients. Thus therapy is not invariably ended because the initial goals are met, but when the dynamics of the therapeutic relationship have been explored and resolved, when the pain of losing that relationship is discussed and assimilated, and when therapist and patient have had the opportunity for a meaningful good bye. Sometimes unplanned termination occurs for a variety of reasons, in which case the therapist does the best she can; here we focus on planned terminations.

In general, either therapist or patient may raise the possibility of termination when there is evidence that distress and symptoms are reduced, the patient has begun to make real and adaptive changes in her approach to life that are related to therapeutic goals, and the transference relationship is understood, discussed, and—at least to some degree—resolved. Regardless of whether the possibility of terminating is raised by therapist or patient, there should be a relatively extended discussion that includes reasons why there should or should not be a termination at this time, how the termination will proceed (e.g., how many sessions will remain, whether there will be any changes in spacing between sessions), and what the relationship will be like after termination (whether there will be any contact between therapist and patient posttreatment). Once a plan is made for termination, it is followed closely so the focus can be on consolidating gains, nurturing the transition to a mature relationship untainted by transference dynamics, and a warm (albeit appropriately sad) ending.

Conclusion: The trait-dynamic dialectic

For nearly a century the trait and psychodynamic approaches have evolved synergistically, ostensibly distinct and separate models, but often influencing each other in subtle ways. In this chapter we have emphasized the complementarity of trait and psychodynamic conceptualizations of antagonism. Whereas trait theory focuses on what a person tends to be like, dynamic theory focuses on why she is that way. Both questions are important; neither can be addressed completely without reference to the other. Pairing the ability of quantitative psychology to generate a robust and evidence-based model of individual differences with the psychodynamic focus on interpersonal patterns that are impacted by developmental experiences and unconscious processes provides a powerful integrative model of personality functioning with considerable clinical utility.

Within this integrative approach, personality can be conceived as a configuration of self-other-affect in different relationships, including those in development, the patient's current life, and the psychotherapy dyad. Antagonism can be understood as a major dimension along which aspects of self and other can vary, with therapy aimed at helping the patient understand the reasons for antagonistic behavior across these relationships through a progression of three phases: Establishment of expectations, roles, and goals via a treatment contract; interpretation of transference, countertransference, and resistance to expand the patient's awareness; and a final phase wherein the transference relationship is resolved, gains are solidified, and the therapist and patient say good bye.

References

Ackerman, S. J., & Hilsenroth, M. J. (2003). A review of therapist characteristics and techniques positively impacting the therapeutic alliance. *Clinical Psychology Review*, *23*, 1–33.

Allport, G. W., & Odbert, H. S. (1936). Trait-names: a psycho-lexical study. *Psychological Monographs*, *47*(1), i.

Andersen, S. A., & Przybylinski, E. (2014). Cognitive distortion in interpersonal relations: clinical implications of social-cognitive research on person perception. *Journal of Psychotherapy Integration*, *24*(1), 13–24.

Arntz, A., Bernstein, D., Gielen, D., van Nieuwenhuyzen, M., Penders, K., Haslam, N., et al. (2009). Taxometric evidence for the dimensional structure of cluster-C. Paranoid, and borderline personality disorders. *Journal of Personality Disorders*, *23*(6), 606–628.

Bateman, A., & Fonagy, P. (2006). *Mentalization-based treatment for borderline personality disorder: A practical guide*. Oxford, UK: OUP Oxford.

Beitman, B. D., & Soth, A. M. (2006). Activation of self-observation: a core process among the psychotherapies. *Journal of Psychotherapy Integration*, *16*, 383–393.

Blagys, M. D., & Hilsenroth, M. J. (2000). Distinctive features of short-term psychodynamic-interpersonal psychotherapy: a review of the comparative psychotherapy process literature. *Clinical Psychology: Science and Practice*, *7*, 167–188.

Bornstein, R. F. (2010). Psychoanalytic theory as a unifying framework for 21st century personality assessment. *Psychoanalytic Psychology*, *27*(2), 133–152.

Bornstein, R. F. (2003). The scientific review of mental health practice_ Implications for psychology and psychoanalysis. [Review of the book *Scientific Review of Mental Health Practice*. Edited by S. Lilienfeld]. *Psychoanalytic Psychology*, *20*(4), 717–726.

Bornstein, R. F. (2012). Rorschach score validation as a model for 21st-century personality assessment. *Journal of Personality Assessment*, *94*(1), 26–38.

Bornstein, R. F. (2018). From symptom to process: case formulation, clinical utility, and PDM-2. *Psychoanalytic Psychology*, *35*(3), 351–356.

Bornstein, R. F., & Becker-Matero, N. (2011). Reconnecting psychoanalysis to mainstream psychology: metaphor as glue. *Psychoanalytic Inquiry*, *31*, 172–184.

Bornstein, R. F., & Masling, J. M. (Eds.), (2005). *Scoring the Rorschach: Seven validated systems*. Routledge.
Braver, S. L., Thoemmes, F. J., & Rosenthal, R. (2014). Continuously cumulating meta-analysis and replicability. *Perspectives on Psychological Science*, *9*, 333–342.
Cartwright, N., & Deaton, A. (2016). Understanding and misunderstanding randomized controlled trials. *Social Science and Medicine*,.
Clarkin, J. F., Yeomans, F. E., & Kernberg, O. F. (2007). *Psychotherapy for borderline personality: Focusing on object relations*. Washington, DC: American Psychiatric Publishing.
DeYoung, C. G., Quilty, L. C., & Peterson, J. B. (2007). Between facets and domains: 10 aspects of the Big Five. *Journal of Personality and Social Psychology*, *93*, 880–896.
Eagle, M. N. (2000). A critical evaluation of current conceptions of transference and countertransference. *Psychoanalytic Psychology*, *17*, 24–37.
Goldberg, L. R. (1993). The structure of phenotypic personality traits. *American Psychologist*, *48*, 26–34.
Greenberg, J. R., & Mitchell, S. A. (1983). *Object relations in psychoanalytic theory*. Cambridge, MA: Harvard UP.
Hammond, R. T., & Nichols, M. P. (2008). How collaborative is structural family therapy? *The Family Journal*, *16*, 118–124.
Harkness, A. R., Reynolds, S. M., & Lilienfeld, S. O. (2014). A review of systems for psychology and psychiatry: adaptive systems, personality psychopathology five (PSY–5), and the DSM–5. *Journal of Personality Assessment*, *96*, 121–139.
Hilsenroth, M. J., & Cromer, T. D. (2007). Clinician interventions related to alliance during the initial interview and psychological assessment. *Psychotherapy: Theory, Research, Practice, Training*, *44*, 205–218.
Hopwood, C. J. (2010). An interpersonal perspective on the personality assessment process. *Journal of Personality Assessment*, *92*, 471–479.
Hopwood, C. J. (2018). Interpersonal dynamics in personality and personality disorders. *European Journal of Personality*, *32*(5), 499–524.
Hopwood, C. J., & Bornstein, R. F. (2014). Toward a framework for integrating multimethod clinical assessment data. In C. J. Hopwood & R. F. Bornstein (Eds.), *Multimethod clinical assessment* (pp. 427–441). NY: Guilford Press.
Hopwood, C. J., Zimmermann, J., Pincus, A. L., & Krueger, R. F. (2015). Connecting personality structure and dynamics: towards a more empirically-based and clinically useful diagnostic system. *Journal of Personality Disorders*, *29*, 431–448.
John, O. P., & Srivastava, S. (1999). The Big Five trait taxonomy: history, measurement, and theoretical perspectives. *Handbook of personality: Theory and research* (pp. 102–138). Vol. 2 (pp. 102–138). New York, NY: Guilford.
Kernberg, O. F. (1984). *Severe personality disorders*. New Haven, CT: Yale University Press.
Kernberg, O. F. (1995). *Object relations theory and clinical psychoanalysis*. New York, NY: Jason Aronson.
Kotov, R., Krueger, R. F., Watson, D., Achenbach, T. M., Althoff, R. R., Bagby, R. M., et al. (2017). The Hierarchical Taxonomy of Psychopathology (HiTOP): a dimensional alternative to traditional nosologies. *Journal of Abnormal Psychology*, *126*(4), 454–477.
Leichsenring, F., Luyten, P., Hilsenroth, M. J., et al. (2015). Psychodynamic therapy meets evidence-based medicine: a systematic review using updated criteria. *Lancet Psychiatry*, *2*, 648–660.
Leichsenring, F., & Rabiung, S. (2008). Effectiveness of long-term psychodynamic psychotherapy: a meta-analysis. *Journal of the American Medical Association*, *300*, 1551–1565.

Levy, K. N., Meehan, K. B., Kelly, K. M., Reynoso, J. S., Weber, M., Clarkin, J. F., et al. (2006). Change in attachment patterns and reflective function in a randomized control trial of transference-focused psychotherapy for borderline personality disorder. *Journal of Consulting and Clinical Psychology*, *74*, 1027–1040.

Lingiardi, V., & McWilliams, N. (Eds.), (2017). *The psychodynamic diagnostic manual*. (2nd ed.). NY: Guilford Press.

Luborsky, L., & Crits-Christoph, P. (1998). *Understanding transference: The core conflictual relationship theme method*. Washington, DC: American Psychological Association.

Luyten, P., & Blatt, S. J. (2013). Interpersonal relatedness and self-definition in normal and disrupted personality development. *American Psychologist*, *68*(3), 172–183.

Markon, K. E., Chmielewski, M., & Miller, C. J. (2011). The reliability and validity of discrete and continuous measures of psychopathology: a quantitative review. *Psychological Bulletin*, *137*(5), 856–879.

McWilliams, N. (2012). Beyond traits: personality as intersubjective themes. *Journal of Personality Assessment*, *94*, 563–570.

Messer, S. B., & Wampold, B. E. (2002). Let's face facts: common factors are more potent than specific therapy ingredients. *Clinical Psychology: Science and Practice*, *9*, 21–25.

Ozer, D. J., & Benet-Martinez, V. (2006). Personality and the prediction of consequential outcomes. *Annual Review of Psychology*, *57*, 401–421.

Pine, F. (1990). *Drive, ego, object, and self: A synthesis for clinical work*. New York: Basic Books.

Roberts, B. W., Kuncel, N. R., Shiner, R., Caspi, A., & Goldberg, L. R. (2007). The power of personality: the comparative validity of personality traits, socioeconomic status, and cognitive ability for predicting important life outcomes. *Perspectives on Psychological Science*, *2*, 313–345.

Schafer, R. (1976). *A new language for psychoanalysis*. New Haven, CT: Yale University Press.

Strupp, H. H., & Binder, J. L. (1984). *Psychotherapy in a new key: A guide to time-limited dynamic psychotherapy*. New York: Basic Books.

Vazire, S. (2010). Who knows what about a person? The self–other knowledge asymmetry (SOKA) model. *Journal of Personality and Social Psychology*, *98*(2), 281–300.

Weiner, I. B., & Bornstein, R. F. (2009). *Principles of psychotherapy: Promoting evidence-based psychodynamic practice*. Hoboken, NJ: John Wiley & Sons.

Westen, D. (1991). Clinical assessment of object relations using the TAT. *Journal of Personality Assessment*, *56*, 56–74.

Westen, D., Novotny, C. M., & Thompson-Brenner, H. (2004). The empirical status of empirically supported psychotherapies: assumptions, findings, and reporting in controlled clinical trials. *Psychological Bulletin*, *130*, 631–663.

Wiggins, J. S. (2003). *Paradigms of personality assessment*. Guilford Press.

Williams, T. F., & Simms, L. J. (2018). Personality traits and maladaptivity: Unipolarity versus bipolarity. *Journal of personality*, *86*(5), 888–901.

Treatment of antagonism: Cognitive behavioral therapy

24

Jessica L. Maples-Keller, Carly Yasinski, Callan Coghlan, Abigail Powers
Emory University School of Medicine, Atlanta, GA, United States

The five-factor model (FFM), widely acknowledged as representing the higher order structure of normal and pathological personality traits (Clark, 2007), includes agreeableness (versus antagonism) as one of its five higher order domains. Within the FFM antagonism versus agreeableness domain, facets include trust, straightforwardness, tender-mindedness, modesty, compliance, and altruism. Antagonism is also included as one of five trait domains in the DSM-5 alternative diagnostic model for personality disorders (PDs), with lower order facets including manipulativeness, deceitfulness, grandiosity, attention seeking, callousness, and hostility (American Psychiatric Association (APA), 2013). Antagonism is implicated in several psychiatric disorders and many maladaptive behaviors, suggesting it is a highly relevant personality domain to consider clinically (Miller, Lynam, & Jones, 2008; Ruiz, Pincus, & Schinka, 2008; Samuel & Widiger, 2008).

While historically there was pessimism toward the effectiveness of psychotherapy for treating personality pathology, recent evidence suggests that cognitive behavioral therapy (CBT) shows promise (e.g., Hadjipavlou & Ogrodniczuk, 2010). For instance, in an randomized control trial (RCT) comparing CBT with treatment as usual (TAU) in 106 patients with borderline PD (BPD), the CBT group demonstrated significantly more improvement in levels of distress, maladaptive cognitions, state anxiety, and suicidal acts (Davidson, Tyrer et al., 2006; Davidson, Norrie et al., 2006). A therapy combining elements of CBT and Dialectical Behavior Therapy was compared to TAU in patients with BPD, and patients who received this treatment demonstrated significantly fewer acts of self-harm (Tyrer et al., 2004). Additionally, while intervention studies specifically focused on trait antagonism have not been conducted, the extant literature provides preliminary evidence that antagonism and other pathological traits may be modified within CBT treatment. In an investigation of group CBT for Social Anxiety Disorder, significant improvements in the trust facet of agreeableness (versus antagonism) in addition to neuroticism occurred (Glinski & Page, 2010). In a sample of patients receiving treatment for major depression, PD symptoms significantly reduced over the 18 months of treatment (Mulder, Joyce, & Frampton, 2010). In sum, the extant empirical literature suggests there is promise in the use of CBT for treating personality pathology.

The Handbook of Antagonism. https://doi.org/10.1016/B978-0-12-814627-9.00024-4

Dimensional models and PD treatment

The bulk of the empirical literature has focused on the use of CBT for specific categorical PD diagnoses (e.g., Davidson, Tyrer et al., 2006; Davidson, Norrie et al., 2006; Tyrer et al., 2004). However, it is notable that there is long-standing consensus regarding the limitations of a categorical approach to personality pathology diagnosis and a call to shift to a dimensional model (e.g., Clark, 2007; Frances, 1993; Widiger & Samuel, 2005). Dimensional models provide several advantages, including being more consistent with empirical evidence and representing patterns of comorbidity and providing improved coverage (Krueger & Tackett, 2003; Lynam & Widiger, 2007; Trull & Durrett, 2005). As noted previously, the DSM-5 includes an alternative model of PDs in Section III, which consists of a dimensional pathological personality trait model and a personality impairment rating system (APA, 2013). This model includes five trait domains, including negative affectivity, detachment, antagonism, disinhibition, and psychoticism. Within the model, six DSM-IV PDs are retained: Antisocial, Avoidant, Borderline, Narcissistic, Obsessive-compulsive, and Schizotypal. Each is defined by a specific set of traits and impairments, with three of the six including antagonism traits including Antisocial PD, Borderline PD, and Narcissistic PD. The shift toward dimensional models of personality pathology holds much promise for informing clinical interventions. As such, the approach described in this chapter will describe how a general CBT framework can be used to inform selection of CBT treatment components that can be combined for a patient presenting with clinically significant antagonistic traits.

CBT for antagonism

CBT is informed by Beck's cognitive therapy (1963, 1976) and Ellis' rational emotive behavior therapy (1957, 1994). This approach posits that maladaptive cognitions and negative self-views can result in distress and problematic behaviors. CBT uses the "ABC model," in which A represents an activating event, B represents beliefs, and C represents consequences, which can be emotional, behavioral, or physiological. CBT is a strong model for treatment of antagonism as it has shown promise in treating personality pathology and can be significantly tailored to focus on a variety of cognitions (the "B") and intervention techniques throughout the ABC sequence. This model is typically initially used to identify and intervene upon negative automatic thoughts, which are cognitions or images that occur spontaneously in response to an event or trigger, as well as their causes and consequences. As treatment progresses, CBT focuses increasingly on identifying and intervening on deeper and more generalized cognitions, such as negative core beliefs or early maladaptive schemas (EMSs), which are pervasive patterns of cognitions and associated phenomena (e.g., emotions, bodily sensations, and memories) that integrate and attach meaning to events. Schema therapy, an integrative therapy that utilizes CBT concepts, posits that EMSs arise from early interactions with important others, and produce dysfunctional interpretations and judgments in a broad array of situations throughout life, leading to maladaptive emotional and behavioral patterns. While core beliefs and EMSs are often entrenched, they are thought to be reinforced by behavioral, cognitive, and emotional elements that can be directly targeted and modified within treatment. Patients with antagonism often have complex presentations, and the empirical and clinical literature has not provided a validated treatment protocol for this specific presenting problem. However, within CBT for personality pathology, rigorous assessment and case conceptualization can guide treatment planning and use of multiple CBT components to successfully address therapy goals for individuals high on antagonism traits.

Assessment and case conceptualization

CBT treatment for antagonism should begin with a thorough assessment in order to inform case conceptualization and treatment planning. Assessment should include presenting problems and history of these difficulties, and assessment of the chronicity and severity of antagonism traits. An initial clinical interview should include assessment of the patient's developmental history, including family history, experiences of abuse/trauma, and early life experiences, as well as impairment, including interpersonal and other difficulties in functioning. The presence of comorbidity should be assessed, as depression, anxiety, and substance use symptoms are frequently comorbid with personality pathology (e.g., McGlashan et al., 2000).

It can be beneficial to include a validated self-report measure of antagonism. The most widely used measure of the FFM is the NEO PI-R (Costa & McCrae, 1992), a 240-item self-report measure that provides the 5 domains and 30 lower order facets. Recently, open access measures developed from the International Personality Item Pool have been developed to represent the NEO PI-R and the 60- and 120-item measures demonstrate strong reliability and validity (Maples, Guan, Carter, & Miller, 2014; Maples-Keller et al., 2017). Facet-level antagonism traits may help identify a more specific understanding of problematic behavioral manifestations to inform case conceptualization (Miller et al., 2008; Miller, Flory, Lynam, & Leukefeld, 2003). Another self-report option is the Personality Inventory for DSM-5 (PID-5; Krueger, Derringer, Markon, Watson, & Skodol, 2012), which was developed to measure the DSM-5 alternative PD trait model. This measure is 220 items and includes antagonism facets of manipulativeness, deceitfulness, grandiosity, attention seeking, callousness, and hostility, as well as assessment of the other domains. Twenty-five and 100-item versions of the PID-5 are available if time is limited (Krueger et al., 2012; Maples et al., 2015). Semistructured interviews for personality pathology can be considered within initial assessment (Widiger & Lowe, 2008), as well as self-report measures that assess for dysfunctional beliefs; potential options include the PD Belief Questionnaire (Arntz, Dreessen, Schouten, & Weertman, 2004) or the Young Schema Questionnaire (Young & Brown, 1999).

It is also highly recommended to consider collecting multiple sources of data for the assessment of patients presenting with antagonistic traits. This can include behavioral observations and self- and informant-report on measures. PDs have often been assumed to be characterized by lack of insight, recent research suggests individuals high on antagonism-related personality pathology are capable of reporting accurately when there are not direct consequences of accurate reporting (Miller, Jones, & Lynam, 2011). However, empirical evidence suggests that individuals and informants have access to different types of information (Ready, Watson, & Clark, 2002) so both can be valuable in informing treatment (Oltmanns & Turkheimer, 2009; Ready et al., 2002). Finally, we note that assessment should be ongoing, and ideally symptoms should be monitored periodically over the course of treatment.

A thorough case conceptualization based on assessment results is an important step in informing a treatment plan. CBT for antagonism represents a structured approach based on an individualized case conceptualization focused on specific treatment goals. This conceptualization will include information on how antagonistic and other personality traits manifest in different contexts, how they relate to impairment, as well as problematic behavioral targets and potential current reinforcers, maladaptive cognitions and schemas, and other specific treatment targets. The case conceptualization can be used as a tool to select and link specific CBT strategies to cognitive and behavioral targets. Patient and therapist should discuss and agree on clearly defined, specific treatment goals. This can be particularly relevant to CBT for antagonism, as patients may be focused on acute symptom relief or addressing specific interpersonal difficulties, or on more long-standing personality and behavioral patterns. Given that antagonistic individuals may demonstrate difficulties with compliance, it is important to socialize the patient to CBT as an active and goal-oriented approach that involves regular homework outside of session. Expectations for treatment, homework, and attendance should be made clear from the outset of treatment.

Therapeutic alliance

In all psychotherapy, building rapport and a strong therapeutic alliance is important, but it may be particularly crucial when engaging with individuals high on antagonistic traits who may present with maladaptive interpersonal cognitions and behaviors. Personality pathology generally can bring strain to the therapeutic alliance and antagonistic traits may be particularly impactful on a therapeutic relationship (Bender, 2005). A study of CBT for pain found that higher agreeableness predicted more positive ratings of therapy sessions (Green, Hadjistavropoulos, & Sharpe, 2008). Another study of CBT for Major Depressive Disorder found that lower scores on the trust facet were associated with being more likely to respond to pharmacotherapy than CBT, leading the authors to highlight the importance of the therapeutic alliance (Bagby et al., 2008). Instilling a sense of collaboration and a nonjudgmental therapeutic approach to strengthen therapeutic alliance at the onset of treatment can mitigate the impact of interpersonal dysfunction.

Our conceptualization of effective CBT interventions for antagonism is based on a few different modern CBT approaches: cognitive therapy (CT) of PDs (Beck, Davis, & Freeman, 2015), schema therapy (Keulen-de Vos et al., 2017; Young, Klosko, & Weishaar, 2003), and cognitive behavioral approaches to anger management (e.g., Kassinove & Tafrate, 2006). The primary goal of both CT for PDs and schema therapy is to help the patient identify and modify core maladaptive schemas. These therapies also emphasize the formation of new, healthier schemas to replace or compete with well-rehearsed maladaptive schemas, and the use of cognitive, experiential, and behavioral techniques to aid in schema change. In contrast, CBT approaches to anger management emphasize techniques to reduce the cognitive and behavioral manifestations of problematic anger, which may be an associated feature of some patients high on antagonism. Following, we review major cognitive, behavioral, and experiential techniques from the earlier approaches that may be particularly helpful for antagonistic individuals.

Cognitive techniques

The first, and arguably most important, cognitive techniques to aid patients high on antagonism are those that help them identify and label maladaptive schemas, and associated conditional beliefs, automatic thoughts, and/or schema modes. Beck's CT in general (Beck, 2011; Beck & Freeman, 1990, 2004), and in particular Beck and colleagues' CT for PDs (Beck et al., 2015) conceptualizes maladaptive thinking across three levels: (1) schemas (or core beliefs); (2) intermediate, conditional, or imperative beliefs; and (3) automatic thoughts. Therapists can provide psychoeducation on these cognitive patterns and how they interact at the beginning of therapy. Automatic thoughts are perhaps the easiest for the patient and therapist to identify and to change, and involve cognitions or images that occur spontaneously in response to an event or trigger, and then affect one's emotions and actions. Intermediate beliefs are beliefs/assumptions that one has about oneself, other people, or the world and that spring from underlying core beliefs or schemas. For example, an antagonistic patient may have a core belief, "Other people aren't trustworthy" which could manifest in the intermediate and conditional belief, "If someone is kind to me, I must put my guard up." Schemas or core beliefs are the most difficult to identify and change, and while cognitive techniques can increase intellectual understanding and change, deeper schema change often requires behavioral and experiential methods.

A number of EMSs identified by Young and colleagues (2003) may be relevant when working with antagonistic patients, including the mistrust/abuse schema, characterized by the expectation that others will abuse, hurt, or manipulate you and the entitlement/grandiosity schema, characterized by the belief that you are superior to others, entitled to special rights or consideration, and/or not bound by normal rules of social reciprocity. Other potentially relevant schemas include abandonment/instability, emotional deprivation, defectiveness/shame, social isolation/alienation, failure, insufficient self-control/self-discipline, negativity/pessimism, unrelenting standards/hypercriticalness, and punitiveness (Young et al., 2003). However, Keulen-de Vos et al. (2017) note that patients with aggressive PDs (and therefore likely high on antagonism), such as those with antisocial, borderline, or narcissistic traits, may have so many EMSs that directly focusing on schemas in therapy can be confusing and counterproductive. Instead, these authors suggest helping the patient identify their most common schema modes, defined as momentary emotional states and coping responses emanating from a currently activated schema that temporarily dominate a person's thoughts, feelings, and behavior (Young et al., 2003). They note that schema modes are largely dissociated from one another, indicating a patient may have little awareness of the other modes when he or she is expressing a particular mode. Young and colleagues (2003) group schema modes into four separate categories: child modes, dysfunctional coping modes, dysfunctional parent modes, and the healthy adult mode. Common modes for antagonistic individuals are likely to include the Angry Child mode, which is characterized by rage about unmet emotional needs, the Detached Protector which involves withdrawing psychologically from the pain of the schema by detaching, abusing substances, avoiding others, or escaping in some other way, and the Overcompensator mode, which is characterized by mistreating others or acting in extreme ways in order to disprove a schema. Other authors have identified a number of schema modes that may be more common in antisocial patients, many of which are likely high on antagonism, which include self-aggrandizer mode, predator mode, bully and attack mode, and conning and manipulative mode (Bernstein, Arntz, & Vos, 2007; Keulen-de Vos et al., 2017).

A number of cognitive techniques can be used to increase the patient's awareness of these cognitive patterns and begin to help them counter them. Thoughts records filled out over the course of the week that involve recording and labeling schemas, modes, or other types of cognitive content can aid the patient in identifying these phenomena in their everyday life. In session, Socratic questioning or guided discovery can be used to help the patient uncover underlying schemas and core beliefs that they may not be fully aware of. One method of doing this is the downward arrow technique (Beck, 1979; Burns, 1980), in which the therapist (and later the patient themselves) delves beneath surface-level or automatic thoughts by asking the patient questions such as "if this were true, what would it mean about you?," or "if that were true, what might happen?" repeatedly, uncovering successive layers of intermediate thoughts, and eventually core beliefs.

Once problematic cognitions have been identified, a number of methods can be used to help the patient increase their cognitive flexibility and consider alternative ways of thinking. It is advisable to avoid taking an approach that attempts to prove the patients' thoughts are wrong, as particularly with antagonistic clients this is likely to engender defensiveness and attempts to prove themselves right. Rather, helping the patient consider a variety of alternative explanations or interpretations through brainstorming, and helping them adopt different perspectives is likely to be most helpful. It may be beneficial to discuss pros and cons of believing certain thoughts, or of acting as though such thoughts are true. For instance, an antagonistic individual may believe their negative perceptions of other people may be valid or accurate, but the pros and cons or helpfulness of behavior based on these thoughts might be explored. The therapist can also introduce certain categories of schemas or thought distortions (e.g., overgeneralizing, mind-reading) to aid the patient in identifying how their thinking patterns may not be considering all the information. Like traditional CT, Socratic questioning and comparing the evidence for and against a certain thought can be helpful to increase this flexibility as well. This technique may not result in changing a patient's thought patterns completely, but can help scale back extreme interpretations or decrease cognitive rigidity. Once the patient has identified common patterns of thought distortions or problematic schema interpretations, a technique to help them generalize this knowledge is the use of coping cards or schema flashcards, in which the patient carries one or more cards that aid them in on-the-spot coaching of considering alternative explanations for predictable stressful situations or events.

Behavioral techniques

Insight into the nature of problematic behaviors, as well as their associated thoughts, emotions, and sometimes physical sensations, is usually necessary for effective behavior change. The therapist can aid the patient in gaining this insight through multiple within- and outside-of-session techniques.

Behavioral chain analysis

Behavioral chain analysis (i.e., functional analysis) can be a useful tool to build awareness around the antecedents and consequences of behaviors that have been identified as problematic (Linehan, 1993). This approach includes a step-by-step analysis of the chain of events before, during, and after a problem behavior occurs (e.g., drinking too much) with the goal of determining specific vulnerability factors that increase the likelihood of a behavior occurring and identifying consequences of that behavior. This enables determination of how the behavior may be reinforced and increases awareness of the detrimental effects of the behavior. Chain analyses can help to increase motivation to change unhelpful behaviors and promote problem-solving interventions aimed at behavior change. The use of chain analysis to treat antagonism can help both therapist and client to better understand vulnerability factors and emotional experiences that may precede antagonistic behavior, increasing awareness of the potential motivation behind such behavior (e.g., engaging in attention-seeking behavior to avoid high levels of anxiety). Chain analysis will also aid in identifying previously unknown reinforcers to the antagonistic behavior (e.g., getting more attention from a loved one as a result of a hostile behavior). Importantly, this technique will also highlight unhelpful consequences of the behavior (e.g., feeling shame) and initiate therapeutic discussion around potential alternative behaviors or choices that could have positively altered the outcome. For example, if an antagonistic patient has committed an aggressive act such as an argument or physical fight with another person, the therapist can help them identify antecedent vulnerability factors (e.g., getting little sleep the night before, substance intoxication, recent reprimand from a superior at work), as well as one or more prompting events (e.g., a perceived insult from a co-worker) that preceded the behavior. Subsequently, the therapist can aid the patient in identifying the chain of interrelated thoughts, emotions, physical sensations, and behaviors that led to the target behavior, followed by the consequences, both short- and long-term. It can often be helpful to map the chain visually on a white board or large pad of paper to help the patient visualize the sequence. Together, the patient and the therapist can brainstorm ideas for alternative thoughts and behaviors. This technique can be used regardless of whether the patient sees his or her target behavior as inherently problematic, as long as the patient can agree that their behavior interferes with accomplishment of long- or short-term goals (e.g., being fired from a job, losing a relationship, being incarcerated).

Behavioral experiments

Once problematic target behaviors and behavioral patterns have been effectively identified, multiple behavioral interventions can be used to address these behaviors. Behavioral experiments, or activities designed to help patients' test-out maladaptive beliefs, can be an invaluable tool with antagonistic patients. For example, the belief, "If I help someone else out, they will take advantage of me," could be tested by doing small good deeds for strangers, followed by favors for friends, colleagues, and family members and examining how the results confirm or disconfirm this belief. Ideally, behavioral experiments should be performed in a repeated and systematic manner across multiple contexts to be most effective. Relatedly, in vivo exposure or activities can be planned or performed within or between sessions to aid the patient in confronting avoided situations or responding differently when maladaptive beliefs or schemas are activated. For instance, antagonistic individuals may be more likely to interpret ambiguous events in a hostile manner and thus react aggressively, so the patient can plan to react in a nonaggressive manner to test whether a different outcome than expected occurs. Between sessions, simple homework activities can be assigned, or depending on the nature of the behavior, activity scheduling can be used to help the patient problem-solve when and how often they will engage in planned behaviors. New behavioral patterns are most likely to be maintained if they practiced repeatedly across diverse contexts.

Behavioral rehearsal and role-playing

If behaviors are difficult to perform in a planned manner in real life, imaginal exposure/behavioral rehearsal and/or role-playing can be used to aid in behavioral practice. For instance, if a patient wishes to practice alternative responses when physically provoked or insulted by others, the therapist can "play" the provocateur or aid the patient in engaging in covert modeling (i.e., imagining how they would act). There is some evidence that imaginal exposure to anger-provoking situations can lead to clinically significant reductions in problematic anger responses (Fuller, DiGiuseppe, O'Leary, Fountain, & Lang, 2010; Grodnitzky & Tafrate, 2001). Therapists could guide patients through imagining past anger-provoking situations repeatedly to aid in extinction of classically conditioned anger or aggression. In combination with the previous strategies, therapists can coach the patient in various behavioral skills as needed based on case conceptualization.

Coping skills

An important part of CBT is enhancing one's coping skills for managing distress and effectively handling situations. Building a client's toolbox with many different skills is critical since what skill is useful will vary by context. This will need to be individualized based on the client. Following is a brief (nonexhaustive) list of common coping skills that could be relevant in CBT for antagonism.

Emotion regulation skills

Teaching clients how to identify and label emotions, understand vulnerability factors that impact emotional reactions and behavior, and engage in specific strategies for managing emotions; some examples include perspective taking, problem solving, and acting opposite to unhelpful emotional urges.

Distress tolerance skills

Teaching clients skills to survive strong emotional experiences without making the situation worse; some examples include distraction, self-soothing, grounding, exercise, and focused breathing.

Relaxation skills

Teaching clients various strategies to enhance relaxation during times of distress or to reduce vulnerability to getting distressed; some examples include diaphragmatic breathing, progressive muscle relaxation, and imagery.

Interpersonal skills

For clients with specific difficulties interpersonally, various interpersonal skills may be important (e.g., assertiveness training, psychoeducation about communication styles and effective approaches). This is likely to be particularly relevant for CBT for antagonism. Therapy will be an opportunity for appropriate modeling of communication and interpersonal style; for example, with an overly hostile client, remaining calm and modeling how you may have communicated in a specific situation could enable the client to see alternative ways to approach a situation.

Mindfulness skills

Mindfulness is a technique of bringing one's attention on the present moment, experiencing reality as it is in a nonjudgmental way. Through the practice of mindfulness, clients increase awareness of emotional and physiological states, thoughts, and behaviors. The practice of mindfulness also helps clients to gain more control over where their attention lies and fully participate in life with awareness, rather than getting stuck in the past or the future. In the therapy context, mindfulness can serve as a behavioral exposure to emotions or sensations or thoughts that may usually be avoided by the individual. Over time, exposure to nonjudgmentally observing and experiencing these emotions, sensations, or thoughts can lead to habituation and learning, reducing avoidance behavior over time. In the context of treating antagonism, mindfulness may be helpful in enhancing clients' willingness to feel vulnerable emotions that were previously less tolerable and avoided (e.g., sadness, anxiety, shame).

Once a client has mastered a number of coping skills, it can be helpful to assist the client in planning ahead and creating coping cards that detail the coping skills to use in a given situation. This can be helpful to return to for ideas following a behavioral chain analysis, especially if certain barriers to engaging in coping skills are identified.

Experiential techniques

Traditional cognitive behavioral techniques are important for antagonistic patients, but sometimes not sufficient for deeper belief or personality change. Experiential techniques used in schema therapy and CT for PDs (Beck et al., 2015; Young et al., 2003) can be implemented with antagonistic patients to help patients overcome emotional avoidance and transform maladaptive schemas. Many of these techniques involve evoking imagery from childhood and/or of interactions with early caregivers, when maladaptive schemas begin to be formed. Imagery may be used early in therapy as a method for helping patients identify EMSs by asking them to imagine a situation in which they were distressed in the presence of a caregiver, and helping them identify what developmental needs (e.g., closeness, protection, esteem) were not being fulfilled (Young et al., 2003). Later, imagery rescripting can be used to change the outcome of the memory, with either the therapist entering the image and meeting the patient's unmet need (an aspect of "limited reparenting"; Young et al., 2003), and/or the patient's healthy adult self entering the image meeting the needs of their young self. For example, an antagonistic patient with an emotional deprivation schema, who expects that no one will be able to meet his or her emotion needs, may have memories of his/her emotions being ignored or invalidated by early caregivers. The therapist may have the patient imagine such a memory, and first describe themselves (the therapist) entering the memory and providing emotional validation and support to the patient as a young child. Next, it may be helpful for the patient to imagine their adult self entering the memory and providing such support, whether through kind attention, verbal validation, or supportive physical touch. These techniques can help the patient emotionally process wounds from childhood, and increase felt awareness of how these wounds affect their current functioning. While the "old learning" of the EMS is not erased, new healthier schemas can compete with and inhibit the old (Bouton, 2002; Craske et al., 2008), giving the patient flexibility and control over cognitive and emotional responses.

Another useful experiential technique is two-chair or schema dialog work, therapy techniques inspired by Gestalt therapy and psychodrama. Using these techniques, the therapist helps the patient enact different schemas or different schema modes, switching chairs or positions as he or she "embodies" each mode. This can be used to have the patient role-play the conflict between different schema modes in regard to current difficulties, or to role-play real or created situations that occurred between the patient and a caregiver or within themselves. For instance, an antagonistic individual who experiences intense rage in regard to perceived lack of emotional support from a spouse and also acts in ways to mistreat or be hostile to the spouse following distressing conflict may role-play a recent conflict from both the Angry Child mode and the Overcompensator mode. This technique again helps the patient evoke powerful emotions and "hot" cognitions, and truly feel their schemas or modes, in a way that mere discussion or Socratic questioning often cannot. Similarly, patients can be assigned to write letters to past caregivers, younger selves, or aspects of themselves as homework exercises that are then read and discussed in session.

Potential challenges

Personality pathology demonstrates a high level of comorbidity with other mental health difficulties (e.g., Lenzenweger, Lane, Loranger, & Kessler, 2007), and issues related to antagonism and other personality pathology may demonstrate a chronic history, as such antagonistic individuals may require longer treatment than a typical short-term course of CBT. Due to the key features of antagonism, antagonistic individuals may present to treatment due to pressure from a spouse or family member or due to a legal requirement, which may impact motivation or validity of patient's reporting. Antagonistic individuals may be noncompliant with treatment. If noncompliance occurs, it can be approached from a CBT approach in which the therapist can query regarding specific thoughts surrounding homework completion and treatment. Antagonistic individuals may also be more likely to act out within the therapeutic context (Bennett, Parry, & Ryle, 2006), as such clear and consistent boundaries should be enforced. Antagonistic individuals may be more difficult patients; therapists should be aware of their own emotional reactions during treatment and the potential for burnout (Colli, Tanzilli, Dimaggio, & Lingiardi, 2014). Therapists should consider ongoing self-care and consultation. The therapeutic relationship can be considered within treatment as an opportunity for modeling interpersonal skills and communication strategies within sessions.

Conclusion and future directions

Despite a history of pessimism toward the effectiveness of psychotherapy for personality pathology, recent evidence suggests CBT shows promise in treating personality pathology. Following a thorough assessment and case conceptualization, treatment planning can occur in which different components of CBT are used to address specific treatment goals for individuals high on antagonism traits. Most existing research has focused on CBT for a specific categorical PD diagnosis. With the impending shift to a dimensional model of personality pathology, rigorous studies of treatment outcome in CBT for dimensional personality traits such as antagonism are needed, as these dimensional models hold much promise for informing effective CBT-focused interventions.

References

American Psychiatric Association (APA). (2013). *Diagnostic and statistical manual of mental disorders, 5.*

Arntz, A., Dreessen, L., Schouten, E., & Weertman, A. (2004). Beliefs in personality disorders: a test with the personality disorder belief questionnaire. *Behaviour Research and Therapy, 42*(10), 1215–1225.

Bagby, R. M., Quilty, L. C., Segal, Z. V., McBride, C. C., Kennedy, S. H., & Costa, P. T., Jr. (2008). Personality and differential treatment response in major depression: a randomized controlled trial comparing cognitive-behavioural therapy and pharmacotherapy. *The Canadian Journal of Psychiatry, 53*(6), 361–370.

Beck, A. T. (1963). Thinking and depression: 1. Idiosyncratic content and cognitive distortions. *Archives of General Psychiatry, 9*, 324–333.

Beck, A. T. (1976). *Cognitive therapy and the emotional disorders.* New York: Penguin Books.

Beck, A. T. (1979). *Cognitive therapy and the emotional disorders.* New York: Meridian.

Beck, J. S. (2011). *Cognitive therapy for challenging problems: What to do when the basics don't work.* Guilford Press.

Beck, A. T., Davis, D. D., & Freeman, A. (Eds.), (2015). *Cognitive therapy of personality disorders*: Guilford Publications.

Beck, A. T., & Freeman, A. (1990). *Cognitive therapy of personality disorders.* New York: Guilford.

Beck, A. T., & Freeman, A. (2004). *Cognitive therapy of personality disorders.* New York: Guilford.

Bender, D. S. (2005). The therapeutic alliance in the treatment of personality disorders. *Journal of Psychiatric Practice, 11*(2), 73–87.

Bennett, D., Parry, G., & Ryle, A. (2006). Resolving threats to the therapeutic alliance in cognitive analytic therapy of borderline personality disorder: a task analysis. *Psychology and Psychotherapy: Theory, Research and Practice, 79*(3), 395–418.

Bernstein, D. P., Arntz, A., & Vos, M. D. (2007). Schema focused therapy in forensic settings: theoretical model and recommendations for best clinical practice. *International Journal of Forensic Mental Health, 6*(2), 169–183.

Bouton, M. E. (2002). Context, ambiguity, and unlearning: sources of relapse after behavioral extinction. *Biological Psychiatry, 52*(10), 976–986.

Burns, D. D. (1980). *Feeling good: The new mood therapy.* New York: William Morrow.

Clark, L. A. (2007). Assessment and diagnosis of personality disorder: perennial issues and an emerging reconceptualization. *Annual Review of Psychology, 58*, 227–257.

Colli, A., Tanzilli, A., Dimaggio, G., & Lingiardi, V. (2014). Patient personality and therapist response: an empirical investigation. *American Journal of Psychiatry, 171*(1), 102–108 [Chicago].

Costa, P. T., Jr., & McCrae, R. R. (1992). The five-factor model of personality and its relevance to personality disorders. *Journal of Personality Disorders, 6*(4), 343–359.

Craske, M. G., Kircanski, K., Zelikowsky, M., Mystkowski, J., Chowdhury, N., & Baker, A. (2008). Optimizing inhibitory learning during exposure therapy. *Behaviour Research and Therapy, 46*(1), 5–27.

Davidson, K., Norrie, J., Tyrer, P., Gumley, A., Tata, P., Murray, H., et al. (2006). The effectiveness of cognitive behavior therapy for borderline personality disorder: results from the borderline personality disorder study of cognitive therapy (BOSCOT) trial. *Journal of Personality Disorders, 20*(5), 450–465.

Davidson, K., Tyrer, P., Gumley, A., Tata, P., Norrie, J., Palmer, S., et al. (2006). A randomized controlled trial of cognitive behavior therapy for borderline personality disorder: rationale for trial, method, and description of sample. *Journal of Personality Disorders*, *20*(5), 431–449.

Ellis, A. (1957). Rational psychotherapy and individual psychology. *Journal of Individual Psychology*, *13*(1), 38.

Ellis, A. (1994). *Reason and emotion in psychotherapy: Comprehensive method of treating human disturbances: Revised and updated*. New York, NY: Citadel Press.

Frances, A. (1993). Dimensional diagnosis of personality—not whether, but when and which. *Psychological Inquiry*, *4*(2), 110–111.

Fuller, J. R., DiGiuseppe, R., O'Leary, S., Fountain, T., & Lang, C. (2010). An open trial of a comprehensive anger treatment program on an outpatient sample. *Behavioural and Cognitive Psychotherapy*, *38*(4), 485–490.

Glinski, K., & Page, A. C. (2010). Modifiability of neuroticism, extraversion, and agreeableness by group cognitive behaviour therapy for social anxiety disorder. *Behaviour Change*, *27*(1), 42–52.

Green, S. M., Hadjistavropoulos, T., & Sharpe, D. (2008). Client personality characteristics predict satisfaction with cognitive behavior therapy. *Journal of Clinical Psychology*, *64*(1), 40–51.

Grodnitzky, G. R., & Tafrate, R. (2001). Imaginal exposure for anger reduction in adult outpatients: a pilot study. *Journal of Behavior Therapy and Experimental Psychiatry*, *31*, 259–291.

Hadjipavlou, G., & Ogrodniczuk, J. S. (2010). Promising psychotherapies for personality disorders. *The Canadian Journal of Psychiatry*, *55*(4), 202–210.

Kassinove, H., & Tafrate, R. C. (2006). Anger-related disorders: basic issues, models, and diagnostic considerations. In E. L. Feindler (Ed.), *Anger related disorders: A practitioner's guide to comparative treatments* (pp. 1–27). New York, NY: Springer Publishing Co.

Keulen-de Vos, M., Bernstein, D. P., Clark, L. A., de Vogel, V., Bogaerts, S., Slaats, M., et al. (2017). Validation of the schema mode concept in personality disordered offenders. *Legal and Criminological Psychology*, *22*(2), 420–441.

Krueger, R. F., Derringer, J., Markon, K. E., Watson, D., & Skodol, A. E. (2012). Initial construction of a maladaptive personality trait model and inventory for DSM-5. *Psychological Medicine*, *42*(9), 1879–1890.

Krueger, R. F., & Tackett, J. L. (2003). Personality and psychopathology: working toward the bigger picture. *Journal of Personality Disorders*, *17*(2), 109–128 [Special issue].

Lenzenweger, M. F., Lane, M. C., Loranger, A. W., & Kessler, R. C. (2007). DSM-IV personality disorders in the National Comorbidity Survey Replication. *Biological Psychiatry*, *62*(6), 553–564.

Linehan, M. M. (1993). *Cognitive-behavioral treatment of borderline personality disorder*. Guilford press.

Lynam, D. R., & Widiger, T. A. (2007). Using a general model of personality to identify the basic elements of psychopathy. *Journal of Personality Disorders*, *21*(2), 160–178.

Maples, J. L., Carter, N. T., Few, L. R., Crego, C., Gore, W. L., Samuel, D. B., et al. (2015). Testing whether the DSM-5 personality disorder trait model can be measured with a reduced set of items: an item response theory investigation of the Personality Inventory for DSM-5. *Psychological Assessment*, *27*(4), 1195–1210.

Maples, J. L., Guan, L., Carter, N. T., & Miller, J. D. (2014). A test of the International Personality Item Pool representation of the Revised NEO Personality Inventory and development of a 120-item IPIP-based measure of the five-factor model. *Psychological Assessment*, *26*(4), 1070.

Maples-Keller, J. L., Williamson, R. L., Sleep, C. E., Carter, N. T., Campbell, W. K., & Miller, J. D. (2017). Using item response theory to develop a 60-item representation of the NEO PI–R using the International Personality Item Pool: development of the IPIP–NEO–60. *Journal of Personality Assessment*, 1–12.

McGlashan, T. H., Grilo, C. M., Skodol, A. E., Gunderson, J. G., Shea, M. T., Morey, L. C., et al. (2000). The Collaborative Longitudinal Personality Disorders Study: baseline Axis I/II and II/II diagnostic co-occurrence. *Acta Psychiatrica Scandinavica, 102*(4), 256–264.

Miller, J. D., Flory, K., Lynam, D., & Leukefeld, C. (2003). A test of the four-factor model of impulsivity-related traits. *Personality and Individual Differences, 34*, 1403–1418.

Miller, J. D., Jones, S. E., & Lynam, D. R. (2011). Psychopathic traits from the perspective of self and informant reports: is there evidence for a lack of insight? *Journal of Abnormal Psychology, 120*(3), 758.

Miller, J. D., Lynam, D. R., & Jones, S. (2008). Externalizing behavior through the lens of the five-factor model: a focus on agreeableness and conscientiousness. *Journal of Personality Assessment, 90*(2), 158–164.

Mulder, R. T., Joyce, P. R., & Frampton, C. M. A. (2010). Personality disorders improve in patients treated for major depression. *Acta Psychiatrica Scandinavica, 122*(3), 219–225.

Oltmanns, T. F., & Turkheimer, E. (2009). Person perception and personality pathology. *Current Directions in Psychological Science, 18*(1), 32–36.

Ready, R. E., Watson, D., & Clark, L. A. (2002). Psychiatric patient- and informant-reported personality: predicting concurrent and future behavior. *Assessment, 9*(4), 361–372.

Ruiz, M. A., Pincus, A. L., & Schinka, J. A. (2008). Externalizing pathology and the five-factor model: a meta-analysis of personality traits associated with antisocial personality disorder, substance use disorder, and their co-occurrence. *Journal of Personality Disorders, 22*(4), 365–388.

Samuel, D. B., & Widiger, T. A. (2008). A meta-analytic review of the relationships between the five-factor model and DSM-IV-TR personality disorders: a facet level analysis. *Clinical Psychology Review, 28*(8), 1326–1342.

Trull, T. J., & Durrett, C. A. (2005). Categorical and dimensional models of personality disorder. *Annual Review of Clinical Psychology, 1*, 355–380.

Tyrer, P., Tom, B., Byford, S., Schmidt, U., Jones, V., Davidson, K., et al. (2004). Differential effects of manual assisted cognitive behavior therapy in the treatment of recurrent deliberate self-harm and personality disturbance: the POPMACT study. *Journal of Personality Disorders, 18*(1), 102–116.

Widiger, T. A., & Lowe, J. R. (2008). A dimensional model of personality disorder: proposal for DSM-V. *Psychiatric Clinics of North America, 31*(3), 363–378.

Widiger, T. A., & Samuel, D. B. (2005). Diagnostic categories or dimensions? A question for the Diagnostic and statistical manual of mental disorders. *Journal of Abnormal Psychology, 114*(4), 494.

Young, J. E., & Brown, G. (1999). Young schema questionnaire. In J. E. Young (Ed.), *Cognitive therapy for personality disorders: A schema-focused approach* (3rd ed.). Sarasota, FL: Professional Resource Press.

Young, J. E., Klosko, J. S., & Weishaar, M. E. (2003). *Schema therapy: A practitioner's guide*. Guilford Press.

Addressing antagonism in a Dialectical Behavior Therapy framework

25

*Sarah Fischer**, *Joanna Marino*†
*Department of Psychology, George Mason University, Fairfax, VA, United States,
†Potomac Behavioral Solutions, Arlington, VA, United States

Antagonism can be characterized as low Agreeableness. Antagonistic individuals are described as callous, manipulative, and display low levels of concern for other people (Miller & Lynam, 2001; Ozer & Benet-Martinez, 2006; Widiger, Lynam, Miller, & Oltmanns, 2012). Antagonism or low Agreeableness is a core feature of Cluster B personality disorders (PDs), in particular antisocial, narcissistic, and borderline personality disorders (BPD). As personality traits are best modeled as dimensions, there is a high degree of overlap between PD diagnoses (Kotov et al., 2017; Krueger & Markon, 2014; Livesley & Jackson, 2009). Someone with low Agreeableness may exhibit many features of several Cluster B PDs, and thus may meet diagnostic criteria for more than one. Dialectical Behavior Therapy (DBT) is a comprehensive outpatient treatment model that was developed to address suicidal behavior in women with BPD (Linehan, 1993). Given the high degree of overlap between symptoms and features of Cluster B PDs, DBT may also be used to treat pathology associated with antagonism.

What is DBT?

DBT is an outpatient psychosocial treatment that incorporates cognitive behavioral principles with acceptance-based skills, originating in Buddhist philosophy and meditation practices. It was designed for the treatment of recurrent suicidal or self-injurious behavior in BPD and has been examined in at least eight randomized controlled trials, and several other less methodologically rigorous outcome studies (Koons et al., 2001; Linehan et al., 2006; Linehan, Armstrong, Suarez, Allmon, & Heard, 1991; Verheul et al., 2003). Based on findings that this treatment significantly reduces self-injurious behavior, suicide attempts, and hospitalization, DBT is currently considered the most effective treatment available for BPD.

DBT is based on a dialectical philosophy, and dialectics are woven throughout the treatment protocol and therapist client relationship. The dialectic present in all interventions in DBT is the balance of acceptance and change. Clients are encouraged to accept and tolerate the intense emotions that they experience or thoughts that arise in response to these emotions, while at the same time changing their behavioral response

The Handbook of Antagonism. https://doi.org/10.1016/B978-0-12-814627-9.00025-6

to these experiences. Thus therapists alternate between validating emotions and problem-solving maladaptive behavioral responses to negative affect. The therapeutic components of DBT reflect this underlying philosophy (Linehan, 1993; Linehan & Dexter-Mazza, 2008).

DBT consists of individual therapy sessions, skills group training sessions, coaching calls, a therapist consultation group, and contact with other ancillary treatment providers, such as a physician managing medications. Individual therapy sessions address treatment targets in several stages. Stage 1 treatment targets include suicidal or self-injurious behavior or thoughts, therapy-interfering behavior, quality-of-life interfering behavior, and the building of adaptive skills. The overall goal of therapy is to "create a life worth living." Suicidal or self-injurious behaviors are always addressed first in therapy, and if they occur over the week, first in each session. Therapy-interfering behaviors, which can be defined as skipping skills group, not doing homework, or arriving late to session, are addressed next in priority. If these two issues have been adequately addressed in session or have not occurred, the next treatment target for each session and in Stage 1 of treatment are quality-of-life interfering behaviors. Examples of quality-of-life interfering behaviors include compulsive spending, eating disorder symptoms, other Axis I symptoms, or interpersonal problems (Linehan, 1993; Linehan & Dexter-Mazza, 2008).

Skills group training sessions include acceptance and change-based interventions grouped into four main skills areas. *Mindfulness skills* are reviewed in between every skills module. The goal of mindfulness training is to increase awareness of and acceptance of thoughts and emotions. These skills are necessary in order to utilize change-based strategies; before one can respond to an emotion adaptively one must know what the emotion is. *Emotion regulation skills* consist of strategies for reducing long-term vulnerability to negative affect. *Distress tolerance skills* are also called *crisis survival* skills and consist of skills for managing intense urges to engage in maladaptive behaviors when emotions have already become escalated. Finally, *interpersonal effectiveness skills* are relationship-building techniques for asserting oneself effectively, creating balance, and validating others (Linehan, 1993; Linehan & Dexter-Mazza, 2008).

In-session interventions/strategies consist of a balance of acceptance and change strategies. For example, communication from therapist to client alternates between irreverence and validation. Irreverence consists of bluntness, "calling a spade a spade," and the use of humor and extension (i.e., taking the consequences of a client's extreme or emotionally driven expression more seriously than the client intended). Validation consists of finding the "kernel of truth" in what the client is experiencing and acknowledging it. Therapy is collaborative and has a behavioral focus. The client and therapist work to identify target behaviors that are consistent with Stage 1 goals and monitor these behaviors on a diary card, which the client fills out each week. Functional analysis of target behaviors is utilized as a primary change-based strategy (Linehan, 1993; Linehan & Dexter-Mazza, 2008). Following, we describe why DBT may be an effective paradigm to address pathology associated with antagonism.

Why DBT?

The primary reason that DBT may be an effective treatment for pathology associated with antagonism is that people with high levels of antagonism are already enrolled in treatment trials of DBT and appear to benefit from it. A significant percentage of individuals in some randomized controlled trials of DBT for BPD include participants who also have a diagnosis of antisocial PD (APD), which is characterized by high levels of antagonism. For example, in a 2-year randomized controlled trial (RCT) for BPD comparing DBT to community treatment by experts, 10.2% of participants in the community treatment condition and 11.5% of participants in the DBT condition also had a diagnosis of APD (Linehan et al., 2006). This trial reported all the co-occurring conditions of participants; many trials have not reported the rate of co-occurring PDs. However, it is safe to assume, given the high levels of comorbidity, that at least some participants in other RCTs of DBT have included individuals with APD and/or narcissistic personality disorder (NPD). Individuals in forensic settings (jail or prison) also tend to have high rates of APD, NPD, and high levels of antagonism. DBT has been piloted in forensic and jail settings and appears to yield some improvements in behavior violations and other target behaviors (Berzins & Trestman, 2004; Evershed et al., 2003; Moore et al., 2018; Sakdalan, Shaw, & Collier, 2010). (However, only one study conducted in this type of setting has been conducted with a control group.)

Additionally, substance use disorder diagnoses have high levels of co-occurrence with BPD and APD, and are positively associated with antagonism (e.g., Kotov, Gamez, Schmidt, & Watson, 2010). Although there is not yet one treatment for substance use disorders that appears to increase abstinence at substantially higher rates than another, some data that suggests that DBT may help reduce these symptoms (Linehan et al., 1999, 2002). Individuals in DBT may report their substance use more accurately and honestly than those in other treatment formats (Linehan et al., 2002). As people with substance use disorders and high levels of antagonism are often described as manipulative, these data are particularly notable. The increased level of honesty may be due to several treatment factors which we discuss as follows.

Third, antagonism is associated with relational impairment and people high on this trait do not perceive it as likeable, see it as impairing and desire lower levels (Lamkin, Maples-Keller, & Miller, 2018; Miller et al., 2018; Weiss, Lavner, & Miller, 2018). These data suggest that relational impairment and the perception that some elements of this trait are undesirable may enhance motivation for treatment. Low empathy, a facet of antagonism, likely contributes to relational impairment. There have been inconsistent findings regarding the nature of low levels of empathy observed in BPD, a disorder characterized by high levels of antagonism (Dinsdale & Crespi, 2013; Lazarus, Cheavens, Festa, & Rosenthal, 2014). Affective or emotional empathy refers to one's ability to share or infer the emotional state of someone else, while cognitive empathy refers to one's ability to infer and understand another person's beliefs or perspective (Davis, 1983). For example, some studies find that individuals with BPD have low levels of both cognitive empathy and emotional empathy, while others find that individuals with BPD have low cognitive empathy and high emotional empathy (Dinsdale & Crespi, 2013; Lazarus et al., 2014; Niedtfeld, 2017). Some recent studies offer potential explanations for these discrepancies. One correlational study reported that BPD features may be associated with low empathy because of the overlap between these features and callousness, noting that callousness is strongly (negatively) associated with empathy, but not other facets of antagonism (Lishner, Hong, Jiang, Vitacco, & Neumann, 2015). Another study manipulated the presence vs. absence of acute stress and observed the impact of this manipulation on empathy in BPD and control participants without PDs (Wingenfeld et al., 2018). Data indicate that individuals with BPD display similar levels of empathy as control participants in neutral conditions, but that empathy is reduced in BPD participants in stress conditions (Wingenfeld et al., 2018). This is consistent with several hypotheses articulated by Linehan (1993) and consistent with our clinical observations. Linehan posits that individuals with BPD may have higher baseline levels of arousal and emotional intensity, and are sensitive to triggers for increases in arousal and intensity. Given the frequent crisis-generating behaviors observed in this population, many individuals with BPD experience frequent stress, may not have time to fully recover from spikes in arousal, and thus find it difficult to expand the scope of their attention beyond that of a very narrow range of stimuli (Linehan, 1993). Putting these findings together, if low empathy is due to high stress and resulting hostile attributional biases, this feature of antagonism can be targeted via skills training in DBT.

Both individuals with BPD and APD may display low empathy as a component of antagonism. However, there is one significant difference in the clinical presentations of individuals with BPD and APD, related to callousness (Bateman, O'Connell, Lorenzini, Gardner, & Fonagy, 2016). It has been observed that individuals with BPD are often motivated by eliciting compassion and concern from other people, and want meaningful relationships with other people, while individuals with APD are often highly motivated by some sort of tangible gain in money, power, and so on (Bateman et al., 2016; National Institute for Health and Clinical Excellence, 2009a, 2009b). This is consistent with the finding that callousness is negatively correlated with empathy and suggests that enhancing motivation for treatment may require different skills or interventions depending upon the level of callousness the client displays. Regardless of the cause, a functional analytic approach to this type of behavior that may impair relationships may be helpful.

A full description of all interventions involved in a DBT program is beyond the scope of this chapter. However, we would like to describe some elements of the treatment that may be specifically adapted to the treatment impairment associated with antagonism.

Assessment and commitment phase—Collaboration and nonjudgmentalness

DBT contains an extensive assessment and commitment phase of therapy. In this initial stage, the client participates in an assessment of Axis I and II symptoms. Although this is typical for most treatment programs, what is not perhaps typical is giving the client direct feedback about an Axis II diagnosis. In DBT, a client who meets diagnostic criteria for a PD is given this feedback and these symptoms are reviewed with the client in a collaborative fashion. Several sessions may be devoted to discussing the assessment feedback and, in the process, establishing a commitment to treat symptoms of the Axis II disorder. Many clinicians may feel hesitation about giving a client with PDs direct feedback at the start of treatment about these symptoms. This is understandable given that therapists may fear that a client will react negatively to the diagnosis of a PD. In addition, individuals with high levels of antagonism may express hostility or may not view some PD symptoms as targets for therapeutic intervention. Thus we propose that in addition to giving feedback about the disorder, clinicians solicit information from the client about if and how symptoms are impairing functioning or interfering with the client's goals. Then, treatment can be directed toward those symptoms that the client perceives as impairing in some way. The following case example illustrates this process.

Rose was a white woman in her 20s who presented for treatment for what she described as "depression." Assessment revealed several features of Cluster B PDs. Rose reported that she had unstable interpersonal relationships characterized by hostility and frequent ruptures. She also reported suicidal thoughts and frequent drug use. Rose was open to discussion of DBT as a therapeutic intervention and readily agreed to target suicidal thoughts, behaviors, and difficulties in relationships as treatment goals. She denied, when asked in structured clinical interviews during the intake, any impulsive behavior targets other than drug use.

Following the pretreatment phase, Rose noted a fight with a family member on her diary card. Functional analysis of this fight revealed that Rose had taken a car following the fight and driven extremely fast as a stress relief. The following week she casually mentioned that she had to appear in court for reckless driving charges, but had not reported those on her diary card or mentioned them to her therapist. The week after that, during another functional analysis of a fight, Rose stated "so afterwards I just went to the mall and stole a bunch of stuff. It's a good stress relief because if you take things from the mall it's not really stealing. They're just corporations." At this point, it was apparent that Rose had not fully described several potential target behaviors during her assessment and pretreatment phase of therapy. The therapist initiated a new discussion of diary card targets and brought up reckless driving and stealing as potential points of intervention. It was apparent in this conversation that Rose had not considered these noteworthy because she did not view them as problematic, and instead viewed them as coping mechanisms. The therapist did not attempt to engage Rose in a discussion of the morality of either behavior. Instead, the therapist noted that part of having a life worth living was staying out of jail, and assessed Rose's motivation to stay out of jail. The therapist suggested targeting stealing and reckless driving as targets in order to make sure that Rose did not have further trouble with the law and could live freely. (And the client agreed to do so.) Although Rose exhibited a lax attitude toward these behaviors, it was obvious from ensuing functional analyses that they were preceded by high levels of arousal associated with anxiety, suggesting anxiety as another therapeutic target.

Related to this discussion is the importance of nonjudgmentalness. In DBT, the diagnosis of a PD is presented in a nonjudgmental fashion. Therapists may explicitly address previous statements from other treatment providers (i.e., that the client is "manipulative") or messages that the client may have received about PDs from film or other media. In fact, although it is described as a feature of antagonism, DBT therapists tend not to use the term manipulative to describe their clients as the term "manipulative" infers intent on the part of the client to use artfulness or deception to obtain a desired outcome (Linehan, 1993). However, many clients with high levels of antagonism are not particularly artful. Thus a statement such as "if you don't do X, I may as well kill myself," is actually very direct and blunt. The therapist may *feel* manipulated, but the client has actually been quite explicit in expressing their wishes. (The effectiveness of this type of communication and how it may be reinforced by the environment is another matter.) Thus using descriptive, nonjudgmental language to describe one's clients may help therapists identify explicitly what about the client causes a negative emotional reaction in others. In general, therapists convey that they are not threatened or frightened by PD diagnoses and see symptoms as problems that can be addressed collaboratively.

Our recent work implementing DBT skills in a jail setting illustrates the impact of this collaborative and nonjudgmental attitude on client engagement (Moore et al., 2018). In the most recent DBT skills manual (Linehan, 2014), an exercise exploring values clarification (e.g., Hayes, 2004) has been incorporated into the emotion regulation module. Clients may not engage in this exercise until several weeks or months into treatment in a traditional DBT outpatient setting. In a brief DBT skills group that was implemented in a jail setting, we explored values in the first session (Moore et al., 2018). All the group clients were incarcerated, for a wide variety of crimes, but were not in a long-term prison facility (i.e., jail is considered short term). In the first session, therapists posted a list of potential values and asked the group members to identify which values were important to them. They then used that values discussion as a bridge for identification of goals or behavioral targets for the skills group. For example, if family was identified as an important value, then what behaviors could we target in jail that would prevent us from being able to be with family? Although this exercise could be labeled as a skill exercise, or as motivational enhancement, we consider it part of conveying a nonjudgmental attitude toward clients with potentially high antagonism (Cameron, Palm Reed, & Gaudiano, 2014; Malouf, Youman, Harty, Schaefer, & Tangney, 2013). Many therapeutic interventions for incarcerated individuals may begin with review of what the client did wrong, and whether or not they can accept responsibility for it. We believe that beginning the skills group with a collaborative discussion of common values conveyed a message of respect for clients as human beings who have similar motivations and emotions as people who are not incarcerated (Malouf et al., 2013). Qualitative data provided by inmates at the end of the therapeutic intervention suggested that this exercise was very helpful in setting a nonjudgmental and collaborative tone. Multiple inmates commented on the respect and nonjudgmental attitude that they perceived on the part of the DBT therapists in contrast to other mental health providers in the jail setting. And, clients consistently completed homework (to the best of their ability in a jail setting) and participated in groups (Moore et al., 2018).

Given that clients are asked to commit to at least 6 months of weekly individual therapy and weekly skills group, motivation is extremely important. Some clients with high levels of antagonism may be court ordered into treatment. Earlier trials of DBT excluded clients who were court-ordered into treatment, because of the level of intrinsic motivation required to engage in the treatment program. A client who cannot commit to keeping a diary card, attending skills group, attending individual therapy, and reducing target behaviors is not an appropriate candidate for DBT. However, the assessment and commitment or pretreatment phase is designed to enhance motivation, and it is also assumed that it is the therapist's role to do everything in their power to enhance motivation and obtain commitment. Thus some of the techniques described previously may help enhance intrinsic motivation to engage with treatment, even when "forced" to do so. It is also true, however, that a DBT therapist may not choose to engage in treatment with someone following the assessment and commitment phase. It is never assumed that a client will enter treatment with a therapist during this phase until both the client and therapist have committed to working with each other in the parameters of the program.

Diary cards

Most clinicians collect some form of data on their clients throughout treatment, either via brief written self-report assessments, behavioral observations, or verbal reports in session. In DBT, data are collected each week in the form of a diary card. Clients identify target behaviors on the diary card, adaptive skills use on the diary card, and participate in functional analysis of the target behaviors with the therapist as they occur. As noted previously, some data suggests that clients with substance use disorders are actually more accurate, honest reporters of their use in this therapy program. We believe that this is because the elements of the precommitment/assessment phase described previously enhance rapport and collaboration between the client and therapist. Additionally, if clients do not complete diary cards, this behavior is labeled as therapy interfering and nothing else in the session is addressed until the diary card is completed and a functional analysis of the therapy interfering behavior is finished. This typically increases the likelihood that clients will fill out their diary cards every week, which increases self-monitoring and awareness of behavior.

Interpersonal effectiveness

Given that relationship quality is typically impaired in clients with high levels of antagonism (e.g., Miller et al., 2018; Weiss et al., 2018), interpersonal effectiveness skills may be particularly helpful. This skills module focuses on making requests or saying no effectively, using skills to maintain relationship quality, and acting in such a way in relationships that the client maintains self-respect (Linehan, 2014). The first portion of the module is designed to help the client understand how to prioritize their wants and needs in interpersonal communication. There are three types of skills: objectives effectiveness (DEAR MAN), relationship effectiveness (GIVE), and self-respect effectiveness (FAST) (Linehan, 2014). Prior to using one of these skills, the client is coached to think about their goals for the interaction and prioritize them. For example, is it more important for the client to get what they want in this particular interaction, or is it more important for the client to maintain the relationship? How may those goals be in conflict with each other?

In our experience, it is invaluable to thoroughly review the concept of identifying and prioritizing objectives for an interpersonal interaction prior to teaching the actual communication skill. Many clients have never thought about the distinction between what their tangible objective is an interaction and how the other person in an interaction may feel about them. And, many clients have never considered the possibility that how they actually make a request to another person may impact their desired outcome. The following is one illustration of this difficulty (and is also an illustration of a deficit in cognitive empathy). The client was a young woman on public assistance, who wished to obtain independent housing. In addition to other symptoms of BPD, she tended to have a hostile attribution bias toward others and at the same time had intense social anxiety about interactions with people that she did not know well. The therapist had coached her on making phone calls to her social worker (who had a large caseload) to make requests for assistance with her housing needs. Making the phone call itself required a significant amount of opposite action to anxiety. When she made the phone call, the social worker did not call her back within what she thought was a timely fashion. She made another phone call at the urging of her therapist. She then left the following message "I've called once before and you did not call back. I would like you to call me back to talk about housing. I'm not a hound dog; I don't need to go chasing after you."

The therapist pointed out that the client had actually used two components of a DEAR MAN in the voicemail—she had Described the situation "I've called once before and you did not call back." And, she Asked for what she wanted "I would like you to call me back to talk about housing." However, she had not Expressed her emotion, and more importantly, she had not Reinforced the social worker in advance for helping her. Instead, she had made a hostile comment to the social worker. When reviewing the interaction, the client remarked "I don't understand why I need to thank her or reinforce her for doing her job. She's supposed to do that no matter what." It was very difficult for the client to understand that GIVE skills (being Gentle, acting Interested, Validating…) would likely help her get her housing needs met faster. The therapist finally found an explanation that was helpful—what if that social worker ended up being in a position later to review her housing application? What if that social worker switched positions and had to approve or deny other requests that the client made? Thanking the social worker may ensure that she did not respond negatively to the client during a later transaction that was important to the client.

While we believe that these skills are helpful, it is also important to validate a client's legitimate concerns about expressing vulnerability to others by expressing emotions or using GIVE skills. Many clients in DBT programs have experienced abuse and perhaps adaptively learned not to express their emotions about interpersonal interactions or make themselves vulnerable to others. Coaching the client to use these skills may require a significant amount of validation, as using these skills will be extremely anxiety provoking.

Therapist burnout and consultation

A crucial issue in work with clients with Cluster B PDs is therapist burnout. This is explicitly addressed in DBT through the use of a therapist consultation team. The consultation team is part of the treatment program and is used to both problem solve issues in therapy through peer or direct supervision and to provide support. The intense emotions experienced by clients with Cluster B PDs often leave therapists feeling drained, confused, or frustrated. Clients with high levels of antagonism may also just present as "unlikeable." We propose that therapist burnout is one issue that must be addressed in the treatment of individuals with high levels of antagonism. Therapist burnout is discussed each week during consultation team meetings and other therapists provide validation or problems solving around this issue. One important component of DBT that may help reduce therapist burnout is that therapists and clients establish "personal limits" during the pretreatment assessment and commitment phase. The therapist explicitly explains to the client what behaviors would cause them to "burn out" on the client. For example, a therapist might say that they are more likely to "burn out" on a client if the client does not express willingness to receive coaching when they contact the therapist outside of session. Other forms of therapy refer to personal limits as boundaries, but they are not necessarily explicitly discussed with the client until the client breaks them. When personal limits are discussed upfront, and the consequences of breaching personal limits are described to the client, it facilitates the client engaging in a mutually respectful relationship with the therapist. If the client is less likely to push personal limits, then the therapist is less likely to "burn out" on the client.

It should also be noted that personal limits may be established after the pretreatment stage of therapy; it is just important that they be immediately identified and explicitly addressed with the client. The following two examples illustrate two such cases, both of which resulted in the therapist terminating treatment with the client for refusing to respect the personal limits of the therapist. For example, a client in a recent DBT program began insulting her individual therapist to skills group leaders and staff at the clinic, as well as sending angry emails to the therapist about her incompetence. Functional analysis of this behavior revealed that this behavior was triggered by the client's intense anxiety regarding her improvement in therapy—as she improved, and the therapist encouraged this behavior change, it triggered fears of abandonment, lashing out at the therapist, and then anger when the therapist addressed the lashing out directly in session. The therapist reviewed the insulting comments with the client and reviewed her email communication. The therapist provided specific examples of communication that would break a personal limit for her; these included insulting the therapist to staff, insulting staff, and name calling in emails. The therapist then stated that she would attempt to problem solve this behavior once more, and that if could not be reduced after that, she and the client would have to take a break from therapy for the duration of the remainder of her DBT contract. If the client was willing to change this behavior, then the therapist expressed willingness to renew the DBT contract, with these behaviors added as part of it. In this case, the client was not able to stop the behaviors outlined as ruptures to the relationship. The therapist terminated therapy. Following this, the client profusely apologized and repeatedly requested to return to treatment, expressing willingness to work on the behaviors. This was very difficult for the therapist and she felt urges to renew the contract. At this point, the consultation team stepped in and provided feedback that renewing with the client at this point would ultimately reinforce the target behavior, providing support for the therapist to maintain her limits.

In the second example, the client did not engage in behaviors that were antagonistic toward the therapist, but toward someone else. A young woman enrolled in a local college participated in our DBT program. She signed a 6-month treatment contract. Approximately 3 months into treatment, she revealed that she had created a false social media identity in order to engage in communication with her expartner. She described plans to engage her expartner in a relationship online and then exact some sort of revenge on them. At this point, the specifics of the plan were not clearly outlined by the client. Although the client had not engaged in any behavior toward the therapist herself that broke their contract or ruptured their relationship, the therapist felt very uncomfortable with this behavior. After several discussions in the consultation team, the therapist clarified that the client was violating an important value to the therapist, and she felt that she could not continue therapy unless she was honest with the client about this and described it as a personal limit. In this case, the therapist provided feedback that she felt that she had to address this behavior as a potential therapeutic target in order to behave consistently with her own values, and potentially alert the expartner if she knew that the expartner was in danger in some way. She described this as a personal limit that had not been established in the initial contract, but that she needed to add. The client was receptive to the discussion and was not hostile to the therapist. However, she was not willing to give up the behavior. Thus the therapist ultimately decided not to renew her treatment contract with the client once her initial contract was finished.

Consultation to the client agreement

Within a DBT framework, therapy teams and their clients make a series of commitments and agreements to each other. One agreement that is often foreign to clinicians who work outside of a DBT framework is the consultation to the client agreement. This agreement states that therapists do not discuss their clients with other people or providers without their client present, either by telephone or in person. Therapists on a DBT team together may discuss their clients with members of the team, as part of a consultation team meeting. This agreement often presents challenges to therapists, clients, and providers outside of the team. The rationale for this agreement is that it reduces splitting among providers, because it makes it less likely that the client will disclose different information to different providers. It also conveys a sense of respect and nonjudgmentalness to the client. Again, the therapist is showing that they are not afraid of the client's symptoms and that they do not view the client as fragile or incapable of discussing their own care. In the following example, a provider outside of our treatment team felt particularly challenged by this agreement. The client was a young adult male, who presented to treatment to address symptoms consistent with several Cluster B PD diagnoses, including intense anger and hostility. He also displayed several misogynistic and potentially unsafe behaviors toward women that he was willing to target in treatment. His psychiatrist was not a member of the DBT team. When she requested consultation with the individual therapist, the therapist explained the consultation to the client agreement and asked that the client be present or on the phone. The psychiatrist at first refused, asking "do you know how pathological he is?"

The therapist worked with the client to explain to his psychiatrist that he knew and understood his diagnoses. From our perspective, everything that we thought about the client or had conceptualized related to his symptoms had been discussed with the client, either in the pretreatment phase or on a weekly basis upon review of diary card/target behaviors. Thus the client did not respond in a hostile manner to discussion of his diagnoses and symptoms, as we had maintained an open, honest, collaborative relationship from the beginning. From our perspective, the consultation to the client agreement enhances collaboration and reduces hostility and suspicion on the part of the client. This may be particularly important in clients whose empathic abilities are reduced under stress or who may have hostile attribution biases.

Concluding remarks

In this chapter, we have briefly reviewed the components of DBT. We have provided more detailed explanations and case examples of the specific features of DBT that may be particularly helpful in working with clients with high levels of antagonism. It is important to note that DBT is, ultimately, behavior therapy. Thus multiple behaviors are targeted through skills practice and principles of operant conditioning. However, the elements that we have focused on in this chapter may be particularly helpful in working with clients with high antagonism. These elements all primarily serve to reduce hostility on the part of the client, increase collaborative behaviors on the part of the client, and reduce therapist burnout. It should also be noted that some literature suggests that callousness, a particular facet of antagonism, is actually the trait associated with low empathy. Hence, this may potentially limit engagement and motivation to improve relationships with others. Although DBT appears to be an effective treatment for individuals in forensic settings, or with substance use disorders, or with PDs, some clients may just not engage with the treatment. We hypothesize, however, that increasing collaboration and reducing therapist burnout proactively through DBT principles will increase the odds of positive treatment outcomes with clients with high levels of antagonism.

References

Bateman, A., O'Connell, J., Lorenzini, N., Gardner, T., & Fonagy, P. (2016). A randomised controlled trial of mentalization-based treatment versus structured clinical management for patients with comorbid borderline personality disorder and antisocial personality disorder. *BMC Psychiatry*, *16*, 304.

Berzins, L. G., & Trestman, R. L. (2004). The development and implementation of dialectical behavior therapy in forensic settings. *International Journal of Forensic Mental Health*, *3*, 93–103.

Cameron, A. Y., Palm Reed, K., & Gaudiano, B. A. (2014). Addressing treatment motivation in borderline personality disorder. Rationale for incorporating values-based exercises into dialectical behavior therapy. *Journal of Contemporary Psychotherapy*, *44*, 109–116.

Davis, M. H. (1983). Measuring individual differences in empathy: evidence for a multidimentional approach. *Journal of Personality and Social Psychology*, *44*, 113–126.

Dinsdale, N., & Crespi, B. J. (2013). The borderline empathy paradox: evidence and conceptual models for empathic enhancements in borderline personality disorder. *Journal of Personality Disorders*, *27*, 172–195.

Evershed, S., Tennant, A., Boomer, D., Rees, A., Barkham, M., & Watson, A. (2003). Practice based outcomes of dialectical behavior therapy (DBT) targeting anger and violence with male forensic patients: a pragmatic and non-contemporaneous comparison. *Criminal Behaviour and Mental Health*, *13*, 198–213.

Hayes, S. C. (2004). Acceptance and commitment therapy, relational frame theory, and the third wave of behavioral and cognitive therapies. *Behavior Therapy*, *35*, 639–665.

Koons, C. R., Robins, C. J., Tweed, J. L., Lynch, T. R., Gonzalez, A. M., Morse, J. Q., et al. (2001). Efficacy of dialectical behavior therapy in women veterans with borderline personality disorder. *Behavior Therapy*, *32*, 371–390.

Kotov, R., Gamez, W., Schmidt, F., & Watson, D. (2010). Linking "big" personality traits to anxiety, depressive, and substance use disorders: a meta-analysis. *Psychological Bulletin*, *136*, 768–821.

Kotov, R., Krueger, R. F., Watson, D., Achenbach, T. M., Althoff, R. R., Bagby, R. M., et al. (2017). The Hierarchical Taxonomy of Psychopathology (HiTOP): a dimensional alternative to traditional nosologies. *Journal of Abnormal Psychology*, *126*, 454–477.

Krueger, R. F., & Markon, K. E. (2014). The role of the DSM-5 personality trait model in moving toward a quantitative and empirically based approach to classifying personality and psychopathology. *Annual Review of Clinical Psychology*, *10*, 477–501.

Lamkin, J., Maples-Keller, J. L., & Miller, J. D. (2018). How likable are personality disorder and negatively valenced personality traits to those who possess them? *Journal of Personality*, *86*, 173–185.

Lazarus, S. A., Cheavens, J. S., Festa, F., & Rosenthal, M. Z. (2014). Interpersonal functioning in borderline personality disorder: a systematic review of behavioral and laboratory-based assessments. *Clinical Psychology Review*, *34*, 193–205.

Linehan, M. M. (1993). *Cognitive behavioral treatment of borderline personality disorder*. New York, NY: Guilford Press.

Linehan, M. M. (2014). *DBT skills training manual* (2nd ed.). New York, NY: Guilford Press.

Linehan, M. M., Armstrong, H. E., Suarez, A., Allmon, D., & Heard, H. L. (1991). Cognitive behavioral treatment of chronically parasuicidal borderline patients. *Archives of General Psychiatry*, *48*, 1060–1064.

Linehan, M. M., Comtois, K. A., Murray, A. M., Brown, M. Z., Gallop, R. J., Heard, H. L., et al. (2006). Two-year randomized controlled trial and follow-up of dialectical behavior therapy vs therapy by experts for suicidal behaviors and borderline personality disorder. *Archives of General Psychiatry*, *63*, 757–766.

Linehan, M. M., & Dexter-Mazza, E. (2008). Dialectical behavior therapy for borderline personality disorder. In D. H. Barlow (Ed.), *Clinical handbook of psychological disorders*. New York, NY: Guilford Press.

Linehan, M. M., Dimeff, L. A., Reynolds, S. K., Comtois, K. A., Welch, S. S., Heagerty, P., et al. (2002). Dialectical behavior therapy versus comprehensive validation therapy plus 12-step for the treatment of opioid dependent women meeting criteria for borderline personality disorder. *Drug and Alcohol Dependence*, *67*, 13–26.

Linehan, M. M., Schmidt, H., Dimeff, L. A., Craft, J. C., Kanter, J., & Comtois, K. A. (1999). Dialectical behavior therapy for patients with borderline personality disorder and drug-dependence. *The American Journal on Addictions*, *8*, 279–292.

Lishner, D. A., Hong, P. Y., Jiang, L., Vitacco, M. J., & Neumann, C. S. (2015). Psychopathy, narcissism, and borderline personality: a critical test of the affective empathy-impairment hypothesis. *Personality and Individual Differences*, *86*, 257–265.

Livesley, W. J., & Jackson, D. (2009). *Manual for the dimensional assessment of personality pathology—Basic questionnaire*. Port Huron, MI: Sigma.

Malouf, E., Youman, K., Harty, L., Schaefer, K., & Tangney, J. P. (2013). Accepting guilt and abandoning shame: a positive approach to addressing moral emotions among high-risk multi-need individuals. In T. B. Kashdan & J. Ciarrochi (Eds.), *Mindfulness, acceptance, and positive psychology: The seven foundations of well-being* (pp. 215–239). Oakland, CA: Context Press.

Miller, J. D., & Lynam, D. (2001). Structural models of personality and their relation to antisocial behavior: a meta-analytic review. *Criminology*, *39*, 765–798.

Miller, J. D., Sleep, C. E., Lamkin, J., Vize, C., Campbell, W. K., & Lynam, D. R. (2018). Personality disorder traits: perceptions of likability, impairment, and ability to change as correlates and moderators of desired level. *Personality Disorders: Theory, Research, and Treatment*, *9*(5), 478–483.

Moore, K. E., Folk, J. B., Boren, E. A., Tangney, J. P., Fischer, S., & Schrader, S. W. (2018). Pilot study of a brief dialectical behavior therapy skills group for jail inmates. *Psychological Services*, *15*, 98–108.

National Institute for Health and Clinical Excellence (2009a). *Antisocial personality disorder: Treatment, management and prevention. Clinical guideline 77*. London: The British Psychological Society and The Royal College of Psychiatrists.

National Institute for Health and Clinical Excellence (2009b). *Borderline personality disorder: Treatment and management. Clinical guideline 78*. London: National Institute for Health and Clinical Excellence.

Niedtfeld, I. (2017). Experimental investigation of cognitive and affective empathy in borderline personality disorder: effects of ambiguity in multimodal social information processing. *Psychiatry Research*, *253*, 58–63.

Ozer, D. J., & Benet-Martinez, V. (2006). Personality and the prediction of consequential outcomes. *Annual Review of Psychology*, *57*, 401–421.

Sakdalan, J. A., Shaw, J., & Collier, V. (2010). Staying in the here and now: a pilot study on the use of dialectical behavior therapy group skills training for forensic clients with intellectual disability. *Journal of Intellectual Disability Research*, *54*, 568–572.

Verheul, R., van den Bosch, L. M. C., Koeter, M. W. J., de Ridder, M. A. J., Stijnen, T., & van derBrink, W. (2003). Dialectical behavior therapy for women with borderline personality disorder: 12 month, randomized clinical trial in the Netherlands. *British Journal of Psychiatry*, *182*, 135–140.

Weiss, B., Lavner, J., & Miller, J. D. (2018). Self- and partner-reported psychopathic traits' relations with couples' communication, marital satisfaction trajectories, and divorce in a longitudinal sample. *Personality Disorders: Theory, Research, and Treatment*, *9*(3), 239–249.

Widiger, T. A., Lynam, D. R., Miller, J. D., & Oltmanns, T. F. (2012). Measures to assess maladaptive variants of the five-factor model. *Journal of Personality Assessment*, *94*, 450–455.

Wingenfeld, K., Duesenberg, M., Fleischer, J., Roepke, S., Dziobek, I., Otte, C., et al. (2018). Psychosocial stress differentially affects emotional empathy in women with borderline personality disorder and healthy controls. *Acta Psychiatrica Scandinavica*, *137*, 206–215.

Pharmacologic interventions for antagonism and related disorders

26

*Alex C. Loeks Johnson**, *Lora M.H. Wichser*†, *Katharine J. Nelson*†
*University of Minnesota Medical School, Minneapolis, MN, United States, †Department of Psychiatry, University of Minnesota Medical School, Minneapolis, MN, United States

As conceptions of mental illness were being developed in the early and mid-20th century, diagnosis and treatment approaches were guided by the dominant psychological theories of the time. As such, the leading psychiatric treatment approaches favored psychoanalytic, behavioral, or cognitive therapies. However, it was noted in certain subsets of patients, these approaches were associated with clinical deterioration (Hoch & Polatin, 1949; Millon, 2012). Psychotherapy remained the principal treatment modality for mental illnesses until the later 20th century. At that time, advances in the fields of neuroimaging, cognitive neuroscience, and psychopharmacology allowed the field to more fully understand the neurobiological underpinnings of psychiatric disease. These discoveries paved the way for groundbreaking studies of the pharmacological treatment of mental illnesses such as major depressive disorder (MDD) and psychosis which established pharmacotherapy as the primary therapeutic modality in these disorders (Ferguson, 2001; Shen, 1999).

Despite these gains for many psychiatric diagnoses and symptoms, very few pharmacologic clinical trials have examined the effects of pharmacotherapy specifically on the personality trait of antagonism. Instead, antagonistic behaviors such as interpersonal dysfunction, emotional dysregulation, and aggression have been used as proxies for the study of antagonism in patients with varied mental health diagnoses. Antagonistic traits are exhibited in many neurological and psychiatric illnesses, including neurocognitive disorders, substance abuse, mood disorders, and psychotic disorders. In addition, antagonism is an especially prominent and characteristic feature of specific personality disorders and results in significant personal and interpersonal dysfunction. Patients with antisocial, borderline, narcissistic, and histrionic personality disorders often exhibit debilitating antagonistic behavior (Angstman & Rasmussen, 2011).

Clinical trials examining the efficacy of pharmacotherapy in the treatment of antagonistic traits have generally contained inclusion criteria regarding the presence of specific personality disorder diagnoses. Much of the available data regarding medical treatment of antagonism is in the context of personality disorder treatment. In addition, impulsivity, a component of the externalizing personality dimension (distinct from antagonism), is often examined along with the antagonistic externalizing behaviors in these studies due their frequent overlap within the domains of personality disorders. Thus while some potential conclusions may be drawn from these studies

The Handbook of Antagonism. https://doi.org/10.1016/B978-0-12-814627-9.00026-8

regarding antagonism, one must be aware of the naturalistic conflation of impulsivity with antagonism in a variety of the available research. Antagonism itself is rarely described in clinical pharmacology literature, but rather is probably best represented by an exploration into treatments for aggression. Thus anger and aggression are the closest approximations for antagonistic traits within this literature.

The success of pharmacological therapies for psychiatric disorders such as MDD and schizophrenia led to interest in the medical treatment of personality disorders. As the neurobiological perspective of mental illness was applied to personality disorders, observable differences in brain structure and function became apparent in patients with personality disorders such as borderline personality disorder (BPD; Grant et al., 2007) and antisocial personality disorder (ASPD; Raine & Yang, 2006). The clear majority of clinical trials examining the pharmacological management of personality disorders focus on BPD and schizotypal personality disorder (STPD). Patients with BPD often exhibit marked dysfunction in personal, social, and functional domains, including self-injurious and suicidal behavior, contributing to significant morbidity and mortality (Schulz & Nelson, 2014). In addition, BPD is one of the few ego-dystonic personality disorders. Patients with BPD tend to seek mental health treatment and resources, facilitating diagnosis and enrollment in trials. STPD has recently been conceptualized as a disorder on the spectrum of psychotic disorders (American Psychiatric Association, 2013). Therefore studies of pharmacologic management of this personality disorder naturally followed successful trials of medications for more severe psychotic disorders such as schizophrenia.

This chapter will review the evidence for the utilization of several classes of psychiatric medication in the treatment of antagonistic traits, primarily in the context of personality disorder treatment. Findings of recent meta-analyses, studies examining combined pharmacotherapy and psychotherapy, and international guidelines will also be discussed. Historically, several other directly biological treatment modalities have been utilized in the treatment of antagonism-related disorders, such as electroconvulsive therapy, surgical lobotomies, and surgical or medical castration. For several reasons, not least of which are significant ethical considerations for some of these approaches, these treatments will not be discussed in this chapter. As this evidence is reviewed, it is important to note that the United States Food and Drug Administration (FDA) has not provided approval for any pharmacologic agent for the indication of *antagonism* or *personality disorder*.

Antipsychotic medications

In the early 1950s, first-generation antipsychotic agents (FGAs), such as haloperidol and chlorpromazine, showed significant antipsychotic effects in patients with schizophrenia and other psychotic disorders (Shen, 1999). The success of these medications in psychotic disorders spurred interest in their applicability in personality disorders, specifically BPD and STPD, due to the prominent cognitive-perceptual symptoms in these disorders. Several early trials showed modest clinical improvements in both groups, although improvements primarily occurred in cognitive-perceptual domains

(Goldberg et al., 1986; Serban & Siegel, 1984; Soloff et al., 1989). Antagonistic traits such as interpersonal dysfunction, affective instability, and impulsivity often did not show significant improvements. In addition, follow-up studies generally failed to replicate the positive findings of earlier trials and emphasized prominent side effects seen with use of these medications (Cowdry & Gardner, 1988; Hymowitz, Frances, Jacobsberg, Sickles, & Hoyt, 1986; Soloff et al., 1993).

Further studies called into question the benefits of the use of FGAs in the treatment of BPD and STPD and demonstrated significant side effects, which tended to reduce patient adherence to recommended medication regimens. FGAs function primarily as dopamine receptor antagonists. Dopamine antagonism in the mesolimbic and mesocortical pathways is thought to result in antipsychotic effects. However, dopamine antagonism in the basal ganglia motor centers can result in debilitating movement side effects known as extrapyramidal symptoms (EPS) such as acute dystonia, akathisia, Parkinsonism, and tardive dyskinesia, the latter of which can be irreversible. Dopamine antagonism in the hypothalamic tuberoinfundibular pathway can also result in hyperprolactinemia, causing decreased libido, galactorrhea, and menstrual irregularities and infertility in women. Most importantly, sudden reduction in central nervous system (CNS) dopaminergic tone has also been implicated in neuroleptic malignant syndrome (NMS), a potentially fatal condition (Muench & Hamer, 2010). As such, FGAs are generally not a first-line recommendation for the treatment of personality disorders.

In the 1990s the second-generation antipsychotic agents (SGAs) were introduced and demonstrated efficacy in the treatment of psychotic disorders with improved side-effect profiles compared to FGAs (Shen, 1999). Similar to FGAs, SGAs' antipsychotic effects are believed to lie in the antagonism of dopamine receptors in various brain regions; however, SGAs also block subsets of serotonin receptors to varying degrees. These dual effects are believed to mitigate some of the EPS seen with FGAs. Trials of SGAs in the treatment of personality disorders began with clozapine. Patients with BPD treated with clozapine generally exhibited improvements in global functioning and externalizing traits such as affective instability and impulsivity (Benedetti, Sforzini, Colombo, Maffei, & Smeraldi, 1998; Frankenburg & Zanarini, 1993). However, clozapine is unique among the SGAs in conferring a significant risk for neutropenia, a potentially fatal form of immunosuppression, necessitating frequent monitoring of white blood cell counts (Miller, 2000). Because of clozapine's risk of significant and potentially fatal side effects with frequent required white blood cell monitoring, it is not routinely used for treatment of personality disorders, except in extreme instances.

Clozapine's efficacy in reducing symptoms of severe personality disorders promoted interest in further research into this class of medications. Many trials of SGAs including risperidone, olanzapine, quetiapine, and aripiprazole were completed primarily in patients with BPD and STPD and demonstrated similar improvements in global functioning and reductions in antagonistic traits such as aggression, and externalizing traits, such as impulsivity, and affective instability (Adityanjee et al., 2008; Black et al., 2014; Bogenschutz & Nurnberg, 2004; Keshavan, Shad, Soloff, & Schooler, 2004; Koenigsberg et al., 2003; Nickel et al., 2006; Nickel, Loew, & Gil, 2007;

Rocca, Marchiaro, Cocuzza, & Bogetto, 2002; Schulz, Camlin, Berry, & Friedman, 1998; Schulz, Camlin, Berry, & Jesberger, 1999; Schulz et al., 2008; Zanarini & Frankenburg, 2001; Zanarini, Frankenburg, & Parachini, 2004; Zanarini et al., 2012). In addition, several case series have examined the use of SGAs for the treatment of antagonistic traits in patients with ASPD, noting modest decreases in aggression and impulsivity (Hirose, 2001; Walker, Thomas, & Allen, 2003).

SGAs showed particularly notable reduction of psychotic or cognitive-perceptual, affective, and impulsive or aggressive symptoms. In addition, SGAs exhibit a side-effect profile with lower risk of EPS and hyperprolactinemia (except for risperidone) compared to FGAs. However, all SGAs carry some risk of EPS, NMS, tardive dyskinesia, and a significant risk of weight gain with metabolic side effects. Prescribing guidelines require baseline and follow-up measurements of weight, waist circumference, blood lipids, and blood sugar. Therefore prescribing decisions (as with all medical therapies) must consider the individual therapeutic goals, disclose "off-label" usage, weigh risks and benefits of pharmacotherapy, and obtain informed consent from each patient in the use of these medications.

Mood-stabilizing medications

The element lithium was initially found to be highly effective as a mood stabilizer in the treatment of affective symptoms in bipolar disorders. Because symptoms of bipolar disorder overlap with affective reactivity and impulsivity observed in several personality disorders, interest developed in the use of lithium for treatment of PDs. Early studies revealed that lithium tended to reduce affective symptoms and impulsivity in BPD (Links, Mitton, & Steiner, 1990; Rifkin, Quitkin, Carrillo, Blumberg, & Klein, 1972). A trial involving prison inmates with histories of chronic impulsive aggression showed that daily lithium use reduced aggressive and violent behavior (Sheard, Marini, Bridges, & Wagner, 1976). Despite these promising studies, research regarding the use of lithium to treat personality disorders has not been extensively pursued. One potential reason is a side-effect profile which can include long-term kidney or thyroid dysfunction, and potential toxicity in the case of elevated blood levels or overdose (Gitlin, 2016). Additionally, lithium is a naturally available element and inexpensive as a pharmacologic agent and has not been the focus of clinical trial investment by the pharmaceutical industry.

During the 1970s, it was discovered that anticonvulsants originally used to control seizures showed significant effects, comparable to lithium, in reducing affective symptoms in bipolar disorder (Okuma, 1983). In patients with personality disorders (primarily BPD), trials of carbamazepine, divalproex sodium (DVP), topiramate, and lamotrigine have shown efficacy in reducing antagonistic traits such as anger and aggression, in addition to externalizing traits, such as impulsivity and interpersonal dysfunction (Cowdry & Gardner, 1988; Frankenburg & Zanarini, 2002; Hollander et al., 2001; Hollander, Swann, Coccaro, Jiang, & Smith, 2005; Nickel et al., 2004, 2005; Pinto & Akiskal, 1998; Reich, Zanarini, & Bieri, 2009; Tritt et al., 2005). In addition, transdiagnostic trials of phenytoin, carbamazepine, and oxcarbazepine have shown reductions in aggressive behavior in populations with chronic aggression (Jones et al., 2011; Mattes, 2005; Stanford et al., 2005).

A notable benefit of the mood-stabilizing anticonvulsants is that they avoid many of the prominent side effects of the antipsychotics and lithium. Anticonvulsants are not known to increase risk of EPS associated with FGAs and SGAs, they have a lower risk of weight gain and metabolic side effects compared to SGAs, and are significantly safer than lithium in an overdose. However, each anticonvulsant does exhibit a characteristic side-effect profile that warrants careful monitoring. For example, carbamazepine and oxcarbazepine are associated with blood and electrolyte abnormalities. Common side effects of DVP include weight gain and sedation, although the most significant side effect is a risk of neural tube defects and other congenital anomalies in fetuses exposed to DVP in the first trimester of pregnancy. When initiating lamotrigine, the dose must be slowly titrated to lower the risk of the potentially fatal dermatologic condition, Stevens-Johnson Syndrome. The most studied side effect of topiramate is dose-dependent cognitive slowing (Loring, Williamson, Meador, Wiegand, & Hulihan, 2011; Perucca & Gilliam, 2012).

Antidepressant and anxiolytic medications

The prominent affective symptoms, including emotional dysregulation, present in several personality disorders naturally led to trials examining the use of antidepressants in personality disorders. Initial studies of antidepressant medications for personality disorders centered on the earliest antidepressant medications, tricyclic antidepressants (TCA) and monoamine oxidase inhibitors (MAOI). Studies of the TCA, amitriptyline, noted either little to no improvements in BPD symptoms, or a paradoxical increase in suicidality, paranoia, and aggression in BPD patients (Soloff et al., 1989; Soloff, George, Nathan, Schulz, & Perel, 1986). In addition to low benefit and a risk of paradoxical worsening in BPD patients, TCAs are also potentially fatal in overdose due to significant anticholinergic and cardiotoxic effects. Trials of several MAOIs in BPD patients noted superior efficacy compared to TCAs, although MAOIs can increase risk of serotonin syndrome and hypertensive crises, requiring substantial dietary and medication restrictions (Cowdry & Gardner, 1988; Soloff et al., 1993). As such, these two older classes of antidepressants are not routinely recommended for the treatment of PDs.

The success of selective serotonin reuptake inhibitors (SSRIs) and serotonin norepinephrine reuptake inhibitors (SNRIs) in the treatment of mood and anxiety disorders led to interest in their use to treat affective symptoms in personality disorders. Trials of women with BPD or patients with a personality disorder diagnosis and a history impulsive aggression have shown that fluoxetine treatment results in a significant, although modest, decrease in anger, irritability, and aggression (Coccaro & Kavoussi, 1997; Salzman et al., 1995). In addition to their demonstrated efficacy in reducing antagonistic traits in PDs, a significant benefit to the SSRI/SNRI antidepressants is their safety profile in the case of overdose making them suitable for patients with suicidal behaviors. The most bothersome side effects of SSRIs include headaches, nausea, and sexual side effects including decreased libido and anorgasmia, and they can confer a risk for the induction of mania in vulnerable individuals.

Other medications of interest

Interestingly, omega-3 fatty acids, dietary supplements known for possible cardiovascular benefits, have been the subject of several trials for personality disorder treatment (Mohebi-Nejad & Bikdeli, 2014). A 2003 trial involving BPD patients, supplementation with omega-3 fatty acids resulted in reduced depressive and aggressive symptoms compared to placebo (Zanarini & Frankenburg, 2003). More recent trials in BPD patients have shown that omega-3 fatty acid supplementation decreased risk of psychotic symptoms, impulsivity, and anger (Amminger et al., 2013; Bellino, Bozzatello, Rocca, & Bogetto, 2014). Although evidence supporting the use of omega-3 fatty acids in personality disorders is at an early stage, initial evidence is promising, and the previous trials made no note of any significant side effects associated with this supplement.

Sympatholytic medications such as beta-blockers and alpha-2 agonists, more commonly used as antihypertensive agents, have also shown efficacy in the treatment of aggression. Sympathetic nervous system hyperactivity has been hypothesized to contribute to aggressive behavior. The sympathetic nervous system is responsible for the limbic system-mediated "fight, flight, freeze" response to a perceived threat and is implicated in several DSM-5 diagnoses including posttraumatic stress disorder (PTSD; Sherin & Nemeroff, 2011). Beta-blockers, such as propranolol, inhibit postsynaptic beta-adrenergic receptors, thereby decreasing sympathetic nervous system tone. Trials in both adult and pediatric age groups have shown modest success in reducing aggressive behavior caused by both neurologic and psychiatric conditions such as psychotic disorders, personality disorders, and intellectual disability (Prado-Lima, 2009; Ward, Tharian, Roy, Deb, & Unwin, 2013). Alpha-2 agonists, such as clonidine, stimulate presynaptic alpha-2 adrenergic receptors, activating a negative feedback loop that results in decreased sympathetic nervous system tone. Alpha-2 agonists have shown reductions in aggressive behavior primarily in pediatric psychiatric disorders such as attention-deficit/hyperactivity disorder, autism spectrum disorder, conduct disorder, and oppositional defiant disorder (Prado-Lima, 2009).

Meta-analyses of medication efficacy and tolerability in the treatment of antagonism

Most studies examining pharmacological management of personality disorders have been case series or small trials of short duration. There are very few large, high quality randomized trials or comparison studies to guide medical management. Additionally, several factors may complicate study design and interpretation of results.

For example, within a single personality disorder diagnosis there can be marked heterogeneity in symptom presentation. In addition, there exists a notable overlap of symptom domains between personality disorders, such as impulsivity and aggression shared between BPD and ASPD. Finally, as discussed previously, most personality disorders are ego-syntonic, making trial recruitment for many personality disorders difficult. As such, clinical trial design has favored a transdiagnostic approach in which symptomatic improvement across several symptom domains common to the personality disorders involved is assessed. This section will review recent meta-analyses of pharmacological studies in which patients with varied personality disorder diagnoses have been pooled and responses of distinct symptom domains were evaluated.

A meta-analysis published in 2006 reviewed 20 randomized placebo-controlled trials examining the effects of several medication classes on symptom domains in patients with BPD diagnoses. This review showed mood stabilizers and antidepressants had beneficial effects on affective instability and anger, with mood stabilizers having a stronger effect. Neither class demonstrated an effect on aggression, impulsivity, interpersonal problems, or suicidality. Antipsychotics showed beneficial effects on impulsivity, aggression, interpersonal relationships, and global functioning (Nose, Cipriani, Biancosino, Grassi, & Barbui, 2006).

A 2010 meta-analysis examined 21 placebo-controlled randomized studies with a combined 837 patients with BPD or STPD in which pharmacological management with antidepressants, antipsychotics, and mood stabilizers was examined. The symptom domains common to both BPD and STPD evaluated in this study were cognitive-perceptual, impulsive-behavioral dyscontrol, and affective dysregulation (including anger, depressive, and anxiety subdomains). Antipsychotics from both classes (FGAs and SGAs) were found to have a moderate improvement on cognitive-perceptual symptoms, a moderate-to-large effect on anger, and a small improvement in global functioning. Antipsychotics showed no effects on impulsive-behavioral dyscontrol or other affective dysregulation subdomains. Mood stabilizers, including lithium and anticonvulsants, showed a very large improvement in both impulsive-behavioral dyscontrol and anger, a large effect on anxiety and global functioning, and a moderate improvement in depressed mood. Mood stabilizers showed no effects on cognitive-perceptual symptoms. Antidepressants, including MAOIs, TCAs, and SSRIs, showed only an isolated small improvement in anxiety and anger with no effects on global functioning, cognitive-perceptual symptoms, impulsive-behavioral dyscontrol symptoms, or depressed mood (Ingenhoven, Lafay, Rinne, Passchier, & Duivenvoorden, 2010).

Likewise, a 2010 Cochrane Review of pharmacological management of BPD examined the efficacy of antipsychotics, mood stabilizers, antidepressants, and omega-3 fatty acid supplementation on similar symptom domains. A total of 28 studies with 1742 pooled patients were analyzed in this review. FGAs showed improvements in only the anger subdomain of affective dysregulation. SGAs showed significant improvements in cognitive-perceptual, impulsive-behavioral dyscontrol, and affective dysregulation domains, as well as suicidality and interpersonal relationships. Mood stabilizers exhibited improvements in impulsive-behavioral dyscontrol, affective dysregulation, and interpersonal problem symptoms. Antidepressants only showed improvement in the depressed mood subdomain of affective dysregulation, and omega-3 fatty acid supplementation improved depressed mood and suicidality Stoffers et al., 2010).

As described previously, this early and limited evidence favors the targeting of medications to the treatment of transdiagnostic symptom domains that are common to severe personality disorders. Regarding the treatment of externalizing traits, mood-stabilizing medications consistently show the strongest reductions in domains such as interpersonal dysfunction, affective instability, and impulsivity.

Clinical trials assessing combined pharmacotherapy and psychotherapeutic approaches

As is the case with most psychiatric disorders, a comprehensive treatment and support plan addressing the psychological, biological, and social needs of each patient is ideal for patients with antagonism-related disorders. Psychotherapy is considered the primary treatment modality for all personality disorders and every patient with a personality disorder should receive regular, structured psychotherapy (Angstman & Rasmussen, 2011; Bateman, Gunderson, & Mulder, 2015). Research is now beginning to examine the efficacy of a combination of psychotherapy and psychiatric medications in patients with personality disorders.

A 2005 trial of women with BPD examined the treatment response of dialectical behavioral therapy (DBT) combined with low-dose olanzapine, a SGA, versus DBT combined with a placebo. Each group showed significant reductions in BPD symptoms; however, the group that received olanzapine showed stronger reductions in symptoms of depression, anxiety, impulsivity, and aggressive behavior. The olanzapine group also showed a lower dropout rate than the placebo group (Soler et al., 2005). A 2008 trial of women with BPD with high levels of irritability and anger compared 6 months of DBT plus low-dose olanzapine with 6 months of DBT plus placebo. Both groups showed significant improvements in symptoms of irritability, depression, aggression, and self-injurious behavior. The olanzapine-treated group tended to have a more rapid decrease in symptoms, although these results were not statistically significant (Linehan, McDavid, Brown, Sayrs, & Gallop, 2008). Interestingly, initial studies of combinations of DBT and either SSRIs or mood stabilizers have not shown similar advantages over DBT alone (Moen et al., 2012; Simpson et al., 2004).

Although the evidence base is at an early stage, this small set of trials indicates combining psychotherapeutic and pharmacologic treatments could enhance or accelerate therapeutic responses. Because psychotherapy is the primary treatment modality of personality disorders, the decision to initiate a psychiatric medication depends upon the presence of severe or debilitating symptoms from a domain observed to be targeted by psychiatric medications and should be based on patient preference and the presence of medical or psychiatric comorbidities.

Clinical best practices for pharmacotherapy in patients with antagonism

Prior to prescribing any psychiatric medications, a thorough psychiatric evaluation must be performed to accurately diagnose personality disorders and any comorbid psychiatric and/or medical illness. Psychiatric disorders such as MDD, bipolar disorder, and anxiety disorders frequently co-occur in patients with personality disorders and other antagonism-related disorders, and the optimal treatment for each disorder will likely differ. The presence of a comorbid personality disorder often makes treatment of psychiatric illnesses such as MDD more difficult (Gunderson et al., 2004). Therefore both psychiatric illnesses and personality disorders must be addressed in treatment. Furthermore, patients and their families should be educated regarding the intended target of individual treatments to avoid confusion and demoralization if treatment does not produce the desired effects. For example, a patient with MDD and comorbid STPD should be counseled that antidepressant medications will likely improve depressive symptoms but not cognitive-perceptual symptoms of STPD.

The presence of a psychiatric illness with primarily pharmacological management, such as bipolar disorder or schizophrenia, can influence pharmacological treatment of any prominent personality disorder symptoms. For example, a patient with bipolar disorder with comorbid BPD and prominent impulsive-behavioral dyscontrol symptoms would likely benefit from a mood-stabilizing agent. However, psychotherapy for the personality disorder must also be pursued. As stated previously, psychotherapy is the first-line treatment for all personality disorders. The presence of comorbid psychiatric illness treated primarily with medications does not negate the need for psychotherapy in these patients.

When deciding to prescribe a psychiatric medication for a personality disorder, a psychiatric evaluation of the patient is performed to determine the most prominent and dysfunctional symptom domain to target. The patient must then be counseled of the specific desired effects and goals of the medication, and which symptoms will likely not be affected by the medication. Research on the pharmacological management of personality disorders has been conducted via short-term trials; therefore very little is known about long-term use of medications in this population. End goals should be decided and discussed with the patient, and when these goals are met the medication should be discontinued.

It is generally not recommended to prescribe or alter medications during a crisis. Patients with personality disorders are expected to experience acute crises, manifesting as panic, agitation, depersonalization/derealization, and so on. There is some evidence that medications may be useful in acute crises, but these medications should be promptly discontinued as crisis symptoms resolve (Shaikh et al., 2017). Adding long-term medications during crises can lead to polypharmacy and unintended drug interactions and should be avoided. There are several evidence-based nonpharmacological techniques to assist patients by improving distress tolerance during acute crises, such as cognitive-behavioral or mindfulness-based techniques, or vagal maneuvers such as paced breathing (Linehan, Suarez, & Allmon, 1991; Saeed & Bruce, 1998).

As our understanding of how biological and psychosocial factors influence development, personality, and psychopathology expands, we continue to discover improved and more comprehensive interventions for the unbearable and debilitating symptoms endured by our patients. Although psychotherapy remains the principal treatment modality for antagonistic behaviors mediated by maladaptive personality traits, modern evidence continues to support the pharmacological treatment of debilitating symptom domains, including antagonistic, seen in personality disorders. Discoveries across neurological and biological disciplines have opened new doors in the thoughtful pharmacological treatment of antagonism-spectrum disorders. As such, a comprehensive evaluation of psychiatric comorbidities, medical illnesses, and biologically mediated contributions to illness is warranted in every patient. In the following decades, further research is needed to develop more specific and effective interventions to expand treatment options for patients and their families.

References

Adityanjee, Romine, A., Brown, E., Thuras, P., Lee, S., & Schulz, S. C. (2008). Quetiapine in patients with borderline personality disorder: an open-label trial. *Annals of Clinical Psychiatry*, *20*(4), 219–226.

American Psychiatric Association. (2013). *Diagnostic and statistical manual of mental disorders* (5th ed.). Arlington, VA: American Psychiatric Publishing.

Amminger, G. P., Chanen, A. M., Ohmann, S., Klier, C. M., Mossaheb, N., Bechdolf, A., et al. (2013). Omega-3 fatty acid supplementation in adolescents with borderline personality disorder and ultra-high risk criteria for psychosis: a post hoc subgroup analysis of a double blind, randomized controlled trial. *The Canadian Journal of Psychiatry*, *58*(7), 402–408.

Angstman, K. B., & Rasmussen, N. H. (2011). Personality disorders: review and clinical application in daily practice. *American Family Physician*, *84*(11), 1253.

Bateman, A. W., Gunderson, J., & Mulder, R. (2015). Treatment of personality disorder. *The Lancet*, *385*(9969), 735–743.

Bellino, S., Bozzatello, P., Rocca, G., & Bogetto, F. (2014). Efficacy of omega-3 fatty acids in the treatment of borderline personality disorder: a study of the association with valproic acid. *Journal of Psychopharmacology*, *28*(2), 125–132.

Benedetti, F., Sforzini, L., Colombo, C., Maffei, C., & Smeraldi, E. (1998). Low-dose clozapine in acute and continuation treatment of severe borderline personality disorder. *The Journal of Clinical Psychiatry*, *59*(3), 103–107.

Black, D. W., Zanarini, M. C., Romine, A., Shaw, M., Allen, J., & Schulz, S. C. (2014). Comparison of low and moderate dosages of extended-release quetiapine in borderline personality disorder: a randomized, double-blind, placebo-controlled trial. *American Journal of Psychiatry*, *171*(11), 1174–1182.

Bogenschutz, M. P., & Nurnberg, H. G. (2004). Olanzapine versus placebo in the treatment of borderline personality disorder. *The Journal of Clinical Psychiatry*, *65*(1), 104–109.

Coccaro, E. F., & Kavoussi, R. J. (1997). Fluoxetine and impulsive aggressive behavior in personality-disordered subjects. *Archives of General Psychiatry*, *54*(12), 1081–1808.

Cowdry, R. W., & Gardner, D. L. (1988). Pharmacotherapy of borderline personality disorder alprazolam, carbamazepine, trifluoperazine, and tranylcypromine. *Archives of General Psychiatry*, *45*(2), 111–119.

Ferguson, J. M. (2001). SSRI antidepressant medications. *The Primary Care Companion to The Journal of Clinical Psychiatry*, *03*(01), 22–27.

Frankenburg, F. R., & Zanarini, M. C. (1993). Clozapine treatment of borderline patients: a preliminary study. *Comprehensive Psychiatry*, *34*(6), 402–405.

Frankenburg, F. R., & Zanarini, M. C. (2002). Divalproex sodium treatment of women with borderline personality disorder and bipolar II disorder: a double-blind placebo-controlled pilot study. *The Journal of Clinical Psychiatry*, *63*(5), 442–446.

Gitlin, M. (2016). Lithium side effects and toxicity: prevalence and management strategies. *International Journal of Bipolar Disorders*, *4*(1), 27.

Goldberg, S. C., Schulz, S. C., Schulz, P. M., Resnick, R. J., Hamer, R. M., & Friedel, R. O. (1986). Borderline and schizotypal personality disorders treated with low-dose thiothixene vs placebo. *Archives of General Psychiatry*, *43*(7), 680.

Grant, J., Correia, S., Brennan-Krohn, T., Malloy, P., Laidlaw, D., & Schulz, S. (2007). Frontal white matter integrity in borderline personality disorder with self-injurious behavior. *The Journal of Neuropsychiatry and Clinical Neurosciences*, *19*(4), 383–390.

Gunderson, J. G., Morey, L. C., Stout, R. L., Skodol, A. E., Shea, M. T., McGlashan, T. H., et al. (2004). Major depressive disorder and borderline personality disorder revisited: longitudinal interactions. *The Journal of Clinical Psychiatry*, *65*(8), 1049.

Hirose, S. (2001). Effective treatment of aggression and impulsivity in antisocial personality disorder with risperidone. *Psychiatry and Clinical Neurosciences*, *55*(2), 161–162.

Hoch, P., & Polatin, P. (1949). Pseudoneurotic forms of schizophrenia. *The Psychiatric Quarterly*, *23*(2), 248–276.

Hollander, E., Allen, A., Lopez, R. P., Bienstock, C. A., Grossman, R., Siever, L. J., et al. (2001). A preliminary double-blind, placebo-controlled trial of divalproex sodium in borderline personality disorder. *The Journal of Clinical Psychiatry*, *62*(3), 199–203.

Hollander, E., Swann, A. C., Coccaro, E. F., Jiang, P., & Smith, T. B. (2005). Impact of trait impulsivity and state aggression on divalproex versus placebo response in borderline personality disorder. *American Journal of Psychiatry*, *162*(3), 621–624.

Hymowitz, P., Frances, A., Jacobsberg, L., Sickles, M., & Hoyt, R. (1986). Neuroleptic treatment of schizotypal personality disorders. *Comprehensive Psychiatry*, *27*(4), 267–271.

Ingenhoven, T., Lafay, P., Rinne, T., Passchier, J., & Duivenvoorden, H. (2010). Effectiveness of pharmacotherapy for severe personality disorders: meta-analyses of randomized controlled trials. *Journal of Clinical Psychiatry*, *71*(1), 14–25.

Jones, R. M., Arlidge, J., Gillham, R., Reagu, S., van den Bree, M., & Taylor, P. J. (2011). Efficacy of mood stabilisers in the treatment of impulsive or repetitive aggression: systematic review and meta-analysis. *The British Journal of Psychiatry*, *198*(2), 93–98.

Keshavan, M., Shad, M., Soloff, P., & Schooler, N. (2004). Efficacy and tolerability of olanzapine in the treatment of schizotypal personality disorder. *Schizophrenia Research*, *71*(1), 97–101.

Koenigsberg, H., Reynolds, D., Goodman, M., New, A., Mitropoulou, V., Trestman, R., et al. (2003). Risperidone in the treatment of schizotypal personality disorder. *The Journal of Clinical Psychiatry*, *64*(6), 628–634.

Linehan, M. M., McDavid, J. D., Brown, M. Z., Sayrs, J. H., & Gallop, R. J. (2008). Olanzapine plus dialectical behavior therapy for women with high irritability who meet criteria for borderline personality disorder: a double-blind, placebo-controlled pilot study. *Journal of Clinical Psychiatry*, *69*(6), 999–1005.

Linehan, M. M., Suarez, A., & Allmon, D. (1991). Cognitive-behavioral treatment of chronically parasuicidal borderline patients. *Archives of General Psychiatry*, *48*(12), 1060–1064.

Links, P. S., Mitton, J. E., & Steiner, M. (1990). Predicting outcome for borderline personality disorder. *Comprehensive Psychiatry*, *31*(6), 490–498.

Loring, D. W., Williamson, D. J., Meador, K. J., Wiegand, F., & Hulihan, J. (2011). Topiramate dose effects on cognition: a randomized double-blind study. *Neurology*, *76*(2), 131–137.

Mattes, J. A. (2005). Oxcarbazepine in patients with impulsive aggression: a double-blind, placebo-controlled trial. *Journal of Clinical Psychopharmacology*, *25*(6), 575–579.

Miller, D. D. (2000). Review and management of clozapine side effects. *The Journal of Clinical Psychiatry*, *61*(Suppl. 8), 14–17.

Millon, T. (2012). On the history and future study of personality and its disorders. *Annual Review of Clinical Psychology*, *8*(1), 1–19.

Moen, R., Freitag, M., Miller, M., Lee, S., Romine, A., Song, S., et al. (2012). Efficacy of extended-release divalproex combined with "condensed" dialectical behavior therapy for individuals with borderline personality disorder. *Annals of Clinical Psychiatry*, *24* (4), 255–260.

Mohebi-Nejad, A., & Bikdeli, B. (2014). Omega-3 supplements and cardiovascular diseases. *Tanaffos*, *13*(1), 6.

Muench, J., & Hamer, A. M. (2010). Adverse effects of antipsychotic medications. *American Family Physician*, *81*(5), 617.

Nickel, M. K., Loew, T. H., & Gil, F. P. (2007). Aripiprazole in treatment of borderline patients, part II: an 18-month follow-up. *Psychopharmacology*, *191*(4), 1023–1026.

Nickel, M. K., Muehlbacher, M., Nickel, C., Kettler, C., Gil, F. P., Bachler, E., et al. (2006). Aripiprazole in the treatment of patients with borderline personality disorder: a double-blind, placebo-controlled study. *The American Journal of Psychiatry*, *163*(5), 833–838.

Nickel, M. K., Nickel, C., Kaplan, P., Lahmann, C., Mühlbacher, M., Tritt, K., et al. (2005). Treatment of aggression with topiramate in male borderline patients: a double-blind, placebo-controlled study. *Biological Psychiatry*, *57*(5), 495–499.

Nickel, M. K., Nickel, C., Mitterlehner, F. O., Tritt, K., Lahmann, C., Leiberich, P. K., et al. (2004). Topiramate treatment of aggression in female borderline personality disorder patients: a double-blind, placebo-controlled study. *The Journal of Clinical Psychiatry*, *65*(11), 1515–1519.

Nose, M., Cipriani, A., Biancosino, B., Grassi, L., & Barbui, C. (2006). Efficacy of pharmacotherapy against core traits of borderline personality disorder: meta-analysis of randomized controlled trials. *International Clinical Psychopharmacology*, *21*(6), 345–353.

Okuma, T. (1983). Therapeutic and prophylactic effects of carbamazepine in bipolar disorders. *Psychiatric Clinics of North America*, *6*(1), 157–174.

Perucca, P., & Gilliam, F. G. (2012). Adverse effects of antiepileptic drugs. *The Lancet Neurology*, *11*(9), 792–802.

Pinto, O. C., & Akiskal, H. S. (1998). Lamotrigine as a promising approach to borderline personality: an open case series without concurrent DSM-IV major mood disorder. *Journal of Affective Disorders*, *51*(3), 333–343.

Prado-Lima, P. (2009). Pharmacological treatment of impulsivity and aggressive behavior. *Revista Brasileira de Psiquiatria*, *31*, S58–S65.

Raine, A., & Yang, Y. (2006). Neural foundations to moral reasoning and antisocial behavior. *Social Cognitive and Affective Neuroscience*, *1*(3), 203–213.

Reich, D. B., Zanarini, M. C., & Bieri, K. A. (2009). A preliminary study of lamotrigine in the treatment of affective instability in borderline personality disorder. *International Clinical Psychopharmacology*, *24*(5), 270–275.

Rifkin, A., Quitkin, F., Carrillo, C., Blumberg, A. G., & Klein, D. F. (1972). Lithium carbonate in emotionally unstable character disorder. *Archives of General Psychiatry*, *27*(4), 519–523.

Rocca, P., Marchiaro, L., Cocuzza, E., & Bogetto, F. (2002). Treatment of borderline personality disorder with risperidone. *The Journal of Clinical Psychiatry*, *63*(3), 241–244.

Saeed, S. A., & Bruce, T. J. (1998). Panic disorder: effective treatment options. *American Family Physician*, *57*(10), 2405–2412.

Salzman, C., Wolfson, A. N., Schatzberg, A., Looper, J., Henke, R., Albanese, M., et al. (1995). Effect of fluoxetine on anger in symptomatic volunteers with borderline personality disorder. *Journal of Clinical Psychopharmacology*, *15*(1), 23–29.

Schulz, S. C., Camlin, K. L., Berry, S. A., & Friedman, L. (1998, May). A double-blind study of risperidone for BPD (NR270). In: *151st Annual Meeting of the American Psychiatric Association*.

Schulz, S. C., Camlin, K. L., Berry, S. A., & Jesberger, J. A. (1999). Olanzapine safety and efficacy in patients with borderline personality disorder and comorbid dysthymia. *Biological Psychiatry*, *46*(10), 1429–1435.

Schulz, S. C., & Nelson, K. J. (2014). Somatic treatments. In J. M. Oldham, A. E. Skodol, & D. S. Bender (Eds.), *The American Psychiatric Publishing textbook of personality disorders* (2nd ed., pp. 321–343). Arlington, VA: American Psychiatric Publishing.

Schulz, S. C., Zanarini, M. C., Bateman, A., Bohus, M., Detke, H. C., Trzaskoma, Q., et al. (2008). Olanzapine for the treatment of borderline personality disorder: variable dose 12-week randomised double-blind placebo-controlled study. *The British Journal of Psychiatry*, *193*(6), 485–492.

Serban, G., & Siegel, S. (1984). Response of borderline and schizotypal patients to small doses of thiothixene and haloperidol. *The American Journal of Psychiatry*, *141*(11), 1455–1458.

Shaikh, U., Qamar, I., Jafry, F., Hassan, M., Shagufta, S., Odhejo, Y. I., et al. (2017). Patients with borderline personality disorder in emergency departments. *Frontiers in Psychiatry*, *8*, 136.

Sheard, M. H., Marini, J. L., Bridges, C. I., & Wagner, E. (1976). The effect of lithium on impulsive aggressive behavior in man. *The American Journal of Psychiatry*, *133*(12), 1409–1413.

Shen, W. W. (1999). A history of antipsychotic drug development. *Comprehensive Psychiatry*, *40*(6), 407–414.

Sherin, J. E., & Nemeroff, C. B. (2011). Post-traumatic stress disorder: the neurobiological impact of psychological trauma. *Dialogues in Clinical Neuroscience*, *13*(3), 263.

Simpson, E. B., Yen, S., Costello, E., Rosen, K., Begin, A., Pistorello, J., et al. (2004). Combined dialectical behavior therapy and fluoxetine in the treatment of borderline personality disorder. *Journal of Clinical Psychiatry*, *65*(3), 379–385.

Soler, J., Pascual, J. C., Campins, J., Barrachina, J., Puigdemont, D., Alvarez, E., et al. (2005). Double-blind, placebo-controlled study of dialectical behavior therapy plus olanzapine for borderline personality disorder. *American Journal of Psychiatry*, *162*(6), 1221–1224.

Soloff, P. H., Cornelius, J., George, A., Nathan, S., Perel, J. M., & Ulrich, R. F. (1993). Efficacy of phenelzine and haloperidol in borderline personality disorder. *Archives of General Psychiatry*, *50*(5), 377.

Soloff, P., George, A., Nathan, S., Schulz, P., Cornelius, J., Herring, J., et al. (1989). Amitriptyline versus haloperidol in borderlines: final outcomes and predictors of response. *Journal of Clinical Psychopharmacology*, *9*(4), 238–246.

Soloff, P. H., George, A., Nathan, R. S., Schulz, P. M., & Perel, J. M. (1986). Paradoxical effects of amitriptyline on borderline patients. *The American Journal of Psychiatry*, *143*(12), 1603–1605.

Stanford, M. S., Helfritz, L. E., Conklin, S. M., Villemarette-Pittman, N. R., Greve, K. W., Adams, D., et al. (2005). A comparison of anticonvulsants in the treatment of impulsive aggression. *Experimental and Clinical Psychopharmacology*, *13*(1), 72.

Stoffers, J., Völlm, B. A., Rücker, G., Timmer, A., Huband, N., & Lieb, K. (2010). Pharmacological interventions for borderline personality disorder. *The Cochrane Database of Systematic Reviews*, *6*, CD005653.

Tritt, K., Nickel, C., Lahmann, C., Leiberich, P. K., Rother, W. K., Loew, T. H., et al. (2005). Lamotrigine treatment of aggression in female borderline patients: a randomized, double-blind, placebo-controlled study. *Journal of Psychopharmacology*, *19*(3), 287–291.

Walker, C., Thomas, J., & Allen, T. S. (2003). Treating impulsivity, irritability, and aggression of antisocial personality disorder with quetiapine. *International Journal of Offender Therapy and Comparative Criminology*, *47*(5), 556–567.

Ward, F., Tharian, P., Roy, M., Deb, S., & Unwin, G. L. (2013). Efficacy of beta blockers in the management of problem behaviours in people with intellectual disabilities: a systematic review. *Research in Developmental Disabilities*, *34*(12), 4293–4303.

Zanarini, M. C., & Frankenburg, F. R. (2001). Olanzapine treatment of female borderline personality disorder patients: a double-blind, placebo-controlled pilot study. *The Journal of Clinical Psychiatry*, *62*(11), 849–854.

Zanarini, M. C., & Frankenburg, F. R. (2003). Omega-3 fatty acid treatment of women with borderline personality disorder: a double-blind, placebo-controlled pilot study. *American Journal of Psychiatry*, *160*(1), 167–169.

Zanarini, M. C., Frankenburg, F. R., & Parachini, E. A. (2004). A preliminary, randomized trial of fluoxetine, olanzapine, and the olanzapine-fluoxetine combination in women with borderline personality disorder. *The Journal of Clinical Psychiatry*, *65*(7), 903–907.

Zanarini, M. C., Schulz, S. C., Detke, H., Zhao, F., Lin, D., Pritchard, M., et al. (2012). Open-label treatment with olanzapine for patients with borderline personality disorder. *Journal of Clinical Psychopharmacology*, *32*(3), 398–402.

Volitional change in antagonism

27

Nathan W. Hudson
Department of Psychology, Southern Methodist University, Dallas, TX, United States

In the opening scenes of Charles Dickens's (1843) celebrated classic, *A Christmas Carol*, Ebenezer Scrooge was a bitter, antagonistic old miser. He had few friends and treated his business associates with cruelty. Rather than sympathize with the poor, he expressed disdain for them and disregard for their hardships. Indeed, the antagonism so deeply rooted in Scrooge's heart has been memorialized in his iconic catchphrase—"bah humbug"—words he used to openly mock both his own nephew's passion for life and the excitement and joy those around him felt during the holiday season.

One lonely Christmas Eve, however, the grace, redemption, and hope associated with the holiday coalesced and manifested itself to Scrooge as three ghosts. In attempt to redeem his soul, these spirits elucidated all that his antagonism had cost him—and might continue to steal from his future. The first apparition surveyed how Scrooge's personality had robbed his past of romantic love and the joy of fathering children. The second ghost revealed the relational connectedness absent from Scrooge's present. The final spirit prophesied that, should he remain unchanged, Scrooge would die a lonely, unmourned—perhaps even celebrated—death.

Terrified of these revelations, Scrooge vowed to change himself and upload the virtues of Christmas in his heart: love, generosity, kindness, relatedness, and joy. And true to his word, in the novella's final pages, Scrooge transformed from a bitter old man into a loving, generous father figure. In short, Scrooge changed his personality.

But fiction and holiday magic aside, can real people change their own personality traits? Is it possible to follow Scrooge's footsteps and become less antagonistic? Within the past several years, an emerging body of research on *volitional personality change*—people's desires and attempts to change their traits—has begun to grapple with this question. The purpose of this chapter is to review this literature, especially emphasizing findings pertaining to antagonism—operationalized via the big five personality trait of agreeableness (Goldberg, 1993; McCrae & Costa, 1987).

As an important preface, in both the personality and clinical literatures, *antagonism* and big five *agreeableness* simply represent opposite poles of the same unidimensional construct (in the same way that introversion and extraversion are opposite poles of a single continuum; McCrae & Costa, 1987; Suzuki, Samuel, Pahlen, & Krueger, 2015). When used in clinical contexts, *antagonism* refers to maladaptively low agreeableness. Ironically, however, item response theory analyses suggest that typical personality measures of agreeableness are more sensitive to variation on the extreme low end of the dimension than are clinical measures of antagonism (Suzuki et al., 2015). In other words, big five personality measures are adequate—and perhaps even ideal—

The Handbook of Antagonism. https://doi.org/10.1016/B978-0-12-814627-9.00027-X

for studying antagonism. Thus this chapter exclusively reviews research on people's desires and attempts to increase in *agreeableness*, with the understanding that "increasing in agreeableness" is synonymous with "decreasing in antagonism." Readers should bear in mind, however, that most research described in this chapter utilized convenience samples and thus may or may not generalize to individuals with clinically meaningful levels of antagonism.

Do people want to become more agreeable?

Scrooge was motivated to change his personality by spectral revelations that his antagonism would lead him to a lonely death. Along these lines, scholars have theorized for more than two decades that at least some people might want to change their personality traits if they are deeply dissatisfied with their lives (Baumeister, 1994; Kiecolt, 1994). But are *change goals*—desires to change personality traits—relegated to only the most dissatisfied and desperate individuals? Or do people in less dire circumstances also want to change their traits?

Despite the compelling nature of these questions, researchers have only recently begun to systematically investigate the prevalence and correlates of change goals. Nevertheless, multiple studies in this nascent body of literature have consistently found that the majority of people want to increase in agreeableness, as well as each of the other big five personality traits—extraversion, conscientiousness, emotional stability, and openness (Baranski, Morse, & Dunlop, 2017; Hudson & Fraley, 2016b; Hudson & Roberts, 2014; Robinson, Noftle, Guo, Asadi, & Zhang, 2015). For example, as depicted in Fig. 1, when change goals are measured via structured questionnaires (e.g., by adapting standard personality measures to assess how much people want to increase or decrease with respect to each item; see Hudson & Roberts, 2014), approximately 85% of people express desires to increase in agreeableness (Hudson & Fraley, 2016b). The distributions of change goals are similar for the other big five traits, as well (see Hudson & Fraley, 2017).

One limitation of structured change goals questionnaires, however, is that they may *impose* goals upon participants. For example, there may be social demand to indicate that one wants to become more "helpful and unselfish" when directly asked—irrespective of whether one truly desires this change. Partly addressing this issue, one study found that approximately 70% of people answer "yes" when asked whether they would like to change an aspect of their personality. When subsequently prompted in an open-ended fashion to list *an aspect* (i.e., only one) that they wish to change, approximately 20% of participants freely volunteer attributes related to agreeableness (e.g., "hold grudges less"; Baranski et al., 2017). Although this study found somewhat lower prevalence of goals to change agreeableness (e.g., ~20%) than is typically found using structured questionnaires (e.g., ~85%; Hudson & Fraley, 2016b), it is possible that if participants were prompted to create a more exhaustive list of desired changes (rather than only one) that a greater proportion would volunteer desires to change attributes related to each big five trait—as they do with structured questionnaires (Hudson & Fraley, 2016b).

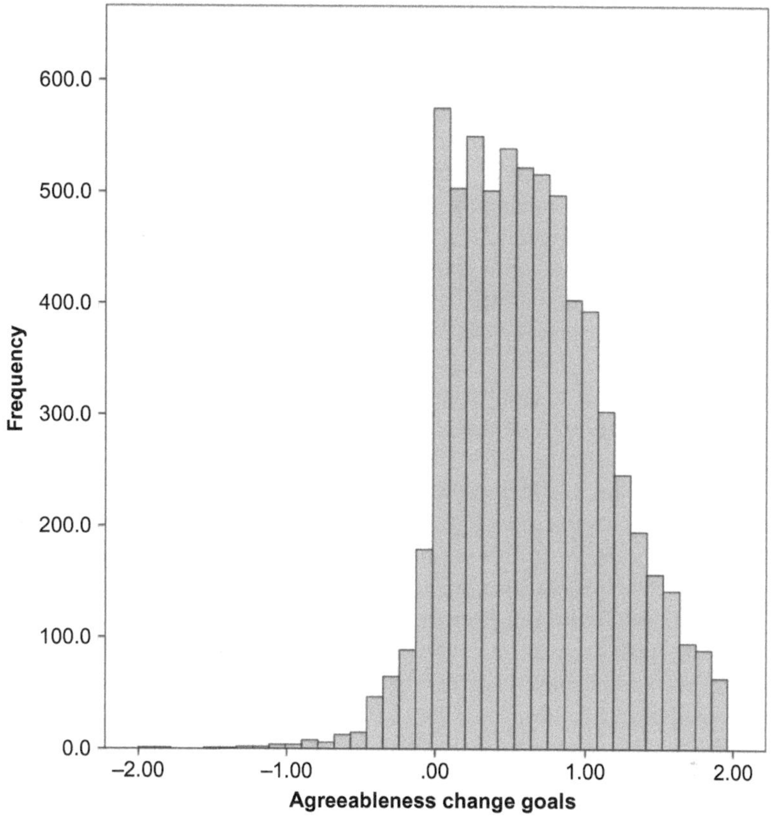

Fig. 1 Histogram of participants' agreeableness change goals, as measured via the 9-item agreeableness subscale from the Change Goals Big Five Inventory (Hudson & Roberts, 2014). Positive values represent goals to increase. Negative values represent goals to decrease. Zero values represent goals to remain the same. Eighty-five percent of people desire to increase in agreeableness.
Data from Hudson, N.W., & Fraley, R.C. (2016b). Do people's desires to change their personality traits vary with age? An examination of trait change goals across adulthood. *Social Psychological and Personality Science*, *7*, 847–856.

In sum, research suggests that it does not require circumstances as dramatic as Scrooge's to motivate change goals. Rather, change goals are normative: Most people want to change their personality traits—and it appears that most people mirror Scrooge's desire to increase in agreeableness.

Why do people want to become more agreeable?

Broadly, scholars have argued that change goals can be both intrinsically and extrinsically motivated (Hennecke, Bleidorn, Denissen, & Wood, 2014; Hudson & Roberts, 2014; Kiecolt, 1994). With respect to intrinsic motivation (see Deci & Ryan, 2000), high levels of agreeableness per se—and each of the other positively keyed big five traits—are widely valued and socially desirable (Dunlop, Telford, & Morrison, 2012; Hudson & Roberts, 2014; Lamkin, Maples-Keller, & Miller, 2018). Moreover, high agreeableness is a component of psychological maturity—as are conscientiousness and emotional stability (Roberts & Mroczek, 2008; Roberts, Wood, & Caspi, 2008). Thus people may wish to increase in desirable traits such as agreeableness for the value those traits inherently have in and of themselves (e.g., to become a "better person"). Supporting this idea, in general, nonclinical samples, trait agreeableness is negatively correlated with goals to become more agreeable. In other words, it is the most antagonistic individuals who express the greatest desires to become more agreeable—perhaps because they wish to possess a valuable trait they lack (Hudson & Roberts, 2014).

With respect to extrinsic motivation (see Deci & Ryan, 2000), like Scrooge, people may desire to increase in traits that they perceive to have utility value in assuaging specific sources of dissatisfaction in their lives or facilitating the attainment of desired outcomes (Baumeister, 1994; Hudson & Roberts, 2014; Kiecolt, 1994). For example, Scrooge wanted to become more agreeable because he believed doing so would help him avoid a lonely death. In this case, empirical research suggests that reality may mirror fiction: Real people also seem to want to change traits they believe will improve their lives (Hudson & Roberts, 2014; Quinlan, Jaccard, & Blanton, 2006).

Studies have most strongly illustrated this phenomenon for extraversion. For example, students want to increase in extraversion if they fear becoming boring persons in the future (Quinlan et al., 2006) or if they believe extraversion will help them in future career endeavors (Stevenson & Clegg, 2011). Similarly, college students who are dissatisfied with their friendships or recreational activities report desires to increase in extraversion—perhaps because they reason that being more extraverted would improve their social lives or enable them to better capitalize on exciting hobbies (Hudson & Roberts, 2014).

In contrast to extraversion, it is less clear from existing research what types of extrinsic motives might underlie goals to increase in agreeableness. Although research suggests that antagonistic individuals recognize that their antagonism impairs their lives (Miller et al., 2017), only one study to date has explicitly examined the correlations between satisfaction with various life domains (e.g., friendships, recreational activities) and change goals. This study used a college sample and found that dissatisfaction with seemingly relevant life domains was *not* correlated with goals to become more agreeable (Hudson & Roberts, 2014). For example, college students who were dissatisfied with their social lives did not indicate goals to increase in agreeableness. Rather, such students tended to express goals to become more *extraverted.* Although agreeableness is certainly relevant for social success (e.g., Ozer & Benet-Martínez, 2006), college students may intuit that popularity is determined to such a great extent by extraversion that they overlook other important determinants, such as agreeableness (Hudson & Roberts, 2014). Thus it is not clear what types of life domains laypersons mentally link to agreeableness.

Subsequent studies have provided hints, however, that people may desire agreeableness partially for its utility value in performing generative roles, such as contributing to one's community and investing in subsequent generations. For example, Hudson and Fraley (2016b) recruited an online sample of more than 7000 participants with ages ranging from 18 to 70. They found that agreeableness is one of the least valued traits among younger, college-aged adults. As people age, however, the relative importance of agreeableness (vs other traits) appears to increase. In fact, among older adults, agreeableness is the second most-valued trait (emotionally stability is the most valued trait irrespective of age). Based on these findings, Hudson and Fraley (2016b) theorized that agreeableness likely has higher utility value for the types of generative roles that characterize middle-to-late adulthood (e.g., caring for romantic partners, children, and aging parents; contributing back to one's community; see Erikson, 1974; Hutteman, Hennecke, Orth, Reitz, & Specht, 2014) than it does for the roles that are more typical for younger adults. Thus older adults may value agreeableness because they perceive it would facilitate performance in generative roles and smooth their ability to handle common problems (e.g., effectively providing love to difficult children). In contrast, younger adults' concerns may focus more upon their academic/career and social endeavors—and they may intuit that conscientiousness and extraversion, respectively, are most relevant to those domains (Hudson & Roberts, 2014).

To summarize, people want to increase in agreeableness—and each of the other big five traits—both for intrinsic and extrinsic reasons. Agreeableness is socially desirable in and of itself. Moreover, agreeableness may have utility value in helping people succeed and thrive in generative roles.

Can people volitionally increase in agreeableness?

Scrooge did not stop at vowing to become more agreeable; rather, he followed through on his word and actually changed. In fact, according to the penultimate paragraph of *A Christmas Carol*, "Scrooge was better than his word.... He became as good a friend, as good a master, and as good a man, as the good old city knew, or any other good old city, town, or borough, in the good old world" (Dickens, 1843). Admittedly, the changes that Scrooge experienced to his personality were extreme. Nevertheless, an emerging body of research suggests that Scrooge's story may contain trappings of truth: Ordinary people may also be able to change their traits in desired ways, albeit to a much more moderate degree.

To date, five intensive longitudinal studies have examined the associations between change goals and growth in agreeableness over time. In these studies, students' change goals were measured at the beginning of a college semester. Over the following 4 months—the full semester—participants' personality traits were repeatedly measured on a weekly basis. Across all five studies, goals to increase in agreeableness consistently predicted subsequent trait growth (Hudson, Derringer, & Briley, 2018; Hudson & Fraley, 2015, 2016a, in press-b). In other words, people who indicated greater desires to increase in agreeableness at the beginning of the semester experienced more positive growth in agreeableness over time, as compared with their peers who did not wish to change. For example, as seen in Fig. 2, which depicts data from Hudson and Fraley's (2015) original volitional change study, participants who reported relatively high desires to increase in agreeableness tended to experience positive growth in trait agreeableness. In contrast, participants who did not wish to change did not experience positive growth in agreeableness over the same period of time. Similar findings have been observed for extraversion, conscientiousness, and emotional stability.

Notably, the personality changes that people experienced in each of these studies were relatively modest. For example, as Fig. 2 depicts, people with relatively strong agreeableness change goals were predicted to increase approximately 0.16 standard deviations in agreeableness across 4 months. In fact, the largest effect size in any of Hudson and colleagues' studies was that in one study, with the aid of an effective intervention, people who wanted to become more extraverted were expected to increase, on average, 0.45 standard deviations in extraversion across 4 months (Hudson & Fraley, 2015, Study 2). Thus in stark contrast to Scrooge's literal overnight transformation from extreme antagonism into radiant agreeableness, personality changes appear to occur slowly and moderately for nonfictitious individuals. Nevertheless, people do appear to change in ways that align with their desires.

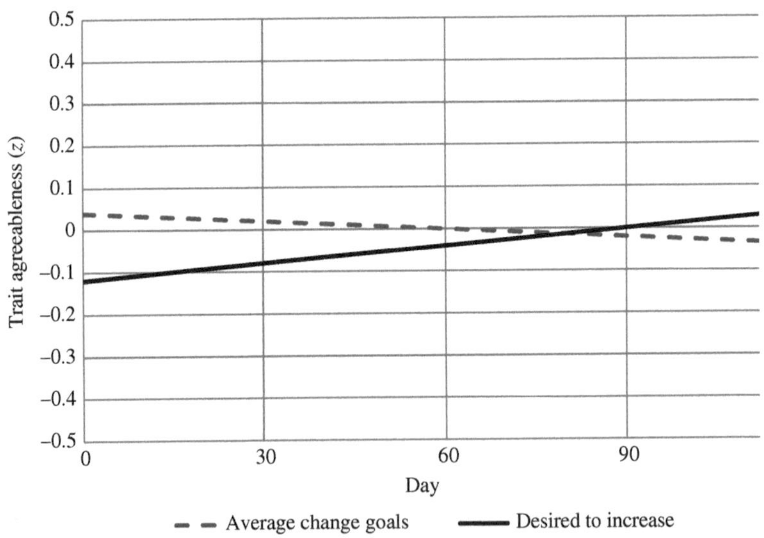

Fig. 2 Agreeableness change goals predicting subsequent growth in trait agreeableness. People with higher change goals tend to experience more positive growth in agreeableness. The "average change goals" line is plotted at the sample mean in agreeableness change goals (original scale score = 0.58). The "desired to increase" line is plotted at one standard deviation above the mean in agreeableness change goals (original scale score = 1.03).
From Hudson, N. W., & Fraley, R. C. (2015). Volitional personality trait change: can people choose to change their personality traits? *Journal of Personality and Social Psychology, 109*, 490–507. Study 1 data.

Mechanisms underlying trait change

How might people be able to change their traits in desired ways? Before considering this question, it is useful to overview how personality change occurs more generally. According to modern personality theory, trait development occurs whenever people change their state-level thoughts, feelings, and behaviors and maintain those changes over an extended time (Hudson & Fraley, 2015; Magidson, Roberts, Collado-Rodriguez, & Lejuez, 2012; Roberts & Jackson, 2008). For example, studies have found that people who intentionally engage in elevated levels of extraverted, conscientious, or emotionally stable behaviors for several months tend to actually increase in the respective traits (Hudson, Briley, Chopik, & Derringer, 2018; Hudson & Fraley, 2015). Similarly, multiple studies have found that regularly practicing techniques to reduce anxiety regarding one's attachment relationships (e.g., expressively writing about one's insecurities) can lead to lasting increases in trait-level attachment security (Carnelley & Rowe, 2007; Gillath, Selcuk, & Shaver, 2008; Hudson & Fraley, 2018).

Why do chronically maintained changes in thoughts, feelings, and behaviors eventually lead to trait-level changes? There are at least three possibilities. First, changes to thoughts, feelings, and behaviors that are maintained for sufficient time may eventually become learned, automatized, and habitual (Hennecke et al., 2014; Hudson & Fraley, 2015). Thus in the same way that children can be trained to be habitually more agreeable (e.g., saying "please" and "thank you") or conscientious (e.g., regularly brushing their teeth), adults may be able to incorporate a variety of new behaviors into their relatively automatic behavioral repertoire.

Second, changes to thoughts, feelings, and behaviors may influence people's identities. For example, a person who chronically engages in kind, tenderhearted behaviors may come to view him- or herself as a fundamentally agreeable person. Individuals may then strive to pull their thoughts, feelings, and behaviors into alignment with newly adopted identities (Burke, 2006; Roberts & Wood, 2006). Thus an individual who views him- or herself as agreeable may strive to behave in kind, tenderhearted manners—producing a self-reinforcing cycle of behavior and identity change.

Finally, scholars have postulated that chronically maintained changes to thoughts, feelings, and behaviors may affect people's biology. These physiological changes may serve as the underlying "biological code" that facilitates lasting trait change. For instance, Roberts and Jackson (2008) argued that changes to thoughts, feelings, and behaviors may alter the epigenome. These epigenetic changes, in turn, educe enduring trait change. As one concrete example, studies with lab rats have found that chronic experiences of emotional stability lead to epigenetic changes (e.g., methylation) that reduce the animals' reactivity to stress hormones (e.g., cortisol). Lower reactivity to stress hormones, in turn, facilitates enduring gains in emotional stability (Weaver et al., 2004). In humans, research suggests that chronic stressful experiences can also alter the physiological structure of the nervous system (e.g., the brain), leading to lasting gains in neuroticism (McEwen, Eiland, Hunter, & Miller, 2012).

In short, chronic changes to state-level thoughts, feelings, and behaviors can eventually coalesce into trait change. Historically, these processes have been used to explain how people's personality traits are passively changed by their life circumstances and social roles (e.g., Lodi-Smith & Roberts, 2007). As one example, successfully committing to social roles typically requires one to internalize and adhere to certain behavioral standards. Excelling in one's career, for instance, often requires one to behave in a conscientious manner (e.g., being punctual, thorough, hardworking; Judge, Higgins, Thoresen, & Barrick, 1999). Thus committing to one's career can lead to enduring gains in conscientious behaviors and, in turn, trait conscientiousness (Hudson & Roberts, 2016; Hudson, Roberts, & Lodi-Smith, 2012). Similarly, romantic relationships can serve as strong, consistent presses to behave in agreeable and emotionally stable manners—perhaps evoking growth in these traits over time (e.g., Lehnart, Neyer, & Eccles, 2010). In sum, people's life circumstances and social roles can shape their thoughts, feelings, and behaviors—eventually producing corresponding trait change.

Volitional personality change

Recently, scholars have begun to question whether strong, external presses (e.g., social roles) are necessary to consistently evoke new thoughts, feelings, and behaviors and eventually spur trait change. Instead, they have postulated that intrapsychic factors, such as the self's volition, might also be sufficiently strong to facilitate trait development (e.g., Hennecke et al., 2014; Hudson & Fraley, 2015; Hudson & Roberts, 2014). In other words, as in Scrooge's story, people might be able to manually modify their thoughts, feelings, and behaviors to volitionally change their personalities.

As reviewed before, preliminary correlational longitudinal data seem to support the idea that people can volitionally change their traits. Across five intensive longitudinal studies, participants tended to change in ways that aligned with their desires (Hudson et al., 2018; Hudson & Fraley, 2015, 2016a, in press-b). For instance, participants who wanted to become more agreeable tended to actually increase in agreeableness at a faster/more positive rate than did their peers who did not wish to change (see Fig. 2).

Moreover, research suggests that attaining desired changes may improve people's well-being. In one intensive longitudinal study, participants who experienced trait growth aligning with their change goals tended to report simultaneous gains in life satisfaction (Hudson & Fraley, 2016a). As depicted in Fig. 3, for example, participants who desired to become more agreeable *and then actually increased* in agreeableness tended to experience larger gains in life satisfaction, as compared with their peers who experienced equivalent growth in trait agreeableness despite not wanting to change. Thus attaining *desired* changes (i.e., volitionally changing oneself) appears to predict heightened subjective well-being, above and beyond the effects of trait growth per se.

The fact that people appear to change in ways that align with their desires—and that doing so may increase their well-being—has naturally raised questions about the processes through which volitional change might occur, as well as whether interventions may be able to help people attain desired changes. To that end, at least three longitudinal experiments have tested interventions designed to (1) explore the mechanisms underlying volitional change, and (2) help people change (Hudson et al., in press; Hudson & Fraley, 2015). All three interventions were premised on the idea that

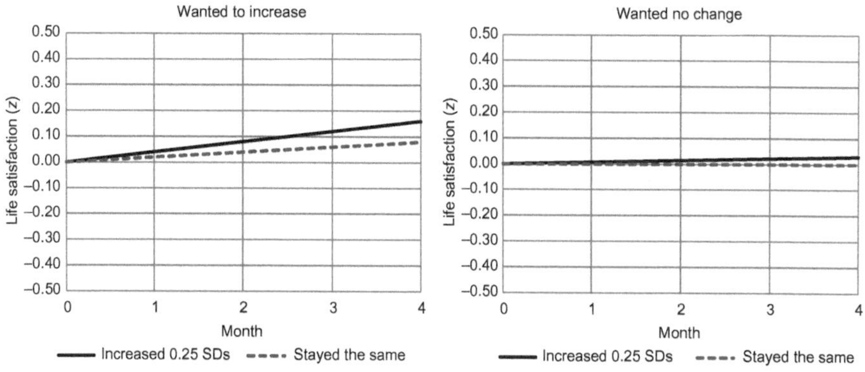

Fig. 3 Growth in life satisfaction as a function of the interaction between agreeableness change goals and experienced growth in trait agreeableness. The "wanted to increase" lines are plotted at a scale score of "1" on the original change goals scale ($z = 1.02$). The "wanted no change" lines are plotted at a scale score of "0" on the original change goals scale ($z = -1.06$). The "increased 0.25 SDs" lines represent individuals who reported increasing 0.25 *SDs* in trait agreeableness across the study. The "stayed the same" lines represent individuals who experienced zero growth in trait agreeableness. Both graphs are plotted with a starting score of 3.66 ($z = 0$) in agreeableness.
Reproduced from Hudson, N. W., & Fraley, R. C. (2016a). Changing for the better? Longitudinal associations between volitional change and psychological well-being. *Personality and Social Psychology Bulletin*, *42*, 603–615.

prolonged changes to thoughts, feelings, and behaviors might promote trait growth. Thus all three interventions were designed to help participants plan, organize, and implement cognitive, affective, and behavioral changes on an ongoing basis.

Hudson and Fraley (2015) tested two very similar interventions. Participants in two intensive longitudinal studies were randomly assigned to receive a weekly goal-setting intervention or to participate in a control task. Participants in the intervention group were asked to generate three concrete, small steps they could take each week to pull their thoughts, feelings, and behaviors into alignment with their desired traits. The original intent was that a person who wanted to become more agreeable, for example, might generate goals similar to, "Send an encouraging text message to a friend this week," or "Donate $5 to a charity this week."

In their first study, Hudson and Fraley's (2015) intervention backfired—producing growth *opposite* people's desired changes in agreeableness, conscientiousness, and emotional stability. That is, a person in the intervention group who wanted to become more agreeable was likely to experience *less positive/more negative* growth in agreeableness, as compared with a person with equivalent change goals in the control group. In reviewing participants' written weekly goals, Hudson and Fraley noticed that many participants had generated abstract, vague intentions that prescribed little concrete action, such as "help others," or "improve my social skills." Hudson and Fraley speculated that these type of goals provided insufficient guidance and structure for behavioral change—and thus it was likely that many participants who authored these vague intentions were not actually changing their behavior (the presumed active ingredient for trait change).

Moreover, simply participating in the intervention may have been construed by participants as making progress toward their change goals, undermining motivation for them to take other steps that might have actually produced change (Gollwitzer, Sheeran, Michalski, & Seifert, 2009). In other words, even sans experimenter intervention, people appear to naturalistically take steps to change their own personality traits (see Hudson & Fraley, 2015; Quinlan et al., 2006; Stevenson & Clegg, 2011). Declaring intentions to change and participating in an intervention per se may have been construed by participants as progress toward their goals. This may have undermined their motivation to take other steps to change their traits—even steps they would have naturalistically taken without any sort of external intervention (Gollwitzer et al., 2009).

To overcome these limitations, in a second study, Hudson and Fraley (2015) more thoroughly coached participants to generate concrete, realistic, attainable goals they could *actually do* each week to pull their thoughts, feelings, and behaviors in alignment with their desired traits (e.g., "I will thank my instructor for her lecture on Tuesday"). Moreover, participants were explicitly warned against generating vague, nonspecific goals. This revised intervention appeared to be efficacious. Participants who were randomly assigned to the improved goal-setting intervention experienced much larger changes in extraversion, conscientiousness, and emotional stability—but not agreeableness or openness—as compared with their peers in a control condition.

Finally, Hudson et al. (in press) tested a slightly different intervention in which participants were provided with prewritten (by the researchers) cognitive, affective, and behavioral "challenges" that they could accept and attempt to accomplish each week. As with Hudson and Fraley's prior interventions, the challenges were designed to pull participants' thoughts, feelings, and behaviors into alignment with their desired traits. For example, prototypical agreeableness challenges included, "If someone asks you for a favor, do it" and "Send a friend an encouraging text."

By providing prewritten goals, this intervention ensured that all participants were implementing concrete behavioral changes. Moreover, unlike Hudson and Fraley's (2015) prior interventions, in which participants all wrote three weekly goals, in Hudson et al.' (in press) intervention, participants were free to accept between 1 and 4 challenges per week. Thus there was individual variation in the extent to which people were attempting to change their behavior. Finally, participants also reported whether they had completed each accepted challenge or not. Thus Hudson et al. (in press) were able to isolate the extent to which people's personality traits changed as a function of (1) participating in an intervention (accepting challenges), and (2) actually changing their behavior (completing challenges).

In this study, completing more numerous challenges predicted growth in extraversion, agreeableness, conscientiousness, and emotional stability—although the effect for agreeableness fell just short of statistical significance. This finding supports modern personality theory that changes to state-level behavior have the potential to coalesce into trait growth (e.g., Magidson et al., 2012). Moreover, accepting *but not completing* challenges backfired: Participants who accepted but failed more numerous challenges tended to experience trait growth in the *opposite* direction of their desires. For example, persons who accepted many challenges pertaining to agreeableness *and then failed those challenges* were predicted to *decrease* in agreeableness across time. This finding appears to align with Hudson and Fraley's (2015) explanation that merely making intentions to change—and declaring those intentions, even to a computer screen while completing an online study—may be construed as goal progress and undermine effective goal pursuit (Gollwitzer et al., 2009).

To summarize, three interventions have tested whether making small cognitive, affective, and behavioral changes has the potential to catalyze trait growth. These studies have converged on the finding that regularly pulling one's thoughts, feelings, and behaviors into alignment with one's desired traits can, in fact, produce trait change. For example, a person who wants to become more agreeable may be able to do so by simply engaging in increased levels of agreeable behaviors over the course of several months. Moreover, interventions that help participants thoughtfully plan and implement concrete, specific, attainable changes to their behavior can facilitate volitional change efforts. Collectively, these findings align with and support theory that prolonged changes to state-level thoughts, feelings, and behaviors can eventually coalesce into enduring trait-level changes (Hennecke et al., 2014; Hudson & Fraley, 2015; Magidson et al., 2012; Roberts & Jackson, 2008).

Interventions and agreeableness. As reviewed before, three interventions have been tested to help participants make desired changes to their personality traits. These interventions appeared to be effective in helping people increase in extraversion, conscientiousness, and emotional stability. Notably, however, none of the interventions had a statistically significant effect in facilitating growth in agreeableness.

Why did these interventions fail to help people change with respect to agreeableness? There exist at least two possibilities. First, it may be the case that participants in Hudson and colleagues' studies were not pursuing changes in agreeableness as enthusiastically as they were pursuing changes in other traits. Specifically, across all interventions, participants were asked to nominate which traits they wanted to work on changing over the course of the semester. For instance, a participant might indicate that s/he wanted to work on changing extraversion and emotional stability during the study. The interventions were then tailored to individuals' goals: Participants were prompted to change behaviors relevant only to the nominated traits.

Likely due to the college-aged samples used in each study, participants were more than twice as likely to nominate that they wanted to work on extraversion, conscientiousness, and emotional stability, as compared to agreeableness (see Hudson & Fraley, 2016b). For example, in Hudson and Fraley's (2015) successful intervention study, only 11% of participants chose to work on changing agreeableness—as compared with more than 25% of participants choosing each of extraversion, conscientiousness, and emotional stability. Similarly, in Hudson et al.' (in press) intervention, only about 20% of participants chose to work on agreeableness—whereas closer to 50%–60% of participants nominated each of extraversion, conscientiousness, and emotional stability. Thus it may have been the case that sample sizes of participants actively working on changing agreeableness were too small in each of these studies to reliably detect effects. In other words, the interventions may have failed to produce statistically significant findings for agreeableness due to low statistical power and sampling error.

Similarly, although the majority of college students do express desires to become more agreeable, they express even greater desires to increase in the other four traits (Hudson & Fraley, 2016b). In other words, agreeableness is the trait for which college students *least* desire changes. Thus the college-aged participants in Hudson and colleagues' intervention studies may have lacked sufficient motivation to consistently change their agreeable behaviors. It may be the case that, if Hudson and colleagues' studies were replicated with older adults—who tend to value agreeableness to a greater degree than do younger adults (Hudson & Fraley, 2016b)—that a greater portion of participants would choose to specifically work on changing agreeableness, that they would be more motivated to change their agreeable behaviors, and that the intervention would consequently exhibit greater efficacy in changing agreeableness.

Alternatively, it may be the case that agreeableness is simply more difficult to change via pure volition alone, as compared with extraversion, conscientiousness, and emotional stability. Prior research suggests that more systemic interventions (such as committing to a career) can produce changes in agreeableness (e.g., Hudson & Roberts, 2016). Thus it may be the case that more powerful interventions would be required to change agreeableness, as compared with the other traits. Future research is needed to elucidate which strategies are most effective in helping people grow in agreeableness—as well as the other four traits.

To summarize, most people want to change their personality traits—including agreeableness. Moreover, people tend to change in ways that align with their desires. Goal-setting interventions that help people effectively plan changes to their thoughts, feelings, and behaviors appear to facilitate growth in extraversion, conscientiousness, and emotional stability—but not necessarily agreeableness. Future research is needed to determine whether this lack of efficacy in interventions targeting agreeableness is due to low participant motivation to change agreeableness—or whether the strategies utilized by existing interventions (e.g., setting weekly behavioral goals) are insufficient to change agreeableness.

Future directions

Ebenezer Scrooge was able to change his antagonistic personality—and in doing so, dramatically improve his well-being. Preliminary research suggests that real people can follow Scrooge's footsteps and volitionally change their personality traits, as well—potentially improving their well-being in the process. However, the emerging body of literature on volitional change is still in its infancy. Thus many critical questions remain unexplored.

Two of the most crucial immediate questions concern (1) the extent to which individuals can change their personality traits, and (2) whether volitional changes can be maintained over extended timeframes (e.g., years). With respect to the former, all intensive longitudinal studies examining volitional change to date have used relatively short timeframes—approximately 4 months. During these spans of time, participants experienced relatively linear growth in their personality traits. However, it seems unlikely that people can change their traits ad infinitum; rather, it seems likely that most individuals will eventually experience diminishing returns in their efforts to change. Future research is needed to understand the boundaries of change—and individual differences that might influence the amount of trait growth people can experience.

With respect to the latter, it remains an open question whether people can *maintain* changes to their personality traits across time. A recent meta-analysis of how personality changes in response to psychotherapy suggest that "real" trait growth can occur quickly (e.g., within 6 weeks) and last for years after interventions are discontinued (Roberts et al., 2017). However, it is unclear whether self-driven efforts to change one's own personality can similarly produce enduring trait growth—or whether people might revert to their baseline levels of each trait after they stop "working on" changing. Future studies using longer timeframes are necessary to disentangle these possibilities.

Focusing specifically on volitional change in antagonism, future research needs to explore the generalizability of the findings described within this chapter. Namely, most of the work described here utilized convenience samples of college students or internet users. Thus little is known about volitional change processes in samples with clinically meaningful levels of antagonism. For example, although relatively disagreeable college students tend to desire increases in agreeableness (Hudson & Roberts, 2014), it is unclear whether persons with extreme levels of antagonism necessarily want to become warmer, kinder, more tenderhearted persons (although preliminary research suggests they may; Miller et al., 2017). Similarly, although interventions designed to help college students become more agreeable were less efficacious than interventions targeting extraversion, conscientiousness, and emotional stability (Hudson et al., in press; Hudson & Fraley, 2015), it is unclear why this phenomenon occurred. As one possibility, college students may be insufficiently motivated to change their agreeableness. Consequently, interventions targeting agreeableness may be more efficacious among older adults who tend to exhibit greater motivation to become more agreeable (Hudson & Fraley, 2016b), or among samples with extreme levels of antagonism (who have more "room" to grow). Thus the work described in this chapter could be replicated with extremely antagonistic samples to test whether the findings generalize.

Conclusion

Recent research suggests that Ebenezer Scrooge's journey of self-change reflects a kernel of truth. Like Scrooge, most people are motivated to become more agreeable. Moreover, an emerging body of studies suggests that people can, in fact, follow Scrooge's footsteps and actually increase in agreeableness. Future research should continue to elucidate more fully which strategies and circumstances best enable individuals to realize their change goals—and the extent to which those findings generalize to clinical and/or older adult samples.

References

Baranski, E. N., Morse, P. J., & Dunlop, W. L. (2017). Lay conceptions of volitional personality change: from strategies pursued to stories told. *Journal of Personality*, *85*, 285–299.

Baumeister, R. F. (1994). The crystallization of discontent in the process of major life change. In T. F. Heatherton & J. L. Weinberger (Eds.), *Can personality change?* (pp. 281–297). Washington, DC: American Psychological Association.

Burke, P. J. (2006). Identity change. *Social Psychology Quarterly*, *69*, 81–96.

Carnelley, K. B., & Rowe, A. C. (2007). Repeated priming of attachment security influences later views of self and relationships. *Personal Relationships*, *14*, 307–320.

Deci, E. L., & Ryan, R. M. (2000). The "what" and "why" of goal pursuits: human needs and the self-determination of behavior. *Psychological Inquiry*, *11*, 227–268.

Dickens, C. (1843). *A Christmas Carol*. England: Chapman & Hall.

Dunlop, P. D., Telford, A. D., & Morrison, D. L. (2012). Not too little, but not too much: the perceived desirability of responses to personality items. *Journal of Research in Personality*, *46*, 8–18.

Erikson, E. H. (1974). *Dimensions of a new identity*. New York, NY: Norton.

Gillath, O., Selcuk, E., & Shaver, P. R. (2008). Moving toward a secure attachment style: can repeated security priming help? *Social and Personality Psychology Compass*, *2*, 1651–1666.

Goldberg, L. R. (1993). The structure of phenotypic personality traits. *American Psychologist*, *48*, 26–34.

Gollwitzer, P. M., Sheeran, P., Michalski, V., & Seifert, A. E. (2009). When intentions go public: does social reality widen the intention-behavior gap? *Psychological Science*, *20*, 612–618.

Hennecke, M., Bleidorn, W., Denissen, J. J. A., & Wood, D. (2014). A three-part framework for self-regulated personality development across adulthood. *European Journal of Personality*, *28*, 289–299.

Hudson, N. W., Briley, D. A., Chopik, W. J., & Derringer, J. (2018). You have to follow through: attaining behavioral change goals predicts volitional personality change. Advance online publication. *Journal of Personality and Social Psychology*. https://doi.org/10.1037/pspp0000221.

Hudson, N. W., Derringer, J. L., & Briley, D. A. (2018). *Does the motive for wanting to change one's personality matter? I: Intrinsically motivated volitional change goals predict greater trait change*. (unpublished manuscript).

Hudson, N. W., & Fraley, R. C. (2015). Volitional personality trait change: can people choose to change their personality traits? *Journal of Personality and Social Psychology*, *109*, 490–507.

Hudson, N. W., & Fraley, R. C. (2016a). Changing for the better? Longitudinal associations between volitional change and psychological well-being. *Personality and Social Psychology Bulletin*, *42*, 603–615.

Hudson, N. W., & Fraley, R. C. (2016b). Do people's desires to change their personality traits vary with age? An examination of trait change goals across adulthood. *Social Psychological and Personality Science*, *7*, 847–856.

Hudson, N. W., & Fraley, R. C. (2017). Volitional personality change. In J. Specht (Ed.), *Personality development across the lifespan* (pp. 555–571). San Diego, CA: Elsevier.

Hudson, N. W., & Fraley, R. C. (2018). Moving toward greater security: the effects of repeatedly priming attachment security and anxiety. *Journal of Research in Personality*, *74*, 147–157.

Hudson, N. W., & Fraley, R. C. (in press-b). To what extent do beliefs and expectations moderate volitional change processes?

Hudson, N. W., & Roberts, B. W. (2014). Goals to change personality traits: concurrent links between personality traits, daily behavior, and goals to change oneself. *Journal of Research in Personality*, *53*, 68–83.

Hudson, N. W., & Roberts, B. W. (2016). Social investment in work reliably predicts change in conscientiousness and agreeableness: a direct replication and extension of Hudson, Roberts, and Lodi-Smith (2012). *Journal of Research in Personality*, *60*, 12–23.

Hudson, N. W., Roberts, B. W., & Lodi-Smith, J. (2012). Personality trait development and social investment in work. *Journal of Research in Personality*, *46*, 334–344.

Hutteman, R., Hennecke, M., Orth, U., Reitz, A. K., & Specht, J. (2014). Developmental tasks as a framework to study personality development in adulthood and old age. *European Journal of Personality*, *28*, 267–278.

Judge, T. A., Higgins, C. A., Thoresen, C. J., & Barrick, M. R. (1999). The big five personality traits, general mental ability, and career success across the life span. *Personnel Psychology*, *52*, 621–652.

Kiecolt, K. J. (1994). Stress and the decision to change oneself: a theoretical model. *Social Psychology Quarterly*, *57*, 49–63.

Lamkin, J., Maples-Keller, J. L., & Miller, J. D. (2018). How likable are personality disorder and general personality traits to those who possess them? *Journal of Personality*, *86*, 173–185.

Lehnart, J., Neyer, F. J., & Eccles, J. (2010). Long-term effects of social investment: the case of partnering in young adulthood. *Journal of Personality*, *78*, 639–670.

Lodi-Smith, J., & Roberts, B. W. (2007). Social investment and personality: a meta-analysis of the relationship of personality traits to investment in work, family, religion, and volunteerism. *Personality and Social Psychology Review*, *11*, 68–86.

Magidson, J. F., Roberts, B. W., Collado-Rodriguez, A., & Lejuez, C. W. (2012). Theory-driven intervention for changing personality: expectancy value theory, behavioral activation, and conscientiousness. *Developmental Psychology*, *50*(5), 1442–1450.

McCrae, R. R., & Costa, P. T. (1987). Validation of the five-factor model of personality across instruments and observers. *Journal of Personality and Social Psychology*, *52*, 81–90.

McEwen, B. S., Eiland, L., Hunter, R. G., & Miller, M. M. (2012). Stress and anxiety: structural plasticity and epigenetic regulation as a consequence of stress. *Neuropharmacology*, *62*, 3–12.

Miller, J. D., Sleep, C. E., Lamkin, J., Vize, C., Campbell, W. K., & Lynam, D. R. (2017). Personality disorder traits: Perceptions of likability, impairment, and ability to change as correlates and moderators of desired level. *Personality Disorders: Theory, Research, and Treatment*,.

Ozer, D. J., & Benet-Martínez, V. (2006). Personality and the prediction of consequential outcomes. *Annual Review of Psychology*, *57*, 401–421.

Quinlan, S. L., Jaccard, J., & Blanton, H. (2006). A decision theoretic and prototype conceptualization of possible selves: implications for the prediction of risk behavior. *Journal of Personality*, *74*, 599–630.

Roberts, B. W., & Jackson, J. J. (2008). Sociogenomic personality psychology. *Journal of Personality*, *76*, 1523–1544.

Roberts, B. W., Luo, J., Briley, D. A., Chow, P. I., Su, R., & Hill, P. L. (2017). A systematic review of personality trait change through intervention. *Psychological Bulletin*, *143*, 117–141.

Roberts, B. W., & Mroczek, D. (2008). Personality trait change in adulthood. *Current Directions in Psychological Science*, *17*, 31.

Roberts, B. W., & Wood, D. (2006). Personality development in the context of the neo-socioanalytic model of personality. In D. K. Mroczek & T. D. Little (Eds.), *Handbook of personality development* (pp. 11–39). Mahwah, NJ: Lawrence Erlbaum Associates.

Roberts, B. W., Wood, D., & Caspi, A. (2008). The development of personality traits in adulthood. In O. P. John, R. W. Robins, & L. A. Pervin (Eds.), *Handbook of personality: Theory and research* (pp. 375–398). (3rd ed.). New York, NY: The Guilford Press.

Robinson, O. C., Noftle, E. E., Guo, J., Asadi, S., & Zhang, X. (2015). Goals and plans for Big Five personality trait change in young adults. *Journal of Research in Personality*, *59*, 31–43.

Stevenson, J., & Clegg, S. (2011). Possible selves: students orientating themselves towards the future through extracurricular activity. *British Educational Research Journal*, *37*, 231–246.

Suzuki, T., Samuel, D. B., Pahlen, S., & Krueger, R. F. (2015). DSM-5 alternative personality disorder model traits as maladaptive extreme variants of the five-factor model: an item-response theory analysis. *Journal of Abnormal Psychology*, *124*, 343–354.

Weaver, I. C. G., Cervoni, N., Champagne, F. A., D'Alessio, A. C., Sharma, S., Seckl, J. R., et al. (2004). Epigenetic programming by maternal behavior. *Nature Neuroscience*, *7*, 847–854.

Index

Note: Page numbers followed by *f* indicate figures and *t* indicate tables.

B

C

D

FSC
www.fsc.org
MIX
Papier | Fördert
gute Waldnutzung
FSC® C083411

Kolibri 360 GmbH
Ferdinand-Jühlke-Straße 7
99095 Erfurt, Deutschland
produktsicherheit@kolibri360.de